1986

# FUNDAMENTALS
# OF PSYCHOLOGY

# FUNDAMENTALS OF

♣ ADDISON-WESLEY PUBLISHING COMPANY
Reading, Massachusetts / Menlo Park, California / London / Amsterdam / Don Mills, Ontario / Sydney

# AUDREY HABER / RICHARD P. RUNYON

# PSYCHOLOGY

## THIRD EDITION

This book is in the Addison-Wesley Series in Psychology

**Sponsoring Editor:** Merryl A. Sloane
**Developmental Editor:** Linda J. Bedell
**Production Editor:** Mary W. Crittendon
**Copy Editor:** Janis R. Bolster

**Text Designer:** Melinda Grosser
**Illustrators:** Kenneth Wilson, Larry Johnson
**Cover Designer:** Hannus Design Associates (Richard Hannus)
**Cover Illustrator:** The Image Bank (Roy Morsch)
**Art Coordinator:** Robert Gallison

**Production Manager:** Karen M. Guardino
**Production Coordinator:** Peter Petraitis

The text of this book was composed in Palatino by The Clarinda Company.

**Library of Congress Cataloging in Publication Data**
Haber, Audrey.
    Fundamentals of psychology.

    Includes bibliographies and index.
    1. Psychology.    I. Runyon, Richard P.    II. Title.
BF121.H16    1983        150        82-16349
ISBN    0-201-11230-2

ISBN 0-201-11230-2
ABCDEFGHIJ-D0-89876543

DEDICATED TO DAVID SCOTT,
LAURIE BETH, MINDY ANN,
AND LARRY WAYNE
JASSENOFF; MARIBETH,
TOMMY, AND RICH RUNYON;
NANCY STOUT AND
AMY GAIENNIE

In the preface to the first edition, we noted that humanity was experiencing one of the most challenging periods in its history. Now, almost a decade later, we find that the population continues its explosive growth; shortages of key resources are surfacing everywhere; much of humanity goes to bed hungry; nations continue to posture and threaten other nations; and advances in technology appear to be the most impressive testimony to the abilities of our species. Yet we find around us a growing disenchantment with technology and awareness that deep psychological satisfactions do not come with the material gains that technology has brought. What is the answer? The next great frontier may not be outer space, but inner space. Understanding what "makes us tick"—our aspirations and motivations, our capabilities, our limitations, and the reach of our imagination—these are the concerns of the science we call *psychology*.

There is a growing recognition that psychology plays a key role in contemporary affairs, and more and more students are attracted to the study of psychology. Some of you will become psychology majors. For most, however, this course will be your only formal exposure to the principles of behavior.

In this edition, as in the previous editions, we have attempted to present the most recent and exciting work of psychologists in a straightforward and interesting manner, avoiding the jargon that can strangle effective communication. We want you to gain an appreciation of the scope of psychology so that, if you enter other fields, you will recognize the possible applications of psychological methods while remaining aware of their limitations. For those majoring in the field, we have attempted a coverage that is both broad and deep enough to enable you to look toward future courses in psychology with anticipation and confidence.

We have retained many of the features of previous editions that were so well received. But the field of psychology is anything but static. Consequently, we have made an intensive effort to update research and reflect current trends in the field. We have taken a more in-depth look at cognitive, humanistic, and social-learning approaches to psychology; a new

PREFACE

chapter on stress and coping has been added; the material on development is now covered in two chapters to reflect a life-span approach; the topics of motivation and emotion are incorporated in a single chapter; we have reorganized the chapter on abnormal psychology according to the third edition of the *Diagnostic and Statistical Manual (DSM-III)*; the coverage of psychotherapeutic techniques has been expanded into a full chapter, in which a single case example is followed throughout, showing how different therapies might approach the treatment process; and an appendix introducing statistical techniques has been added. In addition, we have added more than 25 new boxed selections covering such topics as endorphins, sexuality among the aged, and ethics in psychological research.

## STUDY AIDS

While we have always tried to make your studying a bit easier by supplying some tools to assist in the learning process, in this edition we have increased the pedagogical aids to help you apply more readily the SQ 3R learning technique. Each chapter opens with a brief outline (survey) of the contents. Where appropriate, we have raised questions for you to consider and have then discussed and summarized the answers. Such questions and summarized answers are identified by the use of colored type and lines. Within each chapter, key terms appear in bold type, and a full definition of each term appears in the margin near the word to reinforce what you are reading. Finally, to help you review and to assure that you have mastered the material, each chapter has a numbered summary and a list of the key terms (in the order in which they appear in the text). A glossary at the end of the book provides definitions for all the terms, in alphabetical order.

## SUPPLEMENTS

We recognize the complexities of the introductory course for both student and instructor. Thus we have also made available a wide variety of supplemental materials.

The student workbook for the new edition contains the following for each chapter: an outline; an expanded chapter summary; a programmed-learning unit; a unit focusing on the key terms, concepts, and names in the chapter; an active participation unit; and a self-quiz. A PSI workbook, which includes learning objectives and a set of flash cards, is also available.

The new instructor's manual provides chapter outlines, expanded chapter summaries, demonstrations, film lists, and annotated references. Two test item banks, each containing an entirely different set of approximately 2000 multiple-choice questions, have been prepared especially for this edition. An instructor's edition of the PSI workbook and a set of transparencies are also available.

## ACKNOWL-EDGMENTS

A textbook is always the result of a collaborative effort by many people, from the researchers and theoreticians who provide the basic information, to the members of the production team who assemble the bits and pieces into a whole book.

Specifically, we would like to give special thanks to our editors at Addison-Wesley, who have made enormous contributions to the success of so many of our books. In particular, we would like to thank our editors for this edition—Merryl Sloane, Linda Bedell, Meredith Nightingale, and Mary Crittendon—who, at various points along the way, have provided useful insights, criticisms, assistance, and encouragement.

We are also indebted to many of our colleagues for their enthusiastic support and guidance during the initial development of this text and its successive editions. Their numerous comments and suggestions have provided invaluable ideas for revising this text. Although our manuscript has been greatly enriched by their thoughtful and conscientious comments over the years, we take full responsibility for the final version. Our thanks are due:

Pietro Badia, Bowling Green State University

Isabel H. Beck, Santa Barbara City College

Michael Bergmire, Jefferson College

Tom Bond, Thomas Nelson Community College

James H. Booth, Community College of Philadelphia

James A. Briley, Jefferson State Junior College

Richard Brislin, Western Washington State College

Sheldon S. Brown, North Shore Community College

Jerry Burger, Wake Forest University

Edward C. Caldwell, West Virginia University

Neil A. Carrier, Southern Illinois University

Pauline Christy, Weber State College

John H. Doolittle, California State University, Sacramento

James Eison, Roane State Community College

Joseph D. Eubanks, San Antonio College

Eleanor Fahle, City College of San Francisco

Judith Farrell, Moorpark College

Jonathan C. Finkelstein, University of Maryland, Baltimore County

Gary B. Forbach, Washburn University of Topeka

Arthur Freeman, University of Pennsylvania

Michael Gardner, Los Angeles Valley College

Mary Elizabeth Hannah, University of Detroit

Richard H. Haude, University of Akron

Lillian B. Hix, Houston Community College System

Sidney Hochman, Nassau Community College

Morton Hoffman, Metropolitan State College

Irene M. Hulicka, State University of New York College at Buffalo

William R. Jankel, Montana State University

Wendell Jeffrey, University of California, Los Angeles

Paul S. Kaplan, Suffolk Community College

Richard R. Klene, University of Cincinnati

Richard M. Lerner, Eastern Michigan University

Joel Morgovsky, Brookdale Community College

George R. Mount, Mountain View College

Barbara S. McClinton, Essex Community College

Kathleen McCormick, Ocean County College

Angela Provitera-McGlynn, Mercer County Community College

Diane McGrath, Illinois State University

Retta E. Poe, Western Kentucky University

Daniel W. Richards, Houston Community College System

Kathryn K. Rileigh, Pembroke State University

Jon E. Roeckelein, Mesa Community College

George C. Rogers, Jr., Massachusetts Bay Community College

Stephen M. Saltzman, Los Angeles Valley College

Audrey Schwartz, Broward Community College

Seymour Siegler, Brookdale Community College

Michael G. Walraven, Jackson Community College

Francine Wehmer, Wayne State University

Nancy P. White, Pine Manor College

Jerry S. Wiggins, University of British Columbia

Finally, without the constant encouragement and support of our spouses, Jerry Jassenoff and Lois Runyon, this book would still be in the "talking stage."

*Tucson, Arizona*                                                          **A.H.**
*October 1982*                                                             **R.P.R.**

# CONTENTS

**PERSONALITY**

**ABNORMAL BEHAVIOR**

**TECHNIQUES OF THERAPY**

# FUNDAMENTALS
# OF PSYCHOLOGY

1

# WHAT IS PSYCHOLOGY?

## WHAT IS PSYCHOLOGY?

How often have you heard someone claim to be a "good psychologist"? Have you ever made this claim? Have you ever "used psychology" or "psyched someone out"? Perhaps you have described someone's problems as "psychological"?

It is virtually impossible to pick up a newspaper or magazine without coming across some claim to psychological insight or some reference to an individual who is a "good psychologist," as demonstrated by sales ability, acumen in human relations, insight into personal problems, and so forth. In addition, newspapers and magazines frequently carry articles that deal with such psychological phenomena as personality, emotional problems, drug use and abuse, racism, violence, and sexuality.

Many people feel that they have some special knowledge of psychology, whether or not they have studied it. It is interesting that this claim is rarely, if ever, made about other scientific fields. How often have you heard anybody who has not studied extensively in the field claim to be a "good biologist," or to "use" chemistry or physics? It is quite natural for people to feel that they have a certain degree of expertise in psychology. After all, everybody has had to grow and interact with other people. In the course of everyday living, we all make observations of ourselves and of other people, frequently allowing these observations to flavor our relationships. For example, we may recognize that a certain acquaintance has a "short fuse" and temper our relationship with her accordingly. Or we may become so sensitive to a friend's pressing problems that we willingly spend hours of our time quietly listening to him "bare his chest." Examples of this sort could be cited almost without limit. The truth of the

Living organisms are always behaving, and the study of psychology is the study of behavior. When we look at behaviors, it is natural for us to add our own interpretations to what we see, but psychologists must strive for objectivity in making their observations.

matter is that we are constantly making decisions based on our expectations about other people. Is this psychology?

**Psychology**
The science of behavior.

**Behavior**
In the most general sense, anything an organism does.

What is psychology? **Psychology** is defined as the science of **behavior**. Let us pause for a moment and reflect on the implications of this definition. What do we mean by behavior?

Is sleeping behavior? Is reading this book behavior? What about thinking, daydreaming, going to the movies, driving a car, attending a lecture, smoking a "joint," "shooting speed"? The answer to all of these questions is "Yes"; these things are all examples of behavior. And, as you can see, not only is behavior a very comprehensive term, but it is impossible for a living organism not to be "behaving." Even when asleep, an organism is behaving. As you read this textbook, you are behaving. We, as authors, are especially interested in this last behavior. Our textbook presents the fundamental principles of behavior, and we are concerned with one specific aspect of your behavior as you read the book: your achieving an understanding of these fundamental principles (see Box 1.1).

Clearly, the basic subject matter of psychology, behavior, is of vital concern to all of us. It is perhaps because of this that "psychology" has become a household word. But the mere fact that we attach the word "psychology" to what we do does not confer any special significance upon our actions, and it does not make us psychologists. Many of us are quite competent to drive a car and maneuver it through heavy traffic, snow, sleet, and rain. Does this mean that we understand the car? The true depth of our understanding may be revealed with shocking suddenness the moment the car breaks down and we are forced to call for service. Likewise, we may become aware of our own limitations as "psychologists" only when our lives, or the lives of others, suddenly become disordered. This does not mean that psychologists are concerned only with "breakdowns"; indeed, much of their interest is directed toward understanding the smooth, integrated functioning of the intact organism.

Two characteristics of the professional psychologist's approach to the study of behavior distinguish it from the casual observations of the nonprofessional. The psychologist's method of inquiry is both *objective* and *systematic*.

## Objectivity

When most of us observe behavior, we tend to inject our own personal biases into any observations we make. We see the world through eyes that are colored by our own likes and dislikes and by the beliefs, attitudes, and motivations that we have developed through a lifetime of experiences. What is more, we tend to make value judgments about the things we observe. Thus if we see a child pull a cat's tail, we are likely to describe the child's behavior with such terms as bad, cruel, sadistic, or brutal. Even a psychologist, outside the professional role, might be tempted to apply the same descriptive labels. When acting as a scientist, however, the psychologist's foremost objective is to *understand* the child's behavior. The scientist realizes that prejudgments are likely to blind one to other possible explanations. For example, the child merely may have been trying to pick up the cat, and the cat's tail may have provided the

## BOX 1.1

### The SQ 3R Method

Many students are probably aware of the fact that their study techniques are inefficient and could stand improvement. Here's one technique that seems to "work." It is called the **SQ 3R method.** This method provides a technique which, if implemented conscientiously, will almost certainly improve your performance. It will, in effect, make you your own instructor. At first, this method may seem to take more time and effort than your previous method did. But remember that the SQ 3R method itself has to be learned, and this learning requires time and effort. With practice, you should be able to use the SQ 3R method as easily as any well-learned and thoroughly practiced skill.

The method consists of five stages: *survey, question, read, recite,* and *review.*

During the *survey* phase, you should look over the main headings of a unit of study to gain an overview of the material and note the major points to be developed. This survey should take just long enough for you to see the main topics around which the material is organized. If there is a summary, reading it is worthwhile, because it may also reveal something about the organization of the chapter.

Your actual work begins with the *question* stage. You should rephrase the first heading into the form of a question. For example, if the first heading in a chapter is "Factors within the Individual," you should ask yourself, "What are the factors within the individual that will influence the efficiency of learning and

remembering?" By questioning yourself in this way, your curiosity will be aroused, you will be able to bring your own previous knowledge into the picture, and you will be more likely to recognize the important points.

Now *read* the material in that section with a view toward answering the question you previously raised. This stage should involve an active search for the answer rather than a passive plodding through the written material.

Once you have read the section, put the book aside and attempt to *recite* in your own words the main points of what you have just read. This recitation can be either oral or written. If you cannot do this, you should reread the section until you are successful at reciting the important ideas. You should aim at brevity, however; do not try to memorize the entire section. The recitation phase is probably the most significant aspect of the SQ 3R method, for it is this behavior that is commonly required in class and on examinations.

After you have repeated this procedure for each headed section, you should *review* the entire lesson by looking over whatever notes you have taken. Reviewing serves as a check on memory and also pinpoints areas for further study.

---

**SQ 3R method**
A method of studying that involves five stages: survey, question, read, recite, and review.

---

most accessible or convenient "handle." Or the child simply may not have developed the rather advanced concept of "inflicting pain." The tail-pulling episode may represent nothing more than the child's insatiable curiosity about the world.

Psychologists recognize the need to stand back from the behavior they study in order to make carefully planned observations calmly and dispassionately, and to consider various alternatives. We speak of these characteristics as **objectivity.** Objectivity does not imply that psychologists lack interest in or concern about the subject they study. Rather, objectivity assures them that their experiments may be *repeated*, and their findings *verified* or challenged, by other scientists at other times and places.

## Systematic Observation

**Objectivity**
One of the characteristics of the professional psychologist's approach to the study of behavior; studying behavior without allowing personal prejudices and opinions to affect one's judgment.

**Systematic observation**
Planning and preparing well in advance and controlling the conditions under which observations are made.

Perhaps the characteristic that most clearly distinguishes the observations of the scientist from those of the nonscientist is the *way* in which the scientist makes observations. Whereas nonscientists typically are casual about observations, professional investigators are **systematic**—they plan and prepare their investigations well in advance of carrying them out, and they strive to control the conditions under which they make their observations. In short, psychology (as well as other sciences) follows rules that dictate how research is done. Let's look at an example.

Suppose we are interested in determining both the extent of marijuana use and the way it affects ongoing behavior. The chances are that the nonscientist's approach to this problem would be significantly different from the trained observer's. For example, a nonscientist who happened to note that most of his or her friends smoke marijuana on occasion might conclude that "practically everybody smokes it." Moreover, in attempting to ascertain the effects of marijuana, this observer might ask several friends to describe their "high." "What does it feel like when you are stoned?" "Do you notice any changes in your behavior?" "Do you find you have difficulty concentrating?"

On the other hand, scientists who wish to obtain information about the extent and effect of marijuana use might begin by carefully listing the behaviors they are interested in observing and then working out systematic ways of collecting relevant information. They might sit in on groups of people who are smoking marijuana and make carefully recorded observations of such things as changes in verbal behavior and alterations in social interactions. They might study, in depth, the backgrounds of a number of marijuana users to see if there are any factors in their histories that could account for their use of marijuana or that would explain certain behavioral effects. They might interview large numbers of individuals and ask them the same questions in order to determine such things as the incidence and frequency of use. When conducting studies of this sort, scientists usually assure the anonymity of the respondents so that the responses are more likely to be honest.

The most precise method that scientists have evolved for studying behavior is the experiment. If they want to know the effect that marijuana has on certain psychological processes, they might study an individual's behavior in a prearranged experimental setting. For example, if they are interested in the effects of marijuana on driving, they might observe how their subjects drive before and after smoking it.

Later in this chapter we shall take a closer look at the various methods used by psychologists in their quest for a scientific understanding of behavior. First, let's glance into the past to see how psychology evolved into the science it is today and then look at the many faces of psychology as it appears on the present scene.

## PSYCHOLOGY: A LONG PAST BUT A SHORT HISTORY

Psychology has been described as a science with a long past but a short history. This means that ever since human beings became a separate species, people have been concerned with problems that are psychological in nature; but the systematic study of behavior and the controlled laboratory observations characteristic of the other sciences developed only in the late nineteenth century. Prior to that time, psychology was largely in the domain of philosophy. Behavior was viewed only in the context of some philosophical position, usually one derived from a religious point of view that included certain assumptions about whether human nature was good or evil. It did not matter if these conclusions were inconsistent with everyday observations. The philosophers tried to define the fundamental nature of the human being. They did not ask how individual people behave and why they do what they do, except from the lofty and detached height of philosophical speculation.

The physical sciences have a somewhat similar past: Philosophical assumptions about the basic nature of the universe determined the way earlier scientists characterized physical reality. But during the Renaissance, a period of great advances in the arts and sciences, scientists began to develop striking theories about the world based, not on philosophical tradition but, rather, on systematic observations of the world and of the interactions among events in physical reality. During this time the physical sciences threw off the shackles of philosophical speculation. The contrast between the old philosophical approach and the new scientific approach is well illustrated in the following excerpt from the writings of Sir Francis Bacon (1561–1626):

Until late in the nineteenth century, behavior was commonly seen from a religious point of view; and during the Middle Ages, people often held demons responsible for madness and possession. In this fifteenth-century painting, St. Catherine is casting out the devil from a possessed woman.

*In the year of our Lord 1432, there arose a grievous quarrel among the brethren over the number of teeth in the mouth of a horse. For 13 days the disputation raged without ceasing. All the ancient books and chronicles were fetched out, and wonderful and ponderous erudition, such as was never before heard of in this region, was made manifest. At the beginning of the 14th day, a youthful friar of goodly bearing asked his learned superiors for permission to add a word, and straightway, to the wonderment of the disputants, whose deep wisdom he sore vexed, he beseeched them to unbend in a manner coarse and unheard-of ways, and to look in the open mouth of a horse and find answer to their question-ings. At this, their dignity being grievously hurt, they waxed exceed-ingly wroth; and joining in a mighty uproar, they flew upon him and smote him hip and thigh, and cast him out forthwith. For, said they, surely Satan hath tempted this bold neophyte to declare unholy and un-heard-of ways of finding truth contrary to all the teachings of the fathers. After many days more of grievous strife the dove of peace sat on the assembly, and they as one man, declaring the problem to be an everlast-ing mystery because of a grievous dearth of historical and theological evidence thereof, so ordered the same writ down.*

**Empiricism**
The theoretical position that behavior is determined by ex-perience and that human na-ture can be understood best by **observing** people and their behavior.

**Tabula rasa**
A "blank slate"; the term used to describe the theory that a baby's mind at birth is blank and that all that appears upon it is "written" by experience.

With the liberation of physical science from philosophical restraints, many philosophers began to question their own approach to the under-standing of the human species. Philosophers were greatly impressed with the tremendous insights provided by looking at experience. As a result, a new school of philosophy called **empiricism** (which means "based on experience") emerged. The empirical philosophers maintained that hu-mans could best be understood by *observing* them and their behavior. One of the great philosophers of that period, John Locke (1623–1704), sug-gested that there is no basic human nature, that our minds are at birth a **tabula rasa,** a "blank slate" which will be written on by experience. Thus if you know the individual's experiences, you understand the individual. This position did not lead, however, to any truly systematic observations of individuals under controlled conditions. It led, by and large, to a great deal of armchair speculation, most of it based on casual observations.

In the mid-1800s a number of investigators were working in areas closely related to, and later integrated into, psychology. These investiga-tors studied the way we see and hear the world, thereby providing us with empirically obtained descriptions of the relationships between sights and sounds and our reception of them. Among the most prominent re-searchers at the time were E. H. Weber and Gustav Fechner, who at-tempted to establish a mathematical relationship between how we expe-rience external events and the characteristics of the events themselves. Figure 1.1 illustrates one of the laws derived by Weber and Fechner.

Weber's research resulted in a startling discovery, which is known as Weber's law. Let's examine two illustrations of this law. Imagine you are given a 1-pound weight to lift with one of your hands. Then you are asked to lift a 2-pound weight with the same hand. You are now asked to say whether the second is lighter, the same as, or heavier than the first weight. You would probably experience little difficulty answering that the second is heavier. Now suppose that the first weight is 50 pounds and

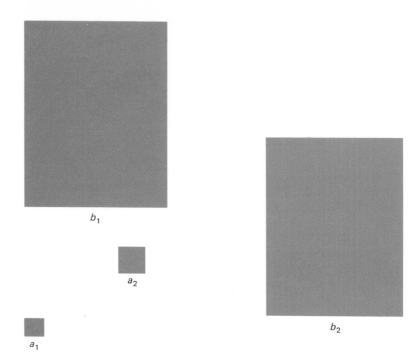

Which member of each pair is larger? Is $a_1$ larger than $a_2$? Is $b_1$ larger than $b_2$? Clearly $a_2$ is larger than $a_1$. However, it requires some examination to see that $b_1$ is larger than $b_2$. Nevertheless, the larger member of each pair is precisely ⅛-inch longer and ⅛-inch wider than its counterpart. Weber and Fechner showed that there is a lawful relationship between the magnitudes of stimulation and our ability to detect differences among them. When stimulation is small or weak to begin with, it requires less of an increase to detect a change than when the initial stimulation is large or strong.

the second is 51. Do you think the discrimination between the two weights would be as easy to make? Not at all. Let's look at another example. You are in a room that, except for 1 candle, is dark. You light a second candle. Do you suppose you would be able to notice an increase in the total amount of light? What if there had been 100 lighted candles at the outset and you added 1 more? Do you still think you would be able to detect the increase? Notice that in both cases the amount of light added is identical. Nevertheless, you would probably answer, "I doubt it," or "That would be difficult." Why would you answer in this way? You might reason intuitively, "A small amount added to a small amount is easier to detect than a small amount added to a large amount." This observation takes us to the core of Weber's law: The stimulus must be increased by a constant fraction of the original value if the change is to be noticed. This constant fraction is the mathematical relationship that Weber sought. In today's highly technological world where space invaders battle on our TV screens, it is difficult for us to imagine the excitement that this observation generated—a precise mathematical relationship between events in the physical world and events in the psychological realm! Later this law was fine-tuned by Fechner, who found a mathematical equation that yields a better relationship between stimuli and sensations throughout the entire range of stimulus values. Fechner's observations,

In 1879, Wilhelm Wundt established the first laboratory for scientific study of the mind. His scientific approach in making observations was the first step in the evolution of psychology as we know it today.

made more than a century ago, form the cornerstone of much present-day thinking about psychological testing scales (see Chapter 12) and about the detection of signals.

We can see the Weber/Fechner law at work in our daily lives. If a person goes from 100 to 70 pounds, the loss is far more noticeable than if one goes from 270 to 240 pounds. An increase of $10 in the price of a new car might not even be noticed, but the same increase in the price of a gallon of oil or gasoline could plunge the world into economic chaos. An increase of $1 million in the portfolio of a billionaire might go undetected by his or her accountant. A similar increase in the fortunes of most of us would surely be the cause of great and prolonged celebration. Fechner's work was so important that some psychologists feel that 1860 marks the birth of psychology as a science. This is the year in which Fechner's *Elements of Psychophysics* was published.

However, the year 1879 is generally accepted as the birthdate of modern psychology. During this year Wilhelm Wundt (1832–1920) established, in Leipzig, Germany, the first laboratory for the scientific study of the mind. Wundt was trained in physiology, physics, and philosophy. His definition of psychology—as the science of conscious experience—was quite different from the one we use today. His idea involved taking some object in the physical world, presenting it to a trained observer, and having the observer describe the fundamental elements of his or her conscious experience. For example, if you presented a red ball, the observer might say, "I see redness, I feel weight, I see roundness." This method of looking within one's conscious experience is known as **introspection.** First you analyze the conscious compound (in this case the red ball) into its basic elements (redness, weight, roundness). How do you recognize a basic element? It cannot be described in terms of other elements. To illustrate, how would you go about describing to a color-blind person what red looks like? Having enumerated the basic elements, you can then investigate the laws that bind these elements together into complex experiences. Wundt maintained that developing a science of conscious experi-

**Introspection**
A method of looking within and describing one's conscious experience.

ence is no different from formulating a science of physical reality. Once you have found the basic building blocks that make up the physical world and have discovered the laws that hold them together, you have constructed a science such as physics or chemistry. Likewise, once you have discovered the basic building blocks of conscious experience and the laws that bind them together, you will have constructed a science of conscious experience. Because it emphasized the structure of the mind, Wundt's position became known as **structuralism.**

As long as psychology was preoccupied with conscious experience, particularly as narrowly defined by Wundt, it remained relatively static. One of Wundt's American students, William James (1842–1910), expanded psychology well beyond Wundt's original conceptions. James wrote an extremely influential and still-admired two-volume treatise entitled *The Principles of Psychology* (1890). In it, he expanded the focus of psychology to embrace such diverse phenomena as learning, motivation, and emotions, as well as other areas that attract psychologists today. His work marked the beginning of a departure from the narrow, structuralist point of view. Because he emphasized the *functions* of such processes as consciousness, learning, and motivation in the individual's adaptation, the school of thought he represented is known as **functionalism.**

By the early twentieth century the scope of psychology had been radically altered to include the study of lower animals, learning, motivation, and abnormal behavior. It was poised, waiting for a new definition. This was accomplished by J. B. Watson, the founder of **behaviorism.** He argued that conscious experiences are totally private and not subject to independent verification. You cannot *really* know what is in my mind, and I cannot know what's in yours. Watson concluded that the science of psychology must be based on publicly observable events, that is, on behavior. He emphasized that one can expose individuals to various kinds of physical events (stimuli) and then observe their behavior. One would have all the elements necessary for a science of behavior, and there would be no need for any reference to conscious experience.

Behaviorism was not the only movement to reject Wundt's position. At the very moment behaviorism was making its debut on the psychological stage, other acts were clamoring for attention. A predominantly German movement known as the **gestalt** school was also rejecting structuralism, but for very different reasons. The gestaltists maintained that a science of behavior cannot be developed by analyzing complex behaviors into simple parts and then combining these parts to produce a whole. The poem "Humpty Dumpty" expresses this view. They maintained that behavior should be studied as organized entities rather than as discrete, independent parts. Hence the word "gestalt" which, in German, means something complete, a whole, a total configuration. The gestalt movement, as we shall see in Chapter 6, has greatly influenced the study of perception.

The schools of thought we have been discussing—structuralism, functionalism, behaviorism, gestalt psychology—evolved in academic settings. Another theoretical school concerned itself with the understanding of abnormal human behavior. Sigmund Freud (1856–1939) is regarded as the founder of **psychoanalysis,** a movement that is at once a theory of

---

**Structuralism**
A school of psychology (associated with Wilhelm Wundt) that emphasized the structure of conscious experience.

**Functionalism**
A school of psychology that raised questions concerning the functions or purposes served by the mind, consciousness, and so forth in the adjusting organism.

**Behaviorism**
A school of psychology (associated with J. B. Watson) that maintains that psychologists should study only what is observable—behavior, not conscious experience.

**Gestalt psychology**
A school of psychology that emphasizes studying behavior as organized wholes rather than as discrete, independent parts.

**Psychoanalysis**
A school of psychology (associated with Sigmund Freud) primarily concerned with the study of abnormal behavior. Psychoanalytic theory stresses unconscious determinants of behavior.

**Cognitive psychology**
A branch of psychology dealing with thoughts, knowledge, and ideas.

**Humanism**
An approach to psychology that emphasizes the self, internal experiences, and natural growth toward good mental health.

Psychoanalysis, a school of psychology concerned with the study of abnormal behavior, arose out of the theories of Sigmund Freud. In general, psychoanalytic theory stresses the unconscious factors that influence behavior.

personality, a philosophical view of human nature, and a method for treating disturbed individuals. In broad terms, psychoanalytic theory stresses the role of early life experiences and sexual factors in human development and the unconscious determinants of behavior. We will discuss psychoanalysis in later chapters, both as a theory of personality (Chapter 13) and as a psychotherapeutic method (Chapter 15).

In recent years, the study of the mental life of the individual has again assumed prominence on the psychological scene. **Cognitive** psychologists, for example, are raising such significant and penetrating questions as: "How is information or knowledge represented and processed in the mind? How do we recognize events, objects, or people when they are never experienced in precisely the same way on different occasions?" Jean Piaget, a leading cognitive psychologist, was originally trained as a biologist, but his fascination with how children think led him to study them closely and to produce some startling conclusions about how children gradually adapt to the environment around them and learn new concepts and thought patterns (see Chapter 11). Cognitive psychology is opening up new and exciting perspectives from which to view the most distinctive of human abilities, language and thought.

Other psychologists, including Abraham Maslow and Carl Rogers, have placed the self at the center of the psychological stage. These **humanistic** psychologists have an optimistic view of humanity. They maintain that we have the ability to control our own destinies and that the self moves naturally toward good mental health. They emphasize that internal states (for example, the content of the mind) are more important in determining our actions than the external realities themselves. If we think that another person dislikes us and is out to get us, our behavior is going to reflect that fearful concern. The fact that the other person is really completely indifferent to us is of minor significance in determining our actions. The humanistic position has led to the, development of a theory of personality, which will be discussed in Chapter 13, and an important form of psychotherapy known as person-centered therapy (see Chapter 15).

## THE MANY FACES OF PSYCHOLOGY

In answering the question, "What is psychology?" it will be helpful to look at what psychologists do. We have already noted that, awake or asleep, behavior is always taking place. Wherever there is behavior, it is appropriate that a psychologist be there to study it. Different psychologists have concentrated their attention on quite diverse aspects of behavior. Few people outside the field of psychology are aware of psychologists' pervasive role in virtually every aspect of our lives.

When you brush your teeth or wash your face in the morning, there is a good chance that psychologists have influenced your choice of toothpaste or soap through their participation in both marketing and advertising. The design of the car you drive may well have the psychologist's imprint on it. For example, psychologists have thoroughly studied the arrangement of the instruments and gauges on the instrument panel in order to maximize driving efficiency and safety. Your admission into college and your choice of a major may have been based, at least in part, on tests designed by psychologists. Psychological research has influenced many aspects of educational instruction. Indeed, the very books you use, the instructional materials employed, and even the way a course is taught probably reflect, to some degree, research by psychologists. Occasionally the problems and pressures of everyday life can so overwhelm us that we seek the professional counseling of a psychologist. Finally, psychologists keep their fingers on the pulse of the nation by engaging in vital research on such contemporary issues as drug use and abuse, alcoholism, crime, divorce, and suicide, to name but a few.

The field of psychology encompasses a broad spectrum of interests and concerns, and so it not surprising that there has been a proliferation of subfields too numerous and complex to classify to everybody's satisfaction. A large percentage of psychologists are employed full-time in educational institutions and practice their specialties within them. Psychologists are found in such disparate settings as business, industry, the military, hospitals, and private practice. Although we discuss the various fields of psychology separately, keep in mind the fact that there is a good deal of overlap between and within fields. Box 1.2 examines a topic as it is explored by the various specialties.

**Counseling psychologist**
A psychologist who focuses on minor adjustment problems or assists in vocational and educational guidance. Counseling psychologists typically work with people whose problems are less serious and less deep-rooted than those treated by clinical psychologists.

**Clinical psychologist**
A psychologist who is involved in diagnosis, assessment, and treatment of emotionally disturbed individuals.

**Psychiatrist**
A medical doctor who has received specialized training in treating emotional disturbances.

**Psychoanalyst**
A psychologist or psychiatrist whose approach to treatment of the emotionally disturbed is based upon psychoanalytic theories.

**Developmental psychologist**
A psychologist who studies the behavior and behavioral changes of the individual from the prenatal period through maturity and old age.

**Social psychologist**
A psychologist who studies the individual's interactions with groups and the ways in which groups influence the individual's feelings, attitudes, and beliefs.

Clinical and **counseling psychology** account for almost 50 percent of all psychologists. Although a number are in private practice exclusively, most **clinical psychologists** work in an institutional setting and are involved in the diagnosis, assessment, and treatment of emotionally disturbed individuals. In this connection they work closely with such allied professions as medicine and social work.

Although it is impossible to draw a fine line between clinical and counseling psychology, counseling psychologists typically work with normal people, focusing on minor adjustment problems or providing vocational and educational guidance. Counseling psychologists must be able to recognize individuals with deep-seated emotional disorders and refer them to the appropriate clinical agencies.

People outside the field frequently confuse **psychiatrists, psychoanalysts,** and clinical psychologists. Psychiatrists are medical doctors. They first obtain their M.D. degrees and then pursue specialized training in psychiatry. They may or may not be well grounded in psychology and research methodology. Because they are medical doctors, they may prescribe medicines and practice surgery or refer patients for surgery.

Psychoanalysts base their approach to the treatment of the emotionally disturbed on psychoanalytic theories of personality. In the past, a psychoanalyst was required to hold a medical degree. However, many psychologists have received training in psychoanalysis and are regarded as psychoanalysts, even without the M.D. degree.

Clinical psychologists usually hold Ph.D. degrees and have received specialized training in normal psychological processes and research methodology as well as abnormal psychology. They may work with individuals or with groups. They use a technique called psychotherapy—the treatment of emotional disturbances by psychological methods. There are a number of different forms of psychotherapy, and many of them have been developed by clinical psychologists. We shall look more closely at these various forms of psychotherapy in Chapter 15. In actual practice, clinical psychologists and psychiatrists use many of the same techniques. Then how do they differ? Because clinical psychologists are not medically trained, they cannot prescribe medicines or practice surgery. They can, however, refer patients or clients for medical diagnosis.

**Developmental psychologists** study the behavior and behavioral changes of the individual from the prenatal period through maturity and old age—literally, from the womb to the tomb. They are interested in describing the ways in which the child gradually develops adult ways of thinking, feeling, and interacting with both the physical and the social environment. They often work in research settings and formulate general principles of intellectual, emotional, motivational, and perceptual growth, which they apply in attempting to understand the individual throughout his or her life span. It is only through the study of developmental psychology that we can fully comprehend the subtleties and complexities of individual behavior.

**Social psychologists** are concerned with the individual's interactions with groups and the ways in which groups influence feelings, attitudes, and beliefs. They seek to understand the dynamics of many of our cur-

# BOX 1.2

## Various Specialties of Psychology Look at Locus of Control

There are times each and every one of us feel that we are controlled by forces outside ourselves, when we do not appear to be masters of our own destinies. In extreme cases, we feel helpless. No matter what course of action we take we feel unable to determine our own fate. It has been found that some people are more likely than others to attribute their successes or failures to forces outside themselves, as if they are being swept along by circumstances. For such individuals, the **locus of control** is seen as external to themselves. **External locus of control** is well illustrated by the following excerpt from *Roots*:

> The old man began to speak. "Fiddler here tell me you run away four times. You see what it got you. Jes' hopes you done learned your lesson like I done. 'Cause you ain't done nothin' new. My young days, I run off so much dey near 'bout tore my hide off 'fore I got it in my head ain't nowhere to run to. Run two states away, dey jes' tell about it in dey papers an' sooner later you gits cotched an' nearly kilt, an' win' up right back where you come from. Ain't hardly nobody ain't thought about runnin'. De grinnin'est niggers thinks about it. But ain't nobody I ever knowed ever got away. Time you settled down and made de best of things de way dey is, 'stead of wastin' yo' young years, like I did, plottin' what cain't be done. I done got ol' an' wore out now. Reckon since you been born I been actin' like de no-good, lazy, shiftless, head-scratchin' nigger white folks says us is."

On the other hand, there are some people who feel confident of their ability to control their own lives. Rather than seeing themselves as passive victims of circumstance, they see the various outcomes in life as a direct consequence of their own behavior. In short, they see the locus of control as **internal.**

The implications of locus of control have captured the imagination of researchers in virtually every area of psychology. Let us look at several of these areas and see how each focuses on different aspects of this intriguing issue.

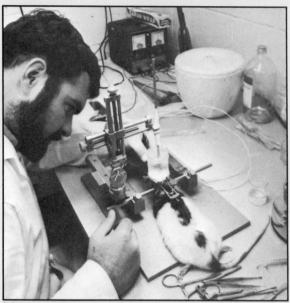

(a)

(b)

Specialties within psychology vary widely in their focus. Experimental psychologists conduct scientific experiments to investigate psychological phenomena, whereas clinical psychologists use a variety of therapeutic techniques to treat their clients' psychological problems. (a) Using an anesthetized rat, an experimental psychologist determines the effect of cooling the brain and spinal cord. (b) By observing his client's reactions during a Thematic Apperception Test, a clinical psychologist hopes to arrive at a better understanding of the client's behavior.

Some *clinical psychologists* have directed their attention to the relationship between locus of control and various clinical problems such as depression. It has been found that depressed patients are more likely than others to perceive their lives as being shaped by external rather than internal forces. As one investigator has noted:

*The depressed patient is peculiarly sensitive to any impediments to his goal-directed activity. An obstacle is regarded as an impossible barrier. Difficulty in dealing with a problem is interpreted as a total failure. His cognitive response to a problem or difficulty is likely to be an idea such as "I'm licked," "I'll never be able to do this," or "I'm blocked no matter what I do." . . . In achievement-oriented situations depressed patients are particularly prone to react with a sense of failure. (Beck, 1967, pp. 256–257)*

*Developmental psychologists* may inquire into the factors that are responsible for the development of internal or external orientations. For example, one researcher (Chance, 1965) found that boys who rated high on internal control were more likely to have mothers who expected them to achieve independence early in life.

The study of group processes lies within the domain of *social psychology*. One broad area of investigation involves the impact of racial prejudice on minority-group members. In locus-of-control studies, it has been found that blacks are more likely to be fatalistic about their prospects in life than are whites. One leading theorist on locus of control has observed:

*When one acquaints himself with the massive literary outpourings regarding the lives of impoverished peoples, displaced persons, and of members of denigrated minority groups, a common characterization is that of abject helplessness and a sense of despair. To people who live in continuously adverse circumstances, life does not appear to be subject to control through their own efforts. Only through some outside intervention do events seem to be alterable, and such intervention is a rare occurrence. . . . In general, it may be concluded that perceived control is positively associated with access to opportunity. Those who are able, through position and group membership, to attain more readily the valued outcomes that allow a person to feel personal satisfaction are more likely to hold internal control expectancies. Blacks, Spanish-Americans, Indians, and other minority groups who do not enjoy as much access to opportunity as do the predominant caucasian groups in North American society are found to hold fatalistic, external control beliefs. (Lefcourt, 1976, pp. 15, 25)*

It has often been observed that the school performance of minority-group members generally deteriorates each year. *School psychologists* might feel that this declining school performance is related to the attitude, "It doesn't matter how hard you study, you're still not going anywhere." They may attempt to change these fatalistic attitudes in the hopes that academic performance will improve. One investigator (deCharms, 1972) initiated a training program aimed at increasing the perception of internal control among minority-group members. Students who underwent this training did not show the same decline in academic performance as a similar group with no special training.

The vastness of modern computerized business and industry often leaves employees with the feeling that they are nothing but cogs in an enormous impersonal machine. *Industrial psychologists* would recognize that such attitudes are likely to lead to poor work habits and inefficient performance. In order to counter these adverse perceptions, they might design various programs aimed at involving employees in the decision-making processes, providing incentives for exceptional performance, and improving the flow of communication among the various elements of the business.

---

**Locus of control**
A broad concept that relates to the point at which controls are exercised over an individual's life.

**External locus of control**
The orientation that the various outcomes in life are determined by forces outside the individual.

**Internal locus of control**
The orientation that the various outcomes in life are a direct consequence of forces within the individual.

rent social problems—for instance, prejudice, crime, and violence. Box 1.3 presents some of Bibb Latane's findings following years of studying a phenomenon he calls "diffusion of responsibility."

**School psychologists** work in educational settings where their responsibilities include evaluating learning and emotional problems, administering and interpreting various psychological and educational tests, and advising both teachers and parents concerning ways to improve the academic and social adjustments of schoolchildren.

**Industrial psychologists** probe many of the problems created by the explosive technological changes characteristic of our times. The scope of their inquiry encompasses such diverse areas as working conditions, personnel problems, environmental concerns, and the interaction between people and the increasingly complex systems they must originate, operate, and maintain.

**Experimental psychology** is both a field of specialization and a method of research. Although the experimental method is employed to

## BOX 1.3

### Psychologist Has People Figured
By Patrick Young, Newhouse News Service

COLUMBUS, Ohio—Do you speak with ease before a small group but panic at addressing 100 people? Will you tip more when dining alone than when eating with others? Are you more willing to aid someone when no one else is there to help?

For most people, the answer to these questions is "yes." And psychologist Bibb Latane of Ohio State University thinks he can explain why.

He's even advanced a theory that predicts how people will react in a variety of situations—from tipping in a restaurant to "accepting Christ" at a Billy Graham crusade.

"As social animals, we are drawn by the attractiveness of others and aroused by their mere presence, stimulated by their activity and embarrassed by their attention," Latane says. "We are threatened by the power of others and angered by their attack. Fortunately, we are also comforted by the support of others and sustained by their love."

His theory, he says, "helps us to understand and predict a number of social-psychological phenomena."

Latane became intrigued by why people act differently in crowds after Catherine "Kitty" Genovese

was murdered in New York in 1964. Thirty-eight people—aware that others were watching—looked on from apartment windows as a man stalked and killed her. None of them called the police.

Latane's study of that event with psychologist John Darley led to their "**diffusion of responsibility**" concept—the idea that people are less likely to respond if they know other people are available to help—and to their book, "The Unresponsive Bystander: Why Doesn't He Help?"

The concept isn't limited to violent events. If five people—rather than only one—are home when the phone rings, each is more likely to wait for someone else to answer it until the caller quits and hangs up.

Based on his work and other studies since the Genovese slaying, Latane offers what he calls "three principles of social impact" to explain how the behavior of individuals is affected by others around them.

■ First, the more people and the more important their status, the greater their impact on an individual. Thus, a person feels more stage fright before a large audience and more nervous addressing upper management than clerical workers.

Also, "immediacy" plays a role. "In general, we're going to be more affected by things close to us [*sic*]," Latane says.

some extent in all subfields of psychology, some psychologists use the method so extensively that they are referred to as experimental psychologists. They usually work in academic settings where they conduct laboratory research in addition to teaching. Their activities cover a broad range of interests in both animal and human subjects. Many of the basic principles of behavior presented in this book have been formulated in the laboratories of the experimental psychologist. Learning theorists focus on the learning process; others, known as physiological psychologists, study the relationship between organic processes and behavior; and yet others, the comparative psychologists, have devoted their attention to comparing the behaviors of a variety of organisms.

Experimental psychologists are most likely to engage in basic or pure research. However, their findings are often utilized by other specialists in applied settings. If there is any controversy surrounding the work of experimental psychology, it usually centers on the specific applications of research findings rather than on the value of pure research.

■ Second, although impact keeps increasing as the crowd size grows, the impact is less for each person added to the group. If, for example, one person stands and stares up at a building, some passersby will stop and stare. If 15 people stare at the building, more passersby will stop and gawk, but not 15 times more.

■ Third, a single person can influence a crowd, but the larger the crowd, the smaller the individual impact. Thus, an individual is more likely to be influenced by a provocative speaker in a small gathering than if that person heard the same talk as part of a large audience.

Latane has compared behavior predicted by his theory against actual human reactions.

For example, the diffusion of responsibility concept suggested that individuals in a group of diners will tip less than a person eating alone. So with the aid of some students, Latane looked at the tipping practices at a Columbus restaurant.

"Single diners left tips (averaging) over 19 percent," he says. "Parties of five or six left about 13 percent."

The theory also predicted that evangelist Billy Graham would be more effective with small crowds than with mass audiences. So Latane examined results of 37 single-night Graham crusades, including one attended by more than 150,000 people, using data supplied by the Graham organization.

The basis for determining effectiveness was how many people signed cards that would allow local ministers to contact them later. Latane's finding: "The fewer people in the audience, the more likely people are to come forward."

"What I like about the theory," Latane says, "is it leads to obvious implications for how we should handle social events."

For example, he suggests, students should start their public speaking before small groups and work up to larger audiences as they build confidence, to avoid stage fright.

Source: *The Arizona Daily Star*, Tucson, Ariz., Thursday, December 3, 1981.

**Diffusion of responsibility concept**
A theory to account for the observation that we become less likely to help a person in distress as the number of other people available to render assistance increases.

Although these various areas of specialization in psychology differ in the focus of their interests, they often examine the same broad areas, albeit from a different perspective.

## METHODS OF PSYCHOLOGY

Regardless of the area of specialization, all psychologists have one thing in common: They all strive to understand behavior. Their methods of studying behavior have evolved over a long period of time in response to people's seemingly insatiable desire to predict and control those forces that shape their destiny.

The first attempts to understand behavior were speculative and abstract. The idea of using scientific methods involving controlled observation stemmed largely from the successes enjoyed by the physical and biological sciences. It is not always easy to apply these methods to psychological phenomena, for it is difficult to be objective about ourselves and about others. This problem, perhaps more than any other, has delayed the emergence and acceptance of psychology as a bona fide science. Nevertheless, psychology has developed a number of techniques for studying behavior. Let's examine a few of these methods.

### Experimental Method

Various devices advertised in the newspaper and in magazines promise to teach you while you sleep—a foreign language, the principles of economics, and so forth. Because the learning process is so frequently laborious and time consuming, the temptation to invest in a "sleep-learning machine" can become quite great. Imagine spending your afternoon and evening hours engaged in some totally enjoyable activity! But before committing your money, you would like to know if there is any truth to the advertising claim: "Now you can learn while you sleep." If it is possible to learn during sleep and if the gains are substantial, you might reason, "A few dollars spent on a sleep-learning device would be a worthwhile investment which, if spread over a lifetime of learning, would amount to less than pennies a day."

The question whether or not learning occurs during sleep seems easy enough to answer. Just conduct an **experiment:** Present unfamiliar learning materials to subjects while they are asleep and then test them after they awake. If their knowledge has improved, we can conclude that learning can occur during sleep. This is precisely what was done in early investigations of sleep-learning. The results of these studies supported the view that learning can occur during sleep. But two investigators (Simon and Emmons, 1956) regarded these findings with a healthy, scientific skepticism. They raised such penetrating questions as: "How can we be certain that the subjects were asleep? Is it possible that the subjects were awake at least part of the time and that the learning observed in prior studies had actually occurred during periods of wakefulness?"

Questions such as these go directly to the heart of psychology as a science. As we shall see throughout this book, much of what we study in psychology is not directly observed but rather must be inferred from various sources of evidence. We study motivation, but motivation is not directly observed. We do not see hunger, thirst, or a "desire to learn." Instead, we infer these states from several lines of evidence, including the behavior of the organism. Similarly, we do not directly observe learning; we infer it from changes in behavior.

But what about sleep? Surely sleep is directly observed and unambiguous. A person is either asleep or not asleep. If you are lying quietly in bed with your eyes closed and your breathing rhythmic and even, it seems reasonable to assume that you are asleep. But think for a moment. When you retire at night, isn't there a period of time when you lie quietly with your eyes closed but still remain alert and responsive to external sounds and smells? You may even have noted a brief interval during which you are in transition between wakefulness and sleep. If someone asks you a question during this period, you will still be able to respond, albeit drowsily. A few moments later, the question may go unanswered.

Because of an inability to define sleep unambiguously, the early sleep studies were inconclusive. To obtain a definitive answer to the question whether or not we are able to learn during sleep, we must first be able to state clearly what we mean by sleep and then show how its presence or absence can be ascertained. Fortunately, as is often the case in science, a seemingly unrelated development in another field came to the rescue by providing a tool that enabled us to define sleep and to ascertain whether or not a person is asleep. Engineering advances in electronic circuitry made it possible to amplify the minute electrical impulses, or "brain waves," that are produced constantly by the brain, whether we are awake or asleep. We shall have more to say about these brain waves in Chapter 5. For the moment, it is sufficient to note that they allow us to determine whether a person is really asleep and also how deeply a person is sleeping. A device called an electroencephalograph (which yields a record called an EEG) can measure these brain waves and enables us to define the stages of sleep in terms of the types of brain waves produced. Such a definition is known as an **operational definition:** The term or concept is defined by the way in which it is measured. Thus sleep is defined in terms of certain types of brain waves observed on the EEG. You are already familiar with some common measurements that are operationally defined. An inch and an ounce, for example, are operationally defined in terms of a platinum rod and a weight housed in the National Bureau of Standards.

Having arrived at a satisfactory basis for confirming that someone is asleep, it was next necessary to define and measure learning. At the outset of the Simon and Emmons sleep study, the subjects were given 96 questions that were repeated on a tape recorder, with answers, while the subjects supposedly were asleep. If subsequent testing showed improved scores, the researchers assumed that learning had occurred.

The results of the study were quite conclusive. Analysis of the EEG records revealed that the subjects did not sleep uninterruptedly throughout the night. There were occasional periods of wakefulness. What is of particular interest is the fact that the subjects learned about 80 percent of

**Experiment**
A scientific method in which the experimenter systematically alters a variable so that observed changes in another variable (behavior) may be attributed to changes in the first.

**Operational definition**
A definition of terms or concepts by the way in which they are measured.

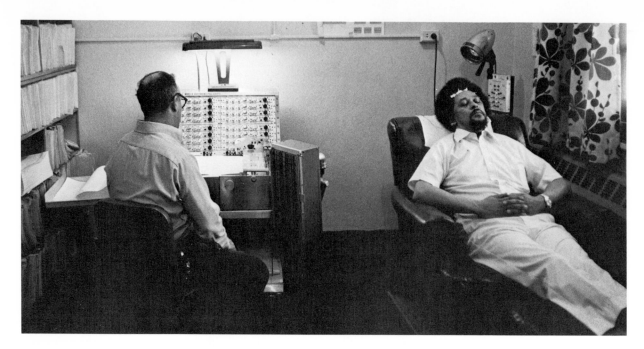

The patient shown here is undergoing an electroencephalogram (EEG), a test that measures the electrical impulses generated by the brain. EEGs help phychologists learn about the relationship between these brain waves and behavior and aid health professionals in diagnosing physiological disorders.

the material that was presented during the *waking* periods. In contrast, there is no evidence that learning took place during the periods when the EEG records indicated sleep. It appears safe to conclude from this study that learning does not take place during sleep; it occurs only during the waking portions of the sleep cycle. The advertisement that promises to teach you while you sleep may be accurate but for the wrong reasons: It may, indeed, teach you, but only if it succeeds in disturbing your sleep sufficiently to keep you awake!

We have gone to some pains to present this illustration of the experimental method. Unlike the other methods we will discuss, the experimental method permits us to control the variables that affect behavior. A **variable** is a characteristic or phenomenon that may take on different values. For example, in the experiment we just discussed, both the level of sleep and the scores on the learning task are variables, for both may take on different values. Many variables affect behavior at any given time. The experimental method permits us to study systematically a single variable at a time (in this case, the level of sleep) to determine what effect it has on observed behavior (here, the learning scores).

The variable that is examined to determine its effects on behavior is called the **independent variable.** The behavior that is being observed and measured is known as the **dependent variable.** In the previously cited example, the level of sleep is the independent variable, and the learning score is the dependent variable. When experimental manipulations of the independent variable leads to consistent changes in the dependent variable, we are usually able to draw strong conclusions, such as, "Changes in the independent variable cause changes in the dependent variable." For example, changes in hunger cause changes in the activity level; ad-

**Variable**
A characteristic or phenomenon that may take on different values.

**Independent variable**
A variable that is examined in order to determine its effects on behavior (the dependent variable).

**Dependent variable**
Behavior that is being observed and measured that depends upon changes in the independent variable.

**Organismic variable**
Such naturally occurring characteristics of the organism as sleep levels, age, and gender.

**Sample**
That part of a population (all possible subjects) selected for study.

**Experimental group**
In an experiment, that group of subjects given the independent variable.

**Control group**
In an experiment, that group of subjects *not* given the independent variable.

**Placebo**
An inactive substance used instead of an active substance and given to the control group in an experiment.

**Double blind**
An experimental design in which neither the experimenter nor the subjects know what treatment is being administered.

**Placebo effect**
An improvement or change resulting from faith or belief that a given substance has curative powers.

ministration of a tranquilizer causes the anxiety level to decrease; or the degree of task difficulty causes us to take more time to complete a task.

The independent variable is usually some aspect of the environment that can be manipulated—for instance, the intensity of the light, the number of practice trials in a learning task, or the dosage level of a drug. The independent variable can also be a naturally occurring characteristic of the organism—sleep levels, gender, or age, for example. We refer to these naturally occurring characteristics as **organismic variables.** The dependent variable, however, is always some measurable aspect of behavior. See Table 1.1 for a listing of representative independent and dependent variables used in psychological experiments.

Another example might serve to clarify the elements of an experiment. Surely you have heard commercials on television making claims such as "Nimbos have been proven clinically effective in the treatment of nagging back ailments." On what basis might this claim be made?

Let's start out by using Nimbos as an example and see how we might evaluate its effectiveness. First, we identify a **sample** of people with chronically aching backs. We *randomly* assign half the patients to the **experimental group** that receives the independent variable (Nimbos). The remaining half of the subjects are assigned to the **control group** that receives a **placebo,** an inactive ingredient that appears to be the same as the drug being tested. We also employ a **double blind** study in which neither we nor the subjects know what treatment is being administered. The purpose of the double blind aspect of the study is to defeat the **placebo effect,** an improvement resulting from faith or belief that a given substance has curative powers. Subsequent testing reveals that the individuals getting the drug actually experienced relief from pain in the lower back, whereas relatively few of the subjects in the placebo or control group evidenced similar relief. Moreover, an analysis of the probabilities

Table 1.1

**Representative Examples of Variables Used in Psychological Experiments**

| Independent variable | Dependent variable |
| --- | --- |
| Administration of a tranquilizer | A measure of anxiety |
| Amount of freedom of choice in an experimental setting | Locus-of-control score |
| Age at which toilet training begins | Time required to achieve success |
| Hours of deprivation of food | A measure of bodily activity |
| Exposure to a propaganda message | A measure of attitude |
| Noise in an industrial setting | A measure of work efficiency |
| Degree of task difficulty | Amount of time required to learn task |
| Method of instruction | A measure of learning |
| Introduction of a sudden signal, such as a light or sound | Time required to react to the signal |

## BOX 1.4

### Conducting Research

People don't usually do research the way people who write books about research say that people do research. . . . In short, books about research (to mix a metaphor) are white tie and tails, research itself is a pair of blue jeans. . . .

Let me give you a personal example. . . . In research some of my associates and I were doing on verbal behavior in human subjects, we were looking for some sort of reinforcer to use as a reward for speaking. Our subjects were equipped with individual microphones and we were studying the verbal patterns of individuals and of these same individuals in group interaction. They were paid by the hour for this. But it seemed to us, as we were sitting around talking about the experiment, that this was not an adequate reward for our purposes inasmuch as it did not matter how much or how loud the subject spoke during the session. He received the same amount no mat-

ter how much he talked. So we wondered what would happen if we tried to get him to speak louder or faster by rewarding him for such verbalization. Recognizing that money is a very good reward in our culture, we decided that it would be a fine idea to see what would happen if we paid the subject in money as he was speaking, so that each impulse spoken into the microphone would be rewarded. What would happen if we paid him by the spoken impulse? We thought that a coin dropping into a chute each time he spoke above a certain amplitude would be a good reinforcer to produce and maintain such behavior.

But then we started counting up the number of such impulses during an hour session and found that there would be several hundred. It would be financially impossible to use coins unless we were to use pennies. In the couse of this informal discussion, it was decided that pennies are not really very good rewards in our culture because of an informal test which everyone has experienced. Even a $25,000-a-year executive is likely to stoop down and pick up a nickel if

forces us to the conclusion that the higher improvement rate of the experimental subjects was not likely to be due to chance factors. To our satisfaction and that of our fellow scientists, we feel justified in claiming that the drug is effective.

Box 1.4 presents some interesting sidelights on the way in which research is sometimes conducted.

### Naturalistic Observation

Naturalistic or field studies involve careful observations of behavior in a natural setting. Although there is usually no attempt to manipulate the situation systematically, this form of observation is by no means casual. Much prior thought must be devoted to such questions as: What behaviors shall I study? How shall I record the observations? What are the characteristics or features of the situation in which I shall do the observing? **Naturalistic observation** has been employed in the study of both animal and human behavior. Because the subject is usually unaware of the observer (or the observer is made as unobtrusive as possible), we may assume that the behavior is not affected by the presence of the observer. This technique is illustrated by Fig. 1.2.

Notable success has been achieved with this method in the study of animals and insects in their natural environments. The results of these observations have often contradicted popular beliefs. For example, do

**Naturalistic observation**
A scientific method that involves careful observations of behavior in a natural setting.

he sees it, but is likely to pass a penny by. There seems to be more than five times the rewarding value of a penny on a nickel. So the minimum successful financial reward in the form of a coin would probably be a nickel. This would become so expensive as a reward in such an experiment that if we did use the nickel the chances are the experimenters would try to change places with the subject!

Someone suggested that we might try using poker chips which the subjects could exchange for money at the end of the session. In this way they would be working for a symbolic monetary reward, which is very strongly reinforced in our culture. We talked about the meaning of poker chips and the images that poker chips conjured up in the minds of various people in a group. Stacks of poker chips in front of a gambler in a smoke-filled room and the various dramatic associations of poker chips in the folklore of our culture were discussed. Of course there was a lot of joking about this and someone wanted to know if we would have to wear green eyeshades and roll up

our sleeves and put garters on them, whether we would have to use a round table for the experiment with a green felt cloth over it and so on, invoking the humor of the gambling situation. We finally decided to use chips.

The above account is merely a capsule record of the many hours of discussion on an informal level which went on during this particular part of the experiment. When the paper was finally written up for publication in professional journals, it merely reported that "because of the generalized reinforcing nature of poker chips, they were used as a reinforcement for verbal behavior as a substitute for monetary reward (but symbolic of such secondary monetary reinforcement) and to be exchanged for money." Nothing about the green eyeshade, the green felt cloth, the sleeve-garters, the smoke-filled room—remarks which would be inappropriate for a scientific paper.

you believe that the gorilla is a hostile, aggressive, combative animal? This commonly held view is contrary to evidence compiled from Schaller's observations of the mountain gorilla in its natural habitat:

> *My technique of habituating the gorillas was simple but essential, for I could only obtain unbiased data on their behavior if they remained relatively unaffected by my presence. I usually attemped to approach the group undetected to within about 150 feet before climbing slowly and in full view of the animals onto a stump or the low branch of a tree where I settled myself as comfortably as possible without paying obvious attention to them. By choosing a prominent observation post not only was I able to see the gorillas over the screen of herbs, but, reciprocally, they could inspect me clearly, which was the most important single factor in habituating the animals. Under such circumstances they usually remained in the vicinity to watch me, and even approached me to within 5 feet. I found it remarkably easy to establish rapport with the gorillas. This process was greatly facilitated by the placid temperament of the animals, and by certain conditions which I imposed on myself: (a) I carried no firearms which might imbue my actions with unconscious aggressiveness; (b) I moved slowly, and used binoculars and cameras sparingly at the beginning to eliminate gestures which could be interpreted as threat; (c) I nearly always approached them alone, leaving any companions behind and out of sight at the point where the animals were first noted; (d) I*

Figure 1.2
Jane Goodall observed
chimpanzees in the Gombe
Stream Chimpanzee Reserve in
Tanzania, while Hugo van
Lawick kept a careful
photographic record. The entire
staff was very careful not to
disrupt the chimps' lives and
their habitat. In this photo,
Ms. Goodall refrains from
responding to a chimp
searching for bananas under
her shirt.

*wore the same drab olive-green clothes every day; and (e) I almost never
tracked the gorillas after they had voluntarily moved out of range. This
last point was, I believe, of special value, for at no time were they subjected to pursuit, an action which could easily frighten them as well as
increase the chance of attacks. By adhering to my conditions I not only
habituated six groups to my presence quite well but also was never
attacked, even though I inadvertently stumbled into the middle of a
group or nearly collided with animals several times. (Schaller, 1963,
pp. 22–23)*

One of the outstanding examples of the use of this method with humans is found in the study of the linguistic abilities of black children
(Labov, 1972). When tested under standard laboratory conditions by a
"large, friendly, white interviewer," black children typically respond with
inadequate speech. If the same children are studied in their natural environments, however, they reveal a sentence structure and a fullness of
vocabulary that is anything but deficient. It may be argued that any laboratory procedures intended to assess the capability of individuals should
first be checked for their **ecological validity** in a natural setting (Ginsburg
and Koslowski, 1976).

Naturalistic observation is a valuable tool through which we gain information and insights about the behavior of organisms in their natural
settings. Moreover, in the course of these observations, investigators develop hunches about which factors are of critical importance and which
can largely be ignored. Indeed, they may develop certain hypotheses, or
informed guesses, that they will later subject to systematic investigation
in the laboratory.

**Ecological validity**
Taking into account the natural setting in which the behavior being interpreted occurs.

**Case-history method**
Data assembled about the past
history of an individual or
group in order to understand
present behavior.

**Survey method**
A method of collecting data
through the use of interviews
and questions.

## Case-History Method

Often situations arise that require knowledge of the past history of an individual or groups of individuals in order to understand present behavior. This method is commonly employed by clinical psychologists in order to gain insight into a patient's present problems. The following excerpt illustrates the use of the **case-history method** in clinical practice:

> *The patient was the oldest of seven children. For the first five years of her life she had been the only child, indulged and overprotected by her mother. Then came the second child, a girl, and the patient was abruptly cut off from the fondling, petting, praise and attention which had formerly been hers. Later in childhood, the younger sister consistently excelled her in school and made friends more easily than she. In adolescence the sister enjoyed pretty clothes, dancing and the company of boys, which the patient herself characterized as "having a good time in a wicked way." Throughout her life, the patient compared herself unfavorably with her sister, calling herself "dumb," shy and "old-maidish." She had few boy friends, went to college dances alone, and was always critical of any young man who came to call on her. Her fantasies and dreams, however, centered around love affairs, marriage and child-bearing. Her younger sister became engaged and then married six months before the patient came to the clinic—the time at which . . . the patient began her voracious eating. (Cameron and Magaret, 1951, p. 39)*

## Survey Method

The **survey method** is commonly employed when the investigators wish to obtain information from a large number of people in a relatively short period of time. Typically, a set of questions is prepared and attitudes, feelings, or opinions are obtained on some issue through the use of mail, telephone, or direct interview. These questions are constructed with great care so as not to bias the outcome of the survey. For example, there is a great deal of difference between these two questions: "Are you in agreement with the political philosophy of John Doe?" and "Do you agree with the radical left-wing stance of John Doe?" A good survey will avoid questions such as the latter one.

We are all familiar with public opinion surveys of the sort conducted by Gallup and Harris. The results of these polls are regularly reported in newspapers and popular magazines. They provide valuable insights into how segments of the public feel about various current issues, and they inform us of the extent to which the public engages in certain practices. By repeating surveys at different times, it is possible to gauge how attitudes, opinions, beliefs, and practices change over a period of time. For example, a survey taken in 1975 reported that 61 percent of males aged 20 had engaged in sexual intercourse one or more times. If we compare this finding with the results of a similar survey conducted in 1948, which reported that 73 percent of males had had intercourse by age 20, we see evidence of an actual decrease in sexual activity by young men—despite the so-called sexual revolution. But the results of similar surveys of young women in 1953 and 1975 show a quite different trend. Table 1.2 presents the results obtained by these surveys.

Table 1.2

**Percentage of Males and Females Having Intercourse Before Age 20**

|      | Males (in%) | Females (in%) |
|------|-------------|---------------|
| 1953 | 73          | 23            |
| 1975 | 61          | 64            |

Note: Results of surveys show a decrease in the percentage of males having intercourse before the age of 20 but an increase in the percentage of females having intercourse by this age.

Source: Kinsey *et al.*, 1948, 1953; Wilson, 1975.

## Assessing Information Gathered through Psychological Methods

Once information has been gathered through one or more psychological methods, we need means of evaluating that information. Often we must use numbers to describe our information (for example, the number of subjects studied, the number of times a behavior was observed, etc.), and we may need to apply a variety of mathematical formulas to these numbers in order to determine just what those numbers mean and what (if any) conclusions we can draw from our study. Psychologists use **statistics** (see Appendix) to perform such analyses.

## AN APPLICATION OF THE METHODS OF PSYCHOLOGY

**Statistics**
The use of mathematics to describe and analyze information.

Now that we have discussed some methods used to study behavior, let's look at a concrete application of these methods to a specific problem.

Imagine you are the director of rehabilitation at a large medical facility. Each year you receive several patients who have been blinded as a result of industrial accidents. Rehabilitating such individuals is extremely difficult, particularly because of their pervasive sense of helplessness following their loss of sight. You think, "If there were only some way to remove that feeling of helplessness, the process of rehabilitation might be eased." You have heard that people born blind frequently show an extraordinary ability to move about in their dark world and somehow avoid obstacles that lie in their path. You begin to wonder how they accomplish this feat and ask yourself whether their techniques could be taught to people who have lost their sight as a result of accidents. Put your book down for a moment and consider how you would go about determining how blind people are able to avoid obstacles in their path. Then continue reading the text, and compare your approach to the one scientists take.

## Naturalistic Observation

Scientists do not accept commonly held beliefs at face value. A necessary and desirable skepticism underlies their approach to all problems. Scientists would not ask, "How are blind people able to avoid obstacles in their paths?" Instead, they would eliminate the word "how" from the question and would ask, "Are blind people able to avoid obstacles in their paths?"

The scientist's approach to this problem might first involve careful observations of blind people in their natural settings. On the basis of these observations, the scientist would find that blind people do, in fact, successfully avoid obstacles in their paths. Even in naturalistic settings, the investigator may occasionally modify some aspect of the environment in order to test a hunch or hypothesis. For example, unfamiliar obstacles could be placed in the paths of blind people. After repeated observations of their success in avoiding even these obstacles, the investigator would probably be ready to conclude that blind people really possess this ability. Note that the investigator has not explained *how* blind people are able to get around but merely that they are *able* to do so. Typically, naturalistic observations permit us to uncover how people behave but not why they behave as they do.

## Case-History Method

Scientists might approach the preceding problem by studying case histories of people who were blind at birth as well as those blinded later in life. If these studies consistently revealed that the ability to avoid obstacles improved with experience, we might begin to suspect that learning is involved. The following excerpt is from the case history of a young man who had been blind throughout his life and was suddenly thrust into an unfamiliar situation:

> When John J. came to the university, he was completely dependent on others for support and guidance. He had to be led from place to place. One day his newly made friends decided to withdraw this constant support and supervision—they were determined that John "stand on his own two feet." They walked John around various parts of the campus, urging him to memorize directions and numbers of steps between points. In time, John became extremely proficient in moving unaided throughout the entire campus. The remarkable thing about John's accomplishment was that, once he achieved a degree of independence, he was able to successfully avoid collisions even when unfamiliar obstacles appeared in his path. (Author's files)

Case histories can be valuable for generating hunches about why people behave as they do. However, because significant life variables are not manipulated in a controlled fashion, we cannot usually make the strong statements of causality that are possible with experimental research.

## Survey Method

The investigator might possibly gain some insight into the way blind people avoid obstacles by interviewing them. Such a survey was, in fact, conducted in 1923. Soldiers blinded in the war were asked about the ways in which they avoided obstacles. The results were as follows: 25 percent of the soldiers thought that they detected obstacles by the sense of hearing; 25 percent by the sense of touch; and 50 percent by a combination of the two senses.

Although the survey method does not establish cause-and-effect relationships, it may generate ideas for more systematic investigation. The results obtained in this survey revealed that blind people felt that they were avoiding obstacles by using their other senses. These results provided the hypotheses for the experimental studies summarized next.

## Experimental Method

The experimental method permits us to evaluate systematically the effect of selected variables on some dependent measure. The question, "How are blind people able to avoid obstacles in their paths?" was, in fact, answered through an experimental approach (Supa *et al.*, 1944).

In a series of experiments, blind people were systematically deprived of the use of touch, smell, taste, and hearing; and they were then tested for their ability to avoid obstacles. Hearing, for example, was blocked by having the subjects wear earplugs. The deprivation of each sense separately and in succession constituted the independent variable, and the measure of obstacle avoidance was the dependent variable. The results of the study were illuminating. Only when the subjects were deprived of the sense of hearing were they unable to avoid obstacles.

Further experimentation established the precise mechanism that was at work. When blind subjects walked on a carpeted floor in their stocking feet so that their movements made no sounds, their ability to avoid obstacles was seriously impaired. It was concluded that blind people avoid obstacles on the basis of echoes from their own footsteps.

Although this method of avoiding obstacles in a dark world could not be considered normal behavior in sighted humans, research has established that a number of animal species use echoes as a primary means of avoiding obstacles or locating food. The bat, for example, emits a steady stream of high-pitched tones that echo off solid surfaces. The reception of these echoes permits the bat to avoid large objects. By using a similar mechanism, porpoises are able to go directly to food even though the water may be too cloudy for them to see the food directly.

These studies on the avoidance of obstacles both by human subjects and by lower animals illustrate how psychologists, through the use of scientific methods, were able to reach very meaningful conclusions (with significant practical consequences) about this particular aspect of behavior. These conclusions do not necessarily correspond to "common sense."

## Summary

1. Psychology is defined as the science of behavior. Behavior is an all-inclusive term that refers to everything we do.
2. The psychologist's method of inquiry is both objective and systematic.
3. Psychology emerged as a science relatively recently. Formerly, it had been largely in the domain of philosophy. In the mid-1800s, studies concerned primarily with our sensory capabilities paved the way for the scientific study of human beings. E. H. Weber and Gustav Fechner showed that there is a lawful relationship between the magnitudes of stimulation and our ability to detect differences.
4. In 1879, Wilhelm Wundt established the first laboratory for the scientific study of psychological events. Wundt's position, called structuralism, defined psychology as the science of conscious experience. By employing the method of introspection, Wundt tried to discover the basic build-

ing blocks of conscious experiences and the laws that bind these elements together into complex experiences.

5. William James expanded the definition of psychology to include more than conscious experience. He delved into such phenomena as learning, motivation, and emotions. Because he emphasized the functions and structures of the mind in the adaptation of the organism, the school he represented was known as functionalism.

6. J. B. Watson asserted that science must deal only with publicly observable events. Because consciousness and the contents of the mind are, by their very nature, private events, he rejected their study in the science of psychology. Behavior is observable and public, and so it is the only appropriate target for psychological study.

7. The gestalt school of psychology objected to both structuralism and behaviorism, maintaining that complex behavior cannot be analyzed into simple parts and recombined, "Humpty Dumpty" style, to produce meaningful wholes.

8. Sigmund Freud developed psychoanalysis, which was at once a theory of personality, a philosophical view of human nature, and a method for treating disturbed individuals. Psychoanalytic theory stresses sexual factors and unconscious determinants of behavior.

9. In recent years, cognitive psychologists have been raising penetrating questions concerning our thought processes. Humanistic psychologists have emphasized the concept of the self and the role of internal mental states as determinants of behavior.

10. Many subfields of specialization have developed within the field of psychology. Among them are clinical, counseling, developmental, social, school, industrial, and experimental psychology.

11. A major area of interest in psychology today concerns our perception of the controls over our lives. As a result, the various fields of psychology must study the concept of locus of control.

12. Psychologists can employ the following methods of study: the experimental method, naturalistic observation, the case-history method, and the survey method.

13. Because most of what psychologists study cannot be observed directly, it must be inferred from what can be measured. In the typical experimental study, an independent variable is manipulated in order to see how it affects behavior. The independent variable is often some aspect of the environment.

14. Many variables other than the independent variable may affect behavior. The effects of these extraneous variables are usually controlled by dividing the subjects into at least two groups that are comparable with respect to the extraneous variables and that differ only with respect to the independent variable.

## Terms to Remember

| | | |
|---|---|---|
| Pyschology | Clinical psychologist | Experimental group |
| Behavior | Psychiatrist | Control group |
| Objectivity | Psychoanalyst | Placebo |
| Systematic observation | Developmental psychologist | Double blind |
| Empiricism | Social psychologist | Placebo effect |
| Tabula rasa | School psychologist | Naturalistic observation |
| Introspection | Industrial psychologist | Ecological validity |
| Structuralism | Experimental psychologist | Case-history method |
| Functionalism | Experiment | Survey method |
| Behaviorism | Operational definition | Statistics |
| Gestalt psychology | Variable | SQ 3R method |
| Psychoanalysis | Independent variable | Locus of control |
| Cognitive psychology | Dependent variable | External locus of control |
| Humanism | Organismic variable | Internal locus of control |
| Counseling psychologist | Sample | Diffusion of responsibility concept |

**LEARNING**

Compare the following behavior of two very different species. One is the stickleback, a small, freshwater fish commonly found in European rivers and streams; the other is the human being, found in virtually every habitable location on the face of the earth.

During certain times of the year, the male stickleback engages in a complicated series of responses culminating in the construction of a nest in the riverbed. It excavates a hole in the sand bottom, carrying the sand, mouthful by mouthful, to another location to be dumped. When it has hollowed out a depression of about 4 square inches, it collects a mass of weeds and algae, piles this mass over the depression, coats it with a sticky substance secreted by its own kidneys, and shapes the mass into a mound. Finally, the stickleback bores through the material to create a tunnel. It has contructed its nest.

When people build their "nest," they usually first study a set of blueprints. Then they select the materials appropriate to the home they have in mind. A wide selection is available, and they may choose virtually any structural material or combination of materials—bricks, brush, wood, steel, and even ice. Then, step by step, and making careful measurements, they join these materials together to conform to the requirements of the blueprints. When they have finished, the humans, like the stickleback, have produced a habitable structure.

What do the activities of the stickleback and the human have in common? Both are highly complex and skilled performances. Both are directed toward the achievement of a goal—the construction of a habitat. But how do these activities differ? The stickleback's behavior represents *unlearned*, complex patterns of responses characteristic of all male members of the species. These responses vary little from member to member and are presumably inborn. Such behavior is usually described as **instinctive.** What about the behavior of humans? Their behavior is certainly complex, but by no means can we describe it as inborn and unvarying. While lower organisms adapt to their environment largely through instinctive behaviors, higher animals, particularly humans, cope with the demands of their environment primarily through *learned* modes of adjustment.

## WHAT IS LEARNING?

We all use the word **"learning"** on many different occasions. Yet if you were to ask for a definition of this word, you would probably get as many different answers as the number of people you asked. Psychologists generally define learning as a relatively permanent change in behavior resulting from experience or practice. Note the two qualifying parts of this definition: The behavioral change must be *relatively permanent,* and it must *result from experience or practice.* These qualifications are necessary in order to exclude changes in behavior that do not result from learning.

Let's consider the first qualification, that a relatively permanent change be produced. This excludes from the definition any changes in behavior due to temporary conditions resulting from motivation, fatigue, illness, or the use of drugs.

(a)

(b)

If you've seen one gannet's nest, you've seen them all. Why is this not true of humans' "nests"? (a) Instinctive nest building. (b) Learned nest building.

**Instinctive behavior**
Unlearned patterns of behavior characteristic of every member of a species or every member of a sex within a species. The behavior appears to be inherited and conforms to a complex, fixed pattern.

**Learning**
A relatively permanent change in behavior resulting from experience or practice.

**Construct**
A term that refers to a set of ideas, not directly observed, by which we organize and interpret the world. Many of the terms used in psychology are constructs. For example, learning, attitude, personality, and intelligence are not directly observed; but we use these terms to organize the ways we think about people and events.

The second qualification in the generally accepted definition of learning is that changes in behavior must result from experience or practice. This rules out changes due to biological growth, accident, or disease. It should be noted that we do not necessarily profit from this practice or experience. Are you profiting from experience when you learn to smoke or to bite your nails? We learn poor study habits just as we learn good ones. Children may learn to cry or to throw tantrums to gain attention, just as they may learn to behave in a way the parents find more desirable. Thus learning may have undesirable as well as desirable consequences. As we shall see in later chapters, we learn to hate as well as to love; we learn distorted as well as accurate ways of perceiving the world; we learn prejudice as well as tolerance; and we learn how to get "high."

We ought to point out here that learning is a **construct.** We can never directly observe learning; we can only infer it from some measure of performance. For example, from your performance on a test, your instructor may infer how much you have learned in class and from your reading over the past few weeks. The distinction between observed performance and inferred learning is extremely important and will reappear throughout this book. Although we are completely dependent on performance measures as the basis for inferring learning, we must recognize that other factors beside learning may affect performance. We are left with an interesting paradox: Performance that shows a change in behavior resulting from experience permits us to conclude that some learning has taken place; failure to perform does not necessarily mean that no learning has taken place. Many students have had the experience of "bombing" on a test for which they felt prepared. Such temporary factors as lack of sleep,

We all learn through experience and practice. Imitation is one important part of the learning process.

the influence of drugs, or an intolerably high state of anxiety may impede performance, even though learning has occurred.

Try to imagine what life would be like if you were totally incapable of learning. Without learning—and its companion, memory—every situation you encountered would be completely new and alien. You would never be able to profit from experience and would make the same mistakes over and over again. You could never recognize places, people, or things, no matter how frequently you were exposed to them. You could accomplish nothing. Thought would be impossible, and so would language. Past and future would be meaningless terms. The beauty of the arts and the stimulation of the sciences would be beyond your reach. You could never even learn to avoid the common dangers of everyday existence. On the other hand, you would escape the many tensions and anxieties that are the lot of the civilized human being.

It is no exaggeration to say that learning is so pervasive that it influences every aspect of our lives. Even turning the pages of this book, an activity we tend to take for granted, requires that we learn to coordinate and integrate a complex pattern of muscle movements.

Clearly, an understanding of the principles of learning is basic to the study of human behavior. We learn our attitudes, likes and dislikes, fears, and emotions. We learn how to perceive and react to the environment around and within us. This chapter deals with some of the basic principles and forms of learning. It will provide a foundation for appreciating more fully the following chapters, which deal with such topics as emotions, personality, mental illness, and social behavior.

## CLASSICAL CONDITIONING

**Physiology**
The study of functions of bodily systems.

**Classical conditioning (Pavlovian conditioning)**
A type of learning in which a previously neutral stimulus, through repeated pairings with an unconditioned stimulus, acquires the capacity to evoke the response originally made to the unconditioned stimulus.

In the late 1890s a Russian physiologist, Ivan Pavlov, was engaged in the most exhaustive studies of the digestive system undertaken to that date. For this work, he received the Nobel Prize in **physiology.** During the course of his investigations he developed surgical techniques that permitted the direct observation of many digestive processes. A simple operation on a dog's cheek enabled him to expose part of the salivary gland and to collect and measure saliva produced under varying experimental conditions. While he conducted his experiments, he noted that the dogs salivated not only in response to the presence of food in their mouths but also to the sight of food, the sound of the food trays, and even the approach of the experimenter. This observation in itself is not unusual. You may have noticed that the sight of food, the rattling of dishes, or even the mention of food may increase your flow of saliva. What made Pavlov's observations important was his recognition that he was observing two different situations that gave rise to salivation. What, you may ask, could possibly be the significance of distinguishing between salivation to food and to the sight and sound of food trays? Salivation to food in the mouth is an inborn, unlearned response. But there is no inborn association between salivation and the sight and sound of food trays. The latter case must therefore involve some form of learning.

Let's look at another example, which may be quite familiar to you. Have you ever had an instructor with the annoying and exasperating habit of screeching the chalk while writing on the chalkboard? Did this screeching make you cringe and give you gooseflesh? If so, you may have found that after a while you would cringe and get gooseflesh at the mere sight of the instructor approaching the chalkboard. In this example we see several key elements of the learning process. You will recall that we defined learning as a change in behavior that results from experience. We can safely assume—we hope—that the sight of this instructor *initially* did not have you "climbing the walls." Therefore, the change in your behavior must have occurred as a result of your experience with the instructor's annoying habit.

Both of these examples involve a type of learning known as **classical conditioning.** Because Ivan Pavlov pioneered the investigation of this relatively simple form of learning, it is frequently referred to as Pavlovian conditioning. Let's look at a typical example of Pavlov's work in order to illustrate both the techniques employed in classical conditioning and the learning principles that have emerged.

## Conditioning Procedure and Acquisition

The apparatus that Pavlov used is shown in Fig. 2.1. In the typical experimental situation, a hungry dog is placed in the apparatus. If a stimulus such as the ticking of a metronome (a device used by musicians to establish tempo) is presented to the animal, it will prick up its ears, but it will not salivate. This is not surprising, because a dog does not ordinarily salivate to the sound of a metronome. Yet when meat powder is placed in the dog's mouth, its saliva flows freely.

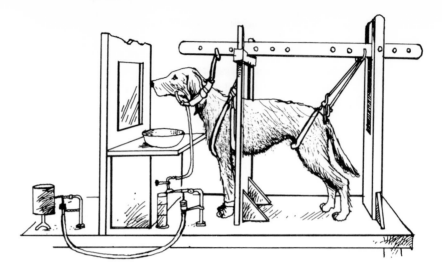

Figure 2.1
**Apparatus used by Pavlov for conditioning salivation in a dog**

Note the main features of the experimental setting. The dog is in a restraining harness that prevents it from seeing events other than those specifically selected by the experimenter. The tube runs from its salivary glands into a graduated cylinder and permits a precise measurement of the saliva. The experimenters can view the dog's behavior through a one-way mirror and deliver food and selected stimuli by remote control. Thus distractions within the chamber are minimized.

Pavlov systematically attempted to connect the salivary response to the sound of the metronome. First, he placed food in the dog's mouth while the metronome was beating. The dog, of course, salivated because food was present in its mouth. After several pairings of these two stimuli, Pavlov sounded the metronome but did not present any food. The dog salivated to the sound of the metronome alone (Pavlov, 1927). Thus the dog *learned* to salivate to the sound of the metronome.

Let's look at the essential elements of the classical conditioning process as it applies to the preceding example. Because the food naturally and automatically elicits salivation, we refer to the food as the **uncondi-**

Figure 2.2
**Classical conditioning**

In order for classical conditioning to take place, there must be (1) an unconditioned stimulus (US) that elicits an unconditioned response (UR); (2) a neutral stimulus that does not initially elicit the unconditioned response; and (3) a pairing of the neutral stimulus and the unconditioned stimulus. After repeated pairings of these two stimuli, the neutral stimulus gradually acquires the capacity to evoke the desired response. We now refer to the originally neutral stimulus as the conditioned stimulus (CS) and the obtained response as the conditioned response (CR).

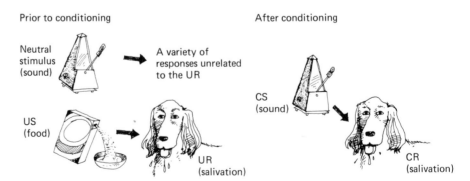

Prior to conditioning

Neutral stimulus (sound) → A variety of responses unrelated to the UR

US (food) → UR (salivation)

After conditioning

CS (sound) → CR (salivation)

**Unconditioned stimulus (US)**
A stimulus that naturally and automatically elicits an unconditioned response.

**Unconditioned response (UR)**
A response that automatically occurs to an unconditioned stimulus without any learning being required.

**Conditioned stimulus (CS)**
A stimulus that, through repeated pairings with an unconditioned stimulus (US), acquires the capacity to evoke a response it did not originally evoke.

**Conditioned response (CR)**
The learned response to a conditioned stimulus.

tioned stimulus (US). The salivation in response to the meat powder, which occurs automatically without any learning, is called the **unconditioned response (UR).** The sound of the metronome, however, is *neutral* with respect to the salivary response, for it does not naturally elicit the UR. We say that conditioning has occurred when the previously neutral stimulus acquires the capacity to evoke salivation. The previously neutral stimulus (the sound of the metronome) is then called the **conditioned stimulus (CS),** and the salivation that occurs to the sound of the metronome is known as the **conditioned response (CR).** Figure 2.2 is a diagram of the classical conditioning process.

The period during which the organism learns the association between the US and the CS is called the **acquisition** stage of conditioning, and each pairing of the CS and US is customarily called an "acquisition trial." Response to the CS increases rapidly during early acquisition trials and remains relatively stable thereafter.

## Extinction and Spontaneous Recovery

**Acquisition**
The stage of conditioning during which the organism learns the association between the US and the CS.

**Extinction**
The reduction in response that occurs in classical conditioning when the conditioned stimulus (CS) is presented *without* the unconditioned stimulus (US).

**Spontaneous recovery**
The recurrence of the previously extinguished conditioned response following a rest period.

We have seen that conditioning involves the association of a response (CR) with a previously neutral stimulus (CS). One of the ways to test for the acquisition of this response is to present the CS alone, without the US. What do you suppose would happen if we continued to present the CS alone? Do you think the animal would continue to salivate indefinitely? Pavlov investigated this question in the following way: He took an animal that had acquired the conditioned salivary response to a conditioned stimulus (in this example, a light) and repeatedly presented the light alone. Each time Pavlov presented the CS alone (a procedure that is called an **extinction** trial), the dog's secretion of saliva diminished. Note that as the extinction trials were repeated, the conditioned response continued to decrease in strength.

What happens to a conditioned response after it has been extinguished? Has it been forgotten or wiped out in some way? Apparently not. There are two lines of evidence bearing on this question. First, if a rest period is introduced following the extinction of a conditioned response and the CS is then presented again, the response will show evidence of recovery. This recovery of the previously extinguished CR following a rest period is called **spontaneous recovery.** It will require several more extinction trials to bring the response down to zero again. If another rest period is then introduced, a smaller degree of recovery will occur.

The second line of evidence involves the time required in order to recondition the response. After a conditioned response has been successfully extinguished and we begin conditioning trials all over again (that is, we pair the CS and the US), it requires less time to reestablish the response than was needed for the original conditioning. In the typical situation, very few trials are required to bring the conditioned response back to full strength. The relationship among acquisition, experimental extinction, spontaneous recovery, and reconditioning is shown in Fig. 2.3.

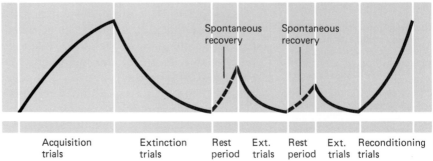

Strength
of
response

| Acquisition trials | Extinction trials | Rest period | Ext. trials | Rest period | Ext. trials | Reconditioning trials |

Spontaneous recovery        Spontaneous recovery

Figure 2.3
**Establishing and changing conditioned responses**

**Note that spontaneous recovery occurs during the rest period and is less after each extinction period. Note also that the CR is quickly reinstated when the CS and US are again paired (reconditioning trials).**

What does this mean in real life? In short, once you have extinguished either a desirable or an undesirable conditioned response, you must be prepared for the possibility that it will recover unexpectedly. If your love for a person has been partially extinguished over a period of time, do not be surprised if it undergoes spontaneous recovery after separation (absence sometimes really does make the heart grow fonder). When you have conquered fear in a given situation, you should not be surprised if it returns at a later date. Patients in therapy often experience temporary setbacks when former fears, anxieties, or hostilities return. Fortunately, spontaneous recovery is at a lower intensity, and so extinction can usually proceed fairly rapidly. The critical factor is whether or not later experiences continue the extinction process or reintroduce the US. If the US is again introduced, classical conditioning of the response has resumed. If a fear of snakes spontaneously recovers and the person is then bitten by a snake, the setback may be longer than temporary.

## Stimulus Generalization

It is difficult to trace the origin of many of our learned emotional reactions. For example, suppose that a child, seeing a horse for the very first time, begins to whimper, cry, and show other signs of acute emotional distress. How would you explain this behavior? Does the sight of a horse automatically elicit fear in young children? This is not likely. The child must somehow have learned the association. Suppose you find out that this child had previously been bitten by a dog. Does this additional information shed any light on the origin of the child's fear of the horse? In a word, yes. Almost a century of research has established a phenomenon known as stimulus generalization.

Once we are conditioned to a specific stimulus or stimulus situation, we tend to make the conditioned response to similar stimuli. This phenomenon, known as **stimulus generalization,** is extremely important in understanding how emotional responses spread from one stimulus situation to another. A child bitten by a dog or scratched by a cat, thereafter is likely to be afraid of all dogs or cats and, to a lesser extent, even all four-legged, furry creatures.

Not all learned emotional reactions are aversive in nature. Suppose that you enjoy the company of a particular person. It is quite possible that your positive feelings could be conditioned to a previously neutral stimulus, for example, a song that you both adopted as "our song." Thus even in that person's absence, the song could come to evoke pleasant feelings. If we have experienced pleasant emotions in one setting, we will find that similar situations also elicit pleasant emotions. The more similar the new stimuli are to the original conditioned stimulus, the greater the intensity of the reaction will be. The fact that the intensity of the behavior generally decreases as the new stimuli become less similar to the original CS can be seen in many real-life situations. For example, suppose that a girl's father is domineering, overly strict, and generally mean to her. He is a highly competitive and successful businesssman whom she views as valuing money more than anything else in life. When she begins to select male companions in her teenage years, she may show a distinct aversion to anyone who appears highly committed to materialistic goals. The less materialistic the boy, the less aversion she may feel. Therefore, she may develop a marked penchant for unambitious, nonmaterialistic young men—the very opposite of her father. Figure 2.4 illustrates the generalization of feelings and emotions from the original conditioned stimulus to similar stimuli.

Have you ever been in a totally new setting and felt overwhelmed by the feeling that you had been there before? "I know I have not been here before, but this strange feeling tells me I have." The experience is rather eerie and may start you wondering about the possibility of a previous existence. Actually this been-there-before feeling is so common that there is a name for it—déjà vu, which means "previously seen." The déjà vu feeling can be explained, at least in part, as a form of generalization. The new situation has some elements that are similar to others you have experienced over a lifetime. This is not surprising, for we undoubtedly encounter untold billions of stimulus situations in a lifetime. These generalized stimuli elicit the emotional responses and feeling tones you previously had learned. You recognize that you have had these feelings before, but you are unable to recall the situations in which they were originally experienced. Unable to account for this sense of having been there, you start looking elsewhere, including the realm of the psychic, for an explanation of the "mystery."

**Stimulus generalization**
Once an organism has learned to associate a given behavior with a specific stimulus, it tends to show this behavior toward similar stimuli.

**Semantically related**
Stimuli are semantically related if the words representing them share similar meanings (for example, "like" and "love," "dislike" and "hate").

An additional point is important. At the human level, the generalized stimuli need not be *physically* similar to the conditioned stimulus. Generalization can also occur when stimuli are symbolically or **semantically related** to the conditioned stimulus. Many contemporary parents respond negatively to "punk rock." Through semantic generalization, they may also look with disfavor upon "hard rock" or just plain "rock." In the following classic case, a young woman acquired a fear of church bells through direct conditioning. However, through semantic and symbolic generalization, her fear spread to concepts, events, and objects that were associated with and reminded her of churches and church bells.

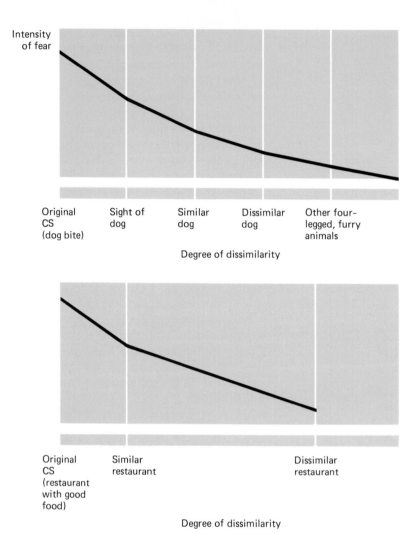

Figure 2.4   Feelings and emotions conditioned to one situation generalize to similar situations. Thus fear at the sight of a dog, based on prior experience with a dog bite, spreads to other dogs and even to four-legged, furry animals in general. Similarly, pleasant feelings evoked by one restaurant may generalize to other restaurants.

*A patient came to her therapist with complaints of a disabling and uncontrollable fear of church bells and church towers. Indeed, she could not even walk past a church when the bells were silent and there was no danger of their sounding as she passed. In a word, her fear had spread to other stimuli associated with church bells and church towers. She had no explanation for this mysterious and crippling fear. During the course of therapy, she recalled the event that caused her emotional turmoil. Earlier in her life, as her mother underwent serious surgery, the patient waited in a hotel room for the news of her progress. The daughter was in a state of extreme agitation, unreasonably blaming herself for her mother's illness. Looking out the window of the room, she viewed a church tower in which the bells pealed every fifteen minutes. When she received word of her mother's death, her guilt and anxiety became conditioned to the bells and tower. Through symbolic generalization, she became fearful of churches and other things associated with churches. It required additional therapy before she would accept the fact that she was in no way responsible for her mother's death. When she did, her anxiety attacks ceased. (Prince, 1921)*

Without generalization, learning would be meaningless. Because no two situations or stimuli are ever identical, we would be forced to learn a new response to every new situation. Imagine the difficulty an infant would have in learning to recognize his or her own mother. Without generalization, every time she appeared in a new outfit or hairstyle, she would be strange and unfamiliar. Clearly, the ability to generalize has adaptive value. For example, it is desirable that a child who has learned to be afraid of fire in a specific situation should generalize this response to other situations. There are many situations, however, in which we must inhibit the tendency to generalize. For example, it is not desirable that we respond in the same way to all people who wear pants, to everyone with long hair, or to all cards in a deck. Learning to make distinctions among similar stimuli is known as **discrimination** learning.

**Discrimination**
Learning to respond differentially to similar stimuli.

## Discrimination Learning

It is often observed that a child who has learned to fear a hot stove will generalize this response to similar stimuli (that is, to *all* stoves). This generalization occurs spontaneously. The only way the child will narrow down this response is through learning to discriminate between hot stoves and cold stoves.

As people mature, they learn to discriminate. One might observe, for instance, that a great variety of people—not all of the same sex— wear skirts. (a) In the movie *Some Like It Hot,* Tony Curtis and Jack Lemmon donned dresses and joined an all-female band in an attempt to elude the mobsters on their trail. (b) On their honeymoon at Balmoral in Scotland, Prince Charles and Princess Diana both wore skirts. Prince Charles's kilt is the traditional costume for men of the royal family during stays in Scotland; Britons consider it a very masculine garment, a symbol of virility and strength. (c) Pope John Paul II in the long white gown that has long been traditional papal dress.

(a)　　　　(b)　　　　(c)

Ellipse

Circle

**Figure 2.5**
**Stimuli used in
discrimination training**

When the ellipse closely
resembled the circle (the shorter
axis was eight-ninths as long as
the longer axis), the dog could
no longer discriminate.
Continued presentations led to
behavior that Pavlov described
as "experimental neurosis."

This type of learning, whether it occurs in a natural setting or in a laboratory situation, involves the techniques employed in both acquisition and extinction training. The subject learns to respond (with fear, for example) to one stimulus, the *positive* stimulus (the hot stove), and to inhibit that response to a similar stimulus, the *negative* stimulus (a cold stove). In discrimination learning, the US (pain) is associated with the positive stimulus and not with the negative stimulus. In a laboratory situation, this type of training is accomplished by pairing the positive stimulus with the US throughout training and by withholding the US when the negative stimulus is presented. By the use of these procedures, many organisms, including humans, have been trained to discriminate between similar stimuli.

In discrimination training, the subject tends to respond to the negative stimulus as a result of stimulus generalization. Thus the more similar the two stimuli are to each other, the more difficult the discrimination training is. When the two stimuli are extremely similar, discrimination behavior may break down, and the subject's behavior may change dramatically. Pavlov first noted this phenomenon in the course of training a dog to discriminate between an ellipse, which is an oval, and a circle (Pavlov, 1927). When the circle and the ellipse were markedly different, the discrimination was readily acquired. Pavlov then gradually changed the shape of the ellipse to resemble the circle more closely. When the ratio of the axes was 9:8 (see Fig. 2.5)—that is, when the ellipse was 9 units high by 8 units across, or 8 units high by 9 across—the dog could no longer discriminate. It then salivated to both stimuli. Continued presentations led to further deterioration of performance, culminating in behavior which Pavlov described as **"experimental neurosis."** Whereas the dog previously had been compliant and placid, it now barked violently, wriggled about, and bit its restraining harness. This phenomenon has since been observed in a variety of different species, including humans. For example, a father may encourage his child to sit on his lap. As a consequence, the child may develop positive emotional reactions to his father. But attempting to crawl onto the father's lap while the father is driving a car may lead to a severe reprimand, and the reprimand will produce fear in the child. To the father, these two situations are clearly different. The child, however, may find it difficult, if not impossible, to discriminate between these similar situations. Repetition of similar incidents may leave the child confused when in the presence of the father.

## Higher-Order Conditioning

Another phenomenon of considerable practical and theoretical significance is **higher-order conditioning.** As we have already discussed, in the typical classical conditioning experiment, a response (CR) is conditioned to a previously neutral stimulus. This conditioning is accomplished by pairing the neutral stimulus with a US that consistently elicits the desired response. In higher-order conditioning, a previously conditioned stimulus is employed in much the same way as the US.

An experimental demonstration of this phenomenon is found in Pavlov's work. In the first stage of the experiment, a dog was conditioned to

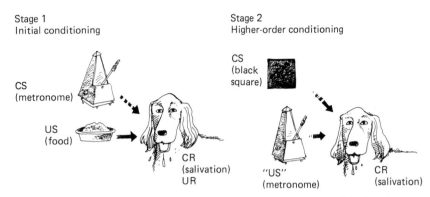

Stage 1
Initial conditioning

Stage 2
Higher-order conditioning

CS
(metronome)

US
(food)

CR
(salivation)
UR

CS
(black
square)

"US"
(metronome)

CR
(salivation)

**Figure 2.6**
**Higher-order conditioning**

Schematic diagram of the two stages in establishing higher-order conditioning. The quotation marks around the US in stage 2 indicate that the metronome is now acting like an unconditioned stimulus.

**Experimental neurosis**
Disturbed behavior in animals that results when they are required to make extremely difficult discriminations.

**Higher-order conditioning**
Conditioning of a response to a stimulus by pairing the neutral stimulus with another stimulus that was previously conditioned to elicit the response.

salivate (CR) at the sound of a metronome. The metronome, which was originally the CS, served as the US in the second stage of this experiment. Recall that an unconditioned stimulus regularly elicits the desired response without prior training. As a result of training during the first stage, the metronome now regularly elicited salivation. In the second stage, the black square served as the CS, and the metronome as the US. Figure 2.6 shows a diagram of both stages in the establishment of higher-order conditioning.

You might suppose that higher-order conditioning could be carried out ad infinitum. In other words, it might seem reasonable to use the black square as a US to condition another stimulus to salivation, and then use this new stimulus to condition still another stimulus, and so on. This process is, however, limited to only two or three additional CSs, for at each additional stage of conditioning, the metronome's power to elicit salivation undergoes experimental extinction.

**Practical Implications of Classical Conditioning**

You may have noticed that all of our examples of classical conditioning have involved the conditioning of some naturally occurring response to various stimuli (for example, salivation to food in mouth; fear to a sudden, loud noise). It should be clear that stress and nonstress reactions can both be conditioned to virtually any stimulus that precedes their occurrence. Many emotional disorders may be the result of accidental pairing of some neutral stimulus and an emotional response. Through generalization and higher-order conditioning, emotional disorders can become conditioned to a wide variety of stimuli. It is believed that many unreasonable and irrational fears (phobias) arise in just this way. The following example illustrates these points:

> . . . the man . . . feared red skies at evening. Like most phobic persons, this patient was unable to explain why red skies had come to be anxiety-provoking for him. Only after expert behavioral analysis did he recall that

*as a boy he had been terrified at the red flames of a tenement fire in which he had thought at the time his mother was being burned to death. (Cameron and Magaret, 1951, p. 313)*

Using the principles discussed in this chapter, how can we explain the man's seemingly irrational fear of red skies? We might speculate that the thought of losing his mother acted as a US that evoked terror. This US was immediately preceded by the sight of the fire. Thus after a single pairing, the fire (CS) acquired the capacity to elicit this strong emotional response. Finally, through generalization, the man came to fear red skies because they resemble fire.

Single-trial classical conditioning is not common. However, when the US is capable of eliciting a strong emotional response, it can and does occur. One of the authors can well remember when, as a boy, he tried one of his father's cigars. The experience burned such a bitter taste in his memory that the mere thought of a cigar still evokes unpleasant feelings.

Experimental extinction is used in many real-life situations to reduce the impact of the acquisition of such negative emotional states as fear, anxiety, or guilt. However, this is not as readily accomplished as the extinction of a salivary response. The reason for this is that we tend to avoid situations that produce undesirable feelings and emotions. To illustrate, imagine that you have a great fear of speaking in public. What do you suppose you would do if you were asked to join an organization that requires you to address various community groups? In all likelihood, you would decline the invitation. This is a serious problem with fear and guilt, for these emotions drive us away from the very situations that would enable us to overcome them. We fear an approaching test, so we cut class; we feel guilty about the way we treated a friend, so we avoid situations that might bring us into face-to-face contact; we fear snakes, scorpions, and tarantulas, so we stay away from the desert. In each case, the emotional state continues to "protect itself" against engaging in the very behavior that could extinguish it.

What can we do under such circumstances? One technique, called **desensitization** therapy, combines stimulus generalization with experimental extinction. Although it doesn't work with everybody, it can claim considerable success in helping people who are overcome by irrational fears, anxiety, guilt, or other negative emotional states. Let's see how this works.

Mark A. is terrified of snakes. He can't go near a zoo because they keep those crawly reptiles in glass cages. In fact, even the thought of them sends shivers up and down his spine. He is not happy about the whole situation. He is acutely aware of the camping, fishing, and boating trips he has missed and will continue to miss unless he can bring his fear under control. A friend advises him to see a **behavior therapist.** He does, and his life changes.

At first, however, he is skeptical. The therapist tells him to imagine standing outside a room that contains a live snake. He shudders a bit but complies with the request. Notice that Mark is not suddenly thrust into a pit of snakes. Imagining a snake safely behind locked doors elicits a small amount of fear but not nearly as much as the real thing would. He can

**Desensitization**
A therapeutic technique that involves training an individual to relax in the presence of a situation that previously aroused anxiety or fear.

**Behavior therapy**
A therapeutic technique based primarily on the application of the principles of conditioning to the modification of maladaptive behavior.

**Operant conditioning**
A type of learning in which the response is instrumental in obtaining rewards or in escaping (or avoiding) aversive stimuli.

handle it. In short order, this small amount of fear is extinguished. He next imagines unlocking the door and entering the room containing the snake. This arouses more discomfort. But again he is capable of handling it. The fear aroused by this imagined situation is extinguished. He is now capable of moving a bit closer to the snake in his imagination. Successive extinctions permit him to get closer and closer to the snake in his imagination. Soon he is even able to imagine holding the snake. He has already come a long way toward gaining control over his irrational fear.

Mark next goes through the sequence all over again, except this time it is not in his imagination. He stands outside a room containing a realistic-looking rubber model. He unlocks the door and sees the snake. Bit by bit he is brought to the point where he can handle the rubber snake. Then he starts on the real thing. The therapy will continue until he is able to approach and touch a live snake. He may even reach the point where he is able to pick it up and handle it.

Of course, not all fears are so readily identified and overcome, but the results of behavioral therapy in treating such problems have been impressive. We will discuss this approach in more detail in Chapter 15.

## OPERANT CONDITIONING

We have thus far concerned ourselves exclusively with classically conditioned responses. But not all behavior is classically conditioned. For example, a dog learns to sit up at a signal from its master. It is then rewarded by its master with either food or praise. This is an illustration of **operant conditioning** (also referred to as instrumental learning or instrumental conditioning). How does this situation differ from conditioning a dog to salivate at the sound of a metronome?

In classical conditioning we can specify the US that elicits the response (in this case, salivation). When a dog learns to sit up, what US elicits this response? In this situation, unlike the classical-conditioning situation, we cannot specify the US for the response. The food or praise used as a reward is not the US, for it does not elicit the behavior in the first place. The food or praise *follows* the desired response, whereas in classical conditioning the US (the food that causes the dog to salivate) both precedes and elicits the desired response.

Unlike classical conditioning, in which the response conditioned is often thought of as involuntary, operant conditioning involves behavior in which the individual *operates* on the environment in order to achieve certain goals. The learning in classical conditioning is typically passive. Because of events over which we may exercise little or no control, we become fearful of certain things and favorably inclined toward others. In contrast, operant conditioning involves motivation, active pursuit of goals, and reinforcements. Note that a specific unconditioned stimulus elicits the response in classical conditioning (for example, food in the mouth causes us to salivate). Operant conditioning does not involve a comparable stimulus. We learn to press a button to ring a doorbell, but there is no unconditioned stimulus that naturally causes this bell-pushing behavior. Rather, the likelihood of making the response is influenced by

Table 2.1

**Classical and Operant Conditioning Compared**

| Classical | Operant |
|---|---|
| *Type of response* | |
| Involuntary response that is elicited by a stimulus | Voluntary response that is initiated (emitted) by the organism |
| *Stimulation* | |
| Unconditioned stimulus naturally elicits the unconditioned response | No identifiable unconditioned stimulus |
| Neutral stimulus acquires capacity to elicit conditioned, involuntary response | Voluntary response becomes more probable in the stimulus situation |
| *Nature of reinforcer* | |
| The US is merely the occasion for the UR; it doesn't reinforce the UR | The *presentation* of certain stimuli (e.g., food) increases the probability that the response preceding it will occur; the *removal* of other stimuli (e.g., painful stimulation) increases the probability that the response preceding it will occur |
| *Time relation of response to reinforcer* | |
| The unconditioned stimulus precedes the unconditioned response and causes it to occur again | The reinforcement follows the operant response and increases the likelihood that the response will occur again |

the consequences of the behavior. In other words, we perform acts to get desirable things done and to escape undesirable events or to prevent them from happening. We think of operant responses as being voluntary. Table 2.1 contrasts several of the factors of classical and operant conditioning.

## A Laboratory Model of Operant Conditioning

Have you ever attended a county or state fair, a carnival, or a circus and wondered how the animal trainers were able to achieve such precise control over the behavior of their animals? Have you been humiliated by a chicken that you were unable to defeat in a game of tic-tac-toe? Embarrassing? Not really, if you understand what was being done.

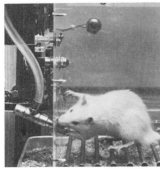

**Figure 2.7**
**A rat in an operant conditioning chamber, an apparatus used to investigate operant learning**

When the rat depresses the bar, a pellet of food or a drop of water is automatically released.

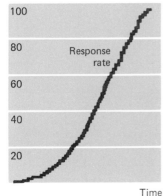

Cumulative responses

Response rate

Time

**Figure 2.8**
**Cumulative record of a rat's response as it occurred in the operant conditioning chamber**

A rat deprived of food for 30 hours at first pressed the food lever only by accident. As it learned the connection between the lever and food, the rat's rate of response accelerated, producing the steep slope shown.

But before we turn our attention to the case of the high-IQ chicken, let's observe the procedures by which operant behavior is established in laboratory animals. First the animal is placed in an operant conditioning chamber, an apparatus that provides a minimum of distracting stimulation. There may be only two features inside—a bar and a receptacle into which pellets of food can be delivered. When sufficient force is exerted on the bar, a food-delivery mechanism is activated. Food is delivered into the receptacle (see Fig. 2.7).

Before an animal is placed in the apparatus, it is deprived of food for a period of time. This assures that the animal is hungry and will, therefore, be sufficiently active to explore the interior of the cage. During this exploratory period, the bar-pressing apparatus may be disconnected from the food-delivery mechanism. This provides a baseline figure for the rate of bar-pressing prior to the introduction of conditioning procedures.

Then the food-delivery mechanism is activated. Now when the bar is pressed, a pellet of food is delivered. If you are observing the proceedings, you will note that some responses are diminished. Thus the animal does not spend much time sniffing and exploring the side of the cage opposite the bar and food receptacle. In fact, it will soon focus almost all of its activity in the area where the food is delivered. Following a few more responses and food rewards, the bar-pressing behavior is well established. The animal will now spend most of its time depressing the bar and consuming food pellets (see Fig. 2.8). In this situation, the bar pressing response is called an *operant*. The word "operant" refers to any activity that operates on an organism's environment to produce a reinforcement. The **reinforcement** is, in turn, an event that strengthens a response that precedes it.

Many studies involving operant conditioning have shown that reinforcement is most effective when it immediately follows the response to be learned. The longer the delay between the response and the reinforcement, the less efficient the learning is. The principle of *immediacy* of reinforcement has many practical implications. If an infant says "da-da" and is rewarded several minutes later, that infant is less likely to learn to repeat "da-da" than if we had provided the reward immediately after the first "da-da." The importance of this principle is often overlooked in many traditional educational settings. If we assume that a good grade serves as a positive reinforcer, then a long delay between the occurrence of the desired behavior (doing well on an exam) and the attainment of the reward (getting the exam back with a good grade) runs counter to the principle of immediate reinforcement. Recent innovations in educational techniques emphasize immediate reinforcement as a means of enhancing the efficiency of the learning process. **Teaching machines, programmed,** and **computer-assisted instruction** are all positive examples of the application of this principle (see Box 2.1)

## Reinforcement

**Positive reinforcement.** There are two types of reinforcers—positive and negative. A **positive reinforcer** strengthens a response by virtue of its presentation. Food following the pressing of a bar and a drink follow-

## BOX 2.1

### Programmed Instruction

Think for a moment about the traditional tools of classroom instruction: the teacher and the textbook. To what extent is either of these geared to take advantage of what we know about learning? In the typical classroom situation, the student is generally a passive recipient of information rather than an active participant in the learning experience. The instructor has little or no control over factors that are vital for effective learning. He or she has no way of ensuring that the

**Figure 2.9**

**Programmed learning**

Work through this program yourself. As you actively participate in the learning experience, note that the program proceeds by finely graded steps. Note also that the material has been prepared in such a way that you will rarely make an error. Moreover, because the correct answer is available, you are provided with immediate knowledge of results.

| | |
|---|---|
| 1 Learning should be fun. <br> However, in the early stages of learning a subject, students often make many errors. <br> Most people (do/do not) like to make errors. | |
| do not <br> 2 When a student makes many errors in learning, he often decides that he does not like the subject. <br> He would be more correct to decide that he does not like to make _____. | |
| errors <br> 3 For a long time, educators, psychologists, and people in general thought it was impossible to learn without making a large number of <u>errors</u>. <br> In fact, they even had a name for this kind of learning. They called it "trial-and-_____" learning. | |
| error <br> 4 Recent developments in the psychology of learning have cast serious doubts as to the necessity of "trial-and-error" learning. If the learning material is carefully prepared, or PROGRAMMED, in a special way, the student can master the subject while making very few errors. The material you are reading right now has been prepared, or _____ in this special way. | |
| programmed <br> 5 The basic idea of programmed learning is that the most efficient, pleasant, and permanent learning takes place when the student proceeds through a course by a large number of small, easy-to-take steps. <br> If each step the student takes is small, he (is/is not) likely to make errors. | |
| is not | |

**Reinforcement**
An event that strengthens the response that precedes or produces it.

**Teaching machine**
A device for presenting programmed instruction.

ing the filling of a glass are both examples of positive reinforcers. The high-IQ chicken that never loses at tic-tac-toe was trained by the use of positive reinforcers. How was it done? With a great deal of skill and a bit of trickery. The chicken was placed in an operant-conditioning chamber. Initially it was trained to peck at the lighted panel situated over the food receptacle. After the response was well established, it was placed in a discrimination-learning situation. In *discrimination* learning, the subject is rewarded when it makes the operant response to one stimulus, whereas

student is paying attention and cannot provide reinforcement when the student has grasped a principle or concept. In general, the typical classroom situation provides little or no reinforcement that is contingent upon the student's responses. With the usual testing situation, reinforcement or feedback is so delayed that it probably has little or no effect on learning. Moreover, the instructor must pace the lecture for the "average" student, thereby boring the brighter student and leaving the slower one behind.

In recent years efforts have been made to overcome the difficulties inherent in the traditional classroom setting. One of the most important developments has been the emergence of programmed instruction, which systematically applies the principles of operant conditioning to the learning situation (see Fig. 2.9).

Several key features characterize programmed instruction. The information is presented in a finely graded series of *small steps*. At each step, the students are required to provide answers to specific questions and thus are actively involved in the learning situation. This *active participation* capitalizes on the advantages of recitation as opposed to passive reading. Moreover, the correct answer appears immediately after each step. Thus the students receive *immediate feedback* on the answer, and this enables them to discover and correct any mistakes they have made. Each step of the program is constructed in such a way that the learners will probably obtain a correct answer. Consequently, they are rewarded at each step along the way. Presumably, this constant reinforcement makes learning a positive and pleasant experience.

Figure 2.9 reproduces part of a learning program designed to teach the elements of programmed learning. In a program of this sort, each student proceeds through every step of the sequence without deviation. A program constructed in this way is called a linear

**Figure 2.10**
**The active participation feature of programmed instruction allows the student to receive immediate feedback.**

program. In contrast, programs that allow students who make errors to branch out to additional and more detailed material are called branching programs. Branching programs take into account wide differences in rates of learning by permitting each student to proceed at his or her own pace. Thus students who make few errors are permitted to go directly through a learning sequence, whereas students who are having difficulty can get the more detailed explanations and steps they need.

Programmed instruction may take a number of different forms. It can be put into book form (as programmed texts) and into teaching machines. It can also be put into a computer; in that case it is called computer-assisted instruction (see Fig. 2.10).

**Programmed instruction**
A method of instruction that systematically applies the principles of operant conditioning to the learning situation.

**Computer-assisted instruction**
Programmed instruction in a computer.

reward is withheld for any response made in the presence of a different stimulus. In other words, it is a combination of acquisition and extinction trials. Thus if the chicken pecked the illuminated panel, it received a grain of food (acquisition). If it pecked when the panel was not illuminated, food was not delivered (extinction). It soon learned to discriminate a lighted panel from an unlighted panel. Then the panel was replaced with another in the form of a tic-tac-toe game. Only one of the nine squares was lighted at a time. The chicken was trained to peck the lighted square.

*Funky Winkerbean by Tom Batiuk © 1981, Field Enterprises, Inc.*

**Positive reinforcement**
An event that strengthens the response that precedes it by virtue of its *presentation*.

**Negative reinforcement**
An event that strengthens the response that precedes it by virtue of its *removal* or *termination*.

**Escape conditioning**
A form of aversive conditioning in which the organism can terminate an aversive stimulus by making the appropriate response.

**Avoidance conditioning**
A form of conditioning in which the organism can avoid an aversive stimulus by making the appropriate response to a warning signal.

The chicken was now ready to accept all challengers. The trickery comes in at this point. Both the challenger's and the chicken's response panels are wired to a one-function minicomputer. When the challenger selects one square, the computer calculates the next move and lights that square on the chicken's panel. The chicken, only following orders, obediently pecks that square. To the outsider, the chicken appears to have made a "voluntary" choice. Now here's the rub. If the program is properly designed, it is impossible to beat a computer at tic-tac-toe. The best you can hope for is a tie. So if you were unable to defeat the high-IQ chicken, do not despair. The world champion tic-tac-toe player couldn't.

Negative reinforcement and escape conditioning. Unlike a positive reinforcer, which strengthens a response by virtue of its *presentation*, a **negative reinforcer** will strengthen the responses that precede the removal of a negative or aversive stimulus. Whereas many students study for the *positive* reinforcement of good grades, perhaps just as many study to *avoid* the unpleasantness of a D or an F.

Negative reinforcement is exemplified by the familiar joke:

*Question:* "Why do you keep hitting your head against that brick wall?"
*Answer:* "Because it feels so good when I stop!"

Suppose we place a laboratory animal in an operant-conditioning apparatus. We then introduce a mild but painful electrical shock through the grid floor. In this situation, the animal must learn to jump over the barrier in order to turn off the shock. Will it learn? Yes, in remarkably few trials. By combining classical- and operant-conditioning procedures, the animal can learn to avoid the shock altogether. That is, it acquires a conditioned **escape** response. Here's how it is done. An animal is placed in an operant-conditioning apparatus. A while later, a neutral stimulus is introduced (a tone, buzzer, flashing light, etc.). Let's use a buzzer in this example. The sound of the buzzer is immediately followed by a shock. When the animal jumps the hurdle, the shock (the negative reinforcement) is terminated. The buzzer is again sounded, and another shock follows. Again, jumping the hurdle permits the animal to escape the shock. In short order, the animal jumps the hurdle as soon as the buzzer sounds, thereby avoiding the shock altogether.

A leading learning theorist (Miller, 1944) has proposed that learned **avoidance** involves a two-stage process—learning to fear the stimulus paired with the aversive stimulus (classical conditioning) and learning to respond to an internal state (fear) by making the avoidance response. In this situation, the reduction of fear becomes the negative reinforcer. Figure 2.11 shows in diagrammatic form learned escape based on shock termination and learned avoidance based on fear reduction. Many human situations involve escape and avoidance learning. Let's return briefly to the example of a child touching a hot stove. It should be clear that the child will eventually learn to avoid the hot stove. The "warning signal" will be the sight of the hot stove. We learn to avoid many dangerous situations in this way. A particular object acts as a warning signal by reminding us of our past experience.

Let's suppose that after a long, hard day you finally have the opportunity to relax over a home-cooked meal. You are extremely hungry, and the bowl of soup placed before you looks and smells particularly inviting. Without hesitation, you take a spoonful. To your dismay, the soup is extremely hot and scalds your tongue. You erupt with a few profane expletives, bang your spoon against the table, and push back your chair. None of these reactions does anything to lessen the pain. You realize that *escape* or "getting away" *after* the pain has begun is not really good enough. It would have been better to *avoid* the pain entirely. You must learn what behavior is adaptive here, that is, what behavior will lead to avoiding the pain. As you sit glowering at the soup, you notice a small cloud of water vapor rising from the bowl. If you are an intelligent person, you will learn that the water vapor is a "warning signal" telling you that the soup is too hot to eat. You will, we hope, learn to avoid future pain by responding to this signal.

Figure 2.11   **In (a), a dog learns to leap a barrier (an operant response) in order to escape the pain and fear engendered by a shock (negative reinforcement). In (b), a dog that has learned through classical conditioning to fear a shock leaps the barrier as soon as it is placed in the apparatus and before the shock is administered. By so doing, the dog avoids pain and is thus positively reinforced (operantly conditioned) for the action.**

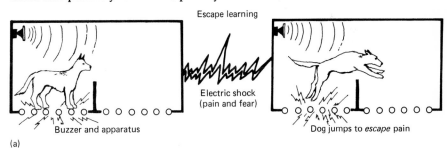

Escape learning

Electric shock (pain and fear)

Buzzer and apparatus

Dog jumps to *escape* pain

(a)

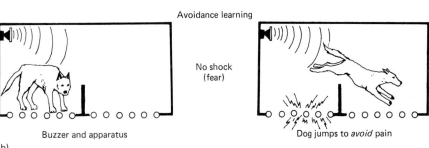

Avoidance learning

No shock (fear)

Buzzer and apparatus

Dog jumps to *avoid* pain

(b)

## Shaping of Operant Behavior

**Shaping**
Modifying behavior by reinforcing only those responses that successively approximate the final desired behavior.

**Contingent reinforcement**
Reward or reinforcement that is dependent upon making a given response.

Many learned behaviors have a very low initial probability of occurrence. For example, a rat will not normally press a bar when it is first introduced into the operant conditioning chamber. As we indicated earlier, we can wait until the animal accidentally presses the bar, or we can "shape" the bar-pressing response. **Shaping** involves the reinforcement of a series of small steps leading to the desired response. As was the case with the couple at the beginning of this chapter who were about to build a house, we must first decide what we want the final product to look like. In other words, we must select in advance the behavior we want the organism to perform. We then place the organism in the learning situation and reward any behavior that is recognizable as an approximation of this desired performance. When the organism has learned these approximations, we set higher standards that are successively closer approximations to the desired behavior. Finally, we reward only the desired behavior.

Let's look at an example of how we can shape bar-pressing behavior in a rat. First, we place a hungry rat in the operant conditioning chamber and allow it to explore the box. We then deliver food when the animal is standing near the food-delivery mechanism. It soon learns to go to the mechanism to obtain food. Now we begin to shape the bar-pressing response. We initially reward the animal for merely approaching the bar.

**Figure 2.12**    Researchers trained Barnabus to perform a complex sequence of responses by reinforcing each behavior in the chain. The investigators worked backward from the last response in the chain to the first. By the end of training, Barnabus was able to perform a long series of responses to obtain a single food pellet. Here we see Barnabus (a) climbing a spiral ramp, (b) crossing a bridge, (c) climbing a ladder, (d) pedaling a toy car, (e) climbing a staircase, (f) crawling through a glass tube, and (g) riding an elevator to return to the starting point. There Barnabus pressed a lever to obtain his food pellet. (Pierrel and Sherman, 1963)

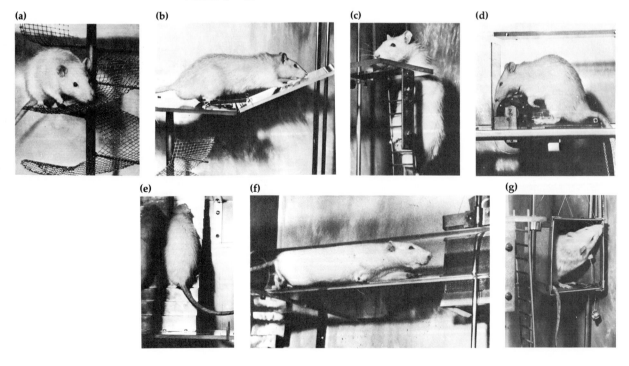

(a)          (b)          (c)          (d)

(e)          (f)          (g)

Figure 2.13    **These elephants have been taught the tricks in their routine through operant conditioning.**

After the rat has learned this step well, we begin to reinforce it only when it touches the bar or a nearby area. Finally, we reinforce it only when it presses the bar. From this point on, reward is **contingent** upon pressing the bar with sufficient force to activate the mechanism.

In addition to shaping a single response such as bar-pressing, investigators can shape a whole series of responses individually and then chain them together to form a complex series of responses (see Fig. 2.12).

The use of positive reinforcement to shape a desired behavior is illustrated in the following example:

> *A three-year-old boy refused to wear his glasses and broke pair after pair. The technique of shaping was decided upon to deal with the problem. Then training was begun with empty eyeglass frames. First the boy was reinforced with the candy or fruit for picking them up, then for holding them, then for carrying them around, then for bringing the frames closer to his eyes, and then for putting the empty frames on his head at any angle. Through successive approximations, he finally learned to wear his glasses up to twelve hours a day. (Coleman, 1979, p. 426)*

Animal trainers have obtained some dramatic results in shaping operant behavior. Figure 2.13 shows examples of behaviors that have been shaped in this way. We can probably all think of examples of shaping behavior in our everyday lives—in bringing up children, in the learning of attitudes, and even in the training of our pets.

Imagine that you have an instructor who paces back and forth across the room as he lectures. Suppose that you wanted your instructor to lecture from a certain location in the room, say, in front of his desk. How would you go about shaping his behavior? First you must decide what to use as reinforcement for the desired behavior. Many things can act as reinforcers, particularly for humans. In this situation, taking notes, paying attention, and showing interest would probably serve as effective reinforcers. Of course, you would need the cooperation of the entire class for this experiment. In the beginning, you would reinforce any activity approximating the final desired response (standing in front of the desk). You would reinforce (by paying attention or by taking notes) any movement toward the selected area. Whenever the instructor moved away from the designated area, you would withhold reinforcement (that is, you would stop paying attention, would talk, or would stop taking notes). Soon you should have the instructor standing close to the desk area. Now you reinforce him only when he stands in front of the desk, and you withhold reinforcement for all other movement. If your entire class has cooperated, your instructor should now be lecturing from in front of his desk. Thus you will have succeeded in shaping his behavior.

**Superstitious behavior**
Behavior learned simply by virtue of the fact that it happened to be followed by reinforcement, even though this behavior was not instrumental in producing the reinforcement.

**Extinction**
The reduction in response that occurs in operant conditioning when the conditioned response (CR) is no longer followed by reinforcement.

**Superstitious behavior.** Sometimes behavior is shaped accidentally. Because reinforcement strengthens the response that precedes it, any response followed by reinforcement tends to be repeated. Consequently, a response may be learned simply because it happens to be followed by reinforcement, whether or not this response was instrumental in obtaining the reinforcement. Behavior learned as a result of this coincidental pairing is called **superstitious behavior**.

Suppose that you used a particular pen while taking an exam and got a high grade; and the next time you took a test, you used a different pen and did poorly. On the basis of these two experiences, you might come to believe that there was something ''lucky'' about that first pen. You are now well on the way to developing superstitious behavior. Such behavior is remarkably resistant to extinction, for failure to engage in the behavior involves a certain degree of risk. If the pen is *really* lucky, then you are

Figure 2.14       A useful measure of learning in the operant-conditioning situation is the rate of response, which is shown in a cumulative response curve. Note that the acquisition curve is steep, indicating a high rate of response. When the line becomes horizontal, the animal is no longer responding (extinction). Notice how the rate of response picks up after a rest period (spontaneous recovery).

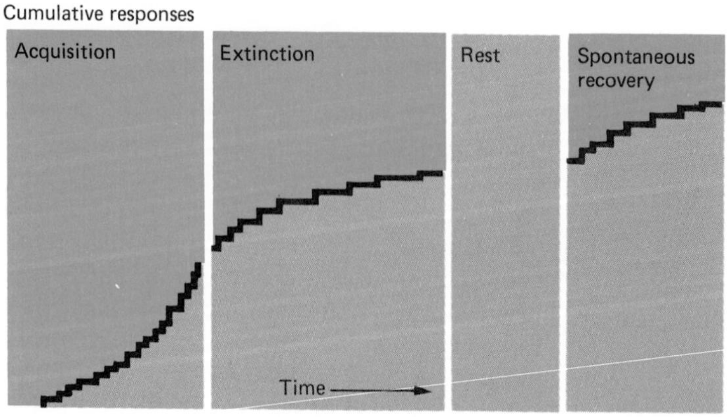

Cumulative responses

taking a chance by not using it. Even a few poor performances with the lucky pen may not discourage you. You may think, "I'd have completely bombed the test if it weren't for my lucky pen." In fact, if you really believe that using that particular pen is crucial to your success, you may actually do poorly if you take the test with another pen.

Superstitious behaviors are common in everyday life; most of us can think of examples in our own behavior as well as in the behavior of others. Have you ever noticed the gambler's rituals before throwing the dice, or a ballplayer's insistence on using the same bat or wearing the same shirt? Do you know people who knock on wood, avoid black cats, or throw salt over their left shoulder?

Analogous superstitious behavior has been observed in the laboratory in experiments with lower animals. For example, a rat may scratch itself before it presses the bar to obtain reinforcement. The animal is learning a chain of responses (scratching and then bar-pressing) that leads to reinforcement, even though only the bar-pressing response is instrumental in producing this reinforcement. The superstitious scratching behavior will persist as long as reinforcement appears to be associated with it. Superstitious behavior will disappear only if the organism tries and gets reinforced for the appropriate behavior without first making the superstitious response, that is, if the rat is reinforced for pressing the bar without first scratching.

## Extinction, Spontaneous Recovery, and Stimulus Generalization

As we indicated earlier, operant conditioning follows the same laws as classical conditioning. In classical conditioning, when the US is no longer paired with the CS, the CR undergoes experimental extinction. In operant conditioning, experimental **extinction** will occur if the operant response is no longer followed by reinforcement. For example, if the rat is no longer rewarded for pressing the bar, it will eventually stop pressing it. If the rat is removed from the apparatus and returned at a later time, it will start pressing the bar again. Thus *spontaneous recovery* also occurs in operant conditioning. Figure 2.14 shows the cumulative records obtained during acquisition, extinction, and spontaneous recovery of the bar-pressing response in rats.

Consider the following case:

*Shari is an exemplary employee. She always arrives a bit early, and never complains if she must stay late. Her work is always done neatly and efficiently. She is extremely well organized. Everyone knows they can "count on" Shari to get the job done. She is rewarded with annual pay increases, bonuses, and lots of praise. Then one day her company is taken over by a large conglomerate. Somehow Shari is "lost in the shuffle." No one seems to notice or even pay attention to her work habits. Since no one else seems to care, Shari starts to lose interest. She begins arriving late and her work becomes slovenly and undisciplined. Thus, due to the withdrawal of positive reinforcement, Shari's superior work habits have gradually extinguished. When she returns from her annual two week vacation, there is a brief interlude during which the "old" Shari reappears (spontaneous recovery). However, this is short-lived and Shari decides to change jobs. She is offered a job with a small company, much like her company used to be. In this new but similar environment, Shari generalizes her original work habits and once again becomes the "ideal" employee. (Haber and Runyon, 1983)*

Extinction procedures have many applications in real-life situations. Parents sometimes have to use extinction procedures when they find that they have inadvertently reinforced behaviors that they consider undesirable. For example, some children quickly learn that the only way to gain their parents' attention is to cry, throw temper tantrums, or engage in other forms of disruptive behavior. These behaviors are learned operants: They are instrumental in obtaining parental attention. One way to extinguish them is to withdraw reinforcement (attention) whenever the undesired behavior occurs. Optimally, extinction should be accompanied by

Drawing by Opie; © 1961, The New Yorker Magazine, Inc.

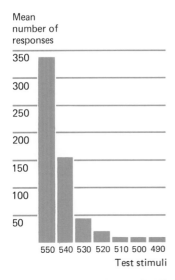

Mean
number of
responses

Figure 2.15

**Stimulus generalization
curve for six test stimuli**

Pigeons were conditioned to
respond at one light
wavelength (550 nm) and then
tested for stimulus
generalization at different
wavelengths. (Haber and
Kalish, 1963)

reinforcement of the desired behaviors. That is, parents should pay particular attention when the child does something constructive.

The following case illustrates an application of extinction procedures. A five-year-old girl had become a serious medical risk as a result of constantly scratching her face, neck, and other parts of her body. In fact, her body had become a mass of open sores, wounds, and large scabs. Her mother then received training at a mental health clinic and learned to withhold all reinforcement, including attention, whenever the child engaged in scratching behavior. She also learned to provide liberal reinforcements (praise, gold stars, goodies, refreshments, and doll clothes) when the girl engaged in desirable behaviors while *not* scratching herself. Within a period of six weeks the girl stopped scratching entirely, and the wounds on her body healed (Allen and Harris, 1966). Box 2.2 presents several techniques for getting rid of undesirable habits.

In our discussion of classical conditioning, we indicated that as soon as an organism has learned to associate a given behavior with a specific stimulus, it tends to show this behavior toward similar stimuli. We referred to this phenomenon as *stimulus generalization.* Such stimulus generalization also occurs in operant conditioning. To illustrate, recall that when Shari changed jobs and went to work at a company similar to the one in which she had compiled an enviable work record, she generalized her fine work habits to the new situation.

In a study of stimulus generalization, pigeons were placed in a modified Skinner box and trained to peck at a panel of a specific color. After conditioning had been established, the color of the panel was varied systematically (Haber and Kalish, 1963). Figure 2.15 shows the results obtained in this study. Note that the number of responses decreases as the stimuli become increasingly different from the original stimulus.

## Discrimination Learning

The procedures for establishing *discrimination* in operant conditioning are similar to those we discussed in relation to classical conditioning. We reinforce the response when it occurs in the presence of the positive stimulus, and we do not reinforce the behavior in the presence of the negative stimulus.

Suppose that you wanted to determine whether a one-year-old child is color-blind. Because the youngster is incapable of sophisticated language at this age, you cannot use any of the conventional color-blindness tests that are available for older children and adults. However, you could set up a color discrimination task. You could design this task in many different ways. You could, for example, use a panel displaying two geometric designs that are identical in every respect except their colors (red and green). When the child touches one color (green), you provide reinforcement in the form of candy. When the child touches the other color (red), you withhold this reinforcement. You must systematically vary the position of the colors, from left to right, in order to be sure that she is responding to color and not to location. If this discrimination is learned, you can assume that the child is not color-blind (at least with respect to red and green).

## BOX 2.2

### Habit Breaking

There are many instances in which we learn some undesirable response or habit and then wish to weaken it. For example, how many of you have tried to kick the nicotine habit? How many of you have fears that you find intolerable? Many techniques for breaking habits have been employed, with varying degrees of success. In a sense, we have already discussed the weakening of learned responses, or habits, in our discussion of experimental extinction. We saw that withholding reinforcement following a learned operant response led to extinction of that response. Most methods of habit breaking rely upon extinction to some extent.

#### Incompatible-Response Method

One of the most effective techniques for habit breaking is called the **incompatible-response method.** It involves the extinction of an undesirable response and the acquisition of a new response in its place. The new response is incompatible with the original, undesirable response; that is, the two responses cannot occur simultaneously. In effect, we are substituting the new response for the old one.

A classic experiment, involving a three-year-old boy's fear of rabbits, made use of the incompatible-response method. The experimenter gave the boy some candy and showed him a caged rabbit at the same time, in the hope that his pleasurable responses to the candy would be incompatible with, and would therefore cancel, his fear of the rabbit. There is, of course, some risk in using this technique. Because the two responses cannot occur simultaneously, the child may have learned negative responses to the candy instead of positive responses to the rabbit. It is important that the desired reaction be more intense than the one we wish to eliminate. In this experiment, the rabbit was kept caged in order to minimize the intensity of the fear reaction. Thus the experimenter successfully substituted the desirable responses originally made to the candy for the undesirable fear of the rabbit (Jones, 1924).

#### Toleration Method

There are two different strategies for simply extinguishing an undesirable response. We have already seen that the incompatible-response method requires that the desired reaction be more intense than the one we wish to eliminate. Another technique, the **toleration method,** involves introducing very gradually the stimulus that elicits the undesired response. By the time it is presented at full strength, the undesired response has been extinguished or greatly reduced in intensity.

The toleration method has been particularly successful in eliminating undesirable emotional responses such as fear. Suppose you have a younger brother who is afraid of the dark. How could you eliminate this fear response? You might install a dimmer switch in his bedroom. In the beginning, you might leave the light sufficiently bright so that his fear responses are minimal. You could gradually reduce the intensity of the light over a period of time, making sure that his fear responses remain minimal. Finally, it should be possible to turn the light off altogether. The effectiveness of this technique might be improved by combining it with the incompatible-response method. You could put some favorite toy, such as a

---

### Secondary Reinforcement

Let's slightly modify the bar-pressing experiment. Before placing a hungry rat in the operant conditioning chamber, we sound a buzzer and then provide food immediately. We repeat this sequence a number of times. We then place the animal in the operant conditioning chamber. Instead of rewarding the bar-pressing response with food, we sound the buzzer immediately after the rat presses the bar. We find that the animal learns the bar-pressing response.

Remember that we defined reinforcement as any event that strength-

teddy bear, into bed with him each night. His favorable responses to the teddy bear might gradually come to replace his fear of the dark.

## Exhaustion Method

A second technique for extinguishing the undesired response, the **exhaustion method,** requires the individual to make the undesired response—in the presence of the stimuli that normally evoke it—so often that the response is eventually extinguished. The exhaustion method is sometimes called the sink-or-swim method, for the stimuli that elicit the undesired response are introduced and maintained at full strength. Thus the exhaustion method involves a single, continuous attempt to extinguish a response, and it is either a resounding success or an outright failure.

The exhaustion method is typically used to break horses. The rider tries to stay on the horse's back until the horse stops bucking. In other words, the bucking is exhausted. At that point, other responses replace the original one.

An interesting clinical case illustrates the successful application of the exhaustion method in a mental hospital. A woman patient would beg, borrow, or steal towels from all conceivable sources. The staff attempted various techniques to break this disruptive habit, including punishment and coercion. None of these methods worked. Finally, they decided to try the exhaustion method. No attempt was made to interfere with the woman's undesirable habit, and towels were made available almost everywhere she turned. She eventually accumulated so many towels in her room that there was barely any space to move around. After a few experiences of this sort, the un-

desired response was exhausted and did not occur again (Ayllon, 1963).

## Change-of-Environment Method

In certain situations it is possible to isolate the individual from the stimuli that evoke the undesirable behavior. In the absence of cues that normally elicit the behavior, the individual will not make the undesired response. This technique is known as the **change-of-environment method.** In most situations, however, it is not possible to achieve the degree of isolation necessary to make this method permanently effective. For instance, you can put alcoholics in an environment where liquor is unavailable for a period of time. During that time they obviously won't drink. When they return to their old environment, however, all of the stimuli that elicit their drinking behavior will still be present, and they will probably return to their former habit almost immediately. The change-of-environment method is generally unsuccessful because no desirable behaviors are substituted for the undesirable one.

**Incompatible-response method**
A method of breaking habits that involves the extinction of an undesirable response as well as the acquisition of a new response that is incompatible with the original undesired response.

**Toleration method**
A method of breaking habits that involves the gradual introduction of the stimulus that is eliciting the undesired response.

**Exhaustion method**
A method of breaking habits in which the individual makes the undesired response, in the presence of the stimuli that normally evoke it, so often that the response is finally extinguished.

**Change-of-environment method**
A method of breaking habits in which the individual is removed from all cues that normally elicit the undesired behavior.

ens the response that precedes it. In terms of this definition, the buzzer reinforces the bar-pressing response. How has the buzzer acquired reinforcement properties?

Food for a hungry animal and water for a thirsty animal are **primary reinforcers,** for their reward value depends little, if at all, on previous learning. Research has demonstrated that any event regularly associated with a primary reinforcement also comes to acquire reinforcing properties. Such events, or stimuli, are known as **secondary reinforcers.** Because

**Primary reinforcement**
Any event that has reinforcing properties that directly fulfill physical needs and that depend little, if at all, on previous learning.

The ability to discriminate can be learned through positive reinforcement. This pigeon was able to tap the correct sign when a light of a certain color was turned on, after the experimenter had trained it by reinforcing only desired responses.

Yale Joel, *Life Magazine*, © 1950, Time, Inc.

**Secondary reinforcement**
Any event that acquires reinforcing properties through association with a primary reinforcer.

the buzzer was regularly associated with food (a primary reinforcer), it became a secondary reinforcer for the bar-pressing behavior. Secondary reinforcers do not have the permanence of primary reinforcers. They are subject to extinction if they are not reassociated at least occasionally with the primary reinforcer.

Some of the most powerful reinforcers of human behavior are secondary in nature. Consider money. We commit ourselves to employment for almost half our adult waking hours. Our reward consists of money, which has acquired reinforcement value because of its association with other reinforcers (for example, food, drink, and entertainment). Some

Secondary reinforcers are events an individual learns to associate with either positive or negative outcomes. After a victorious doubles match, laurels, a trophy, a £40,000 prize, and a kiss from husband John Lloyd serve as secondary reinforcers for Chris Evert Lloyd to win her next competitive event.

people will spend hours perusing racing forms or calculating odds in a game of chance in the hope of "hitting it big." Professional football players and boxers regularly submit their bodies to violence for a bit of praise and large sums of money. Also consider *praise*. This is an extremely powerful secondary reinforcer. We may volunteer for charitable work, study long hours, and put in more time and effort than is required by the job. Why? In part, perhaps, because we want to be praised. Praise can take many forms: It can be verbal ("That was a beautiful forehand shot"), a medal (for heroic action beyond the call of duty), a testimonial (for 30 years of dedicated service), or a good grade on a quiz.

In the example discussed earlier, what was the nature of the reinforcement we used to shape the instructor's behavior so that he would stand in front of his desk? Paying attention, taking notes, and appearing to be interested are all secondary reinforcers. A good grade on an examination certainly has reinforcing value. In many ways, secondary reinforcers are more convenient to use than primary reinforcers. If you had to provide a primary reinforcer—for instance, food or candy—every time a child did something desirable, your pockets would have to be perpetually filled, and you would wreak havoc with the child's feeding schedule and nutrition. Praise is frequently used as a secondary reinforcer with children, loved ones, and pets.

**Figure 2.16**

Chimpanzee inserting token (secondary reinforcer) into a vending machine to obtain primary reinforcement (food).

In humans, one of the strongest secondary reinforcers is money. A somewhat similar phenomenon can be observed in lower animals. In one study, chimpanzees were trained to work for poker chips. These poker chips served as tokens that the animals could later insert into a vending machine (Cowles, 1937). Figure 2.16 shows a chimpanzee inserting a poker chip into the vending machine to obtain food, the primary reinforcer.

One form of therapy, which has been quite successful with certain types of emotionally disturbed patients, is called behavior therapy or behavior modification. We have already looked at an example of this type of therapy in the section on the Practical Implications of Classical Conditioning. Box 2.3 describes the use of behavior modification with a mentally retarded child.

Some forms of behavior therapy rely heavily on the use of tokens (secondary reinforcers) to bring about desired behavioral changes. Let's see how tokens were used in a hospital setting in order to condition operant behaviors.

Patients in mental hospitals typically display a wide variety of disorganized behaviors. Some are sloppy about their personal hygiene: They may not shave, bathe, or change their clothing. Often it is difficult to get them to the dining room in time for meals. Some mope listlessly around the ward and show little interest in their surroundings.

In one study, the experimenters wanted to condition such behaviors as getting to the dining room on time, maintaining personal hygiene, and performing simple household duties. Because the experiment was performed in a hospital setting, the experimenters had to use reinforcers that were available there. Such variables as food, sleeping and dining conditions, and television-viewing privileges could all be controlled by the experimenters and thus could serve as reinforcers. Instead of rewarding de-

## BOX 2.3

### Behavior Modification with a Mentally Retarded Child

By Mary Jo Roberts
Marcia Canfield

As students in a behavior modification course, we used the operant principles of modeling—imitation, stimulus, response, reinforcement, and withholding to modify the eating behavior of Mary C., a four-and-one-half-year-old child with **Down's syndrome.** Mary has been institutionalized since birth in the mental retardation unit of a small hospital run by a religious order. She was tiny, with prominent clubbing of fingers and toes. She was not toilet trained and walked with the aid of an infant walker. She exhibited several modeling behaviors, such as playing "patty-cake" and waving "bye-bye." She could mimic the experimenters and repeat the words "shoe," "patty-cake," and "bye."

Mary had severe learning disabilities, but we believed she was capable of acquiring certain new behaviors, such as independent self-spoon feeding.

We first watched and recorded what Mary did (base rate behavior) for four days during the evening meal. The first day, Mary finger-fed herself. On the second day, she picked up her spoon twice but only to pound her food, her tray, and other children. The third and fourth day, Mary was spoon-fed by attendants.

A behavior modification program was begun. We took turns working with Mary, Monday through Friday, during the evening meal. We used her favorite game, "patty-cake," as a reinforcer. Each time Mary swallowed a bite of food, we gave her small amounts of grape juice with a medicine dropper. Praise was abundantly used during the shaping process. Raisins were an added reinforcer. Mary was fed in the playroom, away from all distractors.

There was little improvement that first week. On the fourth day of therapy, 11 bites of food were swallowed. On the fifth day, however, the number of bites of food swallowed dropped to zero. Mary had caught a head cold, which could explain a loss of appetite.

During the first week, crying behavior decreased from 10 minutes the first day to 5 minutes the second day to 3 minutes on the third. Uncooperative behaviors such as throwing the spoon, the cup, and the food increased during this time.

---

sired behavior directly with these reinforcers, the experimenters rewarded patients with tokens. These tokens could then be exchanged for various special privileges that were important to individual patients (Gericke, 1965).

As a result of the introduction of the **token economy,** many patients showed dramatic changes in behavior. Many who had been passive and inactive for years now took a sudden interest in their surroundings. One woman who had previously refused all food except milk eventually added other foods to her diet, including bacon and eggs for breakfast.

A number of similar studies have reported equally favorable results. Nevertheless, several investigators (Levine and Fasnacht, 1974; Deci, 1972) have expressed reservations about the indiscriminate use of tokens. When interest in a task is high to begin with, the introduction of rewards (tokens) may actually cause the subjects to devalue the task itself. For example, college students in one study (Deci, 1972) were given a puzzle consisting of various blocks that can be assembled into different shapes. Most students find this task interesting in and of itself. One group was promised monetary rewards for solving all of the puzzles, whereas a control group of subjects was promised nothing. During a postexperimental

**Token economy**
A reinforcement technique, sometimes used in hospitals, in which the individual is rewarded for socially accepted behavior with a token that can be exchanged for a desired object or activity.

Uncooperative behaviors diminished as a result of withholding procedures. Whenever Mary cried or threw something, we either turned our backs or went to the opposite end of the room and ignored the unacceptable behavior for 10 seconds.

During the second week, Mary's eating behavior improved greatly. She ate most of her meals, and she began autonomously picking up her spoon and putting food into her mouth. Her dexterity improved so that she could hold a cup and drink from it.

The fourth day of the second treatment week, Mary was moved back into the dining room. Because of Mary's tendency to drink fast and then spill her milk, we made sure that she only had one swallow at a time in the cup. During this dinner session, one other child joined Mary at the far end of the dining room and commended her loudly for each self-feeding response. On this day, Mary fed herself 37 bites of food and successfully drank from her cup 18 times.

Mary got a staph infection on the fifth day of the second week and was isolated from the dining room and playroom. Mary maintained her self-feeding behavior, however, even in isolation.

Sixteen months after completion of the project, Mary, who had students continuing to work with her using behavior therapy, initiated **self-ambulation**, had a vocabulary of 20 words, and colored in a coloring book. Her self-feeding behavior also continued. She now attends a school for exceptional children.

Mary Jo Roberts, R.N., M.S., is an instructor at the Veterans Administration Hospital, Nashville, Tenn. She was an instructor in psychiatric nursing at Troy State University School of Nursing, Montgomery, Ala., when she wrote this article.

Marcia Canfield, M.Ed., was a family case worker at the Elmore County Department of Pensions and Security in Wetumpka, Ala., when she wrote this article. She now is a social worker at the Montgomery County Department of Pensions and Security in Montgomery, Ala.

**Down's syndrome**
A genetic defect resulting in mental retardation and slowed motor development.

**Self-ambulation**
The ability to walk on one's own.

period, subjects were free to engage in a variety of different activities. It is interesting that the rewarded subjects actually spent less of this free time working on the puzzles than the control subjects. The following explanation has been proposed: "If one is doing activity X without a reward, then activity X must be worth doing. If one is getting a reward for activity X, it must not be worth doing without the reward" (Levine and Fasnacht, 1974, p. 818). These findings have caused some investigators to raise the question, "Can positive reinforcement undermine motivation?" For a discussion, see Box 2.4.

The use of behavior modification as a therapeutic technique is discussed in Chapter 15.

## Partial Reinforcement

In the laboratory experiments that we have discussed so far, every correct response was reinforced. In real-life situations, however, reinforcement follows the conditioned operant responses some and not all of the times that they occur.

Parents are not always available to reward their infant for saying "da-da"; gamblers do not win every time they put two dollars "on the nose";

## BOX 2.4

### Can Positive Reinforcement Undermine Motivation?

So far we have seen that reinforcement is at the core of much of our learning. In addition to strengthening operant responses, positive reinforcers have motivational or incentive value. We strive for praise from someone we respect or love, and beam when it is forthcoming; we work many hours a week either for the monetary rewards that climax our efforts or for the self-satisfaction of a job well done. Indeed, the promise of reinforcers in exchange for desired behavior is a transaction with which we are all familiar: "Eat your supper and you can have ice cream for dessert," "Be a good child and teacher will award you a gold star," "Keep your nose to the grindstone and you'll receive a promotion before you know it."

The promise of a positive reinforcer is such a commonplace aspect of our everyday social interactions that we are even tempted to generalize: When applied to desired behavior, positive reinforcement improves the likelihood that this desired behavior will be learned and practiced. But is this necessarily the case? Consider the following. Little Johnny, a nursery school child, loves to draw with felt tip pens. Desiring to encourage the activity, the teacher promises him that, if he continues to draw with them, he will receive a "Good Player" award. Then, during a free play period, the pens are again made available to Johnny. Is he likely to show an increased interest in drawing with them because he has previously received positive reinforcement for doing so? Surprisingly, the answer is "No." In fact, he will probably have less of an interest than previously. It appears that, somehow, positive reinforcement has undermined Johnny's motivation to play with the pens (Lepper *et al.*, 1973; Lepper and Greene, 1978).

To understand this finding, we must distinguish between **intrinsic** and **extrinsic motivation.** We en-

gage in some activities because they are inherently interesting rather than because we expect external rewards. Such activities as reading for pleasure, drawing, solving crossword puzzles, and hiking are typically intrinsically motivated. Contrast these activities with reading for a grade, working for compensation, or engaging in sport for money. In these, the goal of the activity is to obtain an external reward. Such activities are said to be externally or extrinsically motivated.

Now, what happens if we offer external rewards for intrinsically motivated behavior? Apparently, we undermine the intrinsic motivation. Turning play into work seems to make the activity less attractive. Moreover, even the quality of the performance may be reduced (Kelley and Michela, 1980).

The importance of this finding stems from the fact that we tend to look for prescriptions that apply to all people at all times. Thus we may sincerely believe that efforts should be made to provide all people with both incentives to engage in certain activities and rewards when they do. But what if the activity is intrinsically motivated? In some people, such a prescription may undermine the very behavior we wish to encourage. The implication is clear. Perhaps not all primary school children should be offered a gold star as a reward for achievement. This reward might better be reserved for children who are motivated by a desire for external signs of approval. The child who enjoys reading, for example, for its own sake might better be left to pursue the activity without imposition of external motivations and rewards.

| Intrinsic motivation | Extrinsic motivation |
|---|---|
| Desire to perform a behavior based on factors other than external rewards. | Desire to perform a behavior based on the expectation of external reward. |

students are not always rewarded for studying with high grades; parents are not always successful in directing their children's behavior. Yet in spite of frequent nonreinforcements, these behaviors show considerable persistence. These situations involve **partial** rather than **continuous reinforcement.** In partial reinforcement, the response is reinforced only some of the times that it occurs.

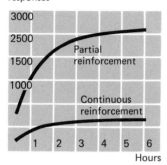

Average cumulative number of responses

Figure 2.17
Resistance to extinction following continuous versus partial reinforcement. (Jenkins, McFann, and Clayton, 1950)

**Partial reinforcement**
Reinforcement of a response only some of the times that it occurs.

**Continuous reinforcement**
Reinforcement of a response every time it occurs.

**Schedule of reinforcement**
An established plan for allotting reinforcements under partial reinforcement.

Operant responses are usually acquired more rapidly under continuous reinforcement than they are under partial reinforcement. Intuitively, we might expect this superiority to carry over into extinction. In other words, *even after the reinforcement has terminated* (extinction), the subject should persist longer in making the stronger response (that is, the one that was continuously rewarded) than the response that was rewarded only part of the time. But when comparable levels of learning are achieved under both conditions, the extinction data are in sharp contrast to the acquisition data. Subjects successfully trained under partial reinforcement typically show a greater *resistance to extinction;* that is, more extinction trials are required to extinguish the behavior.

Figure 2.17 compares extinction data for continuously and partially reinforced learned operant behaviors. Note the greater resistance to extinction following partial reinforcement. The number of responses required to extinguish the partially reinforced operant response was almost five times as great as the number required to extinguish the continuously reinforced operant response. Upon reflection, these findings are not surprising. Under partial reinforcement, it is difficult to identify the termination of reward. This is not the case with continuously reinforced responses. Thus with partially reinforced responses, we may continue to respond because we are not quite sure if or when the reinforcement ended.

These experimental findings have many practical implications. Behaviors persist even though they are not always reinforced. The baby learns to say "da-da" despite frequent nonreinforcement; gamblers continue betting even though they may seldom win; most students continue to study in spite of an occasional low grade; and parents continue to direct their children's behavior despite frequent lack of success.

There are many different ways in which to allot reinforcements. When they are administered according to some plan, they are ordinarily referred to as **schedules of reinforcement.** At one extreme, we may reinforce each correct response (continuous reinforcement); at the other extreme, we may offer no reinforcement at all (a condition of nonreward in which little, if any, acquisition will take place under normal conditions).

**Schedules of reinforcement.** Schedules of reinforcement can be based either on the time between reinforcements or on the number of nonreinforced responses that occur between reinforcements. The first is called an *interval* schedule; the second is called a *ratio* schedule. The reinforcements can also be administered according to some regular or fixed plan, or according to some irregular or variable plan. The combination of these two dimensions yields the following four schedules:

|  | Interval | Ratio |
|---|---|---|
| **Fixed plan** | Fixed interval | Fixed ratio |
| **Variable plan** | Variable interval | Variable ratio |

Number of responses

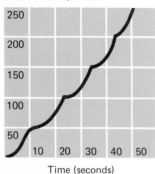

Time (seconds)
(a) Fixed-ratio schedule

Number of responses

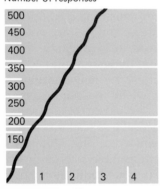

Time (minutes)
(b) Variable-ratio schedule

Number of responses

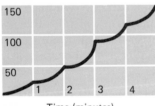

Time (minutes)
(c) Fixed-interval schedule

Number of responses

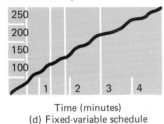

Time (minutes)
(d) Fixed-variable schedule

Figure 2.18
**Schedules of reinforcement**

Figure 2.18 shows the characteristic cumulative response patterns produced by these schedules.

**1. Fixed interval (FI).** In what are termed **fixed-interval schedules,** reinforcement is administered after a fixed period of time, for example, every 40 seconds. Regardless of how much the animal responds between reinforcements, 40 seconds must elapse before the next response is reinforced.

The response rate under a fixed-interval schedule is usually less than it is under the other schedules. Ordinarily, the response rate drops immediately after a reinforcement and then slowly builds up just before the next reinforcement. This results in a "scalloping" effect on the cumulative response record. This schedule has been successful in determining how well various organisms are able to discriminate time intervals.

Many parents employ a fixed-interval schedule. When parents refer to a "two o'clock feeding," they are using this schedule. Some parents will awaken a child from a deep sleep in order to keep to the schedule. People who feed their dogs on schedule will testify to the pets' increased activity level just before feeding time.

Wage earners who receive a weekly salary are on a fixed-interval schedule. However, their response rate does not usually show the scalloping effect (with a slowdown after the weekly "reward"), because their employers generally will not permit them to decrease their work output after they get their paycheck. (It is interesting that Friday is the most common "payday." Most employees are permitted to "slow down" on weekends.)

**2. Variable interval (VI).** In the **variable-interval schedules,** reinforcement is administered after a variable interval of time. For example, reinforcement may be given 40 seconds after one reinforcement, then 5 seconds later, and then after 75 seconds, and so on. We define this schedule in terms of the average interval between reinforcements.

The response rate under a variable-interval schedule is generally greater than under a fixed-interval schedule. Most students spend more time studying when they know an instructor will give a surprise quiz from time to time (variable interval) than they do when regularly scheduled examinations are announced (fixed interval). Moreover, the amount of time spent studying will be more evenly distributed when surprise quizzes are given. Many students will show a spurt of studying activity just before an announced examination and relatively little between exams.

**3. Fixed ratio (FR).** Another variation, the **fixed-ratio schedules,** require that the organism emit a fixed number of responses before receiving reinforcement. The schedule is usually described as a ratio between the number of nonreinforced responses and the number of reinforced responses. Thus if reinforcement occurs after every fifth response, the schedule is described as a 5:1 fixed-ratio schedule. The fixed-ratio schedule is employed in industries where workers are paid on a piecework basis.

**Fixed-interval schedule (FI)**
A schedule for reinforcing operant behavior in which reinforcement is administered after a fixed period of time.

**Variable-interval schedule (VI)**
A schedule for reinforcing operant behavior in which reinforcement is administered after a variable interval of time.

**Fixed-ratio schedule (FR)**
A schedule for reinforcing operant behavior in which reinforcement is administered after the organism emits a fixed number of responses.

**Variable-ratio schedule (VR)**
A schedule for reinforcing operant behavior in which the number of responses required for each reinforcement varies.

The response rate under a fixed-ratio schedule is generally steady and quite high. Pigeons have been trained on a fixed-ratio schedule in which the total number of reinforcements received is barely enough to keep them alive. It has been shown that the higher the ratio, the higher the response rate. Migrant workers are frequently paid on a piecework basis, which constitutes a fixed-rate schedule. Each time they harvest a fixed amount of produce, they receive monetary reinforcement. The total pay is generally hardly sufficient to maintain life. Thus most migrant workers must work at a consistently fast pace just in order to survive.

**4. Variable ratio (VR).** In the **variable-ratio schedule,** as in the fixed-ratio schedule, reinforcement is delivered after a specific number of responses. However, in the variable-ratio schedule, the number of responses required before a reinforcement varies. For example, reinforcement may occur after 7 responses, then after 20 responses, then after 2 responses, and so on. We define this schedule in terms of the average ratio of nonreinforced to reinforced responses.

Variable-ratio schedules characteristically produce an extremely high and steady rate of response. Moreover, responses acquired under variable-ratio schedules are extremely resistant to extinction. If you think for a moment about the characteristics of variable-ratio schedules, the reason should become clear: The organism never knows whether its very next response could be the one that is reinforced.

Gambling is reinforced on a variable-ratio schedule. Inveterate gamblers continue to respond (place bets) at a very high rate, always hoping they will make a killing or hit the jackpot on the very next bet. Figure 2.19 shows a woman operating the one-armed bandit or slot machine, which pays off on a variable-ratio schedule.

Figure 2.19    **The one-armed bandit puts the gambler on a variable-ratio schedule under which rate of response and resistance to extinction are very high.**

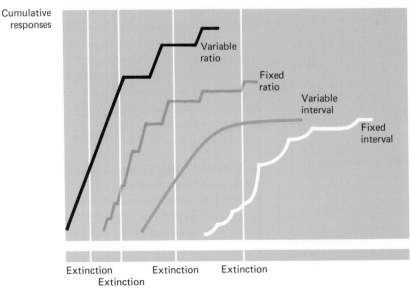

Figure 2.20     **Acquisition, maintenance, and extinction of responses are shown under four schedules of reinforcement. Responses in an operant-conditioning chamber are recorded cumulatively. Thus each response is added to all previous responses. As long as the responses are made, the cumulative curve rises. The steeper the rise, the greater the rate of responding. Horizontal lines indicate periods of nonresponding. (Reynolds, 1968)**

To summarize, schedules of reinforcement can vary in terms of two dimensions. One involves time versus the number of responses, and the other involves regularity of responses (that is, fixed versus variable).

Why are schedules of reinforcement important? To answer briefly, schedules of reinforcement dramatically affect the rate of acquisition of behavior, the rate at which the behavior occurs while on a particular schedule, and the resistance of that behavior to experimental extinction.

Figure 2.20 compares the rates of response during acquisition, maintenance of responding, and extinction under four different schedules of reinforcement. Note that a variable-ratio schedule produces the highest rate of response during acquisition and maintenance. It also produces the highest rate of response during extinction. In fact, the response rate does not decrease during extinction. Rather, bursts of high rates of responding alternate with periods of nonresponding until extinction finally occurs.

Fixed-interval schedules produce the lowest rates of responding during acquisition and maintenance and require the fewest responses to extinguish. Note the scalloping effect on the cumulative response record. The subject has learned to stop responding immediately after being reinforced and to begin again at about the time another reinforcement is due.

## Punishment

Perhaps no question arouses more emotional reactions and less illuminating discussion than the debate over the use of punishment, especially with children. Advocates of punishment vehemently proclaim, "Spare the rod and spoil the child." The opponents reply, with equal conviction, that punishment is a throwback to the primitive stages in our development as a species, that it is as outmoded as the dodo bird, and that it leaves in its wake psychological wounds that never completely heal. The truth probably lies somewhere between these two extremes. We say "probably" because the issue is extremely complex and is currently the subject of intensive investigation. Our tentative conclusions must be tempered by the recognition that we do not yet have all the answers and probably will not have them for many years.

Before we discuss some of the things we *do* know about punishment, we must establish a working definition of it. We shall define two classes of punishment, positive and negative. These two types of punishment are described in Table 2.2.

Punishment may be physical—for instance, a shock to a rat's feet or a rap on a child's bottom. With some organisms, punishment often can be verbal ("bad dog," "naughty boy"). In some cases, punishment may consist of removing something desirable. An example would be restricting an adolescent to his or her room as a consequence of some misbehavior.

When we speak of punishment in reference to animal studies, we usually mean physical punishment that inflicts pain. For obvious ethical reasons, laboratory studies involving punishment in humans rarely employ physical punishment. If such punishment is used, it is restricted to mild levels, at which the threat of punishment is often "worse than its bite."

Let's now look at some of the things we know about the effects of punishment upon behavior. Its most general effect is to suppress the re-

Table 2.2

**Summary of the Differences Between Positive and Negative Punishment and Positive and Negative Reinforcement**

| Punishment | Reinforcement |
| --- | --- |
| (Goal: decrease the probability of the undesired response) | (Goal: increase the probability of the desired response) |
| *Positive (adding something)* | |
| Adding something "bad" following the undesired response (e.g., spanking) | Adding something "good" following the desired response (e.g., praise) |
| *Negative (subtracting something)* | |
| Removing something "good" following the undesired response (e.g., taking away privileges) | Removing something "bad" following the desired response (e.g., terminating shock) |

Note: By "positive," we mean adding something; and by "negative," we mean subtracting something.

One study indicates that punishment, with positive reinforcement for acceptable behavior, has the effect of only *temporary* suppression. How might you relate this to the current policies of our prison system and the high rate of recidivism among former prisoners?

sponse that preceded it. However, *timing, consistency,* and *severity* are crucial elements. Punishment must immediately precede or follow the response in order to achieve maximum suppression (Parke, 1969). The more severe the punishment, the greater the suppression effect is (Reynolds, 1968). Human studies typically use noise as an aversive stimulus and have revealed that punishment is effective even after a delay of a few seconds, provided that the stimulus is sufficiently strong. Weaker aversive stimuli must be applied immediately if they are to be effective.

Delay of punishment may explain some of the difficulties in housebreaking a dog. Punishment is often delayed because the owners are not there when the prohibited act occurs. They may punish the dog when they arrive home, but this may be several hours too late. Because punishment suppresses the response immediately preceding it, the dog may learn instead to suppress tail-wagging and other greeting responses.

Recall what we previously learned about extinction and schedules of reinforcement. If a behavior is not consistently reinforced or suppressed, it becomes more resistant to extinction. Thus if a person engages in some undesirable behavior that is punished on some occasions but not on others, this behavior might become very difficult to extinguish. Unwittingly, we may be establishing variable schedules of reinforcement for the learners that will promote and entrench precisely those behaviors that are least desired. Moreover, inconsistently administered punishment can lead to confusion. For example, suppose your son Ali eats junk food while watching television. He makes a mess all over the floor. You are too involved with other activities to pay much attention to what Ali is doing. Consequently, you fail to reprimand him at this time. A few days later, the scene is repeated. This time, however, you become very angry and scream, "Don't you ever do that again!" Don't be surprised if Ali is confused.

With children, punishment seems most appropriate when it is used to suppress potentially harmful behavior. For example, if a child has a tendency to dart into the street without looking at the traffic, punishment will *temporarily* inhibit that response and, we hope, alert the child to the street's dangers. Punishment is most effective when it is used to suppress an undesirable response while at the same time increasing the likelihood that desired behavior will occur and be positively reinforced. Thus when the street-darting behavior has been suppressed, the parents should take the opportunity to positively reinforce their child for avoiding the street altogether.

Furthermore, research with children suggests that punishment is more likely to be effective if it is administered by a warm and accepting person rather than by a cold and hostile person (Sears *et al.*, 1957; Parke and Walters, 1967). Nevertheless, the administration of punishment is a very tricky affair. Punishment, particularly when it is severe and frequent, may lead to the development of many undesirable emotions, including fear, hostility, anxiety, anger, and hatred. Children who are punished often by a parent, either physically or verbally, may come to fear and hate that parent. As a result, the parent's ability to guide the child's behavior through the use of punishment or through positive reinforcement may be forever undermined by the child's attitude.

Strong punishment may also induce so much anxiety that an individual will not be able to cope with everyday life situations. In one study, six- and seven-year-old children were required to learn a stimulus discrimination task under low-intensity punishment in the form of a loud noise. They had to avoid selecting stimuli similar to those associated with punishment. The children readily mastered the task under low-intensity punishment, but they experienced much greater difficulty when the punishment was "severe." The investigators hypothesized that the high-intensity punishment may have produced anxiety levels that were too high to permit adaptive learning to occur (Aronfreed and Leff, 1963).

The continued use of punishment in an environment from which escape is impossible (for example, in class with a teacher who scolds incessantly) may also cause the child to withdraw psychologically from the situation (for example, by daydreaming) and to become passive (Seligman *et al.*, 1969). It is quite possible that many children are school "dropouts" long before they physically leave school.

The threat of punishment is often used by society as a means of suppressing undesirable behavior (for example, the possibility of a prison term if one commits violent behavior). One study suggests that the threat

Table 2.3

**Summary of Differences Between Reinforcement and Punishment and Their Effects on Human Behavior**

| Effects on preceding behavior | Conditions for maximum effectiveness | Information provided | Emotional consequences |
|---|---|---|---|
| Reinforcement strengthens | Immediately after desired behavior | Continue the desired behavior | Feeling of well-being |
| Punishment weakens | a) Before or immediately after undesired behavior | Stop the undesired behavior | Possibility of fear, anger, hatred, and other negative emotional reactions |
|  | b) When alternative response may be rewarded | Stop the undesired behavior | Possibility of fear, anger, hatred, and other negative emotional reactions |

of punishment may not be an effective deterrent to antisocial behavior when the motivation for the behavior is high. Subjects who were not highly motivated to express aggression successfully suppressed their aggressive responses when they were threatened with punishment. In contrast, even the threat of extreme punishment was ineffective when there was strong motivation to behave aggressively (Baron, 1973).

Table 2.3 summarizes some of the different ways in which reinforcement and punishment affect human behavior.

## Practical Implications of Operant Conditioning

One of the most intriguing concepts to come out of contemporary learning research is that the same principles of learning that guide the acquisition of adaptive behavior also apply to the acquisition of maladaptive behavior. Any behavior, whether adaptive or maladaptive, that leads to reinforcement is likely to be learned in a given situation. Some students learn to study in order to reduce the anxiety associated with an upcoming test, whereas other students learn to avoid this anxiety by engaging in activities (for instance, going to the movies) that take their minds off the impending examination. Both of these forms of behavior intended to alleviate anxiety are learned. The students who study, however, have learned adaptive behavior that is likely to culminate in passing the course, whereas students who go to the movies to take their minds off the upcoming test are engaging in maladaptive behavior that, if practiced chronically, will increase the probability that they will not pass the course.

Many treatment procedures have been developed recently to modify maladaptive behavior through the judicious application of learning principles. We have previously referred to these techniques as behavior modification. Consider the following case involving a compulsive gambler.

A 37-year-old married man, the father of two, had frequently recurring episodes, lasting several months at a time, during which his entire life became dominated by compulsive betting on racehorses. Each morning he would open the newspaper to the racing page and engage in a series of time-consuming and ritualized activities leading to the placing of his bets. During these episodes, he completely neglected his family and marital obligations. His sexual activities declined to zero. He was referred to a behavior therapist after his wife, deeply concerned over steadily mounting debts, complained that she could no longer keep the home together.

The treatment of this man consisted of the random administration of unpleasant electrical shocks during his ritualized, daily betting activities. There were nine treatment days over a two-week period, during which he received almost 700 shocks. By the fourth day, he reported that he had to force himself to open the daily papers. By the end of the treatment, he had lost all desire to buy the morning paper and to follow the races. Follow-up observations, extending more than a year after treatment, have shown no renewed interest in gambling. Indeed, the man's family and marital situation, including his sexual behavior, underwent dramatic improvement during this period (Goorney, 1968).

## OBSERVATIONAL LEARNING

Knowledge of the principles of classical and operant conditioning is extremely important in understanding many aspects of behavior. However, at the human level (see Box 2.5), many of the most important lessons we learn arise from our ability to observe and imitate the actions of others. When children learn to speak, they observe and imitate both the facial expressions and vocal sounds produced by their parents. Subsequently, they learn to ride bicycles, drive cars, read novels, throw baseballs, and smoke cigarettes largely through observing others and imitating their ac-

Imitation sometimes leads to undesirable consequences.

## BOX 2.5

### Learning and Unlearning by Observation

Many of the things we have learned to fear have never actually hurt us. Rather, much of our fear and avoidance learning results from observing evidence of fear in others. Such social learning is quite efficient because it means that one can learn from other people's misfortunes. A common example of such fear learning, although one that is not necessarily advantageous, is the **vicarious** conditioning that takes place by hearing, reading, and watching suspenseful drama. After a childhood diet of entertainment in which various fear-producing things happen at night, one can hardly escape a conditioned apprehension of dark places.

The fact that emotional reactions can be conditioned through vicarious experiences raises the intriguing possibility that existing maladaptive fears might be eliminated in a similar manner. Such a possibility is of more than casual interest because of the obvious therapeutic possibilities. Fears are usually difficult to eliminate. Feared situations tend to be avoided, and contact with feared objects is minimized, with the result that even unfounded fear will be unlikely to be extinguished or supplanted by positive feelings. If, however, it were possible to unlearn the apprehension through vicarious rather than direct

experience, the therapeutic problem would clearly be simpler.

Children three to five years old who displayed a fear of dogs were used as subjects in an experiment to test just this possibility (Bandura and Menlove, 1968). The extent of their fear was determined by a standardized behavioral test. Interestingly, the more fearful subjects were more likely to come from a family in which one or both parents also reported a fear of dogs.

Over a period of several days after the pretesting phase, the children saw eight different three-minute films. For some of the subjects, the movies pictured a five-year-old boy in progressively closer contact with a cocker spaniel. This *single-model* group saw a variety of scenes, such as the dog drinking from a baby bottle, eating a sucker held by the model, and jumping for food in the model's hand. On the final day the last films showed the model's approach responses to the dog in the playpen, interspersed with several humorous sequences. A second group of children in a *multiple-model* condition saw similar scenes, but instead of only one child and one dog, several male and female models of various ages were shown interacting with different kinds and sizes of dogs. Finally, a third group, serving as a *control* condition, watched irrelevant movies about Disneyland and Marineland that were equal in length to the experimental films.

tions. The expression "like father, like son" implies that children may behave like their parents as well as look like them.

**Observational learning**
Learning that takes place by observing models.

There is considerable evidence that incentives and reinforcements do not play the same crucial role in **observational learning** that they do in operant conditioning. Instead, the important elements in observational learning appear to be identifying with the model, setting up personal achievement goals, and administering self-reinforcement for achieving these goals. Self-reinforcement may be as simple as saying, "See—I *can* do it!" Several studies have shown that learning through the use of models (other people with whom the subject identifies) depends more upon the characteristics of the model and the motivations of the learner than on the use of incentives and reinforcers as such (Rosenthal and Carroll, 1972; Rosenthal and Kellogg, 1973). In one study, an attempt was made to teach disadvantaged Mexican–American second graders to raise questions in a classroom setting. When praise alone was used, there was only a slight increase in questioning behavior. But praise combined with mod-

On the day after the sequence of movies was completed, the avoidance test was readministered to all groups. Compared with their pretest behavior, both the single- and the multiple-model group displayed significantly less fearful avoidance of the dog, but the control subjects remained unchanged. In addition, to determine the durability of these changes, the test was conducted a third time one month later. As Fig. 2.21 shows, the children's increased ability to approach the dog was still apparent after a month.

Although both kinds of films were effective, children who had seen the multiple-model films continued to improve even after the posttest. By the follow-up session, they were significantly more bold than they had been just after treatment. In addition, the groups were compared on the number of children who completed the most difficult task (remaining confined with the dog in the playpen). In the follow-up, twice as many in the multiple-model condition as in the other two groups completed this final task. Thus observing more than one model interacting with more than one dog was superior in eliminating all avoidance behavior to observing one model and one dog. Finally, the investigators stress the importance of having a graded series of scenes progressing from harmless to ordinarily fear-producing situations, rather than confronting the child initially with an active, jumping dog.

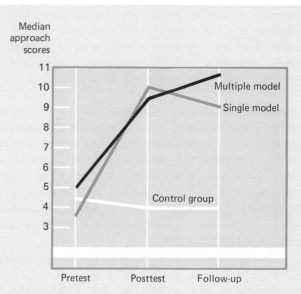

**Figure 2.21**
**Median approach scores obtained by children in each of three conditions at different phases of the experiment.**

**Vicarious**
Experienced through imagining the experience of another.

eling led to large increases in question-asking behavior (Zimmerman and Pike, 1972). Clearly, human learning can occur even without reinforcement, if others are simply watched while they perform.

In some instances, observational learning may have desirable consequences, such as when children learn to manipulate eating utensils as a result of watching their parents. It has also been used successfully in therapeutic situations. For example, someone with a fear of snakes might first view another person handling snakes, then imitate the model's behavior. At other times, the consequences may be undesirable. Children may readily learn from their parents such behaviors as excessive fear of insects, use of foul language, or playing with matches.

The negative aspects of observational learning are of deep concern to many who view the contemporary scene. To what extent does watching violence on television and in the movies lead to imitations of this violence in real life? There is little question that the mass media provide an almost continuous menu of violence. On television alone, a typical child will

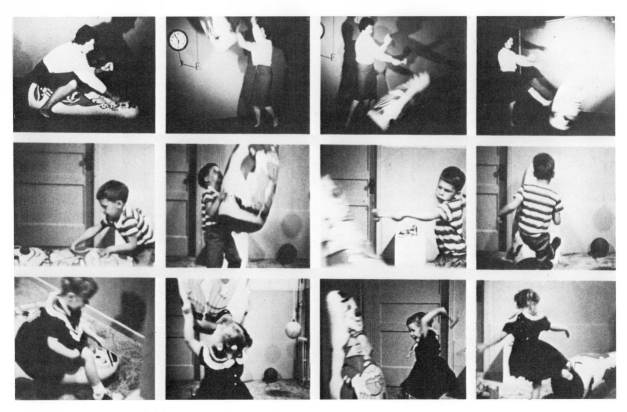

Figure 2.22
Imitating aggressive
behavior

**Nursery school children viewed a film in which an adult was seen throwing, hitting with a hammer, and kicking a clown doll. Afterward the children were observed displaying the same forms of aggressive behavior.**

have been exposed to at least 12,000 violent deaths by age 14 (Buckhout *et al.*, 1971). A series of studies has suggested that viewing violence may increase the likelihood that the viewers will themselves become aggressive if they are frustrated and if they feel that the violence they viewed was justified (Berkowitz, 1968). But Bandura has suggested that prior frustration is *not* a necessary condition for aggression:

> *In short, people do not have to be angered or emotionally aroused to behave aggressively. A culture can produce highly aggressive people, while keeping frustration at a low level, by valuing aggressive accomplishments, furnishing successful aggressive models, and ensuring that aggressive actions secure rewarding effects. (Bandura, 1973, p. 59)*

Several interesting experiments were conducted in order to determine the extent to which models influence the display of aggressive behavior in children. In one study, nursery school children were placed in a room, one at a time, with an adult model. Each child played with a toy on one side of the room while the adult played with toys on another. In the "aggressive model" condition, the adult picked up a clown doll, hit it, punched it, hammered it, and shouted such expressions as "Sock him" and "Pow." In the control condition, the adult played quietly with tinker toys. After this session, all of the children were moved to another room and were frustrated by having some toys taken away. In the second session, only the children exposed to the aggressive model responded with aggression (Bandura *et al.*, 1961).

The type of aggression viewed also has an effect on the aggressive tendencies of children. After children viewed a film in which aggression was realistically portrayed, they engaged in more destructive play than when the aggression was shown in a stylistic fashion (Noble, 1973).

In another experiment, children were found to imitate the aggressive behavior of adult models even when they were presented on film rather than in real life (Bandura *et al.*, 1963). Moreover, the behaviors of the children were very similar to those of the adult models (see Fig. 2.22). In this connection, a leading theorist observes:

> *When a parent punishes a child physically for having aggressed toward peers, for example, the intended outcome of this training is that the child should refrain from hitting others. The child, however, is also learning from parental demonstration how to aggress physically. And the imitative learning may provide the direction for the child's behavior when he is similarly frustrated in subsequent social interactions. (Bandura, 1967)*

We shall discuss other aspects of aggression in Chapters 8 and 9.

It is important to note that in observational learning the model is not merely mimicked. In many cases, the behavior of the imitator will expand upon and modify what was observed. Indeed, children can learn creativity through observation as long as the model exhibits creativity. Imagine the following: Children watch a model name various ways to use a cardboard box (for example, as a container, a house, a hat, or a paperweight). They are then asked to suggest uses for a tin can. It was found that the creativity scores of the children improved even though they rarely used the model's words. Rather, they seemed to have learned the message, "Use your imagination" (Navarick, 1979).

## Summary

1. Learning is defined as a relatively permanent change in behavior resulting from experience or practice.
2. In one of the two basic forms of learning, classical conditioning, a neutral stimulus is paired with another stimulus (the unconditioned stimulus or US) that naturally gives rise to a given response (the unconditioned response or UR). The neutral stimulus acquires the capacity to elicit this response. The previously neutral stimulus is now called the conditioned stimulus (CS), and the response is called the conditioned response (CR).
3. When the CS is presented alone on a number of successive trials (extinction trials), the strength of the CR gradually decreases.
4. If an organism that has undergone experimental extinction is brought back into the experimental setting at a later time, the presentation of the CS alone may lead to the occurrence of the CR. This is called spontaneous recovery.
5. When a response to a given stimulus has been learned, the organism tends to make that response to similar stimuli as well. This is called stimulus generalization. Usually, the greater the

similarity of the other stimuli to the original CS, the greater the tendency is for the CR to occur.

6. Learning to make distinctions among similar stimuli is called discrimination learning. In discrimination learning, the US is associated with the positive stimulus and not with the negative stimulus.

7. In higher-order conditioning, the CS is paired with a neutral stimulus, so that the neutral stimulus gradually acquires the capacity to elicit the CR. However, the ability to achieve higher-order conditioning is limited by the fact that the CS used in place of the US undergoes experimental extinction if it is not occasionally paired with the US.

8. The principles of classical conditioning have many practical implications. Unreasonable and irrational fears can be conditioned and, through generalization and higher-order conditioning, spread to a wide variety of stimuli.

9. In the other basic form of learning, operant conditioning, the organism typically operates upon its environment in order to bring about reinforcement. Reinforcement is most effective when it immediately follows the response to be learned.

10. The principle of immediacy of reinforcement has many practical applications in everyday life as well as in educational settings. Teaching machines, programmed learning, and computer-assisted instruction are some of the educational applications based on the principle of immediate reinforcement.

11. There are two types of reinforcers—positive and negative. Both strengthen a response that precedes it, positive reinforcement by its presentation and negative reinforcement by its removal.

12. Escape conditioning occurs when a subject learns a behavior in order to escape an unpleasant consequence (negative reinforcement). When the same subject then performs that learned behavior prior to the reinforcement's being administered, we say that avoidance learning has taken place.

13. Many responses initially have a low probability of occurring; but by reinforcing successive approximations of the desired behavior, it is possible to "shape" the final response. Moreover, a whole series of responses can be shaped individually and then chained together to form a complex sequence of responses.

14. Extinction, spontaneous recovery, and general-

ization occur in operant conditioning just as in classical conditioning.

15. To establish a discrimination during operant conditioning, we reinforce the response when it occurs in the presence of the positive stimulus and do not reinforce the behavior in the presence of the negative stimulus.

16. Food for a hungry organism and water for a thirsty organism are primary reinforcers, for they directly fulfill physical needs and their reinforcement value depends little, if at all, on previous learning. Nevertheless, any event regularly associated with a primary reinforcer comes to acquire reinforcing properties (that is, it becomes a secondary reinforcer).

17. Some forms of behavior modification rely heavily on the use of tokens as secondary reinforcers. Recent evidence suggests that tokens and rewards should not be used indiscriminately. It appears that rewards may undermine intrinsic motivation while strengthening extrinsically motivated behavior.

18. When reinforcement is applied to a given behavior only a portion of the times that it occurs, the behavior becomes more resistant to experimental extinction. Four different schedules of reinforcement have been studied: fixed interval, variable interval, fixed ratio, and variable ratio.

19. There are two classes of punishment. Negative punishment consists of removing something "good" following the undesired response, whereas positive punishment consists of adding something "bad" following the undesired response. The most general effect of punishment is to suppress the response that preceded it. Timing, consistency, and severity are crucial factors in the administration of punishment.

20. An intriguing concept arising from research on operant conditioning is that the same principles of learning that guide the acquisition of adaptive behavior also apply to the acquisition of maladaptive responses. *Any* behavior is likely to be learned if it is reinforced.

21. Many aspects of human behavior are acquired primarily through observation and imitation rather than through reinforcement and punishment. Such behaviors include the use of language, smoking, and reading. Negative behaviors, including aggression, are also learned through observation.

# Terms to Remember

Instinctive behavior

Learning

Construct

Physiology

Classical conditioning (Pavlovian conditioning)

Unconditioned stimulus (US)

Unconditioned response (UR)

Conditioned stimulus (CS)

Conditioned response (CR)

Acquisition

Extinction (classical conditioning)

Spontaneous recovery

Stimulus generalization

Semantically related

Discrimination

Experimental neurosis

Higher-order conditioning

Desensitization

Behavior therapy

Operant conditioning

Reinforcement

Teaching machine

Programmed instruction

Computer-assisted instruction

Positive reinforcement

Negative reinforcement

Escape conditioning

Avoidance conditioning

Shaping

Contingent reinforcement

Superstitious behavior

Extinction (operant conditioning)

Primary reinforcement

Secondary reinforcement

Token economy

Partial reinforcement

Continuous reinforcement

Schedule of reinforcement

Fixed-interval schedule (FI)

Variable-interval schedule (VI)

Observational learning

Fixed-ratio schedule (FR)

Variable-ratio schedule (VR)

Incompatible-response method

Toleration method

Exhaustion method

Change-of-environment method

Down's syndrome

Self-ambulation

Intrinsic motivation

Extrinsic motivation

Vicarious

3

# REMEMBERING AND FORGETTING

Have you ever been introduced to a person at a party and found that you couldn't recall his or her name a short time later? You probably attributed this failure to poor memory. Perhaps you were right. On the other hand, you may never really have learned the name to begin with.

There is an old German proverb: "He lies like an eyewitness." Capable attorneys never accept an eyewitness report at face value. They know that the original observations may have been inadequate and that memory itself is subject to distortions. A striking proof of this has been unwittingly provided by a group of scientists well trained in observation. During a professional meeting, two men rushed into the meeting room, shouting and scuffling. One of the men was dressed in a clown suit; the other was wearing white pants, a red tie, and a blue jacket.

This incident had been carefully planned in advance. The scientists were asked to write reports, allegedly as part of a police investigation. Of the 40 scientists reporting, 35 misstated some of the facts. The suit of the second man was variously described as brown, striped, coffee-colored, or red. Some scientists reported on the details of the second man's hat, although in fact he wore no hat (Whalen, 1949).

Is this a demonstration of faulty memory? Not necessarily. Any discussion of memory presupposes that some learning has taken place. It is only after we have learned something that we can legitimately begin raising questions about the storage and retrieval of learned materials. In the case of the 40 scientists, it is wrong to conclude that memory is at fault when, in fact, the failure was probably caused by the ineffectiveness of the original learning. If something is not learned well to begin with, there will obviously be difficulties in retrieval.

## WHAT IS MEMORY?

The definition of **memory** poses a problem. So far, we have been making references to memory as if it were an object. In everyday speech, we continually refer to memory in this way. We speak of a good memory, a poor memory, a better memory for faces than for names. We worry about failing memory and seek aids to improve it, as if it were a part of the body. Memory is not something that can be seen or felt. It is a construct; that is, it is inferred from certain behaviors of the individual. Consider the following examples: (1) You have read a novel and, at a later date, can write an essay on it. (2) You make some new acquaintances at a party, and when you see them again, you recognize their faces. (3) As a child you learned to play a musical instrument, and when you take it up again years later, you are surprised at how easily you relearn fingering exercises which caused so much consternation in childhood.

There are three main stages in each of these illustrations. The first stage involved some experience, or learning: reading a novel, meeting people, learning to play a musical instrument. The third stage (retrieval stage) involved some activity or behavior that was clearly influenced by the first stage: writing the essay, recognizing the people, relearning the instrument. The middle or intervening stage involved retention of the prior experiences in such a way that they influenced later behavior. Be-

**Memory**
Retention of prior experiences in such a way that they influence later behavior.

**Recall**
A method of measuring retention whereby the individual must reproduce a previously learned response with a bare minimum of cues.

havior during this intervening time may not reflect the prior experiences at all. However, when you are able to write the essay, recognize the faces, and relearn the instrument, we may infer that you have somehow retained the prior, learned experiences. It is this retention stage that we refer to as memory. To the extent that you are unable to perform these activities, we infer that forgetting has taken place.

Because memory is unobservable, it must be inferred from the retrieval stage. For this psychologists have devised different measuring techniques: recall, recognition, and relearning. As you will see, each of these ways of measuring retention may provide a somewhat different estimate of how much has been retained.

## MEASURES OF RETENTION

### Recall

**Recall** is the method whereby the subjects are required to reproduce from memory what they have previously learned. If we were to ask you to name all the presidents of the United States, recite the Pledge of Allegiance, or sing a popular song, we would be using the recall method for testing your retention. The most common type of recall test used in schools is the essay examination. If your instructor were to ask you on an exam to distinguish between classical and operant conditioning, he or she would be asking you to recall (without references or aids) previously learned material. Try the following demonstration. Without making use of any resource except your own memory, compile a list of all presidents of the United States. Do not be concerned about placing them in the order in which they served. Keep a record of your list so that you can later obtain a score of number correct.

As the opening eyewitness report demonstrates, recall is subject to distortions and error. Box 3.1 presents an excerpt of a classic study that shows some of the distortions that can take place.

The three stages of memory: (a) learning, (b) remembering, (c) retention.

(a)                                (b)                                (c)

## BOX 3.1

### Distortions in Recall

The most famous experiment on reconstruction in story recall was reported in 1932 by the late British psychologist Bartlett. He presented Oxford students with a legend that originates with a Pacific Northwest Indian culture, and then asked the students after varying intervals to recall the story. By comparing the recall version to the original, Bartlett was able to examine how the story was reconstructed. Story (a) presents the original legend, *The War of the Ghosts*, while story (b) presents the recall protocol of a 1977 Rutgers undergraduate, taken five days after hearing the story.

### Story (a)
### The Original Version of Bartlett's *The War of the Ghosts*

One night two young men from Egulac went down to the river to hunt seals, and while they were there it became foggy and calm. Then they heard war-cries, and they thought: "Maybe this is a war party." They escaped to the shore, and hid behind a log. Now canoes came up, and they heard the noise of paddles, and saw one canoe coming up to them. There were five men in the canoe, and they said:

"What do you think? We wish to take you along. We are going up the river to make war on the people."

One of the young men said: "I have no arrows."

"Arrows are in the canoe," they said.

"I will not go along. I might be killed. My relatives do not know where I have gone. But you," he said, turning to the other, "may go with them."

So one of the young men went, but the other returned home.

And the warriors went on up the river to a town on the other side of Kalama. The people came down to the water, and they began to fight, and many were killed. But presently the young man heard one of the warriors say: "Quick, let us go home: that Indian has been hit." Now he thought: "Oh, they are ghosts." He did not feel sick, but they said he had been shot.

So the canoes went back to Egulac, and the young man went ashore to his house, and made a fire. And he told everybody and said: "Behold I ac-companied the ghosts, and we went to fight. Many of our fellows were killed, and many of those who attacked us were killed. They said I was hit, and I did not feel sick."

He told it all, and then he became quiet. When the sun rose he fell down. Something black came out of his mouth. His face became contorted. The people jumped up and cried.

He was dead.

### Story (b)
### Recall Protocol of a Rutgers Undergraduate Taken Five Days after Hearing the Story

Two young men were by a river when they saw a canoe coming downstream. They hid behind a log but were still seen by the people in the canoe. They asked the two men if they wanted to come along. The one replied that he couldn't because none of his family knew where he was, but he told the other man to go ahead, while he went home. The men in the canoe said they were going to war. When they reached the village they shot their bows and arrows till one man said "We've got the Indian." Then they turned around to go back home. When the young man got home everyone was there. Even though he thought he had been shot, he wasn't dead. The next morning something black came out of his mouth and his body became contorted. He was dead.

The important thing to note in comparing the two versions of the story is not just how much was not recalled, but how much was invented to fill in the gaps around the material that was left out. Details like the names of places were omitted. But other details, like the shooting of bows and arrows during the fight, were added. The remarkable thing is that the recall protocol is quite a logical story, with a beginning, a simple plot, and a conclusion. In some ways it seems more logical than the original Indian legend, which comes from a culture very different from our own. But note, too, that the recall protocol is really a different story. The ghosts have even become men. The person was unable to distinguish the logical connections that were in the story from those that were not.

---

Glass *et al.*, 1979, pp. 115–117.

## Recognition

Some of you may at one time or another have learned the names of the presidents of the United States. When you attempted to recall them in the preceding section, how did you do? The odds are that you could not remember all of them. You might erroneously conclude that you had completely forgotten the names of some of the presidents. Box 3.2 contains a list of 67 names. Check off those names you recognize as presidents. Then turn to the answers on page 90. Find the number correct when you used the recall and the recognition method. Although this demonstration lacks the elements necessary for scientific proof, do not be surprised to find that your score on this test is considerably higher than it was when you tried to recall the names. This method of testing retention is known as **recognition**.

**Recognition**
A method of measuring retention whereby the individual must demonstrate the ability to identify previously learned material.

Our capacity to recognize previous events and experiences is often astounding. We meet thousands of people in a lifetime, read countless books, and learn hundreds of thousands of bits of factual information. Yet somehow we can sift the familiar from the unfamiliar. For example, you may not be able to recall the name of your third-grade teacher, but chances are you would recognize it if you heard it. Similarly, how often have you seen a movie and been unable to recall the title later? Yet if you were to see it listed, you would certainly recognize it. Look at Figs. 3.1 and 3.2 to test your powers of recognition.

**Figure 3.1**
**Recognition**

Look at the faces in this picture for about 10 seconds. Then turn to Fig. 3.2 and see if you can recognize which of the faces reappear.

## BOX 3.2

### Recognition Test

| | | |
|---|---|---|
| Harry S Truman | Andrew Johnson | Charles Curtis |
| Garret A. Hobart | Eugene McCarthy | John Quincy Adams |
| John Adams | John C. Calhoun | Woodrow Wilson |
| Calvin Coolidge | Richard M. Johnson | Martin Van Buren |
| Henry Wilson | George Clinton | James Sherman |
| Ulysses S. Grant | Henry Ford | Abraham Lincoln |
| Millard Fillmore | Thomas A. Hendricks | Alben W. Barkley |
| William King | John Tyler | Zachary Taylor |
| Gerald Ford | John C. Breckenridge | James Monroe |
| Charles Fairbanks | Richard Nixon | Lyndon B. Johnson |
| Chester A. Arthur | Steven G. Cleveland | Warren G. Harding |
| George Washington | John N. Garner | William McKinley |
| Aaron Burr | Franklin Pierce | Henry A. Wallace |
| Benjamin Harrison | Charles Dawes | James A. Garfield |
| John F. Kennedy | Grover Cleveland | James Buchanan |
| William H. Harrison | William Wheeler | Franklin D. Roosevelt |
| Tom Dewey | Thomas Jefferson | Andrew Jackson |
| Herbert C. Hoover | Theodore Roosevelt | James K. Polk |
| Leve P. Marton | Ronald Reagan | William H. Taft |
| George M. Dallas | Dwight D. Eisenhower | Daniel D. Tomkins |
| Rutherford B. Hayes | James Madison | Benjamin Franklin |
| Elbridge Gerry | Thomas R. Marshall | Jimmy Carter |
| Adlai E. Stevenson | | |

Check off the names you recognize as presidents of the United States.

Compare your score on this task with your recall score. See the answers on p. 90.

Under most circumstances, recognition is superior to recall at all age levels (Baltes *et al.*, 1980). However, the superiority of recognition over recall diminishes as the number of alternatives is increased (Davis *et al.*, 1961). You may have noticed that a multiple-choice test with five or six alternatives for each question is usually more difficult than a similar test with fewer alternatives. The recognition task also becomes more difficult when the alternatives are quite similar to one another (Bahrick and Bahrick, 1964).

These experimental findings can be illustrated by an experience many of us have had. You may be able to recall, without difficulty, that a friend's phone number is 836–6720. But suppose someone asks you, "Is Beth's phone number 836–6720, 863–6720, or 836–6702?" At this point, you may just give up trying to remember the right number and look it up in the phone book.

## Relearning

We have all had some experience in relearning material that we thought we had forgotten, and probably found that it was easier to learn the second time around. **Relearning** may detect evidence of retention, even though other methods suggest that nothing has been retained. For example, sometimes children born in one country emigrate to another, where a different language is spoken. Years later they may seem to have forgotten everything they knew about their native language, and they may be unable to recall or even recognize words from it. But if they attempt to relearn it, they are often surprised at how quickly it comes back to them.

Relearning is sometimes referred to as savings, because we save time and effort when we relearn previously learned material. To illustrate, let us imagine that you required 15 trials to learn something in the original learning situation. At a later time, you relearned this material and required only 10 trials. By subtracting the number of trials required to relearn from the trials required for original learning, we obtain a **savings score.** In the present example, the savings score is 5. We may express this savings as a percentage by using the following formula:

$$\text{percentage of savings} = \frac{\text{original learning score} - \text{relearning score}}{\text{original learning score}} \times 100.$$

**Relearning**
A method of measuring retention whereby the individual relearns material that has been partially or completely forgotten. The difference in the amount of practice required to achieve the original point of mastery provides a measure of the degree of retention.

**Savings score**
A measure of retention, this is the percentage score indicating the time saved in relearning material.

Figure 3.2

Answer to Box 3.2

| | | |
|---|---|---|
| Harry S Truman | John Tyler | Zachary Taylor |
| John Adams | Richard Nixon | James Monroe |
| Calvin Coolidge | Steven G. Cleveland | Lyndon B. Johnson |
| Ulysses S. Grant | Franklin Pierce | Warren G. Harding |
| Millard Fillmore | Grover Cleveland | William McKinley |
| Gerald Ford | Thomas Jefferson | James A. Garfield |
| Chester A. Arthur | Theodore Roosevelt | James Buchanan |
| George Washington | Ronald Reagan | Franklin D. Roosevelt |
| Benjamin Harrison | Dwight D. Eisenhower | Andrew Jackson |
| John F. Kennedy | James Madison | James K. Polk |
| William H. Harrison | John Quincy Adams | William H. Taft |
| Herbert C. Hoover | Woodrow Wilson | Jimmy Carter |
| Rutherford B. Hayes | Martin Van Buren | |
| Andrew Johnson | Abraham Lincoln | |

In the example just given, the percentage of savings is

$$\frac{15 - 10}{15} \times 100 = 33.3\%.$$

Although relearning is the most sensitive method for testing retention, it is not frequently employed in any real-life situation because it is so difficult to use. The relearning method requires us to compare an original measure of learning. For example, if you were to relearn the names of the presidents of the United States, you would probably require far less time than it took you originally. But because there is no way of knowing how long it took you originally, it is impossible to make a comparison.

In a laboratory, where accurate measures of original learning are routinely obtained, the relearning method is often used to test retention. The relearning method was used by Hermann Ebbinghaus (1850–1909), a German psychologist who conducted the first systematic studies on remembering and forgetting.

Curve of forgetting.   Ebbinghaus was interested in studying the process of memorizing in its simplest and purest form. He recognized that the memorizing of prose, poetry, or other meaningful materials is influenced by past experiences and by emotional and personality factors. Therefore he designed learning materials that were essentially free of the influence of these factors. These materials consisted of three-letter combinations known as **nonsense syllables.** Each nonsense syllable was formed by putting a vowel between two consonants, for example, ZEB, NOV, KUL. Ebbinghaus constructed lists of these nonsense syllables and memorized

**Nonsense syllables**
Three-letter combinations that do not make a word—for example, ZEB.

Hermann Ebbinghaus

Percentage remembered

100
80
60
40
20
1  2  3  4  5  6  7  30

Days after learning

Figure 3.3
**Ebbinghaus's curve of forgetting**

Using himself as a subject, Ebbinghaus memorized lists of nonsense syllables and then noted how long it took him to relearn these lists. Notice that most of the forgetting took place within one day and that forgetting remained relatively stable thereafter. (Ebbinghaus, 1913)

them himself. He was careful to maintain the strictest possible experimental controls. He standardized the material to be memorized, and used exactly the same procedures throughout his investigations. As he memorized each list, he carefully recorded how long it took him. Then he set his lists aside for a specfied interval. At the end of that time, he relearned the same lists, again recording the amount of time required. The difference between the original learning time and the relearning time gave him a measure of retention.

Figure 3.3 presents the results that Ebbinghaus obtained with varying intervals of time between original learning and relearning. Notice that most of his forgetting took place within the first few hours; however, even after 30 days he retained some of his prior learning. This curve is sometimes referred to as the typical curve of forgetting, and much forgetting probably does follow this course. However, recent evidence challenges the generality of the Ebbinghaus forgetting curve. Using pictures, instead of nonsense syllables, several investigators (Erdelyi and Becker, 1974; Erdelyi and Kleinbard, 1978) have found *increased* retention with the passage of time. Figure 3.4 presents "forgetting" curves for picture and word lists based on the averages of six subjects. For the pictures, there is a surprising net gain of 44 percent between the first few minutes of recall and recall almost 7 days later. In contrast, the recall of the words remained relatively stable throughout the period. Thus it appears that the very sharp drop in remembering observed by Ebbinghaus may result from the use of nonsense syllables (Erdelyi and Kleinbard, 1978).

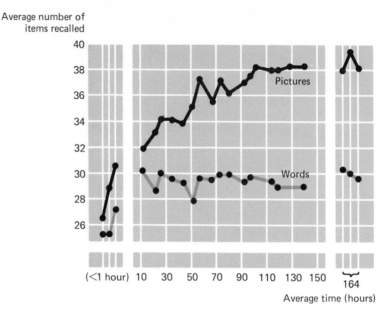

Figure 3.4
Average "forgetting" curves
for picture and word lists
**Note that the word "forgetting," in this context, refers to the amount recalled. (Erdelyi and Kleinbard, 1978)**

However, in the actual world of day-to-day learning, forgetting does take place. For example, if someone were to ask you immediately after class what a lecture was about, you would probably be able to give a pretty complete summary. But one day later, you might be hard pressed to provide more than a scant outline of the material covered. Why does this happen? Does the mere passage of time make us forget, or are more active processes responsible? Is forgetting selective? Are some things remembered better, and if so, why?

These are some of the challenging questions for which psychology has sought and is still seeking answers. The following section is concerned with the various theories that have been proposed to explain why we forget. Keep the questions just raised in mind as you read.

## THEORIES OF FORGETTING

### Disuse Theory

The theory of **disuse** holds that learning produces a **memory trace** that automatically fades or decays with the passage of time. On the surface, this theory appears quite convincing. We have already observed that our retention of events is much better just after the event has occurred and seems to dissipate with the passage of time. In many ways the fading of the memory trace resembles the channels formed on sandy beaches after a rainstorm. With disuse, the memory trace tends to fade away, much as the channels on the beach disappear when water no longer runs through them.

Many of our everyday experiences seem to support the disuse theory. The body-builder's magnificently muscled body turns to jelly after a

**Disuse theory of forgetting**
The theory that learning produces a memory trace which automatically fades or decays with the passage of time.

**Memory trace**
A modification of nervous tissue presumed to underlie memory. This is a construct used to explain retention.

weight-lifting program is abandoned. Students who have studied a course in school report later that, unless they have practiced some of the knowledge or skills they acquired in the course, they seem unable to remember any of the content. Similarly, medical doctors who specialize in a particular field frequently find it difficult to remember aspects of medical practice that fall outside their specialty. On the other hand, a person who is studying a course in which immediate applications are possible is likely to find that he or she retains much of what was learned.

As attractive or appealing as this theory seems, there is much evidence that forgetting involves far more complex processes than the mere fading of memory traces as a result of disuse. If all forgetting simply involves decay of memory traces, why are some things better remembered than others, even though the amount of practice is comparable? Why do we often fail to remember events exactly as they occurred? Obviously, disuse theory cannot explain questions like these. There must be more to forgetting than merely spontaneous decay of a memory trace.

## Trace Transformation

Some theorists accept the notion of a memory trace, but suggest that there is a change in the pattern of the trace rather than a weakening of it. Such changes may account for many of the distortions in memory.

In many social situations, we tell about daily events in our lives. We recount news, gossip, and conversations we have had. We talk about books we have read and movies we have seen. How accurate are our reports? At the beginning of this chapter, we described an experiment in which scientists could not report accurately the details of an event they had witnessed. And what is more to the point, the reports contained

Waitresses and waiters can generally recall an order without writing the details down—until the customer pays the bill. Once the transaction has been completed, the order is forgotten, a phenomenon known as the Zeigarnik effect. Apparently, our ability to remember unfinished tasks is related to the tension created by our desire to complete the task well.

many distortions of remembered "facts." Supporters of the **trace transformation theory** say that these distortions result from transformations of memory traces that occur as time passes. Critics of both the disuse and the transformation theories point out that memory traces have not been demonstrated to exist. They also argue that both the fading and the distortions that occur in memory can be explained in terms of other processes.

## Interference Theory

A more widely held theory maintains that it is not merely the passage of time that produces forgetting. This view holds that events intervening after the original learning may interfere with the retention of this learning. This **interference,** rather than time itself, is what causes forgetting.

A classic experiment demonstrated the effect of intervening activity on retention of previously learned material. Two undergraduates at Cornell University learned lists of nonsense syllables. Following the learning of each list, the subjects were tested to find out how much they recalled one, two, four, and eight hours later. Some of the lists were learned in the morning and some before going to sleep. Thus the period intervening after learning involved either sleep or normal waking activity. Figure 3.5 shows that when the subjects were tested with sleep as their intervening activity, they retained more of what they had learned than when they spent their time in waking activities. If the mere passage of time were the only variable of importance, we would expect the two curves of retention to be the same. Because they were not the same, we conclude that the intervening activity is a determining factor in retention (Jenkins and Dallenbach, 1924).

Although the investigators in this study established the importance of interference in forgetting, they were not able to specify which features of the intervening activities were responsible for the interference. Most subsequent studies have focused on determining the relationship between the type of intervening activity and the amount of forgetting.

**Retroactive interference,** often called **retroactive inhibition,** refers to the interfering effect of an intervening activity on retention of previous learning. The typical experimental design for investigating retroactive interference is as follows:

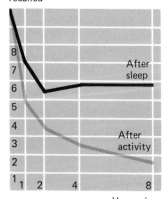

Number of syllables recalled

After sleep

After activity

Hours since learning

**Figure 3.5**

This graph shows that more of the learned material was retained when sleep was the intervening activity. (Jenkins and Dallenbach, 1924)

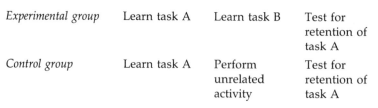

| *Experimental group* | Learn task A | Learn task B | Test for retention of task A |
| --- | --- | --- | --- |
| *Control group* | Learn task A | Perform unrelated activity | Test for retention of task A |

In a typical retroactive interference study, the two groups are compared with respect to their performance on the retention task. If the retention scores of the experimental group are lower than those of the control group, we may infer that the difference is due to interference by the intervening activity. Various investigators have established the conditions under which this interference is greatest. Perhaps the best way to under-

**Trace transformation theory of forgetting**
The theory that explains distortions in memory in terms of changes in the pattern of the memory trace.

**Interference theory of forgetting**
The theory that events intervening after the original learning may interfere with the retention of this learning.

**Retroactive interference (retroactive inhibition)**
Loss in retention caused by the nature of the activity intervening between learning and remembering.

**Proactive interference**
The interference of one task with the retention of a second.

stand retroactive interference is to try the following experiment. For task A, require your subjects to learn to operate a combination lock. Then have half of these subjects (the experimental group) learn a different combination for a similar lock. Have the remaining subjects (control group) rest for an equivalent amount of time. Test both groups for retention of task A. The experimental group should show retroactive interference.

This simple experiment demonstrates an important aspect of retroactive interference. When a subject is required to learn in sequence different responses to similar stimuli, learning of the second response interferes with retention of the original response. The greater the similarity of the stimuli, the greater the retroactive interference will be. It should be pointed out that the retention of the second task may also be similarly affected by the prior learning of task A. The interference of one task with the retention of a second, later, task is called **proactive interference.**

Proactive and retroactive interference have considerable predictive value for many behaviors. For example, imagine the foyer of a large apartment house, with hundreds of mailboxes labeled with people's names. The mail carrier who makes the delivery every day has probably learned the location of everyone's name. Now suppose someone switched all the names to different boxes. How do you think the prior experience with task A would affect the ability of the mail carrier to remember the new order of names? It seems very likely that remembering the new order would be confusing and difficult, owing to proactive interference (see Fig. 3.6).

Interference theory has many practical implications for classroom study and learning. Because similar learning materials (e.g., two different foreign languages) are likely to interfere with one another, it is advisable not to attend similar classes back-to-back or to study a subject immediately after studying a related one.

We cannot dispute the fact that these interference effects occur. But whether the interference theory constitutes an adequate explanation for forgetting remains to be seen.

**Figure 3.6**
**Proactive interference**

After the mail carrier learns to master the order of names on the mailboxes (task A), all of the names are changed to different positions (task B). Remembering task B has been made more difficult by the prior learning of task A (proactive interference).

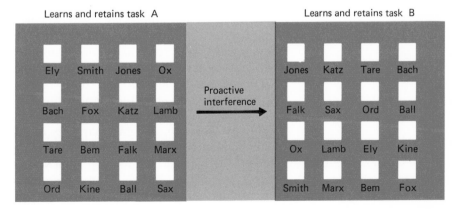

Learns and retains task A · Learns and retains task B

## Motivated Forgetting

One theory that attempts to account for the selective nature of forgetting (that is, the fact that we forget certain things and remember others) maintains that we forget certain events or experiences because we are unconsciously **motivated** to do so.

Indeed, a cornerstone concept of psychoanalytic theory is a form of motivated forgetting known as **repression** (the ejection of anxiety-arousing material from the consciousness). As stated by Freud, "The essence of repression lies simply in the function of rejecting and keeping something out of consciousness" (Freud, 1957, p. 105). Although Freud looked at repression as a means of defending ourselves against guilt, shame, and unfavorable self-evaluations, numerous researchers extended the concept to apply to all painful experiences. Thus some investigators (e.g., Glucksberg and King, 1967) have used painful shocks as a means of experimentally demonstrating repression. However, one critic (Holmes, 1972) has concluded that the experimental attempts to demonstrate repression are flawed, because it is difficult to separate repression from conditioned avoidance.

It is important to note that Freud did not consider all painful experiences as candidates for repression. Rather, only thoughts that were psychologically painful, such as "intolerable ideas," "unbearable affect," "anxiety," or "guilt," were eligible for repression (Erdelyi and Goldberg, 1979, p. 361). We discuss the concept of repression in greater detail in Chapter 13.

In this section we have discussed four different theories of forgetting. It is important to recognize that *each* theory may have a piece of the truth. We do not yet know enough to choose among these theories or to find the "true" theory.

**Motivated forgetting**
A theory which maintains that we forget certain events or experiences because we are unconsciously motivated to do so.

**Repression**
A block in retrieval caused by anxiety associated with the blocked memory.

**Sensory receptors**
Specialized surfaces that are sensitive to particular types of stimuli.

**Sensory register**
A system for holding stimulus information in its original form (sound as sound, vision as image, etc.) for brief periods of time. It is presumed that there is a separate sensory register for each sense modality.

## INFORMATION PROCESSING: THE TWO TYPES OF MEMORY

At any given moment in time, our **sensory receptors** are being bombarded by an incredibly broad assortment of stimuli. There are sounds in profusion—the blowing wind, an airplane overhead, a dog barking, a child playing, and a bird singing. As you turn your head, thousands of images pass rapidly across your visual field. And then there are odors from cooking, or from the plant that is flowering on your desk. Moreover, the clothing on your back and the pen in your hand provide a continuous array of touch sensations. For the most part, these many stimuli fleetingly move across your sensory field and then disappear, never to be heard from again. They have had little or no impact on you and there is little reason to believe that they have left any permanent records in your brain. Nevertheless, it does appear that traces of these stimuli linger long enough for you to attend to them, if the need develops. This brief holding of information about a stimulus is known as a **sensory register** (Klatzky, 1975). To illustrate, imagine that a cry of distress is included in the stimulus bombardment. The sensory register holds a trace of this stimulus sufficiently long for you to drop what you are doing and shift your attention to the distress signal. During the brief period of time the raw sensory information remains in the sensory register, it can be evaluated. Once it is recognized, and meaning is associated with the stimulus, the memory in sensory register ceases (Di Lollo, 1977). Information processing can now move into the next stage of the information-processing system.

## Short-term Memory (STM)

**Short-term memory (STM)**
A type of memory of extremely short duration and limited capacity.

**Memory span**
The amount of information that an individual can absorb in short-term memory and recall immediately.

Most of the earlier studies of memory were concerned with assessing retention over relatively long periods of time—hours, days, and even months. However, in 1959, Peterson and Peterson conducted a landmark study that unleashed a flood of experimentation and speculation about forgetting that takes place within a matter of seconds (see Fig. 3.7). In this study, the experimenter spelled a three-unit nonsense syllable that the subject was asked to remember. To prevent rehearsal, the subject was required to count backward by threes or fours from a three-digit number. The counting was paced by a metronome. At a given signal, the subject was asked to recall the three-unit nonsense syllable. Forgetting was extremely rapid; the ability to remember fell to less than 10 percent after an interval of only 18 seconds. Results obtained in this and subsequent studies have led many researchers to postulate a type of memory of extremely short duration called **short-term memory (STM).**

In this stage, the information is stored briefly, as in sensory register. But it is no longer in sensory form. Usually it is transformed into an acoustic form; that is, we code it into sound. Thus, if we look up a number in the telephone directory, it is first seen as a visual image. It is held in this form long enough to be transformed into acoustic symbols. We say to ourselves: five five five one two one two. But the number will quickly fade into oblivion unless we repeat it again and again.

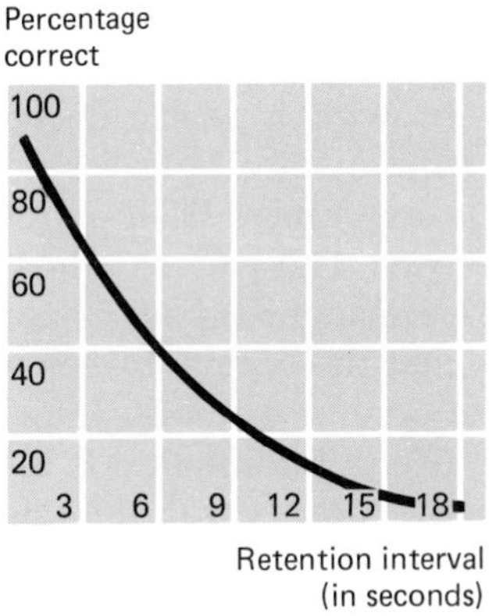

One of the outstanding characteristics of STM is its extremely limited capacity, in terms of the amount of information that can be temporarily stored at any given time. We use the term **memory span** to refer to the amount of information that an individual can absorb in STM and recall immediately. Memory span appears to be limited to seven items, give or take two (Miller, 1956). One of the leading researchers in human memory (Wickelgren, 1981) has proposed that the attentional span is the only distinctive form of STM. Wickelgren refers to this form of memory as *active memory*. He has cautioned:

> *It is unreasonable to tell a co-worker or friend in a five-minute period ten things you want that person to do and expect him or her to remember it all without mistakes. . . . One source of friction in personal relations and of inefficiency in job performance could be eliminated if we remembered that the capacity for learning and memory is limited. (Wickelgren, 1977, p. 4)*

It has been fairly well established that memory span increases during childhood, peaks in early adulthood, and declines thereafter (Baltes *et al.,* 1980).

Short-term memory holds information just long enough for it to be acted upon in some immediate way. When you call directory assistance and ask the operator for the number of a person living at a certain address, the operator has to retain the information only briefly. By the time

Percentage correct

Retention interval
(in seconds)

**Figure 3.7**
**Short-term memory**

As can be seen in this figure, the subject's ability to recall a three-unit nonsense syllable diminished rapidly, falling to less than 10 percent after an 18-second interval. The results of this landmark study prompted much interest in short-term memory. (Peterson and Peterson, 1959)

Short-term memory is short-lived and limited. President and Mrs. Reagan use short-term memory on the campaign trail. They shake hands with and chat with hundreds of people but remember each face only until they move on to the next person.

the next request comes in, he or she has probably already forgotten the name and address you had mentioned. This speed of forgetting in short-term memory is often advantageous. Telephone operators would be utterly confused if they retained all the names, addresses, and numbers they heard during the course of a day.

The impact of most events on STM is like throwing a pebble into a lake. It produces no more than a ripple, which fades away and leaves no permanent record. Obviously, some information that enters STM is not lost, but rather is permanently stored in some way. The way in which information gets transferred from STM to some permanent storage is not yet clearly understood. We do know, however, that there must be some interaction between STM and a more permanent type of memory. Information must be filtered in such a way that the useful information is retained and the useless information is discarded. When you read this book, you do not remember every word. Somehow you are able to select those words and thoughts that are important, compare them with what you have previously learned and retained, and transfer some of the new information into more permanent storage.

## Long-term Memory (LTM)

There are many memories that seem to be stored within the brain for long periods of time—a day, a year, or a lifetime (see Box 3.3). Our own names and addresses, the vocabulary and structure of the language we speak, and significant past events all exemplify **long-term memory (LTM).** One of the leading authorities on human memory (Wickelgren, 1981) refers to LTM as associative long-term memory. According to him, associative

**Long-term memory (LTM)**
A type of memory of extremely long duration.

**RNA (ribonucleic acid)**
A complex molecule presumed to play an important role in the physiological basis of memory.

long-term memory includes a component that decays rapidly because of interference effects. In his view, this component plays an important role in speech recognition, articulation, and reading.

There is a great deal of research going on to determine the underlying mechanisms for short- and long-term memory. Much of the research concerned with LTM has focused on a complex molecule called **RNA (ribonucleic acid)**. RNA is produced in the nucleus and then moves into the remaining portions of the cell. It has been suggested that RNA is capable of encoding the type of information involved in human memory (Hyden, 1969).

## BOX 3.3

### Storage Capacity of Long-term Memory

It is easy to overlook the incredible storage capacity of the human brain. Alex Haley's twelve-year search for the roots of his ancestral line could never have succeeded were it not for the extraordinary memorizing feats of elder villagers in the land of his origins. The following excerpt from *Roots* describes the training of these *griots* as well as their enormous capacity to store information.

*Then they told me something of which I'd never have dreamed: of very old men, called griots, still to be found in the older back-country villages, men who were in effect living, walking archives of oral history. A senior griot would be a man usually in his late sixties or early seventies; below him would be progressively younger griots—and apprenticing boys, so a boy would be exposed to those griots' particular line of narrative for forty or fifty years before he could qualify as a senior griot, who told on special occasions the centuries-old histories of villages, of clans, of families, of great heroes. Throughout the whole of black Africa such oral chronicles had been handed down since the time of the ancient forefathers, I was informed, and there were certain legendary griots who could narrate facets of African history literally for as long as three days without ever repeating themselves.*

*Seeing how astounded I was, these Gambian men reminded me that every living person ancestrally goes back to some time and some place where no writing existed; and then human memories and mouths and ears were the only ways those human*

*beings could store and relay information. They said that we who live in the Western culture are so conditioned to the "crutch of print" that few among us comprehend what a trained memory is capable of. . . .*

*The old man sat down, facing me, as the people hurriedly gathered behind him. Then he began to recite for me the ancestral history of the Kinte clan, as it had been passed along orally down across centuries from the forefathers' time. It was not merely conversational, but more as if a scroll were being read; for the still, silent villagers, it was clearly a formal occasion. The griot would speak bending forward from the waist, his body rigid, his neck cords standing out, his words seeming almost physical objects. After a sentence or two, seeming to go limp, he would lean back, listening to an interpreter's translation. Spilling from the griot's head came an incredibly complex Kinte clan lineage that reached back across many generations: who married whom; who had what children; what children then married whom; then their offspring. It was all just unbelievable. I was struck not only by the profusion of details, but also by the narrative's biblical style, something like: "—and so-and-so took as a wife so-and-so, and begat . . . and begat . . . and begat. . . ." He would next name each begat's eventual spouse, or spouses, and their averagely numerous offspring, and so on. To date things the griot linked them to events, such as "—in the year of the big water"—a flood—"he slew a water buffalo." To determine the calendar date, you'd have to find out when that particular flood occurred.*

There is some support for this view. Research suggests that anything leading to increased RNA production may improve memory, and that any inhibition of RNA production may interfere with memory. Much of the evidence comes from exciting and still controversial research on *planaria* (flatworms). When *planaria* are cut in half, each half regenerates into a whole worm. If the *planaria* are conditioned to make a response, and then cut in two, each new worm retains what the original worm previously learned; however, when one half is treated with a substance that destroys RNA, the new worm which develops from that half shows no memory of the previously learned response (McConnell *et al.*, 1959).

Whatever the underlying mechanisms for LTM ultimately prove to be, every moment of our waking lives testifies to the existence of the permanent repository of information. When we read, speak, or drive a car, we constantly draw upon this repository to guide our ongoing behavior.

It should be noted that other investigators have not always successfully duplicated the *planaria* results. Because *planaria* are difficult to condition, other laboratory animals have been used, including rats, mice, and gerbils. With these animals, the results have not been clear-cut (John, 1967).

In recent years, interest has shifted away from RNA as a memory substance to a startling and bewildering array of chemical compounds (Dunn, 1980). To illustrate, the injection of a brain substance, vasopressin, appears to improve the memory of learned behaviors of laboratory animals (Iversen, 1979). Chemical tests of this substance on human beings

**Singer Linda Ronstadt calls upon long-term memory during her performances, when she is on-stage for hours at a time without written lyrics or music.**

Lynn Goldsmith, Inc. © 1980

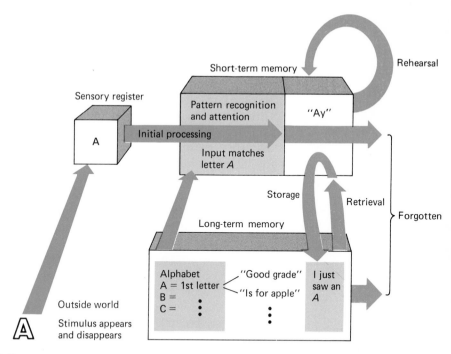

Figure 3.8
**A model of the human information-processing system**

A stimulus from the external world passes into the sensory register, where it is either deemed "unimportant" and forgotten or judged "significant" and coded in short-term memory. Unless displaced by new information, the content is rehearsed and stored in long-term memory, from which it can be retrieved through a search process. (Klatzky, 1975)

are presently in progress, with promising results (LeGros *et al.*, 1978; Oliveros *et al.*, 1978). Vasopressin appears also to reverse amnesia (Pfeifer and Bookin, 1978).

If long-term memory is, in fact, a permanent storehouse of information and past experiences, then how can we explain such things as a student's mind "going blank" during an examination for which he or she had studied quite diligently? Much of what we ascribe to forgetting may actually be a failure in **retrieval** (Shiffrin, 1970). Retrieval is the process whereby we somehow manage to sift through the complex filing system of LTM, find the specific information we need, and bring it into consciousness. Figure 3.8 summarizes the human model of the information-processing system.

Studies of patients who have sustained head injuries have shown that these patients remember very few of the events that occurred just prior to their accident, whereas their retention of earlier events is relatively intact. For example, in a study of 1000 patients suffering head injuries, it was found that approximately 75 percent of them had forgotten events immediately preceding their accident, whereas only 16 percent had forgotten earlier events (Halstead and Rucker, 1968).

Analogous results have been obtained in the laboratory. In the typical experiment, an electrical current—sufficient to produce convulsions—is applied to the brains of laboratory animals at varying time periods after they have learned a task. Little or nothing is retained when the shock

**Retrieval**
The process of sifting through materials in long-term memory to find the specific information needed at a particular time.

immediately follows the learning. With longer time periods between learning and electroconvulsive shock, there is greater retention of the task (Hudspeth *et al.*, 1964).

Studies of this sort have led some psychologists to hypothesize that a period of time is required between STM and LTM for the information to become consolidated (McGaugh and Herz, 1970). Anything that interferes with consolidation, such as an injury to the brain, will prevent information from becoming part of LTM. In other words, events require an undisturbed period of time to be absorbed and integrated. The presumed functioning of the consolidation period may be compared to the action of plaster of paris after it has been poured into a mold. A period of time must pass before the plaster of paris hardens and can be said to be permanently fixed. If the hardening process is interrupted—for example, by overturning the mold—the plaster of paris never achieves the form destined for it by the mold.

A striking example of what happens when consolidation is prevented is the case of a man (known to science as H.M.). He had undergone brain surgery in an effort to alleviate severe, recurrent epileptic seizures. At the time of the operation, he was 27 years old. When he was examined 2 years later, he still gave his age as 27. The following observations were made by the psychologist who examined him:

> *As far as we can tell this man has retained little if anything of events subsequent to his operation, although his IQ rating is actually slightly higher than before. Ten months before I examined him, his family had moved from their old house to one a few blocks away on the same street. He still has not learned the new address, though remembering the old one perfectly, nor can he be trusted to find his way home alone. He does not know where objects constantly in use are kept; for example, his mother still has to tell him where to find the lawn-mower, even though he may have been using it only the day before. She also states that he will do the same jigsaw puzzle day after day without showing any practice effect and that he will read the same magazines over and over again without finding their contents familiar. (Milner, 1959, p. 49)*

In this man's case, we see that both STM and preoperation LTM remained intact. He was still able to perform tasks like mowing the lawn that required him to draw on the long-term memory he already had. He could also remember the location of the mower long enough to find it from his mother's directions, but could not remember it from day to day. After surgery, the consolidation of new information from STM to LTM was impossible.

The memory deficits displayed by H.M. are similar to those observed in patients suffering from Korsakoff's syndrome. This syndrome is usually found in the later stages of severe alcoholism. One of the most serious consequences to this disorder is profound amnesia.

> *To get a feeling for just how devastating this memory loss is, let us consider a specific case. Imagine that you are introduced to a pleasant man in his mid-fifties. A few minutes of conversation indicate that the man is of normal intelligence. To confirm this impression you could ad-*

*minister an IQ test, on which the man might score slightly above the normal range. You ask him about himself, and he tells you about his wife, children, and job. There is no apparent memory deficit. At this point you leave him. Five minutes later you happen to run into the same man again. He shows no sign of knowing you and, in fact, denies ever meeting you before in his life. Now imagine that you continue to meet with the man every day. You rapidly discover that at every meeting you must reintroduce yourself. He never has any memory of the previous meetings. In addition, you may find that his wife had left him years ago and his children are grown up! How long can this go on? There are Korsakoff patients who spend many years in the same hospital and never learn to recognize the people in attendance on them daily, or to find their way from their ward to a canteen two floors below.*

*But contrary to first impressions, Korsakoff patients do encode at least some new information. They can learn a fairly complex rule for generating a series of numbers, but without being able to remember having learned it (Wood and Kinsbourne 1974). Similarly, if you hide a joy buzzer in your hand when you shake hands with a patient one day, on the following days the patient is likely to refuse to shake hands with you, even though having no recollection of meeting you and hence being unable to give a reason for the refusal. (Glass et al., 1979, pp. 126–127)*

## FACTORS AFFECTING LEARNING AND REMEMBERING

Suppose that your psychology professor has scheduled a midterm examination to take place in 10 days. What would be the best strategy to pursue in preparing for this test? Should you wait until the last moment, and then study intensively for a 10-hour period just before the exam? Or would you be better off studying each day for an hour? Should you read through all the material several times, or would it be wiser to pause periodically and recite aloud what you have just read? Should you read through previous tests or the self-tests provided in your workbook? Or would it be better to actually take these tests, making sure to check your answers against the ones provided?

In all probability, students have sought the answers to questions such as these since the first examination appeared on the scene. In a broader sense, the issues implied in these questions underlie some of the fundamental factors associated with human learning and remembering. In the following sections we will focus on the practical management of these principles in order to achieve maximum benefits from our learning experiences.

When we discuss learning, it should be clear that we are not concerned with some abstract or esoteric subject. Learning is the survival instrument of the species; it is the survival instrument of the individual. Unlike lower organisms, which rely largely upon inherited bases for adaptation to the environment, we humans are capable of acquiring an almost unlimited range of responses to meet the demands of the environment. Through learning and cultural transmission of what we have learned, we are capable of reshaping the environment to meet our needs.

Clearly, the student who is able to take advantage of what we know about learning and remembering is more capable of surviving in the academic environment.

There are many factors that affect learning and remembering. In addition to our practical interest in taking advantage of these factors for the everyday management of learning, as students of psychology we also have a broader interest in understanding the learning process. The factors that affect human learning and remembering can be put in three general groups: (1) factors within the individual, (2) characteristics of the material, and (3) the methods used in learning.

## Factors within the Individual

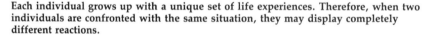

Psychologists are forever seeking general principles that permit understanding, prediction, and control of behavior. When attempting to apply general principles, however, we must never lose sight of the fact that each individual is unique. The way in which each person responds to any given situation is influenced by many factors, both past and present. Because no two individuals have had identical sets of experiences, we should not be surprised when two people, confronted with the "same" situation, display enormously varied and diversified behaviors. For example, we have seen that any response followed by positive reinforcement tends to be repeated. In our culture, grades are commonly employed as reinforcers for study behavior. Students with high motivation to achieve scholastic success will work tirelessly to obtain a high grade in

Each individual grows up with a unique set of life experiences. Therefore, when two individuals are confronted with the same situation, they may display completely different reactions.

a course, completing every assignment, attending all classes, taking copious notes, and diligently preparing for all scheduled quizzes. Students whose achievement motivation is low may cut many classes, rarely open the textbook, and engage in minimal preparation for upcoming examinations—in short, appear to be completely unmotivated by the incentive of a good grade. How do we explain the fact that one student behaves in accordance with the principle of reinforcement, whereas the other's behavior appears to contradict this principle?

Grades are a learned or secondary reinforcer. The use of grades as a positive reinforcer presupposes that, through prior experiences, grades have acquired reinforcement value. Yet what is an effective reinforcer for one individual may not be for another. Students who will not exert any effort to obtain a good grade may work for some other kind of reinforcement. They may demand something more tangible, such as a monetary reward, for their efforts. Or they may be persons for whom the learning experience itself is sufficiently rewarding to motivate them to diligent study. In each of these cases, reinforcement is effective, but the nature of the reinforcement depends upon the unique characteristics of the person. Clearly, for the proper management of the learning process, it is vital that we take into consideration individual differences such as these. Before we can successfully apply specific prescriptions for effective learning and remembering, we must first discover what makes an individual "tick"— why he or she is successful in certain types of learning situations and unsuccessful in others. For example, the same student who flinches at the thought of any course dealing with numerical concepts may be a "whiz" when it comes to calculating baseball batting averages.

We should not overlook the value of self-reinforcement in advancing the learning process. There is much to be said in favor of an occasional pat on your own back accompanied by such thoughts as, "Good work. You set your goal to develop a computer program for writing checks and balancing your checkbook and you did it. Congratulations! Keep up the good work."

Although it is difficult to make general statements when you are dealing with individuals, there are certain personality factors that are known to affect the learning process adversely. Anxiety is one of the most common deterrents to efficient learning and subsequent performance on retention tests. It is, however, a double-edged sword: It can either facilitate or disrupt performance. For example, some people learn to reduce their anxiety about upcoming tests by organizing effective programs of study and preparation. For these people anxiety serves to enhance performance. In other people, however, anxiety leads to diffuse, disorganized, and chaotic behavior. They find that they cannot study effectively under the constant tension of worry about how well they will perform on the test.

Many students experience overwhelming levels of anxiety when confronted with a test situation. Even when they have studied long and hard for an exam, their performance can be so eroded by anxiety that their grades do not reflect their actual level of learning. When this happens repeatedly, it becomes difficult to keep trying in the face of continued frustration. Indeed, each failure to perform well on a test provides additional fuel for their anxieties about tests. Just as success breeds success, so does failure breed failure.

It should be pointed out that this crippling anxiety may occur during the learning stage, the remembering stage, or both. When it occurs during the learning stage, anxiety may lead to behavior that is antagonistic to effective study. For example, the thought of studying for a test may be so anxiety-inducing that the person escapes the learning situation altogether—by daydreaming instead of studying, or by watching television or engaging in social activities with a group of friends. Naturally, one who does this will not perform well on an examination because, as we have already seen, what is not well learned is not well retained. In contrast, another student may study efficiently and learn well but be assailed by attacks of anxiety only during the remembering phase (the test itself). This is perhaps the most exasperating and discouraging circumstance, not only because it usually causes feelings of self-doubt and inadequacy, but also because the instructor may erroneously conclude that the student has failed to study and to learn the assigned materials. We return to this topic in Chapter 8, where we present a technique that has been useful in helping alleviate test-related anxiety in students.

Few would dispute the conclusion that anxiety is one of the most common and pervasive elements in the learning and remembering process. But there are many other variables operating within the individual that also exert profound influence on learning and remembering. Motivation, prior experiences, and, of course, intellectual abilities are among the most important. An individual may have an enormous amount of talent, but if that talent is not directed along efficient and productive lines, it may go wasted. There are many procedures that can be used to achieve better management of both learning and remembering. We will discuss several of these in the remainder of this chapter. For any of these procedures to be effective, however, they must be implemented by the learner. The acquisition of improved learning techniques requires dedication and effort on the part of the learner, similar to the professional athlete's conscientious adherence to training rules in order to achieve and maintain proficiency.

**Serial-anticipation learning**
A type of learning in which the subject is required to memorize a list of words or syllables in a fixed order.

**Paired-associate learning**
A type of learning in which items (words, syllables) are learned in pairs. The subject must respond with the appropriate word or syllable when presented with the associated stimulus.

## Characteristics of the Task

Over the course of a lifetime, we acquire an incredibly large and complex repertoire of learned behaviors. Rarely do we pause to reflect on the remarkable diversity of skills, knowledge, and accomplishments over which we have achieved mastery. Every moment of our waking lives provides mute testimony to the wide range of behaviors of which we are capable: reading the newspaper, buttoning our jackets, writing a letter, memorizing a part in a play, or calculating the correct change after making a purchase at the supermarket, to name but a few.

Learning tasks vary in many ways. They differ in complexity, familiarity, the types of skills they require, and even their degree of pleasantness. When people are confronted with a learning situation, the characteristics of the task itself will certainly influence the strategy they use in attempting to achieve mastery.

**Figure 3.9**
**A memory drum**

The subject is required to learn material that is presented one frame at a time in the small opening.

One of the most significant aspects of human behavior is verbal learning. Most of our everyday learning involves the use of words, and formal education is almost exclusively verbal learning. For this reason, much psychological research is concerned with the study of verbal skills. Experiments in verbal learning generally take one of two forms: **serial-anticipation** or **paired-associate learning.**

In serial-anticipation learning, the subject is required to memorize a list of nonsense syllables (words, digits, or symbols) in a fixed order. Usually the list to be learned is presented to the subject on a memory drum, a device that exposes one word at a time at a rate of speed predetermined by the experimenter. Figure 3.9 shows a memory drum.

The memory drum is also used in paired-associate learning to expose the stimulus materials. A word or syllable (the stimulus) is presented in one frame, and in the next frame the same stimulus is paired with another word or syllable (the response). The subject has to recite the response word whenever the appropriate stimulus is presented. Some typical lists of nonsense syllables used in serial-anticipation learning and paired-associate learning are given in Fig. 3.10. We have purposely used the same syllables in both lists to illustrate the differences between these two methods. In serial-anticipation learning the syllables always appear in the same order, whereas in paired-associate learning the order of the pairs varies from trial to trial.

Learning the alphabet and learning to count are examples of serial-anticipation learning. When you attempt to learn the vocabulary of a foreign language by associating the foreign words with English words, you are experiencing paired-associate learning. Paired-associate learning and the acquisition of a foreign language are in fact so closely related that students who excel in paired-associate learning in the laboratory generally excel in mastering a foreign language (Cooper, 1964).

One of the difficulties in studying verbal learning is that the subjects enter an experimental situation with differing degrees of experience and sophistication in the use of words. Not only that, words have different meanings for different people, and particular words are more familiar to some people than to others. Thus control of the experimental situation is

**Figure 3.10**    **Typical lists of nonsense syllables used in serial-anticipation and paired-associate learning.**

| Serial-anticipation | Paired-associate |
| --- | --- |
| PQJ | PQJ |
| GXK | PQJ–GXK |
| HFC | HFC |
| KHX | HFC–KHX |
| QGJ | QGJ |
| ZHB | QGJ–ZHB |

extremely difficult. It is for this reason that most experiments on verbal learning use nonsense syllables. You might question the applicability of this research to real-life situations. But bear in mind that virtually all of the language symbols that young children encounter are, to them, nonsense materials. To children learning to read, combinations of letters are as meaningful as nonsense syllables are to an adult. Only through long years of almost constant practice do the words appearing on a page of text become invested with the meaning they have for a literate adult. Moreover, many of the other tasks children encounter in school are like nonsense materials because they are unlike any prior experiences.

**Meaningfulness.**   Take a look at the sentence "Me anti meiha dmetan ot herm an." Clearly, it is gibberish. Now put the book aside for a moment and try to repeat the sentence. You are probably experiencing some difficulty. Now do the same thing with the following sentence: "Meantime I had met another man." Surely you had no difficulty repeating this sentence. The difference between these two sentences illustrates one of the most important variables affecting verbal learning: meaningfulness. Material is meaningful because our previous experience with it forms associations in our minds. The second sentence is clearly more meaningful than the first. It consists of familiar words arranged according to the rules of grammar so as to produce a coherent thought. (If you have not already noticed, the first sentence is composed of exactly the same letters as the second, arranged in precisely the same order, but grouped in such a way as to produce unfamiliar combinations.)

The importance of meaningfulness in verbal learning was illustrated by an experiment in which subjects were required to memorize a list of 200 nonsense syllables, 200 numerals in random order, a 200-word prose

**Figure 3.11**   **Meaningful material (poetry and prose) requires less time to learn than nonsense materials. (Lyon, 1914)**

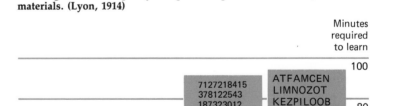

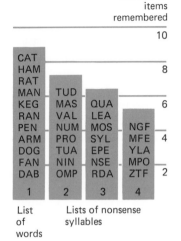

Number of items remembered

| CAT HAM RAT MAN KEG RAN PEN ARM DOG FAN DAB | TUD MAS VAL NUM PRO TUA NIN OMP | QUA LEA MOS SYL EPE NSE RDA | NGF MFE YLA MPO ZTF |
|:-:|:-:|:-:|:-:|
| 1 | 2 | 3 | 4 |

List of words  Lists of nonsense syllables

**Figure 3.12**

Subjects learned one list of words and three lists of nonsense syllables. The nonsense syllables in list 2 had higher association values than those in lists 3 and 4. List 4 contained nonsense syllables of lowest association value. (McGeoch, 1930)

passage, and 200 words of poetry. Figure 3.11 presents the results of this experiment. It is clear that much more time was needed to learn nonsense materials (random numerals and nonsense syllables) than to learn the meaningful materials. Yet even nonsense syllables are not completely devoid of associations with meaningful words. Several experimenters (among them Glaze, 1928, and Archer, 1960) have devised lists of nonsense syllables that vary in the degree to which they suggest meaningful associations. A number of experimenters have used these lists to demonstrate that learning is more efficient as the material is more meaningful. In one study, subjects were required to learn four lists. One of the lists was composed of actual words, whereas the other three lists consisted of nonsense syllables that differed in meaningfulness (McGeoch, 1930). Figure 3.12 presents the results of this experiment. It is clear that the more meaningful the material, the more effective the learning.

You can reproduce these same results by trying the informal experiment in Fig. 3.13 on some of your friends.

Now let us imagine that we are dealing with meaningful material, such as passages of prose. What are some of the factors that influence comprehension and recall? One investigator (Bower, 1978) presents simple stories to groups of subjects and obtains comprehensibility ratings and recall percentages of the story content. Then he systematically investigates the effects of modifying the story. To illustrate, one group of subjects was given a story entitled, "The Old Farmer and His Stubborn Animals." The same story, with a slight reordering of actions, was given to a second group of subjects. The main difference between the two passages was that the goals and motives of the farmer's actions were deleted from the second passage. What is the effect of removing the goal and motive as focal points about which the story is organized? Both the comprehensibility ratings and the percentages of actions recalled fall dramatically. The results are summarized in Table 3.1.

**Figure 3.13**

Study list 1 for 30 seconds. Write down, in order, all of the words you can remember. Repeat this procedure until you have learned all eight items on the list in the proper order. Record the number of trials needed to achieve mastery. Repeat this same procedure for lists 2 and 3. Compare the number of trials required to learn each list. Note that list 1, because it is composed of actual words, is the most meaningful. List 3, which is composed of nonsense syllables of low association value, is the least meaningful.

| List 1 | List 2 | List 3 |
|---|---|---|
| CAT | FAM | FHQ |
| FAN | CEN | KBF |
| KEG | LEM | MZJ |
| NOT | HAZ | BHJ |
| RUG | DOB | ZTF |
| TIP | PIL | LCF |
| DAB | BAL | QJH |
| SEX | MEX | HJC |

Table 3.1

**Comprehensibility Ratings and Recall Percentages of the Coherent and the Themeless Texts**

| Measure | Themeless text | Coherent story |
| --- | --- | --- |
| Comprehensibility rating (of 10) | 5.0 | 9.7 |
| % propositions recalled | 58 | 80 |

**Amount of material.**   In memorizing a set of materials, it is obviously wise not to attempt more than you can accomplish efficiently. We have said that there is a definite limit to the memory span of human subjects. The average memory span is seven or eight items for materials such as numbers or letters. To learn a list of 10 letters or numbers requires about twice as much time as it takes to memorize 7 or 8. Clearly, the amount of material to be learned is a significant factor in the efficiency of learning. The limitations on memory span are of particular importance because of the widespread use of numbers in everyday life—telephone numbers, social security numbers, student identification numbers. Because we learn a series of numbers more easily than a series of letters, it is perhaps fortunate that numbers are used for this purpose.

## Method Variables

"There just aren't enough hours in the day" is a frequent lament of students who are trying to juggle busy schedules in order to accommodate study and social activities and still get a reasonable amount of sleep. For many years, researchers have worked on various aspects of this problem. Many volumes have been written suggesting various strategies that students might develop in order to use their time in the most efficient way possible. In the following sections, we will discuss some of the methods of learning that have been explored both in the laboratory and in the classroom.

It has been suggested that we tend to overemphasize the role of the instructor in the learning process and minimize the role of the student. However,

> . . . it is the student, in the final analysis, who sets the standard of education. He sets this standard by his study behavior. Students are the most important instructors in the college. No matter how brilliant the lecturer or how good the facilities, most students would fail if they did not teach themselves by study outside the classroom. . . . That the student is seldom thought of as an instructor, in the truest sense of the word, is really the most startling indictment of our prevalent educational philosophy. (Fox, 1962)

Repetition. Some things are recalled after only one hearing—a name, an address, a slogan. But these are exceptions. We usually have to read or hear unfamiliar or lengthy material several times before we master it.

Most people have a good memory for things that are associated with their own interests. For example, many of us can give a detailed account of a particularly pleasant vacation long after the events have faded into the distant past. One reason is that we are interested in this material, and so we keep it alive by talking and thinking about it. This repeated rehearsal is, in effect, additional practice, and where learning is concerned there is no substitute for practice. Nevertheless, there are variables that tend to maximize the benefits of practice, as we shall see in the following sections.

Knowledge of results. One of the most important variables that influences learning is feedback, or knowledge of results. When you are trying to learn something and someone tells you that you are on the right track, you feel encouraged to continue along the same lines. On the other hand, if someone says, "No, you are doing it wrong," you are being told that you should pursue an alternative course. Without feedback, we can neither completely enjoy the pleasures of our accomplishments nor profit fully from our mistakes.

Most studies indicate that performance is enhanced when knowledge of results is provided immediately. For example, one study (Sarason and Sarason, 1957) demonstrated that students seem to profit more when

Russian gymnast Nellie Kim performing at an international meet. Years of demanding practice can be endured for the sake of achieving a long-sought-after goal.

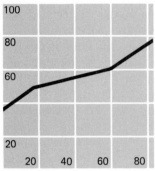

Percentage remembered immediately

Percentage of study time devoted to recitation

**Figure 3.14**
**Recitation**

Subjects spent varying portions of study time in active recitation of a list of 16 nonsense syllables. Subjects who spent more time in recitation showed better immediate recall. (Gates, 1917)

**Recitation**
In learning, active repetition (or recitation) of material one is trying to recall (as opposed to passive reading).

**Massed practice**
Learning material by crowding practice into long, unbroken time intervals.

**Distributed practice**
Learning material with rest periods intervening between practice sessions.

classroom examinations are scored and returned immediately. On the other hand, another study (More, 1969) suggested that older students may profit more when the return of the examinations is delayed for a day or longer. Apparently, older students are more likely to think about, review, and rehearse the materials that appeared on an examination when they are forced to wait for the results. Thus, when feedback is delayed on one examination, their better performance on a subsequent test may reflect the effects of this additional repetition.

You may recall that we raised a question earlier concerning the efficiency of taking self-tests and checking answers. The research on feedback, or knowledge of results, is largely responsible for the popularity of workbooks that include test items and answer keys. If you avail yourself of this source of feedback information, you should note an improvement in your performance. Furthermore, when you know how you are doing, you are more likely to maintain an interest in your work. In other words, knowledge of results enhances the learning process through its effect on motivation.

**Recitation.**   Have you ever had the frustrating experience of reading a page of material and then discovering that you can recall none of its contents? You reread the page several times, and still nothing "sticks." This experience seems to contradict the principle that repetition enhances remembering. But simple repetition is of little value unless you are actively attending to what you are doing. Too often you discover that your mind was drifting while your eyes simply scanned the words on the page. One method of dealing with this problem is to put the book aside from time to time, and try to **recite** out loud what you have just read.

Figure 3.14 presents the results of a study in which the subjects devoted varying percentages of time to recitation. The "zero group" devoted all of its time to reading, wheras the "80 percent group" devoted 80 percent of its study time to recitation and 20 percent to reading. It is clear that recitation led to marked improvements in learning. The groups that spent portions of their study time in recitation learned the material better than the group that spent none of its time in recitation (Gates, 1917).

A wide variety of other studies have shown that reading with recitation is superior to reading alone. Why? When you read something with the knowledge that you must soon recite what you have read, you are more likely to be motivated to remember and less likely to become inattentive. Moreover, recitation provides immediate knowledge of results, so that you can see how well you are doing and can adjust and modify your responses accordingly. Finally, recitation provides active practice in recalling the material you wish ultimately to retain.

**Distribution of practice.**   Like medicine, practice can be administered in large doses at a single time or in small doses distributed over a period of time. When practice is **massed,** all of the learning is crowded into long, unbroken time intervals. When practice takes place in smaller doses with rest periods intervening between practice sessions, it is referred to as **dis-**

Distribution of practice, or spreading practices over a long period of time, aids in retaining the skills or information learned. In an award-winning production of Gershwin's *Porgy and Bess*, Donnie Ray Albert (Porgy) and Clamma Dale (Bess) demonstrate performing excellence acquired through distribution of practice over many months of rehearsals.

**tributed practice.** Distribution of practice usually, but not always, leads to superior performance on verbal learning tasks.

Figure 3.15 presents the results of a study in which subjects were required to learn a list of 12 nonsense syllables. The subjects using massed practice were given a 6-second rest between trials. The subjects using distributed practice were given a 126-second rest between trials. The results show that subjects who used distributed practice required fewer trials to learn the task (Hovland, 1938). Other research in this area, however, has not produced such clear-cut differences between these two types of practice. Occasionally, distributed practice retards or has no effect on verbal learning (Underwood, 1961). For example, if there is a strong response that competes with the correct response, massing practice can inhibit the undesirable response sufficiently to permit the desired behavior to occur. For example, the person who habitually types "hte" for "the" might well be advised to mass the practice of typing "the." On the whole, however, the advantage of spaced over massed practice is quite general. As one reviewer of research in this area noted, "Spaced repetitions almost always benefit memory more than massed repetitions" (Wickelgren, 1981, p. 39).

Many of you have probably developed the study strategy of cramming (massed practice) immediately before an examination. Just how effective is this method of study? Usually, cramming is not as effective as is study with some spacing between sessions. We cannot say exactly how the practice sessions should be distributed to achieve maximum learning efficiency because too wide a range of factors is involved to permit formulation of any hard-and-fast rules. Nevertheless, the research does sug-

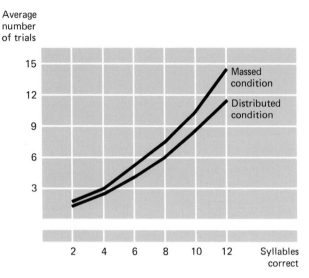

Figure 3.15    **Comparison of massed and distributed practice in learning a list of 12 nonsense syllables. (Hovland, 1938)**

gest certain strategies that will optimize the learning benefits to be derived from study. Students should budget their study time so that they are never faced with the necessity of massing practice just prior to an examination. If the learning has been distributed over a period of time, the night before an examination can be advantageously spent in an intensive review. Distributed practice coupled with review is more efficient than distributed practice without review. In addition, either of these methods is superior to massed practice.

**Whole versus part.**    Suppose that you are expected to deliver a speech approximately 30 minutes long. You have decided to commit the entire speech to memory so that you will not need to refer to notes. What would be the best approach? Would it be better to try to learn the speech as a whole, or should you separate it into parts and learn one part at at time?

There is no simple answer to this question. The advantages and disadvantages of each method depend on several factors, including your motivation, the nature of the speech, and your previous experiences.

The principal disadvantage of learning something as a whole (the **whole-method**) is that it is frequently a long time before you have anything to show for your efforts. Suppose, for example, you decided to memorize the speech as a whole. Presumably, it would take you a considerable amount of time before you accomplished this feat. This long wait for reinforcement may discourage you. On the other hand, if you were to learn only a small part at a time (the **part-method**), you would have something to show for your efforts after only a few minutes' work. Thus one of the advantages of learning one small part at a time is that we receive faster feedback on the progress of our performance. That is, we receive reinforcement when we have accomplished only a part of the task instead

**Whole-method**
A method of learning in which the individual learns the material as a whole unit.

**Part-method**
A method of learning in which the individual separates the material to be learned into parts, and learns one part at a time.

**Rote learning**
Verbatim learning that does not require a logical understanding of the material to be learned.

of having to wait until we have completed the entire task. Trying to learn the whole task at once is likely to be particularly frustrating to children and to adults who have had little experience in memorizing (Garry and Kingsley, 1970).

The part-method is superior when the task can be divided into distinctive units. For example, if you are learning tennis, you can practice your serve at one session and your forehand stroke at another session. The part-method is also superior when the amount of material to be learned is so great that any attempt to attack it as a whole exposes the learner to some of the disadvantages of massed practice.

The whole-method may be more advantageous when the material forms a relatively cohesive unit. With this type of material, the part-method has the disadvantage of requiring not only that we learn the parts themselves, but also that we learn to join them in sequence to form the whole.

**Logic versus rote.**   You have probably all taken courses that involved a great deal of **rote** memorization, for example, a foreign language, biology, or history. On the other hand, most of you have also taken other courses in which the primary emphasis was on understanding certain logical relationships, for example, philosophy, psychology, sociology, or English literature. You probably found that the courses involving rote memory were more difficult to master in the sense that they required more hours of study. The same finding has been demonstrated in the laboratory— that logically interrelated materials are more easily mastered than materials that must be learned by rote.

Try this simple experiment on several of your friends. Ask them to learn the following sequence of numbers: 581215192226293336. Suggest to half of your subjects that they group the numbers into sets of three and then memorize them (call this the "rote memorization condition"). Suggest to the other half that the numbers are arranged in a logical pattern; ask them to find the pattern and then memorize the numbers (call this the "logic condition"). Incidentally, in case you have not already discovered the pattern yourself, the series begins with the number 5 and continues by the alternate addition of 3 and 4 ($5 + 3 + 4 + 3 + 4 + \ldots$). Record the time it takes for the subjects in each condition to learn the numbers. Three weeks later, ask each subject to recall these numbers for you. You will probably find that some of the subjects in the logic group are still able to recall the numbers, whereas none of the subjects in the rote memory group will be successful.

An actual experiment employing these same procedures found a clear difference in the retention of these materials. When tested three weeks after the original learning, 23 percent of the subjects in the logic group recalled the numbers perfectly. In contrast, none of the subjects in the rote memory group were able to remember the numbers at all (Katona, 1940).

It should be clear that the educational process is concerned not only with the immediate learning situation, but also with long-term benefits. Although it may be possible to learn different facets of a subject equally well, long-term retention may differ markedly with the type of material. To investigate this question, one study used the content of a college zoology course. Students were tested on four different aspects of the course on a final examination and again 15 months later. The results of the study are shown in Fig. 3.16. It is clear that the students performed about equally well on all four facets of the final examination. However, there were marked differences in their retention scores obtained 15 months later. Material that was meaningfully related (applications of principles, interpretations of new experiments) was remembered best (Tyler, 1933).

**Mnemonic devices.**   In view of the fact that some facets of many courses require rote memorization, are there any techniques that you can use to maximize your efficiency in retaining rote materials? There are, and they are known as **mnemonic devices.** One technique should be obvious: Try to organize the material in some way that establishes meaningful relationships among otherwise unrelated materials.

A laboratory study has demonstrated that organizing rote materials in meaningful ways is an effective mnemonic device. Subjects were required to learn 12 lists of 10 unrelated nouns. The control subjects were asked to learn the words in each list in their correct order; they were given no further instructions. The experimental subjects, on the other hand, were told to construct stories in which the nouns appeared in the correct order. Here are stories constructed by two of the subjects:

**Mnemonic devices**
Techniques for organizing material to be learned in order to maximize efficiency in remembering.

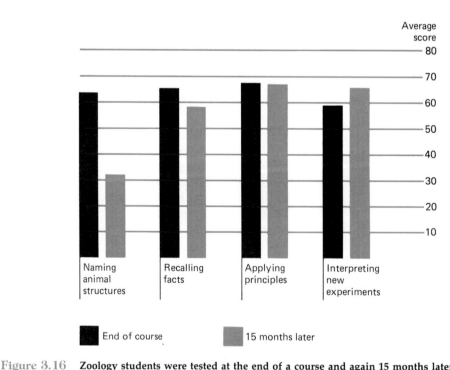

Figure 3.16    **Zoology students were tested at the end of a course and again 15 months later. The graph shows that they retained best the material that was logically interrelated (applying principles and interpreting new experiments). Rote materials were not retained as well. (Tyler, 1933)**

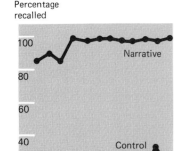

Narrative

Control

List position

**Figure 3.17**
**Meaningfulness**
**and retention**

Subjects who had constructed
stories that incorporated the
words to be remembered
showed dramatically superior
retention over the control
group. (Bower and
Clark, 1969)

*A* lumberjack darted *out of the forest,* skated *around a* hedge *past a* colony *of* ducks. *He tripped on some* furniture, *tearing his* stocking *while hastening toward the* pillow *where his* mistress *lay.*

*One night at* dinner *I had the* nerve *to bring my* teacher. *There had been a* flood *that day, and the rain* barrel *was sure to* rattle. *There was, however, a* vessel *in the* harbor *carrying the* artist *to my* castle. *(Bower and Clark, 1969)*

The results were dramatic, as can be seen in Fig. 3.17. Subjects in the experimental group recalled 94 percent of the words from all the lists, whereas the control subjects recalled only 14 percent (Bower and Clark, 1969).

You are probably familiar with a number of mnemonic devices. For example, if you have studied music, you may have used "Every Good Boy Does Fine" to learn the names of the lines of the treble clef (E, G, B, D, and F), and you may have used the fact that the letters of the spaces form the word *face*. How many of you have been introduced to Roy G. Biv? He's the fellow whose initials represent the colors of the rainbow in the order in which they appear: red, orange, yellow, green, blue, indigo, and violet.

Mnemonic devices have been the subject of renewed interest in recent years. Formidable and rather formal procedures have been devised which permit individuals to retain a remarkable amount of information. Indeed, in one study, subjects were able to memorize lists of 700 paired words in an incredibly short period of time (Wallace *et al.,* 1957).

Nightclub entertainers are frequently able to enthrall audiences with their uncanny feats of memory. A nightclub comedian may be able to rattle off one joke after another without seeming to pause for breath. Other so-called mental gymnasts can be shown hundreds of items by members of the audience and then repeat, from memory, all the items presented. How are these incredible feats accomplished? Are such individuals blessed with supernatural powers of memory?

Recent research has revealed that these entertainers generally use various mnemonic systems. Although the systems vary from one to another in details, they have several features in common. For example, many use visual imagery to aid recall. In one widely advocated mnemonic system, a set of peg-words is first associated with a set of numbers, as in the following jingle:

*One is a bun, two is a shoe, three is a tree, four is a door, five is a hive, six is sticks, seven is heaven, eight is a gate, nine is wine, ten is a hen. . . .*

Then the material to be recalled is associated with these peg-words through the use of bizarre imagery. For example, suppose you wanted to learn the following list of words, in order: pig, fly, run, dog, milk, doll, cup, cheese, chair, book. You might make the following bizarre associations with the peg-words: a pig sleeping in a bun, a fly wearing a shoe, a stocking with a run hanging on a tree, a dog opening the door, and so on (see Fig. 3.18). Presumably, once you have formed these associations,

Figure 3.18    **How can bizarre images such as these aid in recall? See the text for an explanation.**

further learning is unnecessary, because the peg-words readily elicit the bizarre images, which, in turn, contain the critical response words.

Though we do not necessarily label them as such, we all use mnemonic devices to aid recall. You may recall the SQ 3R method that we presented in Chapter 1. The designation of the method is, in itself, a mnemonic device for remembering the sequence: survey, question, read, recite, and review. Mnemonic devices appear to be most successful when the associations stem from the individual's personal experiences (Paivio, 1969). Our memory banks differ, and what is meaningless to one person may arouse a wealth of associations for another. The following verbatim account describes how one student devised a mnemonic device to aid recall:

> *Sometimes you have to be inventive when you want to remember things. I remember once I tried so hard to learn the date 1874. It was the year the first ice cream soda was invented, and I wanted to remember it so I could impress my friends later. But somehow it kept slipping from me. I tried everything—I tried repeating it—I closed my eyes and I said it. Still, I couldn't seem to remember it a few minutes later when I tested myself. So finally I thought about the number 1874 and I saw it was 26 years before 1900. I don't know why that helped me, but later I had no trouble remembering it. (Author's files)*

Although mnemonic devices may be useful for learning certain kinds of rote material, not all tasks lend themselves to their use. For example, there is probably no substitute for straight memorization when one is learning such things as the multiplication tables or the alphabet.

**Overlearning.** We have already said that what is learned poorly is likely to be poorly retained. Similarly, what is learned well is likely to be well retained. Are there any benefits to be derived from continued practice on material already well learned? Continued practice after mastery has been achieved is called **overlearning.** A classic study on overlearning showed that retention is indeed improved with a moderate amount of overlearning (Krueger, 1929).

> **Overlearning**
> Continued practice after mastery has been achieved.

Subjects learned lists of single-syllable nouns to the point where they were able to recite them without error. Subsequently, they were divided into three separate groups. The first received no additional practice. A second group continued to practice the lists for half again as many trials as was required for one perfect repetition (50 percent overlearning). The third group received 100 percent overlearning; that is, they continued to practice for an equal number of trials beyond that required for original mastery of the lists. The results of this study are illustrated in Fig. 3.19.

**Figure 3.19**
**Overlearning**

After subjects had learned a list of words to the point at which they were able to recite them without error, they were subdivided into three groups. One group received no additional practice (zero overlearning); another group practiced half again as long as it took for the original learning (50 percent overlearning); and the third group practiced for as many trials again as were required for the original learning (100 percent overlearning). The effect of overlearning was to improve the retention of the learned materials; however, by the twenty-eighth day, retention was low for all groups. (Krueger, 1929)

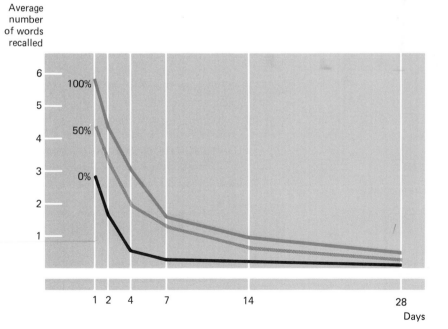

You may note that overlearning did lead to superior retention. There is a point of diminishing returns, however; the gain in retention achieved by 50 percent overlearning, as opposed to zero overlearning, was greater than the gain achieved by going from 50 percent overlearning to 100 percent. More recent research indicates that continued practice not only will improve retention but will speed up the retrieval speed (Corbett, 1977; Wickelgren, 1977). Taken together, the results of all of these studies suggest that we should not discontinue practice at the moment we have barely mastered the material. Rather, continued practice will provide additional benefits in terms of both retention and the time it requires to extract information from memory. Many of you who have memorized and practiced the multiplication tables over several years will recognize how rapidly answers to multiplication problems come to mind.

## CONSTRUCTIVE MEMORY

**Constructive memory**
The transformation of a memory to reflect the inclusion of new information.

When you think about the remarkable capacity of the human brain to store and retrieve information over long periods of time, it is tempting to think of memory as a process involving some sort of tape recorder in the brain. Although this is an appealing concept, a few moments of reflection will bring you to the realization that information in memory is not etched in stone. Nor should it be. To be maximally useful to us, memory should be modifiable to reflect new inputs, new information, and new experiences—a process sometimes called **constructive memory**. These events may supplement or alter memories. If they contain false information, the memories may be transformed to reflect this false information (Loftus, 1979). The following excerpt illustrates the effect of false information on recollection.

. . . *subjects saw a series of 30 color slides depicting successive stages in an accident involving an automobile and a pedestrian. The auto was a red Datsun traveling along a side street toward an intersection at which there was a stop sign for half of the subjects and a yield sign for the remaining subjects. Figure [here, Fig. 3.20] shows the two critical slides used in this experiment. The rest of the slides show the Datsun turning right and knocking down a pedestrian who is crossing at the crosswalk.*

*Immediately after viewing the slides, the subjects answered a series of 20 questions. For half the subjects, question 17 was "Did another car pass the red Datsun while it was stopped at the stop sign?" The other subjects were asked the same question with the words "stop sign" replaced by "yield sign." The assignment of the subjects to one of the two conditions produced a design in which half of the subjects received consistent, or correct, information, whereas the other half received misleading, or incorrect, information.*

*All subjects then participated in a 20-minute irrelevant activity, which required them to read a short story and answer some questions*

Figure 3.20    These photographs were used in an experiment designed to test the accuracy of recollection of two groups of subjects. The only difference between the two photos is that there is a stop sign in one and a yield sign in the other.

*about it. Finally, after this "filler" activity, a forced-choice recognition test was administered. Fifteen pairs of slides were presented with two slide projectors, each pair for approximately 8 seconds, and the subjects were asked to select from each pair the slide they had seen earlier. The critical pair was a slide depicting the red Datsun coming to a stop sign and a nearly identical slide depicting the Datsun at a yield sign. The results indicated that when the intervening question contained information consistent with the first series of slides, 75% of the subjects responded accurately, while with an inconsistent question only 41% did so. (Loftus, 1979, pp. 312–313)*

**Positive transfer**
The facilitation of learning in a new situation by prior experience in another situation.

Studies of this sort remind us that later events can color our recollections of prior experiences. Providing misleading information after the slides had been viewed seriously impaired the ability of the subjects to report accurately what they had seen. These results emphasize the urgency that applies to obtaining eyewitness reports as soon as possible after the witnesses have seen a crime or an accident. If too much time passes by, there is an increased risk that other events and experiences will intervene to distort memories of the original events.

## TRANSFER OF TRAINING

**Negative transfer**
The interference of prior experience in an earlier situation with learning in a new situation.

**Learning how to learn**
Developing certain strategies that can be transferred from one situation to comparable situations.

**Learning set**
A general approach to the solution of similar problems.

In the broadest sense, we might say that the whole purpose of education, formal or otherwise, is to impart knowledge and skills that the individual may apply (transfer) from one situation to another. When we teach children to avoid a hot stove, we expect that they will transfer this learned avoidance behavior to other, similar situations. When people learn to add numbers, we expect that they will transfer this knowledge to courses that require the manipulation of numerical values (algebra or physics, for example) and to real-life situations (changing money in a foreign country, or doubling a recipe, for example).

This transfer of training is the very basis for our capacity to benefit from our past experiences. It is probably fundamental to our ability to recognize familiar faces, places, and things; to develop abstract concepts; and to utilize past experiences to build up a storehouse of learned behaviors that can be applied to many different situations.

There are two different types of transfer. If a prior experience facilitates learning in a new situation, we say that **positive transfer** has occurred. But prior experience does not always lead to facilitation of new learning. Whe prior learning interferes with learning in a new situation, we say that **negative transfer** has occurred.

Positive transfer is illustrated by the ease with which a person who has learned to drive a particular car with an automatic transmission can transfer this learning to an almost unlimited variety of other cars with automatic transmissions. Similarly, if you learned to tell time on one kind of watch, you can easily tell time on other watches in spite of differences in size, shape, and the numerical designations on the face of the watch (see Fig. 3.21). It should be clear that a key factor in positive transfer is the similarity of stimuli in different situations. When the stimulus situations are similar and the same behaviors are required, as in reading the dials of two different watches, positive transfer usually occurs. This is precisely what is expected on the basis of stimulus generalization.

Negative transfer will typically result when people are required to learn new responses to stimuli to which other responses have previously been learned. The negative transfer will be maximal when the new responses are incompatible with the previously learned responses. If you have learned to drive a car with an automatic transmission and then drive a car containing a standard transmission, you will appreciate the problem of negative transfer, for in all probability you will grind the gears and make the owner of the car wilt with apprehension.

**Figure 3.21**
**Positive transfer**

Even if the numerical designations on the face of this watch are unfamiliar to you, you probably have no difficulty telling the time from it.

The items shown in Fig. 3.22 provide an example of both positive and negative transfer in translating words from Spanish into English.

## LEARNING HOW TO LEARN

| SPANISH | ENGLISH |
|---------|---------|
| POPA | STERN |
| INTIMAMENTE | NEARLY |
| SUSPENSO | FAILURE |
| FRUTO | PROFIT |
| OCUPADO | OCCUPIED |
| DOBLE | DOUBLE |
| EDICIÓN | EDITION |
| INSTANTE | INSTANT |

**Figure 3.22**

**Transfer of training in language**

Try to guess the English meanings of the Spanish words while covering the right-hand column. After you check your answers, note that the first four cases involve negative transfer and the last four positive transfer.

It is a common observation that students who take many standardized psychological and educational tests show progressive improvement as they take test after test. They are obviously learning how to take these tests; that is, they are learning how to deal with the types of problems presented. Instead of learning specific responses (answers) to specific stimuli (test questions), they are learning general ways of thinking about and approaching the types of problems that come up in test situations. Or to put it another way, they are **learning how to learn:** They are developing certain strategies that can be transferred from one situation to another.

The classic experiments demonstrating learning how to learn have been performed on monkeys. The typical experiment involved a discrimination task in which a monkey was required to choose between two different stimuli (Fig. 3.23). The monkey was shown two objects, such as a cube and a cup. A raisin was hidden under one of the objects. The monkey had to learn to select the object with the raisin under it, even when the object was moved in a systematic way from trial to trial. Initially, the monkey required a number of trials to master this task. Once it was mastered, two different objects were introduced, a funnel and a cylinder.

**Figure 3.23**

**The monkey is required to learn which of the two stimuli is correct, that is, which one has the raisin hidden beneath it. The stimuli were varied from task to task, but the problem always required learning which stimulus concealed the raisin.**

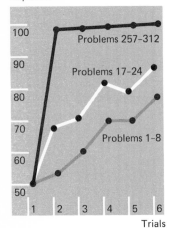

Percentage of correct responses

Problems 257–312

Problems 17–24

Problems 1–8

1  2  3  4  5  6

Trials

**Figure 3.24**
This graph shows the performance of monkeys on a series of discrimination tasks. The animals perform at a chance level on the first trial and show improvement on each successive trial. However, the rate of improvement increases markedly as the animals are given more and more problems.

Again a raisin was hidden under one of the objects, and the position of that object was systematically varied. The monkey required fewer trials to learn the solution to this task. The same procedures were repeated for each subsequent task, each time using different stimulus objects. Eventually the monkey was able to select the correct object after only a single trial. If its first choice was correct it would repeat its choice in the second trial. If its first choice was wrong, it would select the other stimulus object on the second trial (Harlow, 1949).

In this experiment the monkey formed a **learning set;** that is, it developed a general approach to the solution of similar problems. Figure 3.24 shows the progressive improvement in the performance of a group of monkeys as more and more tasks were mastered. The monkeys were clearly *learning how to learn.* Learning sets have been demonstrated to exist in a wide variety of higher organisms, including cats, rats, and humans.

Human society is extremely complex, and in order to function successfully in it, we must learn a staggering amount of information. Thus learning to learn—in essence learning which aspects of a situation are critical and which are not—is particularly important for humans. Fortunately, we are very good at learning to learn, and even at devising new ways to assist this process. For example, the SQ 3R method we discussed in Chapter 1 provides a framework for learning the material in this book by helping you focus on the key issues. Other learning-to-learn programs, such as specialized "cram" courses geared to improve your score on the SAT, also owe much of their success to teaching students what to look for and concentrate on.

## Summary

1. Memory is a construct inferred from certain behaviors of the individual. There are three stages involved in memory: learning, remembering, and retention. Memory, which refers to the retention stage, must be inferred from the remembering stage, during which the individual performs some activity or behavior that was influenced by the learning stage.
2. There are three commonly employed measures of retention: recall, recognition, and relearning.
3. Failure to perform well at the remembering stage may be due to poor original learning, inadequate retention, and/or circumstances occurring during the remembering stage that adversely affect performance.
4. Several theories have been formulated to account for forgetting: the disuse theory, the trace trans-

formation theory, and the interference theory.
5. Retroactive interference occurs when an intervening activity interferes with the retention of prior learning.
6. Proactive interference occurs when the prior learning of a response to a given stimulus interferes with the retention of a new response to the same or similar stimuli.
7. Psychoanalytic theory postulates a form of motivated forgetting, called repression, in which people tend to repress memories of events that are psychologically painful.
8. Present evidence suggests that there are two types of memory: short-term memory (STM) and long-term memory (LTM). There is also a sensory register in which sensory information is held sufficiently long to be evaluated.

9. Learning and remembering are the survival instruments of the human species. Some factors that affect human learning and remembering include (a) factors within the individual, (b) characteristics of the materials to be learned, and (c) the methods of learning.

10. Personality factors, such as anxiety, may affect the efficiency of learning and subsequent performance on retention tests.

11. Much research on the acquisition of verbal behavior involves serial-anticipation or paired-associate learning. It has been found that learning and retention are better as the material that must be learned becomes more meaningful. In addition, limitations in the memory span limit the amount of material that can be assimilated during any given time interval.

12. Several of the method variables that affect both the learning and the retention of materials are (1) repetition, (2) knowledge of results or feedback, (3) active recitation, (4) distribution of practice, (5) whether the material is learned as a whole or piecemeal, (6) whether the learning materials are logically interrelated or involve rote learning, and (7) overlearning.

13. Human memory is adaptable. It may be supplemented and altered by new inputs and experiences. But sometimes the new experiences may introduce distortions in recollections, known as constructive memory.

14. In the broadest sense, the purpose of education is to impart knowledge and skills that the individual can apply or transfer from one situation to another. Prior experience may either facilitate or interfere with learning in a new situation. Facilitation is referred to as positive transfer, and interference as negative transfer.

15. Through an ability to learn how to learn—that is, to determine which elements of a situation are critical and to focus on them—humans and other animals are able to develop general ways of thinking about things and solving certain types of problems.

## Terms to Remember

Memory

Recall

Recognition

Relearning

Savings score

Nonsense syllables

Disuse theory of forgetting

Memory trace

Trace transformation theory of forgetting

Interference theory of forgetting

Retroactive interference (retroactive inhibition)

Proactive interference

Motivated forgetting

Repression

Sensory receptors

Sensory register

Short-term memory (STM)

Memory span

Long-term memory (LTM)

RNA (Ribonucleic acid)

Retrieval

Serial-anticipation learning

Paired-associate learning

Recitation

Massed practice

Distributed practice

Whole-method

Part-method

Rote learning

Mnemonic devices

Overlearning

Constructive memory

Positive transfer

Negative transfer

Learning how to learn

Learning set

# LANGUAGE AND THE THOUGHT PROCESS

## WHAT ARE COGNITIVE PROCESSES?

Have you ever paused to reflect on the marvel of the human being? There is a world outside us that we call the external world. Over eons of time, we have developed specialized cells and organs that provide some sort of "picture" of that world. Moreover, throughout our lives we acquire information or knowledge about this world, we store this information in a permanent form, and we modify this stored knowledge in the light of changed circumstances. And all that the brain receives are electrical impulses from receptors delicately tuned to physical energies! The brain does not see, feel, hear, or smell. Nevertheless, it is somehow able to sort out the billions of electrical impulses, construct a coherent representation of our environment, and store it in such a way that it can be retrieved and used at a later date. (In Chapters 5 and 6 we explore the intricacies of the brain and sensory experiences.)

More astonishing yet, we have developed the ability to organize sounds and symbols to represent our experiences and to communicate them to others. Indeed, language and thinking are perhaps the most significant of all human activities. They account for our ability to conceptualize the world around us, communicate with one another, and solve the problems of our everyday existence. In general, the various events involved in thinking, reasoning, and problem solving are referred to as **cognitive processes.** In this chapter, we examine various aspects of our cognitive behavior, including language, concept formation, and the thought processes.

## WHAT IS LANGUAGE?

Monkeys, living in the wild, have evolved a complex system of warning calls. If one monkey sees a snake, it makes a "chutter" sound. Other monkeys will then approach the snake to observe it, maintaining a safe distance. If a "chirp" is sounded, the other monkeys will run for trees and climb to the highest elevations. Why? The "chirp" sound means that a leopard is near. But if a "rraup" is sounded, the monkeys will leave the trees or scurry from open fields into dense thickets. The "rraup" sound is the warning of the appearance of an eagle (Marler, 1967).

There is little question that the natural sounds made by these monkeys are part of a communication system. They communicate the fact of danger as well as the source. But is this language? Let's examine a few characteristics of human language and find the extent to which the monkeys' communications share some features with that language:

1. Naming. The warning calls of monkeys appear to share this characteristic. Thus "chutter" means "snake," "chirp" means "leopard," and "rraup" means "eagle." Moreover, the monkeys respond in the same way to the "word" as they do to the feared source of danger, much as humans respond to the shout "Fire!" as they would to seeing a fire out of control.

2. The arbitrariness of the association between the "words" and the objects to which they refer. Thus a chirp in and of itself does not appear

to possess any characteristic that is in any way like a leopard, any more than the English word "leopard" bears a resemblance to the actual animal.

3. The use of speech. Both humans and monkeys communicate with vocalizations. However, speech is not a necessary requirement for language. People born deaf can learn to use gestures, and some societies have developed a complicated language based on whistles.

4. Range of meanings. We might translate the "chirp" of a monkey to mean "I see a leopard," or "Yikes, a leopard!" That is about the limit of what monkeys say about leopards. However, humans have been observed to say such things as "I do not see a leopard," "A leopard is a symphony in motion," "A leopard cannot change its spots." The tremendously broad range of meaning of which humans are capable stems from the fifth and most important feature of language: The finite elements of language can be combined in infinite ways to generate new thoughts.

5. Combination of the basic units of language (words, gestures, etc.) in various ways to generate new meanings. This feature, more than any other, sets us aside from other animals. Monkeys simply do not say, "There is no eagle in the sky." In contrast, humans have developed a **grammar,** which is a set of rules for combining words in ways that communicate meaning. Birds, whales, and porpoises have been observed to combine basic sounds into varying patterns, but there is no convincing evidence that these different arrangements convey different meanings. In other words, there is no evidence that any species other than humans has devised a grammar.

**Cognitive process**
The mental process involved in thinking, reasoning, and problem solving.

**Grammar**
The rules that determine how to combine words into meaningful sentences.

**Symbol**
Anything that stands for something else.

Moreover, unlike communication among lower organisms, human language involves the learning and use of an incredibly large and varied array of abstract **symbols.** A symbol is anything that stands for something else. A flag can stand for a nation, a series of letters can represent a lion, and a name can represent you.

Words are among the most commonly employed symbols, and can be used to represent various aspects of experience. For example, the English word "chair" stands for an object, usually with four legs and a back, specially designed for us to sit on, one at a time. We cannot sit on the word "chair," but we can use the word to represent the object we sit on. We call the physical chair the referent for the word "chair." Effective communication among individuals is based upon some general acceptance of the meaning of words and symbols. Difficulties in communication often arise because people attach different meanings to the same words, gestures, and other symbols of their language.

Some words have such clearly defined referents that they evoke relatively similar images and associations in different people. Thus when someone uses the word "chair" in conversation, there is unlikely to be any misunderstanding about the referent—the referent is an object that you can point to. However, many words cannot be defined merely by pointing to an object, but rather must be defined through the use of other words. "Freedom," "democracy," and "radical" are words for which there are no commonly agreed-upon referents. When we use the word "free-

**Human language is characterized by the use of symbols—sounds, letters, or signs that stand for something else. In this ancient wall painting, Egyptians used hieroglyphics, a complex system of symbols and pictures, to record their history and religious beliefs.**

The Metropolitan Museum of Art

dom,'' can we be sure that we are evoking the same chain of associations in all our listeners? One person's idea of freedom may be someone else's idea of prison, as in the following example:

> *The parents of a 17-year-old girl require that she be home by 10 P.M. on weekdays and no later than one A.M. on the weekends. The parents feel that the girl is given a great deal of freedom, and support their view by pointing to some of her friends who are not permitted out on weeknights and must observe earlier curfews on weekends. "You have more freedom than we had at your age," is their clinching argument. The girl, for her part, is able to identify friends whose parents invoke no restrictions whatsoever. She concludes, "I am kept a prisoner in my own home." (Author's files)*

The problem of meaning in language is further complicated by the fact that language is constantly growing and changing. Many people today believe that the expression "The exception proves the rule" means that a rule is confirmed when an exception is found. This logical absurdity stems from the fact that the word "prove" originally meant "put to a test." Thus the original meaning of the expression was "The exception tests the rule," and if we were inventing the expression today, we would have worded it, "The exception disproves the rule." The word "awful" provides another example. Two hundred years ago, a dramatist would have been ecstatic if a critic said his play was "awful." Today the same review might well plunge a playwright into a deep depression. The word "awful" previously meant "inspiring great awe," but today the same word evokes a disagreeable and unpleasant association.

> *Words can fall into bad company and be dragged down by their associates. When St. Paul's Cathedral in London was finished the architect displayed it to the king on the state occasion and the king called it amusing, awful, and artificial. The architect was overjoyed at the royal compliment for in those days "amusing" meant "amazing," "awful" meant "awe-inspiring," and "artificial" meant "artistic." (Fosdick, 1941)*

If people who speak the same language have problems communicating, imagine the difficulty that arises when two people try to communicate in two different languages. This problem is compounded by the fact that many words cannot be translated directly from one language to another. For example, Eskimos have a variety of words to describe different types of snow. Some of these words have no counterparts in the English language (Brown and Lennenberg, 1954). Similarly, the Arabic language contains about 50 different words to describe what in English we would call simply a "pregnant camel" (Thomas, 1937).

Language is more than a means of communication. Rarely do we pause to reflect on the pervasive and dominant role it plays in our everyday lives, but it is involved in virtually all of our ongoing daily activities. When we think and reason, we manipulate the symbols of language. We use language to organize our daily lives. We wake up in the morning at 7:30 in order to make a 9:00 A.M. class. Language provides the symbols both for representing time and for ordering events in time. If we drive, we encounter hundreds of traffic signs directing us to turn left, merge right, or stop. Buying gas requires language, and so does listening to the radio, reading the paper, talking to yourself, and, of course, reading this book.

Language can be the source of both pleasure and pain. A compliment can make your day, but a cutting remark can distress you greatly. In the past, bearers of bad tidings were sometimes executed as soon as they had delivered their message. On the other hand, we enjoy a well-told story and react with pleasure to words of affection and tenderness.

Does language also play a role in the way information is represented in memory? Apparently it does. The memory code need not be in the form in which the information was originally presented. Memory is often coded in the brain in languge symbols (Schachtel, 1959; Conrad, 1964). In one study, college students were presented with a test of six written letters. After they read the letters silently, they were asked to report them in order. The errors they made during recall were most revealing. If they had visually coded the list, we would expect them to have confused letters that are similar in appearance, like X and V. Rather, it was found that the subjects tended to confuse letters that *sounded* alike (e.g., B and

Signs surround us in the modern world. Their words and symbols attract our attention and tell us what to do.

*V*). Thus it appears that, when reading the list, the subjects were recoding the letters from visual to speech symbols (Conrad, 1964).

Presumably we recode information into speech code because of the vast amount of experience we have had with naming and remembering letters. But what would happen if we presented these lists of letters to deaf people who have not learned to speak? Unlike the normal-hearing students, the deaf subjects in an experiment tended to make errors involving visual rather than auditory substitutions (Conrad, 1972). Thus it appears that deaf and hearing people code letters in different ways.

Until recently, some aspects of language study were thought to be outside the province of psychology. The study of the structure of language, for example, was formerly relegated to linguistic specialists. Now, however, psychologists recognize that all aspects of language constitute behavior. Therefore a new field, **psycholinguistics,** has emerged. Psycholinguists study language acquisition and use, and the formal structure of language.

## The Structure of Language

Consider the following:

> *are damned and lies there statistics lies*
> *the flessing sherded over the raufing wall*
> *there are lies, damned lies, and statistics*

These word combinations illustrate two of the three basic characteristics of language: Language has a structure or grammar, and there are rules for deriving the meaning of statements **(semantics).** Unless we follow the rules of grammar, there is neither structure nor meaning, as the first construction illustrates. Even though the individual words have meaning, the haphazard combination of these words does not produce a meaningful idea. The second word combination has a structure and appears to be a legitimate sentence. However, it is gobbledygook because three of the key "words" are meaningless. Finally, the last construction is a meaningful sentence. If follows the rules both of grammar and of semantics. Many of you may recognize it as the words of the nineteenth-century British prime minister, Benjamin Disraeli. Few of us would have any difficulty discerning the meaning of the sentence or interpreting the exasperation with which the words were uttered.

The third characteristic of spoken language is that there are rules for combining the elements of speech sounds into pronounceable words. The basic units of speech are called **phonemes.** Although there are only about 30 phonemes in the English language, they can be combined in countless billions of ways to produce the words of English. However, they are not combined in a random fashion. There are statistical rules for combining phonemes into words. Thus, although "flessing," "sherded," and "raufing" are not words, most of us would agree that they could well be words. Such constructions as "jqwd," "rdan," or "xuzyd," are a different matter. We may safely predict that these latter combinations would never find their way into an English language dictionary.

**Psycholinguistics**
The study of language acquisition and use, as well as the formal structure of language.

**Semantics**
The study of meanings in language.

**Phonemes**
The basic sounds that constitute the building blocks of language.

## The Acquisition of Language

From the moment we are born, we are literally immersed in a sea of language. When newborns arrive home from the hospital, they may be inundated by a wave of chatter from well-wishing friends and relatives. Conversations go on all around them. Strange faces hover over them making unintelligible sounds. They may hear radio or television in the background while their brothers and sisters play beside them. In many ways their situation is like that of an adult who is suddenly exposed to an unfamiliar language. Consider the following observation of a veteran of World War II:

> *G.I.s in the European theater occasionally experienced periods when we could visit with city dwellers and local townspeople. On one of these occasions, I was accompanied by a friend who was raised in the remote hill country of the United States. Although he had not completed the eighth grade, he possessed a searching curiosity concerning the world about him. He constantly asked questions and looked for answers when things mystified him.*
>
> *After observing a group of French children engaged in play, a look of wonderment lighted the face of D.J. (the initials were his name; they didn't stand for anything). He then observed, "These French kids must be awful smart."*
>
> *"Why do you say that, D.J.?"*
>
> *"Do you hear the way they jabber? I been here almost a year and I ain't git'n the hang of their lingo. Kids just gotta be smart to talk French." (Author's files)*

In truth children must be smart to speak any language. To be truly impressed by the complexity of language, do as D.J. did: Listen to a conversation in a language with which you are unfamiliar. Everyone seems to be speaking so fast and with such ease that you marvel at their accomplishments. How can they possibly understand one another? Take heart from the fact that, if foreigners do not speak your native tongue, they will be similarly impressed with your linguistic prowess. Given that language is so complex, how do most children essentially master the fundamentals by the time they are six years of age?

To begin with, newborn infants are capable of only a limited range of vocalizations—crying, gurgling, and coughing. However, even those early vocal productions contain many phonemes. Indeed, during the first few months of life, the child produces all the basic speech sounds of which the human organism is capable (Osgood, 1953). Moreover, these same speech sounds are found in children of all geographical regions and cultures. It is somewhat sobering to realize that the young infant produces without effort or contemplation such exotic sounds as the German gutturals ("ch") and the French "u"—sounds that cause so much frustration in college students learning these languages for the first time.

Many of these vocalizations rapidly drop out of the child's repertory of vocal responses as parents reinforce sounds characteristic of their native language (as in "ma-ma" and "da-da") and provide models of speech sounds for the child to imitate. Thus a child born into an English-

During the first few months of life, a child makes all the basic speech sounds that humans can produce. It is only through parental reinforcement that certain sounds drop out of a child's repertoire and others are repeated, until eventually an intelligible language emerges.

speaking home will soon stop making the German gutteral sounds, because these sounds are not heard in daily conversation and their production is not reinforced.

Between the ages of about three weeks and five months, even crying sounds will undergo subtle but significant modifications that herald the beginnings of communication. At this age crying changes in duration and pitch, and the parents soon learn to distinguish a cry of discomfort from a cry of pain or anger.

During the latter half of the first year, children begin to produce enormously varied, continuous, and patterned sounds which we refer to as "babbling." These sounds are apparently reinforcing to the children, and this may account, at least in part, for the fact that babbling tends to dominate their vocalizations as they approach one year of age.

At about this time, the first sounds that can be identified as true speech appear. Children speak their first recognizable words and attach these symbols to the appropriate referents, although with a high degree of generalization to similar objects. Thus children may respond appropriately with the word "da-da" when they see their fathers, but may embarrass their mothers by saying "da-da" to many different men.

Children's first sentences are typically single words and refer to specific objects (ball) or actions (eat). Gradually, two- and three-word sentences evolve. Thus the child may say, "Want milk," or "cat meow," and later progress to "Bring milk here." But there is an enormous gap between understanding and producing two- and three-word sentences. Understanding comes first, speech later. How do children learn to understand? Do they begin by listening in on the conversation of adults? Wouldn't that put them in the same position as D.J. trying to understand French by listening to the jabber of children? Indeed it would.

But we know now that the language acquisition of children does not happen in this way. In fact, children learn language by being spoken to. Even before infants are able to talk, they are brought into the conversation by adults. For example, a parent may speak to an infant as if they are engaged in a two-way conversation. If the infant burps, yawns, or gurgles, the adult frequently treats these sounds as the child's "turn" in the conversation (Snow, 1977). Moreover, adults make an effort to gain the child's attention, using the child's name frequently and increasing the pitch of their voices (Shatz and Gelman, 1973; Garnica, 1975). Perhaps of greater significance is that they simplify their speech when talking to children. They tend to speak slowly, more distinctly, and in shorter sentences than usual (Sachs, Brown, and Salerno, 1976). Surprisingly, even four-year-olds simplify their speech when talking to younger children (Snow, 1972)!

As a result of all of these modifications, speech becomes more readily understood. The following observations were made by an American psychologist whose mastery of French was rather limited:

*I observed a French woman talking to a 10-month-old baby. She would say slowly and clearly, "red," "yellow," "orange," or "look, this one has a hole," holding appropriately colored and shaped toy objects. Furthermore, she repeated the whole sequence two or three times. I could understand everything she said in French to the baby, but could catch only odd words or messages when she was talking to the baby's mother in rapid, normal French. (Taylor, 1977, p. 231)*

The importance of this adult–child interaction can be gleaned from observing the speech learning of normal-hearing children of deaf parents. Because the parents are unable to converse with their children, they often go out of their way to expose their children to a great deal of radio listening and television viewing. In this way, they hope to compensate for the lack of exposure to parental speech. Nevertheless, by the time their children enter school, they are usually considerably behind the other children in language skills. On the positive side is the fact that they rapidly catch up with their peers (Sachs and Johnson, 1976).

Even after the use of the words is learned, there is no guarantee that children are using these words in the same way as adults. Children who refer to the family pet as "kitty" may restrict the word's use to that one animal. They may not have yet learned that the word "kitty" may be applied to a class of four-legged animals that say "meow." In other words, they have not learned the concept "kitty." A little later in time they may correctly say "kitty" when shown a variety of different cats but may also identify a dog, a squirrel, or a rabbit as a "kitty." In time, children learn that a kitty is defined by more than its general shape. They note such features as the sound the animal makes, the types of fur, the coloration, and the claws.

On occasion, children may call another animal a kitty simply because they don't know the word for the other animal. For example, they may call a rabbit a kitty even though suspecting that each is a different type of animal. If shown a picture of a cat and of a rabbit and asked to pick out the kitty, they will correctly select the picture of the cat. Presumably, when children learn the word "rabbit" or "bunny," they will restrict their use of the word "kitty."

Beyond the age of two years, children's acquisition of speech grows by leaps and bounds—from about 3 words at one year of age, to 50 by the age of two, and 1000 by the third year (Lennenberg, 1969). By the time they reach college age, they may have more than 180,000 words at their command, or 200,000 if they are highly literate (Miller, 1951).

During the early childhood years, in particular, there is a curious and educationally important discrepancy in the rate at which boys and girls acquire language skills. On the average, girls are more advanced than boys at each level throughout the preschool and early school years (see Fig. 4.1). Failure to take these differences into account, at home and in the classroom, may partly explain why speech disorders are far more common among men than among women. For example, it has been estimated that about four times more men than women stutter. Persistent stuttering (as opposed to the normal hesitations that accompany the acquisition of speech) occurs before the age of six in about 90 percent of all cases (Goldenson, 1970).

The acquisition of speech is but one aspect of the mastery of language skills. Speech requires an orchestration of many complex motor and associative skills. Speaking and writing are called the **expressive functions**

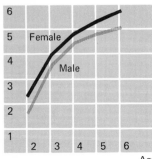

Number of words per sentence

Figure 4.1
**Early language development**

As the graph shows, girls tend to be ahead of boys in their acquisition of language skills.

**Expressive function of language**
Communication of meanings to others, for example, by speech or writing.

**Receptive function of language**
Understanding of language.

of language; they are the means by which we communicate meanings to other people. This ability to use language in a coherent way should not be confused with the ability to understand language (the **receptive function**). Infants demonstrate an enormous capacity to understand human speech long before they are able to reproduce it. Before the age of about one month, infants do not distinguish between speech and other sounds occurring in the environment. At about the age of one month, they begin to smile and respond vocally to the sound of the human voice (Nakazima, 1966). They even develop some rather complex expectations; for example, they "expect" to hear a person's voice come from the spot where that person is standing. When an experimental setting is arranged so that the mother's voice does not appear to come from her face, the infant may become agitated and may even burst into tears (Aronson and Rosenbloom, 1971).

By the age of three months, the child begins to distinguish among the various qualities of human vocalization: An angry tone will evoke withdrawal responses, whereas a friendly tone will elicit cooing and smiling (Wolff, 1963). By eight months, some infants have developed firm ideas of the way their mothers should sound, and show signs of distress when these expectations are violated. If a stranger's voice appears to be coming from the mother, the infant reacts otherwise than if the mother appears to be talking with her own voice (Cohen, 1973). By ten months of age, the child will obey such simple commands as "No" or "Bring me the doll," especially when the commands are paired with gestures.

**Throughout our lives our receptive vocabularly exceeds our expressive vocabulary. This toddler, for example, is able to understand and respond to its mother's words long before it is able to speak the language.**

Throughout our lives, our receptive vocabulary remains far greater than our expressive vocabulary. The receptive function of language can be likened to recognition in memory, and the expressive function can be likened to recall. Just as we are generally more proficient at recognizing prior experiences than at recalling them, we are likewise more proficient at understanding language than at reproducing it. If you have studied a foreign language, you may have observed that you understand far more of the language than you are actively able to use. You may be at a loss to conjure up the Spanish word for "table," but if you hear the words *mesa* and *pesa* spoken, you may well recognize that *mesa* is the correct one. Similarly, a young child may have difficulty pronouncing certain words, but may be perfectly able to recognize the correct pronunciation. One mother told the following story about her 18-month-old daughter:

> *Patty called her bottle "wa-wa." One day when her aunt was playing with her, Patty asked for her "wa-wa." Her aunt picked the bottle up and handed it to Patty saying, "Here's your wa-wa." Patty became very upset, stomping her feet and throwing the bottle on the floor. I'm not sure why, but Patty seems to resent adults speaking "baby-talk" to her. (Author's files)*

## Language in Chimpanzees

Communication systems are not uniquely human. They have been observed in a wide variety of different species, from insects through the primates (see Fig. 4.2). In lower organisms, the communication patterns appear to be established by hereditary factors and are highly resistant to modification. In humans, however, learning plays the dominant role. For many years, investigators have been intrigued by the notion that animals other than man can *learn* complex language systems.

Suppose you are asked to teach language to a chimpanzee. How would you go about doing this? The assignment is by no means easy. For years psychologists have tried to teach chimpanzees to speak. Their early efforts met with extremely limited success.

In one study, a chimpanzee named Gua was raised with a human infant. By the time she was 16 months old, Gua had a receptive vocabulary of about 100 words, but she made no attempts at human speech (Kellogg and Kellogg, 1967). In another study, a chimpanzee was able to employ meaningfully six simple words. The experimenters spent many months of painstaking effort to accomplish this modest feat (Hayes, 1951). Their failure to achieve greater success came as something of a surprise, because many other behavioral measures suggest that chimpanzees are quite intelligent. Indeed, chimpanzees appear to have about the same mental capacity as a three-year-old child. Why, then, are they unable to match the language ability of three-year-olds?

Perhaps our approach is wrong. As humans, we tend to regard all our behavior as intelligent behavior. We look for similar behavior in animals as evidence of their intelligence. It is possible that other animals lack the neural and muscular equipment necessary to produce patterned speech as it occurs in humans. Whether or not the chimpanzee has the

Appeasement posture

Threat posture

**(a)**

**(b)**

Posture inviting play

**Figure 4.2**
## Communication among lower animals

Communication need not involve vocalizations. Many species, including humans, use "body language" to communicate feelings and attitudes such as play, threat, and appeasement.

**(c)**

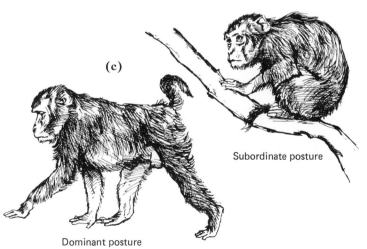

Dominant posture

Subordinate posture

necessary neuromuscular structures to produce human speech is still open to question (Lieberman, 1968). Nevertheless, studies of the chimpanzees have led investigators to conclude that "vocalization is highly resistant to modification in this otherwise highly educable species" (Gardner and Gardner, 1971). It is possible that efforts to teach language to chimpanzees have been unproductive because we have failed to select behaviors that are amenable to modification by learning. Perhaps chimpanzees do have the capacity to learn language, but in another form.

Think for a moment. What do people do who are born deaf? How do they acquire the ability to communicate with the rest of us? Just because they cannot communicate through speech does not mean that they cannot carry on conversations, think, and do all the other things we associate with language. In fact, people born deaf can form concepts, construct sentences, reason, and communicate meaningfully with others through the use of sign language.

Is it possible that a lower animal could also learn to communicate through sign language? Researchers observed chimpanzees in their natural surroundings and noted that they make extensive use of gestures. Even in captivity, chimpanzees spontaneously develop begging and other gestures. These observations led a husband-and-wife team to try to teach sign language to a young female chimpanzee named Washoe (Gardner and Gardner, 1971, 1975).

Washoe was trained in the sign language taught in the United States and Canada. Her training began when she was approximately one year old. She first learned the sign for "come, gimme," which involves pivoting the wrist or knuckles in a beckoning motion. In her first three years of training, Washoe mastered 85 different signs. Two years later, she had increased her "vocabulary" to 175 words. Figure 4.3 shows her making the sign for "drink." (See Table 4.1 for examples of some of the signs

Figure 4.3    Washoe and her trainer making the sign for "drink."

Table 4.1

**Some Signs Learned and Used by Washoe During the First Three Years of Training**

| Sign | Usage | Form | |
|------|-------|------|---|
| | | Place where sign is made (P) | Configuration of active hand (C) |
| 1. Come gimme | For a person or an animal to approach, and also for objects out of reach. Often combined = "come tickle," "gimme sweet" | At arm's length, in front of body | Flat hand, palm up |
| 6. Tickle (touch) | For tickling and chasing games | Back of flat hand, palm down | Index finger extended from compact hand |
| 12. Drink | Used for the object and the action, as in "you drink," "me drink," and "sweet drink," the usual phrase for soda pop. Also used for containers, such as cups and bottles | Lips | Thumb extended from compact hand |
| 16. Please | Asking for objects and activities. Frequently combined = "please open," "please flower." Also, when ordered to "ask politely" | Chest, near shoulder | Flat hand, palm toward signer |
| 23. In | For going indoors, and for indicating locations, as for objects placed inside containers | Palm of curved hand, palm toward signer | Flat hand, palm toward signer |
| 32. Pants (trousers) | For diapers, rubber pants, and trousers | Hips | Flat hands, palms toward signer |
| 40. Look | For the act of looking and peeking, and for optical devices such as glasses, binoculars, and magnifying lenses | Side of eye | Index finger extended from compact hand |
| 48. Bird | For birds and for bird-calls | Lips | Thumb and index finger touch, pointing to signer |
| 59. Dirty | For defecating, voiding the bladder, or their products; for the toilet; and for items that are soiled | Underside of chin | Spread hand, back of wrist, toward underside of chin |
| | | (Usually accompanied by the sound of teeth clacking together) | |
| 71. Bug | For insects and spiders | Nose | Thumb extended from spread hand |
| 84. Yours | Indicating her companion's possessions, when asked "whose that?" | On a person's chest | Flat hand, back toward signer |

Note: The signs are numbered according to the order in which they were learned.

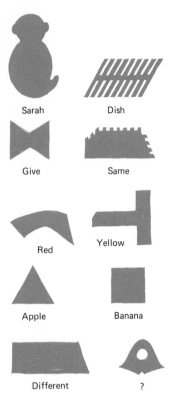

**Figure 4.4**
**Magnetic-backed plastic symbols were selected as the language units to be taught to Sarah. These plastic symbols varied in color, shape, and size. Each symbol stood for a word or concept.**

From "Teaching Language to an Ape," Ann James Premack and David Premack. Copyright © 1972 by Scientific American Inc. All rights reserved.

**Concept**
An abstract idea or representation of the common characteristics of objects that are otherwise different.

Washoe learned.) Washoe also learned to combine signs to form primitive sentences. For example, she learned that by combining "come, gimme" with the sign for "tickle," she could ask her trainers to tickle her.

The problem of language acquisition in lower animals continues to intrigue psychologists. As we said earlier, the chimpanzee is a fairly intelligent animal. Like the human, the chimpanzee is a visual animal. We know that young children can be taught to recognize symbols. You can ask a child, "Where is the spoon?" and the child will point to a symbol that represents a spoon (such as a picture in a book). Why can't we try the same sort of thing on a chimpanzee?

In fact, efforts along these lines are now in progress. In one study, a female chimpanzee, Sarah, began her language training when she was about five years old. During the first five years of training, she acquired an expressive vocabulary of about 130 words. What is more, she could build sentences, could follow written commands, and could ask and answer questions (Premack and Premack, 1972). How did her trainers accomplish this?

The first step was to teach Sarah a basic vocabulary, a process that was done in the following manner. Plastic symbols, each representing a different word or concept (see Fig. 4.4) were constructed and mounted on bases. Once she had learned the basic vocabulary, the next step was to teach her **concepts.** A concept is a representation of the common attribute of objects that are different in other respects. Consider the concept of redness, for example. We would know that Sarah had acquired the concept of redness if she could apply the appropriate symbol to all red objects, even though they differed from each other in other ways. And indeed, Sarah did learn to apply the symbol for red when she saw, for example, an apple and a persimmon at the same time.

Is it possible to manipulate these concepts in such a way as to construct the rudiments of communication? In other words, is it possible to teach a chimpanzee like Sarah certain relational concepts? It is one thing to teach her the concept "red," the concept "yellow," the concept "apple," or the concept "banana." It is another thing to teach her concepts such as "The apple is on the banana," or "The apple is different from the banana." These two statements express the relationships "apple on" and "apple not equal to," a more sophisticated level of conceptualization than "redness."

In order to teach Sarah relational concepts, her trainer taught her symbols for these concepts (see Fig. 4.5). Sarah was so successful at learning these symbols that she even invented her own game and taught it to her trainer. She began a sentence such as, "Banana is on . . . ," and challenged the trainer to complete it. She arranged a number of possible choices (multiple-choice task), and accepted only one as the correct answer, for example, "Banana is on dish."

Investigators continue to work on the challenging problems of language acquisition in chimpanzees. One of the more recent developments involves two-way conversations between two chimpanzees. Figure 4.6 shows two chimpanzees "talking" to each other.

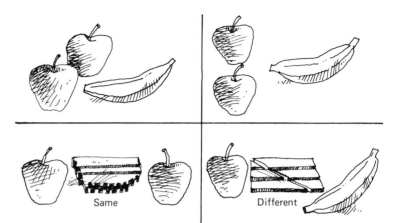

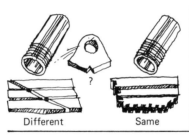

The concepts "same" and "different" were introduced into Sarah's vocabulary by teaching her to pair objects that were alike (*top illustration*). Then two identical objects—for example, apples—were placed before her, and she was given the plastic word for "same" and was induced to place the word between the two objects. She was also taught to place the word for "different" between unlike objects.

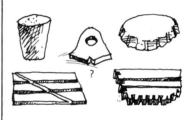

The interrogative was introduced with the help of the concepts "same" and "different." A plastic piece that meant "question mark" was placed between two objects, and Sarah had to replace it with either the word for "same" or the word for "different."

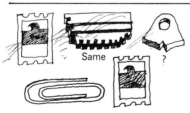

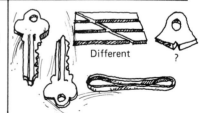

A new version of the interrogative was taught by arranging an object and plastic symbols to form questions: "What is [ object A ] the same as?" or "What is [ object A ] different from?" Sarah had to replace the question marker with the appropriate object.

**Figure 4.5    Materials and procedures used to teach Sarah various relational concepts.**

From "Teaching Language to an Ape," Ann James Premack and David Premack. Copyright © 1972 by Scientific American Inc. All rights reserved.

Although the results of studies of language acquisition among chimpanzees are impressive, there is no evidence that any species other than humans has been able to *invent* a language. Some critics even doubt that the trained chimpanzees are *really* "talking." In fact, one researcher did an about-face in his interpretation of the language acquisition of a chimp named Nim Chimpsky (Terrace, 1979). From the age of about one month, Nim was raised like a human child in an apartment in New York City. His acquisition of vocabulary in American Sign Language was impressive—125 signs in less than four years. Terrace initially felt that Nim had acquired language. However, while carefully reviewing videotape records, he noted some marked differences between the language behavior of chimps and that of human children. The sentences of human children become longer as they grow older, and they imitate the precise statement of their parents less and less. Not so Nim: His "sentences" remained the same length even as he grew older (between one and two words), and he imitated the trainers more and more. Terrace concluded that chimps can learn to use signs but have not demonstrated the ability to learn language (see Box 4.1).

Figure 4.6      **Two-way conversation between chimpanzees. Austin, at right, has signaled a request for bread. Sherman complies with Austin's request (middle panel) and then licks his own fingers (bottom panel).**

## BOX 4.1

### Are Those Apes Really Talking?

*Pupil (rolling on ground): You tickle me.*
*Laura: Where?*
*Pupil (pointing to leg): Here.*
*Laura (after tickling him): Now you tickle me.*
*Pupil (tickling her): Me tickle Laura.*

This dialogue between Laura and her charge might not seem unusual, except for one thing: the pupil was not a human child but a young chimpanzee named Nim. Like several others of his primate kin, Nim had been taught to communicate with humans in American Sign Language, a system of hand gestures developed for the deaf. He eventually learned to make and recognize 125 signs. But the frisky little chimp and other apes who have received such "language" instruction are now the center of a raging academic storm. The issue: can apes really master the essence of human language—the creation of sentences? . . .

No one has done more to stir doubts than Columbia University Psychologist Herbert Terrace in his work with little Nim (full name: Nim Chimpsky, a play on the name of Linguist Noam Chomsky of the Massachusetts Institute of Technology, a staunch proponent of the idea that language ability is biologically unique to humans). The object of Terrace's experiment was to prove Chomsky wrong—to show that creatures other than man could, indeed, conquer syntax and link words into sentences, however simple.

Toward that goal, Terrace, with Laura Petitto, a student assistant, and other trainers, put Nim through 44 months of intensive sign-language drill, while treating him much as they would a child. In some ways the chimp was an apt student, learning, for example, to "sign" *dirty* when he wanted to use the potty or *drink* when he spotted someone sipping from a Thermos. Nonetheless, Nim never mastered even the rudiments of grammar or sentence construction. His speech, unlike that of children, did not grow in complexity. Nor did it show much spontaneity; 88% of the time he "talked" only in response to specific questions from the teacher.

Armed with his new insights, Terrace began reviewing the reports and video tapes of other experimenters. Careful study of the record showed the same patterns with other apes that Terrace had noted in the work with Nim. There were rarely any "spontaneous" utterances, and what had seemed at first glance to be original sentences now emerged as responses to questions, imitations of signs made by the teacher, or as rote-like repetitions of memorized combinations. For instance, when Lana, a chimp at Yerkes, said *Please machine give apple*, the first three words seemed to mean nothing more to her than a mechanical prelude to obtaining something she wanted. Says Terrace . . . "The closer I looked, the more I regarded the many reported instances of language as elaborate tricks [by the apes] for obtaining rewards." . . .

As for the man in whose honor Nim was named, he has no doubts. Says Noam Chomsky: "It's about as likely that an ape will prove to have a language ability as that there is an island somewhere with a species of flightless birds waiting for human beings to teach them to fly."

## Theories of Language Development

Human language is a most extraordinary phenomenon. In spite of wide differences among people all over the world, we all share one characteristic: We have developed ways of describing our environment and communicating with one another. So pervasive is the use of language by humans in all times and places that one might well dwell on the question of how language is acquired.

One view is that language is learned in much the same way as any other operant behavior (Skinner, 1957). We have already seen that any response that is followed by reinforcement tends to be repeated, or learned. When an infant makes a sound that is recognizable as a word or as an approximation of a word (for example, "da-da," for daddy, "ba," for ball), the parents usually show their approval, either verbally ("Good boy," "Good girl") or physically (hugs and kisses), and thus presumably reinforce this behavior. The infant is likely to repeat these sounds, as well as any others that are followed by reinforcement.

Several lines of evidence question the generality of the reinforcement theory of language development. One investigator (Wahler, 1969) made an extensive study of mother–child interaction during the child's first year of life and found, surprisingly, that mothers reinforce virtually *all* the vocalizations their children make, and not only those which approximate adult speech.

Further criticism of the reinforcement theory comes from the observation that, as soon as we achieve some facility with language, we are able to produce an almost infinite variety of meaningful combinations of words that we may never have seen or heard before. Almost every sentence we speak or write is original and may be regarded as a creative act. If we learn language only by being reinforced for uttering specific words and word combinations, how can we account for the rich and varied sentence and paragraph structure of Bob Dylan, James Joyce, or Winston Churchill, or even that of our own personal letters?

One study demonstrated that, even at relatively early ages (seven to eleven years) relationships rather than specific sentences are carried in memory (Paris and Carter, 1973). To illustrate, let us imagine that children are presented with a number of sentences, such as "The bird is inside the cage," or "The cage is under the table." At a later date, investigators test their recognition by providing sentences that are different from the original sentences but that integrate the information contained in the originals. The subjects report recognizing the sentence, "The bird is under the table," even though this particular sentence did not previously appear. On the basis of findings of this sort, Paris and Carter suggested that we carry meanings, rather than sentences, in memory.

Considerations of this sort have led some theorists to suggest alternative explanations for language development. One theorist (Chomsky, 1969) believes that the human brain is highly specialized for language production. He suggests that the brain is prewired to make the various grammatical transformations that occur in any language. This would explain the remarkable capacity children have for generating grammatically correct sentences long before they have had any formal training in grammar.

Suppose you show a picture of a dog to a five-year-old girl and ask her to identify it. You then show her a picture of two dogs and ask her to complete the sentence, "There are two _____." The child will probably supply the correct plural form. You might wonder whether she knows the rules of plural formation, or whether she has simply memorized "one dog, two dogs." What if you show her a completely unfamiliar form, and supply a nonsense word for that form? If she supplies the correct plural form, her response cannot possibly be due to prior memorization. Rather, she must have some knowledge of the rules of plural formation.

This is a wug.

Now there is another one.
There are two of them.
There are two _____ .

Figure 4.7

**Preschoolers and first graders were able to apply the basic rules of grammar to nonsense materials.**

From Jean Berko, "The Child's Learning of English Morphology," *Word* **14**, 1958, pp. 154–155. Reprinted by permission.

When preschoolers and first graders were presented with nonsense materials like those shown in Fig. 4.7, they were indeed able to apply the basic rules of grammar, even though they had received no formal instruction (Berko, 1958). For example, they were able to complete the following sentences:

*This is a man who knows how to rick. He is ricking. He did the same thing yesterday. What did he do yesterday? Yesterday he _____.*

*This is a dog with quirks on him. He is all covered with quirks. What kind of a dog is he? He is a _____ dog. (Berko, 1958)*

No matter what theory of language acquisition we subscribe to, it appears that children are constantly forming **hypotheses** about language and then revising those that prove to be wrong (Clark, 1975). They are in constant pursuit of rules. One of the consequences of this pursuit is a type of error known as **overregulation:** The child applies the rules or strategies more widely than they should be applied (Glass *et al.*, 1979). One frequent problem is the overregulation of the past tenses of verbs. Thus children learn to add "ed" to form the past tense of such regular verbs as want, call, pull, or kick. But when they get to irregular verbs, it is not uncommon to hear such pronouncements as: "I comed," "I fighted," "I breaked," or "I bringed."

We should not be greatly concerned when we observe overregulation in children. It is more important for children to learn rules that usually work than for them to learn rules that are always correct. With time and experience, they will correct their hypotheses to take into account the exceptions to the rule.

## CONCEPT FORMATION

As we have seen, **concept formation** involves attaching a symbol to objects that share a common characteristic and ignoring their differences. Apples come in many sizes, shapes, and colors. In order to learn the concept "apple," you must be able to abstract some characteristic (or characteristics) that all apples have in common. This is not as easy as it might seem. True, "apple" is a concept. But an apple is also a fruit. What is the difference between the concept "apple" and the concept "fruit"?

An apple can also be thought of as "food." Concepts have varying degrees of abstraction. Figure 4.8 presents two examples of different levels of abstraction.

The first concepts we learn are relatively concrete. That is, they are at a low level of abstraction. For instance, we learn the concept "dog" before we learn the concept "animal," and certainly before we learn the concept "living thing." Numerical concepts are the most abstract and have been demonstrated to be the most difficult to learn.

Concept learning has been studied extensively in the laboratory. Because all subjects come into the experimental situation with different language habits and different levels of literacy, experimenters would have to

**Hypothesis**
A proposed explanation of the relationship between events or variables that can be tested.

**Overregulation**
A type of error in which rules are applied more widely than they should be.

**Concept formation**
Learning to attach a symbol to objects that share a common characteristic, while ignoring their differences.

APPLE

FRUIT

FOOD

DOG

ANIMAL

LIVING
THINGS

Figure 4.8    **Concepts vary in level of abstraction.**

control for these differences if they wanted to use an actual language in
the experiment. A more effective way to investigate the acquisition of
concepts is to invent a new language and then study how concepts are
acquired in this new language.

Before reading further, study the names given to each group of objects in Fig. 4.9(a). See if you can discover what the objects in each group
have in common, that is, what the underlying concept is. If you have
succeeded in learning these concepts, you should be able to attach the
correct nonsense word to the appropriate concept in Fig. 4.9(b).

These same symbols were used in a study that investigated three different kinds of concepts: concrete objects, shapes, and numbers. This
study found that subjects learned concepts (that is, learned to attach the
proper symbols) in the following order: concrete objects, shapes, and
finally numbers (Heidbreder, 1947). Other investigators, however, have
found that their subjects had a different experience. Apparently, individuals differ in the ease with which they form different types of concepts.
Try testing a few of your friends on the concepts in Fig. 4.9 and see
whether you observe individual differences.

How do we learn concepts? Reinforcement theorists believe that concepts are acquired through the processes of **generalization** and **discrimination.** When children learn to apply the label "dog" to the family pet,
they tend to generalize this label to all animals they see, for example, to
cats, cows, and horses. Parents usually reinforce their children for correctly calling a dog "dog," and correct them when they use the label in-

**Stimulus generalization**
Once an organism has learned
to associate a given behavior
with a specific stimulus, it
tends to show this behavior
toward similar stimuli.

**Discrimination**
Learning to respond differentially to similar stimuli.

appropriately. Parents may even assist this discrimination by emphasizing a dog's distinctive characteristics (by saying, for example, "Dogs go 'bow-wow,' cats say 'meow'").

An alternative view is that different objects or events are distinguished initially in terms of their functions or useful roles. Thus an apple and a ball may be similar in appearance, but they are distinguished by the fact that one is for eating whereas the other is for playing. It is only after objects or events have entered into stable functional roles that the common attributes are abstracted to define a concept (Nelson, 1974). In other words, it is only when a tennis ball, a baseball, a basketball, and a

**Figure 4.9**   Identify the concepts depicted in (a). Then see if you can label the concepts in (b) with the appropriate nonsense word. (Answer key on p. 150.)

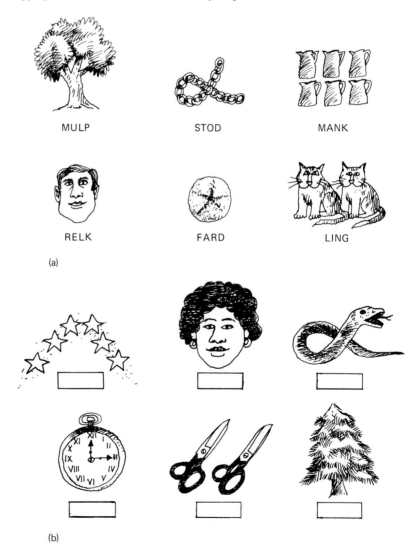

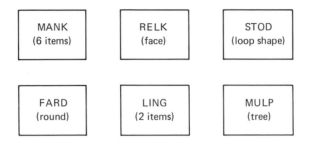

Answers to Fig. 4.9.

football have functioned in the role of playthings that can be thrown, caught, and bounced that the concept "ball" emerges.

Whether we subscribe to the reinforcement or the functional view of concept formation, it appears that concepts involve active rather than passive processes. As with language acquisition, we formulate hypotheses which we then actively test (Horton and Turnage, 1976). To illustrate, when you were learning the names of the concepts in Fig. 4.9(a), your first hypothesis about the concept FARD may have been "a single object." You quickly reject this hypothesis, however, when you note that RELK, MULP, and STOD are single objects. Your next hypothesis may have been "a single, roundish figure." You reject this when you note that RELK is also "a single, roundish figure." Your final hypothesis, "a single roundish nonhuman object," appears to suit the requirements for the concept. You receive confirmation when you correctly apply the name FARD to the watch shown in Fig. 4.9(b).

Cultures do not all conceptualize in the same way our Western tradition does. In the European and English languages, which have common roots, a sentence consists of a subject and a verb. Therefore our very language predisposes us to think in terms of things that *are* (nouns) and things that are *happening* (verbs). You may be surprised to learn that there are languages that do not make distinctions between nouns and verbs. The Hopi Indians, for example, classify things by their duration. Short-lived events (such as lightning and ocean waves) are represented by something that is like our verbs; longer-lasting and more stable events (such as buildings and trees) are represented by something resembling our nouns.

A student of American Indian languages (Whorf, 1956) has hypothesized that the language of a particular culture reflects the experiences of the members of that culture; and the types of concepts a culture forms are, in turn, determined by that culture's language. Specifically, the culture shapes the way its members think about objects and events by providing the words for placing experiences into catagories. To illustrate, in the Hopi language, the same word is used to describe such different objects as flying insects, airplanes, and pilots (Whorf, 1947). In our own country, a study found that black children use relatively more words to describe skin color than do white children (Palmer and Masling, 1969). Moreover, if a particular culture has no word for a particular concept, it will not be able to form that concept. Someone living in the South Sea

Islands, for example, would have no word for snow and therefore would have no way to conceptualize snow. On the other hand, an Eskimo has seven totally different words to describe the various kinds of snow.

Although the hypothesis that language determines concept categories may be interesting, it has not been confirmed experimentally. It is possible that cultures develop their concepts first and then create a vocabulary to encompass these concepts. Moreover, the lack of a word to describe a concept does not necessarily mean that the concept does not exist. A child may call both an apple and a balloon a "ball," but will not try to eat the balloon.

Some people say that there never was a generation gap before this generation. They say, "You never heard anyone talk about it before." Is this because there was no expression in the vocabulary for it, or because it *is* a relatively recent phenomenon?

## THE THOUGHT PROCESSES

**Thinking**
The internal manipulation of symbols.

What do the following behaviors have in common: daydreaming, solving a mathematical problem, reading today's psychology assignment, having a dream, having a nightmare?

All of these behaviors involve **thinking**—the internal manipulation of symbols that represent objects, people, places, events, or relationships. Thinking is unquestionably the most common type of behavior that humans engage in. There is hardly a moment in a person's life when thought processes are not going on. If you really want to see how pervasive these thought processes are, try to stop thinking for even a moment. There have probably been many times when you wished you could turn your thinking *off* and get a bit of respite. For example, when you have had a particularly stimulating evening, you may find that the recurrence of thoughts about the evening's events intrudes upon your efforts to sleep.

On the other hand, thinking is perhaps the most significant activity humans engage in. Thinking frees us from physical restraints, from the necessity of manipulating the physical events in our environment. To illustrate, suppose that you ask a friend how to get to his house. He tells you, "Go three blocks, make a left, proceed to the first stop sign, and make a right. My house is the third house from the corner on the left-hand side of the street." From just these simple directions you will be able to find his house. Imagine how complex our lives would be if we had to see or physically experience each step in the sequence before we could visit a place for the first time. All the great human accomplishments—architecture, mathematics, science, music, art, and literature—involve the manipulation of symbols. We do not have to manipulate two apples and three apples physically to arrive at the conclusion that there are five apples altogether. We can simply manipulate the symbols 2, 3, and 5. Through thinking and manipulation of symbols involved in thinking, we are able to visit the ancient Greeks, solve contemporary problems, and anticipate events that have not yet occurred.

## Imagery in Thinking

Most of the symbols we use in thinking involve language. We have already seen the significant role that language plays in cognitive behavior. Not all symbols are verbal, however. Close your eyes for a moment and think about your psychology classroom. Do you have a visual image of it? Is the image faint or clear? If you say "clear," see if you can count the number of seats.

Individuals vary in the clarity of their visual imagery. Some people can reproduce images with such great detail that we say they have a "photographic memory," or **eidetic imagery.**

A story that is frequently told in this connection involves a law student who was accused of cheating on a final examination. It seems that this student had reproduced, word for word, the details of a case cited in his textbook. The student claimed that he had studied this particular passage and was able to reproduce an exact image of it. In order to test his claim, he was given an unfamiliar passage to study for five minutes. He was then able to reproduce more than 400 words, including the details of punctuation, without a single error.

Study the picture in Fig. 4.10 for 30 seconds. Now put the book down and try to answer the following questions. How many feathers are visible

Figure 4.10    **The Painting *Pine Tree Ceremonial Dance,* by Jose Rey Toledo.**

Courtesy of the Museum of Art, University of Oklahoma, Norman.

on the figures in the painting? What musical instruments are being played by the group in the background? How many bowls are in the picture? What do they contain? If you have answered these questions accurately, you may have eidetic imagery.

Do you wish you had eidetic imagery? Most people wish they did. But it really is not such an advantage. Children often have it, but adults rarely do. Few scientists and mathematicians possess eidetic imagery. The truth of the matter is that clear and persistent imagery tends to interfere with abstract thinking.

## Kinds of Thinking

Although thinking is the most pervasive element in human behavior, it is one of the most difficult to study. By its very nature, it is not subject to direct observation. We must infer thinking from other behaviors. A further problem in the study of thinking is the necessity of distinguishing among different kinds of thinking. Dreaming is certainly a different kind of behavior from purposeful and directed problem solving. For convenience, we shall distinguish between two broad classes of thought processes. One is **nondirected thinking,** which is relatively uncontrolled and includes such activities as daydreaming and dreaming. The other is **directed thinking,** which is more controlled and purposeful and is typified by problem solving and creative thinking.

**Eidetic imagery**
Visual imagery that is so clear and detailed that the objects represented seem to be actually present; sometimes called photographic memory.

**Nondirected thinking**
A form of thinking that is controlled more by the individual's desires and needs than by reality, as in daydreaming.

**Directed thinking**
Controlled, purposeful thinking that is directed toward a specific goal or outcome, as in problem solving.

Nondirected thinking.   At one extreme is nondirected thinking—wishful, symbolic thinking that is influenced by our needs, feelings, and wishes. Examples of nondirected thinking include fantasy and dreams. Nondirected thinking characteristically does not follow the laws of logic and is engaged in primarily for self-gratification. It is effortless, spontaneous, and free from realistic and logical constraints.

We all engage in nondirected thinking. It has recreational value and frequently permits us to tolerate unpleasant circumstances and to achieve, in our imagination, goals that may be impossible in real life. Nondirected thinking can also play a vital role in planning for the future. Premedical students who imagine themselves as highly successful and respected doctors may find themselves better motivated to overcome the many difficult obstacles that lie between them and this goal. Moreover, nondirected thinking may play a significant part in many problem-solving situations, particularly when unusual or novel solutions are required. Many new ideas have come from dreams and freewheeling imagination. The following example was reported by a colleague:

*I had a dream one night in which numbers began to order themselves in columns and then began to subtract themselves from one another. When I awoke, I thought for a moment about what this dream meant. Suddenly I realized that the dream was revealing a new mathematical relationship. In the ensuing thirty minutes I wrote down these ideas as they came to me in fragmentary form from the dream. I prepared a paper which was subsequently published.*

Daydreaming is one familiar kind of nondirected thought. Such self-gratifying, wishful thinking can be helpful in that it gives us a break from unpleasant realities and helps us envision possibilities that logic would defy.

**Directed thinking.** At the other extreme from nondirected thinking is directed thinking—reasoning, problem solving, and creative thinking. Unlike nondirected thinking, directed thinking requires considerable effort, is under the constraints of logic and reality, and is directed toward a specific goal or outcome.

**Problem solving.** We are often confronted by an obstacle that prevents us from reaching a goal. This confrontation stimulates many thought processes. When we concentrate our thoughts upon the anger or frustration caused by the situation, we accomplish little toward reaching the goal. But when we direct our thinking toward overcoming the obstacle, we are engaging in **problem-solving** behavior. Problem-solving behavior has three components: (1) a description of the problem, (2) a set of actions that can be used to reach a solution, and (3) a goal, or a description of what constitutes an adequate solution (Glass *et al.*, 1979).

To illustrate, suppose that you want to go away for the weekend to visit an old friend. You do not own a car so you plan to use public transportation. However, you discover that the busline has canceled its service to the town where your friend lives. So you now have a description of the problem: How do you go from here to there when you lack your own car and no public transportation is available? You might swear at the reservations operator or kick the tires of a bus. Both actions would be nonproductive and neither would carry you closer to the goal.

How would you go about solving this problem? Once you have formulated the problem and identified the goal, you could probably think of

**Problem solving**
Behavior directed toward overcoming an obstacle or adjusting to a situation by using new ways of responding.

**Set**
A readiness to respond in a certain way because of prior experience or expectations.

several possible sets of actions or solutions. These possible solutions, or hypotheses, are an integral part of problem-solving behavior.

The first thing you might hypothesize is that someone else might be driving to the town you want to go to. It is easy enough to test this hypothesis, providing you know of a bulletin board where you can post a notice. And, just in case this attempt proves fruitless, you might formulate another hypothesis. Perhaps there is train or airplane service to that town, with special weekend or student discount rates. Problem solving characteristically involves the formulation and testing of several hypotheses. Either you find a hypothesis that proves to be correct, or you run out of hypotheses and fail to solve the problem. If you are able to verify one hypothesis, you may not be able to do anything about it. For example, suppose you find out that the best way to get to your friend's town is to take a flight that leaves Friday afternoon at the very time you have to be at an important meeting. Because you cannot miss the meeting, you might try to reschedule it, or decide to thumb your way to your friend Saturday morning.

Many different types of problems can be used to investigate problem-solving behavior. Several of these are shown in Fig. 4.11. See how many you can solve before turning to page 160 for the answers.

Our ability to solve problems depends on a number of factors. Past experience, motivation, emotions, and flexibility may all affect our ability to attack and solve a particular problem. One of the most important determinants is **set,** or the tendency to respond in a fixed way.

The game of chess requires directed thinking, which is logical, realistic, and goal-oriented.

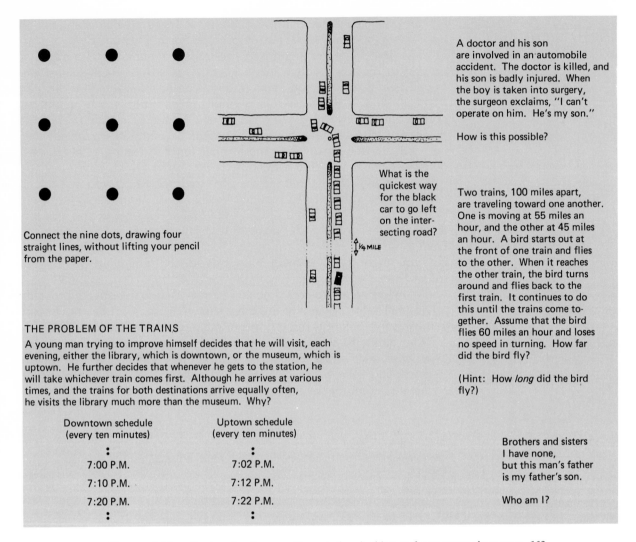

Connect the nine dots, drawing four straight lines, without lifting your pencil from the paper.

A doctor and his son are involved in an automobile accident. The doctor is killed, and his son is badly injured. When the boy is taken into surgery, the surgeon exclaims, "I can't operate on him. He's my son."

How is this possible?

What is the quickest way for the black car to go left on the intersecting road?

Two trains, 100 miles apart, are traveling toward one another. One is moving at 55 miles an hour, and the other at 45 miles an hour. A bird starts out at the front of one train and flies to the other. When it reaches the other train, the bird turns around and flies back to the first train. It continues to do this until the trains come together. Assume that the bird flies 60 miles an hour and loses no speed in turning. How far did the bird fly?

(Hint: How *long* did the bird fly?)

## THE PROBLEM OF THE TRAINS

A young man trying to improve himself decides that he will visit, each evening, either the library, which is downtown, or the museum, which is uptown. He further decides that whenever he gets to the station, he will take whichever train comes first. Although he arrives at various times, and the trains for both destinations arrive equally often, he visits the library much more than the museum. Why?

| Downtown schedule (every ten minutes) | Uptown schedule (every ten minutes) |
|---|---|
| : | : |
| 7:00 P.M. | 7:02 P.M. |
| 7:10 P.M. | 7:12 P.M. |
| 7:20 P.M. | 7:22 P.M. |
| : | : |

Brothers and sisters I have none, but this man's father is my father's son.

Who am I?

**Figure 4.11**      **Try to solve these problems before looking at the answers given on p. 160.**

In problem-solving situations, we tend to respond in ways that were successful in the past. We notice things that we expect to see or are accustomed to seeing. We tend to perceive things in such a way that our perceptions agree with our prior experiences or expectations. In a sense the whole educational process may be described as an effort to provide appropriate learning sets for solving the various types of problems that one encounters in the various disciplines. For the most part, set is desirable, because it permits us to arrive at solutions to problems that we otherwise would not be able to solve. For example, in your math courses you learn multiplication, division, subtraction, and addition. Learning these operations will permit you to solve problems involving quantity in real life.

When a new type of solution is demanded, however, set may interfere with our ability to solve a problem. Under these new circumstances, you might have to "break the set," or take a fresh approach to the problem. You might have to walk away from the problem and then come back and look at it from an entirely new viewpoint. Insightful learning often involves "breaking the set" (see Fig. 4.12). Sometimes the set is so difficult to break that the only way to solve the problem is to call in somebody who does not have the same set. That person can look at the problem in a new and different light and, perhaps, solve it. For example, earlier in this chapter we described how difficult it was to teach language to chimpanzees. Success was achieved only when somebody "broke the set" of trying to teach human speech and recognized that a different approach might be more profitable.

See Box 4.2 for an amusing example of how incorrect sets can result in faulty and, at times, catastrophic solutions.

One of the classic studies involving the effects of set on problem-solving behavior is illustrated in Fig. 4.13. We suggest you try the following demonstration on two of your friends. Ask one of them to write out the solutions to the problems in Fig. 4.13(a). Each problem demands the same indirect solution (B − A − 2C). Then ask this same friend and the friend who has not done the problems in Fig. 4.13(a) to solve the problems in 4.13(b). Record the amount of time they each take. You will prob-

Figure 4.12

**Insight**
A sudden solution to a problem.

**This child is faced with a problem that requires an indirect solution. Because the child is not sufficiently tall to reach his goal, he must discover a relationship between objects in his environment and obtaining the goal. When the solution is novel and comes suddenly, humans typically react with the expression "Aha!" These "aha" experiences are referred to as "insight."**

ably find that the second subject does the task faster than the first subject, who may be trying to apply the formula that solved the problems in 4.13(a). Note, particularly, the comparative performance of your friends on problem 8. Although the indirect solution (B − A − 2C) works for the other problems in 4.13(b), problem 8 can be solved only by a direct solution (A − C). Direct solutions will also work for the other problems (A − C for problems 6, 8, and 10 and A + C for problems 7 and 9).

**Creativity**
Productive thinking that is directed toward novel and productive solutions to problems.

**Creativity.**   What does it mean when we say someone is **creative?** Most people associate creativity with originality. The ability to see things in a novel and inventive way is, indeed, one of the characteristics of the creative individual. But originality is not the only ingredient in creative pro-

---

## BOX 4.2

### Breaking a Set, or How a Set Can Break You

A single water hyacinth is placed in a pond. Each day the number doubles so that at the end of twenty days the entire surface of the pond is covered. How long do the hyacinths take to occupy one half of the pond's surface?

Our first tendency is to blurt out "ten days." This is due to the fact much of the arithmetic of daily living involves straight-line relationships. If we are paid $8 an hour, we can determine how much we are owed merely by multiplying $8 by the number of hours worked. Thus, if we work ten hours, we are owed $80. If we rent an apartment for $600 per month, we can calculate our daily rate merely by dividing by the number of days in a month. If there are thirty days, the daily rate is $20. But anyone familiar with water hyacinths knows that they do not propagate in a straight-line fashion. Rather, their reproduction is more like an explosion in slow motion. One day there is one; the next day there's two; the next day, four; the succeeding day, eight; and so forth. Why, last summer I introduced two into a fish pond with approximately 200 square feet of surface. Within less than a month, the entire surface was cluttered with hyacinths.

The answer to the puzzle? Why, nineteen days, of course. If the number of plants doubles each day, then on the twentieth day the number is double that of the nineteenth day. Consequently, compared to day twenty there are half as many hyacinths in the pond on day nineteen. In fact, there were only one-quarter as many on day eighteen, one-eighth as many on day seventeen, and so forth.

Here's another one. A down-and-out baseball player went to a big-league manager at the beginning of spring training. Joe Aintgotit explained his burning desire to make the big time and offered a contract his manager couldn't refuse. "I'll play for a penny the first day, two pennies the second day. I only ask that you double my salary each day for thirty days. In other words, I want only a 30-day no-cut clause in which I am willing to give my all for just pennies a day. In fact, you may dispense with the usual room-and-board allowance. That's how much an opportunity to make the team means to me. At the end of thirty days, we can negotiate the contract, if you feel I've got what it takes."

The manager happily signed the contract. He was ecstatic at the unprecedented opportunity to get a "free" look at a highly motivated athlete. Only, much to his chagrin, he discovered that his perfect "deal" involved a somewhat greater financial risk than he had bargained for. To be more precise, he paid out $5,368,709.12 on the thirtieth day; $2,684,354.56 on the twenty-ninth day; $1,342,177.28 on the twenty-eighth day; etc. Naturally, the manager was fired by his new owner—Joe Aintgotit, who, sad to relate, never made the club.

---

Runyon, 1981, pp. 59–61.

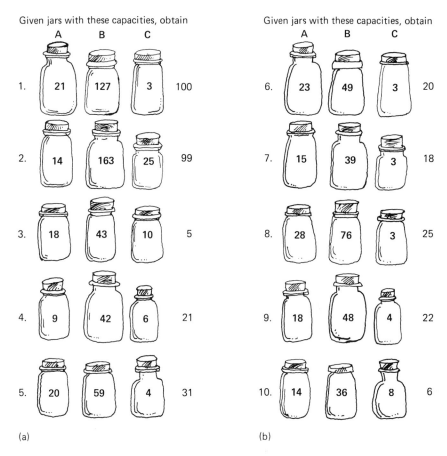

Given jars with these capacities, obtain

Given jars with these capacities, obtain

|     | A | B | C | |
|-----|-----|-----|-----|-----|
| 1. | 21 | 127 | 3 | 100 |
| 2. | 14 | 163 | 25 | 99 |
| 3. | 18 | 43 | 10 | 5 |
| 4. | 9 | 42 | 6 | 21 |
| 5. | 20 | 59 | 4 | 31 |

(a)

|     | A | B | C | |
|-----|-----|-----|-----|-----|
| 6. | 23 | 49 | 3 | 20 |
| 7. | 15 | 39 | 3 | 18 |
| 8. | 28 | 76 | 3 | 25 |
| 9. | 18 | 48 | 4 | 22 |
| 10. | 14 | 36 | 8 | 6 |

(b)

Figure 4.13   **The problem in this figure is to obtain the quantity shown in the last column when given empty jars (A, B, and C) as measures. After you have done this for (a), try the problems in (b). Then try the demonstration suggested in the text. (Luchins, 1942)**

cesses. Simply because an idea is original or different it is not necessarily productive or worthwhile. For example, a publisher may be the first to discover that he can dramatically reduce his production costs by publishing books with nothing but blank pages. But this highly original idea would hardly qualify as a creative act. Creative acts are purposeful, directed toward novel solutions to problems, and productive. Stated another way, creativity is "socially recognized achievement in which there are novel products to which one can point as evidence, such as inventions, theories, buildings, published writings, paintings and sculptures and films, laws; institutions; medical and surgical treatments; and so on" (Barron and Harrington, 1981, p. 442).

Creative acts are generally preceded by intensive study and preparation. Contrary to popular belief, people do not show bursts of creativity in areas they know nothing about. Great mathematicians, artists, or composers must thoroughly understand the basic elements of their fields before they can produce works that we deem creative. On the other hand, creative works are not produced only by the giants of science or art. At

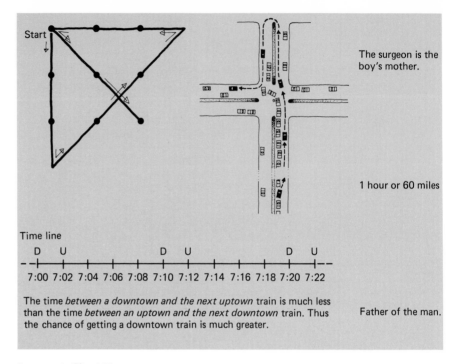

Answers to Fig. 4.11.

one time or another, we are all called upon to produce new and worthwhile creations that need not be earthshaking in their significance. Salespeople may come up with a new way to market a product; cab drivers may find a new shortcut to the airport; camp counselors may make up thrilling new bedtime stories to tell the children in their charge. In fact, any one of us may discover a new approach to some problem we face every day. In Chapter 12 we discuss the relationship between creativity and intelligence.

## Summary

1. The events involved in thinking, reasoning, and problem solving are referred to as cognitive processes.
2. Lower animals often demonstrate communication capabilities. However, there is no convincing evidence that these communication systems constitute language. They lack both a grammar and the range of meaning found in human language.
3. Language is more than a means of communication; it is involved in virtually all of our ongoing daily activities. Moreover, it has been suggested that memory may be coded in the brain in language symbols.

4. The three characteristics of spoken language are its structure or grammar, its rules for deriving the meaning of statements, and its rules for combining the basic elements (phonemes) into pronounceable words.
5. Newborn children are capable of producing only a limited range of vocalizations. Their early vocal productions, however, include many of the basic elements of speech, regardless of the geographical region and language culture into which they are born. Many of these vocalizations will drop from the child's repertory of vocal responses as his or her parents reinforce sounds characteristic

of the culture and provide speech sounds for the child to imitate.

6. During the latter half of the first year of life, the child begins to produce varied, continuous, and patterned sounds referred to as "babbling." At about the age of one year, the first sounds that are recognizable as true speech appear.

7. The first sentences are typically single words that refer to specific objects or actions.

8. Children learn language by being spoken to. Adults simplify their speech when talking to children: They speak slowly, more distinctly, and in shorter sentences than usual.

9. During the early childhood years, girls acquire language skills more rapidly than boys of comparable age.

10. The mastery of language involves the acquisition of both the expressive function (the means by which we communicate meaning to others) and the receptive function (the ability to understand language).

11. Communication systems are not uniquely human. In lower animals, communication patterns appear to be established by hereditary factors; in humans, learning plays the dominant role.

12. In order to investigate whether language is a uniquely human ability, researchers have attempted to teach chimpanzees English via sign language, plastic symbols, and computers. Although some scientists have reported major successes, others have questioned these results.

13. The reinforcement theory, as exemplified by B. F. Skinner, holds that language is learned in much the same way as any other operant behavior: Vocalizations that approximate human speech are rewarded so that a gradual shaping of vocalizations occurs.

14. Opposing the reinforcement position, Chomsky argues that the human brain is an organ that is highly specialized for the production of language. Chomsky suggests that it is prewired for making the grammatical transformations that occur in language.

15. Concept learning involves attaching a symbol to objects that share a common characteristic while ignoring the differences that exist. Concepts have varying degrees of abstraction.

16. Thinking involves the internal manipulation of symbols that represent objects, people, places, events, or relationships. Through thinking, we are freed of having to manipulate physical events in our environment in order to determine the consequences of these manipulations.

17. Most of the symbols we use in thinking involve language. However, not all symbols are verbal. Individuals vary in the clarity of their visual imagery. Some people can reproduce images with such detail that we say they have a "photographic memory," or eidetic imagery.

18. Two broad classes of thinking can be distinguished: nondirected thinking, which is relatively uncontrolled and includes such activities as daydreaming and dreaming; and directed thinking, which is more controlled and purposeful and is typified by problem solving as well as creative thinking.

19. Our ability to solve problems depends on a number of factors including our past experience, motivation, emotions, flexibility, and, most particularly, set.

20. Creativity involves an ability to solve problems in a novel, but productive way.

## Terms to Remember

Cognitive process
Grammar
Symbol
Psycholinguistics
Semantics
Phonemes
Expressive function of language
Receptive function of language

Concept
Hypothesis
Overregulation
Concept formation
Stimulus generalization
Discrimination
Thinking
Eidetic imagery

Nondirected thinking
Directed thinking
Problem solving
Set
Creativity
Insight

5

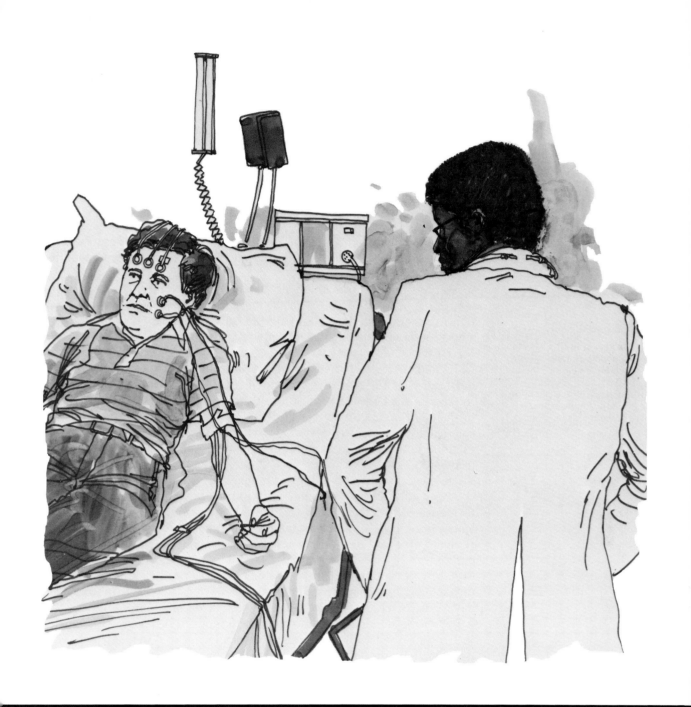

PHYSIOLOGICAL
FOUNDATIONS
OF BEHAVIOR

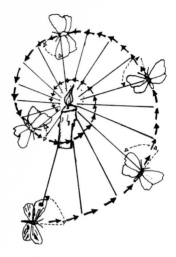

**Figure 5.1**
**The moth and the flame**

As shown in this illustration, the moth pursues a course in which the light of the candle always strikes its eye at a given angle. However, because the light source is so close, the moth flies to its death in a decreasing spiral.

Have you ever attempted to read out-of-doors on a summer night only to find your peace of mind disturbed by an endless array of uninvited guests bombarding your light source? You might have wondered why these winged creatures are so inexorably drawn to the light. The behavior of moths, for example, appears to be senseless and almost suicidal—they constantly batter their frail bodies against light bulbs or fly directly into candle flames. Why?

Let's speculate for a moment on some possible explanations for this apparently meaningless behavior. We might hypothesize that light attracts moths, and accept this as an adequate explanation. But if you think about this "explanation" for a moment, you will realize that it is really not very satisfactory. We have done nothing more than describe their behavior. In effect we are saying that they behave that way because they behave that way.

If **physiological psychologists** were to become interested in this problem, they would attempt to relate the observed behavior to the way in which the organism is put together; in other words, they would look for some correspondence between the structure of the moth and the way it behaves.

Scientists have studied the structure of the moth, and they now understand why the moth flies toward light. Under normal circumstances, the moth uses light from the sun or the moon to guide its flight. It is able to maintain a straight course by flying so that the light of these distant sources always strikes its eye at the same angle. The moth encounters difficulty only when it attempts to use a nearby light source as its guide (see Fig. 5.1).

Success in understanding such relatively simple behaviors has encouraged physiological psychologists to probe ever more deeply into the mysteries of behavior. What are the physiological mechanisms by which learning occurs? Why does forgetting take place? To what extent do abnormal behaviors result from imbalances in body chemistry? These are but a few of the questions that physiological psychologists are now exploring. Even though there is much we do not yet know about the physiological mechanisms underlying behavior, scientists in this field have already made some exciting and significant breakthroughs.

We have defined psychology as the science of behavior. Most of this text is concerned with the fundamental principles of observable behavior. Among the many factors that influence behavior are the structural characteristics of each individual. This structure is intimately related to how the individual responds to its environment, both external and internal. In order to understand many aspects of behavior, it is important to know something about the physiological processes that go on inside our bodies.

## THE NERVOUS SYSTEM

A woman is driving her car. She is deeply engrossed in conversation with a friend. Her favorite song is playing softly over the car radio. She checks traffic moving in both directions, and then passes a slow-moving vehicle. Suddenly a dog runs in front of the car. Although the woman is being

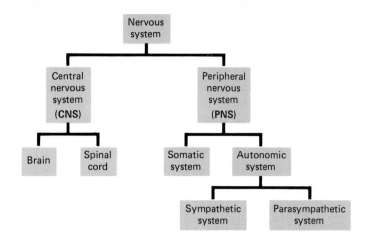

**Figure 5.2**
**The two major divisions of the nervous system and their various branches**

assailed by an almost endless variety of stimuli, she somehow manages instantly to depress the brake, swerve into another lane, avoid the dog, and escape a collision with other vehicles. It is almost miraculous, if you stop to think about it, that the woman is able to integrate information coming from so many different sources and translate this information into a coordinated series of responses. Minor miracles of this sort occur every moment of our lives. At this very instant you are looking at black marks against a white background and deriving coherent meaning from them (we hope). This is, in itself, an awesome accomplishment.

How is it possible to perform these data-processing feats with such apparent ease? Clues are found in the remarkably complex organization of the billions of elements that make up the nervous system.

There are two major subdivisions of the nervous system, the central nervous system (CNS) and the peripheral nervous system (PNS). The central nervous system includes the brain and spinal cord; the peripheral nervous system includes the somatic nervous system and the autonomic nervous system. The somatic nervous system serves the sense organs and skeletal muscles. The autonomic system controls the smooth muscles of the internal organs (those in the stomach and intestines, for example) and the glands. Figure 5.2 diagrams the two major divisions of the nervous system and their various subdivisions. To understand the nervous system and its role in behavior, we must look at some of its basic units.

## BASIC UNITS OF RECEPTION, NEURAL CONDUCTION, AND ACTION

### Receptors and Effectors

Imagine that you are an engineer and are given the assignment of designing a robot. Before you can undertake the many details of mechanical design, you must first decide upon the various functions you want this "organism" to perform. Because physiology is concerned with function, you might say that your first job is concerned with the "physiology" of the robot. At the outset, you decide to keep the robot very simple: Its sole task will be to move away from light. What would be required to enable the robot to perform this task?

First, you would need to develop a specialized surface that would be sensitive to the amount of incoming light: the **sensory receptor.** In the living organism there are many types of sensory receptors; some are sensitive to light (for example, the eyes), others to sound (for example, the ears), and still others to a wide variety of stimuli such as pressure, temperature, and odor. Chapter 6 presents a more detailed discussion of sensory processes. For the time being, it is sufficient to note that receptors usually initiate a sequence of behavior. When receptors are acted upon by stimuli to which they are "tuned," they provide information about the world external to them.

Once you have made the robot capable of light reception, you need a primitive nervous system that will carry messages from the receptor to the "muscles" and thereby permit the robot to move away from the light. The muscles and glands in living organisms are referred to as **effectors**. In the human there are three types of muscles. The striped, or skeletal, muscles are involved in voluntary motor activities such as walking, standing, and swimming. The smooth muscles control such internal organs as the stomach and the intestines. The heart muscles are unlike muscles found in any other part of the body and control the action of that organ alone. The response of effectors permits the organism to make some sort of adjustment to its environment, either internal or external.

In this simplified example we see the three essentials of a behaving organism: a receptor that is "tuned" to some particular source of stimulation, electrical circuits to carry messages to the muscles, and a motor system to move the robot away from light sources. The basic units for the transmission of these messages in animals are the individual nerve cells, or neurons.

## The Neuron

**Effector**
A muscle or gland.

**Neuron**
A nerve cell consisting of a cell body, an axon, and dendrites.

**Dendrites**
Hairlike structures of a neuron that receive nervous impulses from other neurons and carry them toward the cell body.

**Axon**
A long fiber extending from the cell body of a neuron that carries nervous impulses away from the cell body.

**Myelin sheath**
A fatty insulation surrounding many axons.

The **neuron** itself is a remarkable engineering accomplishment. It is distinctive from other cells of the body in three important ways—the shape of the cell, the capacity of the outer membrane to generate and carry nerve impulses, and a remarkable structure for transferring information from neuron to neuron (Stevens, 1979). The brain alone is believed to contain 100 billion neurons. If stretched end to end, these neurons would reach at least to the moon and back. Each is a miniature information-processing center, capable of receiving thousands of messages and, in a fraction of a second, sorting and acting upon them.

Each neuron is a living cell consisting of a cell body and two types of structures, an axon and dendrites. **Dendrites** are delicate, tubelike structures that branch repeatedly. They provide the surface for incoming messages and carry them *toward* their own cell body. The **axon** extends *away* from the cell body and provides the pathway for carrying messages toward other elements of the nervous system. Thus neurons are directional in their operation, and as we will see, so is the entire nervous system.

Some neurons are protected by layers of insulation known as the **myelin sheath.** The intact sheath contains many microscopic gaps along the axons (nodes of Ranvier) where direct contact is made between the cell membrane and fluid outside the cell. Generally, fibers with myelin sheaths transmit impulses faster than fibers without these sheaths. The myelin sheath appears to be involved in conserving the metabolic energy of the neuron. When it breaks down (as it does in multiple sclerosis, for

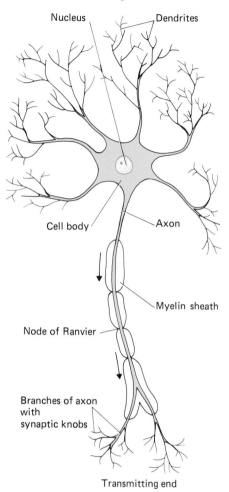

Receiving end

Nucleus

Dendrites

Cell body

Axon

Myelin sheath

Node of Ranvier

Branches of axon
with
synaptic knobs

Transmitting end

Figure 5.3
The neuron

From the main cell body branch numerous nerve fibers that carry impulses toward the cell (dendrites) or away from the cell (axons). Constrictions in the insulating myelin sheath, the nodes of Ranvier, occur at intervals. (Ritchie and Carola, 1979, p. 402)

example), such symptoms as muscular weakness and incoordination develop.

Neurons vary greatly in size and appearance. Some are measured in feet, whereas others are but a fraction of an inch in length. A neuron and its branches may be only a few micrometers from one end to the other, or the branches may be meters long, as in a giraffe's leg. Although the axon depicted in Fig. 5.3 is longer than the dendrites, this is not always the case.

The three classes of neurons. Although neurons may be classified in many ways, a convenient and useful distinction is the following:

1. **Afferent neurons.** These are sometimes called sensory neurons because they transmit messages from the sense organs (eyes, ears, skin) *toward* the central nervous system (spinal cord and brain).

**Afferent neurons**
Sensory neurons that transmit nervous impulses from the sensory receptors to the brain and spinal cord.

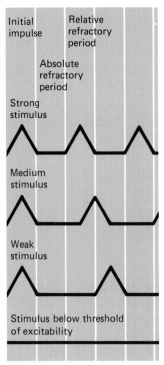

Initial impulse

Relative refractory period

Absolute refractory period

Strong stimulus

Medium stimulus

Weak stimulus

Stimulus below threshold of excitability

Time

**Figure 5.4**

**The characteristics of neural impulses in a single neuron under four different levels of stimulation**

Note that the neuron fires at full charge as long as the stimulation is above the threshold. No discharge occurs during the absolute refractory period. However, firing can occur during the relative refractory period if the stimulus is sufficiently strong. The strong stimulation causes the neuron to fire more often in a given period of time.

2. **Efferent neurons.** These are sometimes called motor neurons because they transmit messages *from* the central nervous system to the motor organs (effectors).

3. **Association neurons.** These neurons are generally within the central nervous system. They may transmit messages to other association neurons, but they also serve as connectors between afferent and efferent neurons; hence the term "association."

The neural impulse.   The "message" we have been referring to is actually electrochemical in nature. Each neuron can generate and hold small electrochemical charges. When sufficiently stimulated, it releases this charge. A popular misconception is that **neural impulses** travel at the same speed as electrical current. As a matter of fact, the maximum rate of conduction of the neural impulse is about 125 meters per second, whereas electric current may travel as rapidly as 300 million meters per second.

Not all stimulation that comes to the dendrites causes an electrochemical reaction within the neuron. There is a certain intensity of stimulation below which the neuron will not fire. This minimum intensity necessary to activate a neuron is known as the **threshold of excitability.** Whenever this threshold is reached or exceeded, the neuron will transmit an electrochemical impulse. Surprisingly, the neuron fires at full charge no matter how intense the stimulation, so long as it is above the threshold. An analogous situation is a fuse in a firecracker. The fuse requires a certain intensity of fire to start it burning. As long as the fire is hot enough the fuse will burn in exactly the same way, whether it is ignited by a match or by an acetylene torch. This characteristic of neural condition is known as the **all-or-none law.**

Given the all-or-none law, how can we explain the fact that a single neuron can distinguish between stimuli of different intensities? A partial answer is provided by the number of impulses the neuron will transmit in a given time period. Let's see how this works. After the neuron fires, there is a short period of time—known as the **absolute refractory period**—during which it will not fire again, regardless of the intensity of the stimulation. Following this, there is another brief interval—the **relative refractory period**—during which the neuron will fire, but only if the stimulation is more intense than is usually required. The more frequent occurrence of impulses under strong stimulation is illustrated in Fig. 5.4.

## The Synapse

How does an impulse get from one neuron to another? There are no direct connections, electrical or otherwise, between neurons. The axon of one neuron is separated from the dendrites of an adjacent neuron by a small gap known as the **synapse.** A single neuron may have anywhere from 1000 to 10,000 synapses and may obtain information from as many as 1000 other neurons (Stevens, 1979). The electrical impulse does not jump across the synapse. Rather, at the synapse, the axon enlarges to form a terminal bud. This bud can hold thousands of molecules of a sub-

**Efferent neurons**
Motor neurons that transmit nervous impulses from the brain and spinal cord to the muscles and glands.

**Association neurons**
Neurons usually found in the central nervous system that connect afferent and efferent neurons.

**Neural impulse**
A temporary electrochemical reaction of the neuron when it has been activated.

**Threshold of excitability**
Minimum intensity of stimulation necessary to activate a neuron.

**All-or-none law**
The principle that a neuron fires at full charge or not at all, no matter how intense the stimulation, so long as it is at or above the threshold level.

**Absolute refractory period**
A short period of time after a neuron discharges a nervous impulse during which it will not fire again, regardless of the intensity of stimulation.

**Relative refractory period**
A brief interval following the absolute refractory period during which the neuron will respond only to intense stimulation.

**Synapse**
The point of transmission of a nervous impulse from the axon of one neuron to the dendrites of another.

stance called a chemical neurotransmitter. There are known or suspected to be 30 different neurotransmitters in the brain, with many more likely to be discovered (Iversen, 1979). When the bud releases this transmitter chemical at the synapse, an electrical impulse is initiated in the dendrite of an adjacent neuron. This means that the nervous impulse can travel only from axon to dendrite, and not in the reverse direction. Figure 5.5 shows the synaptic connection between two neurons.

One investigator has written, ". . . the behavioral effects of many drugs and neurotoxins arise from their ability to disrupt or modify chemical transmission between neurons. It [research] has also hinted that the causes of mental illness may ultimately be traced to defects in the functioning of specific transmitter systems in the brain" (Iversen, 1979, p. 134).

It is interesting that some transmitter chemicals at the synapse are very similar in composition to the well-known psychedelic drug LSD. Apparently LSD produces its bizarre visual and auditory experiences by suppressing a vital neurotransmitter substance (serotonin) in the brain (Watson, 1981).

Not all synaptic connections are excitatory; some inhibit the transmission of impulses. Inhibitory synapses are as important as excitatory ones; without them our higher brain centers would be virtually inundated with useless information.

The activity of the neural elements of the nervous system is not as simple as we have depicted in this brief outline. Thousands of axons may converge upon the dendrites of a single neuron at any given time, so that complex interconnections and interactions result. Indeed, it is estimated that there are as many as 500 trillion synaptic connections in the nervous system of a person. It is this wealth of synaptic connections that makes possible the enormous variety of activities of which we are capable. However, all responses are not necessarily complex. There are a number of relatively simple responses that occur automatically in the presence of certain types of stimulation. These **reflexes,** as they are called, occur when the nervous system functions much as a switchboard does, connecting receptors and effectors.

## The Reflex Arc

**Reflex**
An unlearned automatic bodily response to stimulus.

**Reflex arc**
The pathway from a receptor to an effector that a nervous impulse follows to produce a reflex.

Imagine that you are at a cocktail party and, in the course of conversation, you accidentally touch the lit end of a cigarette. Your response is immediate. Without thinking about what you are doing, you automatically pull your hand away. Only after you make the response do you become aware of the cause for your withdrawal. Many reflexes such as this involve association neurons in the spinal cord as links between sensory and motor neurons. Thus the reflex occurs automatically and does not involve higher brain centers. These automatic responses illustrate the simplest form of an integrated response, the **reflex arc.** Figure 5.6 shows the neural pathways involved in a typical reflex arc.

Reflex responses are inborn, automatic, and often protective in nature. They shield us from the damaging effects of potentially dangerous stimulation. For example, our eyelids close automatically whenever a for-

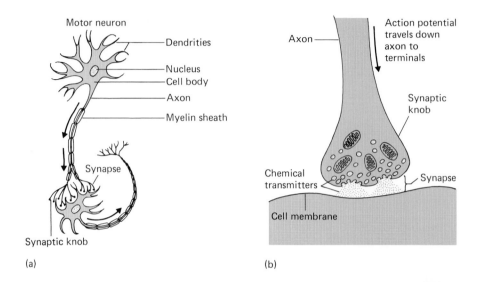

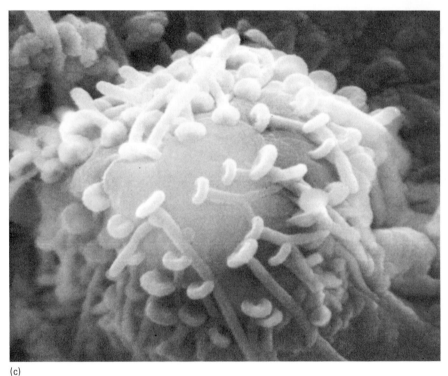

(c)

**Figure 5.5**
**The synapse**

(a) When a neuron is activated, an electrical impulse moves along the axon until it reaches a tiny synaptic knob at the end of each branching fiber. (b) There the impulse causes oval sacs in the synaptic knobs to release a transmitter chemical. This chemical substance travels across the gap, or synapse, and initiates an impulse in the adjacent neuron. (The arrow shows the direction of the impulse.) (c) A scanning electron micrograph of synaptic knobs surrounding the globular cell body.

Fig.5.5(c) source: E. R. Lewis, T. E. Everhart, and Y. Y. Zeevi, *Science* 165, 1140–1143, Sept. 12, 1969.

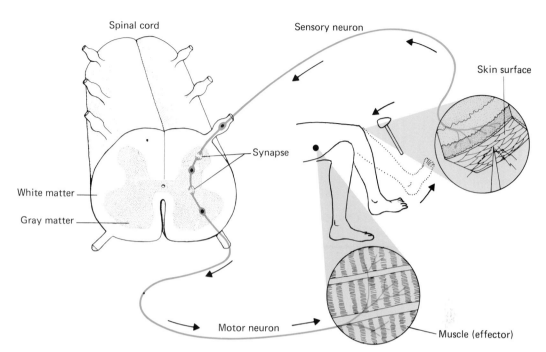

Spinal cord

Sensory neuron

Skin surface

Synapse

White matter

Gray matter

Motor neuron

Muscle (effector)

Figure 5.6
Reflex arc

This figure shows the typical neural pathways involved in the knee-jerk reflex. When the receptor is activated, an impulse travels along a sensory neuron to the spinal cord. In the spinal cord, a synaptic connection is made between the sensory and association neurons. The impulse is then transmitted to the motor neuron, which causes the muscle to contract. Synaptic connections may also be made between sensory neurons and association neurons that carry the impulse to brain centers.

eign object threatens our eyes. Most of our behavior is not reflexive. When we read an assignment, engage in conversation, listen to the radio, or participate in an athletic event, the higher centers of the nervous system are called into play to orchestrate the incredibly complex interplay of sensory information, motor responses, and emotional reactions that constitute ongoing behavior. In popular usage, the term "reflex" is often erroneously applied to any behavior that appears to occur automatically, but may actually involve prior learning. Thus when a driver instanteously applies the brake in an emergency, we might be tempted to classify this response as a reflex. In fact, it is not inborn; it occurs "automatically" only after a great deal of prior experience.

## METHODS OF STUDYING THE NERVOUS SYSTEM

We live in an age of computers—those marvelous complexes of electronic circuitry capable of awesome and sometimes exasperating feats. Yet no created computer even begins to approach the sophistication and capabilities of our own nervous system. We have already seen how incredibly complex the human nervous system is, with its billions of interconnecting components that somehow manage to process and sort thousands of incoming messages and, in a split second, resolve them into unified sequences of action. How remarkable is the human nervous system—at once capable of learning speech and language, remembering thousands of past experiences, recognizing a familiar face, perceiving the beauty of a rose or a great work of art, and crying for joy or sorrow. What is yet more remarkable is that the nervous system is even capable of turning inward and studying itself. Given such complexity, there are obviously many different routes that we may take in seeking to unravel the many mysteries of the nervous system.

**Chemical Methods**

One technique involves the implantation of minute hollow tubes in selected areas of the brain. Through these tubes chemical substances can be introduced directly into the brain and the effects on behavior can then be studied.

## BOX 5.1

### The Body's Own Tranquilizers

When the brain chemicals called endorphins were first discovered, they were dubbed "the brain's own morphine" because of their ability to ease pain and induce a feeling of euphoria. Since then, studies have shown that various endorphins are produced . . . in response to physical stress such as strenuous exercise.

We now have evidence that psychological stress can also induce the release of endorphins. Researchers at the Max Planck Institute in Germany, for example, have found a significant increase in the levels of endorphin in the blood of university students who were about to take important examinations.

Research on the role endorphins play in handling psychological stress grew out of earlier pain studies conducted at the National Institute of Mental Health (NIMH) and elsewhere. In a series of experiments in our laboratory at NIMH, we pinpointed the circumstances under which the brain, in response to pain, produces a natural **analgesia** by activating endorphins in the brain.

We first placed white rats in two chambers with electrified grid floors. The first group received electric shocks every seven seconds for approximately 10 min-

utes. The second group received no shocks. We then tested the rats' sensitivity to pain and found that the ones that had been shocked had developed a greater tolerance for pain. To learn why, we repeated the shock test with other rats and then immediately analyzed their brain and spinal tissues. The endorphin levels were lower than usual in brain areas that register pain . . . Apparently the brain "burns" endorphins in response to pain: it releases the endorphins at a rapid rate, dulling the animal's sensitivity.

The rats we studied were all subjected to physical pain rather than psychological stress. Pharmacologist John Rosecrans and his colleagues at the Medical College of Virginia went further to show that rats also produce endorphins in response to purely psychological stress. The Rosecrans team shocked rats in a chamber just as we did; then, a week or so later, they put the rats back in the same chamber, without shocking them. They found that the rats had a similar increase in brain endorphins—this time, in response to conditioned fear, a type of psychological stress.

Other researchers have shown that psychological stress may cause the brain to increase endorphin output in human beings as well. A French team, led by Jean Claude Willer, placed six healthy men and women in a predicament similar to the rats'. Intermit-

Another chemical technique involves indirect assessment of compounds by the use of blocking agents. To illustrate, researchers recently discovered that the body produces morphinelike substances called endorphines and enkephelins. It has been hypothesized that hypnosis, acupuncture, and direct electrical stimulation of the brain are able to reduce pain by signaling the body to release one of these pain-killers into the brain and/or spinal cord. Evidence supporting this hypothesis was obtained in studies where morphine was administered in combination with a substance known to block the pain-alleviating effect of morphine. It was found that administration of this substance reduced the pain-relieving effectiveness of hypnosis, acupuncture, and electrical stimulation (Iversen, 1979). Analgesia (pain relief) may be only one of several possible functions of the endorphins (Bolles and Fanselow, 1982). Recent studies suggest that endorphins may mediate attention (Lewis *et al.*, 1981) and restrain male sexual performance (Myers and Baum, 1980). Box 5.1 presents some fascinating facts and speculations about the brain's chemistry.

tently, during 90-minute sessions, they were warned that in two minutes they would receive a painful electric shock on their foot. Willer's team introduced the element of psychological stress by sometimes only threatening the shock and not giving it.

The French researchers electronically monitored involuntary flexing of a muscle in the lower leg, a reliable test that is used by researchers to measure foot pain as well as a person's expectation of pain. Halfway through each session, researchers injected the volunteers with either naloxone (a drug that suppresses endorphin activity in the brain), a placebo, or nothing at all. As each session continued, volunteers who had not received naloxone showed the same reaction as had the shocked rats: their muscle reflex became weaker as their pain tolerance increased. But among the men and women who had received naloxone, the muscle reflex increased, showing more sensitivity to pain and stress as time passed. This suggests strongly that human brains release endorphins in response to both psychological stress and physical pain.

The endorphins seem to play a particularly useful role in dealing with psychological stress. Intense stress triggers a fight-or-flight response, increasing the blood pressure, heart rate, metabolism, and other physical functions to mobilize the body for action. That involuntary response was invaluable in fleeing from saber-toothed tigers and is still useful in preparing for a tennis match. But the reaction can be dangerous to one's health if it is produced constantly by situations that call for nonphysical responses, such as an argument with one's boss or spouse. Heart attacks, strokes, and ulcers are among the physical disorders either caused or aggravated by such inappropriate reactions.

The effect of endorphins, fortunately, runs counter to these adrenaline-triggered overreactions. The endorphins slow respiration, lower blood pressure, and calm motor activity throughout the body. Thus the release of endorphins in response to stress seems to have adaptive value for today's men and women.

**Analgesia**
Anything producing an insensitivity to pain.

## Destruction

Sometimes a portion of the brain is destroyed through accident or disease. When brain damage occurs under these circumstances, the investigators have exercised no control over the location or the extent of the damage. Any attempt to relate the loss of brain tissue to resulting behavioral changes is, at best, an educated guess. Even if we knew the location and extent of neurological damage, we frequently have only sketchy information about the patient's past behavior, so that any assessment of behavioral change would be difficult if not impossible. Such accidental damage can, however, provide us with clues to relationships between various parts of the nervous system and behavior. These clues can then be further explored in the laboratory, where it is possible to establish precise experimental controls.

In laboratory studies with animals, the independent variable is the location of the area from which nervous tissue is removed. The dependent variable is some well-identified and measurable aspect of behavior. Control over extraneous variables is commonly achieved by surgical removal (**ablation**) of brain tissue from other areas of the control animals' brains. This procedure allows investigators to assess the possible adverse effects of the surgical procedure itself. Such research may involve the actual removal of nervous tissue, the destruction of connections among different areas, or the production of **lesions** by either surgical or electrical means.

Interpreting the results of neural damage to specific areas of the nervous system is not so straightforward as it might first appear. If an animal performs a specific task prior to surgical removal of brain tissue and then is unable to perform the same task after surgery, we might be tempted to conclude that we have located the area that regulates the performance of this task. As a matter of fact, we may merely have interfered with one of the components necessary for this particular behavior. For example, we may have interfered with the reception of visual cues necessary to perform the task; we may have disturbed the arousal system; or we may have destroyed a part of the system that regulates motivation. A highly elaborate program of research is usually required before a one-to-one relationship between a certain region of the nervous system and a specific behavior can be established, and frequently this research entails the use of techniques other than destruction.

**Ablation**
Surgical removal of a part of the brain.

**Lesion**
Any destruction of or damage to tissue.

**ESB**
Electrical stimulation of the brain.

## Electrical Stimulation

In a sense, the use of destructive techniques to study the nervous system is like firing a cannon to kill a fly. With the burgeoning sophistication of miniature electronic circuitry, many scientists have turned to methods involving the electrical stimulation of the brain (**ESB**). This stimulation can be accomplished in one of two ways. The scientist may explore the brain during surgery, applying a mild electric current to selected areas, or may implant minute electrodes in specific areas of the brain to permit repeated stimulation of the same area. The former method, used primarily with human subjects in the course of surgery, has provided information that has led to the construction of "maps" of the brain. For example, we now

(a)

(b)

Figure 5.7

(a) A rat with a socket implanted in the brain; (b) the plug which is inserted into the socket and through which electrical stimulation is introduced.

know that there is a one-to-one correspondence between specific locations in the brain and sensations arising from specific parts of the body

Direct brain stimulation by surgical exposure of its surface has numerous limitations. In addition to the ever-present risk involved in such surgery, the subject is, of necessity, restrained on a surgical table, and consequently, only a limited number of behaviors can be studied. Moreover, stimulation is often restricted to the readily accessible areas of the brain, so that the depths of the brain remain enshrouded in mystery.

Much of this has changed with the development of minute electrodes that can be precisely inserted in specific regions of the brain and permanently anchored to the skull (see Fig. 5.7). In one use of this technique, any given electrode can be activated by plugging it into a miniature receiver placed beneath the surface of the skin. This device (which does not require connecting wires) permits two-way communication between the brain and a remote radio receiver and transmitter. Because the activity of the subject is unrestricted, it is possible to study a wide variety of behaviors in many different environmental settings.

Some of the ESB results sound like science fiction. Imagine being able to turn rage on or off with the flick of a switch, to control aggressiveness merely by pressing a button, or to alleviate anxiety by turning a knob. Incredible as it may seem, scientists have actually been able to achieve these "miracles" through the use of ESB techniques.

In one particularly impressive study, four monkeys were placed in a soundproofed, air-conditioned room where their social behavior could be exhaustively studied. One male, Ali, emerged as the dominant monkey. He was powerful, aggressive, and quite hostile toward the third-ranking member, a female named Elsa. Stimulation of a specific region of Ali's brain inhibited his aggressive and hostile acts. What do you suppose happened when Elsa was allowed to control the initiation of this stimulation? The results were illuminating. Elsa quickly learned to press the bar that "turned off" Ali's aggressive behavior. In a three-day period she pressed the bar a total of 54 times (Delgado, 1963). Figure 5.8 is a photograph of Elsa pressing the bar to inhibit Ali's aggressive behavior.

Another exciting demonstration of the effectiveness of this technique is shown in Fig. 5.9. Here we see a bull stopped in mid-charge by a radio signal transmitted to an electrode implanted in its brain. It should be noted that one critic has suggested that the effect of the stimulation may be to produce confusion (Valenstein, 1973); that is, Ali's aggressive behavior and the bull's charge may have stopped from confusion rather than from inhibition of aggression.

## Electroencephalograph

We have already noted that the brain never sleeps, but continuously produces rhythmic electrical discharges, the synchronized output of millions of neurons. These rhythmic electrical activities, called brain waves, can be detected by electrodes, which are usually placed on the scalp. Because the voltages produced by brain waves are extremely small, they must be amplified if they are to be recorded. Small recording pens connected to

Figure 5.8     **Elsa (on the left side of the picture) presses the bar to stimulate Ali's brain by radio, thereby inhibiting Ali's aggressive behavior. The fact that Elsa is looking straight at Ali is significant, because looking straight at the "boss" usually provokes retaliation.**

**Electroencephalograph**
An instrument for recording the electrical activity of the brain.

**EEG**
A recording of brain wave activity obtained from an electroencephalograph.

**Alpha waves**
Brain waves typical of a relaxed waking state.

**Amplitude**
The height of a wave, indicative of the strength of a wave.

the amplifier transcribe the brain waves on paper. This apparatus, known as an **electroencephalograph,** yields a record called an **EEG.**

Behavioral scientists have been intrigued by the fact that a number of behavioral states of the organism have been found to be related to EEG activity. For instance, before the development of the electroencephalograph, it was difficult to arrive at a satisfactory operational definition of sleep. Analysis of EEG records taken while subjects were supposedly asleep has established that the brain waves change in a consistent fashion as the individual progresses from wakefulness through four distinct stages of sleep. When people are awake and relaxed with their eyes closed, their brain waves are regular and occur with a frequency of about 8 to 12 per second. These waves are called **alpha waves.** As a person enters the first stage of sleep, the proportion of alpha waves diminishes,

Figure 5.9     **In the experimenter's left hand is a radio transmitter that can send a signal to an electrode implanted in the bull's brain. The photo on the right shows the bull being stopped in mid-charge by the radio signal.**

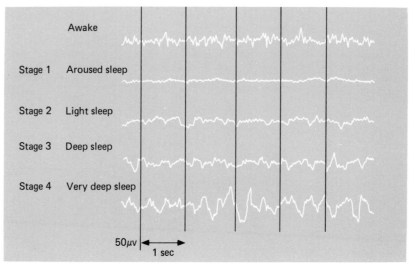

(b) Source: © 1956 United Feature Syndicate, Inc.

Figure 5.10    **(a) Alpha waves and the four stages of sleep as shown by EEG records; (b) the four stages of sleep as shown by Snoopy.**

to be replaced by irregular waves of low **amplitude.** In stages two, three, and four the alpha waves are completely replaced by increasingly high-amplitude and low-frequency brain waves. Figure 5.10 shows alpha waves and the brain waves characteristic of the four stages of sleep. We will look at other aspects of sleep in Chapters 7 and 8.

Much of what we have described in this section is based on the discovery that the brain constantly produces wave patterns that can be recorded on an electroencephalograph. On the surface, it may appear that these brain waves represent a biological phenomenon that is automatic and that is therefore not within the realm of conscious control. In Chapter 7, however, we shall look at some research that appears to contradict this assumption.

## THE BRAIN

Have you ever paused during the course of your daily activities to marvel over the capabilities and complexities of human behavior? Every second 100 million separate messages reach the brain from our senses. We manage to screen out the important messages from those that are less meaningful. Consider conversation. It is so much a part of our daily lives that

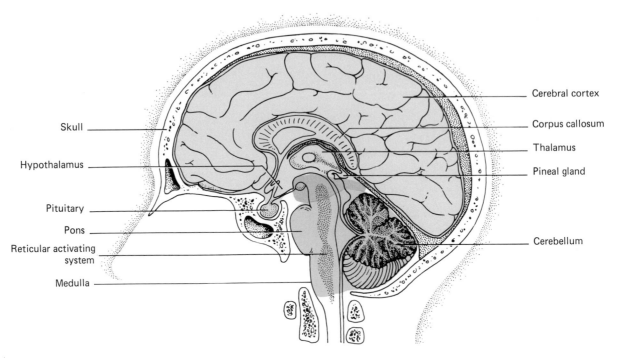

Skull

Hypothalamus

Pituitary

Pons

Reticular activating
system

Medulla

Cerebral cortex

Corpus callosum

Thalamus

Pineal gland

Cerebellum

**Figure 5.11**     This cross-sectional view of the brain illustrates some of the major structures.

**Cerebral cortex**
The layer of nervous tissue beneath the skull that is the outer covering of the cerebral hemispheres and that plays a major role in intellectual processes such as thought and language.

**Cerebral hemispheres**
The two symmetrical halves of the brain.

**Corpus callosum**
Connective fiber bridge through which the two cerebral hemispheres communicate.

we take it for granted. Yet when you analyze all the activities that are required to produce conversation, you must stand in awe at the remarkable engineering feat it represents. A person speaks a sentence. Physically the words are nothing more than pulsating sound waves, which are received by the ear. Here they are transformed into electrical impulses and sent to the brain. In the brain these impulses are processed and somehow translated into coherent and meaningful speech. Meanwhile, the brain is simultaneously sorting other information coming to it through the various sensory channels, suppressing some information that interferes with efficient functioning, and integrating new information with memories stored in the brain over a lifetime. Indeed, it has been estimated that the amount of information in the brain is equivalent to 10 billion pages in the *Encyclopaedia Britannica*!

The body may be awake or asleep, but the brain never sleeps. In addition to sorting information, it constantly regulates the many bodily functions necessary to sustain life—breathing, eating, drinking, and sleeping, to name but a few. In accomplishing these many tasks, it uses 20 percent of the body's total oxygen supply. In contrast, the brain represents only 2 percent of total body weight (Iversen, 1979). If the supply of oxygen to the brain is cut off, the individual loses consciousness within 10 seconds and suffers permanent brain damage.

The human brain may be conveniently subdivided into three major divisions: the cerebral cortex, the subcortical structures, and the cerebellum. The subcortical structures include the hypothalamus, thalamus, medulla, pons, reticular activating system (RAS), and limbic system. A cross-sectional view of the brain is shown in Fig. 5.11. Neither the RAS nor the limbic system is shown, because they are vertically oriented systems widely dispersed among the subcortical structures.

## The Cerebral Cortex

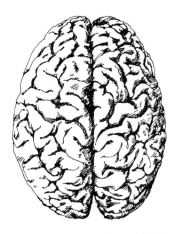

**Figure 5.12**
**Top view of the brain**

The cerebral cortex is divided into two hemispheres. Note the many convolutions and the valleys and ridges formed by these convolutions.

A mass of convoluted, waxy-appearing nervous tissue constitutes the outside layers of the human brain and supervises the many activities that clearly differentiate humans from lower animals. Indeed, the **cerebral cortex** is almost nonexistent in lower animals, whereas it occupies 80 percent of the total volume of the human brain. Imagine folding a sheet of gray matter 3 feet long, 2 feet wide, and ⅛ inch thick into intricate valleys and ridges. Were it not for these many convolutions, the cerebral cortex could not be contained within the skull. As we shall see, we are able to identify the various areas of the cortex by referring to the usual locations of the valleys and ridges.

The cerebral cortex is divided into two hemispheres, the **cerebral hemispheres.** These are similar in size and appearance, as you can see in the top view of the human brain shown in Fig. 5.12. Each hemisphere is further divided into four lobes—the frontal, the temporal, the occipital, and the parietal—that we will discuss in more detail later.

The two hemispheres of the brain exchange information through several different structures, the most important of which is the **corpus callosum** (see Fig. 5.11). Indeed, there is evidence that when information is transferred from one hemisphere to the other, a mirror image is produced in the other hemisphere. For example, *b* received in one hemisphere is recorded as *d* in the other. Children who tend to write and draw in mirror images (see Fig. 5.13) may suffer from interhemispheric interference (Corballis and Beale, 1971).

**Figure 5.13**
**Interhemispheric memory transfer**

**This spontaneous mirror writing is the work of a five-year-old girl in a New Zealand school. The lighter, correctly oriented script is the teacher's; the word order in the pupil's copy is consistently right-to-left, although some words and letters are in the normal left-to-right form.**

Courtesy of Ivan L. Beale.

**The split brain.**    Some of the most illuminating recent research in both animals and humans has involved severing the corpus callosum and other interconnecting structures. This surgical procedure, called the **"split-brain"** technique, eliminates communication between the left and right cerebral hemispheres. The procedure was initially introduced in the treatment of epileptics when all other medical techniques had failed. Epilepsy is characterized by a massive electrical discharge in one of the cerebral hemispheres which then spreads to the other hemisphere through the corpus callosum, resulting in a severe convulsive state (see Box 5.2). It was hoped that preventing the spread of the electrical discharge over both hemispheres of the brain would reduce the frequency and intensity of these convulsions. Following this operation many patients showed marked improvements. For example, one man who had been having severe convulsions for more than 10 years did not have a single major convulsion during a 5-year follow-up period (Sperry, 1968).

What is surprising is that these patients appeared to suffer no behavioral impairment as a result of the operation. Their speech, personality,

> **Split-brain surgery**
> A surgical procedure whereby the structures connecting the cerebral hemispheres are severed.

## BOX 5.2

### Key Types of Epilepsy

Accounts of epileptic seizures are found throughout the recorded history of human beings. They are caused by brain lesions or other pathology which result in a disturbance of the rhythm of electrical discharges of brain cells. Epilepsy affects about 1 person in 100 in the United States—between 2 and 3 million people. Cases occur among all age groups, but more commonly in children and adolescents . . . In over half the known cases, the age of onset is under 15 years.

Epileptic seizures are infinitely varied in form, but for practical purposes they may be classified into three main types described below. . . .

1.  Grand mal: "great illness." The most prevalent and spectacular form of epileptic seizure, grand mal, occurs in some 60 percent of the cases. Typically, the seizure is immediately preceded by an aura or warning, such as an unpleasant odor. During an attack the individual loses consciousness and breathing is suspended. The muscles become rigid, jaws clenched, arms extended, and legs outstretched, and he pitches forward or slumps to the ground. With the return of air to

the lungs the movements, instead of being rigid (tonic), becomes jerking (clonic). Muscular spasms begin, the head strikes the ground, the arms repeatedly thrust outward, the legs jerk up and down, the jaws open and close, and the mouth foams. Usually in about a minute the convulsive movements slow, the muscles relax, and the individual gradually returns to normality—in some cases after a deep sleep lasting from a few minutes to several hours. Another, less common, form of convulsive seizure, much like a modified grand-mal attack, is known as *Jacksonian epilepsy*; here, motor disturbances occurring in one region spread over the side in which they originate, and sometimes over the entire body.

2.  Petit mal: "small illness." In petit-mal seizures there is usually a diminution, rather than a complete loss of consciousness. The individual stops whatever he is doing, stares vacantly ahead or toward the floor, and then in a few seconds resumes his previous activity. In some cases, these seizures, may occur several times a day; and, unlike grand-mal seizures, they rarely have an advance warning or aura. With onset usually occurring in childhood or adolescence, petit-mal attacks are rare after the age of 20.

and intellectual functioning apparently remained unchanged. It was only when special testing procedures were devised that subtle but dramatic effects were uncovered. The most incredible finding was that the operation had produced an individual with two independent thinking centers, almost as if there were two brains in one person.

Figure 5.14 shows one of the techniques employed to demonstrate the presence of two brains in one body. This apparatus tests the subject's use of the right and left hands while his or her vision is blocked. In one experimental setting, a patient is instructed to feel a familiar object with one hand and then to feel three objects with the other hand and indicate which of the three was the original object. Surprisingly, split-brain patients were unable to select with one hand the object they had felt with the other.

In normal as well as split-brain subjects, stimuli presented to the left side of the body are transmitted to the right cerebral hemisphere, and vice versa. When connections between the hemispheres are severed, the left hand literally does not know what the right hand is doing.

3. Psychomotor epilepsy. Psychomotor attacks occur in about 10 percent of child, and 30 percent of adult, epileptics. Attacks usually last from a few seconds to minutes, but in some rare cases they may last considerably longer. Their principal feature is a psychic disturbance, which varies greatly from one individual to another. Despite a lapse or clouding of consciousness, activity continues and the individual appears to be conscious; during his attack he may perform routine tasks or some unusual or antisocial act. A very small percentage of cases may even involve self-mutilation or homicidal assault. The Flemish painter Van Gogh was subject to psychomotor attacks, for which he was later amnesic. On one occasion he cut off one of his ears, wrapped it in a sack, and presented it to a prostitute. In a more serious case, a brain-injured soldier subject to psychomotor epilepsy reported a dream in which he found himself trying to ward off attackers. Actually, he had beaten his 3-year-old-daughter to death, but was completely amnesic for the tragic episode.

Fortunately, drug medication and other treatment measures make it possible to prevent seizures in 80 percent or more epileptics. Often treatment procedures also focus on helping the individual cope with personal problems such as feelings of inferiority associated with the affliction. Educational efforts by professional and lay organizations have succeeded in dispelling many misconceptions concerning epilepsy and in helping epileptics live normal lives. For example, epileptics are no longer branded as poor employment risks—on the contrary, they show a relatively low incidence of on-the-job accidents. Also, legal restrictions on the operation of motor vehicles have been changed, so that epileptics are permitted to drive when it is established that they have been free of seizures (with or without medication) for 2 to 3 years. In general, most epileptics make adequate educational, marital, and occupational adjustments.

Based on Batchelor and Campbell (1969), Flor-Henry (1969), Holvey and Talbott (1972), Jasper (1969), Pryse-Phillips (1969), Rodin (1973), Stearman (1973), and Sutherland and Trait (1969).

Coleman, 1976, pp. 478–479.

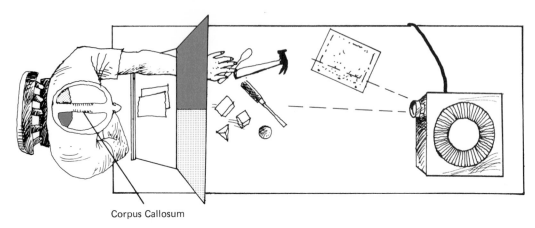

Corpus Callosum

Figure 5.14
**Apparatus employed in
split-brain studies**

This apparatus is employed to present visual and tactual stimuli to subjects whose cerebral hemispheres have been surgically separated. See the text for an explanation.

There is yet another fascinating aspect to the split-brain studies. The apparatus shown in Fig. 5.14 can also be used to direct a visual stimulus to either the right or the left cerebral hemisphere. A distinction must be made between right and left visual fields. This distinction is important because, unlike most other sensory modalities, not all of the optic fibers cross over to the opposite hemisphere; the crossing over is only partial. More specifically, light entering the right side of either eye (i.e., the right visual field) strikes the left side of each retina, forming an image that is inverted and transmitted to the left hemisphere. At the same time, images entering the left side of either eye are carried to the right hemisphere. Because each eye sends images to both cerebral hemispheres, even the split-brain person perceives a "normal" picture when both eyes are functioning. But what happens when visual input is limited to only the right or the left visual field? The answer is: "Some very interesting things."

Let us imagine that you show a patient a picture of an object in such a way that it falls only within the left visual field and therefore is transmitted only to the right hemisphere. The patient will report seeing nothing. But this report does not mean that the individual actually sees nothing. If the same picture, along with several others, is presented to both eyes and the patient is asked to pick out the object supposedly not seen previously, the patient will make the correct selection. If, on a subsequent trial, another picture is presented to the patient so that it falls only within the right visual field and therefore is represented on the left hemisphere, the patient will have no difficulty describing it. Evidence of this sort has led scientists to conclude that the left hemisphere controls the production of speech. Because each hemisphere possesses somewhat independent memories, the left side may verbally deny seeing an object that the right side has perceived. This theory is supported by studies of individuals who have sustained injuries to the left hemisphere. Typically, they have difficulty comprehending and producing language. In summary, then, the left hemisphere appears to play a dominant role in the language function of most people.

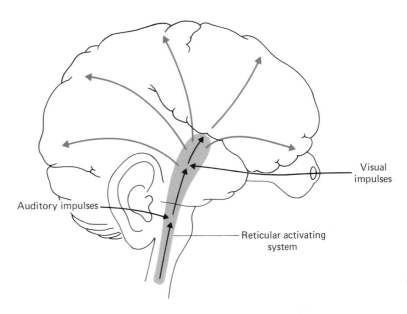

Visual
impulses

Auditory impulses

Reticular activating
system

**Figure 5.21**
**The reticular activating**
**system**

This complex network of nerve fibers extends up from the spinal cord through the brain
stem and into the thalamus. Its primary function seems to be that of a sentry system,
sending "wake-up" signals to higher parts of the brain and screening extraneous
sensory input.

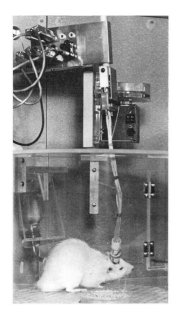

**Figure 5.22**

In this apparatus, the rat can
press a bar to deliver mild
electrical stimulation to its
brain. So-called pleasure and
avoidance areas have been
identified.

the cerebral cortex. In this way, the RAS maintains a state of arousal under conditions of sensory stimulation. When the RAS is severely damaged, the organism goes into a profound coma. Mild electric stimulation
of one part of the RAS will put an animal to sleep, but the same stimulation applied to another area of the RAS will awaken the animal and
immediately produce a state of arousal.

The limbic system.    The area known as the **limbic system** extends
downward from the cerebral cortex and includes a number of subcortical
structures. Three functional parts have been identified: One is involved
with the sense of smell, a second is concerned with emotion and motivation, and a third has no established function.

Tiny electrodes have been implanted in certain portions of the limbic
system to enable investigators to deliver mild electrical stimulation to
these areas (see Fig. 5.22). It may surprise you to learn that mild shock in
certain parts of the limbic system is actually pleasurable. Animals will
work for long periods of time to receive stimulation in these areas (Olds
and Milner, 1954). In some cases, extremely hungry animals preferred to
work for this stimulation rather than to eat (Routtenberg and Lindy,
1965). Even humans report pleasurable feelings when certain areas of the
limbic system are similarly stimulated (Heath and Mickle, 1960). On the
other hand, animals will work to avoid stimulation of other parts of the
limbic system. In humans, stimulation of these other areas produces reactions of either rage or fear.

Other studies have suggested that the limbic system exerts a restraining influence on emotional behavior. Investigators (Bard and Mountcastle, 1947) found that animals in which the cortex had been removed but the limbic system remained intact could be prodded and poked without arousing any apparent emotion. In contrast, when lesions were made in various areas of the limbic system, some animals became extremely ferocious. More recent studies have shown that certain areas of the limbic system serve to excite the organism and others to calm it.

## The Cerebellum

**Cerebellum**
A brain structure located under the rear portion of the cerebral cortex that plays a key role in muscle coordination.

If you hold a cat several feet off the ground and drop it upside down, it will always land on its four paws. This seemingly mysterious behavior can be attributed in part to a structure located under the rear portion of the cerebral cortex, the **cerebellum** (see Fig. 5.11). The cerebellum coordinates muscle movements, such as those involved in walking and swimming. When the cerebellum is damaged, an animal's ability to engage in complex coordinated movements is impaired. For example, a bird with a damaged cerebellum cannot fly, because it is unable to coordinate all the muscle systems involved in flight.

## THE SPINAL CORD

The primary function of the **spinal cord** is to relay messages back and forth between the brain and the other parts of the body, except for the head region. It carries data from sense organs to the brain and relays commands from the brain to the glands and muscles. The spinal cord is also involved in many of the reflex actions we have previously described (for example, the reflex arc).

## HOMEOSTASIS

**Spinal cord**
The part of the central nervous system that serves primarily to relay messages back and forth between the brain and the other parts of the body.

**Homeostasis**
A mechanism whereby the body maintains a state of physiological equilibrium. There are homeostatic mechanisms for virtually every bodily function.

In general, the cerebral cortex appears to be involved in higher-order mental activity, such as thinking and speaking; the structures below the cortex regulate and maintain the organism's internal environment. This regulation of the internal environment is called **homeostasis.** Ordinarily, the body maintains such functions as temperature, pulse rate, breathing, and blood pressure in a more or less constant state. But in unusual environmental circumstances (such as stress), the equilibrium of the body is upset. When this happens, the homeostatic mechanisms serve to restore the equilibrium and return the body to its normal level of functioning. For example, suppose that you opened your wallet and discovered that a badly needed $20 bill was missing. For most people this would be a stress situation. You might note a quickening of your pulse rate, increased perspiration, and disturbed breathing. But your homeostatic mechanisms would be immediately set in motion to restore these processes to their normal state.

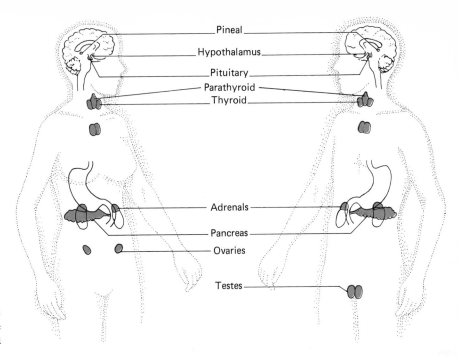

Figure 5.23
The human endocrine
system

Pineal
Hypothalamus
Pituitary
Parathyroid
Thyroid
Adrenals
Pancreas
Ovaries
Testes

## THE CENTRAL NERVOUS SYSTEM AND THE ENDOCRINE GLANDS

**Endocrine glands**
A group of glands that maintain body functioning by secreting chemical substances directly into the bloodstream.

**Hormones**
Chemical substances secreted by the endocrine glands directly into the bloodstream.

**Thyroid gland**
An endocrine gland whose secretions regulate body metabolism.

**Pancreas**
A gland that secretes digestive enzymes into the small intestine and insulin into the bloodstream.

**Gonads**
Sex glands; testes in males and ovaries in females.

**Pituitary gland**
An endocrine gland whose secretions regulate other endocrine glands; sometimes called the master gland.

The central nervous system depends on the body's life-support systems for the maintenance of its many functions. The circulatory system provides it with nutrients and carries away waste products. Any disorder that affects bodily functions may also affect the central nervous system. This is particularly true with the **endocrine glands** (see Fig. 5.23) The endocrine glands release chemical substances **(hormones)** directly into the bloodstream. Too much or too little of one or more of these hormones may seriously affect body functions (Fig. 5.24). For example, the **thyroid gland** regulates metabolism. An insufficient amount of one of its hormones in infancy, if left uncorrected, will cause the child to suffer widespread bodily damages and to become incurably retarded. Failure of the **pancreas** to secrete sufficient insulin (a hormone that controls blood-sugar levels) will cause the individual to suffer from diabetes. And very low levels of the hormones produced by the **gonads** can adversely affect many aspects of sexual behavior and the development of secondary sexual characteristics such as facial hair in males and the breasts in females.

The endocrine glands and the central nervous system function together. For example, there are sensors in the brain that are sensitive to specific hormones. They constantly monitor the level of the hormone to which they are "tuned" and "issue orders" based on the information they receive. Thus the maintenance of hormonal balance involves homeostatic mechanisms. The **pituitary gland,** the so-called master gland, is one of the endocrine glands (see Fig. 5.23). It shares a vast network of interconnecting neural and circulatory elements with the hypothalamus. We have already seen that the hypothalamus regulates many of the life-maintaining functions. In part, it achieves this regulation through its close relationship with the pituitary gland.

The reason the pituitary is called the master gland is that the various hormones it secretes regulate the other endocrine glands. As a broad

**Figure 5.24**     **A severe deficiency of growth hormone may cause a person to develop into a midget, while an excess causes giantism. Such effects are illustrated in this photo of Captain Gulliver (8′1″) and Major Mite (3′), standing with his miniature horse Tiny (24″ high).**

**Adrenal gland**
An endocrine gland, one of whose secretions is adrenalin.

**Adrenalin**
A hormone secreted by the adrenal glands that activates bodily structures and systems during an emergency.

analogy, the pituitary is to the other endocrine glands as the brain is to the body. For example, under conditions of sudden stress, the pituitary secretes a hormone that causes another endocrine gland, the **adrenal gland,** to release **adrenalin.** The adrenalin then activates various body structures and systems to prepare the individual to meet the emergency. It causes the heart to beat faster, so that it pumps more blood and oxygen to the various skeletal muscle systems that are involved in "fight or flight." Adrenalin also activates the various body mechanisms involved in temperature control (for example, perspiration), thus enabling the body to get rid of the excess heat generated by its emergency reactions.

## THE PERIPHERAL NERVOUS SYSTEM

The **peripheral nervous system** is outside the central nervous system. It carries input data from the sense organs to the spinal cord and brain through the afferent neurons, and transmits commands from the central nervous system to muscles and glands through the efferent neurons. The peripheral nervous system has two main subdivisions: The **somatic nervous system,** which serves the sense organs and the skeletal muscles; and the **autonomic nervous system,** which regulates the inner organs of the body such as the heart, the stomach, and the glands (Fig. 5.25).

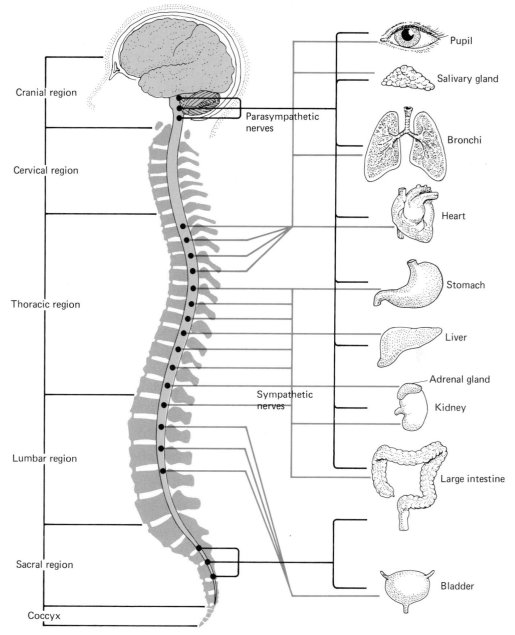

**Figure 5.25**
**The two branches of the autonomic system**

The connections of the sympathetic branch are indicated by the colored lines. The connections of the parasympathetic branch are shown by black lines.

**The Autonomic Nervous System**

The autonomic system and the hypothalamus are closely interconnected. We mentioned earlier that the hypothalamus is important in regulating the organism's internal environment. This regulation is partially achieved by the hypothalamus through its connections with the autonomic system. The autonomic system has two branches: the **sympathetic** nervous system and the **parasympathetic** nervous system. The two often work in opposition to one another, and together they achieve a homeostatic balance under normal conditions.

**Peripheral nervous system**
The part of the nervous system that connects the central nervous system with the receptors and effectors.

**Somatic nervous system**
The part of the peripheral nervous system that serves the sense organs and the skeletal muscles.

**Autonomic nervous system**
The part of the peripheral nervous system that regulates the inner organs of the body, such as the heart, the stomach, and the glands.

**Sympathetic branch**
The division of the autonomic nervous system that mobilizes the body during emergencies by increasing heart rate and blood pressure, accelerating secretion of adrenalin, and inhibiting digestive processes.

**Parasympathetic branch**
The division of the autonomic nervous system that is dominant when the organism is placid. This system decreases heart rate and blood pressure and regulates normal digestive processes.

The sympathetic branch, which is activated under emotional situations such as anger or fear, increases heart rate and blood pressure, stimulates the sweat glands, dilates the pupils of the eyes, and directs many other functions as well.

The sympathetic branch functions somewhat as the adrenal glands of the endocrine system do. For example, under conditions of stress, adrenalin is released by the adrenal glands, and adrenalin produces many of the activities described in the previous paragraph: It increases heart rate, dilates the pupils, and increases perspiration. But whereas the adrenal glands function indirectly through the bloodstream, the sympathetic branch leads to direct neural activation.

The parasympathetic branch is generally dominant when the organism is placid or quiescent. It decreases the heart rate, lowers blood pressure, and allows the normal digestive processes to occur, in addition to other actions shown in Table 5.1. Box 5.3 relates the sympathetic and parasympathetic branches of the nervous system to the practice of voodoo witchcraft.

The sympathetic branch has a profusion of central connections and interconnections. Therefore, when it is activated, it performs in a unified fashion, simultaneously sending its impulses to all the structures that it serves. On the other hand, the structures served by the parasympathetic system are activated by clusters of cells near the structures themselves. Thus any one organ served by the parasympathetic system may be activated independently of another. For this reason, we may say that the parasympathetic branch acts in a piecemeal fashion. Figure 5.25 shows the various connections of the two branches of the autonomic system to bodily organs.

Table 5.1

**Actions of the Two Branches of the Autonomic System**

| Organ | Sympathetic branch | Parasympathetic branch |
|---|---|---|
| Adrenal glands | Secretes adrenalin | None |
| Bladder | Inhibits excretion of urine | Stimulates excretion of urine |
| Blood pressure | Increases | Decreases |
| Body hair | Gooseflesh | None |
| Genital organs (male) | Ejaculation | Erection |
| Heart | Increases heart rate | Decreases heart rate |
| Intestines | Inhibits tone and motility | Increases tone and motility |
| Liver | Releases sugar | None |
| Pupils of eye | Dilates | Constricts |
| Salivary glands | Inhibits salivation | Stimulates salivation |
| Sweat glands | Stimulates sweating | Inhibits sweating |

---

## BOX 5.3

### Voodoo Magic and the Autonomic Nervous System

It is late at night and you are unable to find sleep. After hours of tossing and turning, you give up the effort and turn on the tube. You are not too happy to find that the only program available is that masterpiece of suspense and horror "Voodoo Drums." As you watch these primitive and uneducated people carry out the mysterious rites of voodoo magic, you feel smugly superior. You scoff at the thought that pins stuck in effigies can affect living people. Stupid! Absurd superstition! Yet the rites make you strangely uneasy. You even feel your body hairs stand on end as the victim writhes in terminal convulsion.

Well you might feel uneasy! It is altogether possible that voodoo curses cause death not by some magic spell but by the stimulation of the autonomic nervous system. The critical element is that the victims of the curse believe completely in the power of voodoo. When they learn that they have been singled out by an enemy, a panic reaction sets in, complete with the extreme arousal of the sympathetic branch. The parasympathetic branch attempts to counteract the extreme reaction of the sympathetic branch. It slows all the elements of the emergency response. Apparently, however, it does its job a bit too well. It overreacts and brings the heart to a standstill. Then, the victim dies not from the fear but by the normal actions of the body to quiet itself after an emotional explosion.

---

The autonomic system has usually been described as an involuntary system, primarily because it appears to function without any conscious control. Whether we are awake or asleep, it quietly and unobtrusively directs our life-support functions. And it is always on the alert to be summoned into action in case of emergency. Because it is largely automatic, it frees us to engage in the many activities that require voluntary adjustments to our environment. Imagine trying to master the material assigned in this text, for instance, while at the same time attempting to issue all the orders necessary to digest food, regulate breathing, and control blood circulation.

## Summary

1. Physiological psychologists attempt to relate behavior to the way in which the organism is put together. Their basic assumption is that behavior is intimately related to structure and that, by understanding the structure of the organism, they may better understand the "whys" and the "hows" of behavior.
2. The nervous system has two major subdivisions: the central nervous system and the peripheral nervous system. The central nervous system includes the brain and the spinal cord; the peripheral nervous system consists of the somatic nervous system and the autonomic nervous system.
3. The neuron is the basic unit of the nervous system. It is distinctive in shape, in its capacity to generate and carry nerve impulses, and in its means of communicating with other neurons (synaptic).

4. There are three types of neurons in the nervous system: afferent neurons, efferent neurons, and association neurons.

5. The message carried by the neuron is electro-chemical in nature. The minimum stimulation necessary to activate a neuron is called the threshold of excitability. When a stimulus at or above the threshold is applied to a neuron, the neuron fires at full charge. A neuron never fires at less than full charge. This characteristic is known as the all-or-none law of nervous conduction.

6. A small gap, the synapse, separates adjacent neurons from each other. The axon of one neuron releases a transmitter chemical that initiates an impulse in the dendrites of the adjacent neuron. Approximately 30 transmitter chemicals have already been identified.

7. The reflex arc is the simplest type of connection between sensory inputs and motor responses. Reflexes are innate and automatic and do not involve the intervention of higher brain centers.

8. Four techniques for studying the nervous system are: chemical methods, destruction, electrical stimulation, and electrical recording of brain waves.

9. The brain is divided into three major subdivisions: the cerebral cortex, the subcortical structures, and the cerebellum.

10. The cerebral cortex consists of two hemispheres, approximately equal in size and appearance. Various lines of research, including split-brain studies, suggest that each hemisphere is specialized for different types of functions.

11. Each hemisphere is subdivided into four areas: the frontal, the parietal, the occipital, and the temporal lobes. The body's sensory and motor functions are well localized in the cerebral cortex—patterned vision in the occipital cortex, auditory experiences in the temporal lobes, body feelings in the anterior portion of the parietal lobes, and regulation of fine voluntary movements in the posterior portion of the frontal lobes. Approximately 75 percent of the cortex is involved in the more complex behavioral processes that are referred to as associative.

12. The subcortical structures are responsible for maintaining the many vital life-support functions. In addition, several of these structures—particularly the thalamus, the hypothalamus, the reticular activating system (RAS), and the limbic system—appear to play a major role in behavior.

13. The spinal cord is primarily responsible for carrying impulses from the sense organs to the brain and relaying messages from the brain to the effectors.

14. The maintenance of the organism's internal environment is referred to as homeostasis. Homeostatic mechanisms maintain the balance of the various body functions.

15. The endocrine glands work in close conjunction with the brain, particularly the hypothalamus, in regulating body processes.

16. The peripheral nervous system has two main subdivisions: the somatic nervous system and the autonomic nervous system. The autonomic nervous system includes the sympathetic branch, which is activated under intense emotion, and the parasympathetic branch, which is dominant when the organism is placid.

## Terms to Remember

| | | |
|---|---|---|
| Physiological psychology | Efferent neurons | Reflex |
| Sensory receptor | Association neurons | Reflex arc |
| Effector | Neural impulse | Ablation |
| Neuron | Threshold of excitability | Lesion |
| Dendrites | All-or-none law | ESB |
| Axon | Absolute refractory period | Electoencephalograph |
| Myelin sheath | Relative refractory period | EEG |
| Afferent neurons | Synapse | Alpha waves |

Amplitude

Cerebral cortex

Cerebral hemispheres

Corpus callosum

Split-brain surgery

Frontal lobe

Parietal lobe

Occipital lobe

Temporal lobe

Fissure of Rolando (central fissure)

Lateral fissure

Motor area

Visual area

Auditory area

Associative cortex

Interpretive area

Subcortical structures

Pons

Medulla

Thalamus

Hypothalamus

Reticular activating system (RAS)

Limbic system

Cerebellum

Spinal cord

Homeostasis

Endocrine glands

Hormones

Thyroid gland

Pancreas

Gonads

Pituitary gland

Adrenal gland

Adrenalin

Peripheral nervous system

Somatic nervous system

Autonomic nervous system

Sympathetic branch

Parasympathetic branch

Analgesia

# SENSATION AND PERCEPTION

How many senses are there? Was your answer five? If it was, you are in good company from a historical point of view. Traditionally, we speak of seeing, hearing, smelling, tasting, and touching. As we shall see, however, there are many additional senses.

Try this exercise: Close your eyes and lift your left arm. Where is it? Did you say it is in the air? How do you know? Are you feeling it? Tasting it? Touching it? Because you are obviously not using any of the traditional five senses, some other sense must be operating, the so-called muscle sense. We rely constantly on the muscle sense to tell us where the various parts of our body are, and we usually take it for granted. Only when we are deprived of this sense do we realize its crucial role in our ongoing behavior. For example, in the advanced stages of syphilis, the organism responsible for syphilis attacks many parts of the central spinal column that carry sensations from the leg muscles to the brain. When this happens the patients lose the muscle sense in their legs, so that they literally do not know where their legs are. When they walk, they must continuously watch their legs in order to ascertain their position. If they are distracted for a moment, they may fall flat on their faces.

What about the detection of warmth and cold? Sense of balance? Pain? It is almost impossible to get a consensus about the number of senses we have. Surely there are more than a dozen. It is helpful to distinguish two broad classes of **sensory receptors: exteroceptors,** which provide information about the external world (for example, the receptors involved in seeing, hearing, smelling, tasting, and touching); and **interoceptors,** which monitor and provide information about internal states of the organism (for example, the receptors involved in the muscle sense, pain, and balance). The ongoing behavior of the individual requires the coordination and orchestration of the continuous flow of information arising from both the external environment and the internal environment.

Even looking at the so-called five external senses, we find that many of these can be broken down into separate senses. For example, in vision, we can speak of a black–white sense and a color sense. Even the color sense can be broken down into several separate senses.

It is beyond the scope of this book to discuss the various senses in great detail. It is important to note that our senses do not operate in isolation, but rather function as parts of a total system. All of our senses are linked in one way or another so that our ongoing behavior reflects coordinated rather than isolated sensory activity. At first we examine **sensation**—information taken in by the senses which has not been interpreted. Later we discuss the ways in which we interpret this sensory information (perception). But first, let's examine the ways in which we measure sensitivity to stimulation.

**Sensory receptor**
A specialized surface that is sensitive to a particular type of stimulus.

**Exteroceptors**
Sensory receptors that provide information about the external world (for example, the receptors involved in sight).

**Interoceptors**
Sensory receptors that provide information about internal states of the organism.

**Sensation**
Information taken in by the senses but not yet interpreted.

**Absolute threshold**
The minimum amount of stimulation that can be detected 50 percent of the time by a given sense.

## MEASURING SENSATION

Do you think you could see a candle 30 miles away on a clear, dark night? If it were very quiet, could you hear a watch ticking at a distance of 20 feet? If a bee's wing were to fall on your cheek from a distance of 0.4 inches, would you feel it? If a drop of perfume were diffused into a three-

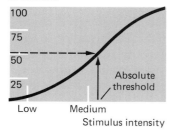

Percentage of correct detection of stimulus

100
75
50
25

Absolute threshold

Low    Medium
Stimulus intensity

**Figure 6.1**
**The absolute threshold**

Stimuli of various intensities are presented to the subject. If the subject reports receiving the stimulus when it is "on," he or she is credited with a correct response. The absolute threshold is identified as the stimulus intensity that is correctly detected 50 percent of the time.

room apartment, do you think you could smell it? Or could you taste 1 teaspoon of sugar dissolved in 2 gallons of water?

For most people, the answers to these questions are "Yes." In fact, these situations describe the minimum amount of stimulation that can be detected by the various senses. In other words, only stimulation at or above these levels is likely to be detected. The minimum amount of stimulation that can be detected 50 percent of the time by a given sense is known as the **absolute threshold** for that sense (see Fig. 6.1).

Even this so-called absolute threshold is not truly absolute. It varies from individual to individual and within the same individual at different times, depending on such factors as momentary changes in the receptors and the conditions under which they function. For example, after exposure to a continuous loud noise, it is difficult to detect a sound that would be readily heard after the ears had rested. The skin senses also show variations from time to time. Their sensitivity depends, in part, on the state of the surface blood vessels and on prior stimulation. After exposure to cold air, we are more sensitive to warmth, and vice versa. Certain illnesses or injuries can have devastating effects on our sensitivity to stimulation. The rubbing of clothing can be agonizing when we have a sunburn, and changes in humidity may be torture to a person suffering from arthritis.

Another aspect of the measurement problem involves the minimum increase or decrease of stimulation necessary to detect a *change* in stimu-

Thresholds of sensitivity are subject to variation, as Helen Keller demonstrated. Because she lacked sight and hearing, her senses of touch and smell were heightened.

**Difference threshold**
The minimum increase or decrease of stimulation necessary for a person to detect a change in stimulation.

**Sensory adaptation**
With most of our senses, continued exposure to a given level of stimulation will lead to an inability to detect that stimulation.

**Iris**
The colored part of the eye; it restricts the amount of light admitted.

**Pupil**
The opening in the eye through which light passes.

**Retina**
Photosensitive surface of the eye; it acts much like the film in a camera.

**Optic nerve**
Those fibers that transmit information about what is seen from the eye to the brain.

**Blind spot**
The spot on the retina where the optic nerve leaves the eye. Because it contains no receptors, it leaves a gap in the field of vision.

**Optic chiasma**
The point at which the optic nerves meet and the fibers from each separate before heading for the left and right hemispheres of the cerebral cortex.

lation. For example, imagine that you are in a room illuminated only by a 10-watt bulb. If a second 10-watt bulb were turned on, you would surely notice the increase in illumination. Suppose, however, that you were in a room illuminated only by a 100-watt bulb. If a 10-watt bulb were turned on, do you think you would notice any difference in illumination in this situation? Probably not. The change in stimulation necessary to detect a difference is known as the **difference threshold**. When the initial stimulation is low, less change in stimulation is required for a person to detect a difference. If you have a three-way lamp, observe how much more noticeable the change from 50 to 100 watts is than the change from 100 to 150 watts.

It is interesting that continued exposure to a given level of stimulation will, with most sense modalities, lead to an inability to detect that stimulation. This is known as **sensory adaptation.** If you enter a room where incense is burning, you will notice it immediately. After a short period of time, however, you will no longer smell it. When you first get dressed in the morning, you feel the clothes on your body. But after a while, you are completely unaware of the clothing, even though it is still stimulating your sensory receptors.

You can easily demonstrate sensory adaptation to light in the comfort of your own home. Some night when you wish to watch the tube for a while, turn on the television and several lights to make the room as bright as possible. Then cover one eye with a towel while viewing your favorite program with the other. After about an hour, go into a darkened room, and remove the towel. You will find that you are completely blind in the eye that viewed the TV. If you wait, you can chart the time it requires for both eyes to see equally well in the darkened room.

The traditional approach to sensation assumes that sensory receptors are normally in a resting state and are activated only when stimulated. In actuality, they are not sitting idly by; they are constantly sending impulses. In fact, what we are responding to when we become aware of a sensation is a *change* in stimulation. Adaptation occurs when there are no further changes in stimulation. You feel as if you were not being stimulated. For example, the clothes you wear provide constant stimulation, but not changing stimulation. That is why you no longer notice them after a while. We have all experienced the kind of adaptation that prompts us to say, "Come on in, the water isn't cold, once you get used to it."

As one observer has noted:

> *If at each moment we were aware of each quantum of energy reaching us, we would probably be overwhelmed by the flood of irrelevant information. We might not be able to discriminate enough to notice impending dangers, a tree about to fall, a truck approaching. Because we must discriminate between continuous "safe" stimuli and survival-related ones, we have evolved sensory systems which respond primarily to alterations in the external environment. The cells in the visual cortex and the retina, for example, are specialized to detect* changes *in input and to ignore constancies. (Ornstein, 1975, p. 43)*

## THE SENSES

### Vision

You have probably heard someone compare an eye to a camera. The eye has a lens to focus an image, a diaphragm to regulate the amount of light entering (the **iris**) through an opening (the **pupil**), and a photosensitive surface (the **retina**) which acts much like the film in a camera (Fig. 6.2.).

It is actually possible to take pictures with the living eye. This has been demonstrated in studies using a rabbit (Kuhne, 1878) and a frog (Garten, 1908) (see Fig. 6.3). It should be noted that insofar as optics are concerned, the eye and camera are quite similar, but beyond the optics, the eye is superior.

The retina contains receptor cells (receptors) that translate light into neural impulses. These impulses are then conveyed to the brain by the **optic nerve.** At the point where the optic nerve leaves the retina there are no receptors. Though we are not normally aware of it, this creates a **blind spot** in our vision. Figure 6.4 provides a demonstration of this effect.

After leaving the eye, the optic nerves of both eyes meet at the **optic chiasma.** There the fibers of each nerve separate, with fibers from the right side of each eye going to the right hemisphere and fibers from the left side of each eye going to the left hemisphere (see Fig. 6.5).

**Figure 6.2**

**The eye is similar to a camera**

Unlike the camera, the image in the retina activates electrical impulses that are relayed to the brain. In a sense, the brain "sees" the image, whereas in the camera the film "sees" the image. Moreover, the eye produces a clear image even when the individual is in motion. The camera must be held steady.

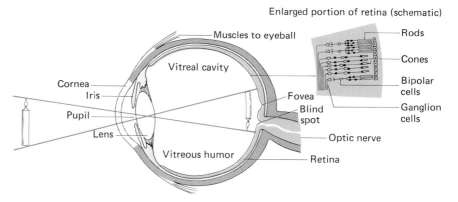

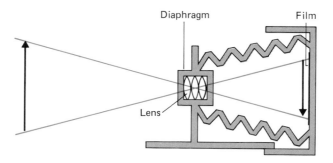

**Figure 6.3**

In a replication of the original experiment, a frog was paralyzed and then put in a box for half an hour and made to look at a pattern of bright stripes crossed at the center by a narrow bar. The retina was then removed and spread upon the knobby end of a white porcelain rod.

**Color vision.** Let's carry the analogy between the eye and the camera one step further. Just as we have to use one kind of film for color pictures and another kind for black-and-white, so the retina has different receptors, **rods** and **cones,** for black-and-white and for color vision.

The rods are extremely sensitive to light. They are so sensitive, in fact, that normal daylight bleaches out the photochemical substance associated with the rods, so that they can function only during periods of low illumination. No color is experienced with rod vision. You have probably noticed, when walking on a moonlit night, that you see the world in shades of gray. The cones, on the other hand, are responsible for color vision. They are far less sensitive to light than the rods, and they function under conditions of brighter illumination. There are three types of cone receptors, each with a different photosensitive pigment. Each is maximally sensitive in different parts of the spectrum, with considerable overlap of sensitivities (Mollon, 1982). The three types of cones are short wavelength, middle wavelength, and long wavelength. They mediate color vision roughly corresponding to blue, green, and red.

Have you ever been driving on a dark night when an approaching car suddenly flashed its high beams in your eyes? The bright light bleaches the photochemical substance associated with the rods and temporarily incapacitates them. When the car passes, there is not enough illumination for the cones to function, and you are momentarily blinded. Many serious accidents have occurred during this brief period of blindness. Thus changing to lower beams for an approaching motorist is more than a courtesy. It can be a matter of life and death.

Although the rods are more sensitive to light than the cones, the nature of their connections with the central nervous system makes them less capable of fine visual discriminations. In contrast to the rods, each cone is directly connected with the central nervous system, so that greater visual acuity is made possible. It is for this reason that day vision is far more acute than night vision. Futhermore, the cones are more prolific in the central region of the retina (the **fovea**), whereas the rods are found in peripheral regions of the retina. Consequently, during daylight, our sharpest vision is located in the fovea; in low illumination, such as in night vision, our sharpest vision is in more peripheral regions of the retina.

The next time there is a clear night, try making the following observation. Pick out a star that is just barely visible. Fix it in the center of your vision. It will probably disappear from view. Move your eye slightly to bring the image into a peripheral region. The star will come back into

**Rods**

One of the two types of receptors for vision located in the retina. No color is experienced with rod vision, only black, white, and gray.

**Cones**

One of the two types of receptors for vision located in the retina; the cones mediate color vision.

**Fovea**

The central region of the retina; it contains only cones.

**Figure 6.4**
**The blind spot**

Close your left eye and focus on the cross with your right eye. Hold your book about 18 to 20 inches from your eye and move it back and forth very slowly until you find your blind spot. To find the blind spot in your left eye, close your right eye and focus on the circle with your left eye.

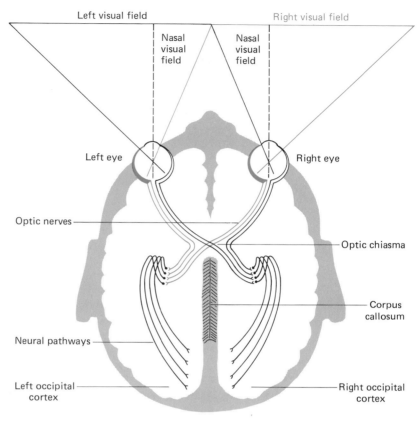

**Figure 6.5**
**Neurological organization**
**of vision**

Incoming light waves from the right visual field form an image on the left half of each retina and are transmitted to the occipital cortex of the left cerebral hemisphere. Images from the left visual field are transmitted to the right hemisphere. Note that bundles of optic nerve fibers meet at the optic chiasma where fibers from the inner, or nose, side of each retina cross over to the opposite side of the brain.

**Nanometer**
A measure of electromagnetic wavelength: one-billionth of a meter.

**Hue**
Scientific term for color; a specific wavelength is seen as a specific hue.

**Brightness**
How dark or how light a color is; it is determined by the intensity of the light at that wavelength.

**Saturation**
The richness of a color; it is determined by the purity of the light at that wavelength.

view. Table 6.1 summarizes some of the differences between the rods and cones.

Light, the physical stimulus for vision, consists of electromagnetic waves of extremely short wavelength. Color Plate 1 shows the entire electromagnetic spectrum and the small region to which the human eye is attuned. As you can see, the visible spectrum consists of a very narrow range of wavelengths, from approximately 400 nanometers to 700 nanometers (a **nanometer** is one-billionth of a meter).

The portions of the electromagnetic spectrum that we respond to as light vary in three important ways: the specific *wavelength,* the *intensity* of the light at that wavelength, and the *purity,* or homogeneity, of the light (that is, the proportion of it that is of one particular wavelength). Three psychological experiences are related to these three physical dimensions: **hue** (what we refer to as color—red, green, orange, and so forth); **brightness** (how dark or light the color is); and **saturation** (how rich the color is). Generally speaking, a specific wavelength is seen as a specific hue of

Table 6.1
**Comparison of Several Aspects of Rod and Cone Vision**

| Conditions for viewing | Color sensitivity | Sensitivity to light | Acuity (discrimination of fine detail) | Maximum acuity | Faulty function |
|---|---|---|---|---|---|
| *Rod vision* | | | | | |
| Dim illumination (dark rooms and nighttime) | Most sensitive to blues and least to red. Provides only white, gray, and black vision | Highly sensitive. Light-sensitive chemical breaks down under bright light | Low acuity. Night vision is poorer than day vision | About 20° outside the fovea. No rods in fovea | Night blindness (helped by vitamin A only if caused by vitamin A deficiency) |
| *Cone vision* | | | | | |
| Normal and bright illumination | Provides color vision | Not highly sensitive to light. Functions best in bright light | High acuity is maximum in fovea | In fovea. Less distributed at increasing distances from fovea | Total color blindness rare (0.003%); partial color blindness sex-related (8% in males and 0.04% in females) |

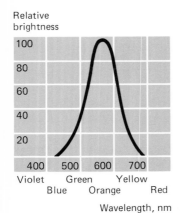

Relative brightness

100
80
60
40
20

400  500  600  700

Violet      Green      Yellow
     Blue      Orange      Red

Wavelength, nm

Figure 6.6
**The cones are not equally sensitive to all wavelengths. The graph shows the relative brightness of equally intense wavelengths under cone, or daylight, vision.**

color. As you can see from Color Plate 1, a wavelength of 400 nanometers is seen as violet and one of 700 nanometers, as red. The perceived brightness of any particular hue is proportional to the amount of physical energy or radiation at that wavelength. A small amount of energy will make the color appear dark, whereas a large amount of energy will make it appear bright. If the incoming light contains only a specific wavelength or a very narrow band of wavelengths (say, between 395 and 405 nanometers), the hue (violet, in this case) will appear rich or saturated. It will appear less saturated when the incoming light contains a wider spread of different wavelengths (say, from 380 to 420 nanometers).

Red and green are probably two of the most important colors in our everyday lives. They are conventionally used as signals, red signifying "stop" or "danger," and green meaning "go." Yet these colors are probably the poorest choices we could have made. Why do you think this is so?

First, rods and cones are not equally sensitive to all points on the visible spectrum. With equally intense lights of different wavelengths, some lights will appear quite bright and others will be barely visible. Figure 6.6. shows the relative brightness of equally intense lights of different wavelengths under cone vision. As you can see, our sensitivity to red is exceptionally poor. Red light must be very intense for us to see it. Red

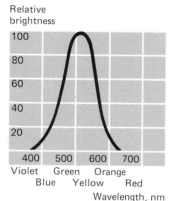

Relative brightness

400 500 600 700
Violet Green Orange
Blue Yellow Red
Wavelength, nm

**Figure 6.7**
The rods are not equally sensitive to all wavelengths. The graph shows the relative brightness of equally intense wavelengths under rod, or night, vision.

light is also less penetrating than is light of other wavelengths. The next time you drive your car in fog, notice how much sooner you can see a green traffic signal than a red one. Many multicar accidents that occur under foggy conditions may be caused by the drivers' failure to see the red brake lights of the cars in front of them in time to stop.

Figure 6.7 shows the relative brightness of equally intense lights of different wavelengths for rod vision. Again, we see that wavelengths in the red region are not very intense. The next time you watch color television, try tuning out the color. You will notice that the red objects appear dark gray or black. Because rod vision operates under conditions of low illumination, red objects will be difficult to see under these conditions, because they will appear dark gray or black. A night hunter who wears a red jacket invites disaster.

We do not see all colors equally well in peripheral vision. For example, red and green do not extend as far into the periphery as do yellow and blue. Thus if you are driving down a street that has a red or green traffic signal on the side of the road, you might not even see it.

You can set up a very simple demonstration to illustrate the relationship of peripheral vision to color. Find some bright blue, green, yellow, and red pencils or pens. Sit in a well-lit room and fix your eyes on some point on the wall in front of you. Cover your left eye. Have a friend bring one of the pencils slowly around from behind your right ear toward the front of your face. As soon as you can tell what color the pencil is, say "Stop." Compare the points at which you say "Stop" for each color. You should find that you see blue first, then yellow, and finally green and red.

A final argument against the use of red and green in warning systems involves color blindness. Color Plate 8 is a reproduction of a color blindness test. Complete color blindness is very rare, but red–green color blindness is not uncommon (approximately 8 percent of the male population and less than 1 percent of the female population have red–green color blindness). People with red–green color blindness can see yellow and blue as well as people with normal vision. Recognizing this fact, some states have designed green traffic lights with a bluish cast and red lights with a yellowish cast.

Knowing that red and green are such poor choices, you might wonder why states persist in using these colors. The answer lies in the risk of making a change. Suppose that purple were to be used to signal danger (or stop) and blue for safe (or go). Millions of people who have been conditioned since childhood to respond almost automatically to the colors red and green would be required to learn a new set of associations and responses to purple and blue. During the learning, many situations with high-risk potential would surely arise.

## Hearing

The organs of hearing are as remarkable as the organs of seeing. Just as the eyes translate portions of the electromagnetic spectrum into visible light, so the ears transform vibrations of air molecules into the experience of sound. These air molecules are set in motion by the vibrations of phys-

(a)

(b)

Organs of hearing vary among animal species. (a) Bats, for example, navigate by a process called echolocation in which the bat emits sounds that reflect off objects. The bat's large, concave ears funnel these high-frequency sounds into its auditory canals, thus permitting it to detect obstacles and prey, even in complete darkness. (b) Dolphins use an underwater echolocation system equivalent to the bat's, emitting clicks, grunts, squeaks, and six different kinds of whistles as they navigate and communicate with one another.

ical objects. Under ideal conditions, our ears can hear vibrations from 20 cycles to 20,000 cycles per second. We can respond to an enormous range of sound intensities: The most intense sound we can hear is approximately 5 million times louder than the softest sound we can hear.

Vibrating bodies may be described in terms of three physical dimensions: **frequency, intensity,** and **complexity.** When you press a piano key, the wire that is struck will vibrate at a given frequency. This frequency is usually described as the number of vibrations, or cycles, per second. If you now strike the same key with greater force, the same frequency will result, but the vibrations will be greater in amplitude (that is, intensity). Few objects vibrate at a single frequency alone. A piano string that vibrates at, say, 400 cycles per second also vibrates, with decreasing intensities, at 800, 1200, and 1600 (and other multiples of 400) cycles per second. This attribute of vibrating bodies is known as complexity.

These physical dimensions have psychological counterparts. Frequency is perceived as **pitch,** intensity as **loudness,** and complexity as **timbre.** The greater the frequency, the higher the pitch; the more intense the vibrations, the greater the loudness; and the more complex the sound, the richer the tonal quality (timbre). It is primarily timbre that gives each musical instrument its distinctive auditory qualities and permits us to distinguish among the thousands of voices we hear in a lifetime.

The ear has three subdivisions: the outer ear, the middle ear, and the inner ear. The **auricle** of modern humans cannot be moved and directed at will in order to collect sounds and direct them into the auditory canal. We move our heads, rather than our auricles, to bring sounds into focus. At the end of the auditory canal is a thin membrane, the eardrum, which is set into vibration by incoming sounds. The vibration of the eardrum activates three bones in the middle ear, which transform the air vibrations into mechanical vibrations. The middle ear is separated from the inner

**Frequency**
The number of vibrations, or cycles, per second; it determines the pitch we hear.

**Intensity**
The amplitude of the sound waves; it determines the loudness of sound.

**Complexity**
The presence of frequencies other than the fundamental frequency; the number and strength of these other frequencies determines the timbre of a sound.

**Pitch**
Highness or lowness of a sound; it is determined by the frequency of the sound wave.

**Loudness**
The hearing sensation determined by the amplitude of the sound wave.

**Timbre**
The richness of a sound; it is determined by the complexity of the sound.

**Auricle**
The external part of the ear.

**Sound threshold**
The minimum sound intensity that can be heard under standardized testing conditions.

ear by another thin membrane, the oval window, which carries the mechanical vibrations into a snaillike structure called the cochlea.

The cochlea is filled with a fluid that is set into motion by the mechanical vibrations of the bones in the middle ear. The movements of this fluid stimulate thousands of tiny hairlike structures, each of which is tuned to a different frequency, like guitar strings. They, in turn, generate electrical impulses that are carried to the brain (see Fig. 6.8).

From this brief description, you can see that the ear is a marvel of engineering. Incoming air vibrations are first transformed into other air vibrations by the eardrum, then into mechanical vibrations in the middle ear, then into vibrations of a fluid in the inner ear, and finally into the electrical impulses that go to the brain.

The human ear is capable of responding to an enormous range of intensities. In fact, the range is so great that it was necessary to devise a special scale to represent the full range of intensity values to which we are capable of responding. Known as the decibel scale, it is quite similar to the Richter scale used to describe intensities of earthquakes. Instead of going up in units of 1, it increases in multiples of 10. An increase of 10 in the decibel scale means that the physical intensity of the sound has increased by 10-fold over the preceding value. Thus an increase from 20 to 30 in the scale shown in Fig. 6.9 represents a 10-fold increase in the intensity of the sound. Between the lowest values that can be heard (the **sound threshold**) and the threshold of pain is an increase of 10 trillion! To describe the difference in the intensities between two sound sources you merely subtract the decibel value of the smaller from the decibel value of the larger. Thus the difference between the noise level of a discotheque (120 decibels) and a soft whisper (30 decibels) is 90 decibels. We can see that a discotheque is 1 billion times more intense!

In recent years, a note of alarm has been sounded by scientists who fear that noise pollution may endanger our sensitive hearing mechanisms. Destruction of hair cells in the inner ear has already been estab-

**Figure 6.8**
**Diagram of the ear**

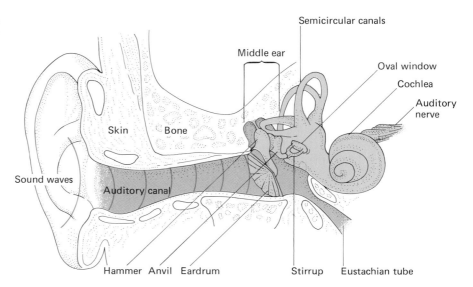

lished as a consequence of overexposure to loud noises, and we know that frequent exposure to intense noise can cause permanent and irreversible damage to our hearing organs. Mechanics working on jet engines have suffered impaired hearing, as have taxi drivers (in their left ears, which pick up the traffic noises). It is feared that men and women who spend a lot of time in discotheques and at rock concerts may, by the time they are 25, have their hearing capabilities reduced considerably. It is ironic that, in their search for louder and more exotic sounds, many peo-

**Figure 6.9**
**The decibel scale of sound intensities**

An increase of 10 in the scale represents a 10-fold increase in the intensity of the sound over the scale value 10 points lower.

| | Db | Sources | Intensity relative to threshold |
|---|---|---|---|
| | 140 | | |
| Uncomfortably loud | 130 | Threshold of pain / Pneumatic riveter | 10 trillion |
| | 120 | Discotheque, power motor | 1 trillion |
| | 110 | Rock band, jet taking off at 600 meters | 100 billion |
| | 100 | Riveting machine, subway station, incoming train, farm tractor | 10 billion |
| Very loud | 90 | Motorcycle at 8 meters, food blender | 1 billion |
| | 80 | Heavy traffic at 5 meters | 100 million |
| Moderately loud | 70 | Vacuum cleaner, noisy office | 10 million |
| | 60 | Conversation | 1 million |
| | 50 | Light traffic at 30 meters | 100 thousand |
| Quiet | 40 | Quiet office | 10 thousand |
| | 30 | Soft whisper at 5 meters | 1 thousand |
| Very quiet | 20 | Interior of broadcasting studio | 100 |
| | 10 | Leaves rustling | 10 |
| | 0 | Threshold of hearing | |

ple may be diminishing their capacity to achieve the very auditory experiences they most value.

Damage to or blockage of any of the structures involved in hearing may lead to hearing loss. Temporary losses may stem from a buildup of wax in the auditory canal or infections in the eustachian tubes. The loss will disappear when the condition is corrected. Any loss caused by destruction of the hair cells on the cochlea is permanent.

There are two primary causes of deafness. When the three bones of the middle ear are injured or diseased, their ability to carry messages to the inner ear is impaired. The resulting form of deafness is known as **conduction deafness.** It may be corrected by surgical replacement or a hearing aid, which simply amplifies incoming sounds.

This is not the case with **nerve deafness.** Amplification of the sound is to no avail once the auditory nerve loses its ability to carry impulses to the brain. This type of deafness is permanent and irreversible.

## Other Senses

In addition to vision and hearing, how many other senses are there? The answer is not as simple as it seems. One thing is certain, however: The senses number well beyond the traditional five. The sense we identify as touch, for example, responds to heat, cold, touch, pressure, and painful stimulation. Each involves highly specialized receptors (see Fig. 6.10).

**Figure 6.10
Various "touch" receptors**

Our "touch" receptors include specialized structures for sensing heat, cold, touch, deep pressure, and painful stimuli. We would not be wrong if we said that there are as many as five distinct senses involving touch. Figure 6.11 shows a similar situation with taste.

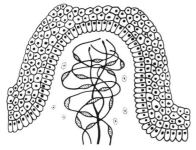

Meissner's corpuscle (touch)

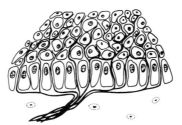

Free nerve ending (pain)

Corpuscle of Ruffini (heat)

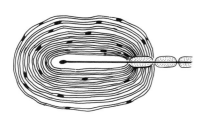

Pacinian corpuscle (deep pressure)

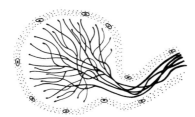

Krause's end bulb (cold)

Gourmets and professional wine tasters have finely tuned senses of taste and smell that allow them to make distinctions among subtle flavors and aromas.

The various receptors are not uniformly distributed throughout the body. For example, **Meissner's corpuscles** are densely distributed throughout the fingertips but are far less common in the palm or back of the hand. There is an interesting demonstration that may be used to map the density of various receptors over the body's surface. Try it yourself. Take two paperclips and make pointers out of them. Note that, when they are very close together as they touch the fingertips, you are able to detect both of them. Applied at the same distance on other parts of your body, you will think that you are being stimulated by a single touch source.

The story is pretty much the same for the sense of taste. Instead of a single type of receptor, there appear to be four different types of taste buds, one each for sweet, sour, salty, and bitter. Although this has not

Figure 6.11
**The distribution of taste buds on the surface of the tongue**

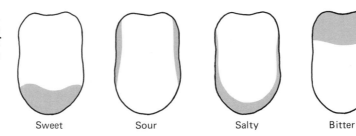

Sweet          Sour          Salty          Bitter

been definitely established, it has been demonstrated that there are four basic taste sensations. What we refer to as the sensation of taste is not restricted to these four types of receptors. In fact, taste is an admixture of odor with these four basic taste experiences. All you need do is close the nasal passages while eating food to appreciate the rich contribution of odor to the sense of taste. Figure 6.11 illustrates the distribution of the taste receptors over the entire surface of the tongue. In infancy, taste buds are densely distributed throughout the tongue, and even in the mucous membranes of the mouth. Each taste bud has a life span of about 10 days. With advancing age, they die more quickly than they are replaced.

## WHAT IS PERCEPTION?

As we sit here writing material for this book, a five-month-old baby girl, Laurie Beth, sits on her mother's lap. Laurie Beth is selectively reaching for objects in her visual field. She grabs at hair, eyeglasses, wristwatches, and the arms of the chairs around her. A few months ago, the faces she saw were unrecognizable, and the objects were just there—they were not meaningful. Now these objects have obviously acquired some meaning for her. They are no longer an unrelated flow of sensory experiences, but are becoming a more structured series of events that can be manipulated and drawn toward the mouth. She reaches out to touch things and seems to respond to textural differences. The feel of a soft teddy bear seems to delight her. She directs her attention to each of us as we speak. Laurie Beth is rapidly changing from a sensory to a perceptual animal. She is learning to organize and interpret her sensory world. We call this activity **perception.**

The rest of this chapter will explore various aspects of the attention and perception processes.

## Attention

Put your book down for a moment, and pay attention to whatever other stimuli you notice in your immediate vicinity. Do your hear a dog barking far away, the radio or television in another room, a clock ticking, cars in the street? While you were reading, you were somehow screening these stimuli out. How did you do it?

This little demonstration illustrates the fact that a constant stream of stimuli are bombarding us at every moment in our lives. We would soon be overwhelmed if we attempted to attend to and react to all of these stimuli at one time. However, we are protected against this "information overload" by two fundamental aspects of the attending process—its limited capacity and its ability to analyze sensory inputs selectively (Glass *et al.*, 1979).

Two types of processes seem to be going on simultaneously: We consciously attend to whatever activity we are engaging in at the moment and unconsciously monitor other inputs. Thus, at this moment, you are engaged in the conscious and voluntary activity of reading. Simultaneously, however, you are unconsciously monitoring other sensory inputs—the barking dog, auto noises, etc. This unconscious monitoring process is absolutely essential to survival. Without it, we would be totally unaware of our surroundings whenever our attention was absorbed by another activity. We would not be able to detect or respond to sudden dangerous and potentially catastrophic situations, such as fire. Thus even though this monitoring process is unconscious, it does not operate in a vacuum. Other cognitive processes—such as perceiving, encoding, remembering, and retrieving—are all facets of the attending process. Figure 6.12 presents a model of the process of attention.

How many different things can you notice at one time? Some people report that they study best in the midst of a constant hubbub of chattering people and blaring music. This would seem to contradict the usual notion that absolute quiet is essential for reading or studying. Libraries, for example, are known for their rules prohibiting any kind of noise. Recent evidence appears to dispute this time-honored practice. One library, located in an urban community, allowed people to talk and play rock music. Many more people began using the library, and they spent more time there reading. Apparently silence can be distracting to those accustomed to noise, as noise is to those accustomed to silence. In fact, we attend to only one thing at a time. When one sensory channel is activated, the activity of others diminishes. Most of us have had the experience of driving with the car radio tuned to the news. Then we approach a busy intersection where we have to pay attention to the traffic. A few minutes later, we realize that we missed several news items.

What are the factors that cause us to pay attention to some stimuli in our environment and to ignore others? Do motivational factors influence this selection? Emotional factors? Previous experience and knowledge? What about the characteristics of the stimuli, that is, intensity, contrast, and movement? These questions are enormously important to teachers, traffic engineers, politicians, publishers, salespeople, and advertising executives, to name but a few (see Box 6.1).

**Figure 6.12**
**Outline of a model of attention**

The inputs, represented by solid arrows, feed into the "conscious decision procedure" and the "unconscious monitoring procedure." The conscious decision procedure initiates and directs voluntary activities. Note that only one input, the *attended* input, goes directly to the conscious decision procedure. All the other *(unattended)* inputs first go to the unconscious monitoring procedures, which detect environmental changes that we are not paying attention to. The unconscious monitoring procedures pass along information (indicated by the dashed arrow) to the "attention controller." The controller determines how much unattended input actually reaches consciousness. (Glass *et al.*, 1979)

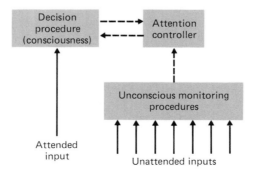

# BOX 6.1

## Psychology, the Law, and Eyewitness Identification

In Chapter 3 we discussed a study in which a convention of scientists was disrupted by the appearance of two men who raised a ruckus on the meeting-room floor. In subsequent interviews aimed at identifying the intruders, the scientists made numerous factual errors (the type of wearing apparel, the physical appearance of the men, etc.). This study was conducted in 1949, but it was neither the first nor the last research on this topic. The initial study was performed shortly after the turn of the century (Munsterberg, 1908). Recent studies have aimed at specifying the variables responsible for faulty identification by eyewitnesses. Such factors as the suggestibility of the eyewitness at the pretrial lineup, attentional factors, motivation, and perceptual distortions have been implicated in judgmental errors (Levine and Tapp, 1973).

Some studies have been conducted in a naturalistic setting for better simulation of the stressful conditions under which most crimes are committed. In one study, a professor was assaulted in front of 141 student witnesses. About 60 percent of the witnesses later identified the wrong man. Even more surprising is the fact that the victim of the assault—the professor, who had a closeup view of his attacker—also made an incorrect identification (Buckhout, 1974).

What has been the impact on the practice of law of this accumulated body of evidence? A recent review concludes:

*Regardless of time or technique then, most sets of data indicated that valid recall is altered by variables such as psychological processes of perception or motivation that mediate reconstruction of a remembered event. Perhaps more discouraging is the evidence that the essential finding on the unreliability of eyewitness testimony was made by Munsterberg nearly 70 years ago. Yet although numerous experiments have verified eyewitness error-proneness, such evidence is still deemed more reliable than other kinds of evidence (e.g., circumstantial). Despite repeated research and educational efforts, psychologists have had little impact on the law's unwarranted reliance on eyewitness reports.*\*

A good case in point is provided by the experiences of the three men shown in the accompanying photographs. The men on the left and right were selected from police lineups by the victims of rape and robbery. They were eventually cleared. The man in the center was arrested and admitted to both crimes.

---

\*Reproduced with permission from the *Annual Review of Psychology*, 1976, p. 388. © 1976 by Annual Reviews Inc.

 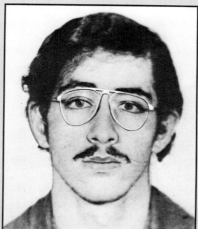 

Certain characteristics of stimuli influence their ability to attract attention. The more intense the stimulus, and the more it contrasts with its background, the more likely it is to attract attention.

**Characteristics of the stimulus.** Modern automobiles are equipped with a red warning light to signal a loss of oil pressure. A warning signal alerts the driver to a dangerous condition. Therefore the signal must be designed to fill this need, that is, to attract attention. How might you improve the design of this warning signal?

Suppose that you have to give a speech. What might you do to attract and maintain the attention of your audience?

Imagine that you are commissioned by a firm to design a billboard to advertise one of its products. How might you design this billboard so as to attract attention to it? Let's look at some of the stimulus characteristics that influence attention.

1. **Intensity.** The more intense the stimulus, the more likely it is to attract attention. The next time you are in a crowd of people, see how your eye automatically picks out people wearing bright colors. Or when you walk into a restaurant, see how your attention is immediately directed to the strong odors coming from the kitchen. The intense siren of a police car, fire engine, or other emergency vehicle is designed to attract immediate attention.

2. **Contrast.** Stimuli that are distinctly different from their background usually attract our attention. This sentence illustrates how small type against a background of larger type attracts your attention. The principle of contrast is widely employed in advertising and in the marketing and packaging of products.

3. **Movement.** One of the best ways to illustrate the role of movement in catching people's attention is to observe an infant's reaction to stationary and moving stimuli. An object that may be completely ignored while stationary is sure to command the infant's attention as soon as it begins to move (see Fig. 6.13). Investigators have recently learned that some receptors in the retina are responsive only to moving stimuli. These receptors are active only when an image moves across the visual field. You may have noticed that more and more billboards use moving stimuli, or the illusion of movement. With this

in mind, you will see that the red warning light on the dashboard might be improved by having it flash on and off rather than remaining in the "on" position.

**Characteristics of the individual.** One of the authors recently visited Disneyland with his family. If you had heard members of the family discuss their experiences afterward, you might have thought each one had gone to a different place. The 16-year-old girl talked about the teenagers she had particularly noticed. The 7-year-old boy found the amusement park full of exciting, and sometimes frightening, animals and prehistoric monsters; he barely noticed the teenage visitors. The 5-year-old girl liked the cartoon characters who talked to all the children and posed with them for pictures. The parents noticed the various family groups who were also visiting (how many children? what ages?), and they paid considerable attention to the prices.

How would you explain the fact that each of these individuals attended to different aspects of the same situation? One possible explanation lies in each individual's motivations. Motivations tend to direct our attention. A hungry person is likely to notice food and related stimuli, such as appetizing odors or advertisements for food. A person walking on a dark, lonely road at night is likely to be alert to any sounds or movements. The same stimuli would not even be noticed during the day.

Advertising agencies are well aware of the effects of motivation on attention. Most agencies have detailed lists of human motivations. In pre-

Figure 6.13     **(a) When the rattle is held stationary over the infant's head, she pays no attention to it. (b) When the rattle is moved, the infant's attention is drawn to it.**

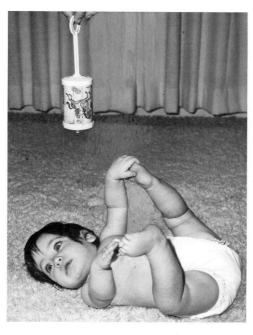

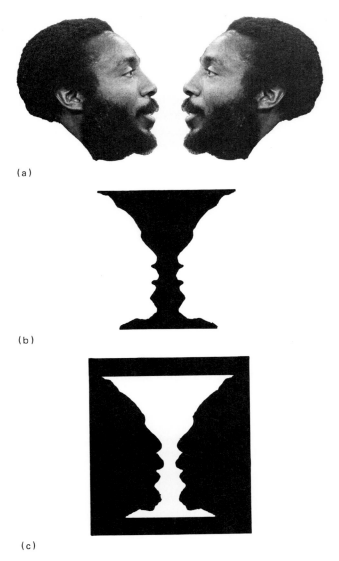

(a)

(b)

(c)

Figure 6.14   **Show one friend the picture in (a) and another friend the picture in (b). Then ask them both what they see in (c).**

paring an advertising message, these agencies seek to identify the relevant motivations in the target audience, and to imply in some way that their product will satisfy these motives. Pick up any two magazines geared specifically for two different audiences, and compare the advertisements in terms of the elements used to attract the readers' attention.

The emotional state of an individual may determine which aspects of the environment he or she will attend to. A person who has just received extremely good news may, in a state of euphoria, fail to notice signs of depression or unhappiness in others. Likewise, a person in a depressed emotional state may selectively attend to stimuli and events that reinforce his or her depression.

**Set**
A readiness to perceive or respond in a certain way because of prior experience or expectations.

**Gestalt psychology**
A school of psychology that stresses the view that we see things as unified wholes rather than as the sum of separate parts.

Previous learning and experience are other factors that affect what is selected for attention. Here is an exercise to try on your friends. Show one friend the silhouettes in Fig. 6.14 (a), covering Fig. 6.14 (b) and (c). Show another friend the vase in (b), covering (a) and (c). Ask them both what they see in (c). In both cases you will have established a **set**, or expectancy, which should influence what each one notices in (c).

You may have observed that people in various occupational groups tend to notice aspects of their environment that are related to their occupations. For example, dentists tend to look at people's teeth; a person who sells cutlery will probably notice the knives and forks at a table setting; and a tailor is likely to notice the cut of a person's clothes.

## Perceptual Organization

Before reading any further, look at Fig. 6.15 (a). What do you see? At first you will probably see a meaningless series of blotches. Look again, and those meaningless series of blotches will take on the form of a tiger: You will see the tiger's head looking at you. Now that you see the tiger, you will no longer see meaningless blotches. In fact, it may be difficult to look at the figure and see it as meaningless. Such organization of our perceptual world is characteristic of our everyday perceptions. We do not see unstructured lines and shadows. We see structured forms—people, animals, objects.

The process of organizing experiences into meaningful and structured perceptions began when we were infants. Now that we are adults, we tend to take the organized world for granted. Rarely do we question the principles underlying this organization. Yet there are principles by which we organize or group physical dimensions into coherent units. These principles were most thoroughly investigated and elaborated by the **gestalt psychologists,** who believed them to be innate. This group maintained that we see things as unified *wholes* rather than as simply the sum of separate parts. The word *gestalt,* in German, means "something complete, a whole, a total configuration." Thus, according to the gestalt the-

**Figure 6.15**    **Look at (a) from all angles. What do you see? See the text for an explanation. See Figure and Ground, a bit further on in the chapter, for a discussion of (b).**

(a)

(b)

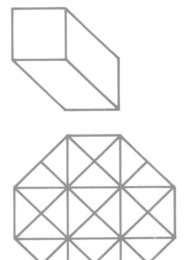

orists, we see these lines not as six separate and disconnected lines, but rather as three pairs of parallel lines:

The gestalt psychologists have contributed much to our understanding of perceptual phenomena. Let's examine some of the ways in which we organize aspects of our visual world into meaningful, coherent perceptual wholes.

**Figure and ground.**    One way we organize our perceptual experiences is to see objects against a background. When there are marked color or brightness differences, we tend to see a patterned **figure** on a **ground.** Look at the design in Fig. 6.15 (b). You probably see a series of black figures against a white background. Continue to look at this design, but reverse the figure and ground. In other words, treat the black as the background and the white as the figure. You should now see the word "Tiger."

In ordinary experience, figure–ground relationships are perfectly clear. We see objects and persons against a background. We almost never have trouble distinguishing figure from ground. A person, a table, a picture on the wall, and a mountain against the sky are all seen as coherent, organized wholes against a neutral, shapeless background. Indeed, as soon as you have seen the tiger in Fig. 6.15 (a), you perceive it as a figure against a shapeless background.

**Figure 6.16**
**Camouflage**

The figure on the bottom contains the one on the top. However, the figure on the bottom is such a tightly organized whole that it is difficult to isolate parts.

**Figure 6.17**
**Reversible figure–ground relationship**

Focus on the top edge of the central rectangle and then on the bottom edge. What seems to happen to the three-dimensional relationships of the various planes as you do this? If you continue to look at this figure, the planes will keep shifting back and forth.

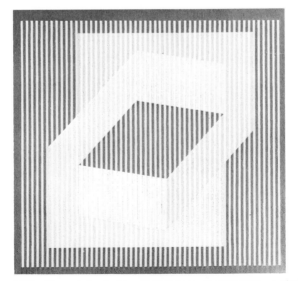

*Neither-Nor,* painting by Hannes Beckmann; German 1907–  ; Abraham Shuman Fund 65.503; courtesy of Museum of Fine Arts, Boston.

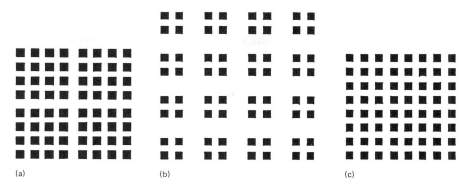

Figure 6.18
Proximity (a) When all of the elements are equally spaced, the entire figure looks like a checkerboard. (b–c) However, when the same elements are arranged so that some of them are placed closer to one another, our perception changes. Note that (c) readily forms a reversible figure–ground relationship. You can see four groups of dots against a white background, or you can see a white cross against a background of dots.

**Figure and ground**
In perception, the tendency to see things as objects against a background.

**Proximity**
In perception, the tendency to see things that are close together as a pattern or an organized whole.

**Similarity**
In perception, the tendency to see objects that are similar as forming subgroups.

**Continuity**
In perception, the tendency to see elements as grouped together if they appear to be a continuation of a pattern.

Camouflage techniques rely heavily upon breaking up these figure–ground relationships. They purposely make it difficult to distinguish figure from ground. The figure is deliberately lost in the background, as you can see in Fig. 6.16.

Several patterns have unstable figure–ground relationships. For an example, refer again to Fig. 6.14 (c). Sometimes you will see faces against a white background, sometimes a vase against a dark background. Note that it is impossible to see both simultaneously. Another example of a reversible figure–ground relationship can be seen in Fig. 6.17.

**Proximity and similarity.** We tend to see stimuli that are close together as a pattern, or an organized whole. Figure 6.18 illustrates the effect of **proximity** on perception.

Objects that are **similar** tend to form subgroups. Figure 6.19 shows how our perception of the checkerboard changes as we vary the shape of some of its "squares."

**Continuity.** We tend to see elements as grouped together if they appear to be a **continuation** of a pattern. Figure 6.20 shows an example in which there appear to be two continuous patterns.

Figure 6.19
Similarity Note how the similar stimuli tend to form subgroups. We perceive different patterns because similar elements go together.

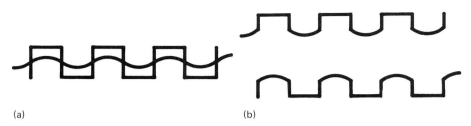

(a)                                                    (b)

**Figure 6.20**
**Continuity**

(a) We see the curved line as one unit and the straight lines as another because of the principles of continuity. (b) Now we see what the figures look like if we do not put them together.

**Closure**
In perception, the tendency to perceive broken lines as continuous, and incomplete figures as complete and closed.

**Perceptual constancy**
The tendency to see the world as relatively stable and unchanging, despite the wide variations in information received by the senses.

**Shape constancy**
The tendency to perceive objects that are familiar to us as retaining their shape, even though a variety of different visual images are received by the retina.

**Closure.**  As we say in our discussion of the eye and the blind spot, there is always a gap in our visual field. Yet we close this gap so successfully that we are virtually never aware of its existence. This is in part because our eyes usually move back and forth, showing us the whole scene, but is also because of our perceptual ability to "fill in the blanks" in what we see.

We tend to perceive broken lines as continuous, and incomplete figures as complete and closed. Fig. 6.21 illustrates this principle of **closure.**

One study nicely illustrates the principles of closure and contrast. Look at Fig. 6.22. In one quadrant of both (a) and (b), the pattern of lines is different from the pattern in the rest of the figure. Find that quadrant.

When subjects were confronted with this task, they took almost a full second longer to identify the different quadrant for (b) than for (a) (Pomerantz *et al.*, 1977). Why is this so? Note that, in (a), the principle of closure applies to the figures in the lower right quadrant. Because of closure, the four patterns in this quadrant appear as circular figures. These figures contrast nicely with the remaining patterns. In (b), however, the curved lines do not form "closed" figures. Consequently, we can find them only by examining the orientation of all the lines in the figure and discovering that the orientation of the lines in the lower right quadrant is different.

**Figure 6.21**
**Closure**

Look at the lines in (a). You will probably see them as three groups of lines plus a single line to the left. This is due to proximity. Now look at (b), in which short horizontal lines have been added. Because of the principle of closure, you should now see three rectangles. The solitary line has moved to the right.

(a)                                                    (b)

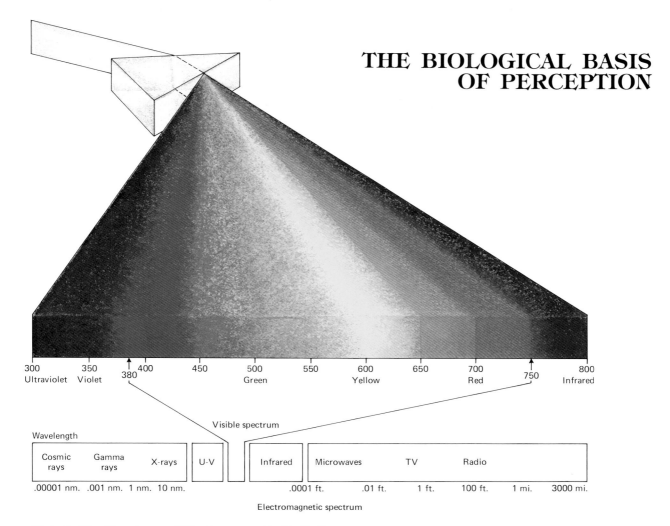

Visible spectrum

Wavelength

| Cosmic rays | Gamma rays | X-rays | U-V | | Infrared | Microwaves | TV | Radio |
|---|---|---|---|---|---|---|---|---|

.00001 nm.   .001 nm.   1 nm.   10 nm.          .0001 ft.          .01 ft.          1 ft.          100 ft.          1 mi.          3000 mi.

Electromagnetic spectrum

## Plate 1  The Spectrum of Electromagnetic Radiation

**By directing sunlight, or white light, through a prism, we can break it down into its component colors—red, orange, yellow, green, blue, and violet. The human eye can perceive only the narrow band extending from 380 to 750 nanometers (the equivalent of 1/1,000,000,000 of a meter).**

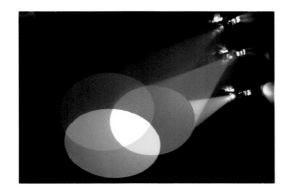

## Plate 2  Additive Color Mixture

**When light beams of different wavelengths are projected together onto a white surface, all wavelengths are reflected back and combine to produce an additive mixture. By mixing selected wavelengths in the correct proportions, all colors of the spectrum can be produced.**

Source: Fritz Goro, *LIFE Magazine*, © 1944 Time Inc.

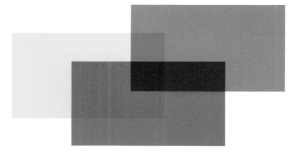

## Plate 3  Subtractive Color Mixture

**Colored paints (pigments) absorb (subtract) colors corresponding to wavelengths different from the wavelengths of the original colors. For example, when red and blue paints are mixed, the first color absorbs nonred hues (green); the second absorbs nonblue hues (yellow). The result is a subtractive mixture that falls between red and blue, that is, violet. In theory, specific wavelengths of the three primary colors (red, blue, and yellow) can produce the entire range of colors.**

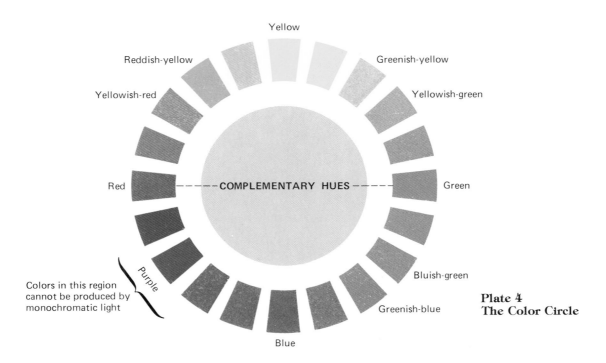

Yellow

Reddish-yellow

Greenish-yellow

Yellowish-red

Yellowish-green

Red — COMPLEMENTARY HUES — Green

Purple

Colors in this region cannot be produced by monochromatic light

Bluish-green

Greenish-blue

Blue

**Plate 4
The Color Circle**

(a)                    (b)

## Plate 5 Red/Green Color Blindness

**A photograph printed as it would appear to someone with normal vision (a) and to someone with red/green color blindness (b).**

Source: D. R. Specker/Animals Animals

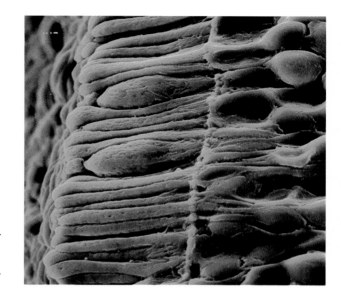

## Plate 6  Photograph of the Rods and Cones

The receptor neurons for vision are the rods—slim, pencil-shaped cells to the left in the photograph. The color receptors, or cones, are the two fat cells squeezed between the rods. In this picture, light would enter the retina from the right, setting off chemical reactions that would in turn trigger a wave of neural firing.

Photograph by Lennart Nilsson from *Behold Man* © 1973 by Albert Bonniers Frolag, Stockholm. Published by Little, Brown & Company, Boston, 1974.

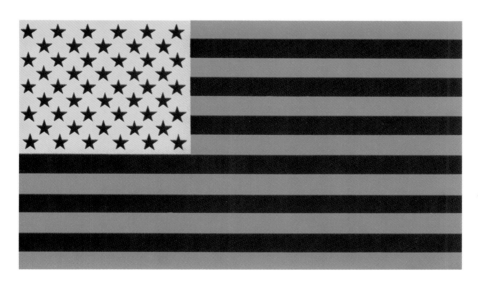

## Plate 7  The Negative Afterimage

Stare at the bottom right-hand corner of the orange square for about thirty seconds and then quickly look at a neutral-colored surface. You should see a familiar picture.

## Plate 8  Tests for Color Blindness

The most common type of color blindness involves a difficulty in distinguishing reds from greens. Less common is an inability to distinguish blues and yellows. Note the numbers depicted in the two circles. People with normal vision see a 75 on the left and a 47 on the right. Others with certain forms of color blindness see something different or no numbers at all.

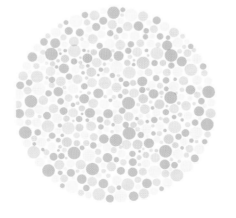
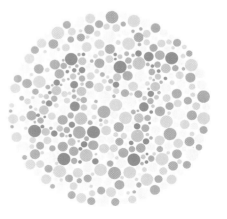

## Plate 9 Recorded Activity of the Human Brain

These actual photographs of brain activity were made using positron tomographic techniques. In each series, the brain is viewed from above, with the frontal lobe at the top and the occipital lobe at the bottom of the photograph. A state of high activity is indicated by the red/white end of the color spectrum and low activity by the blue/purple end.

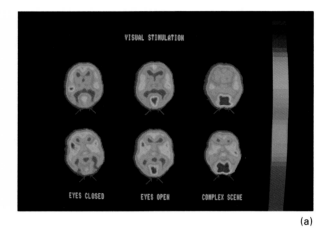

(a)

(a) The first pair of pictures, taken with the subject's eyes closed, shows minimal activity in the occipital area. However, when the subject's open eyes are exposed to a light, the appearance of red hues indicates increased activity in the occipital area. In the pictures at the far right, note the red and white (highest) levels of activity that occur when the subject views a complex scene of a park. This high activity is a reflection of the subject's visual analysis of the scene.

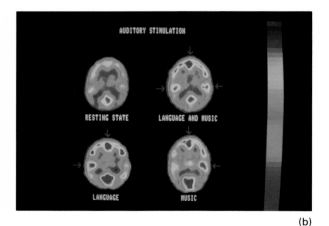

(b)

(b) These pictures show the brain in an eyes-open state. In the top right image, note the activity that occurs when the subject hears both language and music (horizontal arrows); left and right auditory areas are stimulated. The bottom left image shows activity on the left side of the cortex when the subject hears only language. The image at the bottom right shows the right side of the cortex responding when only music is heard. All pictures record activity in the frontal lobes because the subject is interpreting the sensations being received.

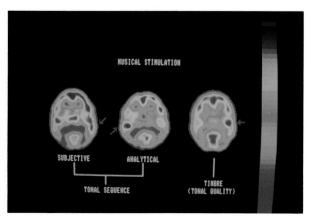

(c)

(c) The left and center pictures depict two subjects' responses to a sequence of tones after they have been instructed to decide whether the tones are alike or dissimilar. The person at the left, who knows little about music, must compare the tones intuitively (right hemisphere), whereas the subject in the center, who has studied music, can analyze the tones logically (left hemisphere). The right-hand picture shows brain activity in a subject who is knowledgeable about music and heard tones presented with no change in the time sequence. Thus the tones could only be compared in terms of complexity and sound quality. Unable to rely on "logical" means of comparing one tone to another, the subject switched to the "intuitive" right side of the brain.

Courtesy of Dr. Michael E. Phelps and Dr. John C. Mazziotta, U.C.L.A. School of Medicine

## The Constancies

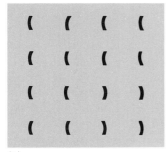

(a)

(b)

Figure 6.22
The different quadrant can be found more quickly in (a) than in (b). See explanation in text. (Pomerantz *et al.,* 1977)

Figure 6.23
Perceptual constancy

Look at Fig. 6.23. Do you realize that when you see a person lying down, this is the image produced on your retina? Somehow, when you look at that person in real life, you do not see extremely huge feet and a distorted body. The camera records the image as it actually is. The perceiving individual makes adjustments in his or her interpretation of the image received so that perceptions are consonant with prior experience and knowledge.

In spite of incredibly wide variations in the conditions under which we view objects in our environment—we see them from many different angles, at varying distances, in different contexts, and under virtually limitless conditions of illumination—we tend to see these objects as relatively stable and unchanging. This is known as **perceptual constancy.** The various constancies discussed here are all based on prior learning and help us make sense out of our environment.

**Shape constancy.** Take a few moments to look at various objects in the room about you. The door—do you see it as rectangular regardless of the angle you view it from? What about the paintings on the wall? The window? Hold a dinner plate in front of you, tilting it in various directions. Does it always look round in spite of the various positions in which you hold it (see Fig. 6.24)? The fact that we usually perceive objects that are familiar to us as retaining their shape in spite of widely contrasting visual images is known as **shape constancy.**

**Size constancy.** Imagine that you are out at night and you are looking at a full moon. You hold a circular object at arm's length so as to cover the moon. What size object do you think would be just large enough to

This is no trick of photography. Here the camera records what it sees. The image made by the feet is much larger than the image made by the head because the feet are closer to the camera. If we were viewing this same scene in real life, we would correct for these discrepancies and the man would not look distorted.

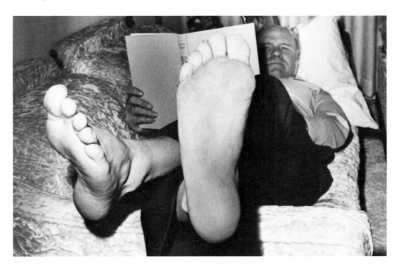

**Figure 6.24**
**Shape constancy**

We have learned that dinner plates are circular and see them that way despite wide variations in the viewing angles. The camera records the plates as we really see them. We interpret these retinal images so that they conform to our expectations of the world.

**Size constancy**
The tendency to perceive objects as their correct size, regardless of the size of the retinal image they produce at varying distances.

**Brightness constancy**
The tendency to perceive objects in their correct brightness, regardless of the conditions of illumination.

cover the image of the moon? A cantaloupe? A tennis ball? A nickel? A pea?

The truth is that an object the size of a pea, when held at arm's length, is sufficient to cover the image of the moon. Yet you perceive a *small* pea and a *large* moon (even though you do not perceive the moon to be as large as it really is). How is it possible for an object the size of a pea, held at a distance of only several feet, to blot out the moon completely? The answer is that objects produce smaller retinal images as their distance from the perceiver increases (see Fig. 6.25).

You can demonstrate this fact with more convenient objects. Take a small circular ashtray and hold it in front of one of your eyes so that it blots out a large painting on the wall. Even though the ashtray covers the painting, you do not perceive both objects as equal in size: You still see the ashtray as small and the painting as large. You have just demonstrated **size constancy.**

**Brightness constancy.** Imagine the following exercise: In a darkened room, put a piece of coal in a box and shine a very bright light on the coal. Then replace the coal with a piece of white paper and shine a very dim light on the white paper. Will the coal look white because it has had a greater amount of light projected on it? Will the paper look dark because it has had very little light projected on it? The answer to both of these questions is "No." The coal will look black even though a bright light is shining on it. The white paper will look white even though it is under very dim illumination. This exercise demonstrates the principle of **brightness constancy.**

We perceive brightness in terms of the proportion of the total light that is reflected. The coal in a bright light reflects only a small portion of the total light falling upon it. In contrast, the white paper reflects a high proportion of the total light shining on it. In general, bright objects reflect more light than dark objects. Thus we tend to see bright objects as bright regardless of the conditions of illumination.

## Distance and Depth Perception

**Monocular cues**
Cues to distance and depth that require the use of only one eye.

**Binocular cues**
Cues to distance and depth that require the use of both eyes.

Think for a moment of the many judgments you are constantly forced to make as you move through this three-dimensional world. For example, when you drive a car, you are continually called upon to estimate the distance of vehicles in front of you. You must be able to judge how soon to step on the brakes as you approach a stoplight. A slight error in judgment could be fatal. Every sport requires extremely fine judgments of depth and distance. It is amazing that we so rarely misjudge distance and depth. In large part, our success may be attributed to the fact that we have so many different cues for making these judgments.

What would happen if you were deprived of the vision of one eye? Could you still judge distance and depth? The answer is "Yes," but not as well as with two eyes. We can obtain many cues to distance with a single eye (these are called **monocular cues**). However, there are other

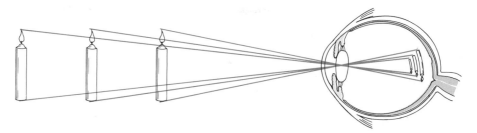

Figure 6.25
**Size of the retinal image**

The closer the object is to the eye, the larger its image in the retina is. Identical objects viewed at various distances will produce retinal images of different sizes. Two objects differing in size and held at the same distance will produce retinal images of different sizes.

cues to distance that require the functioning of both eyes simultaneously **(binocular cues).** Let's look at the binocular cues that help us perceive distance in a three-dimensional world.

**Binocular cues.** Try this simple exercise. Close your right eye. Holding a pencil in front of you, line it up with a corner of the room, or any vertical edge. Now close first your left eye and then your right eye, opening your left as you close your right. Alternate in this way between your left and right eyes. The pencil will seem to move with the opening and closing of each eye. Open both eyes simultaneously and focus on the corner of the room. You will see two pencils in your line of vision. Now focus on the pencil with both eyes and you will see two corners in the background. This simple exercise demonstrates that the two eyes are getting slightly different images, because they are separated. They are actually seeing slightly different views of any object that they focus on. This slight discrepancy between the images reaching each eye is called **retinal disparity.** It is retinal disparity that gives the world its three-dimensional appearance. Retinal disparity is unquestionably the most important binocular cue to depth.

When you look at objects that are close to you, your eyes tend to turn toward each other (or **converge**) in order to focus. If an object is very close, you feel (and look) cross-eyed and you may notice muscular strain. As you look at objects that are farther and farther away, your eyes look in more nearly parallel directions. We presume that the stimuli arising from the activation of the muscles that govern convergence also provide internal cues to depth and distance perception. Convergence typically works in concert with a particular monocular cue, known as **accommodation:** When the eye focuses on a distant object, the lens flattens out; when it focuses on near objects, the lens bulges. We presume that the bulging and flattening of the lens provides an internal cue that informs us of the relative distance of objects. Figure 6.26 shows the eyes viewing near and far objects.

Both of the binocular cues, retinal disparity and convergence, function effectively over only relatively short distances. Convergence, for ex-

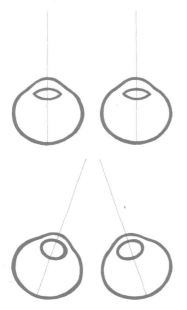

Figure 6.26
**Accommodation and convergence**

Note that, for distant viewing, the lens is flattened (accommodation) and the eyes are on a parallel plane. For near objects, the lens bulges (accommodation) and the eyes turn toward each other (convergence).

**Retinal disparity**
A binocular cue to depth perception; both eyes get slightly different images of an object because the eyes are separated from each other.

**Convergence**
A binocular cue to depth perception; in viewing a near object, the eyes tend to turn toward each other to focus.

**Accommodation**
A monocular cue to depth perception; the lens bulges for near objects and flattens out for far objects.

**Linear perspective**
Distance perception through the apparent convergence of parallel lines.

ample, is useful for judging distance and depth over only a few feet. Even retinal disparity is limited to relatively short distances. There is a far greater disparity between the images your eyes receive when you are 5 feet from an object than between the images they receive when you are 50 or 100 feet away from the same object. Thus, even though we use both eyes, we make many judgments of distance and depth on the basis of monocular cues.

**Monocular cues.**    Close your left eye. Spread your arms out to either side of you so they are parallel to the floor. Now quickly swing your arms around to the front, and see if you can make the index fingers of both hands touch. Do this several times and note your accuracy. Now repeat this procedure with both eyes open. You will probably find that you have no difficulty bringing your index fingers together when your eyes are open. This simple procedure demonstrates the importance of binocular cues in depth perception. Nevertheless, even without three-dimensional cues, our accuracy in judging depth remains relatively good, because there are many cues provided by the environment (see Figs. 6.27 and 6.28). We learn to use these cues to judge distance and depth. Let's look at some of the important ones.

Figure 6.27
**A visual cliff as an illusion**

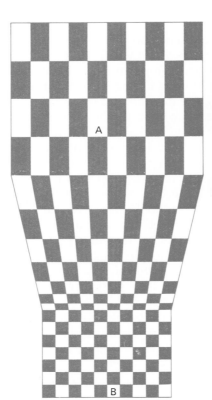

Figure 6.28    **This photo illustrates several monocular clues for judging distance and depth. Note the three-dimensional effect created by shadows, the coarser texture of nearby objects, atmospheric haze, relative size, and the interposition of one object in front of the other.**

1. **Linear perspective.** Parallel lines appear to converge in the distance; you probably noticed this as a child, when you were riding in a car along a straight road or looking down a stretch of railroad track. In general, objects that are nearer the point of convergence appear to be farther away. This is known as **linear perspective.**
2. **Texture.** Closely related to linear perspective is the textural gradient of objects in the visual field. When you look across a long, flat field, for example, nearby objects appear large and, therefore, coarser in texture. As the surface recedes, objects appear progressively smaller and finer in texture.
3. **Atmospheric conditions.** One of the most common cues to distance is the relative clarity of objects that appear in the field of vision. Distant objects seem to be less clear because of atmospheric conditions. The difference in clarity is particularly noticeable in our smog-laden cities, where even relatively close objects are obscured by atmospheric haze.
4. **Light and shadow.** When you look at Fig. 6.29, you clearly see a crater. Turn the book upside down, and the crater suddenly becomes a mound. The reason is that we are accustomed to seeing light coming from above. When light falls upon a crater, the shadows are typically formed on the side of the crater, and the bottom part has a relatively greater amount of illumination. The interplay of light and shadow causes us to interpret what we see as a depression. However, when we turn the picture upside down, we continue to perceive the light

Figure 6.29    **Our perception of light and shadow gives this crater a rounded or hollow appearance, depending on how we hold the photo.**

Figure 6.30
How can you explain the phenomenon of the remarkable shrinking woman? See the text for an explanation.

as coming from above. We now interpret the picture as a mound, because the distribution of light and shadows is the same as occurs when we look at a mountain or a mound in daylight. This perception is instantaneous and does not involve any thought; it is based upon our previous experiences with light and shadow.

5. **Interposition.** Close one eye, and place both hands in front of you in your line of sight so that the right hand partially obscures the left hand. It is easy to judge that the right hand is closer to your eyes than the left. **Interposition** occurs when one object partially obscures another in the field of vision.

6. **Relative size.** We have already seen that the farther an object is from the viewer, the smaller the retinal image will be. If two familiar objects are approximately the same size, but one produces a smaller retinal image, we judge the object with the smaller retinal image to be farther away. Figure 6.30 provides an example of relative size as a cue to distance. As you see in the top photo, the woman is noticeably taller than the man. In the bottom photo, you will judge the woman to be farther away because she appears smaller.

Note that, especially for unfamiliar objects, relative size is an ambiguous cue to distance. When one object appears larger than another, there are two possible explanations: Either the one object is, in fact, larger, or the other object is farther away.

7. **Motion parallax.** Distant objects moving at a given speed seem to be moving more slowly than closer objects that are moving at the same speed. A plane very high in the sky seems to be moving very slowly; when it is closer to the ground, it seems to be moving rapidly. In fact, the opposite is probably true: Planes usually fly at higher speeds when they are at high altitudes. Conversely, if you are in a plane at an extremely high altitude, the plane does not seem to be moving very rapidly because the ground does not appear to be moving rapidly in the opposite direction. Indeed, the ground may appear to be moving slowly in the same direction as the plane. When the plane comes in for a landing, it is actually going at a slower speed. It only seems to be going extremely quickly because the objects in your field

of vision are going by so quickly in the opposite direction. This greater *apparent* movement of near objects is known as **motion parallax.**

## Illusions

So far, we have been discussing many of the factors that allow us to make fairly accurate judgments of the world around us. However, sometimes these judgments become distorted and inaccurately reflect what is going on in the external world. When this happens, we are probably viewing an **illusion.** Illusions contribute enormously to our understanding of the processes of perception. By learning how perception can be distorted in an illusion, it is possible to gain valuable insights into the way perceiving functions under normal conditions.

There are many different types of illusions, and they involve most of the sense modalities. The best known and most thoroughly investigated are the optical illusions and illusions of motion.

**Interposition**
A monocular cue to distance perception; it occurs when one object partially obscures another in our field of vision.

**Motion parallax**
When we move, near objects appear to move across our visual field more rapidly than far objects.

**Illusion**
A perception that is a distortion of an actual sensory experience.

**Phi phenomenon**
An illusion of motion produced by a rapid succession of images that are really not moving, as in electric signs.

**Autokinetic effect**
The apparent movement of a stationary pinpoint of light in a dark room.

*Optical illusions.* Although optical illusions have fascinated people for ages, there are still very few adequate explanations of why they occur. Figures 6.31 and 6.32 present several examples of optical illusions. See how accurately you can answer the questions in Fig. 6.31.

*Illusions of motion.* Have you ever thought of movies as illusions? When you watch a movie, you are really looking at a series of still pictures projected at high speed, so that they blend to produce the appearance of continuous motion.

You can produce a similar illusion of motion by arranging a series of lights in a pattern and turning them on in rapid succession. The lights appear to move through the pattern in a continuous sequence. This illusion of motion is referred to as the **phi phenomenon.** It is widely used in neon signs and billboards.

Another example of apparent motion can be demonstrated very simply. Take a pinpoint source of light into a completely dark room. You can use a flashlight and cover most of its illuminating surface with dark tape, so that only a very small bit of light is visible. Place the flashlight in a fixed position. Now move to another part of the room and stare at the light. To most people, the light will appear to move spontaneously, by itself. This effect is known as the **autokinetic effect** ("auto" means self; "kinetic" means moving).

## Factors Influencing Perception

We have discussed how prior experience, emotions, and motivations influence what we pay attention to in the world around us. The same variables also influence our perceptions of the world.

Even when people pay attention to the same stimuli, they rarely perceive them in exactly the same way. As children, we probably all played

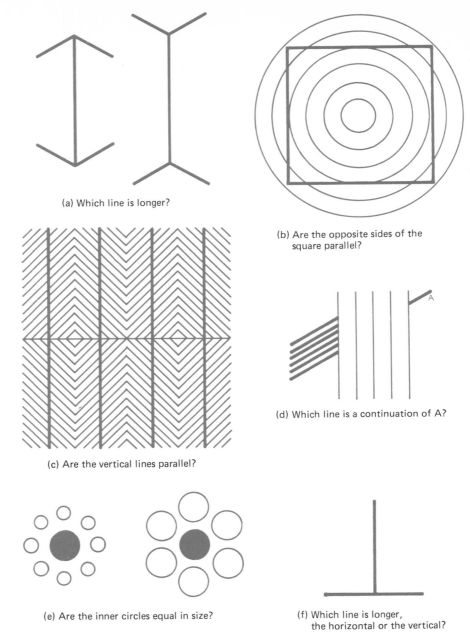

(a) Which line is longer?

(b) Are the opposite sides of the square parallel?

(c) Are the vertical lines parallel?

(d) Which line is a continuation of A?

(e) Are the inner circles equal in size?

(f) Which line is longer, the horizontal or the vertical?

Figure 6.31 (Answers on p. 234.)
Selected optical illusions

the game of looking at cloud formations and telling what we saw. Some of us may have reported a huge monster preparing to devour a small animal, others a king sitting on a throne, and others a variety of plausible or preposterous perceptions. Again we may ask: What are the factors that cause us to perceive stimuli and events in different ways? Why do some individuals perceive and report events in such unusual ways that we call these people emotionally disturbed and hospitalize many of them?

The following excerpt from a conversation between a doctor and his patient in a mental hospital illustrates the extreme distortions in perception of time and space sometimes found among people suffering acute emotional disorders:

> "How old are you?"
>
> "Why, I am centuries old, sir."
>
> "How long have you been here?"
>
> "I have been now on this property on and off for a long time. I cannot say the exact time because we are absorbed by the air at night, and they bring back people. They kill up everything; they can make you lie; they can talk through your throat."
>
> "Who is this?"
>
> "Why, the air."
>
> "What is the name of this place?"
>
> "This place is called a star."
>
> "Who is the doctor in charge of your ward?"
>
> "A body just like yours, sir. They can make you black and white. I say good morning, but he just comes through here. At first it was a colony. They said it was heaven. These buildings were not solid at the time, and I am positive this is the same place. They have others just like it. People die, and all the microbes talk over there, and prestigitis you know is sending you from here to another world. . . . I was sent by the government to the United States to Washington to some star, and they had a pretty nice country there. Now you have a body like a young man who says he is of the prestigitis." (White, 1932, p,228)

**Figure 6.32**
**The Ames room**

(a) Although these three people are actually approximately equal in height, the girl on the right appears to tower over her two companions because of the drastic distortions created by the Ames room in which they are standing. The observer is fooled because, although it looks normal when viewed from a peephole on one side, the room is constructed so that its ceiling is much lower on the right than on the left, none of the angles are right angles, and all the ordinary cues to distance and size are missing or distorted, causing the observer's perceptual system to interpret reality wrongly. This Ames room is located in the Exploratorium, a museum of science and human perception in San Francisco. (b) This drawing of the Ames room shows how the illusion is created.

(a)

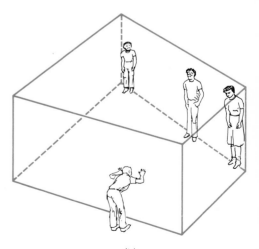

(b)

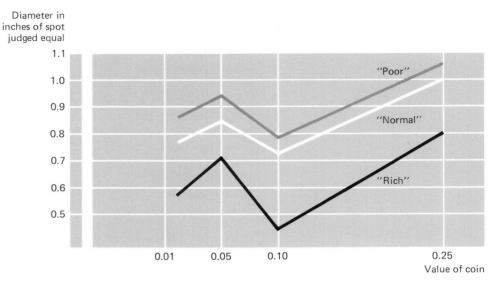

**Subjects were asked to judge the size of coins. This graph shows the results of their judgments in a normal state and after they had been hypnotized to believe they were "poor" or "rich." (Ashley et al., 1951)**

You can probably tell of instances when your own mood, motivations, or expectations influenced the way you perceived a situation. You heard what you wanted or expected to hear, saw what you wanted or expected to see. One of the authors had the following experience as a graduate student:

> The graduate school that I attended was located very near a high crime area of the community. One of the undergraduate students had been stabbed in that area on the previous weekend. While I was returning home, just slightly after midnight, I was thinking about that stabbing. The area was very dark and foreboding. Suddenly, this figure came at me from out of the shadows with an object in his hand. I immediately perceived the object to be a knife and made some defensive movements. At this point, the perceived "would-be assailant" said, "Have a drink." The object in his hand was a bottle of whiskey.

Participants at athletic events are notorious for perceiving all decisions against their team as unjust and obvious errors. "The umpire is blind" is a common expression.

After the final football game of the season between Princeton and Dartmouth in 1951, many charges of foul play were leveled against both teams. The filmed replay of the game was shown to undergraduates from both schools. They were asked to record the number of infractions they detected on both sides. When Princeton students looked at the movie, they saw the Dartmouth team make more than twice as many infractions as their own team. When the Dartmouth students looked at the movie, they saw both teams make about the same number of infractions; that is, they saw their own team make only half the number of infractions that the Princeton students saw them make. Nonetheless, all students saw the same filmed replay of the game (Hastorf and Cantril, 1954).

Much additional research linking motivation and perception has been conducted in the laboratory. In one study, middle-class college students were individually hypnotized on two different occasions. Before they were hypnotized, they were asked to adjust the size of a light so that it would successively equal the size of a penny, a nickel, a dime, and a quarter. During the first session of hypnosis, the suggestion was planted that the students had a prior history of poverty, with insufficient money to buy many of the necessities of life (this was the "poor" condition). In the second session of hypnosis, the same students were told that they came from very wealthy families where there was never a financial problem and never a shortage of either the necessities or the luxuries of life (the "rich" condition). After each session of hypnosis, the subjects were again asked to adjust the size of the light to equal the sizes of various coins. In the "poor" condition, the subjects adusted the light so as to suggest that they saw these coins as larger than they did before hypnosis. In the "rich" condition, the subjects' adjustments suggested that they perceived the coins as considerably smaller than they had before hypnosis (Ashley *et al.*, 1951). Figure 6.33 presents the results of this study.

## EXTRASENSORY PERCEPTION

For several decades, some serious researchers have labored in a controversial area broadly referred to as **parapsychology.** One area that has attracted much attention is **extrasensory perception (ESP),** sometimes called **psi.** ESP is presumed to be a form of perception that does not rely on the use of any of the known senses. It includes: (1) **mental telepathy,** in which an individual "reads" the mind of another person; (2) **clairvoyance,** the ability to perceive things that are not in sight or cannot be seen; (3) **psychokinesis (PK),** the ability to move objects without physically touching them; and (4) **precognition,** the ability to perceive events that have not yet occurred.

ESP studies today are conducted with the same sorts of controls as are used in any other area of research in the behavioral sciences. In a typical experiment on mental telepathy, for example, a "sender" is given a thoroughly shuffled deck of specially prepared ESP cards. The standard deck of cards for these experiments consists of 5 sets of 5 cards. The 5 cards in each set contain the following figures, one on each card: a square, a circle, a triangle, a plus sign, and wavy lines (see Fig. 6.34). The "sender" concentrates on each card in turn, and tries to transmit his or her thoughts to a person seated either behind a screen or at some distance. On the basis of chance, we would expect the "receiver" to be cor-

**Parapsychology**
The scientific study of phenomena such as extrasensory perception that are usually considered outside the realm of scientific psychology.

**Extrasensory perception (ESP)** sometimes called **Psi.** A form of perception that does not rely on the use of any of the known senses.

**Mental telepathy**
A form of extrasensory perception in which one person "reads" the mind of another.

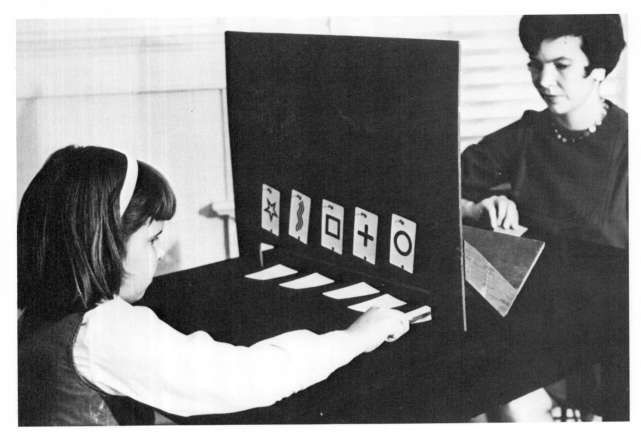

Testing for extrasensory perception is accomplished with a deck of ESP cards.

rect, on the average, five times out of every run through the deck of 25 cards.

In some studies, individuals have achieved remarkable records of success. It is difficult to evaluate these findings, however, because the same person may be successful at one time and unsuccessful at another. Earlier studies of ESP reported striking evidence in favor of its existence. But as more sophisticated experimental controls have been introduced in later studies, the evidence has been less impressive. Nevertheless, some psychologists have been impressed by both the experimental rigor and the number of studies showing positive results. In a major book on the subject (Bowles *et al.*, 1978), the authors attempted to separate the wheat from the chaff in parapsychological research. They found sufficient sound evidence to call for greater efforts to develop a theory of parapsychologi-

Figure 6.34
**ESP cards**

cal phenomena. They noted: "Like Franklin's electricity, Psi may be await-ing its Edison. But even now, we have clues that its possible significance for our lives could be enormous" (p.138).

Nevertheless, psychologists have not generally accepted extrasensory perception as a proved phenomenon. To explain this reluctance to em-brace extrasensory perception in scientific psychology, one reviewer ob-served:

> *One reason for the continuing lack of acceptance may well be that the phenomena studied are difficult if not impossible to demonstrate to skep-tics. People differ in their Psi abilities, and a belief in the reality of ESP and PK seems to be necessary for their occurrence. Since a measure of skepticism is fundamental to the scientific spirit, the majority of psychol-ogists decade after decade have remained unconvinced.*
>
> *A more important reason for the continuing stalemate is probably the lack of any comprehensive theory that would make sense of parapsycho-logical processes in a framework that would also include the other pro-cesses psychologists have studied. (Tyler, 1981, p.11)*

Some investigators have suggested that brain waves might be in-volved. But the electrical power in brain waves is so minute that it seems incredible that they could be transmitted over long distances and sorted out by another person's brain.

Unfortunately for serious-minded investigators, extrasensory percep-tion is commonly associated with stage magicians, charlatans who claim mysterious "psychic" powers, and various mediums who claim to be able to communicate with the dead. Thus when we think of ESP, we tend to think of the occult. As we know, it is difficult to break such a well-estab-lished "set." At present, it seems safe to say that most psychologists favor continued controlled studies of ESP, and have adopted a "wait and see" attitude.

## Summary

1. There are many more senses than the traditional five: sight, touch, hearing, smell, and taste. Other senses include the muscle sense, the sense of pain, and the sense of balance.
2. Two broad classes of sensory receptors may be distinguished: exteroceptors and interoceptors.
3. Measurement of the sensory capabilities of hu-mans has established the degree of sensitivity of various sensory receptors to a broad range of physical energies. The minimum amount of stim-ulation that can be detected by a given sense is known as the absolute threshold for that sense.
4. The change of stimulation necessary for a person to detect a difference in stimulus intensity levels is known as the difference threshold. When the initial stimulation is low, less change in stimula-tion is required for a difference in stimulus inten-sity to be detected.
5. With most sense modalities, continued exposure to a given level of stimulation will lead to a re-duced ability to detect that stimulation (sensory adaptation).
6. Light enters the eye through the pupil, regulated by the iris. It is then focused on the retina by the

lens. Sensory receptors transmit this information to the brain via the optic nerve, which reaches both hemispheres of the brain after splitting at the optic chiasma. Because there are no receptors where the optic nerve leaves the eye, we do have a small blind spot in our field of vision.

7. Two broad classes of receptors are found in the retina: rods, which register only black and white, and cones, which handle colors.

8. The portions of the electromagnetic spectrum to which we respond as light vary in three ways: the specific wavelength, which determines the psychological dimension of hue; the intensity of the light at that wavelength, which determines brightness; and the purity of the light at that wavelength, which determines saturation.

9. Our ears transform the vibrations of air molecules into the experience of sound. The three physical characteristics of the vibrations are perceived as three corresponding aspects of sound: The frequency of the vibrations is experienced as pitch; intensity (amplitude of the vibrations) is experienced as loudness; and complexity (the presence of other frequencies) is experienced as timbre.

10. The ear is composed of three parts: the outer ear, the middle ear, and the inner ear. Conduction deafness results from damage to the bones of the middle ear. Nerve deafness arises from damage to the cochlea or the auditory nerve.

11. The "touch senses" include touch, pressure, hot, cold, and pain.

12. The taste buds provide sensations of sweetness, sourness, saltiness, and bitterness.

13. Perception is the organization and interpretation of sensory experience.

14. There is considerable evidence that we can pay attention to only one thing in our environment at a time. What we pay attention to at any particular time is determined by the characteristics of the stimulus (intensity, contrast, movement) and the characteristics of the individual (prior experiences and motivation).

15. The principles of perceptual organization include figure and ground, proximity, similarity, continuity, and closure.

16. In spite of the incredible diversity of the conditions under which we view objects in our environment, we tend to see these objects as relatively stable and unchanging. The following visual constancies are based on prior experience: shape constancy, size constancy, and brightness constancy.

17. We are constantly forced to make judgments of distance and depth. Some of the cues for depth require only a single eye (monocular cues), and some require the simultaneous operation of both eyes (binocular cues).

18. At times our judgments become distorted and inaccurately reflect what is going on in the external world. We refer to such distortions as illusions.

19. Not all people perceive the same situation in the same way. Moods, motivations, expectancies, and prior experience influence the ways in which we perceive things and events.

20. Extrasensory perception is presumed to be a form of perception that does not rely on the known senses. Although some evidence appears to support the existence of ESP, many psychologists, in the absence of a satisfactory mechanism by which to explain it, have taken a "wait and see" attitude, while encouraging continued controlled research.

## Terms to Remember

| | | |
|---|---|---|
| Sensory receptor | Iris | Cones |
| Exteroceptors | Pupil | Fovea |
| Interoceptors | Retina | Nanometer |
| Sensation | Optic nerve | Hue |
| Absolute threshold | Blind spot | Brightness |
| Difference threshold | Optic chiasma | Saturation |
| Sensory adaptation | Rods | Frequency |

Intensity

Complexity

Pitch

Loudness

Timbre

Auricle

Sound threshold

Conduction deafness

Nerve deafness

Meissner's corpuscles

Perception

Set

Gestalt psychology

Figure and ground

Proximity

Similarity

Continuity

Closure

Perceptual constancy

Shape constancy

Size constancy

Brightness constancy

Monocular cues

Binocular cues

Retinal disparity

Convergence

Accommodation

Linear perspective

Interposition

Motion parallax

Illusion

Phi phenomenon

Autokinetic effect

Parapsychology

Extrasensory perception (ESP), sometimes called Psi

Mental telepathy

Clairvoyance

Psychokinesis (PK)

Precognition

# STATES OF
# CONSCIOUSNESS

Think for a moment. How would you describe your normal state of consciousness? Certainly you know how it feels and can quite readily recognize any qualitative changes in your mental functioning. For example, right now as you are reading this book, your mind is presumably alert and absorbing new concepts. Sometime later you may find yourself fighting a numbing drowsiness. Eventually you will go to bed and perhaps rather swiftly fall into that state in which you lose complete awareness of your immediate surroundings. You call it sleep. You have no difficulty distinguishing between these two familiar states of consciousness. Sleep is sleep and waking is waking. Many people tend to think of all experiences as falling neatly into one or the other of these two categories. But if you reflect for a moment, you will probably recall occasions when you have been awake but sensed a quality of conscious experience that was somehow different from the usual flow of mental activities. Perhaps you have recognized it during a particularly meaningful and moving religious experience or while quietly meditating in splendid isolation. Perhaps you have been frightened by it, as when your train of thoughts contained bizarre images or hallucinations induced by a high fever or a psychedelic drug.

In Chapter 4 we examined cognitive processes at work. Our focus was a state of consciousness that is active when we are involved in problem solving, writing, thinking logically or mathematically, speaking or translating a language, or engaging in scientific ventures. Present thinking ascribes these activities to the dominant cerebral hemisphere. But we also sleep and engage in daydreaming or fantasy activities. Some of us may also have been hypnotized. Others meditate on a regular basis and still others have experimented with or are regular users of mind-altering drugs. The states of consciousness associated with these cognitive activities have a different quality from the state that dominates our business-as-usual consciousness. They are commonly more diffuse and filled with imagery, and they have less language involvement. Thus they are not usually remembered as well as the state of consciousness associated with alert, logical thought. In this chapter we look at states of consciousness found in sleep, meditation, biofeedback, hypnosis, and drugs.

## THE BRAIN AND DIFFERENT MODES OF CONSCIOUSNESS

Recall our discussion in Chapter 5 of split-brain research. We saw that surgical separation of the brain into two independent hemispheres has shed a great deal of light on the functioning of each hemisphere. For most people, the left hemisphere, which controls the right side of the body, appears to specialize in linguistic, logical, sequential thinking. In contrast, the right hemisphere seems to engage in activities concerned with wholes rather than component parts. One leading observer (Ornstein, 1975) has proposed that the two "half-brains" may well underlie, at least in part, the two different modes of consciousness that exist in all of us.

A strong case has been made for the view that, in the Western world, the linguistic, logical, ordered, and sequential left hemisphere tends to dominate the right hemisphere. Nevertheless, we occasionally glimpse the capabilities of the right hemisphere during the course of a dream,

The two hemispheres of the brain specialize in different functions. Creative people who move beyond the confines of logical thought appear to rely on the properties of the right hemisphere. Keith Jarrett, the popular jazz pianist, can improvise on one theme for hours without having ordered beforehand the sequences of notes he will play.

while meditating, or while under the influence of a mind-altering drug. During these moments, we may note that time becomes elastic, there is an almost complete absence of logical thought, and relations among things and events are vastly different from what they appear to be in normal, everyday consciousness.

One fascinating implication of this distinction between the two modes of consciousness is the possibility that a "communications gap" may exist between the left and right cerebral hemispheres. Because the right hemisphere is presumed to lack the ordered, logical language ability of the left hemisphere, "one part of us may simply be incapable of fully understanding the experience of the other part, and may give it a name which reflects this lack of comprehension" (Ornstein, 1975, p. 153).

As you read the remaining pages of the chapter, it is well to keep in mind this broad distinction between left and right hemispheric functioning. It is quite possible that when we experience alterations in our usual consciousness we are delving into the mysterious and largely mute right cerebral hemisphere.

## SLEEP

Have you ever given much thought to sleep? Is sleep really a period during the daily life cycle when the body simply recovers from the physical and mental demands of the waking hours? In other words, is it a little bit like death in that nothing of consequence happens? Although the scientific study of sleep is recent and much is yet to be learned, we can provide a resounding "no" to the last two questions.

By monitoring this man's brain waves with the electrodes attached to his head, researchers will be able to trace the stages of his sleep. Sleep scientists are still seeking to learn what is happening in the brain during the various stages.

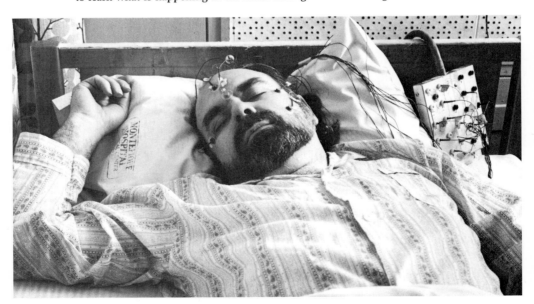

Before delving deeper into sleep, let us consider the following: By the time you are 60 years of age, you will have spent approximately 20 years in sleep (shades of Rip Van Winkle). Moreover, roughly 5 of those years will have involved dreaming. It is also quite possible that, during a substantial portion of the remaining 15 years of sleep, you will have engaged in some sort of mental activity (Foulkes, 1962). Thus, far from being a state akin to death, sleep is a period during which much transpires in your mental life. Indeed, some behavioral scientists speak in terms of three separate states of existence: waking, quiet sleep, and active sleep (Cartwright, 1978). During any of these states, many types of cognitive behavior may be taking place: logical thought, less-organized thought, and thought full of imagery. Thus, in waking as in sleep, we may engage in thought that follows the rules of logic; we may experience periods of thinking that include illogical and unrealistic fantasies; and finally, our thoughts may involve a stream of rich and varied images, including **hallucinations.** The differences are a matter more of degree than of kind. In fact, when subjects lie awake during the day and are interrupted for reports, a relatively large number of reports have a dreamlike and imagistic quality, including hallucinatory images (Foulkes and Fleisher, 1975).

How do we know these things? Historically, sleep has been largely neglected as a target of scientific study. It was not until a method was available for detecting minute differences in the electrical activity of the brain that sleep itself could be objectively defined. Indeed, five different types of electrical activity were described by early researchers (Loomis, 1937, cited in Cartwright, 1978). Loomis and his colleagues referred to these electrical activities as stages A through E.

Then a startling discovery was made in the early 1950s, providing the impetus for sleep research that has continued unabated to this date (Aserinsky and Kleitman, 1953). Eugene Aserinsky, who was studying sleep in infants, noted that periods of quiet sleep alternated with periods during which the eyes moved rapidly under closed lids. Both the eye movements and the accompanying brain patterns were more like a waking that a sleeping state. Yet the infants were clearly not awake. The continuing inquiry into what is happening during the various sleep stages has riveted the attention of many sleep scientists.

**Hallucination**
A sensory impression in the absence of an appropriate environmental stimulus.

**Rapid eye movement (REM)**
Rapid movements of the eyes occurring during sleep. Subjects awakened during the REM stage generally report that they have been dreaming.

## NREM Sleep— from Shallow to Deep

Many people use the expression "I slept like a log," conjuring up the image of profound and motionless sleep. As a matter of fact, a sleeping person remains still only about 11 minutes at a time, on the average (Johnson *et al.*, 1930). Furthermore, sleep is composed of four stages that run cyclically. When adults go to sleep, they progress rapidly to stage four. They remain in the very deep sleep characteristic of this stage for about an hour, and then move back through stages three, two, and one. When they reemerge into stage one, every 90 minutes or so, their closed eyes begin to move back and forth rapidly. This period of **rapid eye movement (REM)** is referred to as stage-one REM sleep (Dement and

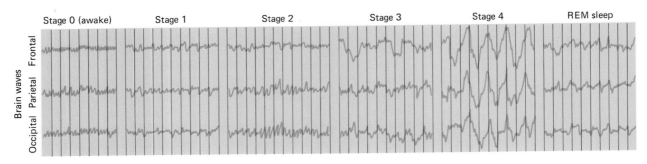

Figure 7.1    **The various stages of sleep are shown above.**

Kleitman, 1957). The remaining stages of sleep are collectively referred to as non–rapid eye movement sleep, or NREM.

When you close your eyes prior to sleep, you may remain in the waking state for various periods of time. If you had electrodes attached to your scalp which, in turn, fed the signals to a machine (the electroencephalograph) that records the electrical activity of the brain, your record would look like the record shown in Fig. 7.1 for stage-zero sleep (i.e., wakefulness). After a period of time that varies from person to person and within the same person from night to night, you enter stage-one sleep. Your eyes roll slowly from side to side but, except for less frequent alpha waves or their disappearance, the EEG pattern does not alter dramatically. Within minutes you pass into stage-two sleep. Two changes occur in the EEG record at this point: A wave pattern appears with the frequency of 12 to 14 cycles per second, and a high amplitude wave (called *K complex*) also appears, with a sharp downward deflection followed by an upward deflection on the EEG record. Gradually, stage-two merges into stage-three sleep. High-amplitude waves with a slow frequency begin to dominate the record. Within about 30 minutes after falling asleep, you enter the deepest stages of sleep. Note that the wave pattern consists of very slow high-amplitude waves in stage-four sleep. It is during this first stage-four sleep that **night terrors** are most likely to occur among those who experience them (see Box 7.1). This is also the stage during which the body restores itself. In fact, among young children the pituitary releases growth hormones during stage four. The heart rate is slowed and regular, the blood pressure lowers, and breathing is deep and slow. After about an hour of stage-four sleep, your EEG pattern returns to stage one, but it is accompanied by the dramatic development we previously referred to as REM. You are now in stage-one REM. Also, your heart rate, blood pressure, and respiration become variable. Physiologically the body is in a state of arousal.

**Night terrors**
A sleep disorder characterized by episodes in which the individual awakens from an NREM state, screaming in terror. The victim frequently is unable to recall the source of the terror and, after returning to sleep, may awaken with no recall of the entire episode.

**Answer to T/F Questions on p. 244**
Present evidence indicates that the odd-numbered statements are false and the even-numbered ones true. (Hayter, 1980 p. 461)

## BOX 7.1

### Night Terrors

It was 11 o'clock at night. Jim and Ellen were going through their nighttime rituals preparatory to sleep. Ellen had just looked in on the children and was struck once again by the contrast between waking and sleeping children. Five-year-old Freddie had looked positively angelic, with no hint of that mean streak that goaded him to tease his three-year-old sister Marie. And cherubic Marie: What a test of patience and endurance she could be. But in repose both looked completely beautiful, innocent, and utterly huggable. She sighed a deep, satisfied sigh. All was well in slumberland.

No sooner had this thought passed through her mind than the night air was shattered by a shriek. Ellen felt the hairs on the nape of her neck stand rigid. "It's Freddie," Jim called out while dashing wildly through the dark toward Freddie's room. He crashed into the night table, swore vehemently, and continued his rush to his son's room. Ellen was not far behind, calling out, "It's all right, Freddie. Mommy and Daddy are coming."

When they entered the bedroom, Freddie was sitting bolt upright on the edge of his bed with his eyes wide open. His appearance sent a chill through both Ellen and Jim. He seemed to be awake but not awake. They asked him what had happened but he did not answer. Frighteningly, he appeared to be looking at a

world of his own invention and listening to a different drummer. Nothing the parents could do seemed to console little Freddie. Then suddenly, about eight minutes after the shriek that split the night air, Freddie put his head down and resumed sleep. He did not awaken during the remainder of the night.

Not so with his parents. They tossed and turned, awoke, listened, and entered into fitful episodes of sleep throughout the night. Both were convinced that something was seriously wrong with their child, so raw and naked was the terror he had displayed. Both were equally shocked the next morning to find that Freddie had no recollection of the previous night's adventure. Indeed, his parents came out of the experience far worse for wear.

For those familiar with *night terrors*, this story does not come as a surprise. Amnesia concerning the experience is quite common. About 3 percent of children between 5 and 12 years of age experience these attacks (Cartwright, 1978). The terror is often attached to a single event, such as being trapped in a dark place or being confronted by an attacking animal. Fortunately, the attacks usually diminish and disappear with increasing age. When they do occur in adults, they are not usually remembered by the individual experiencing the attacks. Thus people witnessing night terrors are probably more frightened than those experiencing the terrors. We shall have more to say about nightmares, a different type of sleep experience.

Stage-one REM sleep has interesting but paradoxical qualities. Both the physiological patterns (elevations of heart rate, irregularities in breathing pattern, increases in blood pressure, penile and clitoral erection) and the EEG patterns closely resemble the waking state (Dement, 1965). Nevertheless, behavioral measures indicate that stage-one REM is deep sleep, similar to stage four. Individuals in stage-one REM are difficult to awaken and are less responsive to external stimuli than when they are in stages two and three. Moreover, the main muscles of the body lose their tonus, and reflexes that can be elicited during other stages of sleep are inhibited.

Research indicates that we enter the REM stage several times a night. If a person is awakened during this period, he or she will almost invariably report a dream in progress. Dreaming is a far more common occur-

**The world of sleep and dreams has intrigued and mystified man throughout recorded history. This painting tries to capture the mystery that is sleep.**

Henri Rousseau, *The Sleeping Gypsy* (1879). Oil on canvas, 51″ × 6′7″. Collection, The Museum of Modern Art, New York. Gift of Mrs. Simon Guggenheim.

rence than most people think. We dream every night, and we have several dreams each night.

In fact, about 80 percent of REM awakenings yield reports of dreams. During NREM periods, this figure varies between zero and 60 percent but averages about 19 percent (Berger, 1969). Moreover, the reports made following REM awakening have a more dreamlike quality than those reported after NREM awakenings, which tend to be more realistic and less hallucinatory. Most of the time we don't remember our dreams because we sleep through them. Occasionally a dream is remembered because the content is sufficiently arousing or frightening. These later dreams, when they occur during REM sleep, are referred to as nightmares, in contrast to stage-four night terrors. Unlike night terrors, nightmares are often remembered the following day. Although both may deal with the same content (e.g., being chased by a monster), the anxiety is better controlled in nightmares. Indeed, both dreams and nightmares may represent safe ways of experimenting with different means of coping with anxiety aroused by the anticipation of future events. Figure 7.2 shows the tracings made by sleep-monitoring equipment before and during a nightmare.

## Possible Functions of REM Sleep

In young children, there may be as many as nine REM periods during a single night. With increasing age, the number of REM periods decreases. In an adult, there are about four or five, each one increasing in length and taking on a more bizarre quality as the night progresses. The final dream is best remembered, perhaps because it is usually the most emotion-arousing dream of the night. Figure 7.3 shows the time periods spent in the various stages of sleep during a typical night for an adult. In adults, approximately 25 percent of the time is spent in REM, 50 percent in stage two, and the remaining 20 percent in stages three and four (Cartwright, 1978).

**REM rebound**
A period of increased REM activity following previous REM suppression or deprivation.

REM sleep appears to be vital for maintaining the well-being of the organism. If adult subjects are awakened every time they go into REM, and thus are deprived of REM sleep, they seem to make up for it by spending longer periods of time in REM sleep the following night. This is called **REM rebound** (Dement, 1965; Kales *et al.*, 1964). Individuals suffering from depression are often treated with drugs, some of which lead to a dramatic reduction in REM sleep. When later withdrawn from such drugs, these patients evidence dramatic REM rebound, often accompanied by frightening dreams (Vogel *et al.*, 1975). A very similar pattern is found with alcohol and alcoholics. REM sleep is suppressed in the presence of alcohol, and alcoholics who are "on the wagon" initially experience the same frightening dreams and high REM levels as those taken off antidepressants.

The behavioral consequences of REM deprivation are less certain. One study found no undesirable side effects (Kales *et al.*, 1964), whereas

**Figure 7.2**
**Tracings made by synchronized sleep-monitoring equipment before and during a nightmare**

The patient, whose deep sleep is reflected in the subdued physical reactions recorded at the far left of the graph, suddenly enters the aroused stage-one REM state. Partially awake, his eyes and brain become active; his heart rate soars. The breath he uses to shout for help distorts the tracing of his respiration, which is also rising. The elapsed time shown in the graph is less than a minute.

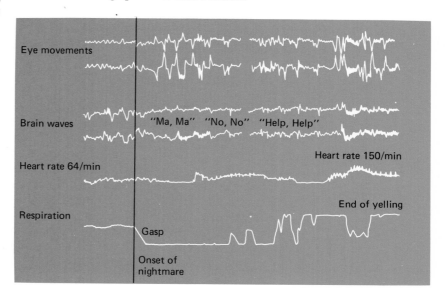

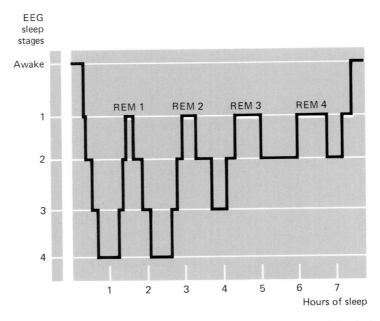

**Figure 7.3**
**A typical night of sleep for an adult**

Note that the first REM period occurs 90 minutes into sleep and is relatively short. Each succeeding REM period is longer in duration. In this record, this individual awoke during the final REM period.

another reported that subjects deprived of REM sleep showed greater tension and irritability during their waking hours (Dement, 1960). Animal research has produced rather dramatic results supporting the notion that REM deprivation leads to undesirable behavioral changes. When specific portions of cats' brains were removed, depriving them of REM sleep but leaving NREM sleep unimpaired, the cats became extremely agitated, occasionally striking at nonexistent objects. Some showed heightened sexual and eating activities. In some instances, REM sleep returned and the behavioral symptoms disappeared, but cats in which REM was permanently eliminated eventually died in a state of agitation and overactivity (Jouvet, 1962).

Exactly what role REM plays is still not known. One researcher (Hartmann, 1973) has proposed that REM sleep provides a restorative function: It permits the replacement of chemical substances that are used by the brain during its normal daily activities. Hartmann's research has suggested that REM sleep is related to our ability to perform psychological functions. For example, it is common knowledge that some people seem to require more sleep than others. Personality testing has revealed that subjects who sleep more than nine hours a night tend to worry considerably more than those who get by on less than six hours a night. They also seem to require about twice as much REM sleep! One may speculate that the greater stress of daily living for these people demands longer REM periods to restore psychological balance.

There are interesting changes in the time spent in REM sleep as we grow older. Figure 7.4 shows the various amounts of time spent in REM and NREM sleep across different age groups. Premature infants spend more than 50 percent—perhaps as much as 80 percent—of their sleep time in REM. At birth, about 50 percent of sleep time is in REM (approximately 480 minutes a day). By the time we are adults, REM sleep de-

**Insomnia**
A sleep disorder characterized by difficulty attaining or maintaining sleep three or more nights a week over long periods of time.

mands only about 25 percent of our sleep time (approximately 100 minutes a day). These facts suggested to several investigators (Roffwarg *et al.*, 1966) that REM is involved in preparing the brain to handle the massive external sensory stimulation that occurs from birth onward. In adults, REM is required to a lesser extent in order to maintain the brain's circuitry in good working condition.

Another possibility is that REM sleep serves a sentinel function (Snyder, 1966). REM sleep represents a state of arousal close to the waking state. To illustrate, it is far easier to wake someone from REM sleep than from stage-four sleep. Moreover, the person who awakes from stage four reacts more slowly, makes a greater number of errors in a vigilance task, and has a weaker hand grip (Jeannaret and Webb, 1963; Scott, 1969). According to the sentinel view, REM evolved as a means of periodically awakening our forebears so that they could scan the environment for potential dangers (e.g., an enemy).

It is also possible that REM is involved in processing new information and shifting this information from short- to long-term memory (Dewan, 1970). This explanation would account for declining of REM sleep with age: An infant must process far more new information than its grandparents.

These three possible functions of REM sleep are not mutually exclusive, nor do they exhaust all possibilities. They just open up some intriguing hunches to be explored on this stimulating frontier of knowledge.

## Disturbances of Sleep

How often have you heard someone complain, "I have not had a good night's sleep in years. I have **insomnia**." The problem with these self-diagnoses is that they are often wrong. It has been established that some people are light sleepers and some are heavy sleepers (Zimmerman,

Figure 7.4
**Changes with age in amounts of total sleep and types of sleep**

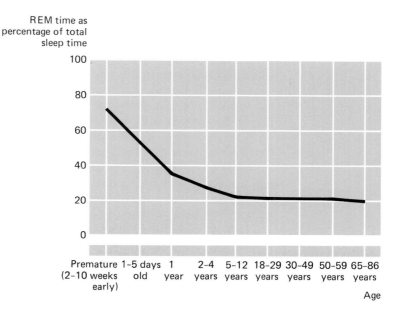

This dog displays the symptoms of narcolepsy. One minute he is wide awake and barking; the next minute he nods and quickly falls asleep.

1970). Light sleepers are more readily aroused by external stimuli. Thus many people who are light sleepers misclassify themselves as insomniacs because of the large number of times they awaken during the night. Similarly, there are short, long, and variable sleepers. A short sleeper can function on about 6 hours of sleep a night, whereas the long sleeper spends, on the average, almost 10 hours a night in sleep (Hartmann *et al.*, 1972). A short sleeper who goes to bed at 10 o'clock at night and awakens fully at 4 o'clock in the morning might easily draw the incorrect conclusion, "I have insomnia." In fact, that person has had sufficient sleep but is simply "ready to go" at the wrong time. In contrast, the typical insomniac experiences difficulty attaining or maintaining sleep three or more nights a week over long periods of time (Cartwright, 1978).

Studies of a large number of people clinically diagnosed as insomniac reveal differences from the normal light and short sleepers. A large proportion evidenced depression patterns. Individuals 30 years of age or older often deny that their psychological problems are related to depression and focus their anxiety around health concerns (Kales, 1972). Insomniacs in all age groups tend to be people who do not have effective means of resolving stress and working off tension. Instead, they carry their problems to bed and pay the price of disturbed sleep.

How well do the various medications available to assist sleep help the insomniac? In a word, they do not help. REM sleep can be suppressed by various drugs such as sleeping pills (barbiturates), heroin, and alcohol. These drugs lead to an abnormal night's sleep. In many instances, when the medication is withdrawn, REM sleep may rebound and greatly increase in proportion to NREM time for several weeks. This pattern may occur after even a *single* sleeping pill (Watson, 1981). If REM sleep is essential for working out emotional problems, as some believe, taking a sleeping pill is depriving the insomniac of a natural avenue of possible relief. Moreover, sleep medications also reduce the total amount of time a person remains in the deepest stage of sleep. In some cases, stage-four sleep is completely absent. To make matters worse, individuals taking sleeping medication rapidly build up tolerance to the drug. The result is that they must keep taking more to get less. They truly have a tiger by the tail. If they suddenly give up the medication, a large increase both in time and in intensity of REM sleep will ensue. The dreams are often disturbing. Thus people continue medication that is no longer effective in promoting sleep in order to avoid the intense dreams of nonmedicated sleep. The best solution is not to go "cold turkey." What is called for is a gradual substitution of a less potent drug that is, in itself, eventually phased out.

In addition to disturbances of sleep, there are disturbances of the waking hours that involve sleep. Narcolepsy is a daytime episode of sleep, lasting no more than 15 minutes. The individual is engaging in some ongoing activity and then suddenly, without warning, goes to sleep. These sleep episodes are often accompanied by a loss of muscle tonus (as in REM sleep) and are often triggered by emotional excitement, such as laughter or anger. Often the episodes appear to involve stage-one REM (Cartwright, 1978). The person goes directly into REM, skipping the 60 to 90 minutes of NREM that usually precede REM. Nonmedical treatment consists of taking one or two naps during the day.

## MEDITATION

**Meditation**
A state of consciousness achieved by concentrating on some repetitive activity and characterized by relaxation, heightened sensory awareness, intense emotional states, and altered perceptions of time and space.

Have you ever sat quietly and totally relaxed in front of a fireplace and let your attention be completely drawn by the sounds of the crackling fire and the sights of the flickering flames? If so, you may have come close to experiencing a stage of consciousness associated with **meditation.**

In meditation, an effort is made to rid the mind completely of all logical processes that appear to be associated with the left cerebral hemisphere. The purpose is to tune out responsivity to the external world and its insistent demands and to tune in levels of consciousness that are normally overridden by the dominant mode. The means of achieving an absence of responsivity to the external world are varied, but they all involve some repetitive activity: continuously viewing a geometrical pattern (see Fig. 7.5), repeating words or meaningless sounds, or listening to one's own breathing. When the meditator achieves a state of total relaxation, free of daily concerns and thoughts, his or her mind is open to increased sensory awareness and expanded consciousness. Verbal reports from meditators indicate that many experience heightened sensory awareness, a sense of well-being, intense emotional states, and a feeling of transcending both time and space (Deikman, 1973). One observer has likened the aftereffects of meditation to a vacation: "We can consider the process of concentrative meditation as similar to that of taking a vacation—leav-

Figure 7.5    **By focusing on a simple visual pattern that continually directs one's gaze to its center, meditators can empty their minds of distracting thoughts.**

ing the situation, 'turning-off' our routine way of dealing with the external world for a period, later returning to find it 'fresh,' 'new,' different . . .'' (Ornstein, 1975, p. 151).

Three popular forms of meditation practiced in this country are Zen, Yoga, and Transcendental Meditation (TM). Of these, the most popular is TM. In brief, TM consists of sitting with the eyes closed for two 20-minute sessions a day and repeating a word called a **mantra.**

> *Mantras are often words of significance, such as names of the deity, but for the psychology of consciousness the important element is that the technique uses a word as the focus of awareness, just as the first Zen exercises make use of breathing. The instructions are to repeat the mantra over and over again, either aloud or silently. The mantra is to be kept in awareness to the exclusion of all else; just as in the first Zen exercise, when awareness lapses from the breathing, the attention is to be returned to it. Mantras are sonorous, flowing words that repeat easily. An example is* Om. *This mantra is chanted aloud in groups or used individually in silent or voiced meditation. Another mantra is* Om mani padme hum, *a smooth mellifluous chant. (Ornstein, 1975, p. 129)*

Each follower of TM is assigned a personal mantra and is asked not to reveal it to anyone else. Deeper states of relaxation are presumably achieved through focusing on the mantra to the exclusion of all other thoughts (Schwartz, 1974).

In a westernized version of TM, the word ''one'' is used as the mantra (Benson, 1975). One researcher has suggested that the word ''one'' has significant meanings to people. It can refer to unity, as in life, God, or even personal unity. In addition, it is similar to the Sanskrit *om,* which has religious connotations for some people (Carrington, 1977).

Some researchers believe that the purpose served by repeating a single meaningless word or phrase is to lull the dominant cerebral hemisphere into relaxing its usual vigilance. Recall that, in most people, this is the left hemisphere. This hemisphere seems to specialize in the logical,

**Mantra**
A smooth-flowing word or phrase, drawn from an ancient Indian language, that is repeated over and over again during a meditative period.

cause-and-effect thinking that dominates our normal business-as-usual state of consciousness. Presumably, by relaxing this hemisphere, we are able to get in touch with the nondominant (usually right) hemisphere, which processes visual and spatial information and appears to be active when we are involved in such aesthetic activities as art, dance, or music appreciation (Ornstein, 1973).

Many benefits have been claimed for meditation, including the achievement of deep inner peace, lowered levels of physiological stress indicators (Wallace and Benson, 1972), and the abandonment of drugs as a means of achieving altered states of consciousness (Gellhorn and Kiely, 1972). Nevertheless, some scientists have questioned whether meditation has any benefits beyond what would be derived from quietly withdrawing, for two 20-minute periods a day, from the strains and stresses of contemporary life (Campbell, 1974). Indeed, one study found that experienced meditators spend approximately 40 percent of meditation time in stages two, three, or four of sleep (Pagano et al., 1976)!

It must be borne in mind, however, that meditation has only recently become a focus of scientific inquiry in the Western world. We are well advised to keep an open mind while a new body of knowledge is in the process of accumulating.

**People who practice meditation claim it has many benefits ranging from relieving stress to altering states of consciousness. Some researchers feel that experienced meditators actually enter certain stages of sleep during part of their meditations.**

© Bonnie Freer

## BIOFEEDBACK

**Biofeedback**
Information about a bodily response from either the senses or an outside source. On the basis of this information, the organism can adjust and modify its bodily responses.

It has long been claimed that Oriental mystics, such as Zen Buddhists, are able to achieve remarkable degrees of control over their bodily functions, willfully effecting changes in heart rate, blood pressure, body temperature, and other biological processes not normally considered to be subject to voluntary control. Most people have regarded these claims as the exaggerated distortions of naive and easily duped observers. Recently, however, the air of skepticism has given way to one of enthusiastic scientific inquiry. Major breakthroughs concerning the voluntary control of internal physiological processes have been made during the past decades. These have come about primarily through the use of a new and powerful tool called **biofeedback.** Unlike meditation techniques, which attempt to screen out environmental interference so that faint body signals can be perceived, biofeedback uses technological advances to amplify these signals (Ornstein, 1975).

Biofeedback may best be explained by describing its relationship to voluntary activities. Complex activities, such as speech, would be impossible were it not for the fact that hearing provides continuous feedback on how well we are performing our language functions. In fact, people who are born deaf are incapable of acquiring speech in the normal fashion because of the lack of auditory feedback. Even with relatively simple movements, such as raising an arm or lifting a leg, we have immediate feedback; that is, we can see and feel the movement in these muscles, and we can adjust and modify subsequent movements in response to this feedback. In contrast, the organs served by the autonomic nervous system provide such imprecise sensory feedback that we do not normally use it to exercise effective control over these organs. For instance, you may occasionally become aware that your heart is beating more rapidly than normal, perhaps because you have been rushing to catch a bus. People who have been diagnosed as suffering from high blood pressure can sometimes sense when their blood pressure goes considerably above normal. But can you do anything to get your heart rate or blood pressure back to normal? Very few people can do anything of this sort with any degree of success. The autonomic system has been regarded as an involuntary system primarily because it appears to function without our conscious control. Biofeedback researchers argue that clear-cut feedback about the actions of internal organs would permit us to exercise a control comparable to that which we have over our voluntary movements.

Much experimentation is under way to test this hypothesis. In one study (see Fig. 7.6), five college students were placed in front of a meter that provided continuous information concerning their blood pressure and were told to decrease the readings on the meter. These subjects constituted the experimental group. Five other students (the control group) were placed in front of the same display but were not told to decrease the readings. The experimental subjects showed a sharp decrease in their blood pressure, while the blood pressure of the control subjects remained at the same level (Brenner and Kleinman, 1970).

Once control is achieved over autonomic functions within a laboratory setting, is it possible to maintain this control outside the laboratory without the use of a complex array of feedback equipment? This question is being raised with increasing frequency by researchers involved with biofeedback techniques. Although the final answer to this question will probably not be known for many years, one study suggests that the answer may well be both "Yes" and "No." In this study, subjects were divided into three groups—those with low, medium, and high perception of their own heart activity. It was found that those subjects with a high perception of their own heart rates were able to achieve control over this function in the absence of laboratory feedback equipment. In contrast, those with medium and low perception of their heart activity were unsuccessful at this task (McFarland and Campbell, 1975).

The possibility that humans may be able to learn to regulate such autonomic activities as blood pressure and heart rate has far-reaching implications (some are discussed in Box 7.2). Biofeedback techniques are now used in a variety of treatment settings. For example, one investigator (Rorvik, 1972) has reported considerable success in the treatment of people suffering from migraine headaches. It is believed that migraine attacks are caused by increased pressure within the scalp's blood vessels, presumably the result of an increased flow of blood in the head. It was thought that if this blood could be diverted from the head to other parts of the body, the pain of migraine might be alleviated. Patients suffering from migraine were given a meter to monitor temperature (and thus blood flow) in their hands. By learning to increase the temperature in their hands, many patients reported dramatic relief from migraine attacks. A more recent study indicates that control of hand temperature alone is not sufficient to reduce migraine attacks. When people suffering from migraine are merely instructed to place their hands in warm water, they obtain no relief. To control migraine attacks successfully, the patients must apparently learn to control some of the mechanisms that regulate the flow of blood throughout the body (Kunzel *et al.*, 1977).

In addition to regulating bodily activities not ordinarily subject to voluntary control, the autonomic system plays an important role in emotional behavior. The possibility that we can learn to control autonomic responses has important implications for the treatment of many disorders—such as high blood pressure, asthma, and headaches—which are often influenced by psychological factors. One of these implications is that self-control via the use of feedback techniques may come to substitute for drugs as a means of treating certain disorders. One study offers considerable promise in this respect (Canter *et al.*, 1975). The subjects were 48 patients under treatment for severe anxiety conditions. Rather than offering tranquilizers for anxiety reduction, the investigators attached to each patient an apparatus that monitored the tension of a muscle in the forehead. When the patients were relaxed, the apparatus produced a low tone; as they became tense, the tone increased in pitch. The patients were instructed to maintain a low-pitched tone by whatever means possible. They were successful. They were able to reduce muscle tension as well as to achieve relief from anxiety symptoms.

Amidst the flurry of hopes and claims concerning the present and future prospects of biofeedback training, one leading investigator has sounded a note of caution. Noting that some claims are based on studies in which experimental controls are inadequate, he advises: "This is a new

Systolic blood pressure

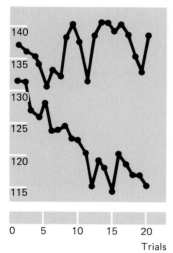

**Figure 7.6**
Human subjects in the experimental group (bottom line) learned to decrease their own blood pressure. The blood pressure of the control subjects (top line) remained relatively stable.

## BOX 7.2

### Practical Implications of Biofeedback

In this chapter, we have seen how biofeedback can apparently allow individuals to achieve a certain degree of control over so-called involuntary functions. In Chapter 2, we saw that an organism can modify an operant response (such as bar-pressing) to receive reinforcement. Can an organism also learn to modify involuntary functions, such as heart rate or blood pressure, to obtain reinforcement?

In a series of ingenious studies, Neal Miller and his associates have demonstrated quite conclusively that operant control over autonomic responses is indeed possible (Miller, 1969). Using a variety of organisms and several different types of reinforcers, these investigators have shown that organisms can learn to control an astonishingly wide assortment of autonomic responses—increasing or decreasing salivary secretion, producing changes in heart rate or blood pressure, modifying intestinal contractions, and even changing the rate at which their kidneys form urine—all to obtain a reward (Miller, 1969).

The practical implications of these studies are enormous. It is quite possible the many *psychosomatic disorders* (physical symptoms resulting from psychological causes) have inadvertently been shaped in real-life situations through operant conditioning. For example, suppose that a business executive is particu- larly harassed by a series of economic setbacks. The resulting tension produces a number of physiological symptoms, among them irregular heart rhythm and increased blood pressure. If business associates become solicitous about the executive's health, they may voluntarily assume some of the upsetting burdens and may even encourage the executive to take it easy for a while. Yet this very release from harassment may serve to reinforce the executive's tendency to respond with these kinds of bodily symptoms any time upsetting circumstances arise.

If it is true that psychosomatic symptoms may be learned through operant conditioning, it is also possible that operant techniques may be employed to relieve these symptoms. Much research is now being conducted along these lines. Figure 7.7 illustrates one of the operant techniques employed to train patients to control abnormal heart rhythms.

In the field of cardiovascular control, researchers have now demonstrated that humans can control blood pressure (Shapiro *et al.*, 1969) and regulate various aspects of heart functioning (Weiss and Engel, 1975; Stephans *et al.*, 1975). These results suggest that we can gain a greater amount of control over our heart and thus may be able to prevent some instances of hypertension and heart attacks.

The possible applications of biofeedback are numerous, and both physicians and psychologists are using these techniques to help people who are suffer-

---

area in which investigators should be bold in what they try but cautious in what they claim" (Miller, 1975). To illustrate, one researcher (Seer, 1979) has suggested that placebo effects may account for some of the results obtained from biofeedback training.

Interest in biofeedback continues to mushroom. National and state societies have been formed; specialized journals, training programs, and certification examinations have been established; and national conferences have been held (Schwartz and Weiss, 1978; Stachnik, 1980). Comprehensive reviews have been written on the subject (see, e.g., Ferguson and Taylor, 1980).

One application of biofeedback techniques that has caught the fancy of scientists and the public alike involves learning conscious control over brain waves. We mentioned earlier that **alpha brain waves** are associated with the relaxed, waking state. Individuals can be trained to "turn on" alpha waves by using biofeedback techniques (Kamiya, 1969; Woodruff,

**Alpha waves**
Brain waves typical of a re- laxed waking state.

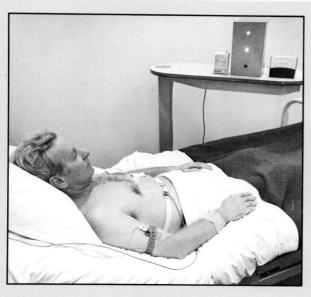

**Figure 7.7**

A technician in the Laboratory of Behavioral Sciences, Gerontology Research Center, Baltimore, Maryland, demonstrates a technique used in attempts to teach patients to control abnormal heart rhythms. A "traffic sign" with red, yellow, and green lights shows the subject how he is doing. An intercom, to the left of the "traffic sign," enables hime to communicate with the doctor. A meter, to the right, shows him what percentage of the time he is accomplishing his task.

ing from a variety of disorders. Some of the conditions being helped are anxiety, tension and migraine headaches, insomnia, epilepsy, paralyzed muscles, asthma, alcoholism, high blood pressure, and the process of childbirth. There are others who feel that biofeedback may also be useful in the treatment of cancer, although at the present time this has not been demonstrated.

Biofeedback techniques have also proven fruitful when applied to disorders of voluntary movement in which muscle functioning is impaired. In this area, information concerning the rate or strength of muscle contractions is fed back to the subject. The subject can then modify these contractions and improve muscle function. Disorders that are included in a muscle dysfunction category include chronic tension and tension headaches (Haynes *et al.*, 1975; Tarler-Benlolo, 1978), rehabilitation of muscles after stroke (Marinacci and Horande, 1960; Johnson and Garton, 1973) and after central nervous system lesion (Brierly, 1967; Cleeland, 1973), and a variety of paralysis conditions (Bird *et al.*, 1977; Jankel, 1977). Taken as a whole, the usefulness of biofeedback in restoring muscle control is the most convincing of all the areas under investigation. This may be due to the fact that we are normally more aware of feedback from our muscles than we are of feedback from other areas of our bodies, and hence the muscles may be more amenable to voluntary control.

1975). Although some subjects report undesirable feelings (loss of control) arising from the alpha state (Sterman, 1973), others describe the state of serenity and well-being as a "high."

Alpha-wave conditioning has prompted a considerable amount of controversy and, in many cases, unjustified claims about the benefits to be derived from biofeedback training. The alpha boom began when a number of laboratories investigating physiological measures associated with meditative states indicated that enhanced alpha activity accompanied subjects' reports of a change in their state of consciousness. The notion of an alpha state was then immediately tied to reports of peacefulness, tranquility, or inner calm, to name a few. Two studies suggest the possibility that the subjective feelings associated with the alpha state may reflect the effects of suggestion resulting from media publicity. In both studies, the experimental subjects received false feedback concerning their brain wave production. They reported significant "alpha experiences'' even though they were not producing alpha waves (Glaros, 1977; Glaros et al., 1977).

The research into the modification of brain electrical activity using biofeedback has led to some potentially useful applications to various conditions and states of consciousness, including insomnia and epilepsy. One study (Sterman, 1973) reported a reduction of convulsive seizures by reinforcing the occurrence of a 12- to 14-cycles-per-second rhythm over the sensorimotor regions of the cerebral cortex. The degree of relief from seizures was apparently related to the abundance of this rhythm. Other researchers have repeated this finding, although there is a growing concern over the possible long-term effects of brain wave modifications.

It has been shown that interesting differences in alpha waves are associated with age. The usual range of alpha is between 8 and 13 cycles per second. The usual alpha frequency in young adults is between 10 and 13 cycles per second, whereas older people (70 years or more) produce alpha waves between 7 and 8 cycles per second (Cherry and Cherry, 1974). Older people generally respond more slowly to the various stimuli in their environment. It has been suggested that the slowing down associated with old age may be related to the production of slower alpha waves (Surwillo, 1963). Indeed, one study provides strong support for this view. When older subjects (average age: 72.5) were trained to produce faster alpha waves, their reaction times improved. In contrast, their reaction times were slower when they were trained to produce slower alpha waves (Woodruff, 1975).

Although the early research on brain waves and various states of consciousness has dealt almost exclusively with alpha waves, more recent research efforts have been directed to other brain wave frequencies. One study has shown that subjects can learn and sustain voluntary control of 40-cycle EEG waves. Rapid wave lengths of approximately 40 cycles per second appear to be associated with problem-solving activity (Ford et al., 1977).

Some researchers have expressed the hope that if we learn to control our brain wave patterns, we may be able to alleviate anxiety, improve memory, facilitate learning, and perhaps someday reduce our dependence on drugs, alcohol, and cigarettes. Much research remains to be done before the claims of today and the hopes of tomorrow receive scientific confirmation.

## HYPNOSIS

**Hypnosis**
A means of achieving a trance-like state of increased suggestibility.

When the word **"hypnosis"** is mentioned, what sort of mental image does it conjure up? A mysterious person in a black cape chanting magical phrases while swinging a pendant back and forth in the field of vision of a willing subject or an unwilling victim? Somebody being forced to commit an act against his or her will? A type of sleep in which your will is placed under the control of the hypnotist?

Many people fear hypnosis because of its association with the occult. Others are distrustful of the loss of personal control that the hypnotic state implies. It is interesting that although some form of hypnosis was

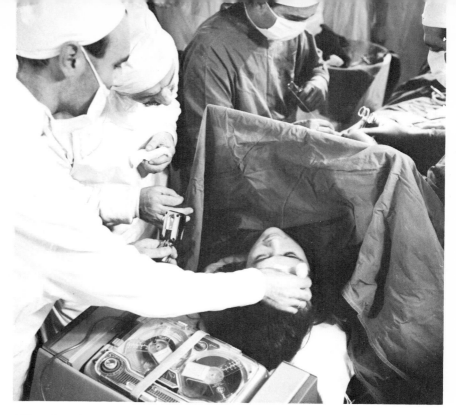

**Although we know little more today than the ancient Egyptians did about hypnotism, we do know that it works. This patient is undergoing an appendectomy under the influence of hypnosis. No anesthetics were used during surgery.**

practiced as long as 7000 years ago by Egyptian priests and seers (Sigerist, 1951), we know little more today about *what* it is and *why* it occurs than the ancient practitioners did. We know it works but we don't know *how* it works. What we do know is that there is no way, at present, to distinguish hypnosis physiologically from wakefulness. The EEG pattern of hypnosis is like that of a waking state. However, an individual who is extremely responsive to hypnosis produces a brain wave of high voltage and greater duration (Nowlis and Rhead, 1968). Heart beat, blood pressure, and other physiological indicators vary according to the condition suggested by the hypnotist. Thus, if told that a lion is about to attack, the hypnotic subject will evidence the physiological signs of fear: pulse rate increase, elevated blood pressure, sweating in the palms of the hands, and so forth.

Some investigators believe that hypnosis is a trance state, different from sleeping and waking, with behavioral laws of its own. Taking their cue from the fact that not all subjects can be hypnotized, others feel that it is a condition of heightened suggestibility in which the characteristics or traits of the subject are the significant factors. Still others attribute hypnosis to role playing (Barber *et al.*, 1974). To illustrate, if subjects are told to pretend that they are hypnotized and asked to act accordingly, they frequently behave like hypnotized subjects, even showing an apparent lack of sensitivity to induced pain. Yet another theory likens the hypnotic condition to a state in which our cognitive controls become segregated or disassociated from one another (Hilgard, 1974).

According to the dissociative view of hypnosis, there are numerous cognitive control systems that function in the human. For example, we may attend to one thing while automatically engaging in other activities. We can drive a car while planning our day's activities because we have successfully segregated or dissociated driving from other cognitive controls. Similarly, hypnosis represents but one means of reordering cognitive controls. Thus a person under hypnosis may successfully "ignore" painful stimulation while attending to other stimuli.

Although the various theorists do not agree on the explanation of the hypnotic condition, most will agree that subjects "under hypnosis" behave and feel differently than when not hypnotized. The following observations have been made:

1. Not all subjects can be hypnotized. We know that the ability to achieve a hypnotic state is related more to the characteristics of the subject than to the techniques of the hypnotist. Such factors as motivation, imagination, and ability to relax and concentrate all favor the achievement of the hypnotic state (Kroger and Fezler, 1976). On the other hand, inability to relax or concentrate and fear of the hypnotist or the hypnotic state interfere with hypnotic induction.

The most prominent feature of persons who can be hypnotized is that they can become immersed in fantasy and imagination (Hilgard, 1979). They are willing to accept distortions in reality as commonplace. For example, a subject will readily accept the suggestion that there is an animal in the room that is capable of speech and will not even think it strange to engage in conversation with this nonexistent animal.

This imaginative involvement appears to be related to the cerebral hemisphere favored by the subject. We previously discussed right and left hemispheric brain functioning (Chapter 5). The left hemisphere appears to be involved in language and logical thought, whereas the right hemisphere seems to be more involved in imagination, fantasy, and holistic thought processes. It is interesting to note that individuals susceptible to hypnotism appear to favor the right hemisphere (Bakan, 1969).

2. Although superficially resembling sleep, the hypnotic state has more in common with the waking state. The subject remains capable of responding to external stimuli (e.g., the hypnotic commands), and the EEG pattern more clearly resembles wakefulness than sleep.

Indeed, it has been demonstrated that hypnosis is also possible during an active alert state. One prominent researcher sees a relationship between "alert hypnosis" and the state athletes call "second wind." There are no known physiological changes associated with second wind. It appears to be subjective. When some of the most successful runners feel they are exhausted, they go into some kind of state that permits them to keep on running; that is their "second wind" (Hilgard, 1979).

3. A third characteristic involves selectivity of attention. Although attention is always selective, under hypnosis it becomes even more so. Thus a hypnotized subject told to hear only the voice of the hypnotist can completely screen out all other voices and sounds. One variation of selective attention is a phenomenon known as the "hidden observer." "A subject who was capable of shutting out all sounds, including pistol shots,

still raised a finger when I asked him in a quiet voice to raise the finger (while he was still psychologically deaf) to let me know if some part of him was hearing me'' (Hilgard, 1973, p. 407). It is as if there is an observer hidden within the hypnotized subject that is capable of responding to and communicating with the experimenter.

4. Hypnosis has been used with moderate success in modifying undesirable behaviors or treating various medical conditions. In one study, habitual smokers were given a single hypnotic session during which they committed themselves to practice self-hypnotic procedures afterward (Spiegel, 1970). It was found that the hypnotically suggestive subjects were more likely to give up cigarette smoking in the short term. However, after a year, only about 20 percent of the subjects were still not smoking.

It has been shown that some subjects verbally report a reduction in pain through hypnosis (Hilgard, 1977). However, these subjects are able to write with their ''unhypnotized'' hand that they are aware of the pain (Brody, 1980).

Hypnosis has been widely accepted as an effective substitute for local anesthetics in certain kinds of minor surgery such as dentistry. In addition, it has been reported that one cancer patient in four will respond well to hypnotic suggestion for relief of chronic pain.

**A sinister side of hypnotism has been popularized in fiction and movies. In the silent film classic** *The Cabinet of Dr. Caligari* **an evil hypnotist exercises absolute control over his zombielike subject.**

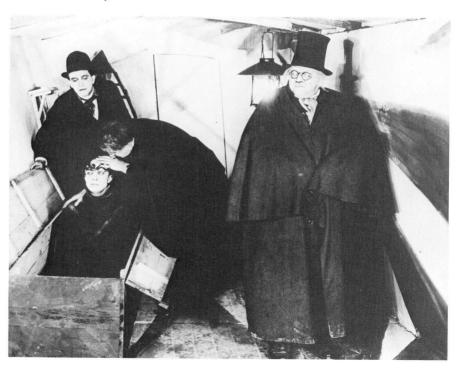

One author (Watson, 1981) reported studies in which subjects with warts on their bodies were hypnotized and were given the suggestion that the warts would go away. Indeed, the warts disappeared, apparently by the mere force of the hypnotic suggestion. Although we must await supportive studies for these results before drawing any firm conclusions from them, these findings certainly raise questions about the power of hypnosis and of the mind itself.

5. Finally, subjects readily respond to the suggestion that they will not remember anything that has transpired during the hypnotic state. Nevertheless, they can be given a posthypnotic suggestion to which they will respond even though they show no recall of the source of the suggestion. One of the most intriguing studies dealing with posthypnotic suggestion induced subjects to talk during their sleep and describe their dream content as it was taking place. Although this seems to work only with subjects who are normally sleep-talkers, it provides an interesting example of posthypnotic suggestion (Arkin *et al.*, 1966).

Contrary to the theme of many grade-B science-fiction movies, neither hypnotic suggestion nor posthypnotic suggestion can be accomplished with an unwilling subject. In fact, not all people can be successfully hypnotized. Studies have shown that somewhere between 5 and 10

Table 7.1
**Depth of Hypnosis**

*I. Memory retained on waking*

*1st degree.* Torpor, drowsiness, or various suggested sensations such as warmth, numbness.

*2nd degree.* Inability to open the eyes if challenged to do so.

*3rd degree.* Catalepsy suggested by the hypnotist and bound up with the passive condition of the subject, but may be counteracted by the subject.

*4th degree.* Catalepsy and rotary automatism that cannot be counteracted by the subject.

*5th degree.* Involuntary contractures and analgesia as suggested by the hypnotist.

*6th degree.* Automatic obedience; subject behaves like an automaton.

*II. Amnesia on waking*

*7th degree.* Amnesia on waking. No hallucinations.

*8th degree.* Able to experience hallucinations during sleep.

*9th degree.* Able to experience hallucinations during sleep and posthypnotically.

From E. R. Hilgard *et al.*, ''The Distribution of Susceptibility to Hypnosis in a Student Population: A Study Using the Stanford Hypnotic Susceptibility Scale,'' Psychological Monographs **75**, 8, Whole No. 512. Copyright © 1961 by the American Psychological Association. Reprinted by permission of the author.

percent of all people are not at all susceptible to hypnotic suggestion. Young people between the ages of 8 and 12 are the most highly susceptible, and no reliable differences between the sexes have been reported (Hilgard, 1965). In addition, not all susceptible subjects achieve the same depth of hypnosis. Some experience little more than drowsiness, whereas others can be induced to experience posthypnotic hallucinations. The various depths of hypnotic induction are summarized in Table 7.1.

## DRUGS

We have seen that achieving a different state of consciousness through the use of biofeedback techniques is, at best, marginally successful, and meditation requires time, patience, effort, and concentration. In other words, neither provides quick and easy relief from daily cares. In contrast, drugs are available for a price, and all that is required of us is that we ingest, inhale, inject under the skin, inject into the muscles, inject directly into a vein, or pour with a spoon into a severed blood vessel. Although some drugs are illegal and must be acquired through illegal channels, many may be obtained in a pharmacy. Some don't even require a prescription. In this section we discuss the major **psychoactive drugs** (see Box 7.3), such as alcohol, LSD, PCP, marijuana, heroin, and amphetamines and barbiturates, also called "uppers" and "downers."

**Psychoactive drugs** Those drugs that have psychological effects—that is, that affect the user's perceptual, cognitive, or emotional state.

## Alcohol

We're a nation of drug users. We use drugs to help us remain wake. We use drugs to put us to sleep. We use them to alleviate anxiety and decrease our level of tension. In recent years we have seen an upsurge in the use of drugs to induce various states of consciousness. Yet when we talk about drugs we tend to forget about one that has been on the scene since the beginnings of recorded history—alcohol.

Have you ever had more than a couple of drinks? If so, you undoubtedly noted a pronounced change in your feelings, your mood, and the way you perceived the world about you. Clearly, the presence of alcohol in the body leads to a different state of consciousness. Although the changes differ from individual to individual and even within the same individual from time to time, some broad generalizations are possible. Low levels of consumption (one to three drinks) generally lead to feelings of warmth, relaxation, and decreased social inhibitions. At slightly higher levels a gap typically develops between an individual's perceived and actual capabilities. Thus after a few drinks people tend to think they are speaking eloquently when, in fact, there may be a slurring of speech. They may be confident of their ability to weave in and out of urban traffic when, in actuality, they probably would have difficulty maneuvering a car into a space large enough for a big truck. Indeed, excessive use of alcohol is responsible for about 30,000 traffic deaths per year in the

## BOX 7.3

### Drugs

Many people use the terms "drug use" and "drug abuse" interchangeably. These terms really have two different and distinct meanings. When a person drinks a cup of coffee, enjoys an alcoholic drink, inhales the smoke from a cigarette or "joint," or swallows a tranquilizer, he or she is a **drug user**. The person who uses these or other drugs to such an extent that he or she is unable to function without them may be considered a **drug abuser**. Figure 7.8 summarizes the lifetime use for a group of high school students of a number of different classes of drugs. Note that the abuse of tobacco and alcohol is far greater than that of any other drug category.

Few people would deny that drug abuse (including alcoholism) is one of the most serious problems we face today. Drug abuse itself is unquestionably a symptom of deeper psychological causes. Unfortunately, at the present state of our knowledge, we are better able to describe the effects of drugs on behavior than to specify the underlying causes of drug abuse.

Some drugs are particularly worrisome because their continued use leads to addiction. For example, chronic heroin abusers find that continued use leads to increased **tolerance**: Their bodies not only can stand (tolerate) more of the drug, but actually require greater and greater dosages to achieve the same effect. Before long, they develop a physiological dependence on the drug; this state of physiological depen-

dence is called **addiction**. Should they try to "kick the habit," their bodies will react violently.

Addiction should be distinguished from **habituation,** which is psychological, rather than physiological, dependence. Withdrawal from habituation is likely to be accompanied by emotional rather than physical distress. People trying to give up cigarettes, for example, are often nervous, tense, and irritable; the physiological symptoms they may have are usually minor.

The chemical nature of a drug determines whether continued abuse will lead to addiction or habituation. Drugs such as heroin, morphine, codeine, and the barbiturates are addicting. Habituating drugs include marijuana, cocaine, and the amphetamines.

---

**Drug user**
A person who uses drugs, but not to excess.

**Drug abuser**
A person who uses drugs to excess and is unable to function without them.

**Tolerance**
The body's ability to withstand a given amount of drug and its need for increased dosages of that drug to produce the desired effects.

**Addiction**
Physiological dependence on (need for) a drug.

**Habituation**
Psychological dependence on (need for) a drug

---

United States (Dusek-Girdano and Girdano, 1980). Figure 7.9 illustrates the effect of number of drinks on responsible driving.

The effects of excessive alcohol on behavior are pervasive. Not only does it affect motor coordination, but it affects the ability to engage in sexual intercourse. In this respect, Shakespeare said it best: "Drink provoketh the desire but taketh away from the performance."

The effect of alcohol on behavior varies with the amount of alcohol in the blood. When the percentage of alcohol in the blood reaches approximately 0.15 (0.10 percent in some states), the individual is considered to be legally intoxicated. He or she loses motor coordination and experiences impairment of speech, vision, and thought processes. Slightly more than 0.5 percent concentration in the blood (about a fifth of 90 proof liquor) can lead to coma, and possibly death.

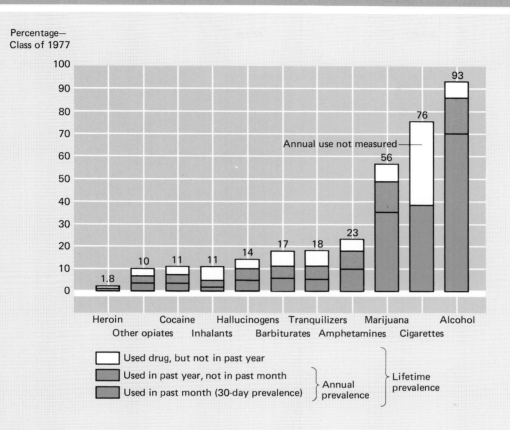

Percentage—
Class of 1977

**Figure 7.8**
**Drug use of U.S. high school students (N = 17,087)**

---

Alcohol does not affect the various brain functions in a uniform way. Relatively small amounts may affect reason and judgment, whereas large amounts must be consumed before the vital life-and-death centers are affected (see Fig. 7.10). Unfortunately, about 10 percent of American adults suffer from alcoholism—a disease in which individuals cannot consistently control their consumption of alcohol (see Box 7.4, p. 270).

**LSD**

There are a number of **hallucinogenic** drugs in use today, including LSD, psilocybin, mescaline, and peyote. The most well known, frequently used, and thoroughly researched is LSD. LSD (lysergic acid diethylamide) is an extremely potent hallucinogenic drug. As little as four-millionths of

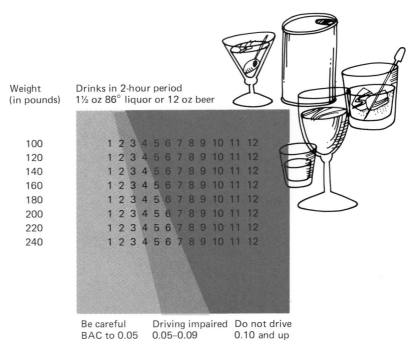

| Weight (in pounds) | Drinks in 2-hour period 1½ oz 86° liquor or 12 oz beer |
|---|---|
| 100 | 1 2 3 4 5 6 7 8 9 10 11 12 |
| 120 | 1 2 3 4 5 6 7 8 9 10 11 12 |
| 140 | 1 2 3 4 5 6 7 8 9 10 11 12 |
| 160 | 1 2 3 4 5 6 7 8 9 10 11 12 |
| 180 | 1 2 3 4 5 6 7 8 9 10 11 12 |
| 200 | 1 2 3 4 5 6 7 8 9 10 11 12 |
| 220 | 1 2 3 4 5 6 7 8 9 10 11 12 |
| 240 | 1 2 3 4 5 6 7 8 9 10 11 12 |

| Be careful BAC to 0.05 | Driving impaired 0.05–0.09 | Do not drive 0.10 and up |
|---|---|---|

**Figure 7.9**
**Effect of number of drinks on responsible driving**

The part of the table to the left of the shaded area shows that, depending on one's weight, one or at most two drinks rarely affect responsible driving. Beyond that, as the blood alcohol count (BAC) rises, the probability of being seriously affected becomes much greater. (Dusek-Girdano and Girdano, 1980)

an ounce produces marked behavioral changes. Stated another way, 1 ounce can provide more than a quarter of a million average doses. An average dose takes effect extremely rapidly, and the effects usually last from 8 to 12 hours. The use of LSD is accompanied by marked physical changes, including elevated blood pressure, temperature, and pulse rate.

Many feel that the Beatles said it all with "Lucy in the Sky with Diamonds." LSD is well known to produce psychic effects that will send people on a trip into the sky (i.e., make them feel high) with diamonds (vivid images and flashes of light). Shortly after ingesting LSD, the individual may feel tingling in the hands and feet, loss of appetite, numbness, and chilliness. The pupils become dilated; and heart rate, body temperature, blood pressure, and blood-sugar levels increase and persist throughout the trip.

Because LSD is chemically similar to a substance occurring at some synapses in the brain, it may block or facilitate relaying of neural messages. This may account for **synesthesia,** the translation of one sensory experience into another—feeling an odor, seeing a sound, or hearing a light. It is not unusual for the user to experience marked changes in sensation and perception, including distorted perceptions of the self. For example, one person, while under LSD, reported: "I don't feel like I'm reacting to my own body now. I feel like I'm away from it. . . . My feet feel like they're a million miles apart" (Pollard *et al.*, 1965). Distorted perceptions of time are also common. Another individual "tripping" on LSD

**Synesthesia**
The translation of one sensory experience into another, such as feeling an odor or seeing a sound.

reported: ". . . I don't know what time it is. I can't even think what time it is . . . it feels like I've been here for weeks and days . . ." (Pollard *et al.*, 1965).

The psychological effects of LSD are not always predictable. They seem to vary in the same person from time to time, and depend on such factors as the amount and purity of the drug taken, the circumstances under which it is used, and the personality characteristics of the individual. In a supportive setting, emotional responses such as laughing or crying are the first behavioral signs that LSD is having an effect.

LSD can produce marked variations in emotional states, ranging from inner contentment and oneness with the world to episodes of unmitigated terror. What is sometimes frightening to users is that they may experience contrasting emotions at the same time, for example, both grief and joy. These mood contrasts are somewhat similar to those found in bipolar disorders (see Chapter 14). LSD may also produce other psychosislike effects—hallucinations, occasional delusions, and feelings of depersonalization or loss of self-identity (Snyder and Lampanella, 1969).

Why do people take LSD? The reasons are almost as varied as the types of effects produced. Some individuals say they take LSD because they are curious, because their friends encourage and sanction it, because they want to experience a high, or because they think they will achieve

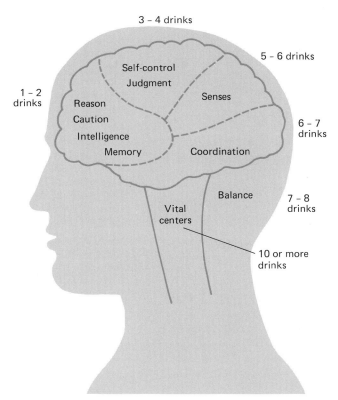

**Figure 7.10**
**Alcohol's effects on the brain**

## BOX 7.4

### Alcoholism

An estimated 100 million or more Americans use alcoholic beverages. The majority of their drinking is moderate, responsible, and socially approved. However, an estimated 12 to 15 million Americans use alcohol excessively and are labeled alcoholics—individuals whose drinking seriously impairs their life adjustment in terms of health, personal relationships, and sometimes occupational functioning. In recent years, alcohol has become the "drug of choice" among teenagers, and the incidence of alcoholism in this age group has risen dramatically. Alcoholism has also increased among women and now approaches that of men.

It might be added that alcohol has been implicated in over half the deaths in automobile accidents, 50 percent of all murders, 35 percent of rapes, and 30 percent of the suicides that occur each year in our society. The life span of the average alcoholic is about twelve years shorter than that of the nonalcoholic. Alcoholism now ranks as the third leading cause of death in the United States, behind only coronary heart disease and cancer.

Contrary to popular belief, alcohol is not a stimulant but a depressant that numbs the higher brain centers and thus lessens their inhibiting control. Aside from this release, which may lead people to say or do things they would normally inhibit, drinkers may find that alcohol provides a sense of well-being in which unpleasant realities are minimized and their sense of adequacy is increased.

Because alcoholism often progresses slowly and by subtle degrees in its potential victim, the line that separates social drinking from alcoholism is not always readily observable. According to the Japanese proverb, "First the man takes a drink, then the drink takes a drink and then the drink takes the man." A general view of the stages which are commonly involved in the development may be outlined as follows:

1. *Initial phase.* The social drinker turns increasingly to alcohol for relief of tension, present or antici-

pated. Toward the end of this period a number of warning signs, including morning drinking, point to approaching alcoholism.
2. *Crucial phase.* Here people lose control over their drinking. One drink seems to start a chain reaction, although they can still partially control the occasions when they will or will not take the first drink. In this phase, people frequently begin to rationalize and make alibis for their drinking. Often they encounter reproof from family and friends.
3. *Chronic phase.* Here the drinkers' control over drinking completely breaks down and alcohol plays an increasingly dominant role in everyday activities. At the same time, their physiological tolerance for alcohol decreases, and they now become intoxicated on far less alcohol than previously. They may also begin to experience tremors and other symptoms while sober—leading to further drinking to control such symptoms. During this period, the alcoholic's life situation usually undergoes serious deterioration.

The causal patterns in alcoholism are not fully understood, but several biological, psychological, and sociocultural factors have been emphasized. One biological possibility which is receiving increasing emphasis is that some individuals—perhaps as a result of genetic factors—develop a physiological addiction to and craving for alcohol much as other do for heroin (Myers & Melchior, 1977). Psychologically, alcoholism has been viewed as stemming from excessive stress, and the learned use of alcohol has been seen as a "crutch" in trying to cope with life's problems. In fact, many investigators view alcoholism as a learned maladaptive response which is reinforced and maintained by tension reduction. Still other studies have emphasized parental models who are alcoholic as well as broader sociocultural conditions that tend to encourage the excessive use of alcohol. For example, alcoholism is rare among Mormons, whose religious values prohibit the use of alcohol.

Coleman, 1979, pp. 198–200.

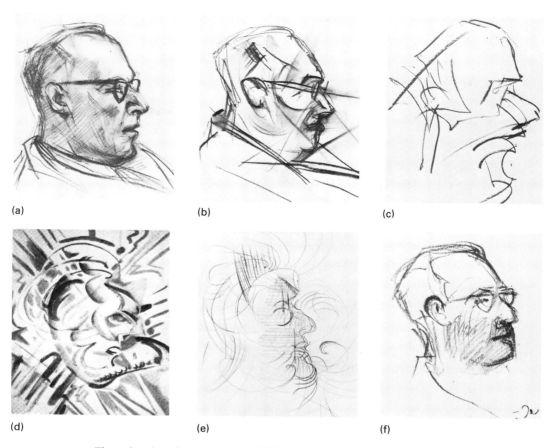

(a)　　　(b)　　　(c)

(d)　　　(e)　　　(f)

These drawings by a man given LSD were done: (a) twenty minutes after a first, apparently inadequate, dose; (b) twenty-five minutes after taking a second dose; (c) after additional time has elapsed; (d) one hour and forty-five minutes after the second dose; (e) four hours and forty-five minutes after the second dose; and (f) seven hours after the second dose, when the effects have largely passed.

psychological, philosophical, and religious insights. Some people, aware of the heightened sensory and perceptual experiences it produces, believe that LSD will make them more creative. In this respect, however, LSD is a complete failure. Artists who have created works while under the influence of LSD have later repudiated the work (Gubar, 1969; McGlothlin and Arnold, 1971).

In any event, most users of LSD tend either to discontinue usage or to restrict their intake vastly after two to three years. The reason appears to be the loss of the uniqueness of the trip experience. "As [the experience] is repeated many times, what was initially unique becomes more commonplace and there is a process of diminishing returns. The effect of hallucinogens is indeed a 'trip' and trips tend to lose their appeal when repeated too often" (McGlothlin, 1975).

How dangerous is LSD? The two most prominent dangers are: (1) obtaining a compound that is not what it is purported to be or is laced with adulterants (e.g., arsenic) that are dangerous to a person's physical health, and (2) triggering memories and/or emotions that can have a devastating consequence on the individual. This latter danger is particularly great if the individual is emotionally unstable to begin with.

In addition, a few people experience *flashbacks* in which—days, weeks, or months after taking LSD—they have a recurrence of some aspects of the LSD experience, usually of a frightening nature, as can be seen in the following examples:

*Patient A:* Now I often see a bright shiny halo around people, especially at the dark edges—sometimes it's rainbow colors—like during the trip.

*Patient B:* Sometimes the sidewalk seems to bend as if it's going downwards—even when I'm not on anything—or it just kinda vibrates back and forth.

*Patient C:* Now I see things—walls, and faces and caves—probably imprinted on my thalamus from the prehistoric past. Sometimes as clear as on a trip, but mostly not.
(Horowitz, 1969, p. 566)

It is interesting to note that approximately 5 percent of LSD users experience flashbacks *despite* the fact that the body appears to rid itself of LSD within two days (Girdano and Girdano, 1976). Thus the cause of flashbacks is still an unanswered question.

## PCP

Phencyclidine hydrochloride (PCP), also called Angel Dust, is not technically a hallucinogen. It was developed as an anesthetic and appears to depress the nervous system. However, it produces the hallucinations and other perceptual distortions associated with the hallucinogens and has, to some extent, supplanted LSD in availability (and thus popularity) on the street.

Unlike LSD, however, PCP is known to have produced convulsions, coma, and even death among users. Also frightening is the unpredictability of its effects. Users may feel euphoric one time and extremely depressed the next. Some individuals who have taken moderate dosages of PCP have felt physical numbness, yet there have been a number of reports of PCP users committing violent assaults and even murder while under the influence of this drug.

Long-term effects of PCP are just beginning to be explored. A recent report from the National Institute of Drug Abuse indicated that as many as 50 percent of those admitted to mental institutions for drug-related problems are suffering from severe mental disorders related to their use of PCP. Whether this finding will hold up and what, if any, problems arise from PCP use must await further studies.

## Marijuana

The chances are that either you or someone whom you know has tried marijuana at least once. Although estimates on its use vary, most experts agree that the use of marijuana has experienced a sharp rise in the past decades, especially among the teenage and college populations. Approx-

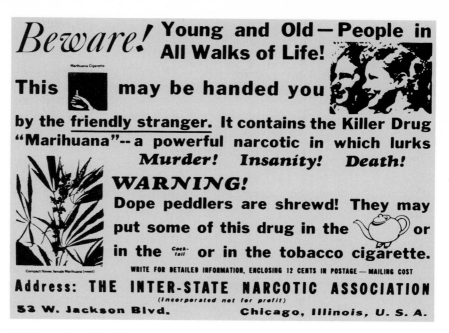

A billboard outside Chicago in the mid-1930s illustrates the intensity of the campaign against marijuana use.

Reprinted with permission from D. D. Girdano and D. A. Girdano, *Drugs, A Factual Account*, 2d ed. Reading, Mass.: Addison-Wesley, 1976, p. 62.

imately 60 percent of high school seniors reported using marijuana. More than 10 percent used it daily (Coates, 1980).

Marijuana was first made illegal in the United States in 1937. It is interesting that the law was passed by Congress more as a result of public clamor and unsupported charges appearing in the news media than because of expert medical testimony. In fact, in committee hearings, one medical authority challenged the validity of most reports indicting marijuana as dangerous. He was severely chastised, browbeaten, and badgered by committee members for "trying to throw obstacles in the way of something that the Federal Government is trying to do" (Snyder, 1970).

A member of the hemp family *(Cannabis sativa)*, the marijuana plant exudes a yellow sticky substance (resin) as a means of protection against hot and sunny weather conditions. In general, the hotter and sunnier the area in which the plant grows, the greater the amount of resin produced by the plant. The resin contains the active ingredient, tetra hydrocannabinol (THC). Thus foreign sources of marijuana (tropical countries such as Colombia, Jamaica, Panama, and Mexico) generally produce plants higher in THC. The strength of various preparations from the cannabis plant also varies widely. Marijuana, which is obtained from the tops of flowering shoots, has from zero to 5 percent THC. Hashish, which is made from pure resin, is 10 times more potent than marijuana and contains 5 to 20 percent THC. Liquid hashish, called hashish oil, is even more powerful, as it is 20 to 70 percent THC.

In the United States, marijuana is usually smoked rather than ingested. The effects are felt more promptly and the smoker can regulate the intake continuously. Smokers also avoid the nausea sometimes experienced by those who ingest marijuana.

Marijuana is generally considered a mild hallucinogen whose effects do not even approach those of LSD. In fact, street grass is so mild and the effects so subtle that the individual must usually be familiar with its use in order to experience a high (Weil *et al.*, 1969). The effects vary according to the user's past experiences and present expectations, the strength and quantity of the drug used, and the circumstances under which it is used. "Turning on" with marijuana involves alterations in sensation, mood, emotions, and perceptions; distortions in time and space; intensification of sensory experiences; and dreamlike thought processes.

Although the long-term effects of marijuana are not known, its immediate effects appear to be much like those of alcohol. While a user is on a high, there is some impairment in time perception, form perception, intelligence test scores, auditory discrimination, number manipulation, and ability to concentrate. Also, as with high levels of alcohol consumption, both judgment and performance while driving are adversely affected. For chronic users, the striving for greater pleasure from each situation leads to a concept of happiness that is defined in terms of immediate pleasure rather than satisfaction of long-term needs (Girdano and Girdano, 1976).

## BOX 7.5

### Marijuana: Does It Damage the Brain?

The possibility that marijuana use may be hazardous has produced a remarkable polarization among scientists. Those who say that marijuana poses no special hazards espouse their convictions with an evangelistic zeal that borders on fanaticism. Those who think there are hazards argue their case with only slightly less fervor, and all too often scientific debate has fallen by the wayside. This polarization is reinforced by the mass of contradictory evidence that seems to lend support to both sides. The naive individual seeking guidance is often hard pressed to know whom to believe.

Enough evidence has accumulated in the past five years, however, to force a dispassionate observer to two conclusions. There is probably little or no hazard associated with the use of a single joint—or even a few joints—but there is enough evidence suggesting potential dangers from long-term, heavy use of marijuana to dictate both caution and concern. These dangers include, among other things (Maugh, 1974a), the possibility that long-term, heavy use of marijuana may produce sharp personality changes that lead to a

marked deterioration in what is normally considered good mental health and may cause potentially irreversible brain injury. If this evidence is corroborated, cannabis (the generic term for marijuana and the more potent hashish) would have to be considered far more hazardous than was previously suspected.

There is little question that cannabis has a number of short-term effects on the brain—it could not be psychoactive if it did not. The consequences of these short-term effects are uncertain, but few scientists seem willing to suggest that these effects are in themselves hazardous. What is of greater concern is the possibility that continuation of these effects over a period of time may produce organic brain damage.

Tetrahydrocannabinol, which is the principal psychoactive constituent of cannabis, has a very high affinity for brain tissues.

### The Amotivation Syndrome

> . . . many scientists argue that the continued presence of tetrahydrocannabinol in the brain induces a set of mental characteristics termed the "amotivational syndrome." This syndrome is familiar to most clinicians who have treated canna-

There are occasional reports of panic reactions, particularly among young users. These reactions, however, may reflect the personality characteristics of the individual more than the effects of the drug: Some people experience panic in any new or changed circumstance. The physiological effects include increased heartbeat, increased thirst, and tingling of the scalp (Becker, 1963). In addition, there appears to be a loss of REM sleep in spite of the fact that total sleep time increases (Tassinari *et al.*, 1974). Withdrawal of marijuana leads to a marked rebound of REM sleep above normal levels (Feinberg *et al.*, 1975).

Marijuana users do not require increasingly large doses in order to experience a high. Marijuana is, therefore, habituating rather than addicting. The term "pothead" is sometimes erroneously applied to anyone who has used marijuana on more than one occasion—a usage equivalent to calling anyone who occasionally takes a drink containing alcohol an alcoholic. The term is best reserved for a person whose psychological dependence on marijuana is so great that its use has become a way of life.

Although some researchers have suggested that heavy and prolonged use of marijuana may be associated with brain damage (see Box 7.5), the jury is still out on the long-term effects of chronic marijuana use. Perhaps

---

bis *users and has perhaps been best described by psychiatrists Harold Kolansky and William T. Moore of the University of Pennsylvania, Philadelphia.*

*Kolansky and Moore treated 13 individuals between the ages of 20 and 41 years who had smoked cannabis three to ten times a week for at least 16 months. All showed the same set of symptoms: The patients were characteristically apathetic and sluggish in mental and physical responses. There was usually a goallessness and a loss of interest in personal appearance. Considerable flattening of affect gave a false impression of calm and well-being; this was usually accompanied by the patients' conviction that they had recently developed emotional maturity and insight aided by cannabis. This pseudoequanimity was easily disrupted if the patients were questioned about their personality change, new philosophy, and drug consumption, or if their supplies of cannabis were threatened. The individuals were physically thin, often appeared tired, and exhibited slowed physical movements. They also showed symptoms of mental confusion, a slowed time sense, difficulty with recent memory, and an incapability of*

*completing thoughts during verbal communication.*

*The stereotyped nature of these symptoms and the apparent psychological stability of the patients prior to cannabis use led Kolansky and Moore to hypothesize that the syndrome was attributable to cannabis. This hypothesis was supported by the strong correlation between the severity of the symptoms and the duration of cannabis use. It was further strengthened by the observation that the syndrome disappeared when the patients abstained from use of cannabis (although some other investigators have attributed this disappearance to the combination of therapy and the power of suggestion). In those patients who had used cannabis most heavily and then stopped, however, the symptoms persisted intermittently for as long as 42 months, and the investigators suggest that these individuals may have suffered irreversible brain damage.*

Maugh, 1974, pp. 775–776.

the most dangerous effects relate to the fact that marijuana is usually smoked. A typical joint is high in tar, approximately four times as much as in a regular cigarette. Moreover, because the inhalation is usually deeper than with tobacco smoking, and the smoke is kept in the lungs a longer period of time, smoking a joint a day may be roughly equivalent to smoking a daily package of cigarettes (Dusek-Girdano and Girdano, 1980). Frequent users often suffer from "joint cough," bronchitis, and other lung complications (Vachon *et al.*, 1976). Also quite noticeable are a reddening of the whites of the eyes (conjunctivae) and speeded-up heart rate.

The most commonly expressed fear concerning marijuana use is that it represents a first step toward the "hard" drugs, which definitely do impair bodily and mental functions. Statements such as "Eighty percent of heroin and morphine addicts had previously used marijuana" raise the specter of millions of youths developing a craving for bigger and better highs as a direct result of their experiences with marijuana. This kind of "evidence" is quite misleading. Using this line of reasoning, we might establish an even greater indictment of milk, because 100 percent of all morphine and heroin addicts have "used" milk at one time or another. Such evidence simply fails to take into account the millions of people who use marijuana on occasion and have no interest in drugs that are clearly dangerous. To date, no direct causal link has been established between marijuana use and addiction to any of the hard drugs. Nevertheless, it is possible that prolonged and continuous abuse of marijuana may pave the way to experimentation with other drugs. As one of the leading authorities on marijuana, William McGlothlin, has observed, "I'm fairly convinced that the *heavy* use of marijuana by an adolescent can contribute to poor judgment and magical thinking—particularly as regards the use of other drugs" (quoted in Gross, 1972). Moreover, because marijuana is often used in a group setting, some people may succumb to group pressure and experiment with a drug that gives them a bigger high.

## Heroin

There can be no question about the dangers of heroin use. What may start out as a desire to experience a new kind of high may progress with extreme rapidity to an almost continuous type of nightmare existence. As one addict expressed it, "Heroin has all the advantages of death, without its permanence" (*Time*, 1970). Many addicts find permanence when they take an overdose.

The heroin user may begin by snorting or inhaling the drug, progress to "skin popping" (injecting it beneath the skin), and end up "mainlining" it (injecting it directly into the bloodstream). If a hypodermic syringe is not available, the user may sever an artery and pour the heroin in with a spoon. Once users are "hooked," their entire lives become centered upon this white powder. They will do *anything*—lie, steal, cheat, even kill—to get that next fix. After a while, they do not even experience a high; they simply need the drug to avoid the terrors of withdrawal. The habit demands more and more, and still more, of the drug. Before long, it may cost more than $100 a day, seven days a week—about $40,000 a

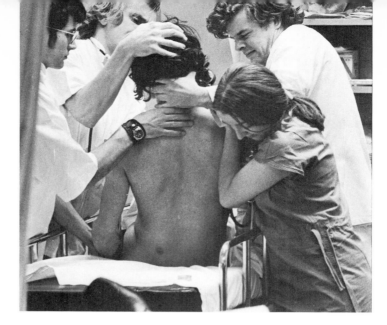

**Thousands of emergency room cases each year can be traced to the abuse of drugs. Overdose is a common cause of death.**

year! Even a highly paid corporation executive would find it difficult to support such a habit. Usually, the only way the addict can get that much money is through crime or prostitution. Thus crime associated with heroin addiction is not a direct effect of the drug, but stems from the need to support the habit. In fact, heroin is an extremely effective depressant, which markedly reduces such motivational states as hunger and sex.

How is it that this innocent-looking white powder can come to dominate the life of the abuser so completely? Within the first minute of heroin injection, there is a sudden, climactic rush of feeling that many users have compared to a sexual orgasm. This extremely pleasurable experience is followed by a high that is characterized by lethargy, emotional detachment, a sense of well-being, and deep feelings of contentment. To illustrate, a heroin abuser may spend hours before a TV set, watching the dancing images on the screen without becoming emotionally involved in the program content. But then comes the crushing aftermath. As the high begins to subside, so also does the sense of well-being. The euphoria of a moment before is replaced by gnawing feelings of apprehension and anxiety. The bizarre cycle culminates in an overwhelming sense of panic as the addict begins a frantic search for the next fix.

The victims of heroin addiction are legion—the addicts themselves, their families, and those they have robbed or otherwise brutalized in their quest for the "big H." In recent years another innocent victim of heroin addiction has come to light, the newborn infant of an addicted mother. Studies of infants born to heroin-addicted mothers have found that more than two-thirds start out life as addicts. Within 96 hours of birth, most will show signs of withdrawal, including extreme irritability, tremors, and vomiting. The incidence of withdrawal symptoms in the newborn depends on how long the mother has been addicted, on the amount of heroin she has taken, and on how close to delivery she was when she took her last dose (Zelson *et al.*, 1971). Traces of drugs taken as little as 10 minutes prior to delivery have been found in newborns.

## "Uppers" and "Downers"

Many of the dangerous drugs in use today are not restricted to the street-corner "pusher" as a source of distribution. They may be obtained legitimately through a doctor's prescription. In fact, one survey showed that about 22 percent of American adults obtained mood-changing drugs through conventional medical channels during 1970–1971 (Mellinger *et al.*, 1972). The main drugs of this sort that are in use today are "uppers" and "downers."

Uppers are stimulants, and include cocaine and the amphetamines (e.g., bennies, dexies, speed). They may or may not be addicting, but they are all habituating. They produce feelings of well-being, elation, and increased energy, and are generally taken to fight fatigue, alleviate mild depression, and curb appetite.

The use of amphetamines was widespread long before their dangers were recognized. Doctors routinely prescribed them for depression, lethargy, and overweight conditions. What is particularly insidious about these drugs is that the user rapidly builds up a tolerance and, within a short period of time, may be taking as much as 100 times his or her original dosage (Girdano and Girdano, 1976). As the dangers of amphetamines were recognized, restrictions were placed on their use, so that the number of those accidentally becoming dependent on or addicted to these drugs was curtailed. At present, amphetamines are obtained largely through illegal sources.

In the past, abusers of these drugs have included people who desired to perform beyond their physiological limits (e.g., athletes) and those who wanted to avoid the profound state of depression that commonly accompanies withdrawal. In more recent years, some individuals ("speed freaks") have started injecting amphetamines directly into their bloodstreams.

**The effects of amphetamine on the web spinning of an adult female spider are evident in this progression of photos.**

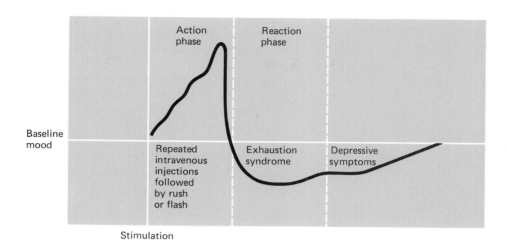

**Figure 7.11**
**The action and reaction phases of the speed cycle**

The action phase involves high levels of activity and mood elevation. Termination of drug use is followed by the reaction phase, which is characterized by exhaustion and depression. (National Clearing House for Drug Abuse Information, 1974)

When speed is injected, the first physical effect is a sudden rush or flash, followed by feelings of well-being and exaggerated activity. As the stimulating effects begin to wear off, the speed freak will again "shoot speed" in order to maintain the high. In fact, injections may be repeated many times in a single day. When continued injections are finally terminated, the reaction phase sets in. The individual lapses into a sleep that may last as long as two days. Upon awakening, the person passes into a severe depression that may continue for weeks. This cycle is shown in Fig. 7.11. Heavy users develop severe physical problems as well. Because they lose their desire to eat and sleep, they rapidly lose weight and become highly susceptible to infection. Viral hepatitis, caused by dirty syringes, is increasingly common. Speed kills.

Speed freaks are sometimes known as "crazies" because they frequently engage in meaningless compulsive activity that exhausts their excess energy. One group of "crazies" undertook a search for "the stone of stones" and dug until they had uncovered an enormous pile of rocks (Fiddle, 1968).

Downers, in contrast to uppers, are taken for their calming effects. The larger group of downers consists of the barbiturates (e.g., Seconal and Nembutal). They are among the drugs most widely prescribed by physicians. In low dosage levels, they are used to treat patients with uncomfortable levels of tension and anxiety. In higher dosages, they are prescribed for bedtime use for people suffering sleep disorders. Unfortunately, the barbiturates have a high abuse potential. A person who uses barbiturates commonly considers them "safe" because they are frequently prescribed by doctors. Nevertheless, they are both addicting and habituating. Moreover, an overdose or sudden withdrawal can lead to death. When taken in combination with alcohol or other drugs, even small amounts can become lethal. Thousand of deaths annually are attributable to barbiturates.

The illegal use of barbiturates and other sedative drugs, such as glutethimide and methaqualone, has been on the upswing in recent years. As two observers have noted,

> Because of the antianxiety and antitension qualities of the sedative hypnotics, their illegal use increased dramatically, and with their misuse and abuse, the dangers inherent in these drugs became apparent. It was found that they created tolerance . . . and psychic and physical dependence, and that abrupt withdrawal after chronic abuse would bring on an abstinence syndrome more severe than that caused by any other drug, because life-threatening convulsions accompanied withdrawal. (Dusek-Girdano and Girdano, 1980, p. 157)

It was largely the dangers of high abuse potential of barbiturates that led to the search for safer compounds which eventuated in the tranquilizers. The tranquilizers may be classified into two broad categories, major and minor substances. The major compounds, such as Thorazine and Reserpine, are used in mental hospitals for the treatment of severely disturbed patients. These appear to offer little danger of dependence or abuse and are not found on the street. The minor tranquilizers, such as Miltown, Equanil, Librium, and Valium, are prescribed for people suffering from tension and anxiety. A greater number of prescriptions are written for Librium and Valium than for any other psychoactive drugs. Unfortunately, like the barbiturates, they have a high potential for abuse. They are depressants that work on the limbic system, which, as we previously saw (Chapter 5), is involved in emotional behavior. They can lead to death from overdose.

Dusek-Girdano and Girdano note:

> The all-out prescribing of tranquilizers has its impact on the street-drug scene in two ways—directly, by supplying legitimate drugs (via theft) to the black market system, and indirectly, through parental example of attitudes toward drugs. Use of illicit drugs by teenagers has been shown to parallel their parents' use of tranquilizers, with children being especially influenced by their mothers' use of these drugs. (Dusek-Girdano and Girdano, 1980, pp. 158–159)

## Summary

1. There are a number of occasions when our mental functioning differs from the normal flow of conscious activities. This reminds us of the fact that there are a number of different states of consciousness.

2. Some of these states are self-induced, others are achieved through the use of chemical agents, and yet others represent natural processes.

3. Several different lines of inquiry suggest that, for most people, the left cerebral hemisphere prevails during normal waking activities. This hemisphere seems to be specialized for linguistic, logical, sequential mental activities. The right hemisphere, on the other hand, appears to be nonlinguistic and perceives events as wholes rather than as parts. A strong case has been made for the view

that some states of consciousness may represent right hemispheric activities.

4. Sleep is composed of four stages that run cyclically. Because of the rapid eye movements in sleepers in stage one, this stage is referred to as REM sleep. Stages two through four are also called NREM sleep.

5. REM sleep, which occurs every 90 minutes, is a period of dreaming. It has been proposed that this kind of sleep provides a restorative function; if an individual is deprived of such sleep on occasion, the body makes up for this loss with increased REM (REM rebound) on subsequent nights.

6. Common disturbances of sleep include insomnia, narcolepsy, and night terrors.

7. In meditation, an effort is made to tune out responses to the external world and to tune in levels of consciousness that are normally overridden by the dominant mode. Many benefits have been claimed for meditation, including a sense of inner peace and the abandonment of drugs as a means of achieving different states of consciousness. These and other claims are the subject of intensive investigation.

8. Much research in contemporary psychology is concerned with biofeedback. It is possible to achieve "voluntary" control over many "involuntary" behaviors when information is provided (feedback is given) about the status of the responses.

9. Biofeedback techniques have been used to control the production of alpha brain waves. Although alpha states have been identified with relaxation and inner calm, it is possible that some of the widely reported effects are the result of suggestion.

10. Hypnosis represents a state of consciousness that has been practiced for at least 7000 years. Various current theorists regard it as a trance state, or role playing, or a state in which cognitive controls are segregated from one another. Although superficially resembling sleep, it has more in common with the waking state.

11. Individuals may achieve various states of consciousness by eating, drinking, sniffing, smoking, or injecting various chemical substances.

12. Alcohol is a depressant which, by interfering with judgment, frequently imbues the consumer with a false sense of well-being and improved capabilities.

13. Today LSD is the most well known and frequently used hallucinogenic drug. The use of LSD is accompanied by marked physical and behavioral changes.

14. PCP (Angel Dust), which has many of the effects of the hallucinogens, is growing in popularity, but appears to pose some additional dangers to users, as compared to hallucinogens.

15. Marijuana is a mild hallucinogen that produces alterations in sensation, mood, emotions, and perceptions. Other stronger hallucinogens are far less predictable in their outcomes, perhaps partly because filler materials may often produce effects of their own.

16. Heroin users get "hooked" on the white powder, in part because it produces a climactic rush of feeling that has been compared to a sexual orgasm.

17. Many mood-altering drugs can be obtained through legal, medical channels. The most common kinds of such drugs are uppers (stimulants), which create a feeling of elation and increased energy, and downers (sedatives and tranquilizers), which are taken for their calming effects. Unfortunately, these drugs can also cause habituation or addiction in users.

## Terms to Remember

| | | |
|---|---|---|
| Hallucination | Mantra | Synesthesia |
| Rapid eye movement (REM) | Biofeedback | Drug user |
| Night terrors | Alpha waves | Drug abuser |
| REM rebound | Hypnosis | Tolerance |
| Insomnia | Psychoactive drugs | Addiction |
| Meditation | Hallocinogens | Habituation |

# MOTIVATION
# AND EMOTIONS

Motivation is unquestionably one of the most important variables affecting behavior. Indeed, most psychologists would agree that *all* behavior is motivated. This idea is so generally accepted that references to motivation occur frequently in everyday conversation. We constantly hear ourselves and others questioning the underlying causes of behavior: "Why does John drink so much?" "Why does Jane want to do such a thing?" "What are you trying to prove?"

Although the questions are easy to raise, the answers are not readily apparent. In trying to pinpoint the motives underlying any given behavior, we are often tempted to jump to conclusions. For example, we see a woman go to a refrigerator, open it, and scan its contents. Her behavior suggests that she is motivated by hunger. But when she produces a container of cold water and proceeds to pour herself a drink, we must revise our inference and conclude that her behavior was motivated by thirst.

To complicate matters, people whose behavior appears on the surface to be similar may, in fact, be prompted by a wide variety of **motives.** Some students study introductory psychology because they are curious about the subject, some are trying to solve their person problems, and some are just fulfilling course requirements.

Because motives cannot be directly observed, we must infer their operation from behavior or from our knowledge of the circumstances accompanying that behavior. Motives have two distinct functions. They *energize*, or activate, behavior, and they *direct* that behavior toward specific goals. As we become increasingly hungry, we become more active and also more likely to direct our activities toward goal objects that will satisfy this hunger—specifically, food.

The language for describing motivated behavior is still not settled. For our purposes, it is convenient to distinguish between two groups of motives: **biological drives,** in which there is clearly a physiological basis such as hunger and thirst; and **learned motives,** those which appear to be acquired from experience. Consider newborn children, whose physiological needs account for all their behavior. They require food, sleep, and water; they must breathe, excrete wastes, and avoid pain or discomfort. As children develop and begin to interact with their environment, learned motives play an increasingly important role in determining their behavior. They seek out playmates on their own, develop interests and skills, and strive for independence from their parents.

There is a third group of motivations, called **stimulus needs,** which function like biological drives but for which no underlying physiological bases have been found. Nor do they appear to be learned. They are inferred from behavior that appears to be motivated by a need to be active and stimulated and to explore and manipulate the environment.

We are often unaware of underlying motivations that operate in ourselves and others. The literature of psychoanalysis provides many examples of the unconscious motivation of behavior. A man who takes care of his invalid father may be so protective that we are led to conclude that his behavior is motivated by love and concern for his father's health. Nevertheless, he may be bothered by a recurrent nightmare in which his father, or a person very much like his father, is repeatedly hurt or killed. Such evidence may lead us to suspect that he harbors considerable un-

---

**Motive**
A condition that serves to energize and direct behavior toward specific classes of goal objects.

**Biological drive**
A motive that stems from the physiological state of the organism, for example, hunger.

**Learned motive**
A motivational state in which learned, rather than biological, factors appear to be the primary determinant.

**Stimulus needs**
A class of motivational states, involving a need for stimulation, for which no underlying physiological basis has been discovered.

conscious hostility toward his father. Clinicians commonly look for indirect indications of unconscious motivation. Such information may be found in the content of some dreams.

People often behave in ways that they themselves do not understand. The explanations they give may seem correct to them; however, a skilled observer may deduce other motives underlying their behavior. Students who claim that they do not study because grades are unimportant may, in fact, have unconscious anxiety about their ability. If they were to study and get poor grades, they would be forced to face the issue of their own incompetence. We shall discuss unconscious motivation at greater length in Chapters 13 and 14.

## MEASUREMENT OF MOTIVATIONAL STATES

It stands to reason that because motives cannot be directly observed, they cannot be directly measured. Nevertheless, four techniques have been developed by which we can measure the strength of a motivational state indirectly.

Motives play an important part in activating behavior and directing it toward a goal. (a) The 1924 Olympic sprinter Eric Leddell was motivated to win by his strong Christian faith and his desire to offer his best for God. (b) Harold Abrahams, Leddell's competitor in the Olympics, was motivated by a strong desire to succeed as a Jew in what he felt was an anti-Semitic world.

(a)                                      (b)

## General Activity Level

We have mentioned that one of the functions of motives is to energize behavior. Thus we can expect that increased motivation will lead to increased restless activity. Because it is usually not practical to observe and measure human activity levels, many of the laboratory studies on motivation use lower animals in situations specially designed for measurement of activity levels. One of the most commonly used devices is the activity wheel, which records running behavior. Various experiments have shown that the more highly motivated the animal is—for example, the longer it is deprived of food—the more it will run. Of course, this observation holds true only within certain limits. If the deprivation is extended over too long a period of time, the animal's activity will diminish as a result of its weakened condition.

## Performance Rate

A habitual gambler will spend hours carefully going over the daily racing form and making selections from it; a baseball enthusiast will spend every spare moment calculating batting averages and studying the latest statistics on individual players and favorite teams; a politician running for office will appear almost indefatigable, shaking thousands of hands, kissing countless babies, and delivering speeches wherever there is an audience to listen. What do all these examples have in common? In each, an individual is responding at a high rate to satisfy a strong motivational state.

Once an organism has learned a response to satisfy a motive, its rate of responding can be used to measure the strength of that motivation. Rate-of-response measures are commonly employed in the laboratory. For instance, a rat that has learned to press a bar to receive food will increase its rate of bar-pressing with increased hunger. Figure 8.1 summarizes the results of one study relating rate of response to increased levels of hunger.

## Overcoming an Obstacle

You have probably observed that a highly motivated individual will sometimes endure a great deal of hardship in order to reach a desired goal. For example, an aspiring concert pianist will endure long and arduous hours of practice in order to achieve his or her vocational goal. A person who hasn't had a bite to eat all day may be willing to drive miles late at night in a snowstorm to get a hamburger. High levels of motivation for a particular goal often enable people to overcome obstacles that stand between them and their goal.

In many laboratory studies, animals are confronted with obstacles that obstruct their goal-directed activities. This obstruction frequently consists of an electrified grid that they must cross to reach their goals (see Fig. 8.2). To illustrate, rats will cross an extremely painful electrified grid to get a pedal that delivers electrical stimulation to the pleasure centers of the brain. Yet, no matter how hungry, not a single rat has ever been willing to cross the same grid to get food ("Mysteries of the Mind," 1979). The stronger the motivation, the more pain the animals will accept to satisfy that motivation.

## Selection Among Goals

In most real-life situations several motivations are operating at once, and behavior is generally determined by the strongest one. Suppose you are motivated to complete a term paper that is due in the morning. Suppose also that you missed your evening meal and are extremely hungry. To make matters worse, you have not had much sleep the past few nights. Which motive will you act on? Presumably, your behavior will be determined by whatever motive is strongest. By observing your behavior, we can assess the relative strength of competing motives.

In the laboratory situation, the relative strength of different motives can be determined by observing which of several goals the organism selects. A rat that has learned to turn left for food and to turn right for water will make whichever response will lead to satisfaction of the motive that is dominant at that particular time (see Fig. 8.3).

## BIOLOGICAL DRIVES

There are certain motivational states that are vital to the survival of all organisms, including humans. These *biological drives* result from the operation of physiological factors, manifest themselves in the same way within a given species, and are not learned. The satisfaction of such drives as hunger, thirst, sleep, and avoidance of pain is essential to the survival of the individual organism. On the other hand, the sex drive may go unsatisfied within an individual organism without threatening its survival. But satisfaction of this drive is crucial if the species is to survive.

## Hunger Drive

Suppose we notice that a little girl who has not eaten for a relatively long while becomes increasingly restless and directs more of her behavior toward finding food. She rummages through the kitchen, hunting for the leftovers from last night's dinner. After she eats, there is a decrease in both her restlessness and her food-seeking behavior. Although we couldn't observe this child's hunger drive directly, we could infer its presence. We observed the condition—the period of food deprivation—which led to the arousal of the drive. We also noted both the *activation* and the *directedness* of the ensuing behavior. Her behavior was directed toward a specific class of goal objects, that is, food. Finally, we observed her eating. This final response in the sequence of goal-directed behaviors, called the **consummatory response,** led to a decrease in the girl's drive level. We could infer the decreased level by observing the decrease in her restlessness and in her food-seeking behavior.

**Consummatory response** The final response in a sequence of goal-directed behaviors.

For a long time it was assumed that the hunger drive was aroused by local physiological causes such as stomach contractions (hunger pangs). But much recent evidence indicates that arousal can occur even when there are no stomach contractions.

It is now well established that the hypothalamus (see Chapter 5) is involved in the arousal of the hunger drive, as well as many other biological drives. There are several lines of evidence for this conclusion: (1) Damage to various areas of the hypothalamus leads to changes in moti-

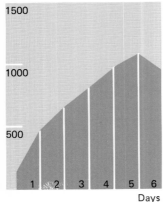

Figure 8.1
**Rate of responding as a measure of drive**

A rat had been trained to press a bar to obtain food. When food was withheld, the rate of bar-pressing increased until the fifth day. After that, the weakening effects of starvation caused the response rate to decrease. (Heron and Skinner, 1937)

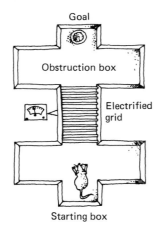

Figure 8.2
The animal must cross an electrified grid in order to reach the goal. The number and intensity of shocks it will accept provide a measure of the strength of the animal's motivation.

vated behavior; (2) different areas in the hypothalamus are involved with different drives; and (3) **excitatory** and **inhibitory nuclei** that control motivation have been identified in the hypothalamus (that is, damage to a specific area of the hypothalamus leads sometimes to activation of some kind of motivated behavior and sometimes to cessation of that behavior).

In the case of hunger, two distinct centers have been identified in the hypothalamus. The *excitatory nucleus* controls the onset of eating behavior. Electrical stimulation of this area causes a satiated rat to start eating; destruction of it causes a rat to stop eating entirely, and finally to die of starvation (Miller, 1958). The other area is called the *inhibitory nucleus.* Electrical stimulation of the area causes a hungry rat to stop eating; destruction of it leads to a dramatic increase in eating behavior (Ehrlich, 1964). Figure 8.4 shows a photograph of a normal rat alongside a rat in which the inhibitory nucleus of the hypothalamus was destroyed.

The results of one study suggested that the effect of the hypothalamic lesions may have been to interfere with fibers transmitting impulses between two different areas of the brain (Ungerstedt, 1971). More recent studies, however, have shown that the effects of hypothalamic lesions are obtained even when these fibers are not interfered with (Stricker and Zigmond, 1976; Grossman *et al.*, 1978).

Both of these nuclei as well as other brain structures (Balagura, 1973) seem to be responsive to the physiological condition of the organism. When biochemical factors produce a state of imbalance in the blood (such as occurs during food deprivation), the excitatory nucleus of the hypothalamus is activated. There is evidence that blood chemistry has an effect on hunger: If satiated animals receive blood transfusions from hungry animals, they show behavioral manifestations of hunger.

It has been proposed that these two nuclei may regulate food intake much as a thermostat regulates temperature. Rather than responding to temperature, however, they react to the levels of free fatty acids in the blood (Sclafani and Kluge, 1974; Sclafani, 1976). When the **lipostat** turns on, it is signaling a weight loss at the lower limit. Thus the organism eats. When the weight gain is approaching the upper limit, the lipostat turns off and the organism stops eating. Sclafani has also proposed that the palatability of the food affects the settings on the lipostat. When the food is tasty, the upper setting is raised so that the organism will eat more. Conversely, when the food is not particularly appealing, the lower set point is decreased. As a result, the organism will undergo greater weight loss before the eating mechanism is turned on (Sclafani, 1976).

Knowing the role of blood chemistry and of the hypothalamus in activating eating behavior, we might be tempted to ask whether obese humans may overeat because of chemical imbalances in the blood or malfunctions of the hypothalamus. In a few instances, one or both of these factors may account for obesity. But present evidence indicates that obesity in most people is determined by a variety of learned, rather than physiological, factors. Obese people do overeat, but not in response to physiological stimuli.

A series of studies on obesity supports the view that obese people are more responsive to external than to physiological stimuli in regulating their food intake. If obese and normal people are given plain, dull, and

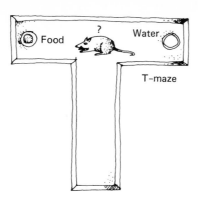

Figure 8.3  If a rat has learned to turn left for food and right for water, and is then deprived of food and water, the goal object it selects presumably indicates which motivational state is stronger.

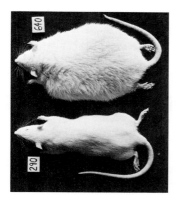

Figure 8.4
**Destruction of the inhibitory nucleus of the hypothalamus leads to excessive eating and subsequent obesity.**

uninteresting food (i.e., food with low palatability), the normal people eat amounts appropriate to their physiological state, whereas obese people eat almost nothing. On the other hand, when food is especially attractive (high palatability), obese people eat huge amounts, regardless of their physiological state. Normal and underweight people eat amounts more nearly appropriate to their physiological states (Schachter, 1965).

One of the most potent environmental cues for eating behavior is time. During waking hours, there is usually a four- to six-hour interval between meals. In one study, subjects were deceived into believing that it was closer to mealtime than it actually was. Presumably, if obese individuals react more to external than to internal cues, they should eat more when they believe it is mealtime, even though they may not be physiologically "hungry" (Schachter and Gross, 1968).

The investigators manipulated two clocks, one running at twice normal speed, the other at half normal speed. Each subject arrived at 5:00 P.M. to participate in an experiment that supposedly concerned "the relationship of base levels of autonomic reactivity to personality factors." They were taken to a windowless room that contained only electronic equipment and a clock. Electrodes were attached to their wrists, their watch was removed ("so that it will not get gummed up with electrode jelly"), and the experimenter left the room for 30 minutes.

Two experimental conditions were employed. In one, the experimenter returned when the clock read 5:20. In the other condition, the experimenter returned when the clock read 6:05 (normal dinnertime for most of the subjects). The experimenter was carrying a box of crackers as he entered the room. He invited the subjects to help themselves after the electrodes were removed. Then he gave the subject a questionnaire to fill out and again left the room, leaving the subject alone with the box of crackers.

The experimenters predicted that obese subjects would eat more crackers when the clock read 6:05 than when it read 5:20, because the eating behavior of obese people is presumably triggered by external environmental cues. On the other hand, normal individuals should eat about the same amount regardless of what time they thought it was, because normal people presumably respond to internal physiological cues. The results are shown in Fig. 8.5. The obese subjects, as predicted, ate about twice as much when they thought it was 6:05. The normal subjects,

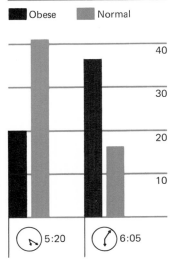

Figure 8.5

**Obesity and eating**

When obese subjects thought it was 6:05 P.M., they consumed twice as many crackers as when they thought it was 5:20 P.M. Normal subjects ate fewer crackers when they thought it was 6:05, presumably not to spoil their dinner.

on the other hand, ate less at 6:05. The experimenters attributed the unexpected behavior of the normal subjects to a desire not to spoil their dinners. Thus it seems that obese individuals must eat when they think it is time to eat, whereas normal subjects are capable of exercising restraint. The results of this study indicate that, contrary to expectations, obese people are not the only ones whose eating behavior is influenced by external factors. Clearly, the normal individuals were also influenced by the external clock. In their case, however, the clock served as a cue to inhibit eating behavior.

Another factor in obesity appears to be daily exercise. In a study comparing both the caloric intake and the daily exercise of overweight and normal girls, it was surprisingly found that overweight girls consumed several hundred calories *less* than their normal-weight counterparts. The difference was that the normal girls engaged in about three times as much daily exercise (Thomas and Mayer, 1973).

The moral of all this research on obesity is clear. If you are overweight and wish to reduce, do not look for quick and magical solutions. Engage in plenty of exercise and try to pay more attention to what your body is telling you about its needs. Also consider the possibility of making high-calorie foods less accessible, limiting the number of locations in which you eat, and cutting down on ''seconds'' by keeping the serving platters off the table (Coates and Thorensen, 1978). The Dieting Rehabilitation Clinic at Duke University has enjoyed considerable success in helping the obese lose weight by applying behavior principles (Musante, 1976). Clients are restricted to 700 calories per day, but the total eating time is increased by use of the following devices: waiting a minute before beginning to eat, putting the eating utensils down between each bite, and slowing down the rate of chewing. The reason for increasing the eating time is to permit the brain to signal the stomach that you are full. This takes approximately 20 minutes. Of those clients who remained in the program between 6 and 11 months, almost 62 percent lost 40 pounds or more, and 85 percent lost at least 20 pounds.

Although hunger is a biological drive and therefore unlearned, its mode of satisfaction is influenced in humans by many learned factors. For example, there are striking differences in the kinds of food people choose when hungry. These choices are strongly affected by cultural factors. Moslems and Orthodox Jews follow religious restrictions against eating pork or shellfish. Many, but not all, societies have a taboo against eating human flesh.

The following story was told by a friend of the authors', a former citizen of Pakistan and a minister of the Moslem faith:

> *Following a long period of trying, American missionaries were finally successful in converting two of my acquaintances, a husband and wife, to Christianity. The missionaries were, of course, delighted, since Moslems are not easily converted. They held a gala affair to celebrate their achievement. Following a veritable banquet, the missionary announced, ''Congratulations, you have just consumed your first Christian meal— pork!'' At this point, the newly converted husband and wife asked to be excused. They proceeded to become violently ill.*

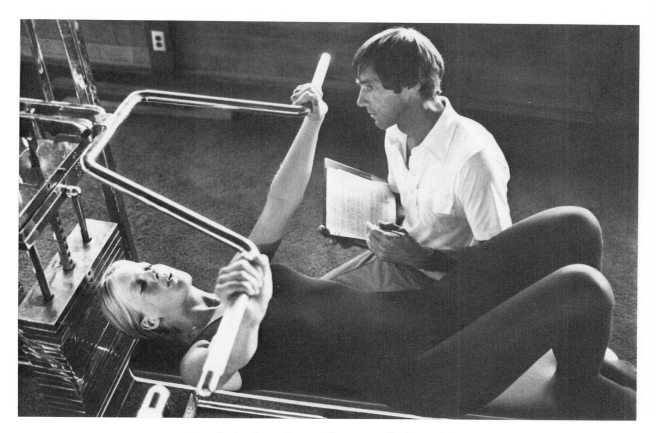

Exercise has been shown to be a very effective weight-loss aid, and more and more Americans are participating in exercise and fitness programs. The woman shown here tests her muscular strength on the bench press at a California fitness center.

The hunger drive in humans is influenced by many other learned factors. (See Box 8.1 for an illustration of a case of undereating in which emotional factors are the underlying cause.) We like to have our food prepared and served in a special way; we consider certain foods to be appropriate for breakfast but not for dinner; we enjoy eating in certain settings and with certain people, despite the fact that the hunger drive can be satisfied in virtually any setting. Learned factors may become so dominant that an individual will prefer to starve rather than eat food that has become repulsive as a result of cultural learning.

## Thirst Drive

Anyone who has been deprived of water for a long time will remember how intense thirst can become. Prolonged water deprivation leads to widespread physical manifestations such as nausea, impaired breathing, and dryness of the mouth, tongue, and throat.

As with hunger, earlier theories about thirst stressed local factors such as dryness of the throat. We now know that the hypothalamus is also involved in the activation of the thirst drive. When a salt solution is injected into the hypothalamus of satiated goats, they will drink water and even urine (Anderson and McCann, 1955). If a tiny quantity of dis-

## BOX 8.1

### A Case of Anorexia Nervosa

The woman in these pictures was diagnosed as suffering from anorexia nervosa, a disorder characterized by severe loss of appetite and weight due to emotional factors. At the age of 18 (left), she weighed 120 pounds, but over a period of years her weight dropped to 47 pounds (center). The photo at right, in which she weighed 88 pounds, was taken after she had undergone behavior therapy.

Treatment of anorexia nervosa is often difficult, and about 10 percent of anorexic patients literally starve themselves to death. The disorder—much more common among females than males—can occur from childhood to adulthood but is seen most frequently among adolescents. The reasons behind the refusal of food hold the key to the etiological puzzle in these cases. As noted above, emotional factors are typically involved, and this view is not negated by the fact that there is often a prior nutritional disorder, for both disorders may result from similar underlying causes. Often obesity precedes anorexia nervosa. Here, the individual reverses previous eating habits, going from one extreme to another, perhaps in reaction to teasing about being "fat." In anorexic children refusal to eat may be associated with unbearable hurt or a desire to get even with parents for perceived mistreatment. Factors implicated among other age groups include depression and sexual conflicts. The latter ap-

pear to lead to an association between eating, sex, and fear of impregnation.

In the treatment of anorexia nervosa, medical procedures typically are required in combination with psychotherapeutic procedures. Liquid feeding—intravenously or by tube—may be indicated for persons whom the disorder has rendered too weak to eat; and with children, forced feeding is sometimes resorted to. Other procedures commonly utilized include chemotherapy, individual psychotherapy, and behavior therapy, with the latter appearing to offer the most promise.

In the case of the woman pictured here, Bachrach, Erwin, and Mohr (1965) utilized a program of environmental control designed to reinforce and shape eating behavior, while denying her pleasures when she did not eat. The program proved effective, and a follow-up report revealed that the woman was working as a nurse at the university hospital where she had undergone treatment.

Based on Bachrach, Erwin, and Mohr (1965); Crisp (1970); Halmi, Powers, and Cunningham (1975); Liebman, Minuchin, and Baker (1974); See (1975); Szyrynski (1973); and Warren (1968).

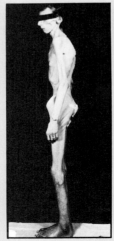

tilled water is injected into the hypothalamus of thirsty cats, they stop drinking, as if they were satiated (Miller, 1957).

In humans thirst, like hunger, is influenced by a variety of learned social and cultural factors. Most Americans prefer to drink cold water even though the temperature of the water has nothing to do with its capacity to satisfy thirst. Moreover, water is by no means the only liquid used to quench thirst, and different societies vary in the liquids they choose for quenching thirst. Nor is drinking necessarily associated with arousal of the thirst drive; there are many occasions when drinking is part of a religious or social ritual.

## Sleep Drive

From time to time various people have proposed that sleep is a form of behavior which, like an undesirable habit, can be broken. To prove their point, they have tried to remain awake for extremely long periods of time. All such efforts have been failures. As the period of sleep deprivation increased, the persons became increasingly irritable and reported sounds and sights that were not physically present. They had to be constantly stimulated and prodded in order to stay awake. Eventually, all efforts to ward off sleep were to no avail, and they fell into deep and prolonged sleep.

The truth is that sleep is not a habit but a drive state, and it shares many of the attributes of other biological drives, like thirst and hunger. Satisfaction of the sleep drive is necessary for the survival of the organism. The longer an organism is deprived of sleep, the greater the need for it is. Deprivation leads to increased irritability. Once the sleep drive is satisfied, the organism will usually not go to sleep again until a certain amount of deprivation exists.

Certain brain centers are intimately involved in sleep and wakefulness. Like the dual mechanism of hunger, there appear to be both excitatory and inhibitory centers for sleep. The hypothalamus, pons, and reticular activating system appear to be involved, but the precise relationships among these structures as they pertain to sleep have not been worked out (Brown, 1976). Destruction of the excitatory, or wakefulness, center leads to profound sleep, from which the organism can be aroused only by very strong stimulation. Destruction of the inhibitory, or sleep, center keeps the organism in a constant state of wakefulness. Further evidence that sleep involves brain centers had come from studies of Siamese twins who share a common blood supply but have separate brains. It has been observed that each twin has separate waking and sleeping cycles.

Most adults need from 6 to 9 hours of sleep each night. The usual pattern is approximately 16 hours of wakefulness during the day and 8 hours of sleep at night; however, like other drives, sleep is subject to modification by learned factors. For example, people who work at night jobs are able to sleep during the day. People in occupations that require shifting back and forth between nighttime and daytime duty are able to do so without great difficulty, although they are often irritable just after each shift from night to day duty or vice versa. It is interesting that in northern Norway, where the sun shines day and night for weeks at a time in summer and does not appear at all during the winter, the population maintains the same pattern of sleep and wakefulness throughout the year.

## Drive to Avoid Pain

The drive to avoid pain is one of the most compelling in all animals. Humans have developed highly sophisticated techniques to eliminate or reduce the intensity of pain and discomfort. Few of us are willing to sit in the dentist's chair without novocaine or some other pain-deadening aid. Indeed, anesthesiology has become a vital specialty in the practice of medicine. In addition, we are inundated with advertisements promising relief of headache, neuralgia, rheumatism, arthritis, and many other kinds of bodily aches and pains.

What do you suppose it would be like to go through life without ever experiencing the throb of a toothache, a migraine headache, or a plain "bellyache"? We might be tempted to regard such a pain-free existence as a life of bliss. But in fact, studies of individuals born without the capacity to experience pain show that their lives are fraught with constant peril. Without pain, virtually all of the cues that we rely on as danger signals are absent. In rare cases, children are born without any sense of pain. If such children were accidentally to touch a hot burner on an electric stove, they would not withdraw their hand from the burner immediately, as normal children would. Instead of receiving a minor first-degree burn, these children could suffer extensive tissue damage from such an incident, perhaps ultimately resulting in serious infection or even the loss of fingers. Many such children do not survive childhood because of their inability to recognize common danger signals arising from within, such as an inflamed appendix.

One 19-year-old girl who was congenitally insensitive to pain was studied extensively by a group of physicians and psychologists. According to her parents, she had never experienced pain, despite numerous accidents resulting in burns, cuts, and fractures. Indeed, she had at one time fractured her ankle in an automobile accident and attended a dance immediately afterward. She did not realize that anything was wrong until later, when she found that her swollen foot would not fit into her shoe (Cohen *et al.*, 1955). She eventually was involved in a fatal accident related to her condition.

Other research has shown that people who survive childhood in spite of congenital insensitivity to pain avoid injuries by learning to recognize other cues (Sternbach, 1963).

## Sex Drive

The satisfaction of the sex drive, unlike the hunger and thirst drives, is not vital to the survival of the organism, but is of utmost importance to the survival of the species. Yet the sex drive does have certain characteristics in common with the other biological drives. When sexually aroused, the organism becomes more active and restless. It learns to make a variety of responses to gain access to a receptive partner. When sexual activity has been completed, the organism shows many of the usual characteristics of satiation. In lower animals, most of the behaviors associated with sex are unlearned and represent unconditioned responses to unconditioned stimuli. Sex hormones secreted by the testes in males and the ovaries in females play an important role in the arousal of the sex drive. When the sex glands of lower animals are removed (by castration—removal of the testicles—in males, spaying in females) before the animals achieve sexual maturity (puberty), the sexual behavior characteristic of the mature animal never emerges. But if removal takes place after sexual maturity, normal sexual behavior continues for a short period in most animals and then disappears. Normal sexual activity can be restored by injecting male sex hormones into a castrated male animal and female sex hormones into a spayed female animal. It is possible to reverse sexual roles by injecting female hormones into a male animal that was castrated before sexual maturity (Whalen and Edwards, 1966).

The effects of removing sex glands are much more variable in humans than in other animals. Castration before puberty sometimes prevents the development of the sexual behavior characteristic of the mature human male and sometimes does not. Castration after the attainment of sexual maturity may have varying effects on sexual behavior: It may decrease or remain the same in some individuals, or increase in others. In women the effects of loss of hormonal functioning (as in menopause) or removal of the uterus (as in a hysterectomy) are equally variable. In some women sexual activity increases after menopause or hysterectomy, possibly because they no longer fear becoming pregnant.

The topic of human sexuality is examined further in Chapters 11 and 14.

## Stimulus Needs

**Hallucination**
A sensory impression in the absence of an appropriate environmental stimulus.

**Sensory deprivation**
A condition in which the individual receives a minimum of sensory stimulation; this condition sometimes leads to hallucinations.

At any given moment the waking organism is bombarded by an indescribably large number of physical stimuli. Have you ever wondered what would happen if we were cut off from all or most of these stimuli? Imagine that you are in a bed in a soundproof room, wearing goggles that allow diffuse light to pass through but remove all patterned vision. In addition, you are wearing gloves that restrict your sense of touch. How long would you last in that situation? What effects would it have on your behavior? If you are like the many undergraduates who have participated in studies of this sort, you would probably last only a few days, even if you were paid a large amount of money each day. In addition, your ability to solve standard psychological problems would be impaired. Most strikingly, with increased exposure to this situation, you would undergo dramatic psychological changes. You might become irritable, begin to **hallucinate,** and experience other changes similar to those occurring in emotional disorders. Figure 8.6 illustrates one type of apparatus used in **sensory-deprivation** studies.

Experimental findings from sensory-deprivation studies strongly suggest that organized, meaningful sensory stimulation is necessary for normal brain functioning. Apparently the brain requires stimulation from the

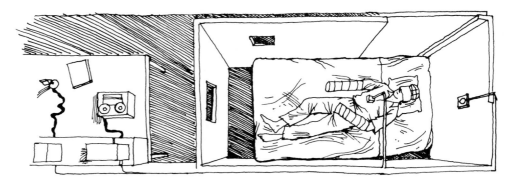

Figure 8.6    **A subject in a sensory-deprivation study is deprived of virtually all sensory stimuli while lying on his back in a soundproofed chamber.**

environment. If the environment fails to provide it, the brain will manufacture its own stimulation in the form of hallucinations and fantasies. The scientists who planned the Apollo missions were aware of this problem and made certain that the astronauts had adequate visual and auditory stimulation.

Not only do we require a certain amount of stimulation for normal functioning, but we actively seek out new forms of stimulation. The need for varied stimulation has been demonstrated with many different organisms, including humans. Rats will spend a long time exploring a new environment. Birds may approach a strange object even though it is po-

Figure 8.7    **Monkeys will learn responses and continue to work for the reward of visual stimulation. Here we see a monkey who has learned to push open a window to see a toy train in operation.**

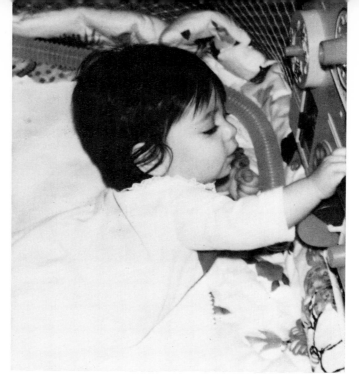

Figure 8.8    An infant shows an almost insatiable curiosity. The five-month-old baby in this photograph will spend many hours playing with a toy for the sole purpose of visual, auditory, and tactual stimulation.

tentially threatening to their lives. Monkeys will learn to manipulate and open a latch when the reward is some form of visual stimulation (see Fig. 8.7). Human infants spend most of their waking hours exploring and manipulating their environment. They are drawn toward any object that is colorful, makes noise, or provides distinctive tactile experiences (see Fig. 8.8). Adults frequently take great pains to set up elaborate light shows and multichannel stereo systems to provide themselves with new and varied stimulation.

Many studies have demonstrated that humans show a preference for patterns and experiences that are variable and unpredictable. In one study, human adults were asked to look at a series of pairs of animal pictures (see Fig. 8.9). One member of the pair of pictures was the same on every trial; the other member was changed from trial to trial. The subjects spent more time looking at the changing picture than at the recurring picture (Berlyne, 1958).

Another aspect of stimulus variability is the *complexity* of the stimulus patterns. Figure 8.10 shows several pairs of patterns in which the right-hand member is more complex than the left-hand member. Adults typically spend more time looking at the more complex of the two patterns.

The need for varied stimulation has obvious survival value for the organism. If an animal does not explore the world around it, how can it find the sources of food? How can it learn what areas are dangerous and must be avoided?

Why do some scientists spend hours in their offices or laboratories, skip meals, miss sleep, and generally risk messing up their social lives beyond all hopes of repair? A skeptic might answer, "The lure of the Nobel Prize." But most scientific investigations are tedious, and the re-

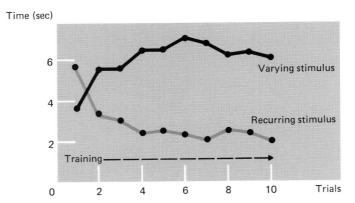

Figure 8.9     **Adult subjects spent more time looking at pictures that changed on every trial (varying stimulus) than at pictures that remained the same on each trial (recurring stimulus). (Berlyne, 1958)**

searchers know that their contributions will probably amount to little more than a single brick in a skyscraper. Nevertheless, the search goes on.

To varying degrees, all humans have an urge to explore their environment and a curiosity about the unknown. The infant in her crib reaching for the mobile hanging above her head, the youth tinkering with the carburetor of his car in order to improve gasoline mileage, the middle-aged couple scouring the valleys in a remote wilderness in search of a rare flower—all exemplify the need to stimulate the cognitive capabilities of the individual.

If farmers do not explore new techniques for planting and harvesting crops, how can they increase production? If veterinarians refuse to try something different when animals are otherwise destined to die, will they be better prepared when similar cases come up? Our need for varied experiences thrusts us into situations that increase our knowledge of the world about us and prepare us to adapt to suddenly changed circumstances. The great achievements of our species have been in response to an insatiable need to know.

Figure 8.10

**Several pairs of stimulus patterns commonly used to investigate preferences for stimulus patterns that vary in complexity**

**The right-hand member of each is more complex than the left-hand member. (Berlyne, 1958)**

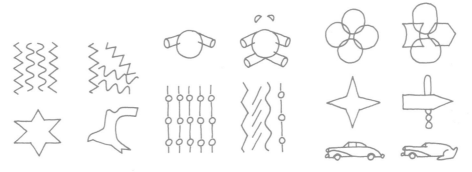

## LEARNED MOTIVATION

There are many motivational states, particularly in humans, in which learned rather than biological factors appear to be the primary determinants. As we have seen, the satisfaction of basic biological drives dominates the experience of newborn children. As they develop and their basic physiological needs are routinely satisfied, learned motives assume a larger and more dominant role in their lives. Humans are preeminently social beings; that is, most of our behavior occurs in a social environment and is, of course, largely shaped by that environment, which includes other individuals, institutions, cultures, values, and ideals. Learned motives are the result of the interaction of the individual with the social environment.

Why do some people strive so desperately for good grades, political office, or social approval? Why do some people stay "tied to their mothers' apron strings" throughout their lifetimes? Why are some teachers so concerned about the outcome of student evaluations? These questions assume the existence of underlying motivational states. It is obvious, however, that they cannot be answered by reference to any of the biological drives or stimulus needs we have already discussed. For answers we must look to the motives that people learn in the course of their interaction with their environment.

Earlier, we discussed some of the measures used to infer the presence and intensity of motivations. When dealing with biological drives such as hunger and thirst, we can be fairly sure that our inferences are correct. Learned motives present more difficulties. There is little agreement on the definition of some of these motives. Even when psychologists can agree on how to define a specific learned motive, they do not always agree on how it should be measured.

There have been many attempts to catalogue learned motives. Some lists are extremely lengthy, and very few agree with one another in all particulars. We shall be discussing some of the more widely accepted of these motives.

**Aggression**
Physical or verbal behavior intended to inflict harm or injury.

**Anxiety**
Fear reaction to unknown or unidentified stimuli; a premonition that something bad will occur.

## Aggression

The question whether **aggression** is a learned motive or a biological drive is still subject to much debate. Although all of the facts are not in, much of the available evidence suggests that in our culture aggression may arise directly as a result of rewarding aggressive behavior, indirectly as the result of modeling the aggressive behavior of others (the aggressive behavior of parents when inflicting corporal punishment, for example, and that of characters portrayed on television and in the movies), and indirectly as a reaction to the frustration of other motivations. We explore the topic of aggression in greater detail in Chapter 9.

## Anxiety

**Anxiety** is one of the most complex concepts in psychology. It is at once an emotional state and a motivational state. As an emotional state, it is frequently described as a vague sort of activation with accompanying undesirable feelings. It also involves physiological activation (often de-

It is unclear whether aggression is a learned motive or a biological drive, but evidence points a finger at our culture for rewarding aggressive behavior on television and in other media.

scribed as a sense of being "churned up") and behavior. As a motivational state it is often regarded as akin to pain, because it is a state that we attempt to escape or avoid.

Anxiety is often described as a vague fear without a specific object to which the person can point as the source of the feeling. Individuals leaving home, entering new life situations, or undertaking new challenges commonly report the presence of feelings identified as anxiety. Anxiety is also frequently regarded as a response to anything threatening in which the danger is not real. For example, if you stand in front of the grizzly bear compound at a zoo and experience negative stirred-up feelings, marked changes in physiological activities, and an impulse to flee, you are anxious. There is no real threat as long as the compound is safe. However, if you were to confront the same bear while hiking in the mountains of Colorado, your emotional response would constitute fear.

## Achievement

American society puts great emphasis on achievement. We are subjected to constant pressures to do well, to do better than the next person, to do our best—in business, in school, in athletics, even in play. This emphasis on doing well and achieving success characterizes the **achievement motive**.

A method that is employed to measure the achievement motive involves a series of pictures. The subject is asked to make up a story about each picture as it is presented—to tell what is happening in each picture, what led to the situation shown, what the characters are thinking, and

**Achievement motive**
The desire to do well and achieve success.

what will happen. The pictures typically suggest situations such as work, study, father–son relationships, and daydreaming. The content of the subject's stories is then analyzed for evidence of the achievement motive.

One study investigated the achievement motive of business executives. Figure 8.11 shows one of the pictures used. Before reading further, follow the instructions given with this figure.

Here is a typical story written by a subject in this study:

*The engineer is at work on Saturday when it is quiet and he has taken time to do a little daydreaming. He is the father of the two children in the picture—the husband of the woman shown. He has a happy home and is dreaming about some pleasant outing they have had. He is also looking forward to a repeat of the incident which is now giving him pleasure to think about. He plans on the following day, Sunday, to use the afternoon to take his family for a short trip. (McClelland, 1962, p. 101)*

None of the content of this story gives evidence of the achievement motive. The subject was completely concerned with the details of the family photograph and the relationships it suggested and made no statement of goals or ways of achieving them.

Contrast the following story written by another subject:

*The man is an engineer at a drafting board. The picture is of his family. He has a problem, and is concentrating on it. It is merely an everyday occurrence—a problem which requires thought. How can he get that bridge to take the stress of possible high winds? He wants to arrive at a good solution of the problem by himself. He will discuss the problem with a few other engineers and make a decision which will be a correct one— he has the earmarks of competence. (McClelland, 1962, p. 101)*

Figure 8.11   **Look at this picture and write a five-minute story suggested by it. Tell what is happening, what led to the situation shown, what the man is thinking, and what will happen. You may get a rough idea of your own achievement motivation by comparing your story with those discussed in the text.**

Source: David C. McClelland, "Business Drive and National Achievement," *Harvard Business Review,* July–August 1962, copyright 1962 by the President and Fellows of Harvard College; all rights reserved, p. 100.

The subject mentioned the family photograph only in passing, concentrating instead upon a specific problem and anticipating the formulation of a successful solution. According to this study, the second individual has a stronger achievement motive than the first (McClelland, 1962).

A variety of studies have investigated a number of variables in relation to the achievement motive. Among these variables are ethnic group, social class, and parental attitudes. In one study, a group of boys was divided into those scoring high and those scoring low in achievement motivation. Their mothers were asked, after the testing, to indicate which of 20 different behaviors exemplifying independence they expected their sons to achieve by the age of 10. Mothers who said that they expected their sons to be independent in life tended to have sons with strong achievement motives (Winterbottom, 1953).

Other studies have shown that other aspects of the family relationship influence the development of achievement motivation. For example, bright, high-achieving adolescents perceive their parents as less restrictive, more trusting, and more likely to encourage achievement than do bright, underachieving adolescents.

## Affiliation

Every now and then a new book, a hit movie, or a television series will burst upon the scene with a central character who is fiercely independent. He or she wants nothing to do with civilized society, seeking instead the peace and solitude of a wilderness inhabited only by the beasts of the forest. This person is usually portrayed as living an idyllic existence, with no pressures from other humans, no obligations, no social expectations to satisfy. You find yourself half believing that all the problems of the world would be solved if we could just keep people away from people. But have you ever thought of what it would be like to be alone, truly alone, for days, weeks, months, and years on end? No one to talk to, laugh with at times and swear at on other occasions. No one with whom to share your disappointments, your hopes, your desires, your dreams. For most of us, it would be sheer hell.

**Affiliation**
The tendency or desire to associate with and form attachments to other people, to depend upon them.

In truth, we need other people. This desire to be with others is referred to as the need for **affiliation.** This need seems to be greater when we are fearful or unsure of ourselves. Nowhere is this more evident than in natural disasters. Whether it's a volcano erupting, an earthquake, or a flood, pictures of the survivors almost always show them huddled together as if the mere physical presence of other people would avert further tragedy. Even when the source of the fear proves to be unreal, as with predictions of the world ending in 1982 when the planets were all aligned on the same side of the sun, those who share such fears band together to await the worst.

There are times when each of us longs for independence and freedom from the obligations to others. There are also times when we actively seek out the company of other people. Not many of us can maintain a sense of well-being when living a solitary and isolated existence; we all need other people.

It has been pointed out that when people feel anxious or unsure of themselves, they find some comfort in the presence of others (Berscheid and Walster, 1969). As the saying goes, "Misery loves company." Try the following:

*Come to a class a few minutes early on a regular school day. You will probably find that few of your classmates approach you. Then sometime when an exam is scheduled in one of your classes, arrive a few minutes early. You may be surprised to see the number of classmates who approach you with friendly remarks or joking comments. . . . Students seem friendlier on days when an exam is scheduled than on days when one is not. (Berscheid and Walster, 1969, p. 32)*

Experimental evidence has supported the notion that anxiety increases the tendency to affiliate. In one study undergraduates participated in an experiment in which they were told that shock would be administered (Schachter, 1959). Some were informed that the shock would be severe and painful (high-fear condition). For others, the role of shock was minimized (low-fear condition). All subjects were told there would be a delay while the experimenter set up the equipment. They were given the choice of waiting either alone or together with other participants. In general, the results showed that subjects in the high-fear group preferred to wait with others, particularly if those others were also to be subjected to high-intensity shock. On the other hand, most of the low-fear subjects either expressed no preference or chose to wait alone. Thus it appears that when people are anxious and under stress they tend to seek out the company of others who are similarly stressed. In contrast,

**Italian earthquake victims display an increased tendency to band together in a time of anxiety.**

when individuals are expecting to be embarrassed in an experimental situation, they prefer the company of others who are completely unaware of their impending humiliation. Thus "misery sometimes loves nonmiserable company" (Firestone *et al.*, 1973).

Knowing these facts about the affiliative motive will, perhaps, allow you to understand why your moods and those of your friends appear at times to be so changeable. In spite of strong affiliative needs, there are moments when we prefer to be alone. We should respect this desire in others and hope that they respect it in us.

## Self-actualization

Imagine the following scenario. You have just arrived in a strange city after days of arduous travel on foot. You have not had a complete meal in several weeks, and so your hunger borders on starvation. You are bone weary from many days on the road. Your clothing is thin and gives little protection against the cold winds that chill you. You are, in a word, totally miserable.

What are your first concerns? To strive for status in your new community so that people will respect you? To identify with the profound problems of humanity? Or merely to get a solid meal into your stomach? Clearly the last of these options would be your first concern. Then you would look for shelter for the night.

Many of the motivations we have discussed in this chapter involve the concepts of maintenance and balance. We attempt to maintain ourselves free of the extremes of hunger and water deprivation. We look for a balanced existence in which such need states as pain or anxiety are not permitted to rise to levels that interfere with ongoing activities. But these motivational states are only part of the total picture. Human motivations are also characterized by strivings that may lead to unbalanced states, sometimes for prolonged periods of time. Some of us attempt to climb unscalable peaks, others to establish new records, and still others to create great works of art. In short, our lives are incomplete to the extent that we fail to achieve our full potentials.

> Human life is a struggle—against frustration, ignorance, suffering, evil, the maddening inertia of things in general; but it is also a struggle for something. . . . And fulfillment seems to describe better than any other single word the positive side of human development and human evolution—the realization of inherent capacities by the individual and of new possibilities by the race; the satisfaction of needs, spiritual as well as material; the emergence of new qualities of experience to be enjoyed; the building of personalities. (Huxley, 1953, pp. 162–163)

Some psychologists have focused their attention on the development of the self (Rogers, 1959; Maslow, 1954, 1971). They explore those aspects of our daily experiences and feelings that give rise to a sense of personal existence. One of the leading proponents of self theory, Abraham Maslow, believed that human beings are fundamentally good. If encouraged rather than suppressed, he argued, we can lead happy, healthy, and fruitful lives:

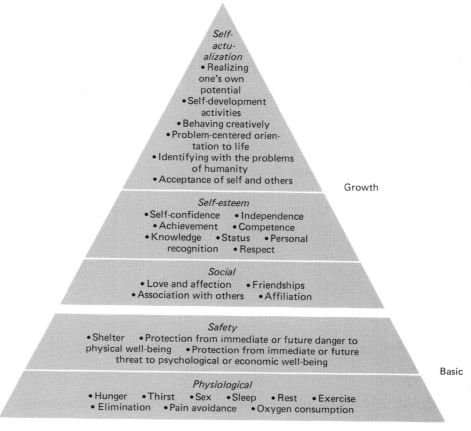

Figure 8.12
**Maslow's hierarchy
of motives**

The basic needs in the hierarchy are dominant. Only when these are satisfied is the individual free to pursue the satisfaction of growth needs.

*Observe that if these assumptions are proven true, they promise a scientific ethics, a natural value system, a court of ultimate appeal for the determination of good and bad, of right and wrong. The more we learn about man's natural tendencies, the easier it will be to tell him how to be good, how to be happy, how to be fruitful, how to respect himself, how to love, how to fulfill his highest potentiality. This amounts to automatic solution of many of the personality problems of the future. The thing to do seems to be to find out what you are really like inside, deep down, as a member of the human species and as a particular individual.* (Maslow, 1962, p. 4)

**Self-actualization**
The tendency to strive to realize one's full potential.

The concept of **self-actualization** is a key element in Maslow's theory. Self-actualization refers to the tendency to strive for the realization of one's full potential. Maslow developed a pyramid that describes an entire hierarchy of human needs. When the needs at the bottom level are satisfied, the individual is free to seek satisfaction of the needs at the next level (see Fig. 8.12). Thus when the basic physiological needs are satisfied, the person may direct his or her attention to achieving safety. Self-actualization needs are at the top of the needs hierarchy. Unfortunately, although many of us may dream of self-actualizing, it remains for most of us a high peak that we only approach and rarely scale.

Self-actualizing individuals strive to realize their full potential. Billie Jean King, tennis champion and publisher of *WomenSports,* has battled aggressively for equality in women's sports, honest professionalism, and a woman's right to be and do what she wants.

The idea of control is crucial in Maslow's theory. Our striving for the achievement of higher goals is extremely fragile, like a delicate flower that is easily bruised by rough handling. Individuals whose lives are burdened with irrational fears and anxieties must first gain control over these states before they can begin to realize their full potential. The highest level of human development is attained when we come to understand and achieve our full potential. Individuals who have reached the point at which they are able to seek satisfaction of their self-actualization motives have reached the highest level of human development. Not everyone self-actualizes, and even those who do on some occasions do not do so at all times.

After intensively studying the biographies of a number of individuals whom he considered self-actualizers, Maslow compiled a list of their characteristics. They are shown in Table 8.1.

Although Maslow's theory has captured the imagination of the general public, a note of caution is in order. A recent review concluded: ". . . need hierarchy as a theory continues to receive little empirical support . . . the available research should certainly generate a reluctance to accept unconditionally the implications of Maslow's hierarchy" (Korman *et al.*, 1977, pp. 178–179).

## EMOTIONS

Most of us expend a great deal of time and energy coping with emotions and trying to bring them under control. We fuss about situations in which the threat is really not that great. We fly into a rage when somebody disappoints us, when we are offended, or when the nail bends under a

Table 8.1
**Characteristics of Self-Actualizers**

Astute and accurate perceptions of reality

Can accept themselves as well as others

Spontaneous in both thought and action, although not extremely unconventional

Problem-centered rather than self-centered

Looks for periods of privacy and solitude

Relatively independent of their immediate environment

Capable of deep appreciation of life's experiences

Capable of deep concern about social issues

Able to achieve satisfying personal relationships

Democratic in attitude, with a good sense of humor

Able to clearly distinguish means from ends but enjoy the means toward their ends

poorly aimed blow of a hammer. Later we feel guilt when we acknowledge how counterproductive the rage has been.

We are grief-stricken at the loss of a pet. We roar uproariously at a well-told joke. We battle valiantly to suppress laughter at a solemn occasion and sometimes lose the battle. We smile, we laugh, we cry, we despair, we love, we hate, we fear, and we experience contentment. At times we seem to be so much hostage to our emotions that we wish we could dispense with them altogether. But when we think about it, we realize that emotions fill our lives with color. We even use color terms to describe our emotions: green with envy, red with rage, yellow with fear, and blue with sadness.

Try to imagine what life would be like if we had no emotions. We would be little more than drab, colorless machines, unable to experience the pride of achievement or the pangs of disappointment. We would derive no happiness from the companionship of others and would feel no grief at their loss. We would neither love nor hate. Nor would we be able to understand the joys and the sorrows of others. Indeed, we would not even envy those emotions we were denied.

## What Is an Emotion?

**Emotion**
A complex state involving cognitions, overt responses, internal changes, and motivational aspects.

If we can't live without emotions, we had better learn to live with them. But what is this thing we call **emotion?** Psychologists are not in complete agreement on the answer to this question. Indeed, there is no generally accepted system for defining, classifying, or even distinguishing one emotion from another.

Though no definition of emotion is completely satisfactory, we may regard emotions as complex states involving cognitions, overt responses, physiological changes, and motivational aspects. Let's look more closely at this description.

**Figure 8.13**
**What emotion is this man**
**experiencing? Turn to Fig. 8.14**
**for a clue.**

First, emotions involve cognitions. Two people confronted with the same situation may interpret it in different ways and therefore respond with different emotions. In other words, our thoughts, beliefs, and prior experiences will color the way we view an event and thus profoundly influence our emotional reaction to that event. For example, someone who is concerned about the energy crisis may interpret the stack emissions of a power plant as an encouraging sign that the lights will stay on, whereas someone who is worried about the ravages of pollution may regard these same stack emissions with disgust.

Second, emotions involve overt responses. What are some of the overt responses that may accompany emotions? We have probably all seen grief-stricken people cry, angry people stomp their feet or kick a chair, and happy people laugh. But does a person's behavior always reveal his or her underlying motivational state?

Let's imagine that, on your way into town on a bus late one afternoon, you catch a fleeting glance of a man. Even though you saw him for only a moment, you noticed that his head was thrown back, his eyes were closed, and his mouth was open (Fig. 8.13). What emotion is the man experiencing? Great anguish? Think for a moment. Don't some people scream when they are very happy? Can you think of any other circumstances that might produce the facial expression shown in Fig. 8.13? Look at Fig. 8.14 for a fuller view of the man. Here we see that we would have misinterpreted his emotional state if we had relied solely upon the information provided by his facial expression.

We saw that it is not always possible to determine motives by observing behavior. Motives are always inferred; they are not directly observed. Similarly, we may not be correct if we assess people's emotional states purely by referring to their behavior. Many other factors must be taken into consideration. For example, we have been taught to conceal our emotions under certain circumstances: The phrase "Don't wear your heart on your sleeve" illustrates this.

Next, emotions involve internal, or physiological, changes. This is particularly true of intense emotional states. But are specific emotions associated with specific physiological states? Can fear and anger, for example, be differentiated on the basis of bodily changes associated with each emotion? Later in this chapter we will look at these and other questions about the physiological bases of emotion.

Finally, emotions involve motivational changes. Most psychologists would agree that there is a close relationship between emotions and motivational states. Satisfaction or frustration of any motive may produce emotions. Pleasurable feelings generally accompany the satisfaction of motives—a good meal when we are hungry, a refreshing drink when we are thirsty, a good grade following intensive study, acceptance into a social group we have striven to join. Even anticipation of satisfaction may be pleasurable. Observe the behavior of someone who has just been told to take the day off, or a child who has been promised a day at an amusement park.

Conversely, frustration of motivated behavior is commonly accompanied by negative feelings. Many of us know, for example, how depressing it is to have to lose weight or stop smoking. Sometimes, the mere anticipation of frustration can lead to fear or anxiety; for example, facing an impending examination when you don't think you are well prepared may produce feelings of anxiety.

The relation between emotions and motivation works both ways. The desire to experience pleasant or to avoid unpleasant emotions provides the impetus to behave in a given way. For instance, a student who is not particularly concerned about an upcoming examination may be motivated to spend many hours preparing for it to avoid the unpleasant feeling that occurs whenever he gets a B grade or lower.

On the other hand: Why do we go to the movies? What motivates us to attend a music festival? Why do we sometimes travel many hours to get to a favorite beach or ski slope? In these cases, our behavior may be motivated by a desire to experience pleasant emotions.

Emotions may also affect our motivation in situations that are unrelated to the emotion we are feeling. If you are sad or depressed, you may find no humor in the antics of your favorite comedian. On the other hand, if you have just received news that makes you excited and happy, you may approach an examination with uncharacteristic optimism.

Emotional behaviors are not engraved in stone. Rather, they are plastic and modifiable. They can serve as well as be served.

As a matter of fact, it is probable that emotions evolved as a means of serving the survival needs of each species. From the perspective of natural selection, virtually all of its characteristics must have survival value in order for a species to survive (Plutchik, 1980a). The case is the same with emotions. Emotions such as fear or terror evolved as a response to danger. The resulting behavior (running or flying away) improved the chances of survival. Similarly, when an individual is endangered by an enemy, anger and rage lead to fighting rather than submission and possible death. Because each emotion presumably served different survival needs, they evolved differently. As one observer stated: "Some emotions are primarily concerned with the maintenance of internal stability; others, such as the **agonistic** and sexual emotions, contribute strongly to the depth of social interactions. Therefore, no one emotion can be taken as a model for all others, rather, each functions within a separate system" (Scott, 1980, p. 35).

**Agonistic**
Agonistic behavior is behavior involving either fight or flight.

Although the various emotional states are sometimes discussed separately, remember that many emotions may be operating simultaneously. For example, a person who is very angry may also be feeling despondent, anxious, or even elated. Indeed, it is not uncommon for emotional states to be in conflict with one another. The question of emotional and motivational conflict will be discussed in Chapter 9.

## PHYSIOLOGICAL BASES OF EMOTION

Probably all of us have experienced and noticed the tremendous range in the level of physiological arousal that accompanies the various emotional states. In the powerful negative emotional states, such as fear or anger, the pupils enlarge to admit more light, the mouth becomes dry as salivary secretions diminish, the heart beats faster to increase the volume of blood

**Adrenalin**
A hormone secreted by the adrenal glands that activates bodily structures and systems during an emergency.

**Noradrenalin**
A hormone secreted by the adrenal glands that produces the physiological changes associated with anger.

**Sympathetic branch**
The division of the autonomic nervous system that mobilizes the body during emergencies by increasing heart rate and blood pressure, accelerating secretion of adrenalin, and inhibiting digestive processes.

flow, the digestive system shuts down to divert blood to the organs and structures of fight and flight, increased perspiration assists the cooling mechanisms to maintain normal temperatures, and sugar is released into the bloodstream to provide quick energy. These and other widespread bodily reactions are initiated and maintained by the release of two hormones, **adrenalin** and **noradrenalin,** directly into the bloodstream. They are all part of the emergency reaction.

The arousal described in the preceding paragraph describes the activities of the **sympathetic branch** of the **autonomic nervous system.** During strong emotions like fear and anger, the sympathetic branch is dominant.

But not all emotions involve an intense generalized mobilization of the bodily structures involved in fighting a potential enemy or fleeing a dangerous situation. There are also placid emotional states in which the bodily processes are slowed down and the individual experiences a sense of well-being. During these times, the **parasympathetic branch** of the autonomic nervous system is dominant. Heart rate slows, blood pressure is reduced, and the pupils of the eyes constrict.

Figure 8.14    **Facial expressions alone may be a misleading clue to underlying emotions. John McEnroe is jubilant after he makes the winning shot that gave him the men's singles title at Wimbledon.**

Intense emotional arousal as a result of anger or fear causes a series of physiological reactions that help an individual cope with emergency situations.

## The Polygraph

**Autonomic nervous system**
The part of the peripheral nervous system that regulates the inner organs of the body such as the heart, the stomach, and the glands.

**Parasympathetic branch**
The division of the autonomic nervous system that is dominant when the organism is placid. This system decreases heart rate and blood pressure and regulates normal digestive processes.

**Polygraph**
An apparatus, commonly known as the lie detector, for recording several physiological measures simultaneously, such as galvanic skin response, heart rate, blood pressure, and rate of breathing.

What is surprising is that the physiological responses themselves do not provide clear-cut clues to the underlying emotion. Knowing that a person's heart is beating faster, that blood pressure is up, and that other symptoms show sympathetic arousal tells us only that some strong emotion is in progress. The physiological signs do not permit us to distinguish among fear, anxiety, guilt, and anger. This is true even when we use the most sophisticated electronic equipment to monitor the emotions. Even the much publicized **polygraph** (lie detector) does not detect lies. It simply reports levels of emotional arousal. More specifically, it records changes in heart rate, breathing rate, blood pressure, and electrical conductivity of the skin (GSR, for galvanic skin response). The GSR is a measure of sweating. The more we perspire, the lower is the resistance to the passage of a tiny electrical current across the surface of the skin.

When the lie detector is used in criminal investigations, a trained operator asks a suspect a series of questions. Many of these questions are neutral—for example, "Is the sun shining today?" or "Is the color of the wall green?" They do not usually result in emotional responses. The responses to these neutral questions provide a baseline against which other reactions can be compared. The key element in administering the lie detector test is to embed critical questions among the neutral items. A critical question might refer to a detail of the crime known only to the police and the actual criminal. An innocent person might be expected to respond to such questions in much the same way as to the neutral questions. The actual criminal, however, might inhale sharply, perspire more, and increase blood pressure and pulse rate.

Is the lie detector test infallible? Advocates of its use claim 90 to 95 percent accuracy. This claim was disputed in research where subjects

This photograph shows a subject taking a polygraph test. The capital letters on the polygraph charts represent the recordings of the following physiological phenomena: *A* is the tracing of the subject's muscular movement during the examination, as picked up by the Reid Movement Chair; *B* and *C* are the tracings for the subject's respiration, as recorded from two pneumographs placed over the subject's diaphragm and chest; *D* is the recording of the galvanic skin response (GSR), as picked up through electrodes on two fingers of the subject's left hand; *E* is the recording of the subject's relative blood pressure/pulse rate, using a standard blood pressure cuff. (The instrument being used is the Reid Five Pen Polygraph manufactured by the Stoelting Company of Chicago. The photo portrays Reid employees Frank S. Horvath as the examiner and Thomas B. Kelly as the subject.)

were instructed to think exciting or disturbing thoughts during the administration of the test (cited in Smith, 1971). By this simple maneuver, they were able to reduce the accuracy rate to 25 percent. Moreover, by simply curling and relaxing their toes, the subjects dropped the accuracy rate to 10 percent.

Although the results of lie detector tests are inadmissible in courts of law, their use in the private sector is increasing. For example, some large corporations use the lie detector test in conjunction with job interviews. Some people consider the use of the lie detector test for this purpose an invasion of their privacy. The legality of this use is presently being tested in the courts.

## The Voice Stress Analyzer

More recently a voice stress analyzer has emerged on the scene. The machine picks up and records tiny tremors in the voice. Like the lie detector test, the stress analyzer detects "nervousness" rather than lies. Like the polygraph, its accuracy is questionable. In one test using individuals accused of committing crimes, it was able to detect, at a level only slightly above chance, those who were later found guilty (Rice, 1978).

If the lie detector test poses a threat to personal rights and privacy, imagine the potential of a stress analyzer. Because the voice stress analyzer does not have to be hooked up to the individual, a voice stress test may be given to people without their awareness. Indeed, a telephone conversation may be taped and later subjected to a voice stress analysis. Some insurance companies are already using the device in the hopes of detecting false claims (Rice, 1978).

## The Pupillometer

**Pupillometer**
A device used to measure changes in pupil size.

The pupils of our eyes have long been known as indicators of emotional arousal. Many magicians have an act that makes use of this response. A subject is asked to pick a card from a deck. After the card is returned to the deck, the subject is shown the cards one at a time. By carefully observing the subject's pupils to see which card produces increased pupil size, the magician is able to identify the correct card. If you try this trick on your friends, do not be discouraged if you don't meet with immediate success. Only a great deal of training will sensitize you to the extremely subtle changes in pupil size. In fact, a special device, called the **pupillometer,** was devised especially to measure changes in pupil size.

The pupillometer was used in an interesting series of experiments to establish the effects of various types of stimulation on pupil size. In one study, male and female subjects were shown a series of images including pictures of a baby, a mother and child, a nude man, and a nude woman. The results of this study are shown in Fig. 8.15. You will note that the pupil size of the female subjects increased markedly in response to the pictures of the baby, the mother and child, and the nude male, whereas the pupils of the male subjects showed their greatest increases in response to the picture of the female nude (Hess and Polt, 1960). Several studies have substantiated these findings. One study, however, found that male homosexuals, as would be expected, showed a greater pupil response to pictures of their own sex (Hess *et al.*, 1965).

**Figure 8.15**
**Changes in pupil size as subjects viewed various pictures**

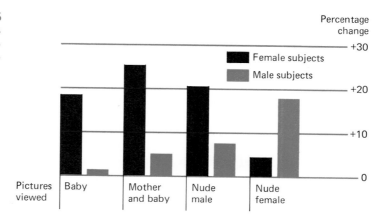

Other studies have established that the pupil size increases with any kind of activating stimulation, not only visual. This suggests that the pupillometer might be useful in situations such as counseling to detect stimuli that are interesting or significant to the client.

## PHYSIOLOGICAL THEORIES OF EMOTION

The strong emotions, such as anger and fear, have attracted the most interest. They are commonly regarded as undesirable because they tend to disrupt ongoing activity and are accompanied by negative feelings. But these same emotions may have survival value, as when they activate adaptive behaviors in a time of emergency. To illustrate, fear causes an increased flow of blood to the peripheral muscles, and this prepares the individual for either fight or flight. The commonsense view of the relation between these emotions and emergency reactions is based on the following sequence of events: A dangerous situation is perceived by the individual, fear is aroused, and the emergency response is activated. Though this sequence does conform to many of our everyday experiences, there are notable exceptions, particularly in cases of extreme emergency.

Consider the following verbal report recounting a student's behavior in response to a sudden and threatening situation:

> When I was an undergraduate student, I lived off campus during my freshman year. I had to take a long walk to school each morning, and found that I could save time by cutting across a field and walking about 100 feet along a commuter railroad track. One morning I was completely lost in thought as I walked along the track, oblivious to the world about me and to where I was at the time. Suddenly the piercing shrill of a train whistle burst into my consciousness. Without thought or hesitation, I plunged headlong from the tracks and landed in a snowbank. The train missed me by inches. It's funny. At the time I jumped, I experienced no fear. The fear came moments later, as I lay in the snow bank and thought about my near miss. (Author's files)

If you think for a moment, many of you can probably tell of similar experiences—for example, avoiding an automobile accident by instantaneously applying the brakes, without thought or fear. Only after the danger had passed did you experience the emotion of fear.

Acknowledging this common experience, one of the earliest physiological theories of emotion maintained that the perception of bodily changes is the critical factor underlying emotional states. This theory, called the **James-Lange theory,** proposed that environmental stimuli give rise to certain bodily changes by a reflex process. It is the subsequent perception of these bodily changes that results in the emotional experience. According to this theory, we see a bear in the woods, run away from it, and simultaneously undergo many physiological changes (increased heart rate, respiratory changes, muscular activities). It is the perception of these muscular and physiological changes that leads us to identify our emotional state as fear. In the words of William James, "We

**James-Lange theory**
The theory that an emotional experience results from perception of bodily changes.

By permission of Mell Lazarus and Field Enterprises, Inc.

feel sorry because we cry, angry because we strike, afraid because we tremble[; it is] not that we cry, strike, or tremble because we are sorry, angry, or fearful, as the case may be" (James, 1890, p. 450).

Perhaps the greatest value of the James-Lange theory was that it unleashed a flood of experimentation concerned with autonomic changes associated with various emotional states. This theory would lead us to expect that each reaction should trigger a different physiological complex which should, in turn, be perceived as different emotional qualities. In other words, certain feelings in our body would be identified as fear, certain others as anger, and still others as love.

How do you know what you yourself are feeling? You should be able to identify your own emotions, because you can feel bodily changes in yourself. But do you always know what you are feeling?

Suppose that your heart is pounding, the palms of your hands are wet and sticky, and your stomach is all churned up. Would you say with certainty that you feel excitement? Fear? Anger? Love?

Numerous attempts have been made to distinguish among the various emotions on the basis of distinctive physiological responses. These studies have met with limited success. In general, stimuli that produce strong emotions will lead to a general stirred-up state in the organism. To date, it has not been possible to assign unique physiological changes to specific emotions. There is one notable exception, however, involving the bodily changes associated with fear and anger.

In a classic study, subjects were made very angry or fearful by a clever manipulation of the experimental setting. Various devices were attached to the subjects to permit the recording of 14 different physiological measures. The technicians were instructed to act in an abusive fashion in the anger-producing condition, and in a clumsy fashion in the fear-inducing condition. Altogether, seven different physiological measures clearly differentiated anger from fear (Ax, 1953). The results of this study are summarized in Fig. 8.16.

The physiological changes associated with anger are known to be produced by noradrenalin, a hormone secreted by the adrenal glands. Fear, however, is accompanied by the secretion of the hormone adrenalin. It is interesting that predators (such as lions) are characterized by high secre-

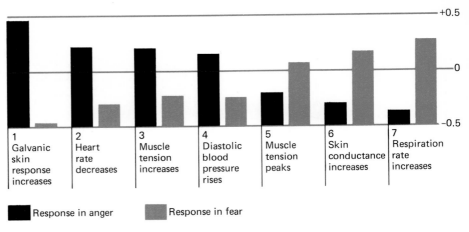

Response in anger        Response in fear

Figure 8.16
**Physiological differences
between anger and fear**

**Shown are seven of the physiological measures that distinguish anger from fear. The graph shows changes from normal (zero). (Ax, 1953)**

tions of noradrenalin, and animals that rely on running away (fear) for survival have large quantities of adrenalin in their systems (Funkenstein, 1955).

In another study, hockey players were given urine analyses both before and immediately after a game. The players who participated actively in the game showed a sixfold increase of noradrenalin levels, whereas those players who were benched because of injury, and thus may have exhibited fear because of lack of control over the situation, showed increased quantities of adrenalin in their urine (Elmadjian, 1959). Recent evidence suggests that stress reduces noradrenalin levels in the brains of experimental animals, a reduction that, in turn, leads to depression. Administration of a drug that prevents the body from breaking down noradrenalin seems to control depression (Weiss *et al.*, 1974).

The James-Lange theory focused on the autonomic changes that take place under strong emotions and on our perception of these changes. Crucial to this theory is the view that autonomic changes are communicated to the **central nervous system,** and that the central nervous system interprets these changes as specific emotions. One of the severest critics of the theory, W. B. Cannon, severed the connections between the autonomic and the central nervous system in dogs and found that the dogs continued to manifest emotional behavior (Cannon, 1929). Moreover, Cannon argued that the autonomic changes that occur in certain emotional states also occur in nonemotional states.

On the basis of the results of his own research, Cannon proposed an alternative physiological theory of emotions, the **Cannon-Bard theory.** This theory maintains that the physiological state and the emotional experience are triggered simultaneously by the hypothalamus. According to this theory, when it receives emotion-arousing stimulation, the hypothalamus activates the autonomic nervous system to produce a state of physiological arousal and, at the same time, sends impulses to the cortical structures so that the individual can interpret the emotional state. The

Cannon-Bard theory says nothing about feedback from the physiological changes, which is the crucial element in the James-Lange theory.

The Cannon-Bard theory is supported by the observation that, as long as the hypothalamus is intact, lower animals display certain emotions and corresponding physiological changes that disappear after the hypothalamus has been surgically removed (Cannon, 1929).

## SITUATIONAL AND COGNITIVE FACTORS

Imagine that you are placed in the following situation. You are standing no more than 20 feet away from a hungry lion. It roars loudly, licks its chops, and glares at you. What emotions would you experience? Fear, terror, panic? Could you possibly feel relaxed and amused?

Either of these extreme opposites is possible. If we encountered the lion in the African veldt and appraised our vulnerability to an attack as high, panic might well be the only behavioral option. In contrast, if we encountered the lion in a zoological park, with a deep moat preventing a closer encounter, our reaction might well be one of amusement and enjoyment.

Cognitive theorists have attributed these differing emotional responses at least in part to situational and cognitive factors.

In 1962 Stanley Schachter and Jerome Singer conducted an interesting experiment. They gave one group of subjects a drug producing arousal and another group of subjects a placebo. When individuals who had received the active drug (and thus experienced physiological arousal) were placed, one at a time, in a room with a confederate of the experimenters who exhibited either lighthearted happiness or hostility, the subjects appeared to experience similar emotions. Those who received the placebo remained neutral when placed in the same situations.

From these results, Schachter and Singer developed a **two-factor theory** of emotion: that in order to feel a specific emotion, the individual must experience physiological arousal *and* interpret the situation to decide which emotion is appropriate. Note that unlike the James-Lange and Cannon-Bard theories, the two-factor theory does not maintain that humans discriminate between different types of arousal. Fig. 8.17 provides a comparison of these three theories.

Although Schachter and Singer's theory sparked much new research into emotions, subsequent replications of this experiment using tighter controls did not produce the same results. Instead, subjects receiving an arousing drug always reacted negatively, regardless of the situation (Maslach, 1979).

Still seeking an explanation of differing reactions to situations, Magda Arnold (1960) developed a theory of **cognitive appraisal.** She saw the determination of emotion as proceeding through a series of steps. At first we *perceive* an external stimulus. Then we *appraise* (evaluate) it, determining if it is good (beneficial) or bad (harmful); this determines which emotion we will feel. Next we enter a stage of *expression*—the physiological state appropriate to the feelings. Finally we *act,* either approaching or avoiding the situation.

**Central nervous system**
The brain and spinal cord.

**Cannon-Bard theory**
The theory that a physiological state and the emotional experience of it are triggered simultaneously by the hypothalamus.

**Two-factor theory**
The theory that an emotional experience is a result of cognitive interpretation of a situation that has produced physiological arousal.

**Cognitive appraisal theory**
The theory that an emotional experience is a result of cognitive interpretation of a situation triggering physiological arousal.

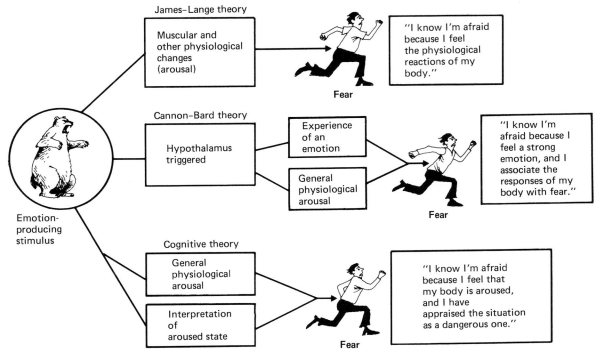

**Figure 8.17**    Three theories of emotion are shown above in a schematic representation.

In some individuals the initial appraisal leads to levels of emotional arousal that interfere with ongoing cognitive processes. As a consequence, these people withdraw from such situations because they are painful or spend too much time in nonproductive worry and too little time in evaluational appraisal. Thus their performance is adversely affected. This situation leads to greater concern and more worry and yet lower performance.

Shortly after the turn of the century, two psychologists formulated a law that relates performance to arousal level. Called the **Yerkes-Dodson law,** it states that there is an optimal level of arousal at which performance is most effective. For simple tasks, a high level of arousal is optimal. For very complex or difficult tasks, low levels of arousal are best. Medium levels of arousal are most effective for tasks that are at a medium level of complexity or difficulty. A graphic representation of the Yerkes-Dodson law is shown in Fig. 8.18.

A more complex variation of this theory was developed by Richard Lazarus, who saw emotion as consisting of both primary and secondary appraisal. Primary cognitive appraisal involves our evaluation of the significance of the encounter for our well-being (Lazarus *et al.,* 1980). If we appraise it as irrelevant, we may ignore it and go on to other things. If we find it benign (positive), we consider the situation beneficial or desirable. We may decide to prolong such encounters. Thus we may spend a considerable period of time observing a lion behind the safety of a moat.

**Yerkes-Dodson law**
A general rule stating that there is an optimal level of arousal at which performance of a task is most effective and that that level is related to the difficulty of the task, with high arousal best for easy tasks and low arousal best for difficult ones.

Even positive changes such as marriage can bring about a state of stress, but the way this young couple responds to emotional arousal—will they call off the wedding, burst into tears, or feel elated—may depend at least in part on their cognitive appraisal of the situation.

Finally, a stressful encounter may involve harm that has already been done, anticipation of harm, or a challenge. It is important to note that challenges are stressful. Thus whenever we accept challenges involving positive gain or personal growth, we are committing ourselves to stressful encounters.

Following this initial appraisal is a secondary appraisal (Lazarus *et al.*, 1980). During this secondary appraisal, we evaluate our own resources and options for coping with stressful encounters. In many ways, this secondary appraisal is more important than the stressful event itself. It will determine, in large part, whether we feel threatened or hopeful in a given encounter. Thus, if we judge our resources to be inadequate or our op-

**Figure 8.18**
**The Yerkes-Dodson law**

(a) For simple tasks, high levels of arousal are best. (b) Medium levels of arousal are best for tasks of medium complexity. (c) For very complex or difficult tasks, low levels of arousal are best. (Martindale, 1981)

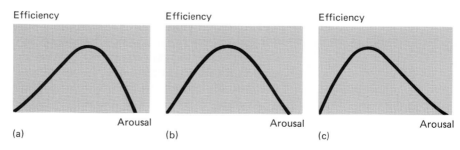

tions severely limited, we may respond to a situation with apprehension. Common examples include: lack of preparation for an examination, competing in an athletic event when we are out of shape, failure to allow sufficient time to travel to the site of an important appointment. In contrast, favorable evaluations of our resources and options lead to feelings of optimism, well-being, and hopefulness.

The appraisal process is not static; rather, it is continuous and dynamic. It involves constant reappraisal as we obtain feedback on the adequacy of our adjustment to the situation. We behave in certain ways and the environment reacts. We appraise both our own behavior and this environmental reaction. We often must change our direction as a consequence of this reappraisal of feedback. These changes are, in turn, accompanied by changed emotions. Thus there is a constant interplay between our cognitions and emotions as we appraise both our own adjustments and the environmental response to these adjustments. This process of appraisal need not be conscious, although it usually is (Lazarus *et al.,* 1980).

## DEVELOP-MENTAL AND LEARNED ASPECTS OF EMOTION

Suppose that you volunteer to babysit for new neighbors while they move into their house. You are left alone with their three-month-old infant while the parents set their house in order. You pick him up and suddenly he starts to cry. How would you interpret his crying behavior? Is he unhappy because you are holding him? Is he afraid because you are a stranger? Is he angry because his parents left him?

We would probably all agree that the baby is exhibiting some form of emotional behavior. On the other hand, it is very unlikely that the infant is actually experiencing as specific an emotion as unhappiness, or fear, or anger. Observations of many infants have indicated that their emotional behavior does not include any specific emotions like grief, disgust, love, hate, or jealousy. When these emotions are "seen" in an infant, it is adults who are labeling them in terms of their own experiences.

In fact, the emotional behavior of newborn babies is vague and undifferentiated. A wet diaper, a sudden loud noise, hunger, and gas pains will produce a state that can be described as generalized excitement. This state can be differentiated from *quiescence,* during which the baby is calm and placid. The excitement state is accompanied by physiological changes, such as increased heart rate and alteration in breathing patterns. As the baby grows, differentiated emotional states begin gradually to develop. The earliest identifiable emotional responses are distress reactions to unpleasant stimuli and, a little later, delight responses to feeding, fondling, and other displays of affection. After three months, there is a rapid differentiation of responses associated with such states as anger, disgust, fear, and elation. Figure 8.19 shows the development of the various emotional states during the first two years of a child's life.

Although different situations will produce different responses, we must learn how to label these responses as specific emotional states. This

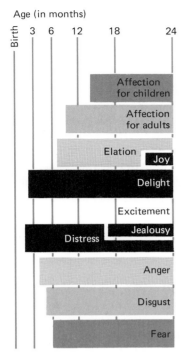

Age (in months)

**Figure 8.19**

**Developmental and learned aspects of emotion**

Development of various emotions during the first two years of life. (Bridges, 1932)

**Affect**
An internal state or feeling.

learning can be exceedingly difficult. This is because, at different times, we apply emotional labels to inner feelings, to the expressive behaviors that we observe, or to situations (Plutchik, 1980a). Each of these is ambiguous. The child may be experiencing more than one feeling at any given time, displaying more than one behavior, and behaving in a situation that has many different aspects. Thus if a hungry child cries when a monster happens to appear on the television screen, the parents may interpret the crying to be in response to the monster. They may say, "Don't be afraid. There really is no monster." In truth, the child was crying because of hunger. Because the parents have labeled the child's feelings as fear, the child may now equate being hungry with being afraid. Only after encountering many different situations in which emotional labels are applied does some core meaning for this label begin to emerge.

When preschool children first learn labels, they are expressed in terms of the external situation. Thus they will say, "I'm happy because we're going on a picnic," or "I'm mad because it's raining." Later, when they are about seven or eight years old, they begin to interpret their feelings in terms of emotional labels. Now they will say, "I feel happy," or "I feel angry." The emphasis has shifted away from the external situation to internal states or feelings, called **affects.**

Children learn not only how to label feelings associated with emotions, but also what emotions are appropriate in a given situation. For example, we don't learn how to cry, but we do learn when and where crying is appropriate. In our culture, boys learn that crying is seldom appropriate, whereas girls learn that their crying is acceptable in any number of situations!

Those who doubt the crucial role of learning in emotion need go no further than to glimpse the expression of emotion in cultures other than ours. Andaman Islanders and the Maori of New Zealand shed copious tears when greeting friends after a long absence and when peace is established between warring tribes. It is reported that Japanese commonly smile after being scolded by a superior or upon learning of the death of a favorite son. Earlier in this century, Chinese girls were provided with a book, *Required Studies for Women,* in which they received such admonitions as, "Do not let your teeth be seen when you smile," or "If your father or mother is sick, do not be far from his or her bed. Do not even take off your girdle. Taste all the medicine yourself. Pray your god for his or her health. If anything unfortunate happens cry bitterly" (Klineberg, 1938).

Observations of this sort have led a number of present-day theorists to view most emotions as cultural inventions that are formed, organized, and constructed according to the rules of the culture. According to one of the leading spokesmen, there is no straightforward relationship between emotions and biological systems: "Biologically determined responses form a relatively small class of emotional reactions. Their primary importance is that they may be incorporated as elements into other kinds of emotion" (Averill, 1976, p. 89). For example, love is probably experienced as a different emotion by members of different societies, depending on which elements are combined with sexual behavior within each society.

## Appraisal of Emotion in Others

Try the following test. Turn your television set to a movie or some drama so that you can see the picture but not hear the sound. How would you label the emotions that the actors are presenting? What cues are you using to make these judgments? How confident are you that you are correct? Now, turn on the sound and listen until you know what is going on. You may feel somewhat more confident in your assessments of their emotional states. But how do you know that your guesses are really accurate? Suppose you try this test again, with several friends present. If most of you agree, does this mean you have made a truly accurate judgment of the emotions the actors are portraying? In everyday situations, how do you know what any person, other than yourself, is really feeling? Because you cannot directly observe other people's feelings, it is obviously difficult to know whether you have made a correct judgment.

When we make judgments about another person's emotional state, we usually rely on outward behavioral signs. To a large extent, we learn the behaviors appropriate for expressing specific emotions. We learn, for example, that a smile or a laugh signifies happiness; and a frown or a grimace, displeasure. Actors capitalize on these learned forms of emotional expression by using gestures, facial expressions, and voice inflections to communicate specific emotional states. Nevertheless, as we saw earlier, judging people's emotional states from their behavior may lead to false conclusions. A wide variety of different situations may elicit the same behavior, and the same situation may give rise to many different behaviors. To complicate matters even further, the same emotional state may arise from a variety of different situations and lead to a variety of different behaviors. Let's look at a few examples.

One Sunday afternoon in 1968, a close football game between the Oakland Raiders and the New York Jets was cut off in the closing seconds so that the broadcast of "Heidi" would begin as scheduled. Although the Jets appeared to have the game in hand, the Raiders scored twice in less than a minute to snatch victory from apparent defeat. Small children and their parents may have been pleased to see "Heidi" start promptly, but football fans—both those who missed seeing their team win and those who wanted to know how their team lost—angrily deluged the local stations and network with protests. As you can see, one event can trigger widely different emotions in different people. Even among those who share an emotion, behavior may differ greatly. Whereas some football fans immediately picked up their phones to vent their anger, others chose to write the network, and still others just banged their fists on their chairs and griped about the switch at work the next day.

Many studies have demonstrated how hard it is to judge the nature of the underlying emotional state by observing behavior. In one study, medical students were asked to judge the emotions of children who had been exposed to various emotion-producing stimuli (for example, a sudden loss of support). When they were unable to see the stimulus situations that provoked the emotional behavior, the medical students were unable to agree on the children's emotions. Only when they were able to see the stimulus situation could they agree (Sherman and Sherman, 1929). It has been shown that we have the same trouble judging the emotions of adults (Coleman, 1949).

(a)

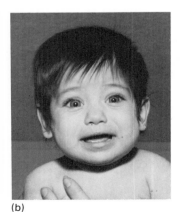

(b)

**Figure 8.20**
The facial expressions of this four-month-old infant clearly reveal the (a) pleasant and (b) unpleasant dimensions of emotions.

Although most studies have shown that we do not make very accurate judgments about the specific emotions of others merely by observing their facial expressions, facial expression can provide valuable clues. For example, some emotions are usually regarded as unpleasant (such as fear and grief) and others as pleasant (such as love and joy). Look at the faces in Fig. 8.20. Clearly, the face on the bottom is expressing an unpleasant emotion, whereas we would certainly judge the face on the top to be expressing a pleasant emotion.

On the basis of a series of studies it has been found that facial expressions can be classified according to three dimensions: pleasantness–unpleasantness, rejection–attention, and intensity (Schlosberg, 1952, 1954). Figure 8.21 shows some of the pictures used to rate facial expressions according to these three dimensions.

There is one serious criticism of the many studies attempting to relate facial expressions to emotions, namely, the experimenters used posed facial expressions that they believed expressed clear-cut single emotions (Plutchik, 1980b). They rarely used spontaneous expressions of emotion. One investigator (Eibl-Eibesfeldt, 1973) made extensive motion pictures of six children who were born deaf and blind. In spite of the fact that they

**Figure 8.21
The Schlosberg circle**

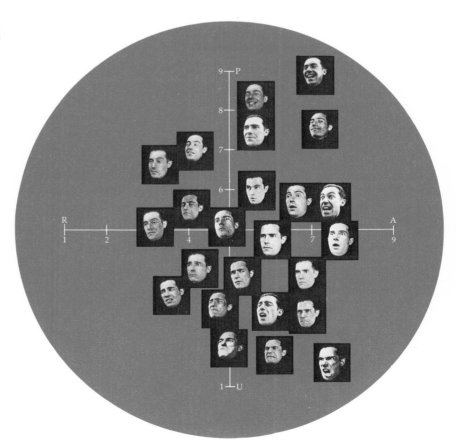

could neither see nor hear and were cognitively impaired, the following observation was made:

> Smiling was observed in all the deaf-and-blind-born studied so far. It occurred spontaneously during play, and in Sabine when she sat by herself in the sun patting her face with the palms of her hands. Smiling could be released by patting, mild tickling, and engaging in social play. The smiling started with an upward movement of the corners of the mouth. At higher intensities the lips opened wide in front, exposing the teeth in the way sighted people do; the eye slits were narrowed, and finally the head was raised and tilted back. (Eibl-Eibesfeldt, 1973)

Because these children could not possibly have learned to smile by imitating the expressions of those around them, these results lend support to Darwin's idea that certain emotional expressions are unlearned, that we are genetically programmed to behave in certain ways, such as smiling when happy.

## Summary

1. Motivational states serve to energize or activate behavior, and to direct the behavior toward specific classes of goal objects.
2. Three broad classes of motivational states can be distinguished: biological drives, stimulus needs, and learned motives.
3. Because motives cannot be directly observed, they must be inferred from behavior and from the circumstances surrounding that behavior. Four measures are commonly used to determine the strength of motivation: (1) activity level, (2) performance rate, (3) overcoming an obstacle, and (4) selection among various goals.
4. Centers for the arousal of several biological drives (hunger, thirst, and sleep) are found in the hypothalamus.
5. The drive to avoid pain is one of the most compelling, in humans and lower animals alike. Rare cases in which children are born without the capacity to experience pain remind us of the importance of this drive for survival.
6. Unlike other biological drives, the sex drive does not have to be satisfied in order for the individual to survive. In humans, satisfaction of the sex drive is overladen with cultural values and learned attitudes.
7. There appear to be motivational states, operating most obviously at the human level, that require new and varied experiences for their satisfaction. We refer to these motivational states as stimulus needs.
8. Studies involving deprivation of sensory stimulation suggest that the brain requires organized and meaningful sensory stimulation for normal functioning. When such input is lacking, the brain will manufacture its own stimulation in the form of hallucinations, fantasies, and other internally produced forms of stimulation.
9. The satisfaction of basic biological drives dominates the lives of lower organisms and of human infants. With growth and development, learned motives assume an increasingly important role in the life of the child.
10. Among the most important of learned motives are aggression and anxiety. Aggression may arise directly as a result of rewarding aggressive behavior or indirectly as the result of modeling the aggressive behavior of others. Anxiety is regarded as a fear reaction to unknown or unidentified stimuli.
11. The achievement motive, with its emphasis on doing well and achieving success, is particularly strong in American society.
12. Affiliation motives are acquired by individuals during the course of their interaction with their social environment.
13. Abraham Maslow described a hierarchy of human needs that he thought were satisfied in order,

from the lowest to the highest levels. These needs ranged from basic physiological needs (the lowest level) to self-actualization (the highest level), which is the striving to realize one's full potential.

14. Emotions may be regarded as complex states involving cognitions, overt responses, internal changes, and motivational aspects. Our thoughts, beliefs, and prior experiences profoundly influence our emotional reactions to events.

15. Many and varied physiological changes are associated with the various emotional states. These changes include skin conductance, heart rate, blood pressure, breathing rate, and pupil dilation.

16. Assessment of changes in several of these measures is at the core of the polygraph or lie detector test. Other measures include those of the voice stress analyzer and the pupillometer.

17. Theorists have differed over the causes of emotion. The James-Lange theory related emotion to the perception of bodily states activated by environmental stimuli in a reflex process. The Cannon-Bard theory maintains that the physiological state and the emotional experience are triggered simultaneously by the actions of the hypothalamus. The two-factor theory of Schachter and Singer holds that arousal occurs and is cognitively interpreted in light of the situation. Arnold's and Lazarus's theories involve cognitive appraisal of the situation triggering physiological arousal and, ultimately, action.

18. The emotions of the newborn child appear to represent an undifferentiated state of generalized excitement. The earliest identifiable responses involve distress reactions to unpleasant stimuli and, shortly after, delight responses to feeding, fondling, and other displays of affection. Beyond three months, there is a rapid differentiation of responses associated with anger, disgust, fear, and elation.

19. It is frequently difficult to judge the nature of the underlying emotional states in others by observing their behavior. In labeling the emotions of others, it appears that knowledge of the stimulus situation is the most important factor determining our judgment.

## Terms to Remember

| | | |
|---|---|---|
| Motive | Anxiety | Polygraph |
| Biological drive | Achievement motive | Pupillometer |
| Learned motive | Affiliation | James-Lange theory |
| Stimulus needs | Self-actualization | Central nervous system |
| Consummatory response | Emotion | Cannon-Bard theory |
| Excitatory nucleus | Agonistic | Two-factor theory |
| Inhibitory nucleus | Adrenalin | Cognitive appraisal theory |
| Lipostat | Noradrenalin | Yerkes-Dodson law |
| Hallucination | Autonomic nervous system | Affect |
| Sensory deprivation | Sympathetic branch | |
| Aggression | Parasympathetic branch | |

# STRESS AND COPING

## STRESS

Imagine the following situation: You have a very important examination scheduled for 9:00 in the morning. You set the alarm for 7:30, which leaves you enough time to dress and review your notes before taking the 15-minute drive to school. Unfortunately, the alarm does not go off and you do not wake up until 8:30. You dash madly around the house trying to get ready to leave. The clothes you wanted to wear are not back from the cleaners, your roommate is in the middle of a shower, and you can't find the keys to your car. At 8:55 you finally get yourself together and dash outside, to find that it is raining, and you have trouble starting your car. You run into traffic and get stopped by a policeman for going through a red light. At school you cannot find a place to park—except for spaces reserved for faculty. Finally you get there, only to find a note posted which indicates that the room has been changed to one on the other side of the campus.

How would you feel? Tense, anxious, upset, angry, and generally out-of-sorts? This is not surprising. What we have described is a series of stressful events. In our daily lives, we are often exposed to situations that produce **stress.** In fact, two psychiatrists have identified important life events that lead to stress. They developed a Social Readjustment Rating Scale (see Table 9.1) that lists 43 life events and the relative degree of stress associated with each. Initially, this scale was devised as a means of predicting the relationship between stress and physical illness. Indeed, several studies have found that individuals who experience many stressful life events run a greater risk of physical illness (see, e.g., Dohrenwend and Dohrenwend, 1974).

Note one important aspect of this scale. Not all the listed events are undesirable. In other words, stress does not consist exclusively of *bad* things that happen to us. It also includes events that are usually considered desirable, such as marriage, vacations, and outstanding personal achievement. As stated in one source, "The important point is that any change in an important area of life can produce stress" (Derlega and Janda, 1981).

We should be careful, though, about concluding that stress is always bad or harmful to us. At least one major researcher in the area of stress, Hans Selye (1978), maintains that some stress—what he calls **eustress**— may actually be beneficial. Just as arousal can be helpful in achieving some tasks (see Chapter 8), so Selye contends that stress can improve our functioning in some situations. However, some of us thrive on tranquility, whereas others require high levels of excitement to be happy in our lives. Thus if we are to take advantage of the benefits of eustress, we must be aware of our individual reactions to stress and adjust our lifestyles to utilize these reactions.

**Stress**
Changes, pressures, threats, and other conditions in life that make physical and emotional demands on a person.

**Eustress**
The "good" stress beneficial to the individual, according to Selye.

**Frustration**
A blocking or thwarting of goal-directed activities.

## FRUSTRATION

How often do you experience **frustration?** You may be surprised to learn that you are frustrated more often than you realize. What is frustration? We may define frustration as a blocking or thwarting of goal-directed ac-

Table 9.1
**Social Readjustment Rating Scale**

| Rank | Life event | Mean value |
|---|---|---|
| 1 | Death of spouse | 100 |
| 2 | Divorce | 73 |
| 3 | Marital separation | 65 |
| 4 | Jail term | 63 |
| 5 | Death of close family member | 63 |
| 6 | Personal injury or illness | 53 |
| 7 | Marriage | 50 |
| 8 | Fired at work | 47 |
| 9 | Marital reconciliation | 45 |
| 10 | Retirement | 45 |
| 11 | Change in health of family member | 44 |
| 12 | Pregnancy | 40 |
| 13 | Sex difficulties | 39 |
| 14 | Gain of new family member | 39 |
| 15 | Business readjustment | 39 |
| 16 | Change in financial state | 38 |
| 17 | Death of close friend | 37 |
| 18 | Change to different line of work | 36 |
| 19 | Change in number of arguments with spouse | 35 |
| 20 | Mortgage over $10,000 | 31 |
| 21 | Foreclosure of mortgage or loan | 30 |
| 22 | Change in responsibilities at work | 29 |
| 23 | Son or daughter leaving home | 29 |
| 24 | Trouble with in-laws | 29 |
| 25 | Outstanding personal achievement | 28 |
| 26 | Wife begin or stop work | 26 |
| 27 | Begin or end school | 26 |
| 28 | Change in living conditions | 25 |
| 29 | Revision of personal habits | 24 |
| 30 | Trouble with boss | 23 |
| 31 | Change in work hours or conditions | 20 |
| 32 | Change in residence | 20 |
| 33 | Change in schools | 20 |
| 34 | Change in recreation | 19 |
| 35 | Change in church activities | 19 |
| 36 | Change in social activities | 18 |
| 37 | Mortgage or loan less than $10,000 | 17 |
| 38 | Change in sleeping habits | 16 |
| 39 | Change in number of family get-togethers | 15 |
| 40 | Change in eating habits | 15 |
| 41 | Vacation | 13 |
| 42 | Christmas | 12 |
| 43 | Minor violations of the law | 11 |

Source: Holmes and Rahe, 1967.
You can measure the amount of stress during a year by the total number of life change units. These units are obtained by adding the mean value associated with the events you have experienced during the year. For example, suppose the following events occurred during the past year: marital separation (65), sex difficulties (39), outstanding personal achievement (28), change in living conditions (25), and vacation (13). Your score would be 170.
To interpret your score, compare the total to the following:
0 to 150: No significant problems          200 to 299: Moderate life crisis
150 to 199: Mild life crisis          300 and above: Major life crisis
This scale is a research rather than a diagnostic instrument. If you obtain a high score, you should not feel unduly alarmed. However, it might be beneficial to consider making some adjustments in your life-style.

tivities. Thus anything that prevents you from reaching some goal is a frustrating circumstance. Did an alarm clock wake you this morning? Did you want to continue sleeping? If so, then the alarm blocked this desire, and you experienced frustration. Did you drive your car to school? Did you get stuck in a traffic jam? If you did, you again experienced frustration. Right now you are reading this textbook. Is there something else you would rather be doing? If you think carefully about your activities during any ordinary day, you will probably discover that you are frustrated a good part of the time.

How do you feel when you are frustrated? Most people think of frustration as an unpleasant emotional state. In this book, we define frustration in terms of the precipitating circumstances rather than the consequences, although we will be looking at some of these consequences later.

There are many circumstances that block us from reaching a particular goal. For example, you may want to remain in college next year, but you might have to take a year's leave of absence so that you can work to earn your expenses. Or suppose your two favorite rock groups finally come to town, but their concerts are both scheduled for the same night. Or perhaps your parents object to the length of your hair or your style of dress and threaten to withdraw financial support unless you make certain changes. These are all examples of frustration arising from environmental circumstances.

**Like these two men, arguing over responsibility for the holdup and damage to their cars, we experience frustration many times every day when we are prevented from doing what we want to do.**

"This is designed to prepare your child for life
in today's world—no matter how he puts
it together, it's wrong."

From *Wall Street Journal,* permission—Cartoon Features Syndicate.

Not all frustrations arise from external barriers. Sometimes, limitations *within* individuals prevent them from reaching their desired goals. For example, an outstanding college basketball star may be rejected by the professionals because he is not tall enough. Or a young man who is overweight may spot an outfit that he really likes but find that he cannot fit into it. Frustrations resulting from personal limitations often involve aspirations to goals that are beyond a person's capabilities.

The frustrations that are the most serious and difficult to resolve are those arising from a source other than external or personal barriers. Conflicting attitudes or motives may prevent us from reaching a desired goal. This third condition is often called motivational **conflict.**

**Conflict**
The simultaneous arousal of two or more incompatible motives or attitudes.

## MOTIVATIONAL CONFLICT

Many different motivations operate concurrently. At any given moment, you may be hungry, be tired, need to go to the bathroom, want to call a friend, and need to study for an examination. Some of these motivations are incompatible with each other. For example, the need to study is incompatible with your desire to sleep. It is easy to think of examples of motivational conflict. An avowed critic of automobile-induced air pollution finds it necessary to drive to work or school. A young woman's desire to go to law school conflicts with her desire to have a baby. A 10-year-old boy wants to go to summer camp, but doesn't want to leave his best friend behind. Some of these conflicts are relatively easy to resolve. Others cause prolonged and profound anxiety and confusion.

**Figure 9.1**    **This schematic representation shows four types of conflict situation.**

Motivational conflicts are subjective in nature and need not reflect the realities of the external situation. A teenaged girl may be apprehensive about starring in the senior play. Although she has appeared successfully in other plays, she may be plagued with self-doubts about taking on the new role. A friend with a more objective view of the situation may find this behavior incomprehensible. The reassurance of this friend—"Don't be silly, you'll be great"—may fall on deaf ears. Whatever the external reality may be, the girl is experiencing what is, to her, a genuine conflict.

Figure 9.1 shows the four basic types of conflict situations: approach–approach, avoidance–avoidance, approach–avoidance, and multiple approach–avoidance (Lewin, 1935; Miller, 1944).

## Approach–Approach Conflict

We often find ourselves simultaneously motivated to approach two desirable but mutually exclusive goals. Because both of the goals are desirable, we refer to this type of situation as an **approach–approach conflict.** Suppose you press the "down" button for an elevator and two elevators arrive at the same time, both going down. Or you must decide which of two appetizing desserts to have after dinner. Or you are faced with a choice between two interesting television shows.

Once you choose between the two goals, you have resolved the conflict. The initial choice is determined by the relative strengths of the two approach tendencies. If one goal is decidedly more attractive, the decision is made rather easily. For example, if an applicant has been accepted by two equally desirable graduate schools, and one school offers a fellowship and free tuition whereas the other does not, the applicant will have little difficulty deciding between the two schools.

In general, approach–approach conflicts are relatively easy to resolve. A slight hesitation may accompany decision making in this type of conflict, but it is usually short-lived.

## Avoidance–Avoidance Conflict

Sometimes we are faced with a choice between two undesirable goal objects—"caught between the devil and the deep blue sea." What we really want to do is avoid both goal objects by escaping the situation altogether; however, the circumstances may be such that we are forced to choose one of the unpleasant alternatives. For example, a child may be forced by his father to choose between spinach and lima beans, both of which he dislikes. A senior in college may need a specific course for graduation, but may learn that the only two instructors who teach it are disliked by everyone who has taken the course. An individual with a throbbing toothache must bear the pain or submit to the dentist's drill.

**Avoidance–avoidance conflicts** generally result in much indecision and hesitation. If the conflict is intense, the individual may try to escape, if this is possible, and/or freeze (that is, take no action). For instance, the college senior may contemplate dropping out of school, petition for waiver of the course requirement, or do nothing because no alternative appears to be viable. The young child faced with two extremely unpleasant alternatives may decide to run away from home, if only for an hour or two.

## Approach– Avoidance Conflict

In the examples of conflict just presented, we discussed the goals as if they produced *either* an approach *or* an avoidance tendency. In fact, most goals have both positive and negative aspects. Ice cream is delicious, but loaded with calories. Smoking may be pleasurable, but carries a potential health hazard. You may love your parents, but find them a nuisance at times. A teenager may disapprove of a proposed action by her peers, but fear censure from the peer group if she objects. When we have both positive and negative feelings about a goal object, we refer to these feelings as **ambivalence.**

**Approach–avoidance conflicts** usually involve much vacillation and indecision. A person who decides to give up smoking may find himself picking up and putting down a cigarette every few minutes. A student who feels inadequately prepared for an examination will be ambivalent about attending class that day. She may get into her car and drive directly to school and then, by the time she has parked the car, start to have second thoughts about going to class. The closer she gets to the classroom, the more real the danger appears to be and the more hesitant she may become in her approach.

Anything that affects the motivational strengths associated with the approach or avoidance tendencies will affect the behavior toward or away from the goal object. For instance, suppose our hesitant student, described in the preceding paragraph, hears rumors that the upcoming examination is unusually easy. If she believes these rumors, her motivation to approach is likely to increase.

In talking about approach–avoidance conflicts, it is helpful to introduce the concept of **gradients** of approach and avoidance. A gradient is a change in the strength of the response tendency with decreasing distance from the goal object. What do we mean by distance from a goal object? Distance can be physical, psychological, or temporal. A lion that is 3 feet away behind bars is physically close but psychologically far away. We have all experienced the effects of temporal distance on approach–avoidance conflicts: At 8:55 A.M., a 9:00 A.M. examination is a lot closer than it was the previous evening.

**Approach–approach conflict**
A conflict in which the individual is simultaneously motivated to approach two desirable but incompatible goals.

**Avoidance–avoidance conflict**
A conflict in which the individual is simultaneously motivated to avoid two undesirable alternatives.

**Ambivalence**
Mixed feelings (both positive and negative) toward a person or situation.

**Approach–avoidance conflict**
A conflict in which the individual is simultaneously motivated both to approach and to avoid a goal object.

**Gradient**
A change in the strength of the response tendency, as shown by a rising or falling curve in a graph.

In approach–avoidance conflict, we experience the conflicting positive and negative sides to a situation. This young cowgirl wants the rewards of participating in a rodeo; but in order to obtain them, she must go through the frightening experience of the ride itself.

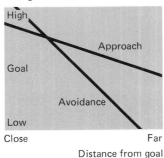

Strength of motive

High

Approach

Goal

Avoidance

Low

Close

Far

Distance from goal

**Figure 9.2**

**Approach–avoidance conflict**

Both the approach and the avoidance motives are strongest nearest the goal; however, the approach motive remains strong even at some distance from the goal.

There are two types of gradients in an approach–avoidance conflict. The **approach gradient** describes the strength of the tendency to *approach* the goal at varying distances from it. In contrast, the **avoidance gradient** describes the strength of the tendency to *avoid* the goal object at varying distances away. In general, the avoidance gradient is steeper than that of approach. This means that, in any conflict involving both approach and avoidance, the strength of the avoidance tendency at the goal is greater than the strength of the approach tendency (see Fig. 9.2). This is why such conflicts are much more difficult to resolve than the other types of conflict just discussed. Unlike the other types of conflict, an approach–avoidance conflict makes it virtually impossible to leave the scene. Individuals trapped in such a conflict cannot get far enough away because the approach tendency draws them toward the goal. At the same time, they cannot reach the goal because the avoidance tendency draws them away. Presumably, the closer they get to the goal, the more anxiety they experience. At the same time, the closer they get to the goal, the more they wish to reach it.

Approach–avoidance conflicts often form the basis of enduring emotional problems that may last throughout life. For instance, a man may have strong homosexual desires. At the same time, he may react with guilt or shame or revulsion to the possibility of a homosexual relationship. If sexually approached by another man, he may experience tremendous anxiety and a strong desire both to approach and to avoid a homosexual encounter.

**Approach gradient**
A change in the strength of the approach tendency with decreasing distance from the goal object.

**Avoidance gradient**
A change in the strength of the avoidance tendency with decreasing distance from the goal object.

How are approach–avoidance conflicts resolved? Think about the last time you had conflict about attending a particular examination. Either you went or you did not; therefore you somehow resolved the conflict. A general strategy for resolving approach–avoidance conflicts is to do something that results in a change in the relative strengths of the two opposing tendencies. Let us suppose that you decided to go to that examination. You may have remembered that the exam covered old material and you would probably do well. Thus the strength of the tendency to avoid was decreased. Or you may have recalled that this instructor never gives makeups, a factor that increased your approach tendency. Suppose, on the other hand, you decided to avoid the examination. You may have resolved this conflict in favor of avoiding by raising the avoidance gradient (realizing how unprepared you were) or by lowering the approach gradient (remembering that the instructor gives makeup exams and that they are reputed to be easier than the original).

## Multiple Approach–Avoidance Conflict

In most real-life situations, any particular goal may have both positive and negative aspects. Think for a moment about some of your own goals and desires in life, and you will find that they are fraught with negative components. When you are studying for a particular career, there are many things you must do that are distasteful. There are long hours of arduous study, many dull lectures to be attended, and many courses that you would prefer not taking. Even a situation that appears to be highly positive may have some negative aspects. We previously discussed approach–approach conflicts as if each goal had only positive elements. In reality, there are some negative aspects to almost all goals in life. For example, those two delicious desserts that you must choose between are both very fattening; and both of those "down" elevators that arrive at the same time have been known to get stuck between floors.

To complicate matters further, a host of motives operates simultaneously within the individual. Each of these motives demands its own goal. The goals may have both negative and positive elements and may be incompatible with each other (see Fig. 9.3).

**Figure 9.3**
**Conflicts in the life of the poor harassed and bedeviled human being**

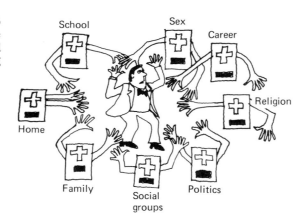

**Multiple approach–avoidance conflict**
A conflict in which the individual is simultaneously motivated both to approach and to avoid two or more goal objects.

**Frustration tolerance**
The amount of frustration that an individual is able to cope with effectively.

An excellent example of a **multiple approach–avoidance conflict** that confronts many of today's youth appeared in an article in *Life* magazine:

*Once last summer Richie had arrived at Jones Beach with a group of "heads." A hundred yards away were two couples who were "straights." Richie waved at the couples, then started walking toward them. But midway he stopped. He glanced back at his "head" friends, then looked forward toward the others. Finally he sat down on a dune mid-distance between them, not able to commit to either side. (Life, May 5, 1972)*

On the surface, this may appear to be an approach–approach conflict. But the fact that Richie had such difficulty in resolving this conflict suggests that there were avoidance elements associated with each goal. In fact, Richie may not have been completely comfortable with either the "straights" or the "heads."

## REACTIONS TO FRUSTRATION

Obviously, individuals differ widely in the variety and intensity of their reactions to frustration. Some people can tolerate enormous amounts of frustration without any disruptive effects on their ongoing behavior. For others, a minor perturbation becomes "the straw that breaks the camel's back." The amount of frustration that an individual is able to cope with is referred to as that person's **frustration tolerance.**

It is not fully understood why some people seem to have high tolerance to frustration and are able to function with remarkable aplomb un-

People deal with frustration in different ways and vary in their ability to tolerate frustration, as illustrated by the different reactions of these two football players.

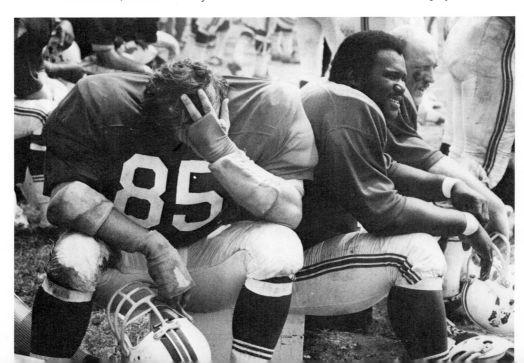

**Figure 9.4**
**Frustration situation**
**The screen separated the children from the more attractive toys and thus presented a frustrating barrier.**
From "Frustration and Aggression," The University of Iowa Press Child Welfare Series.

der circumstances that would drive others to the psychotherapeutic couch. Nor is it clear why other people have such short fuses that they appear to fall apart at the slightest hint of frustration or stress. Although there have been suggestions that genetic factors may be involved, it appears more likely that frustration tolerance involves learning, perhaps starting in infancy. There are as many differences among people in their levels of frustration tolerance as in the kinds of reactions frustration produces. You have probably observed the different reactions frustration produces in others and in yourself.

The different types of reactions produced by a frustrating situation were investigated in an experiment involving nursery school and kindergarten children. In one part of the experiment, the children were individually placed in a room filled with broken or incomplete toys. For example, there was an ironing board with no iron, a chair without a table, various water toys but no water, papers but no crayons. The children were permitted to view a set of complete and more attractive toys in another part of the room. They were separated from these toys by a wire screen (see Fig. 9.4). Presumably, this situation was frustrating, because the children could see the goal (better toys) but were blocked from reaching it. Many of the reactions observed were fairly typical reactions to frustration. In the words of the experimenters:

> *There is a decrease in the happiness of the mood in the frustrating situation; happy emotional expressions decrease in frequency and unhappy expressions increase. In frustration there is an increase in motor restlessness and hypertension as revealed by loud singing and talking, restless actions, stuttering, and thumb sucking. There is an increase in aggressiveness in frustration; hitting, kicking, breaking, and destroying all increase in frequency. (Barker et al., 1943, p. 456)*

## Aggression

The problem of human cruelty and **aggression** toward other humans is most persistent and puzzling. Pick up a copy of today's newspaper. Note the number of articles in which some act of aggression or violence is reported. Many people have expressed great concern about international terrorism. Victims are often selected at random, and their lives are terminated with no other purpose than that of "advertising the cause." History is filled with stories of human violence and aggressiveness, ever since "Cain rose up against his brother Abel and killed him."

Many theories have attempted to explain aggression, but no consensus has been achieved. Some have proposed that, in the course of evolution, aggressiveness was necessary for the survival of some species, including the human species. Because the fittest species (the most aggressive) survived and reproduced, the most successful and populous species would tend to be the most aggressive. Such theories imply that aggressiveness is an inborn trait that had survival value before the development of civilized societies. Furthermore, according to these theories, aggression is outdated in contemporary society and must be inhibited.

Other theorists argue that aggression may be learned in much the same way as operant behavior. If children respond to a frustrating situation with aggressive behavior and are rewarded, they tend to repeat the aggressive behavior whenever they find themselves in that same situation. Imagine the following common occurrence: One child sees another with a desirable toy. The other child refuses to give it up, so the first child hits the second and grabs the toy. Later, in similar situations, the aggressive behavior will probably be repeated.

Most often when we discuss aggressive behavior, we tend to focus on the aggressor. There has also been, however, some interesting research directed at the victim and the role victims play in affecting the aggressive behavior. One study showed that when the victim claimed not to be experiencing pain, the aggressor increased the intensity of the attack (Perry and Perry, 1974). Another study demonstrated that when aggressive behavior is reinforced by the victim (e.g., the victim gives in), the aggressor is likely to select that same victim again as a target for aggressive behavior (Patterson *et al.*, 1967). Victims who fight back, on the other hand, are not likely to be selected again.

Many parents directly instruct their children to be aggressive and reinforce their expressions of aggression. Indeed, many adults consider aggressiveness, particularly in males, to be desirable. In other cases, adults serve as models that children imitate. A little child who points at a playmate and says, "Bang, bang, you're dead," is probably imitating a favorite television hero. Studies have shown that when children see aggressive behavior in others, they tend to act more aggressively themselves (Bandura and Walters, 1963). In fact, following a summary of the effects of violence in television on children, the reviewers concluded that several lines of research "provide relatively convincing evidence that television violence can have an antisocial impact" (Roberts and Bachen, 1981, p. 342).

Other factors in the display of aggression appear to be both the level of the anger in the aggressor and the threat of retaliation. Studies have been conducted in which these two variables have been systematically

Studies have shown that children learn to respond to frustration with aggression when their aggressive behavior is rewarded with compliance.

varied (Baron, 1973, 1974). When anger is low, the possibility of retaliation appears to be an effective barrier against aggression. But when anger is intense, the threat of retaliation has little or no effect on the aggressive behavior. According to Baron,

> . . . this finding appears to suggest that threatened punishment may be much less effective as a technique for the prevention or control of common aggression than has previously been suggested, serving to substantially inhibit such behavior only where aggressors offer no provocation, or very mild levels of this factor. (Baron, 1973, p. 112)

It is interesting that aggression does not appear with equal intensity in all cultures. Indeed, members of some societies are remarkably free of aggressive behavior. Studies of primitive societies suggest that aggression is common when children are specifically trained in aggressive behavior. In one tribe in New Guinea, aggression is encouraged in boys from early infancy. The child cannot obtain nourishment from his mother without carrying on a continuous battle with her. Unless he grasps the nipple firmly and sucks vigorously, his mother will withdraw it and stop the feeding. In his frantic effort to get food, the child frequently chokes—an annoyance to both himself and his mother. Thus the feeding situation

**Some societies display little or no aggression. The Tasaday of the Philippines, for instance, have never possessed weapons of any kind.**

itself is "characterized by anger and struggle rather than by affection and reassurance" (Mead, 1939). The people of another New Guinea tribe are extremely peaceful and do everything possible to discourage aggression. They regard all instances of aggression as abnormal (Mead, 1939). A similar tribe—the Tasaday of the Philippines—has been discovered. These people are extremely friendly and gentle. They possess no weapons for fighting or food-gathering; in fact, they are strict vegetarians who live off the land (MacLeish, 1972). Evidence of this sort has been used to counter the argument that the human being is basically an aggressive animal (Montagu, 1974).

In our culture, we tend to regard aggressive behavior with a great deal of ambivalence.

> *During childhood aggression is discouraged; attitudes toward it are highly restrictive. Yet aggressiveness carries a premium in adult society. The ambitious, hard-driving, aggressive male represents the epitome of success in the competitive, free-enterprise system. His quiet, contemplative, introverted opposite is outdistanced in the race to the top. Aggressiveness appears to be approved in covert, sophisticated forms, but frowned upon in the overt, primitive, physical sorts that characterize children's behavior, except in such formalized events as athletic contests and war. (Medinnus and Johnson, 1976, p. 380)*

Although theorists disagree about the basic causes of aggression, most acknowledge a close link between frustration and aggression. Frustration leads to aggressive tendencies, which may or may not be manifested in aggressive behavior. Conversely, aggressive behavior is frequently, but not always, preceded by frustrating circumstances (Miller, 1941). Some theorists have proposed a modification of the frustration–aggression hypothesis. They suggest that aggression is a function of both the inner readiness to aggress (presumably as a result of frustration) and the nature of the external cues or target of the aggression (Berkowitz, 1965, 1974; Janis *et al.*, 1969). For example, imagine the following scene: You are strolling along the sidewalk in a shopping center when somebody trips you, sending you sprawling on the pavement. Turning around to find the cause, you see a boy of about 15 leering delightedly at you and making no bones about the fact that he was responsible for your present predicament. Are you likely to behave in an aggressive manner?

What if your tormenter turned out to be a large man of about 30 with a sneer on his face and a blunt instrument in his hand that he was waving threateningly? Would the fear of possible retaliation have any effect on your aggressive tendencies?

Finally, what if the other person turned out to be an extremely attractive member of the opposite sex who bore a concerned look on his or her face and whose air was clearly apologetic? Would your perception of the intent modify any aggressive feelings you might have had?

The point of all this is that the stimulus situation alone (the fact that you were tripped) would not necessarily trigger aggressive behavior on your part. Rather, such behavior would depend on a number of other factors, like fear of retaliation and the motive you attributed to the offending party. There is evidence to support the notion that the motives we attribute to others are a critical factor in our aggressive behavior (Nickel, 1974).

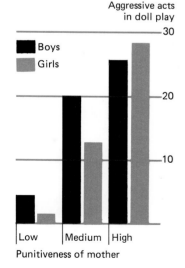

Aggressive acts in doll play

■ Boys
■ Girls

Low   Medium   High

Punitiveness of mother

**Figure 9.5**
**Punishment and aggression**

**The greater the punitiveness of the mother is, the more aggressive behavior the children show in doll play.**

**Punishing aggressive behavior.** What happens when you punish aggressive behavior? Physical punishment of aggression seems to lead to more aggression. Figure 9.5 shows that the more punishment the mother inflicts, the more aggressiveness her child shows in doll play (Sears *et al.*, 1953). In addition, a study of highly aggressive adolescent boys revealed that their fathers were extremely punitive at home. The boys were typically well behaved at home, but were highly aggressive at school (Bandura and Walters, 1959). Note that inflicting punishment provides a model of aggressiveness for the child.

It appears that punishment of aggressive behavior leads to inhibition of that behavior in the presence of the punishing agent, but to an increase of aggressive behavior when the agent is absent. Evidently, the child learns to discriminate between the occasions when aggressiveness is punished and those when there will probably be no punishment.

**Expression of aggression.** Aggressive behavior can take many forms. It may be physical, such as hitting, kicking, shooting, or stabbing. Or it can take the form of a verbal attack—screaming, name-calling, or a vituperative outburst of four-letter invectives.

When aggression follows frustration, the aggression impulse is usually first directed against the source of frustration. In the previously described experiment in which children's access to toys was blocked, the children's first acts of aggression were directed against the wire screen that stood in the path to their goal. Many of you may recall having had a toy taken from you by another child. Did you strike out at that child in retaliation? Perhaps such encounters resulted in a barrage of name-calling as well.

Often it is not possible or not safe to express aggression directly against the frustrating obstacle. The aggressive impulse may be inhibited because of a fear of possible punishment or harmful consequences. Thus workers who are frustrated by their supervisors may be tempted to strike out against the supervisors. They may, however, inhibit this impulse because of the threat of retaliation and instead may go home and start a family argument. We then say that they have **displaced** their **aggression.** When we displace aggression, we direct it toward a source other than the original cause of the frustration.

The following account provides an amusing illustration of displaced aggression by a four-year-old girl whose mother had punished her by shutting her in a clothes closet:

> *After a rather long silence, the mother inquired from her side of the door, "What are you doing?" The child said, "I've spat on your hat, I've spat on your coat, I've spat on your shoes. Now I'm waiting for more spit."*
> (Landreth, 1967, p. 327)

Displaced aggression is aggressive behavior directed toward a source other than the original cause of frustration. Some theorists believe that the violent urban riots of the 1960s were instances of displaced aggression and that rioters were striking out against *symbols* of ghetto oppression. Watts, California, shown here after a fiery outbreak, was a victim of this behavior.

**Displaced aggression**
Aggression directed toward a source other than the original cause of frustration.

**Scapegoat**
An innocent victim who becomes the target of displaced aggression.

Sometimes we displace aggression because we cannot identify the original source of frustration. We may feel angry but have no target against which to direct this anger. Bureaucratic organizations frequently heap frustrations upon individuals. Anyone trying to deal with such an organization usually does not know whom to blame, because the locus of decision making is frequently unspecified. Has this ever happened to you? You register for your courses for the following semester. The registration card comes back and you see that some of the courses you had planned to take are either not assigned or scheduled at the wrong time. You then have to stand in a long line at the registrar's office in order to reschedule your program. When you ask how this mistake was made, no one can give you a reason.

A common form of displaced aggression is **scapegoating.** A scapegoat is an innocent victim who becomes the target of displaced aggression. The term comes from an ancient Hebraic ceremony described in the Old Testament:

> . . . and Aaron shall lay both his hands upon the head of the live goat, and confess over him all the iniquities of the people of Israel, . . . and send him away into the wilderness. . . . the goat shall bear all their iniquities upon him. . . . (Leviticus 16:21–22)

Minority groups are often the victims of scapegoating. Well-known historical examples include the Christians of ancient Rome, the Jews of Nazi Germany, and the blacks in the United States, who, at one time, were lynched at an average rate of one every three days.

**Releasing aggressive feelings.**   Numerous therapy procedures, in addition to the various encounter groups springing up across the country, are based on the assumption that it is undesirable to have pent-up aggressive feelings. These procedures and groups encourage the venting of hostile and aggressive impulses, in the belief that expressing hostility in verbal or symbolic form is a "safe" way of releasing aggressive tendencies and results in a lessening of these feelings.

Research on this point, though not conclusive, is strongly leaning against this release hypothesis. In one study, subjects who were given an opportunity to express their anger against an antagonist ended up disliking the antagonist more, and were more physiologically aroused by his presence, than subjects who were not given the opportunity to vent their feelings (Kahn, 1966). In another study, children showed no reduction in their aggressive feelings even though they were allowed to express physical or verbal aggression against a child who had frustrated them (Mallick and McCandless, 1966). In a major review of the evidence concerning the release of pent-up feelings, the reviewer concluded that watching violent action or behavior or engaging in verbal or physical aggression does not reduce hostile impulses but rather seems to increase them. For example, if we are angry at the time we are watching violence on television, our tendency toward aggression may be increased by what we see (Quanty, 1976). Further research is needed before definitive statements can be made.

## COPING WITH STRESS

One of the most impressive characteristics of humans is our adaptability, our ability to get used to an almost endless variety of different circumstances. We have managed to survive under conditions of semistarvation, dire poverty, daily bombardments, and the incredible brutality sometimes inflicted on us by others. We have learned to cope with virtually all climatic conditions, from the tropical rain forests of South America, to the barren wastelands of the Sahara, to the numbing cold of the Arctic and Antarctic. We are able to adapt to a world that is forever changing, and throwing surprises at us almost daily. At times, however, our exposure to the continual kaleidoscope of changing circumstances has exacted a heavy toll.

## General Adaptation Syndrome

What happens when someone is subjected to chronic and prolonged stress? One investigator has systematically exposed experimental animals to various types of stress, including surgical operations and exposure to extreme cold (Selye, 1956, 1973). He has observed that prolonged stress resulting from emotional pressures, fatigue, or physical suffering produces a three-stage physiological reaction in the body: the alarm stage, the resistance stage, and the exhaustion stage. These three stages have been called the **general adaptation syndrome.**

**General adaptation syndrome**
A three-stage physiological reaction to prolonged stress, consisting of an alarm stage, a resistance stage, and an exhaustion stage.

1. **Alarm stage.** Our first reactions to stress involve such normal bodily defenses as widespread circulatory and digestive changes as well as increased secretions from the pituitary and adrenal glands. The adre-

**Figure 9.6**
**Illustration of the diffuseness of emotional responses under tension**

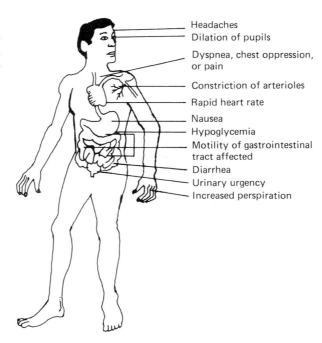

- Headaches
- Dilation of pupils
- Dyspnea, chest oppression, or pain
- Constriction of arterioles
- Rapid heart rate
- Nausea
- Hypoglycemia
- Motility of gastrointestinal tract affected
- Diarrhea
- Urinary urgency
- Increased perspiration

nal glands, you will recall, mobilize many of the body's defense reactions to meet emergency conditions. The increased production of adrenalin is accompanied by an increase in adrenal size and a change in adrenal color. All of these bodily reactions are adaptive in that they permit us to cope with stressful circumstances.

2. **Resistance stage.** If the stress continues, we appear to develop a resistance to the conditions that led to the initial alarm reaction, and many of the symptoms that occurred during the first stage disappear. For example, the adrenals return to their normal size and color. We are, in fact, paying dearly for this seeming resistance. Continued high levels of secretion from the pituitary and adrenal glands are necessary to maintain the appearance of well-being.

3. **Exhaustion stage.** If exposure to stress persists, we pass the point of no return. The pituitary and adrenal glands are strained beyond their limits and can no longer maintain their secretions at this increased rate. Salt levels in the blood diminish markedly and the kidneys undergo damaging changes. Without relief from the relentless assault of stressful circumstances, the organism will die, as if from exhaustion.

## Psychosomatic Disorders

Intense emotions mobilize virtually all the body's systems: the circulatory system (heart, skin, and blood vessels), the endocrine glands (pituitary, adrenals, gonads), the respiratory system (mouth, nasal passages, and lungs), the digestive system (stomach, intestines), and the central nervous system. Figure 9.6 illustrates these diffuse reactions. As you might expect, anything that disturbs our emotional life will have widespread effects on our physical well-being. This is particularly true when emotional responses become classically conditioned to environmental stimuli (Chapter 2). For example, children who are severely punished for not eating will learn to react with fear to the feeding situation. Fear typically leads to inhibition of the entire digestive system. Thus learned fear will interfere with normal digestive processes and may have profound and long-term effects on the organs involved in digestion. Similar parallels may be drawn between emotional conditioning and other bodily systems.

In the not too distant past, the practice of medicine was thought to be concerned primarily with diagnosing and treating the physical symptoms of disease. In contrast, mental and emotional disorders were thought to be the exclusive province of clinical psychologists and psychiatrists. We now recognize that the human organism must be viewed as a totality in which physical and emotional factors constantly interact. Every so-called physical disorder may have a strong emotional component. Thus people seem less resistant to the common cold when they are under stress or suffering unusual emotional duress. Moreover, many doctors have observed that their patients' emotional health significantly affects their ability to recover from a physical illness. For example, there have been many reports of people "hanging on" long after a serious physical disorder should have terminated their lives. On the other hand, some people with relatively minor disorders have succumbed as if welcoming

Because our emotions can affect our health, it is important in treating what appears to be a physiological disorder to consider psychological as well as physical factors. This medicine man may well offer beneficial medical treatment, but in part his treatment is effective because his patients believe he can cure them.

death. As one pioneering investigator of the relationship between emotional and physical factors has observed, it is often "more important to know what kind of patient has the disease than what kind of disease the patient has" (Dunbar, 1943, p. 23). Clearly, then, the physician of today must treat more than merely the physical aspects of disease. Emotional factors should receive at least equal consideration.

Not only are emotional factors involved in many, if not all, physical illnesses, but there are certain disorders in which emotions appear to play the key role. Such conditions are commonly referred to as **psychosomatic disorders.** There is considerable evidence that a wide range of organic disorders (such as ulcers, heart disease, and asthma) have strong emotional components. Indeed, specialists in psychosomatic disorders conservatively estimate that 50 percent or more of many physical disorders have their origins in, or are aggravated by, emotional factors.

Psychosomatic symptoms appear to flare up and subside in relation to the amount of emotional stress the individual is experiencing at any given time. For example, a harassed student may develop severe and debilitating headaches when faced with a deadline on a term paper and two upcoming quizzes, all immediately after the homecoming weekend.

One of the questions that has puzzled investigators in this area is why some people develop ulcers, others develop headaches, and still others develop difficulties with other organ systems. Some investigators

**Psychosomatic disorders**
Physical disorders such as ulcers, asthma, and hypertension that have their origins in, or are aggravated by, emotional factors.

have suggested that the predisposition to certain psychosomatic ailments may be genetically determined. Such disorders as stomach ulcers and asthma have been found to run in families. But because we learn many of our emotional responses by imitating our parents and by being reinforced by them for this imitation we cannot rule out the possibility that learned factors are involved.

Other investigators have speculated that, in a given individual, certain organ systems are more vulnerable to psychosomatic attack than others. For example, people who have a history of severe respiratory ailments are more likely to develop asthma than, say, a stomach ulcer. One study of 1200 asthmatic patients reported that 98 percent of asthmatic attacks were preceded by some respiratory infection (Bulatov, 1963).

Whatever the predisposing factors in psychosomatic illness may be, it is clear that learning plays a key role in the course and development of these disorders. We have already seen (Chapters 5 and 7) that responses of the autonomic nervous system are subject to voluntary control and can be conditioned. If autonomic responses are indeed influenced by circumstances in the environment, it is possible that the specific bodily reactions in psychosomatic disorders are learned in much the same way as any other behavior pattern. One investigator, for example, was able to elicit respiratory patterns that resembled asthmatic breathing by reinforcing certain kinds of breathing (Turnbull, 1962).

It has been suggested that psychosomatic disorders may result from the accidental pairing of physiological responses and reinforcement (Lang, 1970). Here is an example:

> . . . *a child may get little or no attention from crying, but the gasping or wheezing reactions that often follow crying spells may obtain immediate attention and concern for him. If this pattern is repeated, the infant might learn an asthmalike response as a means of obtaining parental attention and alleviating distress. In addition, an asthmatic reaction—as a means of reducing anxiety—might generalize to other types of stressful situations. By virtue of its anxiety-reducing quality, it would continually be reinforced, and hence tend to persist. Even when more adaptive ways of coping with anxiety were later acquired, the individual might still resort to asthmatic attacks under severe stress. (Coleman, 1976, p. 510)*

Although it may be tempting to conclude that a given case of, say, asthma or ulcers is psychosomatic, a note of caution is in order. These same conditions can result from physical causes in which emotions play only a minor role. Emotional stress has been implicated in a wide variety of physical ailments ranging from skin disorders, backaches, headaches, and asthma to hiccoughs, ulcers, and disturbances in menstruation. Let's look at four disorders—asthma, ulcers, hypertension, and heart attacks—in which emotional factors appear to be of paramount importance.

**Asthma.** Asthma attacks are characterized by breathing difficulties—wheezing, accumulation of mucus in the lungs, and irregular contractions of the bronchial tubes. Although an attack is frequently precipitated by inhaling such irritants as pollen and dust, emotional factors are believed to play a role in at least 75 percent of all cases. A person who is allergic to cat hair may, for example, have an attack if he or she sees even a porcelain figurine of a cat. Presumably as a result of prior conditioning, this person responds emotionally to cats and generalizes this response to similar stimuli.

It has also been demonstrated that suggestion and expectation play a role in precipitating asthma attacks. In one study, 40 patients suffering from respiratory disorders inhaled the mist of a salt solution which they were told contained dust or pollen. Of these patients, 19 developed typical asthmatic symptoms. What is more, the 12 patients showing the most severe attacks were "treated" with the very mist that had induced the attack; they were told this time that the mist contained an asthma remedy. Their symptoms disappeared (McFadden et al., 1969).

The following account illustrates the role of expectancy in triggering an asthma attack:

> After moving into a new housing development, a group of men sought to "break the ice" by having weekly poker sessions in their homes. When it was my turn to host the group, I placed my dog in the basement so that he wouldn't interfere with the poker session with his continual begging for food. The cardplaying session went well until about midnight when the dog started to bark at the sound of a disturbance outside. One of the players, Charlie F., called out in distress, "You have a dog? I'm allergic to dogs." Within five minutes he had a full-blown asthmatic attack, with the characteristic wheezing and difficulty in breathing. Clearly, his reaction was not brought about by the presence of dog hairs in his environment (they had been present throughout the preceding three and one-half hours) but by the sudden awareness that a dog was in the house. Presumably this knowledge triggered an emotional response which led directly to the asthmatic attack. (Author's files)

**Ulcers.**    Many people have, at times, experienced acute stomach distress after a particularly bitter family quarrel, worry over finances, or a disappointing love affair. At these times, particularly when anxiety, hostility, and resentment are involved, the stomach becomes churned up. In some people, when these stresses are chronic, the lining of the stomach becomes engorged with blood, excessive acid-containing gastric juices are secreted, the stomach muscles contract, and small lesions are formed. The gastric juices enter these lesions and begin digesting the stomach or intestinal wall itself. These wounds are known as ulcers. Although similar conditions can result from physical causes such as faulty diet or disease, it is generally acknowledged that most ulcers are aided and abetted by internal emotional warfare (Kirsner, 1971).

A particularly dramatic observation of these physiological reactions to stress was provided by a patient who, because of an accident, could not take food through his mouth. It was necessary to expose the interior of his stomach, and it thereby became possible to directly observe the functioning of his stomach. During the course of various interviews, it was

Figure 9.7    The "executive monkey," on the left, was responsible for pressing a lever that prevented electric shocks from being delivered to both animals. The control animal, on the right had no part in the decision making. The executive monkey developed ulcers, while the control monkey did not. However, recent studies have cast doubt on the reasons why this happened.

noted that the patient became anxious, hostile, or resentful. At these times, there was a marked increase in acid secretions and stomach bleeding. It is interesting that when he was afraid, his stomach produced the opposite physiological reactions; that is, it calmed down (Wolf and Wolff, 1947).

Stress has been shown to produce ulcers in many laboratory animals. Figure 9.7 illustrates an experiment in which monkeys who were required to make "executive" decisions developed ulcers. More recent studies have cast doubt on the conclusion that being an "executive," as such, makes an organism more prone to developing ulcers. In the original study, the monkeys were not assigned at random to the experimental and control conditions. Rather, the more reactive and, presumably, more emotional monkeys were assigned to the "executive" condition, whereas the more placid ones were placed in the non-decision-making condition. This flaw in the design of the study was corrected, using rats as experimental subjects. The rats were randomly assigned to experimental conditions, and opposite results were obtained (Weiss, 1968, 1971). The animals in the passive condition did not fare as well as the "executives." They drank less, defecated more, lost more weight, and developed more severe ulcers than their executive counterparts.

Hypertension.    Under normal, relaxed conditions, the heartbeat is regular and the blood is distributed evenly throughout the entire body. Under conditions of stress, however, the familiar emergency reaction is observed: The blood is diverted from the organs of digestion to the muscles involved in fight or flight, and there is a sharp increase in blood pressure. We have already seen that this reaction is adaptive, because it enhances the ability to deal with the emergency. In most people, the body returns to its normal state after the crisis has passed. In some peo-

**Hypertension**
A medical disorder characterized by chronically high blood pressure.

**Defense mechanisms**
Behavior patterns aimed at reducing anxiety in the individual; they are presumed to be unconscious.

ple, however, the blood pressure remains abnormally high during periods of calm as well as periods of stress. The condition of chronically elevated blood pressure is known as **hypertension.**

In only a minority of the cases is the cause of hypertension known and ascribable to physical causes. In most cases the cause is unknown; however, emotional stresses appear to play a dominant role.

The following case illustrates hypertensive reactions in a young man:

> *Mark ————, a senior in law school, evidenced episodes of extreme hypertension whenever he was subjected to stress. He became aware of these episodes when he failed to pass his physical examination for induction into the Armed Forces because of exceptionally high blood pressure. In a later check at a medical clinic, under nonstressful conditions, his blood pressure was normal; however, under simulated stress conditions, his blood pressure showed extreme elevation; and this happened again when he returned for another physical examination at the induction center. Although most people show alterations in blood pressure under stress, Mark seemed to show unusual reactivity to a wide range of stressful conditions. (Coleman, 1976, p. 503)*

**Heart attacks.**   Long-term studies relating personality to heart problems led to the classification of people into two personality types. Type A personalities appear to be driven. They are extremely competitive and success-oriented and will push themselves near the limits of their endurance in order to achieve their goals. In contrast, Type B personalities are more relaxed, less driven, and less competitive than A's. As Box 9.1 points out, Type A and Type B persons appear to differ in more ways than their drive levels.

## Defense Mechanisms

So far in this chapter, we have looked at the various sources of stress and some of the resulting behavior. We have seen that some reactions to stress might be considered constructive, others destructive; still others may represent a compromise. Suppose your car does not start in the morning, so that you are prevented from going to work or school. You might display one or more of several different behaviors. You might call for assistance, kick the car, take an alternative means of transportation, or withdraw from the situation entirely by going back to bed.

There are many stressful situations in life for which there are no appropriate or constructive behaviors. This is particularly true in approach–avoidance conflicts. There are many such conflicts which, for reasons beyond our own control, we cannot satisfactorily resolve. Think for a moment about your own present life situation. Can you think of any conflicts that exist now and have persisted for a period of time? If you are a student now and are dependent on your parents for financial support, you might desire freedom from the various restrictions and controls that they still exercise over you. To repudiate your parents might result in a withdrawal of support. Many students do not resolve this conflict until

# BOX 9.1

## Stress, Competition, and Heart Attacks

Ambitious individuals who set goals and deadlines for themselves at home and at work are called Type A's. Though they may be very successful, their relentless activity makes them prime targets for heart attacks under stress. Type A's set high expectations and push themselves to succeed.

Type B persons are not as competitive as A's. They take work home occasionally, but they do not set goals and deadlines for themselves very often. Type B's are less likely to have heart attacks under stress.

In one study students were asked to walk on a motorized treadmill that had a steeper incline as it went along. A measure was taken of how well the students used their lung capacity to absorb oxygen during the exercise. Type A's used 91.4 percent of their lung capacity. Type B's used only 82.8 percent. Students were often asked how tired they felt during the study. Type A's were less likely to admit being fatigued, even though they had worked harder.

Type A individuals worry about keeping control over what happens to them. It upsets them if they lose control. A study conducted by psychologist David Glass* investigated men hospitalized for heart attacks and other diseases. The men were between thirty-five and fifty-five years of age. Heart-attack victims were more likely to report that they had suffered a great personal loss during the preceding year (such as being fired, death of a close relative, or a financial difficulty) than were a group of healthy, unhospitalized men. Type A persons were more likely to react to such a loss by developing a heart attack. The other men were more likely to develop other diseases.

---

*"Stress, competition, and heart attacks," by D. O. Glass, reprinted from *Psychology Today* Magazine, copyright © 1976, Ziff-Davis. (Adaptation of this material as used in V. J. Derlega and L. H. Janda, *Personal Adjustment*, 2nd ed. Copyright © 1981 Scott, Foresman and Company.)

---

they graduate from college and are able to become gainfully employed on their own. Lifelong ambivalence toward one's parents is not uncommon. To take another example, some form of sexual conflict may start in adolescence and persist throughout the lives of many individuals.

Conflicts like these give rise to prolonged and persistent anxiety. Box 9.2 describes a therapy technique that is used with students for whom the study of mathematics has become stressful.

We have all developed techniques for dealing with stress and anxiety. These techniques protect us against the excessive anxiety produced by the unresolved conflicts. The various anxiety-reducing techniques are generally referred to as **defense mechanisms,** first described in the writings of Sigmund Freud. They defend individuals against their own feelings of inadequacy, guilt, and unfavorable self-evaluations when they are faced with continuing conflict and stress. Although there are individual differences, we all use defense mechanisms to some extent. We have probably all heard a failing student blame his poor performance on the instructor: "She doesn't know how to teach." And we have probably encountered an instructor who attributes the poor attendance in class to the low level of student motivation. Both of these are examples of projection, which will be discussed shortly.

How do we decide whether the student's failure was due to poor instruction or whether he was using a defense mechanism to protect himself from an awareness of his own inadequacy? All defense mechanisms

# BOX 9.2

## Mathematics Anxiety

For many students, courses involving mathematics and numerical concepts evoke high levels of anxiety. One investigator (Suinn, 1971) selected those students who scored high on a "mathematics anxiety" questionnaire and gave them a "treatment" consisting of a short-term course in which they learned to relax in the imagined presence of situations that aroused progressively greater degrees of anxiety. For example, a tape recording described a situation that presumably elicited a relatively low level of anxiety ("Consider two different summer job offers"). This was followed by a description of a neutral situation, one that should have aroused no anxiety. The students were then trained in relaxation techniques. The first scene was presented again, and the students were told to relax. This general sequence was repeated for scenes that became increasingly anxiety-producing. By the time the subjects arrived at the most anxiety-arousing scene ("Imagine you are taking a final examination in mathematics"), they were expected to show considerable skill at relaxing in the presence of anxiety-producing stimuli.

The basic assumption underlying the use of "relaxation" techniques is that relaxation is incompatible with anxiety. If people can learn to relax in anxiety-arousing situations, they can gain a measure of control over their anxiety. In doing so, they can reduce the debilitating effects of anxiety on learning and performance. The results of this study support both expectations. The subjects who received relaxation therapy obtained sharply reduced scores when retested on the "mathematics anxiety" questionnaire, and their performance on a test of mathematical ability improved markedly. Indeed, their performance on the mathematics test was superior to that of nonanxious control subjects. Some of the tape recorded materials used in the first therapy session are presented here.

### Session 1

#### Scene 1

Now as you are relaxing like that I want you to picture a scene. I want you to picture a scene in which you have two different offers for summer jobs. One will pay you a pretty good salary, while the other one pays a lower salary but includes a room and board and travel expenses. Just picture yourself sitting down in a comfortable, relaxed manner. You are beginning to figure out which of the jobs is the most lucrative. As you work out the problem you remain relaxed and at ease. Just picture that scene.

#### Neutral Scene

Now let that scene go. Just let it dissolve away and picture another scene this time. Picture a peaceful scene. Just imagine that on a calm summer's day you lie on your back on a soft lawn and watch the clouds move slowly overhead. Just picture yourself on a lawn or meadow looking up at a blue sky and watching the clouds move slowly overhead. Notice in particular the brilliant edges of the clouds as they slowly pass over you.

#### Relaxation

Now let that scene dissolve away. Just let it completely dissolve away and go back to relaxing. Just concentrate on letting your whole body relax more and more and deeper and deeper. Relax your forehead and your jaws. Relax your neck, shoulders, your chest and back, relax your stomach. Relax your hips and thighs, your knees, your calves. Relax your ankles and feet. Relax your arms, your forearms. Relax your hands and fingers. Just let your whole body relax more and more deeply. Get rid of any tension you might have in your body. Just let the relaxation take over.

#### Scene 1

Now once again as you are relaxing I want you to picture a scene in which you have two different offers for summer jobs and one of them will pay you a pretty high salary while the other one pays room and board, travel expenses, but a lower salary. Now just picture yourself sitting down in a comfortable, relaxed manner and beginning to figure out which of the jobs is the most lucrative, and as you work on the problem you remain relaxed and at ease.

involve some degree of self-deception and may be accompanied by some distortion of reality. To judge the student's behavior accurately, we would need to know something about his underlying motivations and whether or not he was deceiving himself about the cause of his failure.

We can sometimes make inferences about whether people are using defense mechanisms by observing their behavior. If their reactions are inappropriate to the situation (for example, laughing at a failing grade), we can guess that they are probably protecting themselves through the use of a defense mechanism.

Let's look at some of the most frequently used defense mechanisms. Although we will be looking at the "normal" uses of defense mechanisms here, we will examine them in Chapter 14 as they appear in more exaggerated, or abnormal, ways.

**Repression.**   Some of us experience some feelings or impulses that are unacceptable to us and thus produce anxiety. For example, a man might find that he has developed strong sexual feelings toward another man, and consequently feel guilty and anxious. How might he overcome this feeling of anxiety? Psychologists have found that people can **suppress** the anxiety-producing thoughts by consciously trying to think of other things, or by engaging in activities that distract them from the anxiety-arousing impulses. However, another process, **repression,*** operates automatically and involuntarily to cause an individual to "forget" undesirable impulses or feelings. Repression does not occur with all anxiety-producing material. It is difficult to specify all the conditions under which it occurs; however, several facts are clear: (1) The thought or impulse must have great significance to the individual; (2) it must be extremely anxiety arousing, probably involving feelings of guilt; (3) repression must lead to relief of the acute phase of anxiety.

Repression may be described as burying an impulse, or feeling, alive. We say "alive," because banishing objectionable thoughts or impulses from consciousness does not eliminate their dynamic force:

> They continue to lead a subterranean life beneath a conventional surface, yet they are liable to manifest their influence in traits of personality, in special interests, in some system of beliefs or code of values, or in more marked form as neurotic, psychosomatic, or psychotic symptoms. (Noyes and Kolb, 1963, pp. 41–42)

Moreover, the repressed impulses may express themselves in such disguised forms as dreams, fantasies, and slips of the tongue. Repressed impulses may also arouse vague feelings of discomfort or anxiety which, if they work their way toward consciousness, may become quite intense.

Under certain conditions, the repressed material can be brought into consciousness, where the associated anxiety can be dealt with and under-

**Suppression**
Conscious inhibition of anxiety-producing thoughts, feelings, and impulses (contrasted with repression, which is unconscious).

**Repression**
A defense mechanism in which the individual unconsciously excludes unpleasant thoughts, feelings, and impulses from conscious awareness.

---

*Many texts attribute to Freud the view that repression is an unconscious process. In an important paper on repression, two researchers (Erdelyi and Goldberg, 1979) carefully document their claim that Freud regarded repression as a conscious process.

Repression is an automatic process that causes an individual to forget something that causes anxiety or guilt. In *Ordinary People,* Timothy Hutton played the role of a boy who repressed events surrounding a boating accident because he felt guilty for living after his brother died.

stood. Such techniques as hypnosis, sodium pentothal interviews (see Box 9.3), and, as we will see later (Chapter 15), various types of psychotherapy have been used for this purpose.

The following case illustrates the extent to which repression may interfere with memories of unpleasant experiences and may even affect ongoing behavior:

> A young man who had recently become engaged was walking along the street with his fiancée. Another man greeted him and began to chat in a friendly fashion. The young man realized that he must know this apparent stranger, and that both courtesy and pride required that he introduce the visitor to his fiancée. The name of the other man, however, eluded his completely; indeed, he had not even a fleeting recognition of his identity. When in his confusion he attempted at least to present his fiancée, he found that he had also forgotten her name.
>
> Only a brief behavior analysis was necessary to make this incident comprehensible as an example of normal generalized repression. The apparent stranger was in fact a former friend of the young man; but the friendship had eventually brought frustration and disappointment in a situation identical with the one described. Some years before, our subject had become engaged to another young woman, and in his pride and happiness he had at once sought out his friend and introduced the two. Unfortunately, the girl had become strongly attached to the friend and he to her; at length she broke her engagement and married the friend. The two men had not seen each other until this meeting, which repeated exactly the earlier frustrating situation. It is hardly surprising that the newly engaged man repressed all recognition of his former friend, all hints as to his identity, and even the name of the fiancée. (Cameron and Magaret, 1951, pp. 367–368)

## BOX 9.3

A Case of Psychological Amnesia: Disassociation of Memory as the Unconscious Defensive Response to Intolerable Emotional Conflict

### 1. Parental approval vital

Mr. G. R. was a 24-year-old college student. He was the only son of an extremely ambitious father who was a very successful engineer. His mother was perfectionistic, obsessional, and domineering. The young man was in his third year of university study, struggling to get through a pre-engineering course, in which he was not the slightest bit interested. He felt, however, he had to continue, largely as a result of irresistible parental pressure. He had already failed one year in this course.

His third year was further complicated by the fact that he had made a marriage which had been kept secret, in as far as his parents were concerned. He did not feel that he could possibly tell them of his marriage unless at the same time at least, he could also present them with a successful college record. This was impossible. The parental approval which had always been vital to him appeared forever lost!

### 2. Precipitating event

The marriage had involved emotional and time demands, which had still further interfered with his college performance. He had become extremely anxious about the probable results of examinations, which were due to begin in a few weeks' time. One Friday afternoon, after classes, he took part in a "bull session" in the college dormitory. This left him thoroughly convinced that he would not be able to pass his examinations. This served as the precipitating event.

He started for home, but did not arrive there. Late that evening he was found wandering in the streets of a city some two hundred miles away from the site of his college.

### 3. Prompt identification and medical care

He was soon identified by papers in his wallet. There was also a picture of the few people who had been present at his wedding. One of these happened to be recognized by one of the local policemen. This friend had acted as best man at the wedding some six or seven months before. He was called to the police station to identify his friend. This he was quite promptly and positively able to do, although at this time the patient had no conscious memory of ever having seen this man before.

The patient was admitted to the psychiatric service of a general hospital and treated psychotherapeutically. *Pentothal* interviews were accompanied by strong suggestions that he would gradually recover his memory. By the end of the week, things were pieced together and, with the exception of some of the events of the trip from college, the material was returned to consciousness.

### 4. Amnesia an extension of avoidance pattern of defense

Further psychiatric study over a period of time revealed that this man had always been disturbed by his parents' attitudes. His established and usual method of handling these difficulties had been to attempt to ignore them. This was a pattern of avoidance. As he said, "I just pretend they're not there. In this way, I can deal with them. . . ."

His amnesic episode represented an episodic magnification and extension of this established pattern of defensive avoidance. Psychotherapy was able to resolve many of the problems. He accordingly was enabled to make marked improvement, with more realistic evaluation of his assets and future possibilities, . . . partly through some helpful modifications in certain of the parental attitudes.

Reprinted by permission of the publisher, from Laughlin: *The Neuroses*, 1st ed. Woburn: Butterworth Publishers, 1967.

**Denial**
A defense mechanism in which the individual unconsciously denies the existence of events that have aroused his or her anxiety.

**Reaction formation**
A defense mechanism in which individuals protect themselves from unacceptable motives or feelings by repressing them and assuming the opposite attitudes and behaviors.

**Denial.**    One of the simplest mechanisms of defense is **denial,** in which the individual "screens out" disagreeable events or materials by ignoring them. Denial is assumed to operate unconsciously by a protective mechanism of nonawareness; in this way it is different from a conscious effort to suppress or repudiate reality—for example, by lying. People may refuse to discuss topics that make them anxious, look away from unpleasant sights, or faint at times of emotional crisis. By denying the reality, they protect themselves from the associated anxiety. For example, a mother who refuses to admit to herself that her child is incurably handicapped may go from doctor to doctor looking for a different opinion. Or the relatives of a patient with a terminal illness may convince themselves that the patient is getting better.

The following case illustrates the mechanism of denial among the parents and sisters of a dangerous delinquent boy:

> *A large physically mature boy of fourteen was brought to a juvenile court by police officers who reported that his theft of a bicycle was the latest in a long series of minor offenses. . . . His neighbors complained that he struck and injured other children, that he was noisy and disorderly in his general conduct, and that he seemed to be out of control of his family . . . .*
>
> *It was impossible to obtain from the parents reliable evidence concerning the boy's early development. Consistently, in their reports, in their attitudes and in their general treatment of him, his parents and his sisters denied his retardation. . . . The parents explained that their son was "just playing" when in his vigorous activity he knocked the mother down, or nearly chocked to death another child. . . . Over and over again the parents repeated their repudiation of their boy's diagnosis of retardation. His sister expressed the family attitude in her description of her brother. "He's so bright and so good—he is just like Jesus." (Cameron and Magaret, 1951, p. 169)*

A general prescription for mental health, to which many psychologists subscribe, is that we should face the facts: Good contact with reality is necessary if we wish to deal effectively with the pressures and stresses of everyday life. One psychologist, Richard L. Lazarus, has presented convincing evidence that this prescription is not appropriate for all people at all times. Box 9.4 describes some instances in which Lazarus feels denial and illusion are useful in adjustment.

**Reaction formation.**    Individuals may protect themselves from unacceptable motives or feelings by developing conscious attitudes and behaviors that stress *opposite* motivations. Thus a mother who has strong, but unacceptable, underlying hostility toward an unwanted baby may become overprotective and smother the child in affection. People with intense unconscious sexual conflicts may protect themselves from feelings of guilt by devoting a large part of their lives to eradicating smut and pornography and other forms of social "evil," real or imagined. One clue to whether their behavior represents **reaction formation** is the degree of exaggeration that it displays. The famous line from Shakespeare, "The

## BOX 9.4

### A Case for Denial

For many years the traditional wisdom in psychology has been that people should "face facts." People should be able to recognize their own shortcomings, threatening situations, and other unpleasantries. Most mental health professionals believe that efficient perception of reality is an important characteristic of well-adjusted individuals.

Over the past few years psychologist Richard Lazarus at the University of California at Berkeley has been conducting extensive research on the topic of stress that has prompted him to arrive at some surprising conclusions. Lazarus believes that both denial (refusing to "face facts") and illusions (false beliefs about reality) can be important to psychological health—for some people on some occasions. When Skylab was about to fall to earth in 1979, Dr. Lazarus' advice when asked how to deal with the threat was to ignore it—advice that was consistent with his research findings.

Much of his research has been conducted with surgical patients. What he found was that patients who did use denial and who insisted on maintaining their illusions had a better post-surgical recovery than those patients who insisted on knowing all the facts about their surgery and having a detailed account of their prognosis. To illustrate, a patient who uses denial wanted to know very little about his upcoming operation. When asked about the operation, the patient might say, "I'll leave that to my doctor. He's the best in the world." After the operation, such patients have relatively few complaints. They may perceive any discomfort as something to be expected and not even report it to their physician. Furthermore, illusions can speed the recovery process. By believing they can make a speedy recovery, such patients may actually try harder. And physicians have long been aware that the patient's attitude plays an important role in the recovery process.

On the other hand, patients who "face the facts" are likely to be much more anxious about their operations—which can in turn lower the chances for success. Following surgery these patients are acutely aware of every ache and pain. Their inability to have illusions may cause them to be more pessimistic about their chances of recovery. Again, this attitude may interfere with the recovery process.

Lazarus is quick to point out that denial and illusions are not appropriate for every situation. He cited cases of women who denied the potential risk of a lump in the breast until it was too late for treatment. Men who were having heart attacks have begun to exercise to prove to themselves that nothing serious was wrong with them.

It is in situations where one has little control that denial and illusions can be most useful. Certainly Skylab's falling was beyond our control, and ignoring its threat was the best solution. So too, denial and illusions concerning a major operation could lessen anxiety and lead to a quick recovery.

---

"Positive Denial: A Case for Not Facing Reality," by R. S. Lazarus, interviewed by D. Goleman, reprinted from *Psychology Today Magazine,* copyright © 1979, Ziff-Davis Publishing Company.

---

lady doth protest too much, methinks," is a common way of acknowledging reaction formation.

Reaction formation may help people adjust to their situations by preventing them from recognizing tendencies within themselves that they regard as threatening or beneath their dignity. In extreme cases, however, it may lead to a rigidity of behavior and beliefs that seriously complicates their relationships with others. For example, the person who has devoted his or her life to eradicating pornography may inflict excessive punishment on a teenage son for reading books that are only slightly racy, and hardly pornographic.

**Intellectualization.**    Sometimes people defend themselves against the anxiety of a conflict by avoiding or cutting off their emotional involvement. They deal with the situation strictly on an intellectual plane. A man who has been recently divorced may discuss the causes for the breakup in a completely unemotional, detached, and clinical fashion. If we were to take his behavior at face value, we might think that he had no emotional involvement whatsoever.

The process of **intellectualization** is illustrated in the following account by a London prostitute:

> *The act of sex I could go through because I hardly seemed to be taking part in it. It was merely something happening to me, while my mind drifted inconsequentially away. Indeed, it was scarcely happening to me; it was happening to something lying on a bed that had a vague connection with me, while I was calculating whether I could afford a new coat or impatiently counting sheep jumping over a gate. (Cousins, 1938)*

**Rationalization.**    **Rationalization** is probably the most common defense mechanism. We often find plausible reasons for engaging in certain behaviors when we cannot face up to the real reasons. We fool ourselves into believing that our behavior is motivated by feelings and desires that are socially acceptable. For example, we persuade ourselves to watch a television program, instead of doing some unpleasant work, on the grounds that we "need a little relaxation."

We also use rationalization to muffle the disappointment of blocked or frustrated aspirations and desires. If we have difficulty achieving a satisfactory academic record in school, we may excuse ourselves by saying that "grades are not important," "the educational hierarchy is a tool of modern, corrupt society," or "most classroom instruction is not relevant." A well-known example of this type of rationalization is Aesop's fable of the fox who couldn't reach the grapes and rationalized, "The grapes are probably sour anyway."

It is, of course, often difficult to determine the dividing line between rationalization and objective, dispassionate consideration of the facts. We may suspect rationalization if people overreact, that is, if they become upset when their motives are questioned and have difficulty recognizing contradictory evidence.

**Projection.**    When we attribute our own unacceptable desires, impulses, traits, and thoughts to others, or even to inanimate objects, we are **projecting.** At one time or another, most of us have resorted to projection to protect us against an unfavorable self-evaluation. When we have prepared inadequately for an examination, we may attribute our poor performance to the instructor's lack of preparation—"How can I learn anything? He's so disorganized, he never prepares his lectures." Conversely, a disorganized and poorly motivated instructor with many failing students may ascribe their failure to inadequate preparation and motivation on their part. A young woman who is in conflict about her feelings for her

---

**Intellectualization**
A defense mechanism in which individuals defend themselves against the anxiety produced by a conflict by cutting off their emotional involvement and dealing with the conflict on a strictly intellectual level.

**Rationalization**
A defense mechanism in which individuals find socially acceptable but false reasons for their behavior.

**Projection**
A defense mechanism in which individuals attribute their own unacceptable desires, impulses, traits, and thoughts to others.

**Regression**
A defense mechanism in which individuals revert to an immature form of behavior that once brought satisfaction.

**Compensation**
A defense mechanism in which individuals make up for a real or imagined deficiency or weakness in one area by striving to excel in another.

**Figure 9.8
Projection**
Both motorists backed out of their driveways without looking in their rearview mirrors. Who is to blame?

boyfriend may decide to back off because "he really doesn't love me." Or a tennis player who carelessly splinters her racket on the ground may defend herself by sheepishly saying, "It was a lousy racquet." A person who holds hostile attitudes toward a particular social group may attribute this hostility to members of that group, accusing *them* of hating *him*.

There have been many laboratory studies on various aspects of the projection mechanism. One well-known study demonstrated projection among college students. Members of a fraternity were asked to rate themselves and each other on four undesirable traits: stinginess, obstinancy, disorderliness, and bashfulness. Of the subjects who possessed one or more of these traits, some displayed self-awareness, whereas others did not. Those subjects who had the traits but did not recognize them in themselves had a greater tendency to attribute these traits to others than did subjects who either did not have the traits or recognized them in themselves (Sears, 1936).

Projection often involves transferring blame to some object or person other than oneself (see Fig. 9.8). In this way people evade responsibility for their own acts.

**Regression.** We have seen that, as infants, we are completely dependent and relatively helpless organisms. As we progress from infancy through childhood and into adulthood, we gradually cease depending on others for gratification of our needs and begin to function as independent individuals. With increased autonomy come the burdens of greater responsibility. This transition is not an easy one to make, and adults often look back wistfully on the carefree and protected days of childhood. When confronted with overwhelming stress, they may find refuge in behavior that brought satisfaction at an earlier age. For example, an adult who feels neglected and unappreciated may throw a temper tantrum that, in childhood, brought parental attention. This kind of behavior is called **regression.** Children who experience sudden separation from their parents may regress to such infantile behaviors as thumbsucking and bedwetting.

**Compensation.** **Compensatory** reactions are defenses against feelings of inferiority stemming from real or imagined deficiencies or weaknesses. For example, people who see themselves as weak or frail may compen-

An asthmatic, nearsighted child who was teased mercilessly by his peers, Theodore Roosevelt was motivated to build up his body with special exercises. Energetic and adventuresome, he became an avid sportsman, a reform-minded politician, and a forceful chief executive.

sate by engaging wholeheartedly in activities in which physical prowess is not required, such as scholarly or artistic pursuits. In some instances of compensation, the person tries to achieve eminence in an activity in which his or her "deficiency" is most pronounced. The literature abounds with apparent examples of such compensation. For Franklin D. Roosevelt, polio apparently provided the impetus for outstanding achievements in politics. Moses, who was a stutterer, became a great leader. Glen Cunningham became a track star even though he had suffered extensive and severe burns on both of his legs when he was a child. Napoleon Bonaparte, who was extremely short in stature, strove to rise to the heights of military and political power.

**Displacement.** The woman whose boss yells at her and who, in turn, yells at her children; the worker who feels he will never get ahead and blames blacks for the economic woes of the country; the little girl who feels sexual urges toward her father and marries a man "just like dear old dad"—all show what Freud called **displacement,** redirection of reactions or energies from one object to another, "safer" object. Although this process can be beneficial to society, as when children learn acceptable ways to gratify their urges, it can also be detrimental, forming the basis for prejudice. Further, because of the need to find a safer—usually weaker—object on which to displace the reaction, the innocent and the vulnerable often pay for the sins of the powerful. In fact, displacement of frustration is frequently a cause of child and spouse abuse.

**Displacement**
A defense mechanism in which individuals transfer reactions or energy from one object to another, "safer" object.

**Sublimation**
A defense mechanism in which individuals transform "shameful" motives into socially acceptable, creative ones.

Sublimation.   One final defense mechanism is nearly always beneficial to the larger society. By **sublimation,** we transform anxiety-producing (shameful) motives into socially acceptable, creative purposes. For example, Freud believed that all great art was the result of sublimating sexual urges. He also felt that individuals ashamed of feelings of cruelty might sublimate these urges by becoming prosecutors or surgeons or otherwise employing power and inflicting pain for the benefit of others. Of course, sublimation may not be beneficial to the individual. The sublimator may close off many options and opportunities, as when the artist (or workaholic in any area) sacrifices a fulfilling personal life for art.

## Positive Action

The defense mechanisms may be broadly regarded as a means of escaping or avoiding the consequences of conflict and stress. In this sense they are negative forms of adjustment. There are also many positive measures that are available to us when facing life's problems. In this section we consider a few.

The first step in coping with conflict is to recognize that it is an inevitable and inescapable fact of life. Findings ways to adjust to conflict is as much a requirement for emotional well-being as food is for physical health. It is important to bear in mind that there are no easy and pat formulas. Just as a satisfactory diet requires a diversity of foods so also do successful adjustments to conflict demand a variety of coping behaviors. Moreover, what works with one person will not necessarily work with another. Each of us must find the drummer whose beat is uniquely suited to our step. This having been said, let us turn to some broad principles of adjustive behavior that each of us may adapt to meet our own needs.

Appraising the situation.   Imagine you are a woman in her middle thirties (try to do so even if you are a male: The ability to empathize with another's point of view is often a key element in finding solutions to social conflicts). You have been married 15 years, have two children approaching their teenage years, and a husband who commutes to the big city five days a week. You have a nice house in the suburbs, friendly neighbors, and access to the entertainment and cultural facilities of the city. Because this is what you wished for at the time of your marriage, you are unable to comprehend the onslaught of negative emotions that has assailed you in recent weeks. Periods of depression, when you doubt your own worth, alternate with intervals when you have hostile feelings toward your husband and children. There have even been a few worrisome occasions when you were quick-tempered with members of your family. To make matters worse, these antagonistic feelings and behaviors always leave a bitter residue of guilt. This, in turn, plunges you into another cycle of depression and anger.

The first principle of coping is to appraise the situation as calmly and objectively as possible. You should be aware of a natural tendency to defend yourself through the use of defense mechanisms. For example, it is easy to rationalize your negative feelings by telling yourself that your husband doesn't understand you and that your children take you for granted. Ironically, it is also easy to gain a measure of relief by placing the blame at your own footsteps. "I am unworthy of my family," you tell yourself, and you wallow in self-pity. Neither train of thought is likely to lead you out of the quagmire.

The key step in appraising the situation is to raise and calmly evaluate questions that have answers. You are unhappy. Why? You then consider alternative possibilities. "Is it possible that I really dislike my husband and/or children? No. Most of the time I derive pleasure from their company. When I consider the occasions when they irritate me, I realize that my agitated state preceded my encounters with them. Thus they are usually the scapegoats rather than the cause of my dissatisfaction."

Further inquiry may lead you to at least one source of chronic unhappiness. The children are rapidly approaching an age when they will be leaving home, either to attend college or to seek employment. Your husband has continued to grow both intellectually and socially since your marriage. All about you is movement and growth while you feel oppressed by stagnation.

Recalling Maslow's hierarchy of motives (Figure 8.12), you feel mired at the social level of need satisfaction. You have accomplished little toward gratifying the self-esteem motives at the next higher level (self-confidence, independence, achievement, knowledge, etc.).

**Planning a course of action.**   Let us suppose that you have correctly identified a major source of dissatisfaction—a feeling of stagnation in your social and intellectual development. What do you do now? Just as you previously considered alternative explanations of your feelings, you now explore alternative plans of action. Again the passwords are, "Remain calm and objective." The plan you decide upon should balance probability of success, expected satisfactions, and cost (Coleman, 1979).

Imagine that you consider "taking a sabbatical leave," a rather gentle way of expressing a plan to leave home. Will it work? What about satisfaction? Will it help you achieve your goal of social and intellectual growth? Finally, you must consider the emotional cost. Are you capable of cutting off your ties with your family, or will you be trading one cluster of guilt feelings for another? For some women, this may be the only solution that effects a satisfactory balance among the three factors. For others, the cost may be too high, the probability of success too low, or the satisfactions too doubtful. Some women may find a favorable balance by planning a career, returning to college to continue their education, or becoming actively engaged in some community or charitable activity.

**Implementing the action and revising in the light of feedback.** Whatever course of action is taken, the next step is to implement it. It is important not to regard the plan as fixed and unchangeable. Crucial to its success is feedback. Feedback lets you know how well you are doing and suggests revisions necessary to keep you on course.

# Summary

1. Stress is a common aspect of daily life. Individuals who experience many stressful life events run a greater risk of physical illness. However, positive stress (eustress) may be beneficial, depending on individual needs.

2. Frustration, which is a blocking or thwarting of goal-directed activities, may occur as a result of environmental circumstances or limitations within the individual. The most serious and difficult-to-resolve frustrations arise from conflicting attitudes or motives (motivational conflicts).

3. Many different motivations operate concurrently, and at times they are incompatible with one another. Four basic types of conflict situation have been described: approach–approach conflict, avoidance–avoidance conflict, approach–avoidance conflict, and multiple approach–avoidance conflict.

4. People differ widely in the variety and intensity of their reactions to frustration. The amount of frustration with which an individual is able to cope is called the frustration tolerance.

5. One of the common reactions to frustration is aggression. Specific forms of aggressive behavior are learned. Children who observe aggressive behavior in their parents will often imitate it. Moreover, when aggressive behavior is punished, there appears to be less aggressive behavior thereafter in the presence of the punishing agent but greater aggressiveness when the agent is absent.

6. Aggressive behavior may take many forms, physical and verbal, and may be directed toward the frustrating agent or displaced toward a source other than the original cause of frustration.

7. Whether or not we respond to frustration with aggressive behavior depends, in part, upon fear of retaliation and the motives we attribute to the instigator to aggression.

8. When an individual is subjected to chronic and prolonged stress, a three-stage physiological reaction (the general adaptation syndrome) occurs. This reaction includes an alarm stage, a resistance stage, and an exhaustion stage.

9. There are many physical disorders (psychosomatic illnesses) in which emotions can play a key role, including asthma, ulcers, hypertension, and heart attacks. Psychosomatic symptoms appear to flare up and subside in reaction to the amount of emotional stress that the individual is experiencing at any given time.

10. There are many conflict situations that persist over long periods of time—some for a lifetime. Many of these conflicts give rise to prolonged and persistent anxiety. Individuals may adopt various defense mechanisms to protect themselves against the excessive anxiety produced by unresolved conflicts. A few of the most common defense mechanisms are repression, denial, reaction formation, intellectualization, rationalization, projection, compensation, displacement, and sublimation.

11. Positive action when coping with stress includes appraising the situation, planning a course of action, implementing the action, and revising in the light of feedback.

# Terms to Remember

Stress
Eustress
Frustration
Conflict
Approach–approach conflict
Avoidance–avoidance conflict
Ambivalence
Approach–avoidance conflict
Gradient
Approach gradient
Avoidance gradient

Multiple approach–avoidance conflict
Frustration tolerance
Aggression
Displaced aggression
Scapegoat
General adaptation syndrome
Psychosomatic disorders
Hypertension
Defense mechanisms
Suppression
Repression

Denial
Reaction formation
Intellectualization
Rationalization
Projection
Regression
Compensation
Displacement
Sublimation

# DEVELOPMENT I

## DEVELOPMENT: A LIFELONG PROCESS

Today was his fiftieth birthday. Was it a cause for celebration, reflection, or despair? Jim was not sure. All he knew was that, on an intellectual basis, he was certain he would continue to grow older as measured by the calendar. But emotionally, deep down in his gut, he had never really accepted the reality of the aging process as it applied to him. He was embarrassed at some of the thoughts that had passed through his mind these many years: "Maybe I'm different; perhaps it won't happen to me," or "Age is a state of mind. I still have the same thoughts, the same outlook as when I was 20. Sure I'm a little slower, a bit paunchier, and I ache in places I didn't know I had. But my mind is still that of a young man."

He smiled when he thought of a "serious" conversation he had had with his mother when he was a young lad. What was he at the time? Six

Development is an ongoing process, beginning with infancy and continuing through old age. The process is a combination of behavioral and biological growth. Biological maturation sets the stage for adult behavior, but years of learning are necessary in order to bring a human being to adult maturity.

years old, or was it seven? Strange how well he could remember something that happened over 40 years ago—just like yesterday. He grinned broadly at the cliché. But it was true. He could even picture his mother, dressed in her Sunday best and good-naturedly accepting the "condolences" of family and friends. It was her birthday. "How old are you, Mommy?" he had asked during a pause in the festivities. "Why I'm 30 today," she replied. "Thirty? Mommy, you're old. I'll never get that old," he had solemnly promised. At that, his mother picked him up and smothered him with kisses. "Oh yes, you will, my little cherub. It will come much sooner than you can possibly imagine."

How right she was. Now *he* was 20 years older than she had been at the time! If his mother was old at 30, what was he at 50? He didn't try to answer the question. But there were many, many more questions he would be raising on this day he reached the half-century mark. Some would have to be answered. Others he would sweep into the deep recesses of his mind. Of one thing he was certain: This was going to be one of those days. Not much work would reach the "Out" basket today.

This scenario reminds us that life is a time line with a beginning and, with rare exceptions, a definable ending. It begins when a single sperm from the father overcomes many natural obstacles and hordes of competitors to fertilize the ovum of the mother. That single fertilized cell then begins a process of development that will continue throughout the individual's lifetime. Yes, Jim at 50 is still developing, still learning new ways to meet the demands of everyday living, and still acquiring new means of coping with the unforeseen turns and twists of fate that occur with astonishing regularity. Moreover, he will continue to do so throughout the remainder of his life.

Growth and change are inescapable facts of life. At 50, Jim is not the same person he was at 30, nor is he the same person he will be at 60. As we shall see, we do not grow physically, mentally, emotionally, socially, and morally up to a certain age and then undergo a sometimes precipitous and sometimes gradual decline in each of these capabilities. It is true that some processes are slowed with age (e.g., time to respond to the onset of stimulation), but others continue to improve as long as challenges are accepted, motivations remain high, and our physical structures survive the many risks of increasing age.

In this chapter and the next we shall look at some of the highlights in this lifelong process of development.

## GENETICS

Most of you can probably recall remarks such as, "You look exactly like your mother," or "You have your father's eyes." Such observations call attention to the fact that, at least in part, we are all products of our heredity. Each of us is a mixture not only of our immediate parents but of our parents' parents and all the generations that went before. Each of us is unique in our particular assortment of the thousands of traits and tendencies that are transmitted through heredity. We are all different from those in other families, and we are also different from our own brothers and sisters. The principles of genetics provide an understanding of how we can share certain characteristics with members of our families, yet still retain a unique genetic identity.

Each cell in the human body contains complex chemical substances known as **chromosomes** on which the **genes** are located. It is estimated that there are slightly over 1000 genes on each human chromosome and about 50,000 genes in all (Ritchie and Carola, 1979). Genes are the transmitters of hereditary material from parents to offspring. There are 23 pairs of chromosomes in each cell of the body (except the germ cells, which will be discussed in a moment). Normal body cells reproduce themselves by splitting in two so that each new cell is an exact copy of the "parent" cell. Each contains the full complement of 46 chromosomes.

In the female, one of these 23 pairs of chromosomes consists of two X chromosomes; in the male, this pair consists of one X and one Y chromosome. The X and Y chromosomes determine sex.

The sex organs of a mature adult produce **germ cells:** the egg in the female and the sperm in the male. Each germ cell contains one member of each of the 23 pairs of chromosomes. Thus germ cells contain half the usual number of chromosomes. All female eggs (germ cells) contain one X chromosome. Approximately half the sperm cells contain an X chromosome, and the other half contain a Y chromosome. Upon ejaculation of semen into the vagina of a woman who has ovulated (that is, whose ovary has produced a mature unfertilized egg), approximately 200 million sperm cells begin a race to fertilize the egg. If a sperm containing an X chromosome wins the race, the fertilized egg will have two X chromosomes and the egg will develop into a female. If fertilized by a sperm carrying a Y chromosome, the fertilized egg will have the XY combination

**Figure 10.1**
**Sex determination**

Some male sperm cells contain an X chromosome; others contain a Y chromosome. All female egg cells contain an X chromosome and no Y chromosome. If a sperm cell containing an X chromosome combines with an egg, the result will be an offspring with two X chromosomes—a female. However, if a sperm cell with a Y chromosome combines with the egg, the result will be an XY combination—a male.

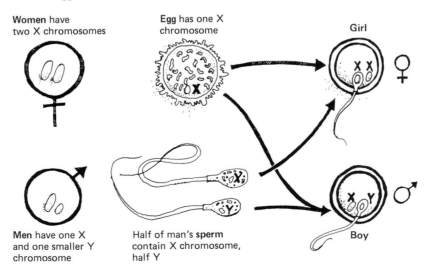

Women have two X chromosomes

Egg has one X chromosome

Girl

Men have one X and one smaller Y chromosome

Half of man's sperm contain X chromosome, half Y

Boy

## Chromosomes
Complex chemical substances within the cell nucleus that carry the determiners of heredity called genes. The normal human cell has 46 chromosomes, arranged in pairs.

## Genes
The basic unit of hereditary transmission, located on the chromosomes.

## Germ cells
The sperm in males and egg in females that unite during fertilization to produce a new organism. Germ cells contain half the chromosomes found in other body cells

## Dominant gene
A member of a gene pair that takes precedence over the remaining gene in determining inherited characteristics.

## Recessive gene
A member of a gene pair that is expressed only when combined with a like gene. If a recessive gene is paired with a dominant gene, the effect of the recessive gene is masked.

## Genotype
The underlying genetic makeup of an individual.

## Phenotype
The characteristics that we can observe, as distinguished from those traits carried genetically but not necessarily displayed.

## Genetic counseling
Providing people information about the risks and consequences of inheriting or transmitting various genetic disorders.

and the egg will develop into a male. Thus the sex of the offspring is determined by which chromosome ($X$ or $Y$) the father has contributed to the fertilized egg. In other words, the sex of the offspring is determined by the father. Figure 10.1 shows how the $X$ and $Y$ chromosomes determine sex.

Each set of chromosomes contains all the genes necessary to impart a given characteristic to the developing individual. The genes may themselves exist in two or more different forms. For example, let us oversimplify somewhat by imagining that there are genes for only two types of eye color, brown *(B)* and blue *(b)*. Children receiving *B* genes from both parents will have brown eyes. Similarly, if they receive *b* genes from each parent, their eye color will be blue. But what is the eye color of children who inherit a *B* gene from one parent and a *b* gene from the other? Now we find that one characteristic dominates over the other. Such children will inherit brown eyes. Brown *(B)* is said to be **dominant** and blue *(b)* **recessive.** Figure 10.2 shows the possible outcomes of different pairings.

The underlying genetic makeup of an individual is known as that person's **genotype,** and the characteristic that we can observe is called a **phenotype.** The genotype cannot always be judged by observing the phenotype. For example, a person with a *Bb* genotype will have the same eye color as another with a *BB* genotype. But only the individual with the *Bb* genotype has the potential of transmitting blue eyes to his or her children. This may occur whenever the person's mate also carries genes for blue eyes.

We have said that each individual has a unique genetic makeup. There is, however, an exception. Identical twins develop from a single fertilized egg. Thus they each receive the same set of chromosomes and are exactly alike in their heredity. Fraternal twins, on the other hand, develop from two separate eggs fertilized by two different sperm (see Fig. 10.3). Therefore fraternal twins are no more alike in their heredity than are ordinary siblings. This difference in the genetic similarity of identical as opposed to fraternal twins has formed the basis for much research aimed at clarifying the relative roles of environmental as opposed to hereditary factors. Data from identical twins studies have been addressed to such questions as: Is intelligence inherited? Are there inherited predispositions to become emotionally disturbed? To what extent are personality variables influenced by genetic factors?

Many people resist the notion that genetic differences may play a critical role in accounting for individual differences in various psychological traits such as intelligence or mental health. One reason for the reluctance to accept the role of genetic influences is the feeling that nothing can be done to improve conditions that are genetically determined. However, through genetic research, we have learned to understand genetic disorders so well that measures can now be applied to treat and prevent some genetic diseases. For example, phenylketonuria (PKU) is a genetic disorder involving an inability to metabolize protein that can result in mental retardation. If the child is immediately placed on a special diet, the effects of this disease can be prevented.

Even where treatment is not yet possible, **genetic counseling** provides a method for preventing genetic disorders. Through counseling,

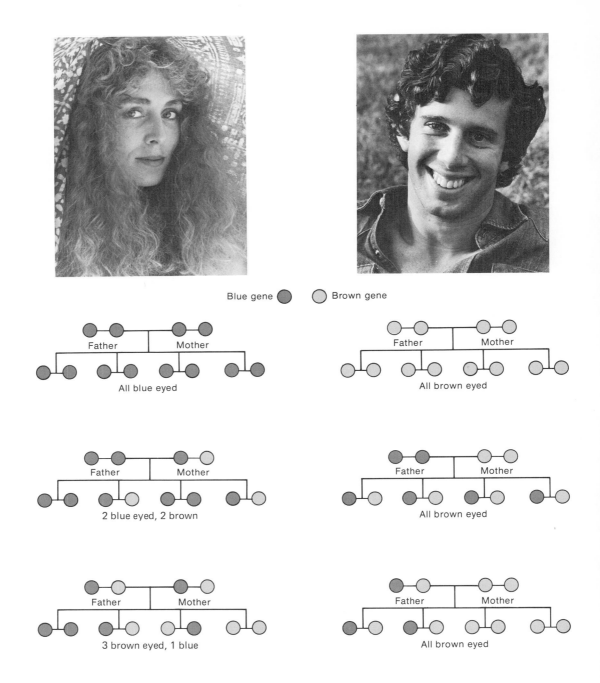

Blue gene ⬤    ⬤ Brown gene

All blue eyed

All brown eyed

2 blue eyed, 2 brown

All brown eyed

3 brown eyed, 1 blue

All brown eyed

Figure 10.2
Heritability of eye color

Because the genes for blue eyes are recessive, two are necessary to produce blue eyes, whereas either one or two of the dominant brown-eye genes will produce brown eyes. Thus it is possible for two brown-eyed parents to have a blue-eyed child, if each parent carries one brown-eye and one blue-eye gene and passes on the blue-eye gene to the child. In contrast, two blue-eyed parents, who must both have two blue genes, will always produce blue-eyed offspring.

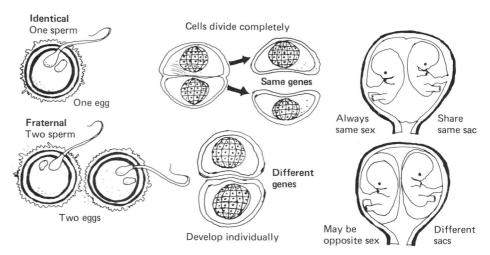

**Figure 10.3**
**Fraternal and identical twins**

Identical twins result from the fertilization of a single egg by one sperm. During the course of subsequent division, the cells divide completely and two separate organisms are formed. They share the same genetic makeup and are, of course, the same sex. Fraternal twins result from the fertilization of two eggs by two sperm. They therefore have different genetic makeup and may be of opposite sex.

parents can learn the risks associated with particular genetic diseases. As one group of authors observed:

> *Until recently, parents usually did not realize that they were carriers of recessive deleterious genes; they did not know that their children were in danger until a child was born with the disease. With recent advances, however, it is possible in many cases to detect whether a parent is a carrier. Such parents still face a difficult decision: either they risk having a child who may be born with a serious disorder, or they decide not to have children at all. Nevertheless, in cases where such a genetic disorder is relatively common among a well-defined group, medical geneticists are now making efforts to screen large numbers of potential parents so that they can be alerted about the dangers of having an affected baby. One example of this procedure concerns* Tay-Sachs *disease (also know as infantile amaurotic idiocy), a serious degenerative disease of the nervous system that usually sets in soon after the infant is born and produces a steady physiological decline, culminating in death when the infant is only a year or two old. The disease is thus an unusually cruel one, as the parents must watch helplessly as their young baby slowly dies. As it happens, Tay-Sachs disease is caused by a recessive gene and primarily affects Jewish children of northern and eastern European ancestry. For this reason, the Jewish medical community has been active in urging all American Jews who are prospective parents to have a simple test to determine whether they are carriers of the gene. Carriers thus could avoid marrying each other, or, if already married or planning to marry, they could adopt children. (Birren* et al., *1981, pp. 123–124)*

Through genetic counseling, potential parents may be alerted to the possible dangers they face if they are carriers of certain recessive genes.

However, although alerted, they must still face the traumatic months of waiting before they know for sure how the baby turns out. Box 10.1 describes a procedure called **amniocentesis** that removes these doubts by determining whether or not the fetus is carrying a genetic defect.

## PRENATAL DEVELOPMENT

Each of us begins life as a single cell. This cell, the product of fertilization of an ovum (egg) by a sperm, contains all the genetic information that will direct the growth of the organism throughout its life. About one day after fertilization, this cell divides into two living cells. Each of these cells,

## BOX 10.1

### Amniocentesis: "Visiting" the Baby before Birth

Amniocentesis is the technique of obtaining cells from an unborn infant (see Fig. 10.4). The procedure is to locate the fetus by bouncing high-frequency sounds off it and recording the echoes. This is a safe method, unlike the use of X-rays, which are potentially dangerous to embryos. Then a hypodermic needle is inserted into the amnion, usually directly through the abdominal wall. The embryo is surrounded by the amnion, and the amnion is filled with fluid in which a number of loose cells float. Some of the cells are from the embryo itself and some from the amnion, but they are all derived from the original zygote and are therefore genetically alike. Some 20 milliliters (0.6 fl oz) of the amniotic fluid are drawn into a syringe and may be grown as tissue cultures. They may be studied directly, but cultured cells can be made to yield more information. However, nearly a month is needed to establish a satisfactory culture, so the delay may be undesirable.

By amniocentesis the sex of the unborn can be determined, but despite possible curiosity of the parents about this, it has no medical importance. What is important is to find whether or not there are chromosome abnormalities, which might indicate possible deformities. Since the chromosome situation can be read with fair accuracy, it is possible to learn, for example, whether some duplication has occurred. If there is an extra chromosome of one of the middle-sized chromosome groups, the prediction can be made that the embryo, if allowed to come to term, will not survive infancy. The parents may decide that the best action is to terminate the pregnancy by having an abortion. On the other hand, if there is a history of abnormality in the family and consequent doubt concerning the unborn child, amniocentesis may show that the chromosomes are normal and that the child should be healthy.

Since the earlier an abortion is performed, the easier it is on the mother, amniocentesis is best done as soon as any question arises. The procedure of amniocentesis is reasonably safe for both embryo and mother, and it is advisable when there is any liklihood of serious fetal abnormality. This would be true if a mother is known to carry a chromosome aberration, or even if she is normal and over 40. Women over 40 have a disproportionately high number of babies with chromosome defects, probably because the eggs ovulated at that age are 20 or 25 years older than the eggs released in the time just after puberty, and the older eggs are more likely to be affected by multiple mutations than were the younger eggs. It is judicious for older expectant mothers to have the cells of their unborn babies checked.

**Amniocentesis**
The procedure used to remove amniotic fluid from a pregnant woman. This fluid is then analyzed to determine whether there are genetic defects in the fetus.

**Embryo**
The developing organism from about the second to the eighth week after conception.

in turn, contains the same genetic information found in the original cell, the fertilized egg. The process of division continues, and after about two weeks a hollow ball has been formed. This ball contains three separate layers of cells, each of which will play a different role in the developing organism. The outer layer will develop into the skin, the nervous system, and the sense organs. Bones, muscles, and blood will develop from the middle layer. The inner layer will become the organs that make up the digestive system.

Between the second and eighth weeks the **embryo's** anatomy begins to take shape. By the end of the embryonic period, the developing organism, though only slightly more than an inch long, already contains such basic anatomical structures as limbs and distinguishable facial features.

**Figure 10.4**

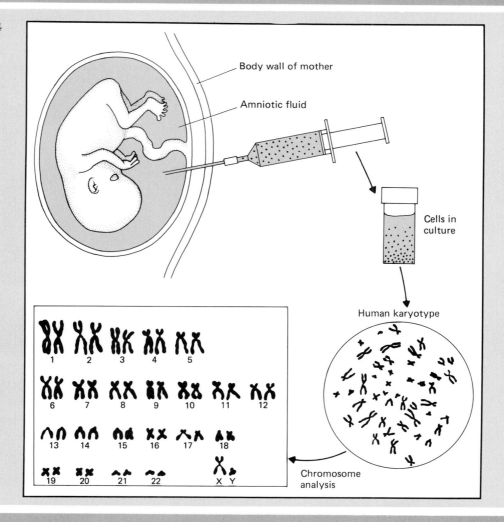

From about the end of the second month until birth, the baby-to-be is referred to as the **fetus.** All the structures required to sustain life as an independent organism are basically formed during the embryonic period and refined and finished during the fetal period. By about the fifth month, the heartbeat can be heard and the mother becomes aware of the spontaneous movements of the fetus. All the body systems are capable of functioning by the twenty-eighth week, and if an infant should happen to be born at this point, it might survive if intensive medical care is provided. Figure 10.5 illustrates some of the landmarks in the prenatal development of the human organism.

It was once believed that if the expectant mother exposed herself to certain types of situations, she could greatly influence what the child would subsequently become. Many expectant mothers became devotees of art museums, opera, and musical concerts in the expectation that these cultural activities would cause their children to appreciate the "finer things in life." When this view was repudiated, the pendulum swung in the opposite direction. For a while, researchers ignored the possibility of

Figure 10.5
**Stages in prenatal development**

(a) Two-cell stage of human ovum 30 hours after fertilization; (b) human embryo at 28 days; (c) human embryo at 8 weeks; (d) human fetus at 14 weeks.

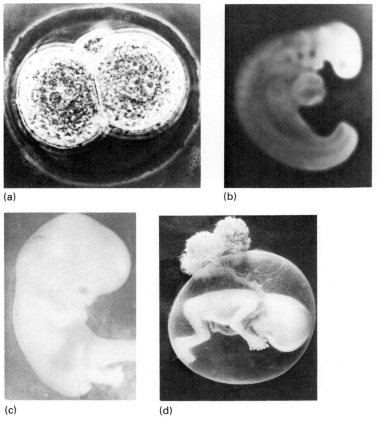

(a)                                              (b)

(c)                    (d)

Courtesy of Dr. Landrum B. Shettles.

**Fetus**
The developing organism from about the end of the second month after conception until birth.

**Prenatal**
The prenatal period is the period of life before birth.

**Intervention procedures**
Attempts to correct unfavorable aspects of a child's environment by modifying this environment at a sufficiently early age.

any form of **prenatal** influence. It became a neglected area of research. We now realize that the child has an environment from the moment of conception, and we know that alterations in this prenatal environment can profoundly affect the developing organism. Some of the following factors may be related to later problems at birth and in infancy: the age of the mother, whether or not she has taken drugs or contracted an illness during pregnancy, her smoking and nutritional habits, and the number of previous pregnancies (see references in Parmelee and Haber, 1973). For example, when the mother contracts rubella (German measles) in the first few months of pregnancy, there is a high risk that her child will be born with an affliction such as deafness.

The developing baby-to-be is completely dependent on the mother for all its nutritional needs. Hence it is reasonable to assume that serious deficiencies in the mother's diet will adversely affect the physical well-being of the baby. It used to be thought that the unborn baby had first claim on the nutritional resources of the mother and that any dietary inadequacies would be inflicted on the mother rather than on the developing child. It now appears that the opposite is true. The mother's body takes care of itself first and then attends to the needs of the organism growing within her. We now know that, for example, if the mother is malnourished, the mother and the unborn child both suffer. However, because the mother already has her organs formed and the child doesn't, it is the unborn baby who may suffer irreparable harm. Research has indicated that malnutrition, particularly during the fetal period, leads to an irreversible loss of brain cells in the unborn child (see Birren *et al.*, 1981, for example). Thus malnutrition in the pregnant mother may lead to permanent impairment of her offspring.

The most vulnerable children are those born into impoverished economic circumstances. Protein, crucial to the development of the unborn child, is typically in short supply because of the prohibitive cost of high-protein foods such as meats. Thus many children of poverty start life with one strike against them. The incidence of malnutrition throughout the world is alarming. If babies born to malnourished mothers do indeed suffer permanent losses of brain tissue, then obviously society must find a way to reduce malnutrition on a worldwide scale. It is reassuring that many researchers are initiating **intervention procedures** during the prenatal period and placing much emphasis on nutrition (see McKay *et al.*, 1978).

After about 36 weeks in the mother's womb, the child is ready to be born. It is fully capable of breathing on its own, possesses a strong sucking response, has well-coordinated swallowing movements, is able to ingest food and excrete wastes, and can regulate its body temperature. Contractions in the mother's uterus signal the beginning of labor. The length of the labor is quite variable, being longer for the first child (about 14 hours, on the average) and shorter for later children (about 8 hours) (Newman and Newman, 1979).

The labor contractions shorten the cervical canal and enlarge the cervix 100-fold, from about 1 millimeter to 100 millimeters (about 4 inches). This provides an opening with a diameter large enough for the child to pass through. Both of these processes occur without any conscious effort

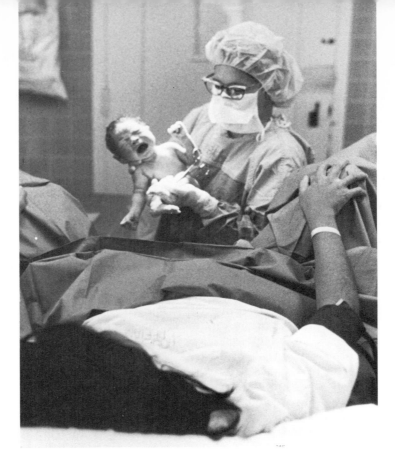

At birth, the human organism is physically ready for life in the world and begins the series of learning experiences that will influence its behavior through maturity.

on the part of the mother. However, she may assist the birth process by exerting pressure on the abdominal walls surrounding the uterus. Even the child can assist in its own birth by squirming, turning its head, and pushing against the birth canal.

Anesthetics are commonly used to reduce the pain experienced by the mother during childbirth and to ease the delivery for the physician. However, because the medication passes from the mother to the fetus, the neonate is frequently born in a semidrugged state. Follow-up studies of babies born with the assistance of drugs compared to those during whose births no medication was used indicate that the drugs may interfere with the coping behaviors of the newborn (Aleksandrowicz, 1974; Scanlon and Alper, 1974). Some of the effects were found to last for as long as 28 days. Although some experts regard these effects as minor (Yang *et al.*, 1976), many mothers currently opt to have their babies by techniques that do not involve the use of medication.

## MATURATION

Have you ever observed the parental delight when a baby takes his or her first step? The parents proudly proclaim that the baby has learned to walk. But has the child, in fact, learned to walk? Or is the first step merely the culmination of months of muscular growth and neural devel-

**Maturation**
Biological changes that occur in the normal course of development after birth.

**Maturational readiness**
The time interval during which the organism is first physically capable of acquiring a particular function or skill.

**Critical period**
The time period during which the capacity to benefit from experiences is optimal.

opment? These questions are not as easy to answer as they might seem. Behavioral changes may result from learning or from physiological changes that occur in the normal course of development **(maturation).** It is often difficult to distinguish changes that occur as a result of learning from those that are due strictly to maturation of the organism. Both kinds of change show increasing approximation to adult behavior over time.

The concept of maturation is of limited use in understanding the diversity of human behavior. Maturation sets the stage on which certain behaviors occur, but the full development of these behaviors is heavily dependent on learning. We do not acquire such skills as ice skating, bicycle riding, or dancing solely through maturation. Nor do we acquire our language skills simply through maturation.

Children must mature before they can engage in many activities that are characteristic of the human species. At birth, the legs are not sufficiently developed to support the weight of the body. The brain, though it possesses the full complement of neurons, is still largely an undeveloped organ. The physical changes necessary for the emergence of language have not yet occurred. A host of interrelated physical developments must occur before children can walk, talk, think, and reason. Once the physical changes necessary for the exercise of a given function have taken place, children are "ready" to benefit from practice.

**Maturational readiness** refers to the time interval during which the organism first becomes physically capable of acquiring a particular function or skill. The term implies that practice prior to this period will be largely wasted. Not all of the evidence uniformly supports this conclusion. For example, one study indicates that practice in walking and foot-placing exercises during the first eight weeks of life facilitates walking later on. Infants receiving this special training walked about 2 1/2 months earlier than a control group that was not exercised (Zelazo *et al.*, 1972).

The concept of maturational readiness is of considerable interest to educators. Is there, in fact, an optimal time to begin teaching such things as reading and arithmetic? The answer to this question is both "Yes" and "No." Many poor educational practices have stemmed from the view that there is a "magic age" at which all children are "ready" to speak, learn to read, and manipulate numerical concepts. The practice of placing children in grades according to chronological age is a reflection of this point of view. We now recognize that the "magic age" will vary from child to child, and from skill to skill within the same child. The inflexible use of time-bound sequences of educational experiences has probably hampered the development of many children. Much of the thrust of education today is in the direction of permitting children to learn at a pace that is consistent with their own maturational development.

## Critical Periods

Some exciting findings in animal studies have suggested that the time of maturational readiness is a **critical period,** in the sense that deprivation of particular experiences during this period may lead to permanent impairment. For example, it has been observed that, shortly after hatching, a duckling or gosling will follow its mother around. This observation is

Figure 10.6    Konrad Lorenz (b. 1903) coined the term "imprinting" and demonstrated that imprinting will happen only during a critical period in the animal's early life. Here Lorenz plays foster Mother Goose to some imprinted goslings.

LIFE NATURE LIBRARY, *Animal Behavior* photograph by Nima Leen, © 1980 Time-Life Books Inc.

**Imprinting**
A learning process that occurs with extreme rapidity during a critical period in the organism's life—for example, the process by which a young duckling learns to follow its mother or any moving object.

not particularly dramatic. What makes it interesting is the fact that newly hatched ducklings will follow almost *any* moving object and become attached to it (see Fig. 10.6). This phenomenon is known as **imprinting.**

Studies on imprinting have revealed that there is a critical period of time in which imprinting can occur (Hess, 1958). For the mallard duckling, this period is between 13 and 16 hours. After the age of 16 hours, the likelihood that imprinting will occur declines rapidly in this species. Figure 10.7 shows the apparatus employed in an imprinting study and the relationship between imprintability and age.

In humans, "the effects of experience become less irreversible and more plastic, so the term 'sensitive' may be more appropriate than 'critical'" (Hunt, 1979, p. 136). This flexibility may be related to our greater capacity to learn. It is also in keeping with the general tendency for higher species to exhibit more behavior resulting from learning and correspondingly less behavior determined by heredity.

## Social Attachment

Under natural conditions, the imprinting response has clear adaptive value for the newly hatched gosling or duckling. The mother provides protection for the young and will lead the young to sources of food.

In natural settings, higher animals also form strong attachments to their caretakers. As with ducklings and goslings, these attachments have obvious adaptive value, because the infant cannot survive unless it is fed and cared for. These attachments may persist for years.

One researcher (Bowlby, 1969) believes that many unlearned behaviors in human infants—crying, clinging, smiling, and sucking—are analogous to the following response in birds. Human infants lack the locomotor capabilities necessary to follow their caretakers physically. But between the ages of about 6 and 20 weeks, they spend a great deal of time looking at things that move or have edges where the contrast is large (Hunt,

1979). It has been suggested that visual rather than physical contact is the basic for establishing human sociability (Rheingold, 1961).

In laboratory settings it is possible systematically to deprive monkeys of contact with their mothers or other members of their species. See Box 10.2 for a discussion of the experiments on contact comfort in which monkeys were "raised" by surrogate cloth or wire "mothers." The initial studies seemed to suggest that the cloth "mothers" were adequate substitutes for the real mother. Infants showed the same sorts of affectional response toward the terrycloth "mothers" as control animals did toward real mothers. For example, when novel fear-producing stimuli were presented, these monkeys ran to their terrycloth "mothers." They clung to them for a few minutes and then went out to investigate the fear-producing stimuli (see Fig. 10.8). Only when these mother-deprived monkeys achieved adulthood did it become apparent that something was wrong. For example, when 18 female monkeys were released on an island along with sexually experienced males, most of them resisted any attempt on the part of the males to engage in heterosexual activity. Indeed, after many months on the island, only four of these monkeys were successfully impregnated (Harlow, 1965). Clearly the deprivation of contact with a real mother during the first few months of life led to a serious impairment in their ability to adjust to a normal adult heterosexual role. Furthermore,

**Figure 10.7**
**Imprinting**

(a) The decoy adult duck in the center of the apparatus could be moved on a circular runway. Groups of ducklings were placed in the apparatus at varying time periods after hatching. (b) The graph shows the percentage of ducklings at each age that showed imprinting behavior. The critical period for imprinting the ducklings used in this experiment appears to be between 13 and 16 hours after hatching. (Hess, 1958)

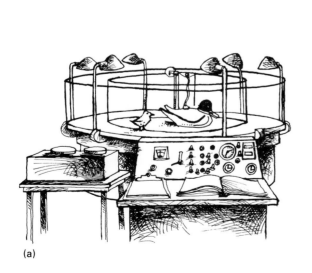

(a)

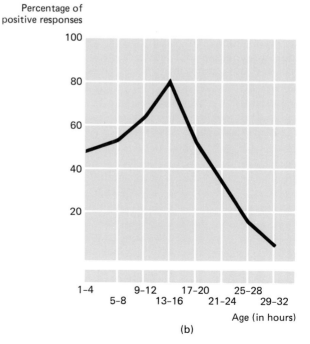

(b)

## BOX 10.2

### Contact Comfort

Until fairly recently, many psychologists believed that children come to love their mothers through a classical conditioning process. The mother, initially a neutral stimulus, acquires the capacity to elicit positive emotional responses in the infant as a result of her continuous association with positive reinforcements: She provides nourishment when the child is hungry, provides water when the child is thirsty, changes wet or soiled diapers, and provides comfort when the child is distressed.

Research on infant monkeys has suggested another possible explanation for the child's attachment to the mother. The investigators, noting that mothers provide a soft, warm surface when they hold or nurse the infant, hypothesized that this contact comfort may be the basis of the child's love for the mother. To test their hypothesis, they provided infant monkeys with various types of substitute "mothers." Some of these provided a soft, warm surface, such as terrycloth; others were made of wire mesh or covered with sandpaper. Given a choice between a soft, comfortable terrycloth "mother" that supplied no food and a hard, uncomfortable wire "mother" that provided a continuous supply of warm milk, the monkeys showed a marked preference for the terrycloth "mother." It would therefore appear that the need for contact comfort was stronger than the hunger drive in determining the monkey's attachment to a substitute mother (Harlow and Zimmerman, 1959; Harlow and Suomi, 1970).

These studies, if they are applicable at the human level, have important implications for child-rearing practices. Although experimental evidence on human infants is lacking, it appears that human infants also have a need for contact comfort. Although hospital practices are changing in response to parents' demands to interact with their newborns, some hospitals still separate child and parents immediately after birth, relegating the child to an antiseptic nursery for most of its stay. If there is, in fact, a comfort need that manifests itself at birth, the mother and father should be free to cuddle their child during the first days of life.

> . . . social attachment is a two-way street: it does little good for an infant to become attached to the parent if the parent does not become attached to the infant. In sheep, for example, the mother becomes imprinted on the scent of her newborn lamb shortly after birth. If the lamb dies, the mother usually will not accept a substitute lamb (Scott, 1962). Some pediatricians believe that there is evidence—still controversial—for a similar phenomenon in human beings, and that a mother more readily forms an emotional bond with her infant if she can see and hold the infant shortly after birth. This is one line of research cited by those who favor drug-free or home delivery, in which the mother is alert and able to experience close contact with her baby after giving birth. (Birren et al., 1981, p. 197)

when a mother-deprived monkey gave birth to her own infant, she withdrew into a corner, completely ignoring the infant. She repeatedly rejected efforts by the new infant to achieve contact with her. Figure 10.9 shows a mother pushing her infant's face into the wire floor.

In another study, infant monkeys were systematically deprived of social contacts for varying periods of time (3, 6, and 12 months). This deprivation was either *partial* (they could see and hear other monkeys, but were allowed no physical contact) or *total* (they could see no animal of any kind). Long-term studies of monkeys released after 3 months of total deprivation revealed that the monkeys made a complete social recovery and showed normal learning and sexual adjustment. But monkeys either partially or totally deprived of social contact for 6 months showed an im-

Figure 10.8
**Attachment behavior in an infant monkey**

When a frightening toy was introduced, the infant monkey ran promptly to its terrycloth "mother" and clung to it. After clinging for a few minutes, the monkey turned to investigate the strange object.

Figure 10.9
**The effects of maternal deprivation**

The mother monkey was separated at birth from her own mother and not given any opportunity to observe and interact with members of her own species. When she herself became a mother, she repulsed all efforts by her infant to establish physical contact. Here we see the mother resisting contact by forcing the infant's face into the wire mesh floor.

pairment in their ability to interact socially with other monkeys. These social inadequacies persisted for many years. Twelve months of total deprivation produced catastrophic results—these monkeys were not able to interact with other monkeys at all (Harlow and Harlow, 1966).

Are the effects of social and maternal deprivation fixed and irreversible? At least for the monkeys deprived for six months, the answer appears to be "No." In a rather amusing study, monkey "therapists" were provided for the socially isolated monkeys. The "therapists" had been trained to cling to and play with the disturbed monkeys. By the time they reached two years of age, the isolates showed almost complete recovery from the behavioral defects that had previously been considered incurable (Suomi *et al.*, 1972). The authors concluded, ". . . we are aware of the existence of some therapists who seem inhuman. We find it refreshing to report the discovery of nonhumans who can be therapists" (p. 392).

These studies show the extreme importance of social contacts during the formative months of life in primates. Indeed, recent research suggests that the attachment-deprived organism may suffer incomplete development of elements of the nervous system, including the brain. As one observer noted:

> *During formative periods of brain growth, certain kinds of sensory deprivation—such as lack of touching and rocking by the mother—result in incomplete or damaged development of the neuronal systems that control affection (for instance, a loss of the nerve-cell branches called dendrites). Since the same systems influence brain centers associated with violence . . . , the deprived infant may have difficulty controlling violent impulses as an adult. (Prescott, 1979, p. 124)*

In human infants, the most critical factors in establishing attachment to the caretaker are the quality of both the care and the interaction between the child and the caretaker. As stated by one observer, "Evidence from longitudinal studies is suggesting that what may be most important for the infant's relationship with its mother is the mutual delight that each takes in their transactions with each other" (Hunt, 1979, p. 126). Though much of the research has focused on the mother–child relationship, recently attention has turned to the role of the father. A study by Sawin and Parke (1979) found that fathers exhibited attachment to their infants even in the first days of life and took more pleasure in holding and feeding them than did the mothers. The father's presence also appeared to provide emotional support for the mother, improving her responsiveness to the newborn.

The pregnancy itself, when wanted, encourages a bonding of the mother to her child in anticipation of the joys she expects to experience after the child is born. When the pregnancy is not wanted, however, this anticipatory joy may be missing, and the initial strength of the mother's attachment to the child may be diminished. Even if the pregnancy is wanted, the child may not live up to parental expectations. Its appearance may not be as imagined; it may cry too much; or it may not be as responsive as desired (Blehar *et al.*, 1977). All or any of these problems can damage the early interactions between parent and child. Some researchers (Brazelton *et al.*, 1975) believe that even the separation that occurs in some hospital settings can hinder the establishment of parental attraction. If so, the plasticity of the human organism appears to enable both child and parents to bounce back from early failures in social attachment.

For obvious reasons, the effects of prolonged social deprivation in human infants cannot be systematically investigated in an experimental setting. Still, we know that children are born into an incredibly wide variety of environments, both physical and social. Some are born in poverty, others in affluence. Some are welcome additions to the family unit and are loved and cherished; others are like an albatross hung around their parents' necks and are met with cold indifference or rejection. A number of investigators have reported observations of children raised in a cold, mechanical manner and deprived of warmth, attention, and personal care. The effects are especially dramatic in institutional settings, where children frequently receive, at best, custodial care.

One study compared children from comparable backgrounds raised in two different types of institutions in Iran. The following is a description of the child-care practices in institution A:

> On the average there were eight children per attendant. . . . The attendants have no special training for their work and are poorly paid. The emphasis on the part of the supervisors seems to be on neatness in the appearance of the rooms, with little attention to behavioral development. In his crib the child is not propped up, and is given no toys. . . . Except when being bathed, the younger children spend practically their entire time in their cribs. (Dennis, 1960)

Contrast with this the care provided in institution B:

> The number of children per attendant is 3–4. Children are held in arms while being fed, are regularly placed prone during part of the time they are in their cribs, are propped up in a sitting position in their cribs at times, and are placed in play pens on the floor daily when above four months of age. Numerous toys are provided. Attendants are coached in methods of childcare, and supervisors emphasize behavioral development as well as nutrition and health. (Dennis, 1960)

Studies have shown that the amount of attention and stimulation given to very young children affects their rate of development. A child born into a loving family environment will be more likely to form those crucial attachments that set the stage for attachments formed later in life.

Dramatic differences were observed in the motor behavior of children raised in these two institutional settings. By the age of two, only 42 percent of the children raised in institution A were able to sit alone, whereas 90 percent of those raised in institution B were able to do so. Only 8 percent of the children in institution A could walk by the age of three. By contrast, 94 percent in institution B could do so (Dennis, 1960).

The results of these studies are consistent both with observations from animal laboratories and with anecdotal reports about children raised in disturbed family settings. Largely as a result of these observations, many hospitals have instituted programs in which nurses who care for children are asked to handle and fondle them and give them the personal care that was previously denied children in these settings. Caretakers can be taught to play games with their infants that bring smiles and laughter into the transaction of the two participants (Hunt *et al.*, 1976; Levenstein, 1976). Even institutions that are seriously understaffed have invited women in the community to visit for a few hours daily to "play mother" to the infants. The decline in infant mortality over the last few decades can probably be attributed in part to these new practices. It should be noted that mothering can be done by anyone. The caretaker does not necessarily have to be the child's mother, nor is it necessary that the caretaker be female.

Children raised in impoverished households often experience deprivation of stimulation not unlike that found in institutional settings that provide only custodial care. In many cases, there is only one parent (usually the mother), who is forced to find employment to maintain her family, which may consist of several children. In order to support them, she has to leave them for long periods of time, sometimes without adequate care or supervision. Yet even under these circumstances, children can make normal progress if the mother devotes what time she can (known popularly as "quality time") to stimulating and interacting with them.

What happens to a child who has been deprived of intellectual, social, and positive emotional experiences during the critical years? The concepts of critical and sensitive periods stress the importance of timing of stimulation, social and otherwise, in the sequence of development. The issue is crucial to programs based on the premise that individuals will catch up,

---

## BOX 10.3

### Influencing Development

Intervention programs are based on the rationale that positive changes can be produced by altering the child's environment at a sufficiently early age. The environment provided by the parent or parents in the United States is not always optimal. Indeed, people who live in relatively comfortable middle-class communities are not always aware of the devastating experiences to which young children living in impoverished areas are exposed.

Most investigators assume that children raised in impoverished environments will inevitably suffer profound and demoralizing behavioral deficits. Efforts are under way to counteract the effects of such deprivation and despair. Progams to provide supplementary outside intervention have been initiated in many major cities (Lally, 1971; Parmelee, 1973; Schaefer and Aaronson, 1970).

The way society is presently structured, the mother seems to be the most important feature in the infant's environment. For this reason, intervention programs usually try to enlist the mother's participation in the program. The hope is that the mother will transfer what she learns in the intervention program to the care of her children at home. One of the most significant effects of intervention has been increased social interaction between the mother and her child.

We now recognize that both the mother and the community play a vital role in the development of the child. Approaches to the care and handling of children with behavioral and intellectual problems have

changed dramatically. We used to isolate these children from their home and community environments by placing them in specialized institutions. Now many of the large institutions are being closed and replaced by smaller facilities located within the communities where they are needed. Members of the communities are becoming actively engaged in the operation of such centers. Professionals, paid staff, and volunteers from the community are currently being trained to work with these children, and the parents in the community are being encouraged to participate actively.

---

Courtesy of Dr. Alice S. Honig and Dr. J. Ronald Lally; photos by Roger Gregoire, Boston.

#### Intervention

**Typical activities at Syracuse University's Children Center program. (a) An activity on a rug in the sensory experience room, which contains reading and listening materials and comfortable places for story time. The child is starting to point to the ballerina's "foot" at the adult storyteller's request. (b) The adult has partially hidden a colorful plastic doughnut under a printed cloth screen. Although the 8 1/2-month-old cannot yet locate the doughnut when it is completely hidden, he is clearly reaching for the partially hidden toy. (c) Lunch room activity. Toddlers eat meals family-style at a table with a teacher. They choose from a wide variety of offerings and have learned to eat and enjoy a great many different kinds of foods. (d) An activity in the small-muscle area. The teacher is helping a couple of completely absorbed toddlers to fit puzzle pieces together. (e) The infant, working with a long link chain, has victoriously found a new bunch-and-drip-into-jar technique for dealing with the problem.**

even though they have been deprived during their critical periods. Probably the best known of these programs is Project Headstart. Recognizing that children from impoverished homes often are inadequately prepared to benefit from the educational system, Project Headstart has tried to provide these children with compensatory education. The children, age four and older, are given an opportunity to experience various forms of intellectual and social stimulation. The hope has been that this intensive preschool educational setting will counteract the deficiencies of earlier years. The rather limited success of Project Headstart has led to attempts to influence the development of deprived children even before the age of four (see Box 10.3).

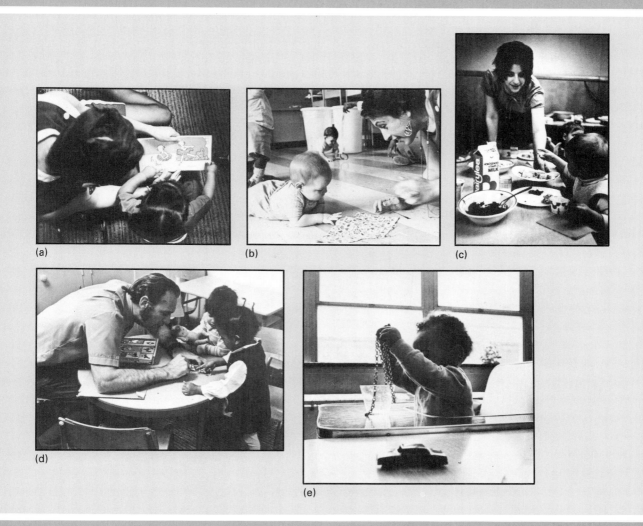

(a)

(b)

(c)

(d)

(e)

**THE DEVELOPING CHILD**

When the child emerges from the warm, moist, somewhat crowded, but usually uncomplicated uterine environment provided by the mother, it is suddenly thrust into a strange and highly variable new world. A thin, reedy cry is typically its first response to this new environment and heralds, by the breathing necessary to activate the cry, its readiness to begin lifelong interaction with the world.

Until recently, many psychologists regarded the infant as little more than a passive recipient of sensory stimulation, reacting primarily to internal stimuli such as hunger and gas pains. We now know the newborn to be a remarkably capable organism. For example, a recent study found that at an average of *nine minutes* of age, newborns responded more frequently to the form of a normal human face than they did to a scrambled face or to a blank form! At *two hours* of age, infants follow a moving light with their eyes. In addition to visual ability, hearing, smell, taste, and touch are all functioning at birth. The newborn exhibits a wide number of reflexes. Furthermore, very young infants display goal-directed behavior in that they work to alter their environment. They will, for example, change their rates of sucking to bring into focus patterns projected on a screen or to move a mobile hanging above them. Finally, newborns display individual differences in temperament. Although personality appears to be influenced by environmental factors throughout life, as we shall see in Chapter 13, there does appear to be some stability of these early reactions evident in later life (Thomas *et al.*, 1970; Thomas and Chess, 1977).

**Like all other human beings, newborns make reflex responses to certain stimuli. (a) A newborn demonstrates the grasping reflex when a doctor places his fingers in the baby's hand. (b) For an infant, the involuntary response to hunger is the sucking reflex, which enables the child to receive nourishment.**

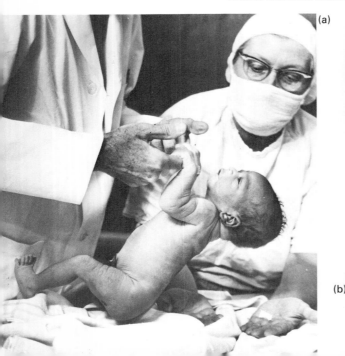
(a)

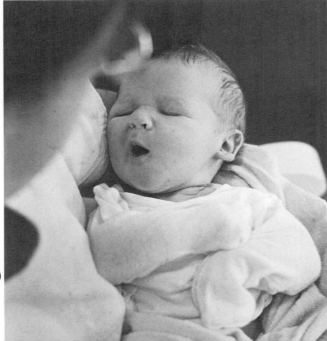
(b)

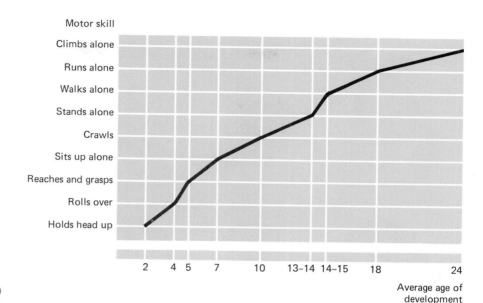

Figure 10.10
**Motor skills and average
age of accomplishment**    Adapted from Newman and Newman, 1979.

## Motor Development

**Rooting**
A reflex in infants: The baby's head turns toward the cheek that is stimulated.

It is hard to believe how rapidly the baby changes. Neonates (newborns) possess weak and largely uncoordinated muscles. They are able to engage in such reflexive behaviors as sucking, grasping, **rooting,** kicking, swallowing, and coughing. But voluntary activities, such as reaching for an object in their visual field, are beyond their capabilities. However, muscular development advances rapidly after birth and follows a head-to-foot order. Thus infants first learn to coordinate activities involving the head and neck (e.g., sucking and raising the head). Before long, they are able to reach for and grasp objects that they see. Using their legs and feet in coordinated activities (such as standing and walking) comes later. However, almost before the parents are aware of it, the helpless infant has become a veritable monkey, climbing into every corner, helping itself to its favorite foods. Before the end of the baby's first year, perceptual and motor coordination have advanced to the point where a favorite toy can be spotted from halfway across the room and retrieved by crawling or running. Figure 10.10 shows some of the motor skills acquired by the child during the first two years of life and the average age at which they occur.

A broad observation made by numerous researchers is that, in general, babies follow the same sequences of behavior. They crawl before they stand, stand with support before they stand alone, and walk before they run. It is as if children must complete one stage of development before they are ready for the next. Although the general sequences of development are similar, none of the achievements are rigidly fixed by the calendar. Parents who have several children will tell you that no two of them developed in exactly the same way. Figure 10.11 shows the general sequence of posture and locomotion in developing infants and the

2 days old

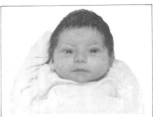

2 months (head up 45 degrees)

3 months

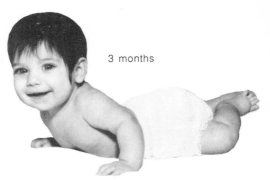

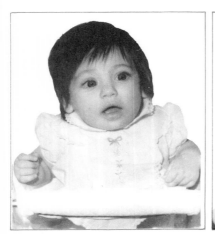

4 months
(sit with support)

5 months
(sit on lap, grasp object)

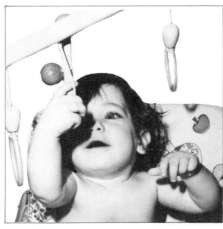

6 months
(sit on high chair, grasp dangling object)

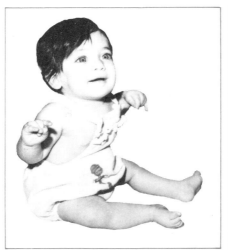

7 months
(sit without support)

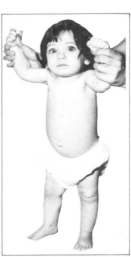

8 months
(stand with help)

9 months
(stand holding furniture)

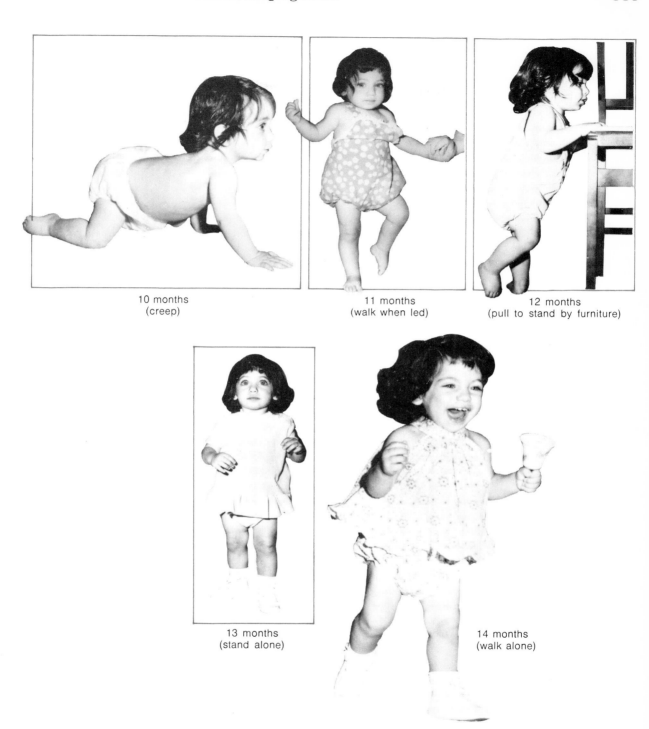

10 months
(creep)

11 months
(walk when led)

12 months
(pull to stand by furniture)

13 months
(stand alone)

14 months
(walk alone)

Figure 10.11
Sequence of posture and
locomotion in infants

The ages shown are meant only to approximate the time at which these behaviors are observed in most infants in the United States. There is a wide range of individual differences.

ages at which these behaviors typically appear. These ages should be regarded as crude guides, because wide differences in development are normal and expected. Parents who are unaware of this wide variability will frequently make comparisons of their own children with those of a neighbor, sometimes with delight and sometimes with dismay. Neither of these reactions is necessarily appropriate. Such reactions typically stem from the notion that a "normal" child will sit up, walk, and talk at specific ages. This is not the case, however. It is the sequence of development rather than the specific timing that is consistently observed. Nevertheless, in order to develop standards by which to judge normal health and development, timetables are kept by psychologists on the ages at which most children achieve control over various motor tasks. Large departures from the norms may then alert observers to possible problems that demand attention.

## Language Development

Like motor development, children's language development follows a sequence of stages, with certain steps common at certain ages but not tied rigidly to those ages.

One of the most dramatic moments in development is a child's first word. Most children speak their first real word by the age of about one year. At about two years of age, these first utterances carry the meaning of an entire sentence. Thus when Johnny says "Milk," he is usually making the request, "I want milk." Shortly after the second year is reached,

Table 10.1
**The First Sentences in Child Speech**

| Structural meaning | Form | Example |
|---|---|---|
| 1. Nomination | that + noun, it + noun | that book |
| 2. Notice | hi + noun | hi belt |
| 3. Recurrence | more + noun, 'nother + noun | more milk |
| 4. Nonexistence | allgone + noun, no more + noun | all gone rattle |
| 5. Attributive | adj. + noun | big train |
| 6. Possessive | noun + noun | mommy lunch |
| 7. Locative | noun + noun | sweater chair |
| 8. Locative | verb + noun | walk street |
| 9. Agent–action | noun + verb | Eve read |
| 10. Agent–object | noun + noun | mommy sock |
| 11. Action–object | verb + noun | put book |
| 12. Conjunction | noun + noun | umbrella boot |

Source: Reprinted with permission of Macmillan Publishing Co., Inc. from *Psycholinguistics* by R. Brown. Copyright © 1970 by The Free Press, a Division of Macmillan Publishing Co., Inc.

there occurs what can only be regarded as a "language explosion" in the young child. In one study, a two-year-old child could speak 14 two-word sentences (such as, "See doggie"), and six months later he was forming 2500 such combinations (Braine, 1963). With the development of two-word sentences, some of the elements of the formal structure of language may be discerned. For example, if Rebecca says, "Daddy shoe," she may be referring to the fact that the shoe belongs to her father or she may be seeking help from him in putting on her own shoe. Twelve different types of relationships between words in two-word sentences have been described (Brown, 1970). Table 10.1 provides some examples of these types of relationships.

This burgeoning language development opens a whole new world to the child. He or she can convey thoughts and feelings to others, interpret and make sense of experiences, play word games, and invent fantasies.

Between the ages of three and five, children learn the transformation rules that permit them to generate negative sentences ("I don't want . . ."; "Corey isn't going") and "when," "what," "why," and "where" questions. By the time they are six years of age, their use of syntax in speech is virtually indistinguishable from that of an adult (Birren *et al.*, 1981). Moreover, during the preschool years, children acquire a rich and varied vocabulary, which they practice with none of the adult's concern for social amenities. In short, they say everything that comes to mind:

> *My four-year-old daughter was riding in the car with a college student. She looked long and searchingly at the student and finally burst forth with an observation she had carefully formulated, "Marcia, you're ugly." "Yes, I know," Marcia replied with consummate patience and an acute awareness of her physical limitations. "God made me that way." The child replied with the candor only found in the preschool years, "God must have hated you." Needless to say, her parents squirmed uncomfortably throughout this exchange.(Author's files)*

Children also exhibit a spontaneous originality in speech, resourcefully linking together two apparently separate concepts. A five-year-old was asked to describe the taste of a carbonated drink. She replied: "It tastes like my foot's asleep."

By the age of six, children find humor in the incongruity of words. They will laugh about equally, however, at two forms of the same joke: "Call me a cab"—"You're a cab" and "Call a cab for me"—"You're a cab." Only when they reach the age of eight and above do they recognize the first joke as more humorous than the second (Shultz and Horibe, 1974).

Although children's language abilities have increased remarkably by the time they enter school, they often use words without any comprehension of their meaning or implications in an adult world. The following story is an amusing illustration of a child's use of words which, because of her limited experience, are meaningless to her:

> *A mother whose children had grown up returned after a lapse of several years to teaching first grade. During her first week she tried to stimulate rapport and conversation by asking the children to tell the group something interesting that had happened at home. "Interesting," to the chil-*

*dren, apparently meant "unusual." They vied with each other in reports of how mother fell off the stepladder, the dog got run over in the drive, and father cut himself with the power saw and had to have stitches. Discouraged by these accounts of carnage on the home front, the teacher changed the conversational topic for the second week. "Today," she said "I'd like you to tell me a happy thought." There was a long silence. Then a little girl stood up; "I think I'm pregnant," she said. As this remark held no possibilities for conversation expansion, the teacher let it pass with a quiet "Thank you." It stayed in her mind, though, and that night she called the little girl's mother, who greeted her account with a gale of laughter. At breakfast that morning as she was shaking the Crispies into the children's bowls, she had said to her husband, "I think I'm pregnant." "That's a happy thought," he muttered. (Landreth, 1967, pp. 202–203)*

## COGNITIVE DEVELOPMENT

From the moment of birth, children begin to interact with the environment. They explore, manipulate, and begin to formulate hypotheses about the nature of reality. Even before the acquisition of formal language, children have developed concepts that guide their interaction with the world. The term **"cognitive processes"** refers to these many activities that constitute the mental life of the individual.

One of the most influential investigators of the cognitive development of children was the Swiss psychologist Jean Piaget. Piaget obtained many of the data that form the basis for his theories by observing his own three children as they developed. He combined naturalistic observation with

**Figure 10.12**
**Testing cognitive development**

The infant in (a) is being tested on a sensorimotor scale. She must pull the pad with the toy on it. In (b), the youngster is learning spatial relationships by stacking rings on a cone.

(a)                                              (b)

Table 10.2
**Piaget's Stages of Cognitive Development**

| Stage | Age | Achievements |
|---|---|---|
| Sensorimotor stage | Birth to 2 years | Motor skills; object permanence; beginnings of symbolic thought |
| Preoperational stage | 2 to 7 years | Symbolic thought; inability to master conservation |
| Concrete operational stage | 7 through 11 years | Logical thought only in relation to concrete (real) objects; mastery of conservation |
| Formal operational stage | 12 years + | Abstract thought* |

*Not found in all persons; often found only in certain situations even in individuals achieving this stage.

**Cognitive processes**
Mental processes involved in thinking, reasoning, and problem solving.

**Schema (plural: schemata)**
Piaget's term for a mental framework for classification or conceptualization of information.

**Assimilation**
Piaget's term for the incorporation of new stimuli into an existing schema.

**Accommodation**
Piaget's term for the alteration of an existing schema to allow for new stimuli.

**Sensorimotor stage**
Piaget's first stage of cognitive development, occurring during the first two years of life, when the child learns to know the world through sensory and motor activities.

the experimental method. Piaget's theory has formed the basis for much of the testing and assessment of children's cognitive development (see Fig. 10.12).

According to Piaget, children attempt to organize the stimuli from the world around them. They begin with the simplest of **schemata** and then modify these schemata to reflect new information. Piaget describes such changes in terms of **assimilation** and **accommodation.** When faced with a new stimulus that does not conflict with our present knowledge, we assimilate it. For example, a child who has learned to pick up a ball can assimilate the picking up of a stuffed animal, as both require a two-handed approach. However, sometimes the new stimulus does not fit into the existing schema. In that case, we accommodate it by altering our schema to include this information, just as the child must learn to accommodate a smaller object by using only one hand and perhaps only the fingers.

In addition, Piaget studied the ways in which children's abilities to process information follow a sequence of predetermined stages (see Table 10.2) from a reliance on reflexes to the development of symbolic thought. Children differ from one another in the rate, but not in the sequence, of progress. For the individual, the timing of a given cognitive development depends on the maturation of the child and the amount and complexity of experience. Generally, increasing complexity of interactions with the environment will accelerate the time at which a given cognitive stage is entered as long as the child is maturationally ready. Let us look at the stages of cognitive development as described by Piaget.

## Sensorimotor Stage (Birth to 2 Years)

During the **sensorimotor stage** of development, children's concepts are largely based on the consequences of their own actions. They explore, they probe, they manipulate objects, and they observe the consequences of these manipulations. When they see a favorite toy resting on a distant towel or blanket, they pull the blanket toward them to acquire the valued goal. They shake toys in order to make sounds, rattle cribs to observe the action of the mobiles attached to them, and suck objects that are given to them. In short, they are learning to know the world through sensory and motor activities, developing the ability to make relationships and undertake intentional activities.

An interesting aspect of the earlier substages of the sensorimotor period is that objects seem to have no permanence: "Out of sight, out of mind." But toward the end of the first year, children develop a "theory" about their environment: Objects *do* continue to exist even though they are not in view. This is known as **object permanence.** To test the age at which children develop this concept, Piaget hid an object by throwing a piece of cloth over it (see Fig. 10.13). If a child did not retrieve the hidden object from under the cloth, Piaget assumed that the child had not yet acquired a concept of permanence—the object ceased to exist once it was out of sight. Piaget found that the concept of object permanence emerges at about the age of eight months.

Once children have developed the concept of object permanence, parents may have to devise new ways of keeping forbidden objects from them. One mother reports:

> Before, when I didn't want Danny to play with something, I simply hid it under a blanket or newspaper. As soon as it was out of sight, Danny seemed to forget about it. I can't do that anymore. Now when I hide something, he either finds it or gets real upset. (Author's files)

By the time children reach the final substage in the sensorimotor period, they are able to make symbolic representations of problems and to invent solutions. The following is an example of sensorimotor invention that Piaget observed in one of his children:

> Jacqueline, at 1 year, 8 months, arrives at a closed door—with a blade of grass in each hand. She stretches out her right hand toward the knob but sees that she cannot turn it without letting go of the grass. She puts the grass on the floor, opens the door, picks up the grass again and enters. But when she wants to leave the room things become complicated. She puts the grass on the floor and grasps the doorknob. But then she perceives that in pulling the door toward her she will simultaneously chase away the grass which she placed between the door and the threshold. She therefore picks it up in order to put it outside the door's zone of movement. (Piaget, 1952, p. 339)

### Object permanence
A concept of Piaget's that refers to the child's realization that an object continues to exist even though it is not physically present.

### Preoperational stage
Piaget's second stage of cognitive development. During this period the child develops symbolic thinking and language but not logical thinking.

## Preoperational Stage (2 to 7 Years)

The outstanding feature of the **preoperational stage** is the emergence of language. In arriving at a better comprehension of their world, children are no longer restricted to the actual manipulation of objects. They can now manipulate symbols. They can also pretend that things are what they are not: Building blocks can become trucks that are moved about, accompanied by realistic chugging sounds. But it is a mistake to think that these symbolic processes are comparable to those of an adult.

One of Piaget's most important contributions was to explode the myth that children think the same way as adults do, only not quite as well. Attempts of adults to produce educational materials for children

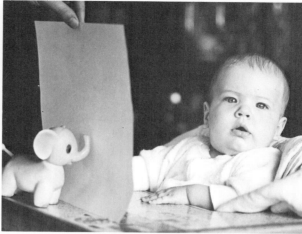

**Figure 10.13**
**Object permanence**

This child has not yet developed object permanence. When the object is hidden by a cloth pad, the child loses all interest.

sometimes go awry as a result of this misconception. They fail to recognize the nature of the thinking process that goes on in younger children. According to Piaget, children's thinking may follow completely different premises from those of adult thinking (see Box 10.4). For example, most children at the preoperational stage are unable to recognize the possibility that behaviors may be caused by more than one factor (Erwin and Kuhn, 1979).

> . . . these limitations restrict a child's interpretation of another person's act to one in which the act is regarded as a direct and probably invariable outcome of a single, necessary, and sufficient determinant. Such a simplistic view of human nature is bound to influence how children conceptually structure interpersonal relationships and how they perceive their own instrumental role in these relations. (Erwin and Kuhn, 1979, p. 353)

Children frequently bombard their parents with questions: "Why?" "How?" "When?" Parents assume that their children are asking for logical explanations when, in fact, they are unable to understand adult logic. If a child asks, "Why is it raining?" he or she may not be asking for a scientific explanation of precipitation. The authors heard this story:

> A mother who had attended adult education classes on sex education for children was well prepared to answer any questions on sex posed by her three-year-old son. One day he asked, "Mommy, where do I come from?" The mother immediately went into a long, detailed explanation of the process of insemination, gestation, and birth. At the end of this discourse, the little boy scratched his head and said: "That's funny. Jimmy says he comes from Chicago."

According to Piaget, children must undergo a sequence of developmental changes in cognition before they can integrate complex concepts

## BOX 10.4

### Stage Theory and the Cognitive Gap

One of the fascinating implications of a stage theory of cognitive development is the inevitability of communications gaps between individuals perched at different cognitive levels. Consider the following account of an encounter among a 2-year-old boy, his 5-year-old sister, and their 45-year-old father.

David is seated on the floor, completely absorbed in play with two hand puppets. Without warning or preamble, Laurie suddenly grabs one of the puppets. David's response is instantaneous and vigorous. He screams, stamps his feet, and displays all of the signs of acute emotional distress. Between sobs and tears, he manages to voice a protest, "Mine! Mine!" Laurie becomes very annoyed with David. "Don't you know you can't have two toys by yourself? You must share." Unimpressed with the force of Laurie's logic, David remains restive. "Mine! Mine!" he continues to shout. Finally, in the role of ombudsman, Daddy decides to intervene. "Laurie, you should not have taken the puppet away from David. He was playing with it."

"But he wasn't sharing," Laurie replies, a tear beginning to form at the edge of her voice. "You always tell me I must share. So I *was* sharing. David wasn't sharing."

"But David's only a baby," Daddy replies placatingly. "He doesn't understand sharing."

"Well, he's supposed to share," Laurie affirms, confident of the basic righteousness of her stand. As she leaves the room, she defiantly displays the trophy she has wrested from David by her obedience to the rule of sharing.

If we look at this transaction from the point of view of a stage developmental theorist, we can make several interesting observations that bear directly on personal–social interaction at many stages of life. David is just beginning to emerge from the sensori-

---

**Conservation**
A term used by Piaget to refer to the ability of the child to recognize that certain properties of objects (e.g., weight, quantity) remain the same despite changes in their appearance.

into a consistent logical framework. Suppose you pour the same amount of water into two identical glasses. By the age of four, children can recognize that the two quantities are the same. Now suppose you pour the water from one of the glasses into a tall, thin glass. Even though young children see you do this, they will report that the taller glass contains more water. Evidently, they judge "more" in terms of height rather than quantity. It is only after the age of six or seven that most children will recognize that quantities remain the same in spite of the way they are divided, shaped, and packaged. This is referred to by Piaget as **conservation** (see Fig. 10.14).

### Concrete Operational Stage (7 through 11 Years)

The acquisition of the concept of conservation is a key step in the cognitive development of children. In distinguishing between appearance and reality, between how things look and how things are, the child must resort increasingly to a cognitive structuring of the world. The manipulation of symbols comes to replace the manipulation of things. However, children at the **concrete operational stage** are not yet able to divorce the symbols completely from the things they represent. In short, they are not yet able to deal with completely abstract concepts. They show an ability to deal with logical relationships, but only if they are stated in concrete terms. Children at this stage would have little difficulty describing how a cat and a mouse are alike. For instance, they can report that they are both

motor period in which the outstanding feature is **ego-centrism**. Egocentrism in the young child shows that he or she has not yet developed a sense of self as a separate being in the world. The baby sees the world as revolving round him- or herself and is unable to take another person's point of view. In fact, the baby is unable to distinguish clearly between self and non-self. To David, not only are the puppets *his* but they are *him*. At least, they are as much him as an arm or a leg.

Laurie's admonition to share is beyond David's comprehension. The gap between Laurie and David is one not of quantity (how much they differ in the *same* point of view) but of quality. The concept of sharing is different in *kind* from the concept "all the world is part of me." But just as Laurie and David are destined to undergo many similar confrontations until both have achieved the blessed state of the same level of cognitive development, so also are Laurie and her father. At Laurie's cognitive stage, rules are treated as

God-given. Rules are rules and must not be violated. She has not yet reached the level of cognitve development in which such rules are recognized as the "inventions" of people, constructed to achieve a degree of social harmony.

In this single real-life situation, we see how stage theory may shed light on several gaps that have captured the imagination of many observers of the contemporary scene—the generation gap, the credibility gap, and the communications gap. We may add the "cognition gap."

**Egocentrism**
An early stage in the child's cognitive development in which he or she does not clearly distinguish between the self and the world other than the self.

animals. But the abstract meaning of proverbs will frequently be beyond them. For example, if you ask them what the proverb "You can lead a horse to water but you can't make him drink" means, they might merely rephrase the proverb in concrete terms, showing no grasp of its broader implications.

## Formal Operational Stage (12 Years and Beyond)

**Concrete operational stage**
Piaget's third stage of cognitive development, in which the child develops logical thinking toward concrete objects.

**Formal operational stage**
Piaget's final stage of cognitive development, in which the child develops the ability to deal with abstract relationships.

During the **formal operational stage** children develop the ability to deal with abstract relationships. They are no longer dependent on the visible or concrete. It now becomes possible for them to imagine rather than experience the consequences of their actions and to deal with hypothetical situations. A whole new world opens to the mind. They can now think in abstract terms, can consider all possible solutions to a problem, can generate and test hypotheses in a systematic fashion. Such activities can be both a source of personal satisfaction and an enjoyable outlet for the mind. The horizons of the child's thinking expand to include word games, crossword puzzles, and complex computer activities.

Originally, formal operations was viewed as the final and inevitable stage in cognitive development. However, Piaget (1972) and others have since revised this view. They suggest that, unlike the other stages, formal operations may not be universal. The attainment of this stage and the degree to which it is attained may depend on aptitude, education, and life experiences. Training in certain areas (for example, science, math, and

Figure 10.14
Conservation

This five-year-old girl spontaneously raised the question, "Do I weigh the same standing up as I do sitting down?" How does this question exemplify the concept of conservation?

logic) is usually associated with greater abstract ability. However, individuals who are unable to reason abstractly in math and science may still achieve the formal operational stage in their areas of specialization. According to Piaget, "The period from 15 to 20 years marks the beginning of professional specialization and consequently also the construction of a life program corresponding to the aptitudes of the individual" (Piaget, 1972, p. 209). Thus mechanics may be able to reason hypothetically when dealing with automobile engines; lawyers may display exceptional logic when handling a legal matter; and electricians may form abstract concepts of electrical circuits.

Although Piaget believed that the final stage of intellectual growth is reached at about 12 years of age, several studies indicate that certain aspects of cognitive development may extend well into adulthood (Rubin *et al.*, 1973; Papalia, 1972). Some cognitive abilities are maintained intact in old age, and some individuals show little or no impairment in any cognitive area even in advanced age (Baltes and Schaie, 1976).

One investigator has proposed that various stages of cognitive development may be distinguished on the basis of how cognitive skills are applied throughout the life span in response to environmental pressures (Schaie, 1979). Childhood and adolescence represent the **acquisition stage.** It is at this stage that we learn the intellectual skills that we will apply throughout our lives. These skills include those acquired in school but are not restricted to them. When we enter early adulthood, we must apply our cognitive skills to real-life problems and situations. Continued

**Acquisitive stage**
According to Schaie, the acquisition of the intellectual skills we will need throughout life; it is characteristic of childhood and adolescence.

**Achievement stage**
According to Schaie, the initial application of cognitive skills to real-life problems and solutions; it is characteristic of early adulthood.

**Responsible stage**
According to Schaie, the improving of cognitive skills in order to deal with the greater complexity of life characteristic of the thirties to the sixties

**Executive stage**
According to Schaie, the development of high-level problem-solving skills not related to day-to-day job or family responsibilities; it is characteristic of the thirties to the sixties.

**Reintegrative stage**
According to Schaie, the refocusing of cognitive skills to deal with the problems of old age and retirement.

cognitive growth will occur among **achieving** adults who find creative applications of these skills.

The **responsible stage** extends from the thirties to the sixties. During this stage, we are faced with complex environmental demands, both at home and at our places of employment. With greater complexity of life and daily decisions come improved skills necessary to deal with this complexity. There is also an **executive stage** in which problem-solving skills are applied to systems that go beyond the family and the day-to-day requirements of the job. According to Schaie, ". . . our studies of life complexity as related to maintenance of cognitive function show that individuals of high social status indeed perform at higher levels and show greater tendency to maintain levels of function over time" (Schaie, 1979, p. 109).

In old age, the same structure of intellect is maintained, but the requirements change. With retirement, some aspects of the environment remain meaningful and relevant. However, we lose interest in others or they become irrelevant. Consequently, we must **reintegrate** our cognitive abilities so they become applied to problems and concerns that are relevant to our status as old and retired citizens. Figure 10.15 diagrams this

The executive stage of development is one in which an individual applies problem-solving skills to systems beyond his or her family and the day-to-day requirements of a job. Sandra Day O'Connor, the first woman to be appointed as a justice of the Supreme Court, makes decisions that become the interpretations of United States' laws.

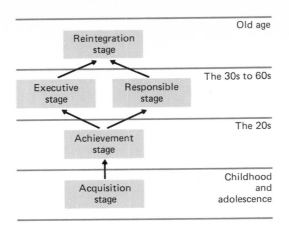

Figure 10.15
**Diagram of a stage theory of adult cognitive development**    (Schaie, 1979)

stage theory of cognitive development. Notice that changes in cognition in old age are a matter not so much of less as of different. The *capacity* of both our sensory and our short-term memory appears to change "little if at all across the life span" (Baltes *et al.*, 1980, p. 84). Moreover, in most of us, the accumulated life experiences remain largely intact.

There is a delightful story told by film director Garson Kanin (1975) showing that wisdom does not come cheap. A town in Connecticut lost its electrical power. After several days and many frustrating attempts to restore power, the engineers could not correct the difficulty. Finally, in desperation, they sent for the retired electrical engineer who had installed the system in his earlier years. After surveying the situation, the engineer grabbed a mallet, tapped it sharply on the equipment, and threw the switch. The lights came on immediately. The town received a bill of $1,000.02 for his services—$0.02 for tapping and $1,000 for knowing where to tap.

# Summary

1. Each of us begins life as a single cell, a fertilized egg, which contains all the genetic information that will direct the growth of the organism throughout its life.

2. Each of us is, in part, a product of our heredity. The principles of genetics provide an understanding of how we can share certain characteristics with members of our family, yet still retain a unique genetic identity.

3. Each cell of the human body contains complex chemical substances, known as chromosomes, on which are located the genes. Genes transmit hereditary material from parents to offspring.

4. The sex of the child is determined by the father. If the sperm that fertilizes the egg contains a *Y* chromosome, the offspring will be male; if it contains an *X* chromosome, the child will be female.

5. Some genes are said to be dominant, and the traits they carry are always evident in the individual. Such observable characteristics are called the person's phenotype. Other genes are recessive, and their traits will appear only if the individual receives two such genes—one from each parent. The complete genetic makeup of the individual, including both dominant and recessive traits, is called a genotype.

6. The field of genetic counseling has grown in recent years as researchers are able to determine the presence of many genetic defects through techniques such as amniocentesis.

7. Prenatal development in humans progresses from a single cell produced by fertilization of an ovum to the embryo state (2–8 weeks) and finally to the fetus stage (8 weeks–birth [about 36 weeks]).

8. A number of prenatal conditions may adversely affect the developing embryo or fetus: For example, faulty maternal diet may lead to an irreversible loss of brain cells in the unborn child; certain drugs or illnesses contracted during pregnancy increase the risk that the child will be born with a deficit such as deafness.

9. Labor, beginning with contractions in the woman's uterus, enlarges the cervical canal and the cervix, allowing the baby to be born. Drugs to reduce the pain of labor are commonly used, although concerns about their effects on neonates are causing many mothers to opt for few or no drugs during childbirth.

10. During the course of growth, behavioral changes may arise from learning or from physiological changes that occur in the normal course of development (maturation). It is often difficult to distinguish between the two.

11. Maturational readiness is sometimes related to a critical period in the development of an organism, when the capacity to benefit from experience is optimal. Although studies have found this period to be common in lower animals, most researchers feel that its applicability to humans is limited and that for humans it is perhaps better defined as a sensitive period.

12. Studies on the formation of attachment between infant and parent have found that contact comfort plays a greater role than feeding and that attention and affection may be still more critical.

13. The newborn is not a passive recipient of external stimulation. From birth onward, the baby is an active shaper of the environment.

14. Motor development progresses rapidly in the first two years of life, transforming the neonate, whose activities are largely limited to reflexive actions, into an active toddler. This form of development appears to follow a sequence of stages that are age-related but not age-fixed. Although norms for motor development can be useful in detecting problems, they should be viewed as guidelines, not rules.

15. The observation that development proceeds in orderly sequences has led some theorists to propose stage theories of development. However, it is the sequence of development rather than the specific timing that is consistently observed.

16. Language acquisition explodes in most children shortly after they enter their second year. The ability to manipulate words and formulate concepts opens up whole new vistas to the developing child, but children's understanding of certain aspects of language often lags behind their use of language.

17. Jean Piaget has formulated a comprehensive theory of cognitive development. The first 2 years of life, called the sensorimotor period by Piaget, are a period of astonishingly rapid physical, motor, cognitive, and social development. The preoperational stage (2 to 7 years) sees the emergence of language. Between 7 and 11 years of age (the concrete operational stage), children are able to deal with logical relationships as long as they are expressed in concrete terms. During the formal operational stage (12 and beyond,) children develop the ability to deal with abstract relationships.

18. Throughout life, cognitive abilities appear to change. Schaie has theorized five stages of cognitive development in adulthood: acquisitive, achievement, responsible, executive, and reintegrative.

# Terms to Remember

| | | | |
|---|---|---|---|
| Chromosomes | Embryo | Cognitive processes | Formal operational stage |
| Genes | Fetus | Schema (plural: schemata) | Acquisitive stage |
| Germ cells | Prenatal | Assimilation | Achievement stage |
| Dominant gene | Intervention procedures | Accommodation | Responsible stage |
| Recessive gene | Maturation | Sensorimotor stage | Executive stage |
| Genotype | Maturational readiness | Object permanence | Reintegrative stage |
| Phenotype | Critical period | Preoperational stage | Egocentrism |
| Genetic counseling | Imprinting | Conservation | |
| Amniocentesis | Rooting | Concrete operational stage | |

**DEVELOPMENT II**

In Chapter 10 we noted that development is a lifelong process that begins with conception and continues until death. In this connection, we examined the biological factors in development (genetics, prenatal growth, and maturation) as well as some of the highlights of motor, language, and cognitive development. But, as we have seen, we grow in many directions at the same time. As we interact with other human beings, we develop standards, including moral judgments, sexual behavior, and sex roles. In turn, these standards affect the personality and social and psychosocial development. In this chapter we will look at these aspects of development.

## MORAL DEVELOPMENT

How often have you heard a parent or a teacher cry out in dismay, ''If I've told you one time I've told you a million times, 'You must not do that. It is naughty' ''? And yet, in spite of constant preaching, sermonizing, rewarding, punishing, begging, and modeling, the undesirable behavior persists. It is easy to slip into the view that children are like obstinate and negativistic demons, actively resisting efforts to mold them into a civilized form.

Two cognitive psychologists, Jean Piaget and Lawrence Kohlberg, have proposed theories that might clarify the reasons for our difficulty in teaching moral judgments. Both theorists believe that moral judgments undergo a sequence of cognitive reorganizations called stages. At any given stage, the child may simply be unable to understand the adult basis for a moral judgment.

Let's look briefly at an example of the techniques used by Piaget to study moral behavior. Children at varying ages are confronted with a moral dilemma. The investigator probes each child's response to the dilemma and analyzes his or her answer. A typical story is as follows:

*A. A little girl named Marie wanted to give her mother a nice surprise and cut out a piece of sewing for her. But she didn't know how to use the scissors properly and cut a big hole in her dress.*

*B. A little girl named Margaret took her mother's scissors one day when her mother was out. She played with them for a while. Then, because she didn't know how to use them properly, she made a little hole in her dress. (Piaget, 1932)*

The reaction to dilemmas such as these appears to vary with age or stage of moral development. Very young children tend to base their judgments on the magnitude of the damage. Thus a five-year-old might say that Marie (story A) should receive the more severe punishment because she did more damage. An older child would be more likely to take the motivations of the guilty person into account. Thus an eight-year-old might judge Marie less deserving of punishment because her intentions were good (Duska and Whelen, 1975).

Kohlberg presents complex stories to his subjects and asks them to judge whether the actors behaved rightly or wrongly. These stories usually feature a conflict between the personal interests of the actors and the greater good of society. In many situations, the individual may see that it is possible to break a law in order to preserve a moral principle. To illustrate, the following is one of the stories used by Kohlberg to investigate moral judgment:

> *In Europe, a woman was near death from cancer. One drug might save her, a form of radium that a druggist in the same town had recently discovered. The druggist was charging $2,000, ten times what the drug cost him to make. The sick woman's husband, Heinz, went to everyone he knew to borrow the money, but he could only get together half of what it cost. He told the druggist that his wife was dying and asked him to sell it cheaper or let him pay later. But the druggist said, ''No.'' The husband got desperate and broke into the man's store to steal the drug for his wife. Should the husband have done that? Why? (Kohlberg, 1969, p. 379)*

In moral dilemmas of this sort, it is possible to develop moral arguments either favoring or rejecting the husband's action. The answers are not scored on the basis of right or wrong, but rather in terms of the underlying *reasoning.*

Using this technique with subjects of all ages and both genders, Kohlberg has described seven stages of moral development organized into three levels (see Table 11.1)—preconventional morality (ages about 4 to 10), conventional morality (ages about 10 to 13), and postconventional morality (ages 13 through adulthood, with many never reaching any stages at this level) (Kohlberg, 1969, 1980).

Stages one and two are at the premoral level of development. The central theme at this level is obedience and avoidance of punishment. At stage one, action is motivated by the fear of punishment and the desire to avoid its consequences. Thus an individual at this stage might respond, ''You shouldn't steal the drug because you'll be caught and sent to jail if you do'' (Liebert *et al.,* 1974, p. 368).

During the second stage, the primary motivation is reward or some benefit. A person might respond, ''If you do happen to get caught you

Table 11.1

**Kohlberg's Levels of Moral Development**

| Level | Stage |
|---|---|
| *Preconventional level* (ages 4–10) | Stage one: Act to avoid punishment<br>Stage two: Act to receive reward |
| *Conventional level* (ages 10–13) | Stage three: Act to avoid disapproval of others<br>Stage four: Act in accordance with law and duty |
| *Postconventional level* (ages 13–adulthood)* | Stage five: Act to achieve and maintain respect of others<br>Stage six: Act to uphold one's own principles<br>Stage seven: Act in accord with universal principles |

Source: Based on Kohlberg, 1980.

*Many individuals never reach any of the stages at this level.

During stage three of moral development, a person's primary motivation is to avoid disapproval. In this stage, disapproval is often punishment enough for any wrongdoing.

could give the drug back and you wouldn't get much of a sentence. It wouldn't bother you much to serve a little jail term, if you have your wife when you get out" (Liebert *et al.*, 1974, p. 370).

Stages three and four are at the conventional level of moral development. During stage three, the central motivation is to avoid the disapproval of others. At this stage, the individual distinguishes disapproval from fear of punishment. A person might advocate stealing the drug on the grounds that the family might judge a husband inhuman if he does not do everything in his power to save the life of his wife. If he did not take action and his wife were to die, the husband would be unable to look anyone in the face again.

By stage four, honor becomes the overriding concern. A person does something because it is the honorable thing to do rather than because of fear of punishment or disapproval. A person at this stage might justify the stealing on the grounds that the husband would feel guilty for causing the death of his wife by his failure to take the honorable course. A person advocating the opposite position might defend the husband's failure to steal the drug on the grounds that he would be doing wrong and that it would be dishonorable to violate the law.

The final three stages of moral development involve the postconventional level of morality. All are based on reason rather than emotions and feelings. As previously noted, many individuals never achieve any of the stages at the postconventional level. At stage five, the primary theme is achieving and maintaining the reasoned respect of one's equals in the community and avoiding the loss of self-respect. Thus a person at stage five might justify stealing the drug by the following reasoning: "I shall lose the respect of my friends if I choose to let my wife die. I must be willing to risk criminal prosecution in order to save her life." Another person might reason, "The long-range goals served by laws against stealing would be violated if I stole the drug in order to save my wife's life. I would lose the respect of the community if I allowed myself to be carried away by my desire to save my wife."

In stage six, the central motivation is to avoid self-condemnation for violating one's own principles. Reasoning at this stage might run: If the man believes that the law provides long-range benefits for society, stealing the drug for his wife would lead to self-condemnation for sacrificing a principle in favor of personal gain. If the man holds life more valuable than laws devised by human agencies, he would condemn himself for failing to break the law. According to Kohlberg, very few people achieve this stage or the next.

The moral reasoning of individuals who have reached the seventh stage transcends the limitations of human frailty and fallibility. Rather, morality is judged in a cosmic perspective. Such great thinkers and leaders as Gandhi, Spinoza, and Martin Luther King, Jr., have reached this stage of moral development (Kohlberg, 1980).

Much research on moral judgment focuses on whether or not an individual commits an act intentionally or by accident. More recent studies

**Martin Luther King, Jr., was one of the rare individuals who reached the seventh stage of moral development. People who attain this stage are able to disregard human limitations and see issues in a cosmic perspective. Here Dr. King is shown speaking to his followers before the 1963 civil rights march on Washington, D.C.**

have manipulated such factors as the type of damage committed. Children tend to judge people as more culpable if they cause harm to others than if they cause material damage (Elkind and Dabek, 1977). In another study, young children judged people who accidentally injured themselves more negatively than those who were uninjured. This distinction disappeared by the fifth grade. Apparently young children operate under the concept of immanent or intrinsic justice. That is, if someone is hurt, he or she must have done something bad to deserve it (Suls and Kalle, 1979).

## PSYCHOSEXUAL DEVELOPMENT AND SEXUALITY

### Psychosexual Stages

The stage theorists we have previously discussed in this and the previous chapter have focused on the cognitive aspects of development—intellectual growth and moral judgment. The father of the psychoanalytic movement, Sigmund Freud, directed his attention more to the motivational and sexual aspects of development. He conceived of development as proceeding along a series of stages that he called **psychosexual stages** (see Fig. 11.1).

Before discussing these stages, it is important to understand Freud's conception of sexuality. Sexuality is the cornerstone of Freud's theory and has generated much controversy, largely because his use of the concept has been misunderstood. According to Freud, the pleasurable feelings that the individual gets from stimulation of the sensitive areas of the body **(erogenous zones)** are basically sexual. As the individual matures and passes through the various stages of development, the focus of pleasure shifts from one erogenous zone to another, essentially from the mouth to the anus to the genitals.

**Oral stage.** The infant's principal source of sexual or erotic pleasure during the first year of life is the mouth. In this first stage of personality development, the **oral stage,** pleasure is derived from sucking and biting. If the infant's experiences during this stage have been particularly satisfying, such oral activities as eating, kissing, and talking will continue in a normal way into adulthood. But if the infant has experienced frustration during the oral stage, it is possible that his or her later personality will reflect this in behaviors such as overeating and greediness.

**Anal stage.** During the **anal stage,** which occurs between the ages of one and three, the infant derives pleasure from both elimination and retention of feces. If the infant is highly frustrated during the course of toilet training, he or she may become obstinate and excessively frugal as an adult.

**Phallic stage.** Somewhere around the fourth year of life, the focus of erotic pleasure shifts to the genital zone. During this so-called **phallic stage,** the child derives pleasure through manipulations in the genital

**Psychosexual stages**
Freud's theory of developmental stages in which the focus of pleasure shifts from one part of the body to another.

**Erogenous zones**
The various sensitive areas of the body.

**Oral stage**
In psychoanalytic theory, the first stage of psychosexual development, during which the mouth is the principal source of sexual or erotic pleasure.

**Anal stage**
In psychoanalytic theory, the stage of psychosexual development during which the infant is preoccupied with sensations from the anal area.

**Phallic stage**
In psychoanalytic theory, the stage of psychosexual development in which the focus of erotic pleasure is the sex organs.

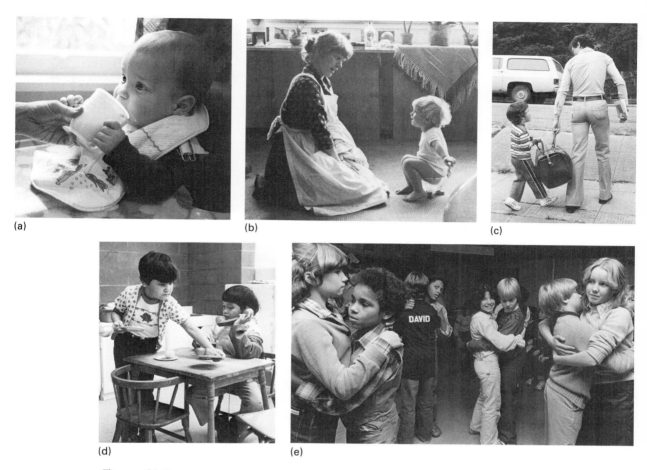

Figure 11.1
**Major developmental tasks in Freud's stages of psychosexual development**

(a) Oral stage—weaning; (b) anal stage—toilet training; (c) phallic stage—identification with same-sex parent; (d) latency stage—reaction formation to opposite sex; (e) genital stage—establishing sexual intimacy.

zone (masturbation). A critical event, which must be resolved at this time if the child is to advance to more mature psychosexual stages, is the **Oedipus complex** in boys and the **Electra complex** in girls.

The boy unconsciously develops strong sexual feelings toward his mother. These feelings are threatening to him because they place him in direct conflict with his father; this conflict is known as the Oedipus complex. The boy fears that his father will retaliate by castrating him. Thus **castration anxiety** develops, perhaps because the boy has observed that females lack a penis. To protect himself against this anxiety, he represses his incestuous urges and identifies with his father.

The situation is somewhat different with girls. The girl blames her mother for her lack of a penis, a condition known as **penis envy.** She shifts her attachment to her father and sees her mother as a direct rival. This is known as the Electra complex. Freud believed that girls never completely lose their attachment to their fathers. He regarded this attach-

---

**Oedipus complex**
Unconscious sexual feelings of a boy for his mother.

**Electra complex**
Unconscious sexual feelings of a girl for her father.

**Castration anxiety**
A boy's fear that his father will castrate him in retaliation for his Oedipal feelings.

**Penis envy**
In Freudian theory, the female's unconscious desire to have a penis.

During the latency stage, which occurs around the age of six, children practice behavior associated with their emerging sex roles.

ment as normal and felt that it would later form the basis for heterosexual relations with a husband. The girl resolves the Electra complex by identifying with her mother and by seeking a substitute father image, a boyfriend.

Latency stage.    Presumably by about the age of six, the normal child has successfully repressed the Oedipus or Electra complex and has entered the **latency stage.** Sexual urges become dormant for the next few years. Reaction formation is a common defense mechanism at this stage and may be inferred from the almost universal plaint of boys at this age, "I hate girls." During this period, children practice many of the behaviors associated with their emerging sex roles. Girls do "girl things" and boys do "boy things."

Genital stage.    With the advent of puberty, the beginning of adolescence, the focus of erotic pleasure returns to the **genital** zone. The individual who has successfully passed through all the preceding stages is well prepared for assuming the normal adult heterosexual role.

## Sexuality

The media often paint the adolescent period with purple prose as one of reckless sexual abandon. One might easily conclude that sex is at the forefront of the minds of most adolescents. One study disputes this view. A total of 430 boys and girls from grades 5 through 11 were asked to list and rank their interest in obtaining more information about certain topics (Kermis *et al.*, 1975). It was found that arts, sports, crafts, and understanding other people were a few of the topics that ranked higher than sexually related topics, such as dating, going steady, birth control, and sexual relations. Of course, sexuality still ranked high as a topic of interest, and it is possible that the adolescents gave the answers they thought adults wanted to hear, but this study certainly seems to indicate that adolescents are less than obsessive about sex.

Sexual activity in adolescence spans the entire spectrum from abstinence, to casual kissing, to "going all the way." The various levels of sexual activity fulfill a number of important needs. Besides sheer pleasure, this activity provides an opportunity for and practice in communicating and investigating the mysteries of love. It may also win peer approval.

However, although sexual intercourse among unmarried adolescents appears to have increased over the past few decades, the picture is not one of a continuous orgy. In many cases, sexual intercourse involves only a single partner with whom marriage is contemplated (Zelnik and Kantner, 1972).

In early adulthood, the typical individual is in search of a sexual partner. Unlike prior generations, however, not all young adults choose marriage as the route. There are more than 50 million single adults in the United States, of whom 15 million have never been married (Francke, 1978). Some of these frequent singles' bars in search of "one-night stands," whereas others enter homosexual relationships. Nevertheless, approximately 80 percent of young adults choose to establish a long-term relationship with a partner of the opposite sex. With the relaxation of attitudes concerning sexual intimacy outside marriage, many couples prefer **cohabitation;** others take the traditional road of marriage.

Relaxed attitudes toward sexuality have also entered the marriage bedroom. One survey reports substantial changes that have occurred in the sexual relationships of married partners. When compared to groups reported by Kinsey in the late 1940s and early 1950s, married partners are engaging in intercourse more often, employing a greater variety of sexual behaviors, and enjoying a fivefold increase in the average duration of sexual intercourse (Hunt, 1974). Moreover, ratings of marital happiness correlate with ratings of sexual pleasure. In one study, almost all couples who described their marriage as emotionally close also reported marital intercourse as pleasurable (Hunt, 1974). On the other side of the coin, 70 percent of the women who rated their marriages as poor reported that their sex lives were also poor (Levin and Levin, 1975).

As adults enter their later years, they frequently deny their sexuality (Crooks and Baur, 1980). This may be, in part, because our society tends to focus on youth, particularly females, as sex objects. To illustrate, *Playboy* magazine presented an article entitled "The Mystique of the Older Woman" (1977), in which the average age of the women was only 33 years! As women grow older, they are commonly regarded as unattractive (owing to the gray hair, crow's-feet, and wrinkles). Recent generations also assumed that women were and should be less sexually active as they aged. On the other hand, men frequently are considered more distinguished as they grow older. Here the wrinkles and the gray hair are

**Latency stage**
In psychoanalytic theory, the stage of psychosexual development in which sexual urgings become dormant.

**Genital stage**
In psychoanalytic theory, the stage of psychosexual development in which the focus of erotic pleasure returns to the genital zone and the individual achieves mature heterosexual relations.

**Cohabitation**
Living together in a sexual relationship without marriage.

regarded as evidence of wisdom and full life experiences. Thus there is a double standard concerning the effects of aging on sexual attractiveness.

Many women attempt to deny the fact of their aging by the use of cosmetics, facial surgery, and specially designed clothing. Susan Sontag suggests a different avenue:

*Women have another option. They can aspire to be wise, not merely nice; to be competent, not merely helpful; to be strong, not merely graceful; to be ambitious for themselves, not merely themselves in relation to men and children. They can let themselves age naturally and without embarrassment, actively protesting and disobeying the conventions that stem from this society's double standard about aging. Instead of being girls, girls as long as possible, who then age humiliatingly into middle-aged women and then obscenely into old women, they can become women much earlier—and remain active adults, enjoying the long, erotic career of which women are capable, for longer. Women should allow their faces to show the lives they have lived. (Sontag, 1972, p. 38)*

In spite of cultural myths, sexual behavior can continue throughout the life span. However, there are changes. Males do not experience sexual tension as often during the middle and later years. Therefore they do not seek sexual contacts as frequently as in their youth. The length of sexual intercourse is extended because they take longer to reach orgasm. However, the amount of sexual activity during their young adult years is a good indicator of the likelihood of continued sexual activity during their middle and older adulthood (Masters and Johnson, 1966).

**Sexual behavior can continue throughout the life span, contrary to popular belief.**

## BOX 11.1

### Sexuality and Aging in Nursing Homes

The double standard, especially as it relates to aging, has been so ingrained in the traditions and assumptions of our society that until recently it has come under relatively little question. The situation in some nursing homes, however, has been the center of considerable controversy in the past decade. A number of practices and attitudes that are beyond the scope of this text have been criticized for their insensitivity to the human rights of aged individuals in some nursing homes. Our own concern is with antisexual prejudice and practices, which are clearly demonstrated in many nursing home facilities. Of the 5 percent of the population over 65 who live in nursing homes at a given time, many are denied the adult rights of sexual opportunity and privacy. One writer describes the situation:

> Their environment is almost totally desexualized. It is considered progress when dining room or recreation halls and residential wings are not sex-segregated. Privacy is virtually nonexistent. . . . [O]nly a minority of institutions make an effort to provide areas where a couple can be alone together even to talk, much less to court. Even married couples may be separated; some state institutions segregate them or permit the sexes to mix only under "supervision." If only one spouse is in a home, the other seldom has the right to privacy during a visit. (Lobsenz, 1974, p. 30)

Because older individuals are often assumed not to be sexual, medications are sometimes prescribed without consideration of their effects on sexuality. Some tranquilizers, antidepressants, and high blood pressure and arthritis medications can have an inhibiting effect on sexual interest and arousal. These factors should be discussed with each person and adjustments made. It is also desirable for concerned parties to be thoroughly educated about the potential effects on sexuality of suggested surgeries, particularly those which involve the reproductive organs (Page, 1977).

Some relatives of nursing home residents and the staffs of such facilities help to perpetuate difficulties such as those just outlined, perhaps in part because of their own lack of knowledge or discomfort concerning sexuality and aging. Some concerned individuals, progressive nursing home personnel, and organizations such as the Gray Panthers and Services to Ongoing Mature Aging are beginning to make some inroads into restrictive situations in nursing homes. Staff education, programs on sexuality for the residents, private lounges, and acceptance of affectional and sexual rights of residents are important elements in such care facilities. Perhaps, as these alternatives are made increasingly available, such policies and practices will help maintain the important option of sexual expression for the aged who are in institutions.

Reprinted by permission from Crooks, R., and Baur, K., *Our Sexuality*, Menlo Park, California, The Benjamin/Cummings Publishing Company, Inc., 1980, pp. 436–437.

With the cessation of menstruation, women are no longer capable of childbearing. However, the physiological changes do not lower the desire for intercourse or substantially change the nature of the sexual response. Indeed, theoretically, the greater surplus of androgens over estrogens should increase the sexual drive (Kaplan, 1974). As an additional factor, one of the psychological barriers to intercourse (fear of pregnancy) is removed. Thus many postmenopausal women report an increased enjoyment of sex.

In view of the fact that sexuality continues throughout life, a cause of grave concern among many experts is that institutionalized older people are almost always deprived of privacy and conjugal rights (see Box 11.1).

**SEX ROLES**
From the moment of birth, forces are set in motion that prepare children for their later adult roles. Many of these influences are direct, as when a father scolds his young son with the words, "You're a boy. Boys don't cry." This theme, repeated time after time with minor variations (e.g., "Boys aren't afraid of the dark; boys are brave"), carries the implication that boys are different emotionally from girls. They should be in constant command of their feelings and emotions and not put them on public display. Moreover, they should be achievement-oriented and competitive. For girls, the emphasis is on achieving and maintaining close interpersonal relationships.

> They are encouraged to talk about their troubles and to reflect upon life, are shown affection physically, and are given comfort and reassurance. Where the issues between parent and son appear to be those of authority and control, the parent–daughter theme at the several age levels reflects an emphasis on relatedness, protection, and support. (Block, 1973, p. 517)

Not only are sex roles learned by direct instruction from caretakers and other adults, but they are learned through observation and modeling. Both boys and girls learn at an early age that there are two types of individuals, each of whom has distinctive anatomical features. Moreover, ev-

Sex roles are usually learned by observation and imitation, as well as by direct instruction. It is likely that a little girl who sees women performing formerly male-oriented tasks will learn that she also is capable of mastering those skills.

eryday observation reveals that these physical differences form the basis for broader differentiations that include expected behaviors or roles. Children have many opportunities to take note of how their fathers and mothers behave toward one another. Boys imitate what they see their fathers do, and girls imitate the behavior of their mothers. Thus girls tend to grow into adults who behave like their mothers and boys to develop into men who behave like their fathers.

The important point is that the roles we perform are dictated not by biological factors but rather by the demands and expectations of the situation. Expectations about how boys and girls should behave are elaborated in virtually all of life's situations, including even the selection of toys. Boys are given guns, erector sets, trains, and chemistry sets. Girls, on the other hand, are encouraged to be passive and submissive, and are given dolls to play with. During the school years, boys are expected to excel in mathematics and the sciences. Girls who develop similar aspirations are frequently discouraged by both adults and their peers.

One study nicely illustrates the effects of role expectations on behavior (Howe and Zanna, 1975). Groups of four subjects (two males and two females) were given the task of forming words from scrambled letters. One male and one female in each group were told that success at the task was related to masculine interests and abilities. The other two subjects were given the opposite information, namely, that the task was appropriate to feminine abilities and interests. During the course of completing the task, the subjects were given feedback on their level of performance. Male subjects who were told they were succeeding on a "feminine" task adjusted their performance to do less well on the task. If they had been told that their task was "masculine," their performance improved. Among female subjects, the opposite results were obtained. They improved when they thought the task was appropriate for females but decreased their performance when the task was regarded as masculine.

One observer of the differences between the roles of male and female (Block, 1973) has made a strong case for the view that the most effective functioning adult (an **androgynous individual**) is one who is free to incorporate the positive aspects of both masculine and feminine sex roles. She finds, however, that "the sex role definitions and behavioral options for women . . . are narrowed by the socialization process, whereas, for men, the sex role definitions and behavioral options are broadened by socialization" (p. 525). Thus men are relatively free to adopt some traditionally feminine concerns, for example, conscientiousness, conservation of resources, and interdependency. Simultaneously, they may renounce such conventional male characteristics as opportunism, restlessness, and self-centeredness. Women, on the other hand, find it difficult to renounce traditional femine characteristics like docility and submissiveness and to adopt conventionally defined masculine characteristics such as self-assertiveness, achievement orientation, and independence.

One of the expectations about androgynous people is that, because they presumably receive more social rewards as a result of their flexibility, they are likely to have developed a strong sense of self-worth. Several studies have supported this position (Bem, 1979, 1980; Spence and Helmreich, 1978, 1979). However, one study found that, whereas both males

**Androgynous individual** An individual who has the ability to express both masculine and feminine characteristics as the situation requires.

and females with high "masculinity" scores generally scored higher on behavioral adaptability, such was not the case with those who had high "femininity" scores (Jones *et al.*, 1978). This may explain why, for many women entering the male-dominated world of business, androgyny (that is, the adoption of both traditional "masculine" and "feminine" traits) is especially desirable (see Box 11.2).

## PERSONALITY AND SOCIAL DEVELOPMENT

Knowledge about our sexual identity and sex roles is just one facet in the complex pattern of social and interpersonal relationships we must learn in order to function in the larger society.

One of the most delightful things to observe during the early years is the infant's changing responsiveness to social stimulation. By the age of two months, the infant may bestow upon its parents its first smile in response to seeing or hearing them ("social smile"). The infant may have smiled at an earlier age, but it was largely in response to internal stimuli (for example, the "gas smile"). Although the social smile has been re-

## BOX 11.2

### Sex Roles

In the 1970s, with-it parents tried to encourage their little boys to be sensitive and to show emotion, and their little girls to be goal-oriented and assertive,

Lately, with the country in a more conservative mood, there has been talk about saving the family by reversing that trend and returning to traditional values and sex roles.

Whatever side of the issue you may be on, the reality is that there are no old roles to go back to, says Janis Stevenson, a specialist in early childhood development at Tucson Association for Child Care.

The family and the roles of women in society have changed too radically, she argues, for us to ever turn back to a time when men were men and women stood behind them all the way.

She has an armory of statistics to back her up: The nuclear family—working father, nonworking mother and 2.5 children—exists today in only 11 percent of America's households.

Ninety percent of the women in this country will work at some time in their lives.

One of every five families now is headed by a single parent; of those, two of five are living—somehow—on incomes below the poverty level.

"Why? Because they are headed by women whose sexual programming didn't prepare them for entering the work force and supporting families.

"Those women know there are no old roles for them. They're out there on their own, frustrated because there are no jobs for them," Ms. Stevenson said.

When she led a recent workshop on sex role stereotyping, sponsored by Enrichment for Parents, Ms. Stevenson began by saying she doesn't consider herself a feminist.

She stressed, too, that she respects parents who want to raise their children to assume the traditional roles of male providers and female caretakers.

"But my own bias," she told the 20 mothers attending the class, "is to be careful about putting limits on kids, because I see the sex roles as limits. It's scary to me that we're lopping off parts of people and limiting what they can do later."

And that, she said, is what we are doing—to give one example—when we tell girls it's OK for them to be afraid of math or mechanical things. "Eighty percent of career choices are shut off to women at the

ported as early as two weeks (Emde and Harmon, 1972), is it usually not until about the age of two months that it can be consistently elicited.

There are large individual differences in the tendency to produce a social smile, however. Some infants are lavish with their smiles; others bestow them with far less frequency. Because the mother usually interprets the smile as a sign of the baby's well-being, the infrequent smiler may cause its mother to worry and doubt her own abilities. These doubts may, in turn, affect the quality of the mother–child relationship.

By the age of 3 months, many infants show a wariness of strangers that indicates a dawning awareness of the difference between the familiar and the foreign (Bronson, 1971). Nevertheless, most children do not clearly distinguish the mother from other familiar adults until sometime after the sixth month. At about this time, many infants display a marked fear of strangers **(stranger anxiety).** Whenever an unfamiliar person appears, the infant cries or screams and clutches at its parent. This reaction is often disconcerting to the well-meaning grandparents who come from out of town for their long-anticipated visit with their grandchild. The intensity of stranger anxiety is markedly diminished if the infant has known many adults from an early age, as in the kibbutzim of Israel (Spiro, 1958).

**Stranger anxiety**
A fear of unfamiliar or strange faces that develops in the infant somewhere around the sixth month.

---

college level because they didn't have the proper math and science training," she said. "That's critical in terms of economics."

To compete in the work world, women need to develop some of the qualities associated with men, such as drive, independence, willingness to take risks, problem solving skills and self-esteem, she said.

"But there are also some beautiful, special qualities our society needs that traditionally are female," added Ms. Stevenson, listing compassion and nurturing as examples. "Men are just as robbed of potential" by sex role stereotyping as women are, she contended.

So, if you buy her arguement, what can you do as parents? "Enrich your child's life by providing a wide range of choices in toys, activities and human relationships," she suggested.

Keep in mind, though, that children "aren't your little pawns," and there is only so much you can do to break the old patterns.

Ms. Stevenson knows a family, for instance, in which the mother always does the driving, even when her husband is in the car. Yet her child drew a picture of dad at the wheel and mom in the passenger seat.

"You know I drive," she pointed out, and her son replied, "Yeah, but that's not the way it's supposed to be."

Kids know how men and women are traditionally supposed to act, Ms. Stevenson said. They pick up on advertising, friends and school.

And they start learning the roles—tough, strong boys and pretty, emotional girls—at an age when their critical faculties are undeveloped and they believe everything they are told.

There are subtle, but significant, differences in the way boys and girls are handled from birth, Ms. Stevenson said.

Boys are usually punished directly and physically, she contended, while girls are often disciplined psychologically, by withdrawal of love. "That's a powerful tool in making women emotionally dependent later in life. They fear that withdrawal."

Boys are encouraged more than girls to venture out of their yards and into the neighborhood . . . the examples go on and on.

---

"Sex Roles" by Norma Coile, *Tucson Citizen,* August 14, 1981, p. 1B.

This reaction reaches its peak at 13 to 15 months of age and is quite rare by the age of 3 years (Kagan, 1979).

Brief separation from the mother or caretaker before 6 months of age produces no greater emotional response than separation from any other adult (Schaffer and Emerson, 1965). At about the age of 10 to 12 months, however, the child will show signs of disturbance whenever separated from the mother. For example, if the child is playing and the mother leaves the room, the child will frequently burst into tears. This is known as **separation anxiety** and usually disappears by the time the child approaches his or her second birthday.

One of the areas in which we see the greatest changes and expansions is play activity. Whereas the young infant plays either alone or with adults, beyond the age of two the child begins to play in the company of other children, all playing side by side with a minimum of interaction. After the age of three, the child begins to engage more in cooperative play, in which interaction is a vital element. A favorite form of play at this time is dressing up and acting like adults.

As children enter the school years, they begin to lose the open and forthright innocence of their earlier days. They start to practice guile and deception, forming small ingroups that revel in the sharing of secrets. During these early school years, peer groups begin to assume greater importance to children than adults do. Many children form closely knit groups or "gangs" that, in many cases, establish elaborate and often secret rules of codes of conduct. The six-year-old is still somewhat of a baby

During a child's early school years, peer groups assume more importance than adults do. These groups are usually formed on a same-sex basis and have little or no contact with groups of the opposite sex.

and is not likely to be a full-fledged member of the gang. He or she is still likely to cry easily and be regarded as a tattletale. But by nine years of age or so, this child has become an integral member. These gangs are usually grouped by sex, and members of the opposite sex are frequently regarded with disdain or indifference.

When we wrote the first edition of this book, Audrey Haber's daughter was on the threshold of life. At birth, Laurie Beth was little more than a bundle of unrealized potential. We have watched that potential take form and direction. We have observed her grow physically, mentally, emotionally, and socially. We have seen and shared in her moments of joy and have felt pain during her periods of distress. But the direction of her growth has always been clear. Step by step she is progressing toward maturity and adult years. In doing so, she is reaching out for greater control over her own life. She recently celebrated her tenth birthday. The birthday party was largely planned and carried out on her own. She remains, however, a delightful package of contradictions. She wants and needs to experience independence but she still has strong needs for love and guidance from the family. At times she is a child in adult's clothing; at other times, she is an adult in child's clothing. Although she spends most of her time with her friends, there is a growing need for intimacy with her mother. They share certain "secrets"—about boys, menstruation, and what it means to be a girl. Many forces are influencing her development at this stage: her home and family life, peer relations, and school. She is now at another of life's thresholds—one that will usher in the abrupt and rather dramatic changes that begin her adolescence.

Adolescence is the time span between childhood and adulthood. Although there are minor disagreements among experts, most would place the onset of adolescence at around age 12 and its end somewhere between 18 and 20.

Adolescence is frequently painted as a period of great storm and stress. This is because massive changes are taking place in virtually every aspect of the adolescent's life. The body undergoes dramatic physical changes; there is an awakening of sexual urgings; the cognitive abilities make a dramatic leap to embrace abstract thought. Whether or not adolescence is experienced as a period of continual stress depends largely on how the individual views and reacts to these changes. Some go through this period as smoothly as a stroll on a quiet beach. Others find themselves caught up in the waves of a raging ocean. Let's look more closely at some of the far-reaching changes that occur during adolescence.

How many of you have visited a seventh- or eighth-grade class recently? If you have, you most surely were struck by the varied assortment of sizes and shapes. Some children will have started to manifest the sweeping physical changes associated with **puberty.** Others will still be very childlike in appearance. You may also have noted a striking difference between the boys and the girls. Typically, the girls will have already begun the growth spurt that heralds oncoming maturity. Consequently, many of the girls are taller and more fully developed than the boys of the same age. On the average, girls begin their growth spurt at around the age of 12. In contrast, the boys may not start until about two years later.

More striking yet are the differences in shapes. Some members of both sexes will already manifest the rapid body changes that accompany emerging sexual maturity.

Physically, girls change much more rapidly than boys during this period. Today both boys and girls achieve sexual maturity earlier than they used to, probably because of better dietary and health practices. Figure 11.2 shows the average ages at which girls in the United States, Norway, the United Kingdom, and Germany have reached the **menarche** (first menstrual period) from 1880 to the present. Many 11- and 12-year-old girls have already reached puberty, and often they find that boys of the same age are too young for them.

In girls the breasts enlarge, the hips increase in width, and body hair starts to appear under the arms and in the pubic area. Of course, one of the most dramatic changes is the onset of menstruation. In boys, the voice deepens, hair begins to sprout in many different parts of the body, and the penis and testes increase in size.

These physical changes can be a source of pride or embarrassment:

*Feeling self-conscious is a common reaction, and individuals who mature early or late often feel particularly self-conscious:*

*"I was the first one to get hair on my chest. At first I would cut it off so I wasn't different from everyone else in the shower room."*

**Menarche**
First menstruation; the beginning of puberty for females.

**Figure 11.2**
**Average age of menarche**

**The downward trend shown here is probably chiefly due to advances in nutrition over the past century. However, it appears to be leveling off in some countries. (Tanner, 1973)**

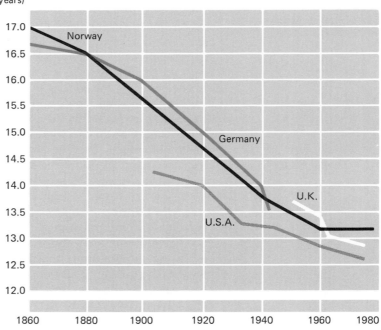

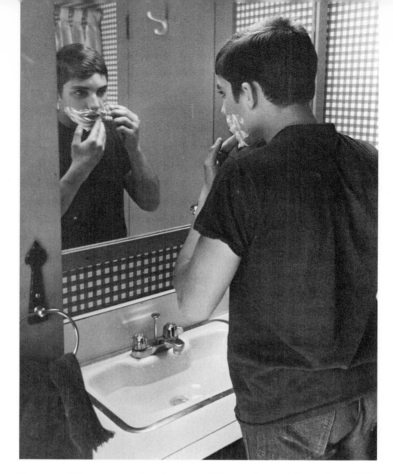

Because adolescents reach puberty at different times, this can be a difficult period for both males and females. Teenagers tend to very self-conscious about their physical development and appearance, and nothing seems less desirable than being different from one's peers.

*"All my friends had started menstruating a long time before and I still had not. I started wearing pads and a belt once a month so I wouldn't feel so out-of-it."*

*These physical changes do not go unnoticed by adolescent peers. Boy–girl friendships often change and adolescents are likely to become— at least temporarily—more homosocial, relating socially primarily with members of the same sex. A young woman clarifies:*

*"When I was growing up a neighbor boy and I were best buddies. We spent our summers exploring nearby fields, wrestling, and building a great tree house. When I started developing breasts, it all changed and we didn't seem to know how to talk to each other any more."\**

The problems of puberty can be especially great for early and late maturers—those boys and girls for whom puberty comes earlier and later than for most of their peers.

For boys, there seems to be a definite advantage in reaching puberty early. Early maturing boys are generally more at ease socially than other

---

*Reprinted by permission from Crooks, R., and Baur, K., *Our Sexuality*, Menlo Park, California, The Benjamin/Cummings Publishing Company, Inc., 1980, pp. 394–395.

boys and are better liked by their peers. As adults, they tend to be successful socially and vocationally, although they often prefer conventional life-styles and careers. Late maturing boys, on the other hand, may suffer rejection from girls their age and show lessened social skills throughout life. As adults, they are often unconventional in their choices of life-style and career.

There do not appear to be consistent benefits or disadvantages for girls in maturing early or late. Some early maturing girls may be subjected to unwanted and frightening attentions from men who mistake their physical development for emotional maturity. Others may comfortably date older boys, gaining social skills somewhat earlier than their peers. Though they may be rejected by some physically mature boys their age who find them less attractive, late maturing girls do not generally seem to be affected either positively or negatively, perhaps because they are maturing at about the same time as average boys their age. Still, as any adolescent can tell you, there is nothing worse than being different from one's peers—regardless of how or why.

## PSYCHOSOCIAL DEVELOPMENT

### Stages of Psychosocial Development

**Psychosocial stages**
Erikson's theory of eight developmental stages, in each of which the individual must resolve a different crisis.

From the moment of birth until death, there is a constant interplay between what a person wants to do and what society demands of the person. At times the interplay is in the form of conflict: Society's expectations and the individual's aspirations are frequently on a collision course. These conflicts constitute life's crises. According to one of the leading stage theorists, Erik Erikson, there are eight major crises (see Table 11.2) that an individual faces in the course of a lifetime (Erikson, 1963). These crises are regarded by Erikson as personal challenges and opportunities for further growth. Erikson's theory of **psychosocial** development may be regarded as an alternative to the Freudian psychosexual stages.

The first crisis arises during the first few months after birth when the infant is completely dependent on adults for nurturance. The crisis involves *trust versus mistrust*. If the care of the child is undependable or inconsistent, he or she may develop a mistrust that persists throughout a lifetime. During the second stage, between the ages of one and three, the child is gaining increasing control over his or her muscles and motivations and the external environment. In Erikson's words, the child is developing a sense of *autonomy*. If not successful in achieving autonomy, the child is afflicted with *shame and self-doubts*. Between the ages of three and five, the child's capabilities are expanding explosively. Control over the environment can be achieved by the use of words as well as by the improved locomotor development. The child runs, climbs, and throws objects. During this stage, the child's desires often come into conflict with the demands of society: "You must not throw rocks at Tommy," or "Don't call Maribeth bad names." If successful in resolving this crisis, the child becomes capable of initiating independent action; if not, he or she may become racked with feelings of guilt.

Table 11.2
**Erikson's Psychosocial Stages of Development**

| Developmental stage | Nature of crisis | If successfully resolved | If not successfully resolved |
|---|---|---|---|
| *Birth–first year* (infancy) | *Trust versus mistrust* Infant utterly dependent on others. Crisis involves learning either trust or mistrust for others. | Develops trust for others. | Becomes suspicious and mistrustful of others. |
| *Ages 1–3* (toddler) | *Autonomy versus doubt* Child is gaining control over musculature and begins to assert individuality, causing some conflict with parents. | Develops a sense of being an individual, with some control over own destiny. | Develops a sense of shame and doubt concerning own capabilities. |
| *Ages 3–5* (preschool) | *Initiative versus guilt* Crisis involves inner desire versus the demands of society. | Develops a sense of initiative. | Develops strong guilt feelings. |
| *Ages 6–11* (middle childhood) | *Industry versus inferiority* Occurs during school years prior to adolescence. Crisis involves competence versus failure. School performance plays a vital role in resolving this crisis. | Achieves competence. | Develops feelings of inferiority. |
| *Age 12 to end of school* (adolescence) | *Identity versus role confusion* Involves the finding of identity versus confusion over roles, sexual as well as social. | Learns what roles to adopt in various life situations. | Remains confused over roles and identity. |
| *End of school to about age 25–30* (young adulthood) | *Intimacy versus isolation* Crisis involves need to establish commitment to another person. | If successful in "finding self," can find another with whom to share intimacy. | Unable to find another with whom to share intimacy. Remains isolated. |
| *Age 25–30 to retirement* (middle adulthood) | *Generativity versus stagnation* As individual settles into routine patterns, faces the crisis of generativity (productivity) versus stagnation. | Continues to generate new ideas and to remain productive. | Stagnates like a pond without an outlet. |
| *Old age* | *Integrity versus despair* Can be achieved only by resolving all prior stage crises. Conflict involves integrity of the self versus despair. | Is able to integrate knowledge of coming death into life's patterns. | Individual is unable to integrate reality of death into life patterns. Sees life as wasted and futile. |

The fourth stage occurs during the school years prior to adolescence. This is a period during which sexual interests lie dormant as the child tests his or her ability to acquire knowledge and put it to use. The conflict during this period involves *industry versus inferiority.* In successfully resolving this crisis, children become productive members of society; they discover that they are capable of achievement. If children fail to develop such feelings of competence, they may instead feel inferior and be afraid even to try doing things.

The fifth stage comes during the adolescent years, when the body is experiencing massive changes. A major and pivotal crisis the individual must solve is one of *identity versus role confusion*—"Who am I and what roles am I to play in the adult society to which I shall soon gain admittance?" There are three disruptions that can occur to adolescents at this time: inability to establish their own personal meaning ("Why am I here?"); a feeling of rejection by the dominant culture ("They neither understand me nor like me"); and the inability to integrate the many roles they are called upon to assume ("One moment they treat me like a kid and the next moment they scold me for not acting like a grownup").

Achieving a sense of identity involves many decisions, including occupational choices. The problem is "how to connect the roles and skills cultivated earlier with the occupational prototypes of the day" (Erikson, 1963, p. 261). In other words, how does one choose an occupation? This is not easy. Many young people become confused when they have difficulty finding roles that fit their interests and abilities. However, finding one's own identity extends beyond the question of occupation. It also includes sexual, political, and religious beliefs.

During adolescence, the individual plays many different roles—son or daughter, student, girlfriend or boyfriend, to name just a few. From all these separate roles, the adolescent struggles to achieve a clearly defined sense of personal identity. According to Erikson:

> *The identity the adolescent seeks to clarify is who he is, what his role in society is to be. Is he a child or is he an adult? Does he have it in him to someday be a husband and father? What is he to be as a worker and an earner of money? Can he feel confident in spite of the fact that his race or religious or national backgrounds make him a person some people look down upon? Overall, will he be a success or a failure? (Erikson, 1951, p. 9)*

Some observers (Douvan and Adelson, 1966) feel that girls find it more difficult than boys to develop a clear sense of self. They suggest that some girls may postpone this task until after marriage. Then they merge their identities with those of their husbands. Thus their sense of self may depend on their husbands' plans and accomplishments. Ironically, failure to achieve an independent sense of personal identity may actually interfere with the marital relationship.

Creating a sense of one's own personal adult identity is a difficult task. The dramatic physical and sexual changes occur so rapidly during this period that many young people are left confused about themselves and their roles in society. It is not surprising to find that many adolescents never establish a clear sense of self. This is one of the reasons that

One reason adolescents turn to cults is their desperate need for a sense of belonging. They seek to become part of a group in order to establish their own sense of identity.

many adolescents turn to causes and cults in a desperate search for a sense of belonging. Others look to the ultimate escape by taking their own lives (see Box 11.3).

During the early adult years, the major crisis involves *intimacy versus isolation*. Once we have established a clear sense of personal identity, we are ready to fuse ourselves with others. However, we may not be capable of making a commitment to another person until we have resolved our own life roles. Many relationships run into problems because one or both partners are dissatisfied with their own personal lives. If we are still striving to "find" ourselves, we are not ready for an intimate, sharing, and give-and-take relationship. Individuals who have not satisfactorily resolved the identity crisis remain like a lighthouse on the ocean, isolated from the mainstream of society.

The developmental tasks facing individuals in early adulthood include the following: finding a mate, learning to live with a partner, starting a family, managing a home, getting started in an occupation, assuming civic responsibilities, and finding a congenial social group (Havighurst, 1972).

The years of middle adulthood are marked by the routine pattern of daily activities. The business person is in danger of performing his or her

## BOX 11.3

### Teenage Suicides: Why Our Children Are Killing Themselves

It wasn't the first time 15-year-old David thought about killing himself, but it was the first time he attempted to go through with it. He took an overdose of tranquilizers following a heated argument with his mother over his frequent curfew violations.

David's trouble had actually begun two years earlier. First there was his parents' separation, and the bitter divorce battle that ensued. Once a B-plus student, David was so disturbed by his parents' breakup that he started doing poorly in school. Then his mother remarried, and that event caused him additional anguish. David's mother had been seeing the man who became his stepfather while she was still married to David's father, and David blames his stepfather for his parents' divorce. Things became even worse when David's grandmother died. He had come to rely on her for the love and support he felt he wasn't receiving from his parents, and he later revealed that he had even experienced fantasies of rejoining his deceased grandmother, who, he felt, was "one person who really loved me." David then sought peer acceptance and companionship from what he termed "a group of losers," and was eventually arrested for breaking and entering and placed on one year's probation. In addition, he occasionally experimented with various drugs, another dangerous activity in which his new peer group was involved. But,

ironically, the pills he ingested during his suicide attempt had been prescribed for his mother.

Yet, despite its tragic beginning, David's story (his name has been changed and all identifying information deleted to protect his family's confidentiality) does have a much happier ending. His suicide failed, and with the help of therapy, he's trying to put his life back together and has shown a marked improvement in his self-esteem, self-image and self-confidence. More importantly, to date, he has not attempted suicide again.

Unfortunately, a growing number of today's teenagers will not get a chance to start all over again. . . . Suicide is now the third leading cause of death among all 15-to-25-year-olds, behind accidents and homicides.

And, like David, an alarming number of the youngsters killing themselves are black.

In a 1978 study on black suicides prepared at the University of Wisconsin at Madison's Institute for Research on Poverty, Dr. Robert Davis, a North Carolina A&T State University sociology professor, found that the suicide rate among nonwhites ages 15–34 is now higher than it has been in more than 50 years. Dr. Davis also cited statistics which showed that blacks between the ages of 15 and 24 commit suicide at a higher rate than that of the total black population of all ages. Although the National Center for Health Statistics of the U.S. Department of Health and Human Services does not list specific ethnic groups in its most recent figures, it did find that from 1968 to 1978, the

---

functions in a mechanical fashion with no infusion of new ideas and no sense of excitement or anticipation. The woman who elects to marry and raise a family can become a prisoner of her daily chores. The crisis of middle adulthood, then, is *generativity* (remaining productive and capable of generating new ideas) *versus stagnation.* Individuals who succumb to the tendency to treat every day in a thoroughly routine manner are in danger of stagnating, like a pond with no outlet.

The following developmental tasks face individuals during their years of middle adulthood: helping teenage children become productive, responsible, and happy adults; achieving and maintaining satisfactory performance in a career; assuming adult social and civic responsibilities; relating to a spouse as a person; adjusting to the physical changes of middle age; and adjusting to aging parents (Havighurst, 1972).

suicide rate for nonwhites ages 5–14 increased 200 percent, from 0.1 suicides per 100,000 people to 0.3. Among nonwhites ages 15 to 24, the rate increased 59 percent, from 5.6 suicides per 100,000 people in 1968 to 8.9 in 1978.

Why are so many young blacks ending their lives?

Dr. Davis says one possibility is the weakening of family and communal ties in the black community. He says that in the past blacks had their families, communities, and institutions to help them cope with stressful situations. "But now, we're not as tightly knitted into the family or community as we used to be," says Dr. Davis. "I've found that the stronger one's relational system—that is, the greater the number of social involvements with family, friends and relatives and the more of a sense of belonging one has—the lower the suicide rate."

Psychiatrist Dr. Wille Hamlin feels current economic trends and governmental policies share some of the blame for the rise in teenage suicides. He says many blacks feel they've been "written off," a situation that he says produces anger, helplessness, and hopelessness. "This in turn filters down to our children, who are the most vulnerable individuals in our society," he says. Dr. Hamlin, who is the assistant director of the Department of Child Psychiatry at Howard University Hospital, further explains that adolescence can be a difficult stage in any youngster's life, "because it's a time when they seek self-identity and peer acceptance. It's also important to them that society sees them as important and worthwhile, but our society gives a negative impression to minority and poor children, especially when one considers current governmental policies."

Dr. Hamlin adds that other "variables" have been known to increase the risk of suicide attempts by adolescents. They include academic failure, the loss of a girlfriend or boyfriend, a family history of suicide attempts, chronic illness, and an unstable home environment, especially in the case of foster or adoptive children. One teenager who attempted suicide, for instance, did so because she did not want to live in a detention center. Abandoned at an early age, she had spent much of her life in and out of foster homes and was finally placed in a detention center because she ran away from all of her foster homes. Adolescents may also commit suicide because they feel unloved and unwanted at home.

"On the personal level," says Dr. Hamlin, "parents need to be a lot more in touch with thier children. They should listen freely to their children, show affection toward them and praise their accomplishments. We have to remember that these are our future caretakers, and how we raise them will reflect on how they treat us in our old age. There's an old saying that goes, 'twice a child; once an adult.'"

Source: "Teenage Suicides: Why Our Children Are Killing Themselves," Marilyn Marshall, *EBONY Magazine*, September 1981. Reprinted by permission of *EBONY Magazine*, copyright, 1981, by Johnson Publishing Company, Inc.

It is during the middle years that we recognize that about half of our life has been lived. Thoughts turn toward death more frequently than before, particularly as parents and older relatives begin to die. However, we are typically at our peak with respect to our influence in our community and place of employment. Thus the impact of thoughts of death is reduced by feelings of effectiveness and well-being.

With old age, the developmental tasks reflect the disengagement of the individual from active participation in many of the activities of earlier years. New roles, such as grandparent and retiree, emerge as old roles disappear. Some individuals even pursue totally new careers at this juncture of their lives. The developmental tasks common to people in this age group include adjustments to decreased physical strength, poorer health, retirement, reduced income, and the deaths of a spouse and friends.

Moreover, the individual commonly must find new age-group affiliations, adopt flexible social roles, and maintain satisfactory living conditions (Havighurst, 1972).

In Erikson's view, this final stage, maturity, can be entered only by those who have resolved the crises at all prior stages of development. The crisis during these final years on earth involves *integrity of the self versus despair*. That is, we can believe in the wholeness or integrity of the self only if we have developed trust and initiative, gained a sense of autonomy, achieved competence, learned our identity, achieved intimate relations, and continued to generate new ideas in our middle years. It is at this stage that we recognize our mortality and that life must end. If able to integrate the knowledge of the inevitability of death into our life patterns, we are able to look over life's accomplishments with a sense of satisfaction (Box 11.4). Otherwise, we regard life as a cruel hoax that is both futile and wasted. We sink into the quicksand of despair.

## BOX 11.4

### Growing Old Can be Graceful
#### By Ellen Hale, Gannett News Service

Washington—Though the Fountain of Youth remains elusive, scientists are finding that growing old isn't as inevitable as it used to be and that there are some ways the aging process actually can be reversed.

Aging may be controlled as much by lifestyle as it is by genetics, a host of new studies shows, leading experts across the country to conclude that people can live longer and better than they have in past generations.

As a result, special clinics and programs for the elderly are springing up across the country, and senior citizens as old as 80 and 90 are getting into shape, some of them for the first time in their lives.

Fully half the effects of growing older—the physical decline that occurs in an aging individual—are caused by lifestyle, by disuse and simply by being out of shape, asserts Everett L. Smith, an expert on the physiology of aging and a member of the Preventive Medicine Department at the University of Wisconsin.

Where 15 years ago physiologists and medical experts wrote off physical fitness programs for the elderly as pointless, in recent years studies have shown that the elderly can be trained into good physical con-

dition and that being in good shape will prevent many old age symptoms.

And only last year did experts finally conclude that proper diet and nutrition are integral for the elderly and, as a result, drew up the first dietary guidelines for the aged.

Here are some of the myths that have been debunked and which prove that the aging process can be slowed down, if not actually reversed in some cases.

- High blood pressure, an ingredient in many diseases of the elderly, does not automatically accompany growing old. It does, however, accompany a diet high in salt. Studies of countries where salt intake is low show that the elderly have the same low blood pressure levels as do young people.
- Stiff joints, muscle deterioration and all the other physical aches and pains that have been credited to growing old don't have to happen. "There is no longer any doubt that the health benefits to be derived by the elderly (by exercise) are entirely similar to the benefits derived by the young and middle-aged," says physiologist Herbert A. deVries, of the Andrus Gerontology Center at the University of Southern California.
- The decrease in bone mass that occurs with age

## Dying and Death

"Getting old," the joke goes, "isn't so bad when you consider the alternative." Yet sooner or later each of us will die, and in this age of increased medical ability to prolong life, many of us will have substantial opportunity to contemplate our deaths before they occur.

In a study involving hundreds of patients who had been informed of their impending death, five different stages of dying were identified (Kübler-Ross, 1969). At first, there is *denial*. The patient rejects the idea that a correct diagnosis has been made. This is usually followed by *anger:* "Why does it have to be me? Why can't it be someone else?" Then the patient starts *bargaining* with God for an extension of life. Many humanitarian services are offered in exchange for continued life. As the patient's health continues to deteriorate, a *depression* sets in. There is a sense of loss and of helplessness, grief over the ending of life. In some patients, this stage is followed by *acceptance* of the inevitability of death. They may not be willing or anxious to die, but they come to recognize that the value

and which causes bones to become brittle and fragile can be reversed, Smith has found in a landmark new study. Generally, everyone begins to lose bone at age 30 at a rate of about 1 percent a year, although the rate is considerably higher for menopausal women. After three years on an exercise program, a group of 80-year-old people in Smith's study increased their total bone mass by over 2 percent, while a group of the same age which didn't exercise recorded a bone loss of over 3 percent—a full 5 percent difference.

All of this is not to say, however, that there aren't inevitable changes that go along with getting old. Scientific evidence proves that "as we grow older, we do suffer losses in functional capacity at the cellular level, at the tissue level, at the organ level and the system level," explains deVries.

For example, the ability of the heart to pump blood declines about 8 percent a decade after adulthood. The chest wall stiffens and breathing takes more muscular effort so suddenly "we must huff and puff at chores that hardly increased our breathing in youth," deVries says. Skeletal muscles also decrease with age, and people lose up to 5 percent of their muscle tissue every decade as they grow older.

These losses, in turn, make it harder for the body to transport oxygen into the cells and use it. By the age of 75, most people have lost 50 percent of their oxygen consumption capability, and, therefore, half of their "pep, vim and vigor," says deVries.

Yet, a person can increase or decrease his chances of suffering seriously from these problems by the way he takes care of himself, experts say.

Fitness and exercise are vital to this, since being in shape has been linked to lower risk of heart disease and other "killer" ailments of the elderly.

It also provides these benefits and more in the elderly: improves temperature adaptation and tolerance, increases blood volume and artery size, lowers the rate and depth of breathing and reduces the tendency for blood to clot.

The evidence also seems to indicate that an older person doesn't have to work all that strenuously to get in shape and stay there, and that what is most important is exercising regularly, perhaps three to five times a week for up to 30 minutes at a time.

But diet, too, plays a vital role in aging healthily, stresses Dr. Myron Winick, director of the Institute of Human nutrition at Columbia University. Some ways are obvious: reducing calories, cholesterol, fat and salt intake.

*Tucson Citizen*, September 14, 1981, pp. 1A, 3A.

In old age, individuals who have developed a sense of autonomy and competence are better able to accept the inevitability of death. Despite such factors as decreased physical strength, poorer health, and reduced income, these individuals often pursue new careers and activities and adopt new social roles.

of their contributions does not depend on their physical presence. Their interest shifts away from concern for the preservation of their lives and focuses more on the improvement of the quality of the term of life that still remains.

Although Kübler-Ross's work has been important in focusing the attention of psychologists on this once taboo area, there is considerable dispute about the validity of her stage theory. One study found that not every individual goes through all five stages (Kastenbaum, 1977). Certainly there is room for argument about the rigidity of the stages, and the emphasis on fixed emotional states has drawn fire from those who point out the ability of a dying woman, for example, to show joy at the sight of her newborn grandchild.

# Summary

1. The individual appears to undergo various stages of moral development during the course of a lifetime. Lawrence Kohlberg has proposed a three-level theory of moral development according to which individuals pass from a preconventional level in which decisions are made on the basis of fear of punishment or hope of reward, to a conventional level in which decisions are based on a desire to maintain conventional values and to conform, and finally to a postconventional level in which decisions are based on self-accepted moral principles.

2. Sigmund Freud proposed a five-stage theory of psychosexual development—oral, anal, phallic, latency, and genital.

3. Although sexual intercourse among unmarried adolescents appears to have increased over the past decades, a false picture of a continuous orgy is often painted. In spite of cultural myths, sexual activity can continue throughout the life-span.

4. In our society, males and females encounter different expectancies concerning their appropriate roles and behaviors. Children learn these roles through imitating the behaviors of adults.

5. Recently there has been a trend for individuals to be androgynous in their behavior. Although men appear to find it easier to adopt positive female traits, some studies indicate that androgyny is more acceptable in females.

6. Some key aspects in the development of personality and social relationships are the social smile, stranger anxiety, separation anxiety, expansion of play activity, and formation of peer groupings. With adolescence come massive physical changes and an increased desire for independence.

7. Erik Erikson has developed a theory of psychosocial development around the concept of eight major crises that the individual faces during a lifetime of growth. These crises involve trust versus mistrust, autonomy versus doubt, initiative versus guilt, industry versus inferiority, identity versus role confusion, intimacy versus isolation, generativity versus stagnation, and integrity versus despair. Only if we resolve the crises at earlier stages of development can we maintain our integrity in old age.

8. Elizabeth Kübler-Ross described five stages among patients informed of their impending death: denial, anger, bargaining, depression, and acceptance. Though these stages are open to question, Kübler-Ross's work has focused psychological attention on the topic of dying.

# Terms to Remember

| | | |
|---|---|---|
| Psychosexual stages | Electra complex | Androgynous individual |
| Erogenous zones | Castration anxiety | Stranger anxiety |
| Oral stage | Penis envy | Separation anxiety |
| Anal stage | Latency stage | Puberty |
| Phallic stage | Genital stage | Menarche |
| Oedipus complex | Cohabitation | Psychosocial stages |

# INTELLIGENCE AND TESTING

## WHAT IS INTELLIGENCE?

You have probably used the word "intelligent" many times in your life. What precisely do you mean when you say that someone is intelligent? Do you think your friends would agree with your concept of **intelligence?** Ask some of your friends, "What do you mean by intelligence?" You may be surprised at the number of different answers you get. Even psychologists have had a difficult time agreeing on a definition of intelligence. Some psychologists stress the ability of the individual to adapt to new situations and to profit from previous experiences. Others regard intelligence as a cluster of various types of abilities, such as reasoning, memory, verbal fluency, and competence with numerical concepts. Still other psychologists view intelligence as scholastic aptitude, the ability to do well in school.

The lack of universal agreement on a scientifically precise definition of intelligence often obscures a fairly basic agreement regarding the nature of the concept. For example, who would doubt that the individual in the following description showed a high level of intelligence?

> At the age of three, John Stuart Mill had learned the entire Greek alphabet and was able to translate long lists of Greek words into their English equivalents. By the age of twelve, he had mastered many of the Greek classics in their original form, including the various philosophical treatises of Plato and the scientific writings of Aristotle. Before he was fifteen, he had studied chemistry, botany, mathematics, Latin and French. As an adult he wrote many scholarly books encompassing such diverse fields as history, law, and logic.

Similarly, most of us would agree that the person described below is *not* intelligent:

> At the age of three, William R. had not yet spoken his first word. By the age of fifteen, he was capable of communicating only simple thoughts and ideas. Moreover, he had difficulty comprehending reading materials beyond the second-grade level. As an adult, he could obtain employment only in situations in which considerable supervision was required. (Author's files)

Note that in neither of these cases was intelligence directly observed. Like so many other phenomena we study in psychology, intelligence is a contruct that we infer from behavior. Often these inferences are based on informal observations of the behavior of others. We listen to a person speak and, for reasons that are often difficult to pin down, we conclude that he or she is bright, average, or dull. A person who does well in school or in business is commonly judged intelligent. Another who experiences difficulties in school or who fails to climb the ladder to success in business is considered less intelligent. However, such informal judgments are usually based on only limited observations of behavior, under widely varying conditions, and do not permit precise comparisons of different individuals at different ages.

In effect, the psychologist formalizes many of the behavioral criteria by which we judge intelligence and provides an objective basis for comparing individuals. The various tests of intelligence represent the culmi-

**Intelligence**
The ability to adapt to new situations and to profit from previous experiences when confronted with new situations or problems; some people define intelligence as what intelligence tests measure.

**Operational definition**
A definition of terms or concepts by the way in which they are measured.

nation of many years of effort along these lines. Although, as we shall see, these efforts have not been an unqualified success, tests of intelligence have had a major impact on education, counseling, and related fields.

Many psychologists define intelligence as what intelligence tests measure. Although this **operational definition** may appear circular, it does take into account all the factors that were investigated in the course of constructing the intelligence tests, and this is a fairly broad range of factors. Before looking at the way in which intelligence is measured, let us look at the requirements of a good test.

## REQUIREMENTS OF A TEST

Every day of our lives we make judgments about people and things. We usually base these judgments on limited information obtained under informal conditions. For example, we may decide to buy a particular car by road testing it. On the basis of this small sample of the car's "behavior," we are, in effect trying to predict future performance. When we meet a person at a party, we observe only a small sample of that person's behavior. Yet on the basis of these informal observations, we typically make judgments about personality, interests, and even intellect. We rely on these observations, despite their limitations, because it is usually not practical to carry out all the observations necessary to provide a firm basis for judgment. For example, rather than take a course with a particular

Various tests are used to measure intelligence. In this test, an educational psychologist monitors a woman's speed and accuracy as she places forms in the appropriate positions.

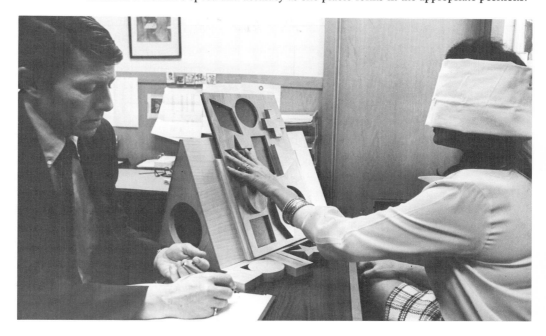

instructor completely "on the blind," most students try to get some information about the instructor and the course in order to predict their own, or the instructor's, future performance. They may ask friends who have had this particular instructor; they may note the grade distributions at the end of the previous semester; or they may even sit in on one of his or her classes.

We are aware of the pitfalls of these informal types of observation. Yet the more formal testing procedures used in psychology and education are much like these informal methods. They also rely on limited samples of behavior in an attempt to predict future performance. However, formal testing is expected to meet several specific requirements.

## Objectivity

A good test must be **objective**. This means that the scoring of the test should be free of the influence of subjective and personal factors. When different people score the same test, they should come up with the same test score for each individual.

## Reliability

Suppose that you rely on your alarm clock to wake you at seven o'clock every morning to get to class on time. If your alarm clock is working properly (and you hear it), it will ring at seven o'clock and wake you up. But what if it is defective? Perhaps sometimes it runs slow. Even though you set it for seven o'clock, it actually rings at eight. At other times, it runs fast and you find yourself getting up at the crack of dawn.

A good test, like a good alarm clock, must be **reliable;** that is, it must yield consistent results. We can determine the reliability of a test in several different ways. We can compare the performance of the same individual on two different occasions, using the same or alternate forms of the test. We can compare the performance on two halves of the same test by comparing the performance on all the odd-numbered items with the performance on all the even-numbered items. If the test is reliable, the scores compared in these ways should be nearly identical.

## Validity

A test is said to be **valid** if it measures what is purports to measure. To illustrate, tests such as the Scholastic Aptitude Test—SAT—claim to measure the potential of the individual to perform scholastically. If the claim is correct, it can be said to be a valid test. However, many so-called aptitude tests have been criticized as measuring verbal and mathematical *achievement,* not *potential*. The definition of validity states that, for an intelligence test to be valid, it must actually measure intelligence. But as we have already pointed out, intelligence is not directly observed but must be inferred from behavior. Consequently, there is no direct method of demonstrating that an intelligence test is *really* measuring intelligence. The best we can do is determine that an intelligence test is measuring some aspect of *behavior* that we generally acknowledge as "intelligent" behavior. For example, an underlying assumption of most early intelligence tests was that intelligence is involved in the ability to do schoolwork. Indeed, many tests of intelligence were validated by showing that IQ scores predicted scholastic achievement. With these considerations in mind, we might say that a test is valid if it predicts performance in a criterion situation.

We will distinguish between two types of validity, both of which relate test performance to some criterion measure. To clarify the distinction, let's look at a hypothetical example. Let's imagine that we have developed a physiological measure that we believe will permit an extremely rapid assessment of intelligence. How might we go about determining the validity of this claim?

**Predictive validity.** It is generally accepted that scholastic performance reflects, in large part, the operation of intelligence. If our physiological measure permitted us to predict the future scholastic performance of subjects, we would have reason to accept the measure as a valid indicator of intelligence; that is, it would have **predictive validity.**

**Concurrent validity.** Suppose we selected three groups of individuals who, we could agree, represented three different levels of intellectual functioning. One group, for example, might consist of college professors; another, of high school graduates; and a third, of high school dropouts. If the physiological measure is a valid instrument for assessing intelligence, we would expect the professors to obtain the highest scores on this measure and the high school dropouts the lowest. This method is called **concurrent validity** because it compares the scores on the new measure with an already existing criterion of intellectual performance (the number of years of education successfully completed).

In order to be valid, a test instrument must be reliable. For instance, suppose that a high score on an intelligence test leads to the prediction of superior school performance, and a low score leads to the prediction of poor school performance. If the test were not reliable, then the same individual might score high on one day and low on the next. How could we make valid predictions about his or her school performance? On the other hand, a test can be perfectly reliable, but have no validity at all. For example, the length of a person's big toe can be reliably measured, but it is unlikely to provide a valid basis for predicting school performance.

## Standardization

A score by itself is meaningless. It takes on meaning only when it can be compared to some known standard. Most tests are **standardized.** They are administered to some large and representative group of people, selected at random and tested under comparable conditions. The resulting scores are subjected to acceptable statistical procedures, and norms, or standards, are devised. Any individual's score can be compared to these norms. The method of selecting individuals to make up the standardization group is extremely important in any application of these norms to specific individuals. Most tests of intelligence in the United States have been standardized on a white, English-speaking, urban school population, and thus their norms are of questionable value for interpreting the scores of persons outside this group. We shall have more to say about this problem in later sections of this chapter.

## MEASURING INTELLIGENCE

### Stanford–Binet Test of Intelligence

Around the turn of the century, the Paris schools faced a severe problem of overcrowding. Moreover, French educators had long been aware that many children did not seem to benefit from traditional educational experiences. These children swelled classroom enrollment and interfered with the progress of the other children. It had been assumed that these children were simply perverse, and the only way to deal with them was to inflict punishment and humiliation. But these methods had not solved the problem. Continued failure of punitive methods prompted many educators to take a different view. Perhaps some children were not capable of benefiting from traditional education. If these children could be identified, they could be placed in special educational settings. A French psychologist, Alfred Binet, devised a test to identify such children. The test met with immediate success and was the precursor of many subsequent measures that have come to be known as intelligence or IQ tests.

In devising his original scales of intelligence, Binet started with the assumption that, on the average, the older a child was the better that child would perform on his test. Moreover, a set of norms could be established defining average performance for each age group. Binet established his norms by grouping together items that a majority of children at a given age could pass. Thus if a four-year-old could pass all the items at the six-year level, the child's **mental age** was six. Because the mental age exceeded the chronological age, this child would be considered bright. On the other hand, if a child with a chronological age of six could pass all the items at the four-year level but none beyond, this child had a mental age of four and would be considered dull.

The original Binet scale has undergone many revisions since it was introduced in 1905. The most famous revisions were accomplished at Stanford University in 1937, 1960, and 1972. The scales resulting from these revisions are known as the Stanford–Binet intelligence scales. Figure 12.1 shows some of the Stanford–Binet materials. Each child is tested individually, and there are a number of items at each age level. The child receives credit for each item he or she is able to answer correctly. The examiner continues to administer the test at progressively higher age levels until the child misses all the items at a particular age level. Table 12.1 shows some of the items from several different age levels.

The concept of **intelligence quotient (IQ)** was introduced in one of the Stanford–Binet revisions. IQ reflects the relationship between chronological age (CA) and mental age (MA). By applying a single formula, it is possible to obtain a score that allows comparison of intellectual functioning among children of the same as well as different ages. Let's calcu-

French psychologist Alfred Binet developed a scale of intelligence that evolved into the modern intelligence quotient, or IQ scale.

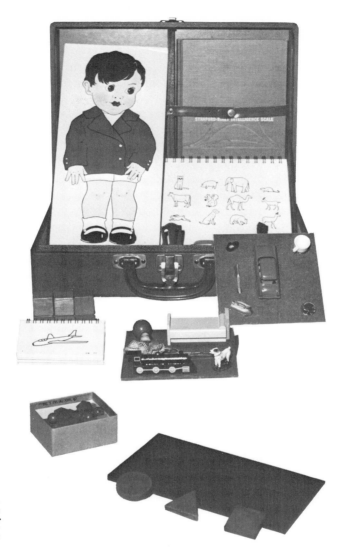

late the IQs of the four-year-old with a mental age of six, and of the six-year-old with a mental age of four. The IQs are obtained from the following formula:

$$IQ = \frac{MA}{CA} \times 100.$$

Thus, for the four-year-old,

$$IQ = \frac{6}{4} \times 100 = 150,$$

and for the six-year-old,

$$IQ = \frac{4}{6} \times 100 = 67.$$

When MA = CA, IQ = 100, which is the average IQ for the population. Figure 12.2 shows the distribution of IQs on the 1937 Stanford–Binet revision.

**Mental age (MA)**
The individual's score on an intelligence test based on a norm; an MA of 7 means that the individual has performed as well as the average seven-year-old child.

**Intelligence quotient (IQ)**
The individual's mental age divided by his or her chronological age and multiplied by 100: IQ = (MA/CA) × 100.

Table 12.1

**Sample Items at Various Age Levels from the Stanford–Binet Intelligence Scale, 1960 Revision**

| Age level | |
|---|---|
| Three-year | Copy a circle |
| Four-year | Why do we have houses? |
| Five-year | Copy a square |
| Six-year | What is the difference between a bird and a dog? |
| Seven-year | In what way are wood and coal alike? |
| Eight-year | What should you do if you found on the streets of a city a three-year-old baby that was lost from its parents? |
| Nine-year | What is foolish about: "Bill Jones' feet are so big that he has to pull his trousers on over his head"? |
| Ten-year | What is grief? |
| Eleven-year | In what way are a knife-blade, a penny, and a piece of wire alike? |

**Derived IQ score**
The average score on an intelligence test for a given age group is set equal to 100; individuals who score on a par with their age level will obtain an IQ score of 100.

Not all intelligence quotients are defined in the same way. For adults and late adolescents, the concept of mental age is no longer appropriate. Some psychologists believe that mental growth, like physical growth, does not continue throughout life. Sometime during the adolescent years, the individual stops growing, both physically and mentally. Other psychologists argue that mental growth continues well beyond adolescence, and that what appears to be stabilization is artificial and merely reflects inadequacies in test construction. Whatever the case may be, there is relatively little growth in mental age beyond the adolescent period as measured by intelligence tests. Consequently, there are several tests with a **"derived" IQ score.** The performance of individuals of the same age is compared, and certain statistical manipulations are performed so that the

Figure 12.2

**Distribution of IQ scores for the 1960 Stanford–Binet Intelligence Scale**

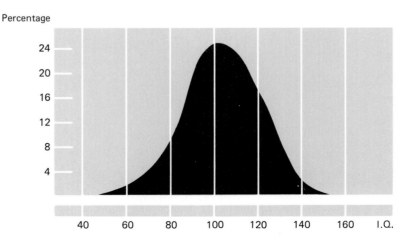

average score is 100. Thus individuals who score on a par with their age will obtain an IQ score of 100. Individuals who perform considerably better than their age peers will have an IQ considerably above 100.

Although the Stanford–Binet remains one of the most widely used and respected instruments for measuring intelligence, it has several limitations. First, it is highly verbal in nature and tends to discriminate against those who have difficulties with the English language. In addition, it is of questionable value when employed with adolescents and adults. Moreover, because it yields only one overall index of intellectual performance, there is no way to assess the specific strengths and weaknesses of the person tested.

## The Wechsler Tests

As we have pointed out, the Stanford–Binet intelligence test tends to discriminate against individuals who have limited use of the English language. The following case illustrates the difficulty of assessing the intelligence of a person who has a pronounced language handicap:

> Martha P., a friendly, highly motivated, and cooperative girl of 12, had emigrated from Russia at the age of 9. Only Russian was spoken in her home. On the Stanford–Binet test, she received an IQ score of 96, well within the normal range. Nevertheless, the test administrator received the distinct impression that her performance did not truly reflect her intellectual ability. A subsequent detailed analysis of the test results suggested that her language handicap might have impaired her performance. A few examples shed light upon the extent of this handicap. In the vocabulary, she made only four correct responses. Approximately one-half of those children with a chronological age of 8 years get at least eight vocabulary words correct. Thus Martha, who was nearly 12 years of age, apparently had an English vocabulary of less than 8 years. The types of errors made were also quite revealing. For "tap" she replied "spinning thing" (obviously thinking of "top"), in spite of the fact that she had the printed word in front of her. Similarly, for "muzzle" she replied "mixed up," obviously thinking of "muddle." On the basis of many examples of this sort, it was concluded that Martha's intelligence was probably much higher than the test score indicated. (Author's files)

Wechsler tests were developed to deal with difficulties of this type. Although the original test was designed to assess adult intelligence, later versions also included separate tests for children of different ages. Like the Stanford–Binet, these tests are individually administered. The Wechsler tests still in use include the Wechsler Adult Intelligence Scale (WAIS-R), the Wechsler Intelligence Scale for Children (WISC-R), and the Wechsler Preschool and Primary Scale of Intelligence (WPPSI). The outstanding difference between the Wechsler tests and the Stanford–Binet is probably the addition of items not dependent on verbal ability (performance items). In fact, the Wechsler tests are constructed to yield separate verbal IQ and performance IQ measures, as well as an overall IQ score. The IQ scores are derived measures, computed from tables. They do not represent a relationship between mental and chronological age. Table 12.2

Table 12.2

**Comparison of Some of the Characteristics of the Stanford–Binet and Wechsler Tests**

| Stanford–Binet | Wechsler tests |
|---|---|
| Individually administered, highly verbal | Individually administered, both performance and verbal measures |
| Primarily for children | Scales for both children (WISC-R) and adults (WAIS-R) |
| Yields one overall score | Yield verbal and performance IQs plus profiles in various categories |
| Based on "mental age" concept | "Derived" IQ |

summarizes characteristics of the Stanford–Binet and the Wechsler scales, and Table 12.3 shows the various subtests of the WISC-R and a sampling or description of items from each subtest.

The WAIS-R and WISC-R contain very similar subtests. The WISC-R, however, is designed for children aged 5 to 15, and the WAIS-R is used for people above the age of 16.

## Group Tests

Many of you probably remember taking a group test of intelligence sometime during your school career. You may have experienced many of the frustrations that are characteristic of any group-testing situation. Perhaps you were not feeling well that day, or perhaps you did not understand some of the instructions. When large groups take a test, it is usually difficult for the individual to get any kind of attention or help. The examiner generally finds it impossible to deal with individual problems that may arise during the test. This is not to say that group tests have no value, but rather to caution you against putting too much weight on any one individual's performance on a group test.

The following story, although not necessarily typical of the problems that may arise when a single group test is used to assess an individual's level of intelligence, may serve as an example of the type of thing that can happen when individual identity is lost:

> *Donald J. was a student in the eighth grade in a large metropolitan school system. At a given time and date, all children throughout the system were administered a group test of intelligence. Just prior to the test, Donald was summoned to the principal's office to discuss his eligibility to receive honors at a forthcoming graduation exercise. When he returned to the classroom, the testing had already been in progress for a period of time. The teacher handed him a copy of the test and told him to complete it before the time limit had expired. Because Donald had not received instructions on taking the test, he doodled on the answer sheet instead of filling in the various alternatives. When he arrived at high school the following year, he was surprised to learn that his request for a precollege*

*curriculum had been disapproved. Instead, he was assigned to a class of children who were experiencing all manner of mental and emotional difficulties. He remained in this special educational setting, in which more emphasis was placed upon the students' deportment than upon their scholastic growth.*

*Two years later, the city again required all of its students to take a group intelligence test. A few weeks later, Donald was again summoned into the principal's office. After checking his signature against the one appearing on the test form, the high school officials acknowledged that a serious error had been made. His test scores of two years earlier had suggested that Donald was severely retarded; his most recent score placed his performance beyond that of most college graduates. When the circumstances of the first test were revealed by Donald, he was immediately placed in a precollege high school program. Subsequently, he graduated with distinction from college and is generally acknowledged as successful in his chosen profession. (Author's files)*

Group intelligence tests are valuable primarily in large screening programs, where it is not possible to adminster an individual test to each person. These tests are often used for selection purposes, such as in a

Table 12.3

**Verbal and Performance Subtests of the Wechsler Intelligence Scale for Children (WISC-R)**

| Verbal scale | Performance scale |
|---|---|
| 1. *Information*—A series of questions to assess the general knowledge of the child beginning with easy items such as, "How many ears do you have?" to more difficult items such as "What are hieroglyphics?" | 1. *Picture completion*—Incomplete pictures are shown, and the child must state what is missing (e.g., teeth from a comb). |
| 2. *Similarities*—The child must identify the quality that two words have in common (e.g., *shirt* and *hat* are both pieces of clothing). | 2. *Picture arrangement*—The child must order a series of pictures so that they tell a story. |
| 3. *Arithmetic*—A series of problems is presented orally, and the child must solve them in his or her head in a fixed amount of time. | 3. *Block design*—Blocks with colored parts must be arranged to match a presented design in a limited time period. |
| 4. *Vocabulary*—A list of words of increasing difficulty must be defined (e.g., "What does *knife* mean?") | 4. *Object assembly*—The child is given the name of an object for which the parts are presented, and he or she must assemble the parts in a fixed time period. |
| 5. *Comprehension*—The child is asked to explain certain phenomena or solve situational problems (e.g., "What is the thing to do when you cut your finger?") | 5. *Coding*—Objects such as a star and a ball are presented with lines through them, and the child must replicate the lines in additional blank stars, balls, and so on in a fixed time period. |
| 6. *Digit span (optional)*—From three to nine digits are read, and the child must repeat them. A second part of this test has the child repeat the digits backwards. | 6. *Mazes* (optional)—Drawings of mazes are presented, and the child must trace through them in a fixed time. |

military setting to identify individuals best suited for training in various specialties. Table 12.4 presents examples of items from several of the more widely used group intelligence tests.

## THE VALUE OF INTELLIGENCE TESTING

Intelligence test results have been used extensively in education. This is reasonable, because the validity of intelligence tests is frequently established on the basis of performance in a formal educational setting. It was recognized early that IQ test scores provide a generally valid basis for ascertaining the individual's *present* level of intellectual functioning. This is particularly true of IQ tests administered individually.

Table 12.4
**Sample Items from Some Widely Used Group Intelligence Tests**

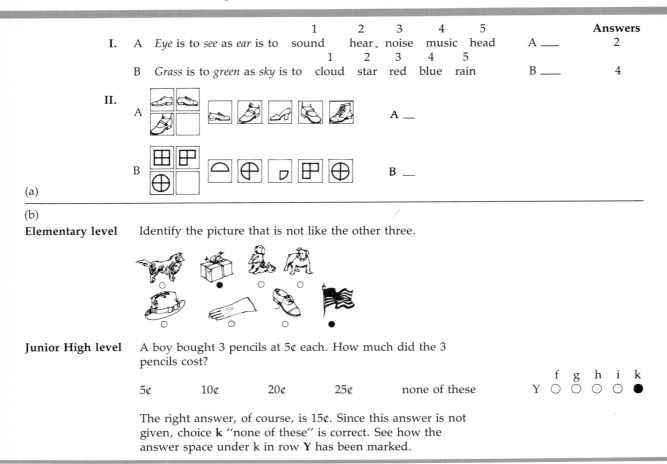

|   |   |   | 1 | 2 | 3 | 4 | 5 |   | Answers |
|---|---|---|---|---|---|---|---|---|---|
| I. | A | *Eye* is to *see* as *ear* is to | sound | hear. | noise | music | head | A ___ | 2 |
|    | B | *Grass* is to *green* as *sky* is to | cloud | star | red | blue | rain | B ___ | 4 |

(a)

(b)

**Elementary level**    Identify the picture that is not like the other three.

**Junior High level**    A boy bought 3 pencils at 5¢ each. How much did the 3 pencils cost?

5¢        10¢        20¢        25¢        none of these

The right answer, of course, is 15¢. Since this answer is not given, choice **k** "none of these" is correct. See how the answer space under k in row **Y** has been marked.

(a) Kuhlmann–Finch junior high school test items. (Courtesy of Dr. Frank H. Finch and Dr. Frederick Kuhlmann, and the publisher, American Guidance Service.) (b) Otis–Lennon Mental Ability Test items for elementary school and junior high school. (Sample items reproduced by permission from the Otis–Lennon Mental Ability Test. Copyright © 1967 by Harcourt Brace Jovanovich, Inc. All rights reserved.)

Resourceful teachers have recognized the value of providing graded educational experiences for children at different levels of intellectual functioning. It is useful to know that particular children are unusually bright, so that they can be stimulated with new and exciting materials at the level they are capable of handling. Otherwise, they may retreat into boredom and view school as a dull, unexciting sequence of tedious exercises. They may start using their intellect to invent ways of avoiding school or, if this fails, they may end up disrupting class routines. On the other hand, if more is demanded of children than they are capable of delivering, they may come to fear school and they, too, may become disruptive.

The various group intelligence tests have been used extensively in education. As we pointed out earlier, the use of group tests for individual

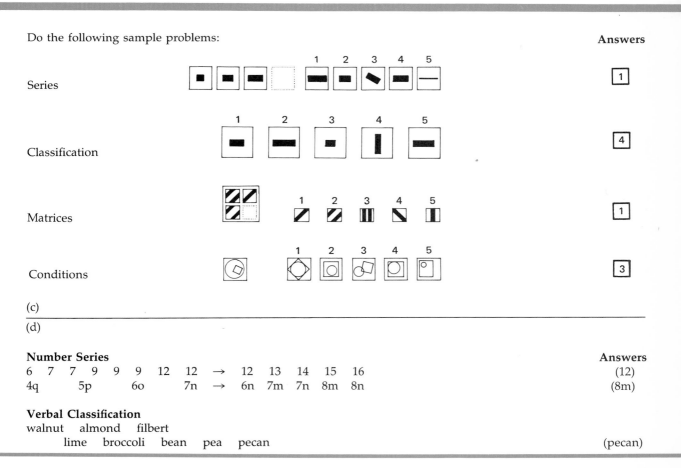

Do the following sample problems:                                          Answers

Series

Classification

Matrices

Conditions

(c)

(d)

**Number Series**                                                            Answers

6   7   7   9   9   9   12   12   →   12   13   14   15   16        (12)

4q        5p        6o        7n   →   6n   7m   7n   8m   8n        (8m)

**Verbal Classification**

walnut   almond   filbert

   lime   broccoli   bean   pea   pecan                        (pecan)

(c) IPAT Culture Fair Intelligence Test items. (Taken from the Culture Fair Intelligence Test, Scale 2, Form A test booklet, © 1949, 1960, R 1977, the Institute for Personality and Ability Testing, Inc. Reproduced by permission of the copyright owner.) (d) Lorge–Thorndike Intelligence Test items. (Reproduced by permission of Riverside Publishing Company.)

Intelligence testing has come a long way since its beginnings in the early 1900s. These World War I recruits, who were among the first to take such tests, obviously had neither a comfortable testing environment nor privacy.

diagnostic purposes is questionable. These tests have often been used, however, to screen large numbers of individuals in order to identify those with possible intellectual problems. Those individuals so identified can then be referred for individual testing.

Both the military and private industry have long recognized the value of group intelligence tests for personnel screening. Some of the earliest success in this area was achieved by the military, starting as early as World War I. In World War II, the Army General Classification Test (AGCT) was employed as one of the bases for selecting candidates for

**Figure 12.3**
**The relationship between the Army General Classification Test (AGCT) and success in Officer Candidate School during World War II**

Note that the higher the score on the AGCT, the greater the percentage of men who were successful in receiving their commissions. (Boring, 1945)

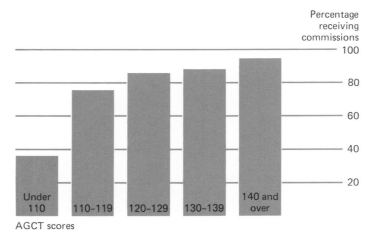

officer training school. Considerable success was achieved, as you can see in Fig. 12.3. You may recall that one way of determining the validity of a test is to see how well it predicts success and failure. The AGCT was particularly good in this respect. A greater percentage of those who scored high than of those who scored low on AGCT were successful in receiving their commissions.

Today many corporations administer group intelligence tests as a standard aspect of personnel selection and classification. These tests are part of a battery of psychological tests. The aim is not necessarily to select the most intelligent person, but rather to provide a match between level of intellectual functioning and the requirements of the job. A person may be overqualified, that is, too intelligent to find the job challenging and stimulating. Many studies have found that people of lower intelligence adapt best to routine, repetitive work such as factory and clerical work. Persons of higher intelligence easily become bored in these jobs and have higher absentee and turnover rates.

Figure 12.4 shows the distribution of IQs for various occupations. It is interesting that, although the average IQ of farm workers and miners is considerably lower than that of accountants and teachers, there is some overlapping. In other words, some farm workers score higher than some

**Figure 12.4**
**IQ and occupation**

The range of AGCT test scores for several occupational groups. Each bar shows the range of scores for the middle 80 percent; the lowest and highest 10 percent are not shown. The line between the darker and lighter halves shows the middle scores for each occupational group. Half score above and half score below this point. (Anastasi, 1958)

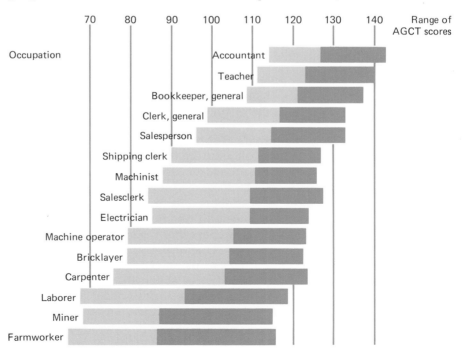

accountants. It appears that a certain minimum intellectual ability is necessary for entering a given occupational field. The fact that some individuals score much higher than the majority of others in the same field suggests that factors other than intelligence operate in job selection.

## THE TYRANNY OF INTELLIGENCE TESTING

In the preceding section, we were careful to emphasize the fact that IQ scores are useful insofar as they provide insight into an individual's present level of intellectual functioning. The IQ score is not some magical number that stays with a person through a lifetime, fixed and immutable. Failure to recognize this fact has led to much misunderstanding and many injustices. Individuals are often pigeonholed early in life—"borderline" IQ, "normal," "potential genius"—and it is often difficult for them to escape. A teacher sees a recent measure of a child's IQ on the transcript and notes that it is low. The teacher adjusts his or her expectations of the child's academic performance accordingly. This is as it should be, except that the teacher should not label the child marginally educable for all time. Indeed, a good teacher recognizes that the score is only an *estimate* (and therefore subject to error) of the student's *present* level of intellectual functioning. Throughout the school year, this teacher will continually reevaluate the child's level of functioning in accordance with careful observations of his or her classroom progress. Once a teacher says, "This child's IQ is too low; I can teach this child little," the teacher is abdicating the responsibility of the teaching profession and is making the child the unknowing victim of a misunderstanding. An IQ score, we repeat, is not a magical number that, like a person's given name, will remain with him or her for life.

A number of studies have confirmed that teachers can have a significant impact on children's later academic performance (e.g., Pedersen *et al.*, 1978). One classic study showed that teachers' expectations can also change IQ scores (Rosenthal and Jacobson, 1968). Teachers were led to believe that, on the basis of tests administered, certain of their students were "late bloomers." Thus they expected these children to show marked progress during the school year. In actuality, these children were selected at random from the class. Several months later the children were retested. Those children designated as "late bloomers" improved more than the other children—presumably because the teachers expected them to.

Students and parents have similar difficulties. One reason for the reluctance of a psychologist or guidance counselor to reveal an IQ score is the awareness that the score will often be misinterpreted and occasionally misused. One of the authors recalls the proud proclamation of an undergraduate acquaintance, an attractive girl of 18: "My IQ is 135; I don't have to study." Her statement was idealistic rather than diagnostic. She received a letter from the dean, at the end of her freshman year, encouraging her to seek admission elsewhere.

There are other characteristics of intelligence tests that limit the generality of their applications. As we pointed out earlier, most IQ tests used in the United States are highly verbal in nature, and they are typically standardized on English-speaking populations. Moreover, they are constructed by middle-class professionals and reflect middle-class values and morality. There is consequently a built-in bias favoring English-speaking, middle-class children.

> *An IQ score, at best, can indicate where an individual stands in intellectual performance compared to others. What others? His nation? His social class? His ethnic group? No intelligence test that has ever been devised can surmount all of these complicating considerations and claim universal validity. (Wortis, 1971, p. 22)*

We shall return to this problem later in the chapter.

## The Constancy of IQ

Earlier we defined reliability in terms of the consistency with which an instrument yields measurements or scores. The fact that IQ tests are reliable (that is, yield similar scores for the same person on two different occasions) has led many people to proclaim that the IQ is constant. If an individual obtains a score of 105 at age 4, it is assumed that he or she will obtain a score of 105 at age 20, plus or minus a few points owing to error in the test. Such an assumption confuses short-term repeatability of measures with long-term predictability. Let's look at an analogy.

If you measure the weight of a two-year-old child on two successive days, you will receive consistent measures; that is, the test is reliable. What is more, the measures will validly reveal differences between several two-year-old children who differ in weight. How successful do you think you would be in predicting their adult weights? Similarly, how accurate do you think you would be in predicting the adult IQ of a child of two? The truth is that neither measure would accurately predict an adult value from a childhood measure. Just as the rate of change in physical growth fluctuates considerably before adult weight is reached, so also does IQ. One way to establish this fact is to measure changes in IQ of a group of individuals who achieved identical scores at an earlier age (see Fig. 12.5). It is readily apparent that gross errors in judgment would occur if we assumed that IQ remains constant throughout life.

Proponents of the position that IQ is constant point to the fact that the IQ score predicts adult intelligence with greater accuracy as the child comes closer to adulthood. This finding is not surprising, but it does not lend weight to the assumption that IQ is constant. Whatever the forces are that determine the ultimate level of adult intelligence, these forces have been at work longer in the older child. If intelligence is negatively affected by an intellectually unchallenging environment, the cumulative effects will be greater in a 10-year-old child than in, say, a 5-year-old. The child's score at age 10 will therefore more closely approach his or her adult score.

The tyranny of IQ testing arises whenever a test result blinds us to the plasticity of the human organism. When we plan the lifelong course of children's education on the basis of an early assessment of their intel-

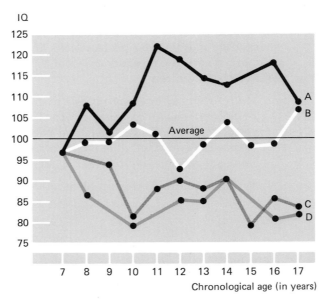

Figure 12.5
Constancy of IQ

**Four children with identical IQ scores at age seven were retested annually over a period of 10 years. Note the fluctuation in IQ for each child and the widespread differences that ultimately emerged. (Lindgren, 1956)**

ligence, we may be doing them a grave injustice. If the IQ score reveals that a child has "low normal" intelligence, the parents, the teacher, and even the child may conclude that there is not much of a future for this child in the intellectual sphere. The child may receive few inducements to intellectual growth, and considerable encouragement to make do with limited abilities. In many cases, his or her later lack of accomplishment is simply a self-fulfilling prophecy.

To observe that the IQ measures of many individuals fluctuate over time is not to deny that some individuals show fairly stable performance over long periods of time. What factors cause some people to show quite dramatic changes with age, while others remain relatively constant? Later in this chapter, we discuss changes in intellectual functioning that occur as a result of changes in the environment.

Much recent research has focused on the intellectual changes that accompany the aging process. The popular belief is that there is a broad, sweeping decline in almost all areas of intellectual functioning. In short, one of the seemingly inescapable facts of life is that some degree of incompetence is an almost unavoidable penalty of aging. This view of aging is simply not supported by the bulk of present-day research. Although the evidence strongly suggests that there is some loss of performance in some areas, the loss is selective rather than across-the-board. It is selective both with respect to the intellectual area assessed and with regard to the general state of health of the individual being tested. Thus tasks that require speed for optimal performance are likely to show a decline with age, but cognitive tasks that reflect cumulative experiences may evidence improvement well into the advanced years (Horn, 1976).

## Intelligence: Nature or Nurture?

Closely related to the view that IQ is constant is the position that intelligence is genetically determined. The reasoning goes something like this: "If IQ is determined at the moment of conception, it must, like eyes, hair, and skin color, remain constant throughout the individual's life." Fluctuations in IQ similar to those reported in Fig. 12.5 must represent testing errors—aberrations resulting from the conditions of testing, the state of health of the person tested, and momentary factors such as mood, anxiety, and motivation. In a less extreme view of the genetic position, IQ is viewed as heavily influenced by inherited genetic potentials. This does not negate the influence of environment. Heredity and environment are seen as inseparable, interacting forces.

More than a hundred years ago, Francis Galton, a pioneer in the study of individual differences, made some observations that became the focus of the nature–nurture controversy. He found that men of accomplishment had many more distinguished relatives than did an equal number of "average" people. He concluded that this phenomenon was a result of heredity, that intelligence "runs in the family." Later studies have reported similar conclusions. Box 12.1 presents a highly controversial graph that has served as a summary statement of the scientific evidence supporting the notion that IQ is inherited.

Support for the role of environmental factors comes from studies which show that city children score higher on IQ tests than do children from rural areas. There are many factors that might explain this differ-

Recent research has shown that most elderly people suffer only small, insignificant declines in cognitive ability. Henri Matisse continued to paint, sculpt, and design until the age of 85.

## BOX 12.1

### IQ and Family Relatedness

Figure 12.6 has been at the center of a heated controversy during recent years. It is frequently reproduced in order to prove that intelligence is inherited. The figure shows an increasing similarity of IQ scores with increasing degrees of genetic relatedness. The degree of relationship is expressed in terms of a statistical measure, the correlation coefficient. The higher the coefficient, the greater is the similarity in IQs. A coefficient of 1.00 means that the IQs are exactly the same; a coefficient of 0.00 indicates no relationship between the IQs of related individuals. The figure shows that the greatest similarity in IQ scores is found among identical twins reared together. Identical twins are as alike genetically as it is possible for two separate individuals to be. The figure also shows some degree of similarity in IQ scores among first cousins. Unrelated individuals would show a zero correlation.

The accuracy of this figure has been subjected to serious scientific challenges in recent years. One forceful critic (Kamin, 1974) has pointed out that the testing procedures were not standardized, the methods of intellectual assessment were subjective rather than objective, and many of the descriptions of subjects in the various studies were not accurately reported. Most of the conclusions concerning the heritability of IQ are based on the work of the late Cyril Burt. One reviewer commented:

*Surely no roguish alchemist selling his royal patrons a fraudulent recipe for turning base metal to gold ever matched the bizarre accomplishments of Sir Cyril Burt recounted by Oliver Gillie (1979). Sir Cyril conjured up subjects and data as needed to support his conclusions that intelligence was mainly (85 percent) genetically determined, whatever that may mean. Gillie details the failure of his*

**Figure 12.6**

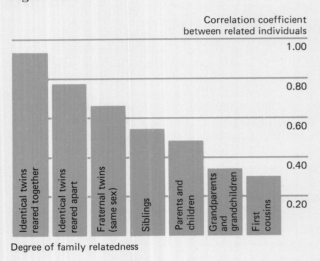

Correlation coefficient between related individuals

Degree of family relatedness

ence. Some psychologists have argued that many intelligence tests contain items that are more familiar to a city child than to a child brought up on a farm. There is also evidence to suggest that the difference in measured IQ may be due to the fact that city schools were generally superior to rural schools at the time these studies were conducted. Both of these possibilities are supported in one study. Southern-born black children who moved to Philadelphia showed significant gains in IQ test scores, whereas the mean IQs of children born and raised in Philadelphia remained about the same (Lee, 1951).

Another study involved the intellectual assessment of 130 black or interracial children who had been adopted by advantaged white families. Although the biological parents of the black adoptees were educationally average, their children adopted by the white families scored above the IQ of the white population. The authors concluded, "The high IQ scores of the socially classified black adoptees indicate malleability for IQ under

intense search for Sir Cyril's two collaborators, Miss Margaret Howard and Miss J. Conway.* Apparently they sprang full-grown from Sir Cyril's brow. These phantoms allegedly assisted Burt with the research that won him knightly spurs in Great Britain and the Thorndike Prize in the United States. Arthur R. Jensen (1969) described the research as the "most satisfactory attempt to estimate the influence of heredity upon intelligence" and Hans J. Eysenck (1971) praised the "outstanding quality of design and statistical treatment of the studies."† Another missing lady—M. G. O'Conner, claimed by Sir Cyril to be an Irish student assistant—could not be located anywhere in Great Britain or Ireland. According to Gillie, Burt claimed that this leprechaun demonstrated that the ability of London schoolchildren had declined between 1914 and 1965. Burt used her data in his attack on the comprehensive (nonselective) schools in 1969. Exactly how Burt could argue that the school environment can depress the ability that he believed to be largely fixed by heredity is not clear. In any case, Gillie concludes that, even if the missing ladies did exist, "the evidence suggests they were not the ladies that Sir Cyril said they were and they could not have done all the things he said they did."‡Gillie closes his letter with this remark:

"The time has now come for us to ask why Burt's work was looked at so uncritically by psychologists and others for such a long time. The answer might tell us something important about the role that power, charisma and wishful thinking can play in bolstering support for scientific theory."**

The wishful thinking is quite clear. The educational establishment wished to have an efficient device to sort out children for various tracks of education: Laborer, tradesman, technician, professional, merchant, chief. They wished the capacity for education to be a fixed immutable quantity so that children could be assigned early to their appropriate educational tracks without need for untidy track switching later on down the line. Since there were some practical difficulties in assigning the master's child to a labor track and his servant's child to a professional track, the educational establishment wished that the capacity of the children would match the socioeconomic status of their parents. Cyril Burt gave them their wish and they knighted him. (Eckberg, 1979, pp. ix–xi)

---

*See Oliver Gillie, "Burt's Missing Ladies," *Science* 204 (1979): 1035–9, for the latest report of this intrigue. As far as we know, Burt never invented men, only women and children.
†Ibid., p. 1038.
‡Ibid., p. 1037.
**Ibid., p. 1039.

rearing conditions that are related to the tests and the schools" (Scarr and Weinberg, 1976, p. 726).

It is clear that environmental factors do indeed play a crucial role in the intellectual development of a child. The most striking evidence comes from studies in which dramatic changes in IQ have occurred as a result of changes in environment. One investigator extensively studied 25 orphanage children. The IQs of these children were ascertained early in life. Thirteen of the children were later moved from the orphanage to a state institution for retarded children. The IQs of the children transferred to the state institution generally showed dramatic increases: Although the average gain was 28 points, in one case the increase was 58 points. On the other hand, those children who remained in the orphanage generally showed significant decreases in their IQ test scores (Skeels, 1966).

It may seem strange to regard a change from an orphanage to an institution for retarded children as a favorable change of environment.

It is dangerous to attribute IQ differences in children from impoverished backgrounds to heredity. Many Americans, like these Apache Indian children, have never been exposed to the language or values of the highly verbal middle class that writes the intelligence tests used in this country.

The fact is that the change was a very substantial improvement in the environment of these children. The children in the orphanage were given little more than custodial care, whereas those in the state institution received individual care from the nurses and even from the older retarded inmates. Although all 25 of these children were originally considered unfit for adoption, 11 of those transferred were eventually adopted, whereas none of those remaining in the orphanage were ever adopted. Moreover, all 13 of the transferred children grew up to lead normal adult lives. Only 4 of the orphanage children could be described as leading somewhat normal adult lives; only one managed to complete high school and obtain skilled employment.

What about the home environment? Bright parents tend to have bright children and dull parents, dull children. On the average, twenty-point differences in IQ have been found between children of professional parents and those of unskilled laborers (McNemar, 1942). This evidence has been regarded as support for the role of heredity. These data can be viewed in another way, however. Brighter parents are more likely to provide stimulating intellectual environments for their children and to stress the acquisition of those abilities that IQ tests measure. For example, children of professional parents are likely to be exposed to a rich and varied verbal environment.

In contrast, children from impoverished backgrounds usually do poorly on intelligence tests. Because many of the poor come from ethnic minorities, it has often been concluded that children from these backgrounds are lazy or stupid. This view is consistent with the notion of racial and ethnic differences in intelligence that are determined by genetic factors. The idea that certain racial and ethnic groups inherit lower intelligence gets apparent support from the fact that, for the most part, these groups do differ in achievement. They generally do not perform very well in school, and they rarely achieve positions of prominence in our society. Can these differences be attributed to genetic factors? If these children had equal opportunities to acquire the skills, experiences, and concepts measured in intelligence tests, we might be justified in concluding that racial and ethnic differences are indeed genetic in origin. But as long as the majority of blacks, Puerto Ricans, Mexican-Americans, and Indians grow up in environments lacking these opportunities, we cannot attribute IQ differences to heredity. The poor performance of these groups may be, in part, a self-fulfilling prophecy: Their parents, their teachers, and the community in general expect them to do poorly, and so they fulfill these expectations.

Family size may also be a factor. After reviewing the evidence concerning the relationship between intelligence, birth order, and family size, one researcher concluded:

> *Intelligence declines with family size; the fewer children in your family, the smarter you are likely to be. Intelligence also declines with birth order; the fewer older brothers or sisters you have, the brighter you are likely to be. (Zajonc, 1975, p. 37)*

Because the 1973 census showed that blacks are much more likely than whites to have six or more children in the family, family size and birth order, not race per se, may be responsible for lower IQ scores among blacks.

There is another bias that bears repeating. Intelligence tests are, for the most part, made up by middle-class people using middle-class language, experiences, and concepts. In other words, IQ tests have a built-in bias that discriminates against children from different subcultures. For example, black children raised in the ghetto acquire concepts and language that are not tested in traditional IQ tests. A black sociologist, Adrian Dove, devised his own IQ test (the "chitling" test) in a half-serious attempt to show that "we're just not talking the same language." Table 12.5 presents 10 items that are included in this test. See how well you can do.

**EXTREMES IN INTELLIGENCE**

When you look at the distribution of IQ scores for a large number of randomly selected people, you usually find a wide range of values. There is a pattern to this distribution. Most people score around the middle of the distribution, and relatively few at the extremes. You can see this pattern in Fig. 12.7, which presents the distribution of IQ scores on the

Table 12.5

### The "Chitling" Test

1. A "Gas Head" is a person who has a: (a) fast moving car; (b) stable of "lace"; (c) "process"; (d) habit of stealing cars; (e) long jail record for arson.

2. If you throw the dice and "7" is showing on the top, what is facing down? (a) seven; (b) "snake eyes"; (c) "boxcars"; (d) "little Joes"; (e) eleven.

3. Cheap chitlings (not the kind you purchase at a frozen food counter) will taste rubbery unless they are cooked long enough. How soon can you quit cooking them to eat and enjoy them? (a) 15 minutes; (b) 2 hours; (c) 24 hours; (d) 1 week (on a low flame); (e) 1 hour.

4. "Bird" or "Yardbird" was the "jacket" that jazz lovers from coast to coast hung on: (a) Lester Young; (b) Peggy Lee; (c) Benny Goodman; (d) Charlie Parker; (e) "Birdman of Alcatraz."

5. Hattie May Johnson is on the County. She has four children and her husband is now in jail for non-support, as he was unemployed and was not able to give her any money. Her welfare check is now $286.00 per month. Last night she went out with the highest player in town. If she got pregnant, then nine months from now how much more will her welfare check be? (a) $80.00; (b) $2.00; (c) $35.00; (d) $150.00; (e) $100.00.

6. A "handkerchief head" is: (a) a cool cat; (b) a porter; (c) an Uncle Tom; (d) a hoddi; (e) a preacher.

7. "Money don't get everything it's true _____
   _____ ." (a) but I don't have none and I'm so blue; (b) but what it don't get I can't use; (c) so make do with what you've got; (d) but I don't know that and neither do you.

8. Which word is out of place here? (a) splib; (b) Blood; (c) grey; (d) Spook; (e) Black.

9. How much does a short dog cost? (a) $0.15; (b) $2.00; (c) $0.35; (d) $0.05; (e) $0.86 plus tax.

10. Many people say that "Juneteenth" (June 10) should be made a legal holiday because this was the day when: (a) the slaves were freed in the USA; (b) the slaves were freed in Texas; (c) the slaves were freed in Jamaica; (d) the slaves were freed in California; (e) Martin Luther King was born; (f) Booker T. Washington died.

*Answers:* 1(c), 2(a), 3(b), 4(d), 5(a), 6(c), 7(b), 8(c), 9(a), 10(b).

Source: From Lewis R. Aiken, Jr., *Psychological and Educational Testing.* Copyright © 1971 by Allyn and Bacon, Inc., Boston. Reprinted with permission.

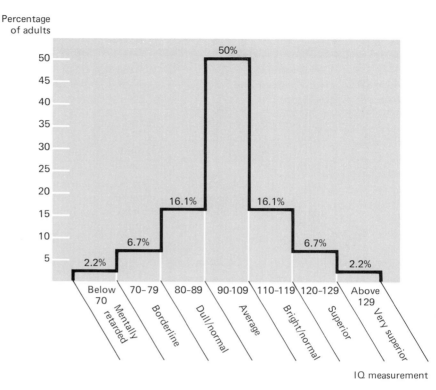

**Figure 12.7
Distribution of adult IQ
scores on the Wechsler
Adult Intelligence Scale**

(Adapted from Wechsler, 1958)

WAIS, with the descriptive terms applied to the various categories. On the basis of this figure, in the population of the United States there should be about 4½ million people who can be classified as very superior and an equal number who can be classified as mentally retarded.

## The Mentally Retarded

Although it is generally accepted that people with IQs below 70 are mentally retarded, there are wide differences in the degree of **mental retardation.** Table 12.6 describes the characteristics of people with various degrees of retardation at different ages.

Take a few moments to contrast the characteristics of people in the "mildly retarded" group with those in the "profoundly retarded" category. Most mildly retarded people are capable of taking care of themselves and even performing some kind of gainful employment; however, people who are profoundly retarded are almost certain to spend their lives under close supervision and custodial care. The fact that mild retardation does not necessarily incapacitate an individual in all areas is strikingly illustrated in the case of a teenage boy with an IQ of about 55 who is a noted concert organist. Although he has some difficulty in performing such everyday activities as dressing and buttoning his clothes, he has

**Mental retardation**
Below normal intelligence;
generally an IQ of 70 or less.

Table 12.6

**Developmental Characteristics of the Mentally Retarded**

| Degree of mental retardation | Preschool age 0–5 (maturation and development) | School age 6–20 (training and education) | Adult 21 and over (social and vocational adequacy) |
|---|---|---|---|
| *Profound* (I.Q. below 20) (1%) | Gross retardation; minimal capacity for functioning in sensorimotor areas; needs nursing care. | Some motor development present; may respond to minimal or limited training in self-help. | Some motor and speech development; may achieve very limited self-care; needs nursing care. |
| *Severe* (20–35) (4%) | Poor motor development; speech is minimal; generally unable to profit from training in self-help; little or no communication skills. | Can talk or learn to communicate; can be trained in elemental health habits; profits from systematic habit training. | May contribute partially to self-maintenance under complete supervision; can develop self-protection skills to a minimal useful level in controlled environment. |
| *Moderate* (36–52) (10%) | Can talk or learn to communicate; poor social awareness; fair motor development; profits from training in self-help; can be managed with moderate supervision. | Can profit from training in social and occupational skills; unlikely to progress beyond second-grade level in academic subjects; may learn to travel alone in familiar places. | May achieve self-maintenance in unskilled or semi-skilled work under sheltered conditions; needs supervision and guidance when under mild social or economic stress. |
| *Mild* (53–69) (85%) | Can develop social and communication skills; minimal retardation in sensorimotor areas; often not distinguished from normal until later age. | Can learn academic skills up to approximately sixth-grade level by late teens. Can be guided toward social conformity. | Can usually achieve social and vocational skills adequate to minimum self-support but may need guidance and assistance when under unusual social or economic stress. |

Source: The President's Committee on Mental Retardation, Washington, D.C., 20201.

achieved proficiency on seven different musical instruments. He has memorized over 1000 different songs and composed about 40 of his own.

What causes mental retardation? Before we try to answer this question, we must first point out that mental retardation is not a single disorder. Rather, it is a symptom of a large number of different conditions that affect the functioning of the individual. Thus there are many causes of mental retardation, and most of them are still poorly understood. There are factors operating before birth that may lead to deficient intellectual functioning; these include infections contracted by the mother during pregnancy and drugs and other toxic agents taken by the mother while carrying the child. Some forms of retardation, such as **Down's syndrome,** are caused by genetic factors. Brain injuries during birth are responsible for a small percentage of cases. Finally, there are factors operating after birth that may lead to retardation. Certain infectious diseases, accidents resulting in brain damage, or diets deficient in substances vital for normal development may cause retardation. As intelligence scores decrease, the known physiological causes of the deficits increase.

**Down's syndrome** Mental retardation associated with genetic factors and manifested in certain physical characteristics as well as deficient intelligence.

**Down's Syndrome is a form of mental retardation caused by genetic factors. This child possesses the physical characteristics of Down's Syndrome: skin fold at the inner corner of the eye, flat nose bridge, and short hands.**

The symptoms of mental retardation are frequently observed in children raised under adverse environmental conditions. Indeed, it has been estimated that 75 percent of mental retardates come from culturally, socially, and economically disadvantaged homes (Coleman, 1976).

> *They are raised in homes with absent fathers and with physically or emotionally unavailable mothers. During infancy they are not exposed to the same quality and quantity of tactile and kinesthetic stimulations as other children. Often they are left unattended in a crib or on the floor of the dwelling. Although there are noises, odors, and colors in the environment, the stimuli are not as organized as those found in middle-class and upper-class environments. For example, the number of words they hear is limited, with sentences brief and most commands carrying a negative connotation. (Tarjan and Eisenberg, 1972, p. 16)*

## The Mentally Gifted

The most comprehensive and long-term studies of the intellectually gifted were conducted under the general supervision of Lewis M. Terman. Approximately 1500 children with IQs of 140 or higher were selected in 1921 and have been studied up to the present. The purpose of the study was to identify the characteristics of the mentally gifted and to follow their progress to see how they developed as adults. This study contradicted many popular misconceptions about the mentally gifted. You have probably heard people talk about "the thin line between genius and insanity." Many people stereotype the very bright as skinny, bespectacled book-worms. Terman's studies revealed that these mentally gifted children were above average in emotional stability, physical health, and height and weight. Moreover, their academic and occupational accomplishments have become legendary. Approximately 90 percent of them attended college. Although they were, on the average, about two years younger than their classmates, they won three times as many honors. When studied 25 years later, 150 out of 700 were judged "very successful" by criteria such as holding responsible managerial positions, or being listed in *Who's Who* or *American Men of Science* (Terman, 1925; Terman and Oden, 1947, 1959).

It is evident that the mentally gifted make important contributions to our society. Yet if you were to look at the names of people of accomplishment in the sciences, literature, politics, and industry, you would find very few women's names among them. Because the distribution of IQs among women closely parallels that among men, there are just as many mentally gifted women as men. Therefore, on the basis of numbers alone, we would expect greater representation of women on the lists of distinguished people than is the case.

The unbalanced representation of women among the distinguished is no doubt in part reflective of differing societal pressures on and expectations of women. Many young girls have been raised to believe that it is somehow "not nice" to compete—especially with boys. This attitude may carry over into adulthood, where they may shy away from entering male-dominated fields, contributions to which are readily measured. The active antipathy of many men in these fields may serve to further reinforce such behavior in women. Most important, even today very bright females may be encouraged to put their career interests second to home and family.

Finally, not all gifted children live up to their potential. Terman and Oden's follow-ups (1947, 1959) also reported that some of the gifted children were extremely unsuccessful in life, dropping out of school or working at menial jobs. Because there was no significant difference in measured intelligence between those who succeeded and those who failed, it seems likely that individual social and personal differences were responsible for the success of some and the lack of success of others.

## CREATIVITY AND INTELLIGENCE

As we have seen, people differ widely in intelligence. Yet many people who score well on IQ tests are not characterized by an ability to come up with new and **creative** ideas. Think for a moment. Do you know people you would call "creative"? Why would you call them creative? What characteristics or abilities do they have? Now think of the people you consider "intelligent." Are they creative? The distinction between creativity and intelligence is an intriguing and difficult one to make. It has often been suggested that there is a curvilinear relationship between intelligence and creativity. In other words, the more intelligent an individual is, the more creative he or she is—up to a point. At the highest levels of intelligence,

**Creativity**
Thinking directed toward new relations and solutions to problems.

**Convergent thinking**
Thinking that involves the ability to arrive at a conclusion "in accordance with truth and fact."

**Divergent thinking**
Thinking that involves seeing new and unusual relationships that are appropriate to a problem situation.

according to this curvilinear hypothesis, creativity and intelligence are no longer related. However, in a major review of the research and literature, the authors (Barron and Harrington, 1981) concluded that there is insufficient evidence to accept this hypothesis.

One of the problems is that there is no general agreement on the definition of creativity. Some definitions require socially valuable products in order to qualify an act or person as creative. Others see creativity as valuable in itself and do not require that it produce anything of social value. Still others regard the level of accomplishment (difficulty, elegance, or beauty) as basic to the definition (Barron and Harrington, 1981).

A noted investigator of creativity (Guilford, 1967) distinguishes two classes of thinking, **convergent** and **divergent.** Convergent thinking involves the ability to arrive at a conclusion in accordance with truth and fact. The IQ tests we have just reviewed stress convergent thinking. Divergent thinking has more to do with the ability to see new and unusual relationships that are nevertheless appropriate to the problem situation. Many people view the creative person as characterized by divergent thinking. A test that is often employed to evaluate creativity involves unusual uses for common objects (Guilford, 1954). For example, what are the various uses of a shoe? A convergent thinker is likely to answer by citing the conventional use of a shoe—to protect your feet when you are walking. A divergent thinker may come up with such uses as a hammer, a bed for a doll, a drinking vessel, an ashtray, or a surface to draw on.

Many tests have been devised to measure creativity. Figures 12.8 and 12.9 show the different types of responses made by creative individuals and by randomly selected subjects on two tests of creativity.

Researchers in creative thinking believe that the conventional IQ test and formal education stress convergent rather than divergent thinking (Wallach, 1970). If convergent and divergent thinking represent different and quite unrelated abilities, it may be argued that individuals with creative talents go unrecognized and largely ignored in our society (see Pankove and Kogan, 1968; Wallach and Wing, 1969). Indeed, an individual

**Figure 12.8**
**Welsh Figure Preference Test**

Subjects are asked to state a preference for a series of drawings. Randomly chosen individuals tend to prefer the figures shown on the left, whereas creative individuals prefer the figures on the right.

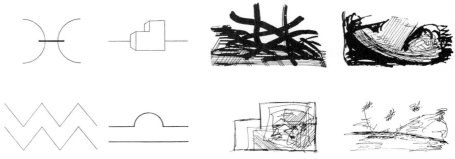

Reproduced by special permission from the Welsh Figure Preference Test by George S. Welsh, Ph.D. Copyright 1949, published by Consulting Psychologists Press, Inc.

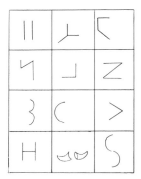 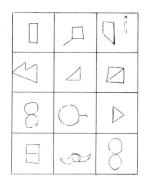  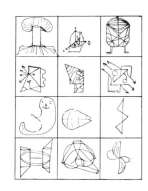

**Figure 12.9**
**Drawing-completion test**

Subjects were asked to elaborate on the set of line drawings shown at the far left. Randomly chosen individuals produced sets of drawings like the one shown second from the left. The two right sets of drawings were produced by creative individuals. (Barron, 1958)

with too many new and unusual ideas may be regarded, in many settings (including the classroom), as a nuisance.

Nevertheless, intelligence appears to be a key element in creativity. Reviewers of 15 years of creativity research arrived at the following conclusion: "Studies of creative adult artists, scientists, mathematicians, and writers find them scoring very high on tests of general intelligence" (Barron and Harrington, 1981, p. 445).

Research on the personality characteristics of creative individuals has located a relatively stable set of characteristics, such as a high value placed on esthetic qualities in experience, broad interests, independence of judgment, intuition, and a sense of the self as creative (Barron and Harrington, 1981). However, there appear to be differences between the personalities of creative scientists and those of creative artists and writers. Compared to the typical individual, scientists appear to be more stable emotionally, more venturesome, and more self-assured. In contrast, creative artists and writers appear to be less stable, less venturesome, and more guilt prone (Cattell, 1971). Even within fields, distinctions should be made. Fine artists differ from applied artists in personality characteristics. Lumping them together in one group may obscure many real differences that do exist (Getzels and Csikszentmihalyi, 1976).

## APTITUDE AND SPECIAL TESTS

"What do you want to be when you grow up?" a doting aunt asks her little nieces and nephews. "A truck driver," "an architect," "a teacher," they reply with little deliberation, and whirl off to engage in the thousand-and-one activities that capture the attention of early school-age children. The same question, with variations, will be repeated on countless occasions throughout their childhood by mother, father, teachers, clergy, relatives, and friends. With each passing year, the question will take on added significance. Before too long, the little nieces and nephews have reached the age of serious decision making. And this very decision may be the most important one they will ever have to make. If they successfully appraise their own skills and motivations and the employment opportunities in whatever line of work they choose, they will receive deep satisfaction from the activities that will occupy approximately one-third of their adult waking hours. On the other hand, failure to obtain a happy match between their abilities and their interests may lead to a lifetime of dissatisfaction, disappointment, and frustration. What is more, chronic dissatisfaction with their work will contaminate every aspect of their lives, social and personal as well as occupational.

Psychologists have labored for many years to devise tests that can help people make career decisions. (Figure 12.10 presents samples from two of the more widely used vocational aptitude tests.) Many people have no need of these tests, because they can arrive independently at choices that are consonant with their own abilities and interests. Other people are confused about their own motivations and are unable to identify areas of strength that relate to job opportunities. Some of these people seek the advice of professional counselors, who, through the skillful use of tests and interviews, may be able to help identify sources of strength and weakness relative to various vocational goals.

The two broad classes of tests commonly used by vocational counselors involve the assessment of aptitudes and of interests.

Figure 12.10
Aptitude tests

(a) One part of a widely used test of manual dexterity. The subject is required to insert a bolt in each hole and place a rivet over the bolt. (b–c) Sample items from a test of vocational aptitude that measures eight different ability areas. The sample items have been taken from two of the areas.

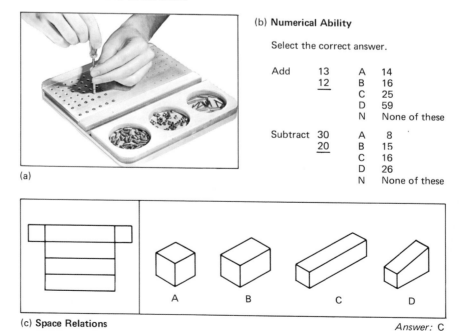

(a)

(b) **Numerical Ability**

Select the correct answer.

| Add | 13 12 | A | 14 |
| | | B | 16 |
| | | C | 25 |
| | | D | 59 |
| | | N | None of these |

| Subtract | 30 20 | A | 8 |
| | | B | 15 |
| | | C | 16 |
| | | D | 26 |
| | | N | None of these |

(c) **Space Relations**                                    *Answer:* C
Which one of the four figures can be made by folding the pattern shown?

**Aptitude tests**
Instruments designed to measure an individual's capacity to achieve proficiency in a given activity or occupational field.

**Aptitude tests** attempt to measure the individual's capacity to become proficient in a given activity or occupational field. You are probably already familiar with the Scholastic Aptitude Test (SAT), which predicts students' aptitude for college-level study. The objective of aptitude tests, when they are used for occupational counseling, is to identify and isolate those skills and abilities required by various occupations. Presumably people whose performances on those tests show them to possess the abilities demanded by a particular line of work are more likely to succeed in that line of work than people who do not show these abilities. Unfortunately, however, aptitude tests have not enjoyed the success in predicting occupational outcomes that intelligence tests have had in predicting scholastic performance.

It is almost a truism that aptitude alone will not guarantee success and satisfaction in a given occupation. Certainly motivations and interests are also of great importance. Many tests are designed to assess interest patterns as they relate to occupational fields. One of the most widely used of these is the Kuder Preference Record. Table 12.7 presents some sample items from this test. Figure 12.11 presents a sample profile from the Kuder Preference Record obtained by a single subject.

Another special test—the achievement test—is widely used. In one sense, every examination you have ever taken has been an achievement test, but this term is more commonly used to refer to standardized tests of more general skills and knowledge. Achievement tests measuring children's abilities to read and do arithmetic have long been a part of many school systems' self-evaluations. With the current emphasis on competency testing at all levels of education, achievement tests are taking on increased significance. In many systems, students must pass such tests in order to be promoted to the next grade, and some cities and states now require high school seniors to pass an achievement test in reading and mathematics before they can graduate.

Table 12.7

**Two Sample Items from the Kuder Preference Record**

|   |   | Most |   | Least |
|---|---|------|---|-------|
| P | Visit an art gallery | ☐ | P | ☐ |
| Q | Browse in a library | ☐ | Q | ☐ |
| R | Visit a museum | ☐ | R | ☐ |
|   |   |   |   |   |
| S | Collect autographs | ☐ | S | ☐ |
| T | Collect coins | ☐ | T | ☐ |
| U | Collect butterflies | ☐ | U | ☐ |

The subject must choose from among three alternatives the one he likes best and the one he likes least.
Source: From *Kuder Preference Record*. Form Bl. Copyright 1948 by G. Frederic Kuder. Reprinted by permission of the author.

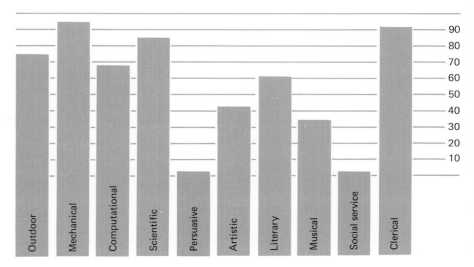

Percentile

90
80
70
60
50
40
30
20
10

Outdoor · Mechanical · Computational · Scientific · Persuasive · Artistic · Literary · Musical · Social service · Clerical

Figure 12.11
**Kuder Preference Profile**

**The Kuder Preference Profile shown was obtained from an adult named Mary. It shows high areas of interest in mechanical, scientific, and clerical categories. If Mary wishes to see how her interests compare with those of males, she can fill in the columns under the M headings in the test profile section.**

From the KUDER PREFERENCE RECORD, Vocational, Form CP, by G. Frederic Kuder. © 1948, G. Frederic Kuder. Reprinted by permission of the publisher, Science Research Associates, Inc., Chicago, Illinois.

Even beyond high school, achievement tests play an important role. Many of you may have taken achievement examinations as a requirement for college admission. Such tests are also common prerequisites for admission to graduate schools (e.g., the Graduate Record Examinations). Finally, most professionals, including doctors, lawyers, architects, and teachers, must take what are essentially achievement tests in order to be certified to practice.

# ASSESSMENT OF PERSONALITY

Suppose you were asked to write a description of your own personality. How objective do you think you could be? We are often not aware of many characteristics within ourselves. Our defense mechanisms operate so well in achieving self-deception that we really cannot see ourselves as others see us. For example, you might say that you are "firm," whereas others would describe you as "stubborn."

Because we cannot be expected to give a fair and accurate assessment of our own personalities, we must look elsewhere for this assessment. But why is it desirable to assess personality in the first place?

There are several reasons why psychologists strive to develop better and better instruments for assessing personality. People are frequently confused about their life goals and about their ability to succeed in various activities. In order to help them make decisions, tests are used in conjunction with vocational counseling, as illustrated in the following case:

> *Frank P. went to the counseling center on campus because he was confused about his life and vocational objectives and his entire life appeared to be without focus. In his first two years at college he had switched his major no fewer than four times—from English literature, to mathematics, to chemistry, to philosophy. Although his academic record was good, he expressed great concern about his inability to find a major that struck a deep responsive chord within him. The results of testing revealed him to have an extremely high IQ with varied interests, including mathematics, science, psychology, and writing. Personality inventories suggested that personal–social relations played a significant role in his motivational makeup. When all the facts were put together, it was recommended that he consider psychology as a major field.*
>
> *He followed the recommendation and has since become a respected professional in the field.*

Potential employers often use test instruments for determining a person's suitability for a job. Individuals with emotional problems may benefit from diagnoses and prognoses based on test results. Finally, psychological instruments are often useful in testing the assumptions and predictions arising from some theory of behavior.

The multitude of techniques for assessing and describing personality attests to the widespread interest in this area. One approach that has fascinated people for ages has been the divination of personality in relation to heavenly bodies. In a book on astrological signs, the following descriptive terms are used to describe the Aquarian personality:

> *The Aquarian is so much a dreamer that he lives on rainbows. But he is basically a realist. He is fascinated by politics, sports, children, horses, automobiles, elderly people, medical discoveries, authors, astronauts, alcoholics, pianos, pinwheels, prayers, and baseball.*
>
> *He loves the security of crowds but he has spells of gloominess when he wants to be left alone. He is fixated on friendship, but does not have many intimate friends. He can empathize with others but enjoys defying public opinion. He stings.*
>
> *Aquarians are so broad in outlook that they are rarely prejudiced, "unless there are severe planetary influences in the natal chart." (Goodman, 1968)*

Criticisms of astrological personality descriptions are aimed primarily at their lack of validity and at the broadness of the descriptions, most of which could fit almost anybody. Can you think of somebody born under Aquarius—or any other sign, for that matter—who does *not* fit this description, at least in part?

Psychologists have attempted to develop sophisticated techniques for the measurement and description of personality. As we saw in our discussion earlier, a good test must have two characteristics. It must be reliable, that is, yield consistent results on repeated testing of the same

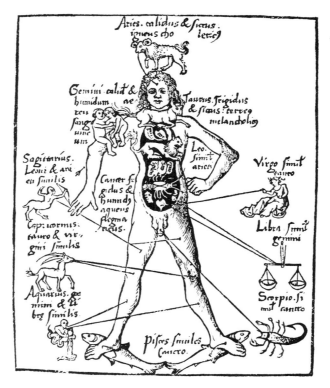

This sixteenth century woodcut of the "blood-let man" shows the supposed influence of stellar positions on various organs of the human body.

individual. It must also be valid, that is, measure what it purports to measure. These same requirements hold for personality assessment.

Let's now look at some of the methods that have been developed for assessing personality.

## Interviews

When you applied to college, were you required to come in for an admissions interview? How often have you been interviewed in the course of seeking employment? Although the interview is not commonly regarded by nonpsychologists as a method of personality assessment, its purposes are usually diagnostic (Does the person have the necessary characteristics?) and prognostic (How well will he or she do?). The interview procedure has much in common with the naturalistic procedures described in Chapter 1.

Interviews may be structured or unstructured. In the *unstructured* interview there is no set pattern of questions. The interviewer remains flexible and is free to explore tangents and probe more deeply whenever he or she feels such inquiry is warranted. In the *structured* interview a standard set of questions is used. Although the structured interview does not provide the variety of information the unstructured interview provides, it has the advantage of permitting more precise comparison of the responses given by different people.

In any interview situation, the outcome may be influenced by the characteristics of the interviewer. Even such subtle behaviors as nodding the head or mumbling "uh hum" may serve as cues to or reinforcers of the behavior of the interviewee.

## Rating Scales

Look at Table 12.8. You will see a number of sample items as they might appear in different types of personality **rating scales.** Think of several people whom you know quite well. Referring to Table 12.8(a), place a check mark at the point that you feel best describes each of these individuals on the trait shown. You have, in effect, made a judgment about a personality characteristic of each of these people. If you were to complete the entire scale, you could then construct a profile of your judgments along a number of different personality dimensions.

The item shown in Table 12.8(a) illustrates one type of rating scale, the graphic rating scale. There are a number of different types of rating scales in common use. Sample items from two other kinds of scales are shown in Table 12.8(b) and (c).

Rating scales are useful only when the people making the judgments are well acquainted with the persons being rated. Incidentally, rating scales can be self-administered, in which case the subjects are making judgments about themselves, as in Table 12.8(d). Besides assuming familiarity with the person being rated, rating scales require that the judgments be objective. A frequent problem with rating scales involves the **halo effect,** in which the judgment of each trait is influenced by the rater's overall impression of the individual. Thus a rater who likes the person being judged might rate him or her high on all traits. Conversely, a rater who dislikes the person being judged may tend to judge him or her low on all traits. Students in colleges and universities all over the country are currently rating the effectiveness of their instructors. If an instructor makes an extremely favorable impression because of one characteristic (for example, because of being a high grader or having a good sense of humor), the instructor may receive high overall ratings. This is an example of the halo effect.

**Rating scale**
A device for making judgments about oneself or others on certain defined traits.

**Halo effect**
The tendency, when making judgments about a particular trait, to be influenced by an overall impression of the individual being rated.

**Inventory**
A series of objective questions designed to measure a single trait or several aspects of personality simultaneously.

## Personality Inventories

Personality **inventories** differ from other types of tests (intelligence, aptitude, and achievement tests) in that there are no "right" or "wrong" answers. The subjects are expected to answer a series of questions about themselves. Like the other types of tests, personality inventories are scored objectively and permit comparison of an individual's standing on a given characteristic with that of some standardization group.

One very serious problem encountered in the construction of personality inventories arises from the fact that individuals, either purposely or inadvertently, may not provide truthful answers. One method that has been used to identify individuals who are not answering truthfully is to insert key items that may reveal inconsistencies in the individual's pattern of responses. For example, if someone answered all of the following items

Table 12.8
**Examples from Different Types of Personality Rating Scales**

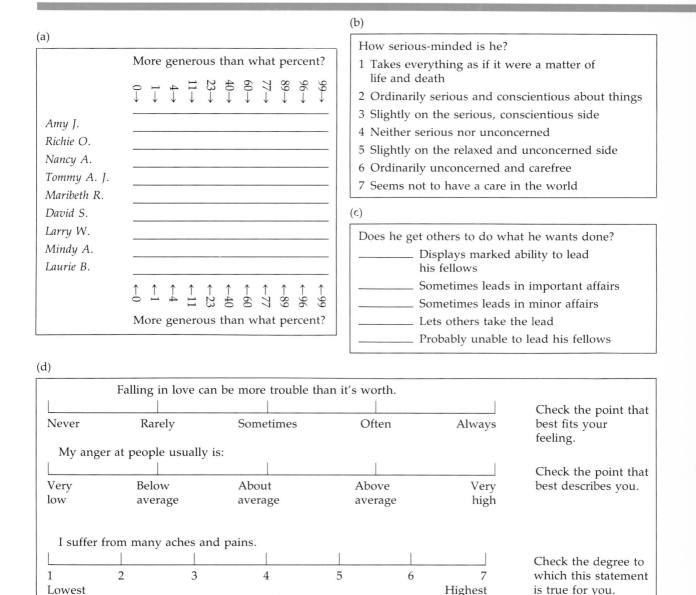

(a)

More generous than what percent?

0↓ 1↓ 4↓ 11↓ 23↓ 40↓ 60↓ 77↓ 89↓ 96↓ 99↓

Amy J.
Richie O.
Nancy A.
Tommy A. J.
Maribeth R.
David S.
Larry W.
Mindy A.
Laurie B.

0↑ 1↑ 4↑ 11↑ 23↑ 40↑ 60↑ 77↑ 89↑ 96↑ 99↑

More generous than what percent?

(b)

How serious-minded is he?

1 Takes everything as if it were a matter of life and death
2 Ordinarily serious and conscientious about things
3 Slightly on the serious, conscientious side
4 Neither serious nor unconcerned
5 Slightly on the relaxed and unconcerned side
6 Ordinarily unconcerned and carefree
7 Seems not to have a care in the world

(c)

Does he get others to do what he wants done?

_____ Displays marked ability to lead his fellows
_____ Sometimes leads in important affairs
_____ Sometimes leads in minor affairs
_____ Lets others take the lead
_____ Probably unable to lead his fellows

(d)

Falling in love can be more trouble than it's worth.

| Never | Rarely | Sometimes | Often | Always |

Check the point that best fits your feeling.

My anger at people usually is:

| Very low | Below average | About average | Above average | Very high |

Check the point that best describes you.

I suffer from many aches and pains.

| 1 | 2 | 3 | 4 | 5 | 6 | 7 |

Lowest      Highest

Check the degree to which this statement is true for you.

(a) The rater places a mark on each vertical line. (b) The rater checks that statement which best describes the person he is rating. Each statement has a numerical value assigned to it. (c) The rater checks that statement which best describes the person being rated. In this case, the rater does not know what numerical value is given to each statement. (d) The individuals rate themselves in terms of the descriptions provided.

Source: Parts a and b are from *Personality* by J. P. Guilford. Copyright © 1959 by McGraw-Hill Book Company. Used with permission of McGraw-Hill Book Company. Part c is from *Theory and Practice of Psychological Testing*, 3rd edition, by F. S. Freeman. Copyright 1926 by Rinehart Press. Used by permission. Part d is from *Introduction to Personality* by Walter Mischel, copyright 1971 by Holt, Rinehart and Winston, Inc. Used by permission.

"False," we might well suspect his honesty on the rest of the inventory: "I sometimes feel angry"; "Sometimes my friends disappoint me"; "I sometimes have thoughts which I am ashamed to share with others."

A personality inventory may be designed to measure a single trait or dimension of personality. In this case, the total score provides a quantitative measure of where the individual stands on that characteristic. Other inventories measure several aspects of personality simultaneously.

There are two ways of standardizing a personality inventory. One is to standardize it on the basis of a group of subjects displaying the characteristic measured by the test. For example, a measure for homosexuality could be standardized on a group of homosexuals; an individual's score would then be compared to this reference group. Another way to standardize a personality inventory is to use a reference group that is "normal" with regard to the particular characteristic being measured. We would then be interested in the individual's deviation from the norm. Such deviations may permit us to identify personality problems.

There are literally thousands of personality inventories in use today. One of the most widely employed is the Minnesota Multiphasic Personality Inventory (MMPI). On this instrument, the individual is required to respond "True" or "False" to 550 statements. The following are sample items from this inventory: "It does not bother me particularly to see animals suffer"; "People often disappoint me"; "My sleep is fitful and disturbed"; "At times I feel like smashing things."*

The MMPI is an example of a test that was developed on the basis of groups of patients with known personality disorders. Scoring of the test yields a profile of scores. The responses of the individual taking the test are then compared with the profiles of various clinical groups.

We have indicated that individuals may distort their responses to items on personality inventories. Many people tend to answer items so as to present a socially acceptable picture of themselves. The level of "social desirability" of an item is a constant source of difficulty for the test constructor. One method of overcoming this difficulty is to force the subjects to choose between two items that are judged to be equal in either social desirability or social undesirability. The Edwards Personal Preference Schedule exemplifies this approach to personality test construction. Based on the assumption that the motivational dispositions of individuals reveal important dimensions of personality, the test attempts to measure 15 basic needs of the subject.

## Projective Techniques

Another problem with personality inventories is that their purposes are generally transparent. Consequently, as we have seen, individuals may distort their answers to present a favorable picture of themselves. They may do this consciously, but unconscious forces may also be at work. We have already discussed defense mechanisms as a way of protecting our-

---

*Reproduced by permission. Copyright 1943, renewed 1970, by the University of Minnesota. Published by the Psychological Corporation, New York. All rights reserved.

selves from anxiety. Being asked to admit to unfavorable personality characteristics may give rise to anxiety and bring defensive reactions into play. **Projective techniques** are an attempt to overcome this difficulty.

A further criticism of personality inventories is that they present a picture of personality that is limited by the structure of the test and of the items. Projective methods are frequently referred to as "unstructured" tests, because the individual is free to respond in an unlimited variety of ways to the test materials. The materials themselves are frequently ambiguous in form; that is, they do not have any obvious meaning. The rationale behind these techniques is similar to the defense mechanism of projection. The assumption is that individuals will *project* their unconscious motives, feelings, and attitudes into the responses and thus reveal something about their personalities.

Unknowingly, you have probably been using projective techniques throughout your life. Have you ever looked at cloud formations or abstract artworks and tried to state what they looked like to you? You may have noted that the wide variety of answers given in these situations seems to reveal more about the beholder than about what is beheld. Projective methods provide a more systematic way of presenting ambiguous types of stimuli.

There are, however, reliability and validity problems. Because projective techniques are difficult to score in an objective manner, most studies fail to show agreement among examiners, internal agreement among the items, and retest reliability (Buros, 1972). The findings of validity studies of these methods have also been largely negative (Liebert and Spiegler, 1978). However, in spite of these problems, projective techniques continue to be used extensively in personality research and in applied settings for diagnostic and evaluative purposes. When they are used in conjunction with other information and tests, many trained observers feel they can provide valuable insights into personality.

**Rorschach test.** Have you ever splattered ink on a piece of paper and then folded the paper over the blot? You may have obtained something similar to Fig. 12.12. What do you see in the blot? Do you see any human figures? Do they appear to be stationary, or are they doing something? Does what you see involve the entire blot or just a portion of it?

Presumably, the responses you are making are revealing certain aspects of your personality. In fact, one of the most widely used projective personality tests, the **Rorschach test,** employs a series of ten inkblots similar to the one shown in Fig. 12.12. The subjects are asked to describe what they see in the blot, or what it looks like.

The responses are scored in a number of different ways. Look again at the questions just asked. They reflect several of the elements of the response that are analyzed. For example, did you see any human figures? Animals? Landscape? Such responses would reflect what is referred to as content, which is one of the scoring categories. Other categories include the popularity of the response, and whether the response involves the whole blot or only a part of it.

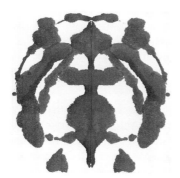

**Figure 12.12**
**An ink blot similar to those used in the Rorschach test**

**Figure 12.13**
**A card similar to those used in the TAT test**

Intensive training is required before an individual is qualified to administer, score, and interpret Rorschach responses. Although some standardized scoring methods are available, the experience of the examiner plays a significant role in the interpretation of the responses.

**Thematic Apperception Test (TAT)**
A projective test of personality in which the subject makes up stories for a set of pictures.

**Thematic Apperception Test (TAT).** Another projective technique, one that is more structured than the Rorschach, is the **Thematic Apperception Test (TAT).** It consists of 20 cards, 19 of which show actual scenes taken from photographs or paintings, and one of which is blank.

The subjects are shown a card and asked to make up a story about it. They are told to describe what is going on, and what the character or characters are doing, thinking, and feeling. They are asked what preceded the events shown and what will be the outcome. In the case of the blank card, they are asked to imagine a picture and make up a story.

The following story was related by a married male adult in response to a TAT card showing a group of casually dressed men lying close to one another in a field (Fig. 12.13):

(Pause) I don't get much from this. If it were in the service, why it's a possibility that they might be just relaxing from the fatigue. (Pause) This gives me the impression that it's just four lazy men. (Pause) It's hard for me to imagine anything out of this primarily because I don't care for (Pause) the relatively—relative closeness there—ah—of how they're lying (Pause) one so close to another with apparently more ground to spread out in. Ah—ah—I don't know why one should—should rest on another. (Pause) It looks like it might be a hobo jungle. (Pause) As far as I'm concerned, it—it's repulsive to me.

*Q:* Why?

Well, ah I—ah I just—ah—something like that doesn't—ah (pause) I get nothing from it. I—I—I can't—I see no reason for men to be bunched up sleeping together like that unless they were cold. Apparently they're not. (Pause) They're not dressed for cold weather. (Pause) They're—there's one lying on one man—no on this—well—all three of them, all three of the fellows are resting on another man, apparently in one form or another, they're touching him. (Pause) It's hard for me to get anything out of the picture. I don't know what would bring it about (Pause; sigh) unless it were—unless it was a hobo jungle. I've never been in one, all I've seen is an ex—is pictures similar to this one. (Rosen and Gregory, 1965, pp. 181–182)

The examiner evaluates the content and formal characteristics of the stories and attempts to discover something about the person's motives and conflicts. As can be seen in this example, the cards can sometimes

**Figure 12.14**
**Different types of projective techniques**

The following types of projective techniques are used in the study of personality. (a) The subject is provided with a number of cardboard figures and asked to create a dramatic scene in front of several different backgrounds. (b) The subject has to complete each sentence. (c) The subject has to supply the missing captions. (d) The subject is asked to choose the two faces he or she likes best and the two he or she likes least.

(a)

(b)　I like
　　　Most people
　　　My greatest worry
　　　Men
　　　Women
　　　My father
　　　This test

(c) Supply the missing captions.

(d) Which two faces do you like best? Which two do you like least?

elicit thoughts and images that are disturbing to the subject, and may reveal unconscious underlying conflicts.

The TAT has also proved useful in research designed to measure the achievement motive (see Chapter 8).

**Other projective techniques.**    There are a number of other projective techniques in common use. Figure 12.14 on page 473 presents examples from some of the more widely used of these methods.

The projective tests are not usually used in isolation. Various test procedures are combined so that the examiner's evaluation is based on a broad sampling of behaviors in different types of situations.

## Summary

1. Intelligence is not directly observed, but must be inferred from aspects of the behavior of people. The psychologist formalizes many of the behavioral criteria by which we judge intelligence and provides an objective basis for comparisons among individuals.

2. The formal tests used in psychology and education attempt to obtain samples of aspects of an individual's behavior from which predictions of future behavior may be made. A good test must be (1) objective, (2) reliable, (3) valid, and (4) standardized.

3. The most famous and widely used revision of the original Binet scale, the Stanford–Binet Intelligence Scale, introduced the concept of IQ as a relationship between chronological age (CA) and mental age (MA). The Stanford–Binet test is individually administered, is highly verbal in nature, and yields a single overall index of intellectual performance.

4. The Wechsler tests are also individually administered, but provide two separate estimates of intelligence (verbal and performance) as well as an overall IQ. These IQ scores are derived measures, however, computed from tables.

5. Group tests of intelligence may best be used in large screening programs, where it is not possible to administer an individual test to each person. Because of the limitations of such tests, their usefulness for individual diagnostic purposes is minimal.

6. IQ tests have been used advantageously in educational, military, and industrial settings. In industry, the intelligence test is frequently used as part of a battery of tests in an effort to find a match between individual interests and capabilities and the requirements of the job.

7. IQ scores must be used carefully. Teachers and administrators can misuse IQ to pigeonhole people and create self-fulfilling prophecies. Individuals aware of their IQs may mistakenly assume their abilities are greater or lesser than is actually the case.

8. The fact that IQ scores are reliable has led many people to proclaim that the IQ is constant. Such a view confuses short-term repeatability of measures with long-term predictability and ignores the plasticity of the human organism.

9. Closely related to the view that IQ is constant is the position that intelligence is genetically determined. The question of the heritability of intelligence is complicated by the fact that most IQ tests are standardized on middle-class populations and use middle-class language and concepts. Moreover, the studies supporting the view that intelligence is inherited have been seriously challenged in recent years.

10. At both extremes of the distribution of IQ scores is a small proportion of individuals whose intellectual functioning is either so impaired that they can be considered retarded or so advanced that they can be regarded as intellectually gifted. Retardation is generally caused by either biological factors or a deficiency of stimulation.

11. Long-term studies of the intellectually gifted have dispelled many popular notions concerning their physical health and emotional stability: Mentally gifted children are, as adults, above average in emotional stability, physical health, and height and weight.

12. Distributions of IQ scores of men and women are closely parallel. The fact that so few women in our society have risen to positions of prominence in the sciences, literature, politics, and industry suggests the operation of cultural factors.

13. Studies of creativity suggest the possibility of two broad classes of thinking: convergent thinking, presumably tested in IQ scales; and divergent thinking, which involves the ability to see new and unusual relationships that are appropriate to a problem situation. Research has shown creative adults to be high in general IQ. Creative individuals appear to share some basic personality characteristics.

14. Psychologists have devised several tests to help people who are assailed by doubts concerning career or vocational objectives. Some of these tests attempt to measure the individual's capacity to achieve proficiency in a given activity or occupational field (aptitude tests). But because aptitude alone will not guarantee success and satisfaction in a given occupation, other tests have been devised to assess interest patterns as they are related to occupational fields.

15. Achievement tests are widely used today both as measurements of material mastered and as a qualification for promotion, graduation, college and graduate school admission, and certification of professional competence.

16. A number of instruments have been designed to assess various aspects of personality. The results of testing are used for vocational counseling, determining a person's suitability for a position, assisting in the diagnosis and prognosis of emotional problems, and testing the assumptions and predictions arising from some theory of behavior.

17. Some of the methods that have been developed to assess personality include interviews, rating scales, personality inventories, and projective techniques, such as the Rorschach test and the Thematic Apperception Test. Despite reliability and validity problems, projective tests are widely used as diagnostic tools, usually in conjunction with other tests.

## Terms to Remember

| | | |
|---|---|---|
| Intelligence | Mental age (MA) | Aptitude tests |
| Operational definition | Intelligence quotient (IQ) | Rating scale |
| Objectivity | Derived IQ score | Halo effect |
| Reliability | Mental retardation | Inventory |
| Validity | Down's syndrome | Projective techniques |
| Predictive validity | Creativity | Rorschach test |
| Concurrent validity | Convergent thinking | Thematic Apperception Test (TAT) |
| Standardization | Divergent thinking | |

PERSONALITY

## WHAT IS PERSONALITY

In popular usage, the word **"personality"** most often occurs in evaluative statements, such as, "He has a good personality," "She has a bad personality," or "He has no personality at all." When psychologists study personality, their purpose is not to make value judgments, but to try to describe those persistent and enduring *behavior patterns* of an individual that tend to be expressed in a wide variety of life situations.

Each person's personality is unique; no two individuals will always behave in precisely the same way even under the same conditions. We all eat, drink, sleep, engage in recreational activities, read, and have conversations with our friends. What differentiates us and provides the basis for personality study is the *way* in which we engage in these various activities. We each have different food preferences and eating habits; different things "turn us on"; we converse in different ways and on different topics.

In spite of these differences, our behavior is highly predictable. Moreover, much of our behavior is based on the assumption that people about us will behave in expected ways. For example, when we drive an automobile, we are constantly making assumptions about the behavior of other drivers—for example, that they will drive on the right side of the road (in this country) and that they will stop for traffic signals. Our survival in spite of the fact that there are thousands of unique personalities behind the wheels of the other cars attests to the predictability of behavior. Indeed, it is when individuals behave in unexpected ways that headlines are made.

**Personality**
Persistent and enduring behavior patterns of an individual, which tend to be expressed in a wide variety of life situations.

## FACTORS AFFECTING PERSONALITY DEVELOPMENT

Why is it that two children born to the same parents and brought up in similar environments may differ widely in their personality characteristics? One may be affable, easygoing, and relaxed, whereas the other is a completely obnoxious brat. One variable that has been offered to explain these differences among siblings is birth order. Investigators studying the effect of this variable have related the individual's sequential position among his or her siblings to the development of various personality traits. Environmental differences exist for firstborn and later children (as well as for only children), and these differences lead to different personality tendencies. Table 13.1 presents the average personality tendencies for children in different birth-order positions.

At birth, differences already exist among children. Some cry quite frequently and are very active; others are more placid. Babies eat and sleep according to different schedules. These variations produce different reactions among adults. A child who is responsive to parental affection will certainly elicit different responses than an infant who squirms and refuses to be held. These inborn tendencies and initial contacts form the basis for the development of those enduring behavior patterns we refer to as personality. But does personality remain stable over the lifespan or does it change? One view is that personality structure is determined by early childhood experiences. Experts taking this position see further develop-

Table 13.1

**Birth Order and Average Personality Tendencies**

*The Firstborn Child*

Uncertainty, mistrustfulness, insecurity, shrewdness, stinginess, dependency, responsibility, authoritarianism, jealousy, conservatism, lack of dominance and aggressiveness, suggestibility, excitability, sensitiveness, timidity, introversion, strong achievement drive, need for affiliation, petulant, spoiled, and prone to behavior disorders

*The Second Child*

Independence, aggressiveness, extroversion, fun-loving, gregarious, adventuresome, dependable, well adjusted

*The Middle Child*

Aggressiveness, easily distracted, craves demonstrations of affection, jealousy, plagued by feelings of parental neglect, inferiority, and inadequacy, and prone to behavior disorders

*The Last Child*

Secure, confident, spontaneous, good-natured, generous, spoiled, immature, extroverted, ability to empathize, feelings of inadequacy and inferiority, resentments against older siblings, envy and jealousy, irresponsible, and happy

Source: From *Child Development*, 5th ed., by E. B. Hurlock. Copyright © 1972 by McGraw-Hill Book Company. Used with the permission of McGraw-Hill Book Company.

ment simply as an extension of personality patterns that have already been established early in life. Certain traits, in particular, show fairly well-determined developmental patterns because of physiological and genetic determinants (Birren *et al.*, 1981). Thus, according to this position, despite unique interactions between the individual and the environment, no further systematic development of personality structure takes place.

In contrast, other experts argue that personality develops and changes throughout our lives. They see the individual as flexible and ever-changing in response to various environmental influences. In this chapter we examine the various theories that take these two very different positions.

As much as two siblings may differ from one another, they share many more personality characteristics than do any two individuals raised in two different cultures. To understand this, we must recognize that different cultures have different values. The various members of each culture—parents, relatives, neighbors, peers—selectively reinforce and shape different behaviors. Children learn to do what is expected of them, and different cultures expect different things. There are even differences among subgroups in the same culture. For example, in the United States, middle-class parents tend to value and reinforce self-direction and independence in their children. Working-class parents, however, appear to be

Every culture in our world is characterized by its own unique personality, as expressed in different values and behaviors. For example, Japanese mothers tend to soothe and quiet their babies more often than American mothers, which in turn encourages Japanese children to be less vocal and active than their American counterparts.

more concerned that their children learn to conform to the expectations of others, particularly those in authority (Kohn, 1963).

During the first few years of a child's life, most of his or her experiences are provided directly by the parents, particularly the mother. Parents are the primary agents for transmitting their culture. They interpret their culture's values in their own way, according to their understanding of these values. There are wide differences in people's understanding of cultural values, and corresponding to these differences are wide variations in child-rearing practices. This is one reason why there is such diversity in the personality development of children, even in the same culture. For example, some parents feel that punishment makes children "good," and therefore inflict a great deal of punishment. Other parents, trying to achieve the same goal ("good" children), use positive reinforcement instead of punishment. Children raised under these different circumstances will inevitably develop different personality characteristics.

As children grow older, their social contacts broaden dramatically to include teachers, neighbors, storekeepers, and members of their peer group. When they learn to read, they become exposed to a wide variety of different values and ideas, some of which may profoundly influence their thinking and behavior.

Critical and largely unpredictable events—such as the death of a parent, an accident resulting in a permanent physical disability, or moving to another state or country—may also have an enormous impact on personality development. The following account by the mother of a teenaged girl is not at all unusual:

> *Karen's changed. I just don't understand it. Ever since we moved out here to _____ somehow—I think—it has something to do with the friends she has here. They have such different ideas about everything— sex, drugs, you name it. They don't have any respect for their parents. Karen didn't use to be like that when we lived in _____. (Author's files)*

## THEORIES OF PERSONALITY

So far, we have seen that although personality is unique, certain consistent patterns of behavior are shared by many individuals. There is also consistency within each individual. Just as we expect most people to behave in certain ways, we expect individuals to behave in ways that are consistent with our past observations of them. Think about some person you know extremely well. You can probably predict how she or he would behave in a wide variety of situations.

As children grow older, their social contacts expand beyond the family to include friends and other members of the community.

There is no universally accepted theory of personality. In some cases, the lack of agreement is due to the fact that the goals of the theorists are different. Some theorists are interested in developing an overall basis for *describing* personality. Others seek to understand *how personality develops.* Even among theorists seeking explanations for personality development, there are differences in the extent to which they emphasize biological as opposed to social and cultural factors.

Let's look first at those theories that emphasize the description of personality.

## Trait Theories

Suppose you wanted to introduce someone to a friend and were asked, "What's his personality like?" Generally, when we think of a person, we think of a combination of things that make up his or her personality. So you might say, "He is very outgoing, a little selfish, and not too dependable."

Can you think of more words that could be used to describe **traits** of individuals? The English language has about 40,000 words that can be used to describe behavioral differences or traits (Norman, 1967). With this seemingly endless list available, how does one decide how many traits are necessary and sufficient to describe personality and predict behavior? R. B. Cattell has made the most thoroughgoing and comprehensive attempt to apply the trait approach to the description of personality (Cattell, 1965). Three sources of information are used to construct a description of an individual's personality characteristics: observers' ratings of information taken from the life record of the individual, information obtained from questionnaires and interviews usually administered directly to the individual, and the results of the administration of objective tests in which the individual is unaware of the aspects of personality being investigated. According to Cattell, we can obtain a complete assessment of the complexity of human personality only by integrating all three of these sources.

Through the use of sophisticated statistical techniques, Cattell came up with a series of personality traits that can be used to describe and assess personality. Many of these traits can be described as opposites—reserved versus outgoing, less intelligent versus more intelligent, emotional versus stable. See Table 13.2 for a listing of 16 trait dimensions. These opposites are regarded as the extreme points on a continuum, with most individuals falling between the two extremes. Moreover, traits tend to group themselves or cluster together. For example, outgoing individuals tend to be good-natured, cooperative, easygoing, attentive to people, softhearted, trustful, and adaptable. In contrast, reserved individuals are likely to be critical, grasping, obstructive, aloof, hard, suspicious, and rigid. Note that only those individuals at the extremes of the reserved versus outgoing dimensions will also be at the extremes of the associated personality characteristics.

Cattell also distinguishes between two types of traits—**source** and **surface.** The first three variables shown in Table 13.2—reserved versus outgoing, less intelligent versus more intelligent, and emotional versus

**Trait**
A characteristic used to describe a basic personality dimension.

**Source traits**
Underlying variables that are determinants of observed behavior.

**Surface traits**
Clusters of behavior that appear to go together.

Table 13.2

**The 16 Major Factors in Cattell's Analysis of Personality**

| Low-score description | | High-score description |
|---|---|---|
| Reserved | vs. | Outgoing |
| Less intelligent | vs. | More intelligent |
| Emotional | vs. | Stable |
| Humble | vs. | Assertive |
| Sober | vs. | Happy-go-lucky |
| Expedient | vs. | Conscientious |
| Shy | vs. | Venturesome |
| Tough-minded | vs. | Tender-minded |
| Trusting | vs. | Suspicious |
| Practical | vs. | Imaginative |
| Forthright | vs. | Shrewd |
| Placid | vs. | Apprehensive |
| Conservative | vs. | Experimenting |
| Group-tied | vs. | Self-sufficient |
| Casual | vs. | Controlled |
| Relaxed | vs. | Tense |

Source: Adapted from Cattell, 1965.

stable—are the most important source traits. Source traits are the building blocks of personality. They both underlie and explain our behavior. As stated by Cattell:

> . . . the source traits promise to be the real structural influences under-lying personality, which it is necessary for us to deal with in develop-mental problems, psychosomatics, and problems of dynamic integra-tion. . . . As research is now showing, these source traits correspond to real unitary influences—physiological, temperamental factors; degrees of dynamic integration; exposure to social institutions—about which much more can be found out once they are defined. (Cattell, 1950, p. 27)

Surface traits, on the other hand, do not underlie behavior. Rather, they result from the interaction or admixture of source traits. Surface traits appeal to common sense because they represent characteristics that appear to go together. They are also in agreement with simple observa-tion. To illustrate, success in business and success in politics might fre-quently be observed to go together. In actual fact, they may not share much in common because each may derive from the interaction of differ-ent source traits. In other words, their association is superficial or surface rather than basic.

Once traits have been identified and measured, using a number of different sources of information, we can construct a profile for an individ-ual or for a group sharing one common characteristic. This profile pre-sumably represents the extent to which the individual or the group in question displays the various traits that make up personality. Figure 13.1

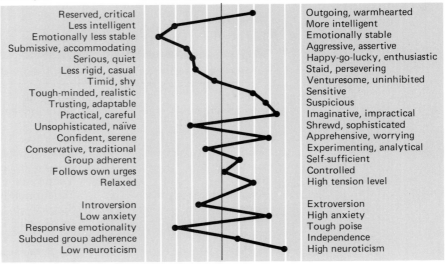

Trait description
for scores on left
side of grid

Percentile rank
0 10 20 30 40 50 60 70 80 90 100

Trait description
for scores on right
side of grid

| Reserved, critical | Outgoing, warmhearted |
| Less intelligent | More intelligent |
| Emotionally less stable | Emotionally stable |
| Submissive, accommodating | Aggressive, assertive |
| Serious, quiet | Happy-go-lucky, enthusiastic |
| Less rigid, casual | Staid, persevering |
| Timid, shy | Venturesome, uninhibited |
| Tough-minded, realistic | Sensitive |
| Trusting, adaptable | Suspicious |
| Practical, careful | Imaginative, impractical |
| Unsophisticated, naïve | Shrewd, sophisticated |
| Confident, serene | Apprehensive, worrying |
| Conservative, traditional | Experimenting, analytical |
| Group adherent | Self-sufficient |
| Follows own urges | Controlled |
| Relaxed | High tension level |
| Introversion | Extroversion |
| Low anxiety | High anxiety |
| Responsive emotionality | Tough poise |
| Subdued group adherence | Independence |
| Low neuroticism | High neuroticism |

Figure 13.1
**Sample personality profile
of a group**

**A personality test was administered to a group of 937 male drug addicts while they were in prison. Note that the addicts tended to be outgoing, emotionally unstable, impractical, and apprehensive.**

is a sample group profile. We have discussed some of the instruments used in personality assessment in Chapter 12.

Many psychologists are not satisfied with the trait approach to personality theory. They argue that merely assigning traits to an individual does not express the full complexity of the personality as it manifests itself in ever-changing life situations. For example, we may describe a person as honest, loyal, and fair-minded. But is this person always honest? Under what circumstances might he or she be dishonest? Is an individual who scores high on aggressiveness always aggressive? Or does the expression of this tendency depend on the situation? For example, a professional football player may be as ferocious as a lion on the field, but gentle as a lamb in his home. In addition, researchers have been unable to agree on the traits that make up personality. This is not surprising when you consider there are so many words in the English language that denote personality traits.

A final objection to trait theories of personality is that they ignore the question how personality is formed. Assigning the label "aggressive," even if it is accurate, gives no insight into how the person may have developed this trait.

**Type theories**
Theories of personality that attempt to classify people into broad categories, using primary characteristics to describe the whole personality.

## Type Theories

It is not uncommon to hear someone described as "the artistic type," "the scholarly type," "the bossy type," "the independent type," or "the nervous type." The idea of classifying people into specific types dates far back into history (see Fig. 13.2). **Type theorists** search for primary characteristics to describe the whole personality. A person either does or does not fit into a specific category. A type is a much broader classification than a trait and may include many trait descriptions.

Figure 13.2   A medieval "type" theory of personality held that each individual was composed of four humors, with one humor dominating the other three. This dominant humor determined the person's physical and emotional character, or temperament. The four humors were (a) melancholic (sad), (b) sanguine (cheerful), (c) choleric (angry), and (d) phlegmatic (impassive).

One of the best-known examples of a type theory is Sheldon's (1940) description of body types and their relationship to temperament. He advocated the position that physical structure is a primary determinant of behavior. Obviously people differ in a number of physical features, sometimes described as their *physique* or *body type.* Sheldon examined the front, back, and side views of 4000 college-age men. He found three "primary structural components" of physique. He called these components *endomorphs, mesomorphs,* and *ectomorphs* and rated them on a scale from 1 to 7. A high rating on endomorphy indicates a preponderance of soft roundness throughout the body. Mesomorphs are muscular individuals with generally hard and heavy physiques. Finally, ectomorphs are slender and flat-chested. Their brains and central nervous systems are most predominant. Figure 13.3 illustrates Sheldon's body types.

Although it is tempting to define these three basic types as fat, muscular, or thin, this is misleading. As one observer noted, "Starve an endomorph and you do not end up with an ectomorph; you simply have an emaciated endomorph" (Engler, 1979, p. 242).

Figure 13.3
**The human body types identified by Sheldon**

Sheldon believed that each body type was associated with a specific pattern of personality.

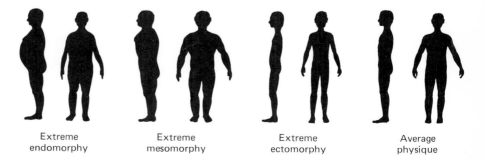

Extreme endomorphy    Extreme mesomorphy    Extreme ectomorphy    Average physique

**Introversion**
The tendency to look inward, to prefer being alone, and to engage in activities in which there is little contact with people.

**Extroversion**
The tendency to be outgoing and to engage in occupations or activities in which there is much contact with people.

**Psychotocism**
As postulated by Eysenck, an ingredient of personality that includes a deficiency in loyalty toward people, groups, or social standards.

**Psychotic**
Displaying a severe form of emotional disturbance that involves loss of contact with reality, disturbed thought processes, and personality disorganization.

**Psychoanalysis**
A school of psychology, founded by Sigmund Freud, that emphasizes the unconscious determinants of behavior; a theory of personality and the diagnosis and treatment of psychopathology.

Because these components rarely exist in a pure form, Sheldon employed a *somatotype* in which each individual was ranked according to the degree to which he exhibited a particular component (1 corresponds to a low rating, 7 to the highest). Thus each individual's physique can be expressed in terms of three numbers—one for the individual's relative position on each component. A 1–7–1 somatotype indicates an individual extremely high in mesomorphy. A somatotype of 4–4–4 characterizes an individual who is "average" on all three components.

Sheldon related three personality patterns to the three components. He postulated that endomorphy is associated with a general love of comfort, relaxation, sociability, food, and affection. The mesomorphs were primarily assertive, interested in muscular activity and a tendency to seek action and power. Finally, the ectomorph was seen as restrained, low in sociability, and inhibited.

Sheldon (1944) found rather high correlations between temperament and body type. He firmly believed that temperament could be accurately predicted from a person's somatotype. His studies have been tested by other researchers, and the results have been mixed. His conclusions have been attacked by various critics. One serious objection is that Sheldon's research involved only males. He believed, but never demonstrated, that relationships exist between physical structure and temperament in women as well as men. Additional criticisms have been leveled as well. As one observer pointed out:

> . . . *environmental responses to a particular type of physique may be more important than Sheldon realized. Commonly accepted stereotypes lead us to expect certain behaviors from certain types of physiques. An identical aggressive act from a strong muscular person and a small frail one usually draws different responses. Many people expect a strong muscular person to behave aggressively and they accept his or her aggressive behaviors as natural. The frail individual, on the other hand, has more difficulty in establishing a pattern of recognized aggressive responses. Thus, individuals with particular physiques may find certain responses ignored or punished in their environment and other kinds rewarded. The consequent similarities in temperament may, therefore, be due to environmental responses as well as to constitutional factors. Components of physique and temperament establish limits and potentialities for adult behavior. Nevertheless, environmental effects may determine to what extent a person is able to fulfull those potentialities. (Engler, 1979, p. 248)*

Because of the historical limitations of type theories, many psychologists feel that classifying personalities into *any* system of single-dimension categories is an inadequate way of describing personality. They feel that personality can be adequately described only by using a large number of dimensions.

Aware of these criticisms of type theory and not wishing to "throw out the baby with the bath water," E. J. Eysenck has developed a theory of personality that includes elements of both type and trait theories (Eysenck, 1967, 1970, 1975). Rather than regard a type as a category in which relatively few people belong, he regards type as being distributed in a bell-shaped fashion, as shown in Fig. 13.4. Very few people occupy

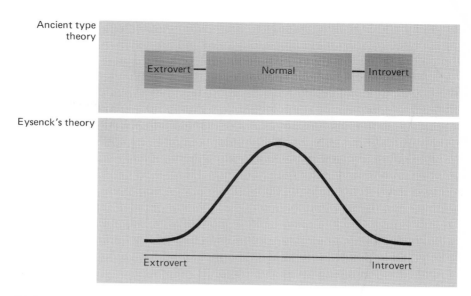

**Figure 13.4**
**Ancient type theories versus Eysenck's theory**

(Liebert and Spiegler, 1978)

the extremes or polar positions in the category shown. Most tend to cluster near the central values. Thus the **introversion–extroversion** dimension applies to everyone to some degree. What differentiates one person from another is the position each occupies on the scale between the two extreme values.

Types are at the very foundation of the personality structure, and they exert the strongest influences on its composition. In Eysenck's view, two dimensions are of major importance: introversion–extroversion and stability–instability. If these are combined in the way shown in Fig. 13.5, individual personalities can be placed in any of the four quadrants. Note that the two structural elements of personality bisect the circle, with various traits occupying varying positions within the circle: A moody person is extremely unstable and introverted; a quiet person is introverted and slightly unstable; a calm individual is introverted and highly stable.

In addition to the two personality types, there is a third factor that is an ingredient in the personality soup rather than a dimension. Referred to as **psychotocism,** it represents a tendency to be **psychotic** and includes a deficiency in allegiance toward people, groups, or social standards. Individuals high in psychotocism are, among other things, solitary, troublesome, cruel, insensitive, sensation-seeking, hostile, foolhardy, irritating, opposed to accepted social customs, and likely to prefer "impersonal" sex (Eysenck, 1975). Eysenck believes this tendency is inherited, is higher among men than women, and is highest among individuals imprisoned for offenses involving sex or aggression.

## Psychoanalytic Theories

**Psychoanalysis** is more than a theory of personality. As we saw in Chapter 11, it is also a theory of development. Moreover, as we will see in the next two chapters, it is concerned with the diagnosis and treatment of psychopathology. In this section, however, we will concentrate on those aspects of the theory that are concerned with the development of person-

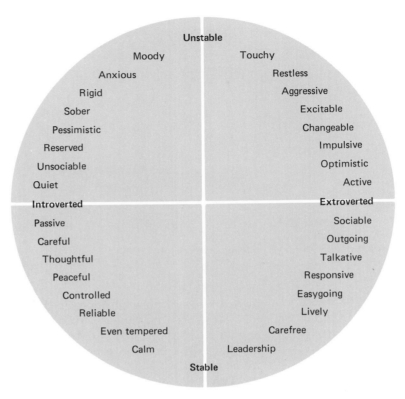

**Figure 13.5**
**Dimensions of personality**      (Eysenck, 1975)

ality. Because Sigmund Freud is the founder of psychoanalytic theory and the most widely known of the psychoanalytic theorists, let's look first at some of the concepts he proposed.

**Basic Freudian concepts.**    A central concept in Freud's theory is that of the **conscious** versus the **unconscious mind.** The conscious mind, for Freud, was not merely awake, but also *aware;* by the same token, the unconscious mind was unaware. Like an iceberg, the mind has only a small tip—the conscious portion—exposed and receptive to the world. The vast remainder—the unconscious—lies beneath the surface, unknown and unknowing.

Freud further believed that personality is divided into three parts: the id, the ego, and the superego. However, it is important to note that these three are parts of an integrated whole and work together so closely that it is difficult to separate the functions of one from those of the others.

The **id** consists of the primitive drives and instincts the individual is born with. The id is completely unconscious; it is visible to us only at second hand, through an examination of our dreams and behavior. For example, you may have heard someone make an interesting slip of the tongue. Freud believed these slips arise from the unconscious and reveal

**Conscious mind**
In psychoanalytic theory, that part of the mind which is aware of the individual's feelings and behaviors.

**Unconscious mind**
In psychoanalytic theory, that part of the mind which is unaware of the individual's feelings and behaviors.

**Id**
In psychoanalytic theory, the primitive and instinctual drives of the individual; the id is concerned only with immediate satisfaction of basic biological drives.

much about the id. Thus this phenomenon is sometimes called a "Freudian slip."

**Pleasure principle**
The tendency to seek immediate satisfaction of basic urges; it is characteristic of the id.

**Libido**
In psychoanalytic theory, the energy of the id, often associated with the sexual drive.

The id operates on the **pleasure principle;** that is, it is concerned only with the immediate satisfaction of basic biological drives. Very young infants are under the complete control of the id, seeking only to satisfy basic needs—"they want what they want when they want it." The infant is responding to one of the basic self-preservation drives (hunger), which also include breathing, thirst, and excretory functions. Other drives include aggression and the **libido**—the psychic energy of sexual behavior—which Freud saw as the most important drive for the development of personality. These drives in turn provide the energy for personality by arousing discomfort in the individual. Because the only outlets for the id are basic physiological reflexes and a sort of wishful thinking that is out of touch with reality, the id needs a way to deal with the real world to gratify its needs. Freud called this portion of the mind the ego.

A black-and-white lithograph of Edvard Munch's work *The Shriek* (1896), which launched the school of Expressionism. Munch had been inspired by a sunset in which he felt the clouds resembled blood. Some claim he was unconsciously creating an image of his mother's fatal hemorrhage. According to Freudian theory, in all of us a vast portion of our minds is beyond the reach of conscious thought.

Collection, The Museum of Modern Art, New York. 20 5/8″ × 15 13/16″. Mathew T. Mellon Fund.

**Ego**
In psychoanalytic theory, the aspect of the personality that regulates and controls the impulsive expressions of the id and deals with the demands of reality.

**Reality principle**
The principle of adapting the demands of the id to the realities of the environment.

**Superego**
In psychoanalytic theory, internal controls and standards derived from early influences; the superego corresponds to the "conscience."

**Ego ideal**
In psychoanalytic theory, the perfect self one would like to be.

**Identification**
The process of incorporating into one's own personality the values and beliefs of another person, usually a parent.

**Psychosexual stages**
Freud's theory of developmental stages in which the focus of pleasure shifts from one part of the body to another.

**Collective unconscious**
In Jung's theory, a portion of the unconscious containing certain shared experiences, predispositions, and symbols that are inherited and found in all members of a given race or species.

The **ego,** which develops during the first year of life, functions on the **reality principle;** it thinks realistically and transforms hunger into a way to get food. The ego also permits the individual to postpone the gratification of basic drives until the "proper" time. A person who is hungry is functioning on the level of the id if he or she demands food immediately. If the person is able to wait some time before eating, the ego is in control. The id and the ego are in constant conflict, because the ego must control the impulsive, and sometimes unrealistic, demands of the id and direct its energy.

The id and the ego are sufficient to gratify our basic needs. But it is the **superego** that permits us to function successfully in society. Freud's description of the superego is analogous to what most people call the conscience: It is the moral director of the ego, comparing the actions of the ego with an **ego ideal** of perfection and rewarding or punishing the ego accordingly. It is important to remember that the super ego is not inborn, but must be developed through children's interactions with their parents and other important people in their lives. Young children, dominated by the id, barely harnessed by the ego, are amoral and see nothing untoward about going after whatever they want by any means, fair or foul. It is only as children begin to perceive the values and beliefs of the significant people around them that they incorporate these values into their own personalities. This process is referred to as **identification.** Eventually the internal restraints of the superego replace the external restraints of other people.

According to Freud, these three parts of the personality are delicately balanced in the normal individual. Dominance by either the id or the superego could lead to serious personality problems. Thus a person with a weak superego may not successfully inhibit his or her id impulses and may thereby come into conflict with society. If the superego is too strong, the person achieves gratification of instinctual urges only at the cost of tension, anxiety, and guilt.

This three-part structure is only a portion of the Freudian conception of personality. As we saw in Chapter 11, Freud also considered personality development. As the individual matures, he or she goes through a number of **psychosexual stages,** each of which is important to the development of the personality.

**Evaluation of Freudian theory.** There is little question that Freud's theorizing had a major impact on the study of personality. The broad range of concepts that he developed has stimulated much investigation of and theorizing on the nature of personality.

Many aspects of his theory are still widely accepted. Few psychologists question the importance of early childhood experiences in the development of personality, and few doubt that Freud made major contributions to the study of personality. Freud was responsible for emphasizing the role of unconscious factors, motivational conflict, and defense mechanisms in behavior.

Much of Freud's work has been the subject of severe criticism. Freud based virtually all of his formulations upon his observations of emotionally disturbed patients who were undergoing psychoanalytic therapy. The setting was Vienna of the late 1890s and the early 1900s, a setting with many of the special characteristics that we associate with Victorian England. Questions have been raised concerning the validity of generalizing observations from this setting to today's population. In addition, many people question the applicability of Freud's findings to other cultures at other times. Indeed, much anthropological evidence has cast doubt on the generality of his conclusions.

Many critics also object to the emphasis Freud placed on sexuality and on biological instincts. These critics think that he tended to gloss over the role of social and cultural factors in the development of personality.

Finally, many of Freud's statements do not readily lend themselves to scientific verification. For example, how would you scientifically determine that a person is assailed by feelings of guilt related to his Oedipal strivings, and that these feelings are the underlying determinants of his behavior?

**Departures from Freud.** It is interesting that some of Freud's severest critics were originally his own disciples. These theorists used Freud's findings as a point of departure, but they departed so far from Freud that they developed their own theoretical schools.

Two of Freud's contemporaries, Carl Jung and Alfred Adler, proposed ideas that shifted the focus of the theory away from sexuality. Jung viewed personality as the resulting balance between conscious and unconscious forces. One of Jung's key concepts was that of the **collective unconscious.** Jung believed that, in the course of evolution, certain shared experiences, predispositions, and symbols became part of the genetic makeup of the human being. For example, one might cite the universality of certain dreams (such as dreams of falling) as evidence of Jung's collective unconscious. Presumably, our ancestors slept in trees in order to reduce the danger from insects and predators. Under these circumstances, falling could lead to tragic consequences. Dreams of falling reflect these unconscious fears.

Indirect evidence favoring the possibility of the collective unconscious comes from the fact that certain phobias are quite common, are readily learned, and are difficult to extinguish. These include the fears of darkness, insects, snakes, and high places. As one observer has noted:

> *All of these are relatively common phobias. And only rarely, if ever, do we have pajama phobias, grass phobias, electric-outlet phobias, hammer phobias, even though these things are likely to be associated with trauma in our world. The set of potentially phobic events may be nonarbitrary: events related to the survival of the species through the long course of evolution. (Seligman, 1971, p. 312)*

Adler viewed the individual as a social rather than a sexual creature. He stressed the role of human society on the development of personality and emphasized its importance on every aspect of our lives. Two forces are at work within the individual: the need to overcome feelings of inferiority and the drive to do so by becoming superior. Adler believed that

In Britain the extreme importance given to social position and the fulfillment of roles may have a strong impact on the development of personality. No matter what his basic personality, Prince Charles, here being invested as Prince of Wales, has developed considerable poise, self-assurance, and social grace in performing his public duties.

"to be a human being means to feel oneself inferior" (Adler, 1964, cited in Liebert and Spiegler, 1978, p. 76). Thus life is a continuous struggle to gain superiority over others. Recall that, in Freud's theory, adults have little or no awareness of their unconscious motives. In contrast, Adler maintained that we are all too aware of our deeply rooted feelings of inferiority. The result is that we overcompensate by trying to become superior. The greater the sense of inferiority, the greater is the tendency to overcompensate. Thus individuals with physical defects often labor long and diligently to become superior athletes.

Adler is responsible for introducing the term "inferiority complex" as a household word. However, in contrast to common usage, Adler regarded the inferiority complex as an abnormal condition, characterized by an unhealthy exaggeration of feelings of inferiority and/or strivings for superiority.

It should be noted, however, that Adler did not view humans as exclusively aggressive or as having no positive motivations. He believed that humans also have an instinct for perfection. He called this striving creative power and saw it as the driving force behind all our behavior.

Other theorists, such as Karen Horney and Erich Fromm, attempted to redress what they felt was an overemphasis on biological determinants in Freud's theory. They focused instead on the role of social and cultural factors in the development of personality.

Karen Horney objected to Freud's relegating social and cultural factors to a minor role in the development of personality. She pointed out that many stresses arise from inconsistencies within the individual's own society (for example, we subscribe to the commandment, "Thou shalt not kill," yet we send people to war).

Erich Fromm maintains that through increased automation and depersonalization, society has deprived individuals of satisfying personal and social relationships with each other. He feels we must find new meanings in life and productive ways of satisfying personal and social motives.

Erik Erikson, whose psychosocial stage theory was presented in Chapter 11, also used Freud's work as a point of departure in developing his own theoretical position.

## Social Learning Theories

Whereas the various psychoanalytic theorists derive their data from observations of patients in clinical practice, other theorists approach the study of personality from an experimental point of view. Learning theorists start out with the basic assumption that personality is learned and that, therefore, the principles of learning are applicable (see Chapter 2). There have been many different groups of social learning theories. In this section, we will look at two of the most prominent.

**Dollard and Miller.** Dollard and Miller point out that there are four basic elements in the learning process: drive, cue, response, and reward. When a drive is active in the presence of various environmental stimuli (cues), responses that serve to reduce or satisfy that drive are acquired. This drive reduction is rewarding. For example, a hungry (drive) rat in an operant conditioning chamber (cues) will learn to press a bar (response) to obtain food that satisfies its hunger drive (reward) (Dollard and Miller, 1950).

At this point, you might be thinking, "This is all very interesting, but how does one develop a theory of personality based on hungry rats learning bar-pressing responses?" Dollard and Miller attempted to apply the principles of learning derived from laboratory experiments to psychoanalytic phenomena. Let's look at some of the similarities in basic concepts between Freud's theory and learning theory. First, both stress the importance of drive as an energizer of behavior. Second, both postulate that drive or tension reduction is rewarding; that is, the organism will act in ways that lead to tension reduction. Third, both have developed elaborate theories of motivational conflict, and both are concerned with the ways in which motivational conflicts are resolved.

It might be instructive to look at a single phenomenon and compare the approach of the learning theorists to that of Freud. Earlier (Chapter 12) we discussed **displaced aggression,** which sometimes occurs under frustrating circumstances. Although the concept of displacement originated in psychoanalytic theory, it can readily be handled by learning theory. Let's look at an experiment in which displacement was demonstrated in human subjects.

A questionnaire that assessed attitudes toward certain minority groups was administered to a group of boys both before and after exposure to frustrating conditions. As a result of the frustration, the boys expressed a greater number of hostile attitudes toward the minority groups. A psychoanalyst might say that the boys were *displacing* their aggression from the source of the frustration (the experimenters) to the minority groups. Learning theorists, however, would say that the subjects were *generalizing* hostile feelings from the experimenters to the minority groups (Miller and Bugelski, 1948).

In effect, Dollard and Miller translated many psychoanalytic concepts into operationally defined terms that permit experimental testing.

**Bandura.**   One of the criticisms of Dollard and Miller's work is that it relies heavily on animal research to develop a personality theory. The major emphasis is on the use of rewards and punishments to mold and modify behavior. Laboratory animals figure prominently in the literature concerned with rewards and punishment. Bandura has pursued an opposing research strategy. He argues that a comprehensive theory of personality can be developed *only* by studying humans, and that interpersonal processes cannot be ignored. Moreover, the use of rewards and punishments constitutes only one facet of human learning. Much of what we learn is based on observing others and using their behavior as a model for our own reactions. Thus we may learn to fear a Doberman pinscher, not as a direct result of experiencing its bite, but as a consequence of observing the fear that the dog arouses in other people.

Bandura has focused on a kind of learning imitation that emphasizes the role of social factors. Let us contrast the ways in which a reinforcement theorist and a social learning theorist like Bandura might evaluate

**Much of what we learn is based on observing others, although we do not necessarily model our own behavior after the actions of others.**

the use of punishment to modify behavior. Imagine the following situation: A child has just engaged in a prohibited act. A parent applies immediate punishment in the form of a sharp slap. The undesired behavior is successfully suppressed. The reinforcement theorist might argue that the suppression of the undesired behavior is a desirable outcome of punishment, because it provides an opportunity for an alternative behavior to occur and be rewarded. Bandura, on the other hand, would point out that the child may be learning many things from this transaction, not all of them desirable. For example, the child may learn that when you are annoyed you strike out against the instigator of your annoyance and that physical aggression is an effective method of control. Bandura maintains that both the parent and the child would benefit if the parent provided a model of prosocial rather than antisocial behavior (Bandura, 1973).

It should be noted that the individual does not necessarily imitate the model. A key distinction must be made between learning and performance. We have learned how to do many things in daily life by observing the actions of others directly; we learn indirectly by reading or hearing about the behavior of others. We may learn how to commit murder, rape, and arson, but we do not necessarily ever perform these learned acts. A comprehensive theory of personality must delve into the reasons why learned acts are *not* performed, as well as why they *are* performed.

Consider the following. Scott observes his older brother Barry go into the kitchen, search in a few drawers and cabinets, and emerge with a chocolate fudge cookie. If he subsequently enters the kitchen and engages in similar search behavior, we may say that he has engaged in direct imitation. But what if he observes Barry suddenly seize the family cat by the tail and immediately scream in pain as the cat sinks its claws into his arm? Does Scott imitate his brother? Probably not. As a matter of fact, he probably avoids the cat like the plague. Does this mean Scott has not learned from the model? Not at all. He has, in fact, accepted the model's behavior and the consequences of his actions as a guide to his own behavior. In short, he has learned what *not* to do. Bandura refers to such learning as *direct counter-imitation*.

Observational learning, then, is seen as a three-stage process. First there is exposure to a model. But mere exposure does not guarantee that the second stage, acquisition, will occur. Acquisition requires both attention to the model and the storing of observations in permanent memory. However, even if the behavior has been attended to and stored in permanent memory, there is no guarantee that the third stage, acceptance of the model, will occur. Unless the individual accepts the model's behavior as a guide for action—what he or she should do or should not do—neither imitation nor counter-imitation will occur.

Bandura also argues that direct imitation is more than a mere copying of the model's behavior. The individual observes the behavior, evaluates it, stores it in permanent memory, and then, at some later date, is able to apply the learning to situations that may be markedly different from the original setting. In short, cognitive factors play a prominent role in imitative learning.

Moreover, this imitation is highly selective, as indicated by a series of ongoing studies (Yarrow and Scott, 1972; Yarrow *et al.*, 1973). A group of nursery school children interacted over a sustained period of time with teachers who served either as nurturant (i.e., warm and supporting) models or as nonnurturant models. It was found that nurturant models facilitated the imitation of nurturant but not aggressive behaviors. In contrast, nonnurturant models increased the imitation of aggressive behaviors (Yarrow and Scott, 1972).

**Evaluation of social learning theories.** Social learning theorists have contributed much to our understanding of human behavior and personality. Their emphasis on the flexibility of personality and the effects of

## Plate 10

This series of drawings, created by one boy over a five-year period, gives insight into cognitive development. Within a short time after birth, the biological components of visual perception are complete; it is the child's ability to organize and communicate his or her perceptions that undergoes dramatic change as cognitive development continues. Here we see how one child dealt with themes of fire and impending disaster at the ages of 5, 7, and 9.

Zachary Nightingale

## Plate 11

A series of paintings, created during therapy, by a patient diagnosed as paranoid schizophrenic. Picture (a) was selected from a magazine for the patient to copy. The patient's fearful, distorted perception of reality and inability to use colors or letters of the alphabet are evident in his first attempt, picture (b). The still life in (c) shows improvement; and one year after therapy began, the patient was able to achieve the realism of picture (d).

Al Vercoutere

(a)

(b)

(c)

(d)

## Plate 12

This yarn painting, created by a member of the Huichol Indian group, was intended to show the kinds of hallucinatory shapes and colors brought on by taking peyote. To the left, an Indian carrying a basket of freshly harvested peyote sees a vision exploding with brilliant color and streaks of light. The peyote cactus is represented at the right.

## Plate 13

Poverty-stricken and despairing over his inability to succeed at various vocations, Van Gogh at age 27 committed himself to his art, deciding that his mission was to bring consolation to humanity through his creative powers. His feelings about his subjects were expressed through simplification and exaggeration and through his use of intense, almost arbitrary color. He suffered from both epilepsy and severe depression, and during the late 1800s, his mental health deteriorated. This series of self-portraits reflects the artist's growing struggle against madness. In his last paintings, elements of mental disturbance and artistic genius merged. The last portrait—with its swirling tension and aura of terror and sadness—was painted two months before his suicide.

Sources: Left top and bottom, Collection National Museum Vincent Van Gogh, Amsterdam. Right, Scala/Editorial Photocolor Archives.

**Plate 14**

Artists have long used their creative abilities to make effective social commentaries. Duane Hanson's superrealistic sculptures of everyday subjects, for example, confront us with familiar material that we are forced to see in new, intense ways.

Courtesy of O. K. Harris Works of Art

**Plate 15**

Ben Shahn is another artist who likes to reconceptualize the everyday world. However, whereas Hanson dwells on minute, realistic detail, Shahn uses imagination and abstraction to create haunting images that transcend objective accuracy.

Ben Shahn. *Willis Avenue Bridge* (1940). Tempera on paper over composition board, 23″ x 31⅜″. Collection, The Museum of Modern Art, New York. Gift of Lincoln Kirstein.

environment on behavior have led to some promising methods for modifying maladaptive behavior. We will discuss these therapeutic techniques in more detail in Chapter 15. Also, the precise descriptions of behavior in social learning theory, in contrast to psychoanalytic theory, lend themselves well to controlled testing of the theories.

However, social learning theories have also drawn criticism. Some have questioned the validity of generalizing from studies of animal behavior to the more complex human condition. Others have criticized social learning theories as failing to explain how a series of learned behaviors becomes an integrated personality. Many have disputed the extremely unstable nature of personality as it is described by social learning theories. But the strongest criticism of social learning theories has been what some see as a failure to consider the role of individual differences and an emphasis on behavior and environment to the neglect of the person. It appears that many current social learning theorists are taking such criticisms seriously, stressing the interaction of the individual and the environment to a greater degree than previously and giving more consideration to the role of genetic factors in human behavior.

## Humanistic Theories

Have you ever tossed a piece of wood into a body of water and then observed its "behavior"? If the water is calm, it will sit placidly on the surface, bobbing with each little ripple that passes by. It will show little movement, little change of position. But if the water is disturbed by, say, tides, wind, or rain, the piece of wood will be tossed about helter-skelter, a hapless victim of changing conditions.

Humanistic psychologists argue that many personality theories equate the individual with that piece of wood. According to these traditional theories, we are, at birth, thrust into an environment over which we have no control. What we become in life is the sum total of the types of environments we encounter. In other words, we are, like the piece of wood, both victims and captives of our environments.

The humanists argue that this traditional view ignores the considerable talents that we, as humans, possess. We are not lifeless objects subject to the whims of storm-tossed seas. We are intelligent, resourceful, and flexible organisms, capable of being masters of our own destinies (Mischel, 1981). If our environments offend us, we can change them. If our lives fall into disarray, we have within ourselves the capacity to restore order and coherence. In brief, personality is not fixed and unchanging; it is alive, dynamic, and flexible.

One of the leading exponents of the humanistic theory of personality is Carl Rogers. The key concept in his theory is that of the self, "an organized, fluid, but consistent conceptual pattern of perceptions of characteristics and relationships of the 'I' or the 'me,' together with values attached to these concepts" (Rogers, 1951, p. 498). The self consists only of perceptions and values that either are conscious or can readily become so (Epstein, 1980). According to Rogers, the individual has one fundamental tendency—to actualize, maintain, and enhance the experiencing organism. The self stands as a bastion that must be defended at all costs. More specifically, we must defend ourselves against experiences and perceptions that lower our self-esteem. Favorable self-esteem is, in turn, acquired in an environment of unconditional positive regard. We accept people for themselves and not for what they can do to us or for us. We accept them with their imperfections, their fallibilities, and their frailties. A parent who insists upon perfection as a condition for favorable regard is likely to raise children with a seriously bruised self-esteem.

Many of you may have seen the film *The Elephant Man*. You may recall that John Merrick grew up with a horrible disease that produced tumors over his entire body and led to a progressive deformity of his physical features. He was exploited as a sideshow freak and was stripped of all vestiges of human dignity. Treated like a dumb and unintelligent animal, he behaved as one, apparently unable to speak and with no sign of underlying intelligence. It was only when the surgeon and the nursing staff of a hospital befriended him and began to regard him positively that John Merrick began to view himself in a favorable light. Only then was he willing to reveal his own intelligence, converse with others, attend concerts, and appear in public without a sack over his head.

The values we learn from direct experience are more reliable guides to ourselves than those we learn from others. To illustrate, one of the authors observed the following transaction between a six-year-old boy and his visiting aunt.

> *"Johnny, how do you like school?"*
> *"It stinks."*
> *"Come now, tell me the truth. How do you like school?"*
> *"It stinks."*
> *"I don't think I can love or bring presents to a little boy who doesn't like school. Tell me, how do you really feel about school?"*
> *"I love it, auntie."*

According to Rogers, scenes like this set the stage for maladjustment. When we experience pain directly, we can learn to label the experience correctly as pain. But when the doctor or parent says, "This won't hurt," when the needle is thrust into Mary's arm, she will experience confusion about applying the label. She has been told it doesn't hurt, but she feels pain. In order to maintain a positive image of herself, however, Mary exclaims, "That didn't hurt a bit," as she stifles a sob forming in the recesses of her mind. She is also told that it is bad to be angry at a younger brother or sister. Thus she avoids labeling her own feeling as anger. Instead she may say, "I love Johnny," while seething with inner turmoil. In this way, the **conscious** self is moved out of phase with the **organismic** self. The stage is set for maladjustment. The lack of agreement between the conscious and organismic selves contributes to anxiety or tension. Moreover, because Mary finds the perception of herself as hating her brother unacceptable, she is forced to misrepresent reality and adopt exaggerated defense mechanisms (Epstein, 1980).

**Conscious self**
That part of the organismic self concerned with individuals' perceptions of themselves and of their relationships with others.

**Organismic self**
In Roger's theory of self, the total, organized awareness, or potential awareness, of the mind.

**John Merrick, popularly known as the "Elephant Man," was able to develop a normal personality in spite of his physical deformity once people accorded him the respect and dignity he deserved as a human being.**

The greater the threat to the self, the greater the defenses that must be organized to defend it. There are times, however, when the defenses are overwhelmed. When this happens, a catastrophic breakdown and disintegration ensues. But even at this point the basic optimism of the humanistic psychologist reveals itself. Rogers believes that, given an open and supportive atmosphere and a self-structure that is not overly threatened, the individual spontaneously moves toward health and actualization of potential.

Another prominent humanistic theory of personality is Abraham Maslow's concept of a hierarchy of needs and self-actualization, which we discussed in Chapter 8 as a motivator of human behavior.

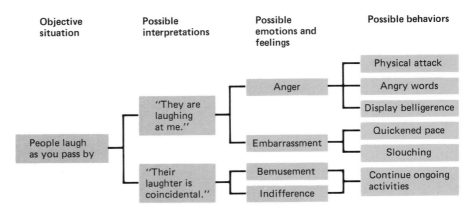

Figure 13.6    This schematic diagram presents the view that our reactions to situations depend on what is "in our heads" rather than on objective reality.

**Evaluation of humanistic theories.**    Perhaps the greatest contribution of humanistic theories is their positive outlook on human behavior—as seen in the concept of self-actualization—and their emphasis on normal, healthy functioning. Furthermore, unlike the social learning theorists, humanists have focused on individual differences, especially variations in perceptions and interpretations of events. Humanistic theories also concern themselves heavily with how personality develops. Out of humanistic theories Rogers developed a type of psychotherapy he calls person-centered therapy (see Chapter 15 for more detail on these techniques). His studies of patients treated by this therapy provide support for humanistic theories of personality.

**Cognitive Theories***

Imagine the following situation. You are walking along the sidewalk in a small community in which you are a stranger. As you approach a group of people, you nod slightly and smile to acknowledge their presence. Just as you pass them, they suddenly burst into laughter. What is your reaction likely to be?

If you think about it a moment, you will probably answer that your reaction depends on the intent of their laughter. If you think they are laughing at you, your reaction will understandably be different from what it will be if you conclude that their laughter has merely coincided accidentally with your passing. Cognitive theorists frequently use examples of this sort to point out the weakness of the behavioristic (social learning) approach. Behavioristic psychologists attempt to describe objectively both the situation and the various resulting behaviors. On the other hand, cog-

---

*This section is based largely on an excellent discussion in Epstein (1980).

nitive theorists, like the humanists, argue that objective reality is often irrelevant. What is in our heads, rather than objective reality, determines our courses of action in the real world. If we think people are laughing at us, our feelings might include anger or embarrassment. We might scowl back at them, say something unpleasant, or even act in a belligerent fashion. Figure 13.6 shows several possible emotional responses and external behaviors resulting from different interpretations of the laughter. But cognitive theorists go one step beyond the humanists by looking at what individuals do as a result of their personal realities.

Cognitive theorists view humans as information processors or scientists, constantly taking in data, weighing it, and using it to support, refute, or alter concepts and behaviors. They maintain that we do not focus on the past, but on the present and future; we are particularly concerned with predicting and controlling our environment.

**George Kelly.**     George Kelly's theory provides a purely cognitive view of personality. Kelly was primarily concerned with how the individual makes sense of the world. As a cognitive theorist, he believed reality to be subjective. As a scientist, he was concerned with evaluating personality objectively. Much of his work was directed at finding ways to define and assess personality, to bridge the gap between the scientific rigor of behaviorism and the subjectiveness of the humanistic approach.

**Personal construct**
Kelly's term for each individual's unique categories for classifying people and events.

Kelly studied the ways in which humans organize their individual realities by sorting people and events into categories he called **personal constructs**—categories that humans then use in evaluating and attempting to control their world. Kelly believed that by examining a person's constructs we can understand the individual's psychological workings.

Kelly also explained the development of personality in terms of constructs. He argued that, just as we master simple cognitive concepts before complex ones, so our constructs become more sophisticated as we mature. Good and bad may be absolutes (though with limited application) to a 6-year-old. A 60-year-old will no doubt have revised that construct many times and may well see more exceptions than absolutes.

Just as we master cognitive concepts by altering our schemes, so we alter constructs by confronting new information. Each time we face a new situation, we first attempt to assimilate it into our current construct of reality. If we can do this easily, we feel no anxiety. Our comfort with the situation will increase the likelihood that we will repeat the experience. This repetition in turn may be reflected in a liking for a person or activity. However, when a situation cannot be easily assimilated into our personal constructs, we may be anxious and may avoid such an environment in the future. Over time, must of us develop a wide range of constructs and generally enjoy new experiences. Those whose constructs are more limited are correspondingly more rigid and restricted in outlook. Still, Kelly believed that it is only when humans fail to reject constructs that they have previously found unworkable—when the behavior is not consistent with even the subjective reality—that individuals suffer from disorders.

**Evaluation of cognitive theories.**   Perhaps the greatest contribution of cognitive theories is their view of humans not as merely subject to or even interacting with the environment, but as active shapers of it. Cognitive theorists' integration of findings from many perspectives gives their theories greater scope and enables them to account for a great many aspects of personality.

The strongest criticism against cognitive theories has come from the behaviorists, who argue that this approach is not sufficiently objective. Kelly developed a test (Role Construct Repertory Test) that has provided psychologists with one way to study constructs objectively, but firm conclusions on such topics as consistency of constructs over time must await more research.

# Summary

1. Personality consists of those persistent and enduring behavior patterns of an individual that tend to be expressed in a wide variety of situations.
2. Even at birth, differences in crying and activity level are discernible, and these variations produce different reactions among adults. Such inborn tendencies and initial contacts form the basis for the development of those enduring behavior patterns referred to as personality.
3. People coming from different cultural settings may manifest widely varying personality characteristics, because the members of each culture selectively shape and reinforce different behaviors.
4. During the first few years of a child's life, the parents act as the primary agents for transmitting their culture. As children grow older, their social contacts broaden dramatically.
5. Trait theorists attempt to use a number of basic characteristics to describe and assess personality. Cattell, a leading trait theorist, came up with a series of traits such as reserved versus outgoing, emotional versus stable.
6. Type theories of personality search for primary characteristics that can be used to describe the whole personality (for example, extroversion versus introversion). A well-known type theory relates body type (somatotype) to temperament.
7. One of the most influential theories of personality, psychoanalytic theory, was initially developed by Sigmund Freud. Freud emphasized the role of the unconscious and the interaction between what he saw as the three parts comprising the personality: the id, the ego, and the superego.
8. Many of those who were influenced by Freud, including Carl Jung, Alfred Adler, Karen Horney, and Eric Fromm, continued in the psychoanalytic tradition, but rejected Freud's emphasis on sexual factors in personality development in favor of social influences.
9. Whereas the various psychoanalytic theories derive their data from observations of patients in clinical practice, learning theorists start out with the basic assumption that personality is learned, and therefore the principles of learning are applicable. In short, we learn behaviors that are positively reinforced.
10. Bandura's research strategy has focused on the role of social factors in personality development. He points out that humans learn much through observation and imitation.
11. Humanistic theories stress the intelligence, resourcefulness, and flexibility of humans in pursuit of their destinies. In the view of Carl Rogers, the individual functions at all times to protect the concept of the self.
12. The cognitive view of personality asserts that humans are concerned with controlling their environment. In the view of George Kelly, they do this by systematically forming and amending constructs of their world.

# Terms to Remember

| | | | |
|---|---|---|---|
| Personality | Psychotocism | Libido | Collective unconscious |
| Trait | Psychotic | Ego | Displaced aggression |
| Source traits | Psychoanalysis | Reality principle | Conscious self |
| Surface traits | Conscious mind | Superego | Organismic self |
| Type theories | Unconscious mind | Ego ideal | Personal construct |
| Introversion | Id | Identification | |
| Extroversion | Pleasure principle | Psychosexual stages | |

# ABNORMAL BEHAVIOR

## WHAT IS ABNORMAL?

**Abnormal**
(1) Those behaviors that fail to comply with cultural values or standards (cultural definition); (2) behaviors that interfere with the individual's ability to achieve goals or to resolve motivational conflicts (adjustment definition); (3) certain types of behaviors, for example, disordered thought processes.

There are many different ways of defining **"abnormal."** Unfortunately, these definitions are often at variance with one another. Legal definitions are frequently in conflict with psychological and psychiatric definitions. In some states, for instance, persons are considered mentally ill only if they are unaware of the consequences of their actions. Thus a person who plants a bomb "to gain revenge against all of the people who are out to get me" might be ruled legally sane if he or she knew that detonation of the bomb might kill people. Psychologists, however, might conclude that the same individual was suffering from some form of a mental disorder because of the severe distortions in the individual's perceptions of the motives of others.

The word "abnormal" means "away from the normal"; thus the question, "What is abnormal?" implies that there is a clearly defined "normal" and that departures from it constitute the abnormal. In many fields of human endeavor, it is not difficult to define what is normal. In medicine, for example, scientists and doctors have a reasonably good idea of the structure and functions of the various parts of the body. The line between normal and abnormal functioning is usually fairly clear. When it comes to psychological functioning, however, we have no established model of normality against which to judge abnormality. This is not meant to imply that no definitions of "normal" have been attempted. Box 14.1 presents some of the characteristics that are thought to describe "healthy" mental functioning. Note that we have not portrayed the normal individual as always happy, contented, and free from conflicts. On the contrary,

*. . . he may often fall short of his ideals; and because of ignorance, the limitations under which an individual lives in a complex world, or the*

---

## BOX 14.1

### Characteristics of the "Normal" Individual

**Attitudes toward self.** Emphasizing self-acceptance, adequate self-identity, realistic appraisal of one's assets and liabilities.

**Perception of reality.** A realistic view of oneself and the surrounding world of people and things.

**Integration.** Unity of personality, freedom from disabling inner conflicts, good stress tolerance.

**Competencies.** Development of essential physical, intellectual, emotional, and social competencies for coping with life's problems.

**Autonomy.** Adequate self-reliance, responsibility, and self-direction—together with sufficient independence of social influences.

**Growth, self-actualization.** Emphasizing trends toward increasing maturity, development of potentialities, and self-fulfillment as a person.

**Interpersonal relations.** Capacity for forming and maintaining intimate interpersonal relations.

**Goal attainment.** Does not strive to achieve perfection but sets goals which are realistic and within the individual's capabilities.

Adapted from Coleman, 1976.

Behavior regarded as normal in some cultures would be considered abnormal in others. This fisherman is demonstrating a method of fishing that is popular in Fiji but that foreigners might consider quite bizarre.

*strength of immediate pressures, he may sometimes behave in ways that prove to be shortsighted or self-defeating. Consequently, he knows something of the experience of guilt at times, and because he tries to be fully aware of the risks he takes he can hardly be entirely free from fear and worry. (Shoben, 1957, p. 189)*

How do we draw the line between normal and abnormal? What are some of the different ways of defining abnormal? One approach would be to define normal as behavior that is approved and accepted within a given culture. Thus those behaviors that fail to comply with cultural values or standards would be called abnormal. This cultural definition of abnormality implies that no behavior is abnormal so long as it is accepted by society. Advocates of this definition would argue that there is no such thing as a "sick society":

*A critical example is whether an obedient Nazi concentration-camp commander would be considered normal or abnormal. To the extent that he was responding accurately and successfully to his environment and not breaking its rules, much less coming to the professional attention of psychiatrists, he would not be labeled abnormal. Repulsive as his behavior is to mid-twentieth-century Americans, such repulsion is based on a particular set of values. Although such a person may be made liable for his acts—as Nazi war criminals were—the concept of abnormality as a special entity does not seem necessary or justified. If it is, the problem arises as to who selects the values, and this, in turn, implies that one group may select values that are applied to others. This situation of one group's values being dominant over others is the fascistic background from which the Nazi camp commander sprang. (Ullmann and Krasner, 1969, p. 15)*

The cultural definition of abnormality has some serious shortcomings. Its critics argue that "it rests on the questionable assumption that socially accepted behavior is never pathological, and it implies that normality is nothing more than conformity" (Coleman, 1972, p. 15).

Another way to define abnormal is in terms of the significance of an individual's behavior. If the behavior interferes with his or her ability to achieve goals or resolve motivational conflicts, we may regard the individual as maladjusted. If a young woman is highly motivated to achieve a satisfying heterosexual relationship but constantly engages in self-defeating behavior (picking arguments, overeating, avoiding social occasions), we may say she is maladjusted and, in a sense, abnormal.

Critics of the adjustment point of view argue that some behaviors may be well adapted to achieving goals, but the goals themselves may reflect abnormality. Hitler was eminently successful in achieving many of his goals, but one would be hard pressed to regard him as normal. Moreover, people who wage unpopular campaigns on political and social issues often encounter significant personal discomfort and loss. From a cultural point of view, they are often considered abnormal. It is important to bear in mind that many of our great statesmen, religious leaders, inventors, writers, poets, and composers have been drawn from the ranks of those who, from the cultural definition, might be judged abnormal.

A third basis for a definition is the one used by many professionals in the mental health field. They classify certain types of behaviors as abnormal—for example, those indicating disordered thought processes, or loss of contact with reality, or irrational emotional outbursts. A person who manifests some or many of these behaviors is deemed abnormal.

The most ambitious and widely used classification system, revised in 1980 by the American Psychiatric Association, is called the *Diagnostic and Statistical Manual of Mental Disorders (DSM*-III). It features clear descriptions of diagnostic categories and provides specific criteria for making diagnoses (see Box 14.2). The goal of the manual is to produce increased diagnostic agreement among clinicians. It does this by emphasizing the description of behavioral or psychological patterns that are associated with either a painful symptom or impairment in one or more areas of everyday behavior. In recognition of the fact that users of the manual come from many different theoretical backgrounds, a thoroughgoing effort is made to avoid theoretical issues that are often the center of controversy among clinicians. In some cases, theoretical differences in ascribing causes to disorders may be an almost unbridgeable chasm. For example, a follower of psychoanalytic theory might attribute a person's fear of snakes to displacement (see Chapter 9) of unconscious anxiety about the penis, which physically resembles a snake. In contrast, a learning theorist might consider the same problem to be merely the result of maladaptive learning. Whatever the theoretical differences, however, field trials have demonstrated that "clinicians can agree on the identification of mental disorders on the basis of clinical manifestations without agreeing on how the disturbances came about" (*DSM*-III, 1980, p. 7).

What causes abnormal behavior? Although theories abound to answer this question, let us acknowledge that, for the most part, we still don't know. Scientists all over the world are struggling with this problem,

## BOX 14.2

### The *DSM*-III: Who and What Is It Good For?

In an article entitled "But Is It Good for the Psychologists? Appraisal and Status of DSM-III," Schacht and Nathan (1977) level a number of criticisms at the DSM-III. They point out that although more than half of the disorders listed are not attributable to known or presumed organic causes and should not be considered medical disorders or diseases, the DSM-III has a definite medical orientation. The suggestion is made that the medical emphasis is due in part to the needs of psychiatrists to define and assert the boundaries of their profession. In other words, professional needs to some extent influenced the formulation of the system.

An article by Garmezy (1978) called "Never Mind the Psychologists: Is It Good for the Children?" followed soon after. Garmezy acknowledged that the DSM-III represented a major advance over its predecessors and agreed that "mental disease" was an appropriate label for certain disorders (such as schizophrenia) and that psychiatric labels (such as "mental patient") carried a certain stigma. Garmezy faulted the DSM-III for defining too many behaviors of children as deficits and mental disorders. For example, *avoidant disorder of childhood* is defined as "persistent and excessive shrinking from contact with strangers." Under this rubric, millions of shy children might be considered to be suffering from a mental disorder; it might, in fact, be more appropriate to characterize these behaviors as a delay in social development. The diagnostic system, he argues, is over-inclusive in labelling certain behaviors of children as mental disorders.

These questioning articles were followed by another that addressed the question, "But Is It Good for Science?" (Zubin 1977/78). He argues that DSM-III is too artificial because it is a product of compromises and practical considerations, such as accommodation of contrasting views of those who were involved in developing the system, utility and ease of application, and general acceptability to practitioners. While acknowledging the importance of these considerations, Zubin believes they can make it difficult to use DSM-III for scientific purposes.

How good is DSM-III? It is a diagnostic system with both strengths and weaknesses. Reliability seems to be higher in this version than in previous ones, and criteria for disorders are better clarified. It is acknowledged to be descriptive, not theoretical; much more information is systematically collected on the five axes than in earlier versions. Hence, research into the meaningfulness of the information can be tested. Although the pervasive medical-model orientation and the implications for childhood disorders are serious shortcomings, overall the DSM-III appears to be a substantial improvement over DSM-I and DSM-II.

Sue *et al.*, 1981, p. 119.

---

**Neurosis**
The term formerly used to denote emotional disturbances characterized by maladaptive behavior aimed at avoiding anxiety.

and many feel that some of the answers are just around the next corner. However, *DSM*-III makes clear the fact that the cause of any disorder (except a few known to be of organic origin) is still a matter of dispute. The new *DSM* reflects an increased commitment to research to help settle conflicts over the causes of some of the disorders. In fact, it was for just this reason that *DSM*-III eliminated the word **"neurosis,"** with its links to Freudian theory and implication of causality.

There are many categories of mental disorders presented in *DSM*-III (see Table 14.1). Although we do not discuss all the disorders in detail here, we adhere to *DSM*-III vocabulary for those disorders that we cover. Where it seems appropriate, we have included the old terminology as well as the new, since you may encounter such descriptions in many of your readings.

## Table 14.1
## Major Disorders Described in *DSM*-III

| Disorder | Description |
| --- | --- |
| Disorders arising in childhood or adolescence | Problems of thought and behavior (for example, mental retardation, stuttering, and bedwetting) that are first identified relatively early in or are peculiar to the precollege or pre–working life period |
| Organic mental disorders | Transient or permanent brain dysfunction attributable to such factors as the aging process or ingestion of a substance that affects the brain |
| Substance use disorders | Personal and social problems associated with use of certain substances (for example, opium) |
| Schizophrenic disorders | Chronic disorganized behavior and thought of psychotic proportions (delusions, hallucinations), incoherence, and social isolation |
| Paranoid disorders | Well-organized system of delusions (often of being persecuted) without the incoherence, bizarreness, and social isolation seen in schizophrenia |
| Psychotic disorders not classified elsewhere | Includes schizophreniform disorders (similar to schizophrenia but currently of less than six months duration), brief psychosis in reaction to a particular stress and schizoaffective disorders (a combination of disorganization and delusional behavior with feelings of depression and elation) |
| Affective disorders | Depression or manic excitement, or both |
| Anxiety disorders | Includes as major aspects anxiety, tension, and worry, with psychotic features (delusions, hallucinations) absent; also includes posttraumatic (reactive, stress-caused) disorders, which may be brief or chronic |
| Somatoform disorders | Physical symptoms for which no medical causes can be found, which are apparently not under voluntary control, and which are linked to psychological factors or conflicts |
| Dissociative disorders | Sudden, temporary change in the normal functions of consciousness (for example, loss of memory, sleepwalking) |
| Psychosexual disorders | Deviant sexual thoughts and behaviors that are either personally anxiety-provoking or socially maladaptive |
| Factitious disorders | Physical or behavior symptoms voluntarily produced by the individual, apparently in order to play the role of a patient, often involving chronic, blatant lying |
| Disorders of impulse control not elsewhere classified | Maladaptations characterized by failure to resist impulses (for example, pathological gambling, chronic stealing of desired objects, habitual fire-setting) |
| Adjustment disorders | Maladaptive reactions to identifiable life events or circumstances that are expected to lessen and cease when the stressor ceases; the reaction may be dominated by depressed mood, anxiety, withdrawal, conduct disorders such as truancy or lessening in work or job performance |
| Psychological factors affecting physical condition | Used to describe what have been referred to as either psychophysiological or psychosomatic disorders; common examples include migraine headache, painful menstruation, asthma, and duodenal ulcer |
| Personality disorders | Deeply ingrained, inflexible, maladaptive patterns of thought and behavior (for example, the tendency to be socially withdrawn) |
| Conditions not attributable to a mental disorder | Various maladaptations (for example, marital problems, antisocial behavior) for which evidence of mental disorder is not available at the time of diagnosis |

Source: Adapted from Sarason and Sarason, 1980.

**A Note of Caution**

Before we proceed further, it is important to point out that abnormal behavior is not always bizarre. Unfortunately, the public's acquaintance with most abnormal behavior comes from the mass media (newspapers, television, and movies), in which only the extreme forms of emotionally disturbed behavior are likely to be depicted. We read about and see rapists, mass murderers, or child abusers. Such accounts tend to portray mental patients as dangerous "raving maniacs" whose behavior patterns are so totally different from the "normal" that they appear to be almost a species unto themselves.

As a matter of fact, the behavior of most emotionally disturbed persons, whether institutionalized or not, is often not distinguishable from the normal. There is no sharp dividing line where normal ends and abnormal begins. Some individuals are in an almost constant state of turmoil, unable to cope with the everyday requirements of living. All of us are, at one time or another, beset with worry, guilt, or self-doubts. Mostly it is a question of degree. The magnitude of the problems as the individual sees them, and the success he or she has in coping with them, may vary by minute degrees from normal to abnormal. In this normal–abnor-

There is no clear dividing line between normal and abnormal behavior. In a televised interview, brilliant comedian Richard Pryor recalled the periodic incidents of violence and drug abuse that had dogged his career. Despite outbursts of what many would label "abnormal" behavior, Pryor's rise in the entertainment industry indicates his ability to function successfully.

mal continuum, even the same person may shift his or her position at different periods of life and under special circumstances. Otherwise well-adjusted individuals may, at times, be so overwhelmed by life's problems that their ability to make effective adjustments may be impaired. Conversely, changes in one's life situation for the better (a job promotion, an improved marital relationship, or an easing of financial burdens) may result in better adjustment.

A final note of caution: As you read this chapter, you may find that you "recognize" many of the symptoms of disturbed behavior in yourself or others. This is not uncommon. Just as many medical students are likely to perceive symptoms of physical illness in themselves as they read about various disorders, so also are students of psychology prone to imagine themselves victims of psychological disorders. If you have such thoughts as you read, you should note them but not push any panic buttons. It is only through increased knowledge and awareness of the factors underlying emotional disorders that we can gain those special insights that permit us to know ourselves. With such knowledge may come a special bonus: We are able to adjust more effectively to our life situations.

## ANXIETY DISORDERS

*A college student appeared at the counseling center with a complaint that he was deathly afraid of examinations. Although he prepared himself well for tests, the mere mention of an exam would rouse fear in him. He had thus far achieved a fair but not outstanding grade point average. He had previously been involved in a confrontation with an instructor whom he accused of having administered an unfair test in that there was not enough time to answer all the questions. It soon became evident that such antagonistic behavior was a displacement of his frustration with himself. He soon realized that the time limit had not been long enough because he had wasted most of his time in attempting to control his anxieties. He had already skipped two other examinations by remaining in bed petrified with his fears of failure. (Suinn, 1970, p. 242)*

**Anxiety disorders**
Emotional disturbances characterized by maladaptive behavior aimed at avoiding anxiety.

**Defense mechanisms**
Behavior patterns, presumed to be unconscious, aimed at reducing anxiety in the individual.

**Anxiety**
A fear reaction to unknown or unidentified stimuli, a premonition that something bad will happen.

**Anxiety state**
A type of disorder characterized by constant anxiety and tension.

This excerpt from a case history illustrates many of the characteristics of **anxiety disorders.** Its victims are almost constantly unhappy, feel threatened and anxious in situations that most people would not consider dangerous, and avoid threatening situations instead of coping with them. They tend to cling rigidly to behavior patterns that are maladaptive because they provide an immediate, though temporary, relief from anxiety. These behaviors, of course, do not solve the real problem. For example, the student in this illustration on two occasions managed to avoid the acute anxiety associated with examinations by staying in bed, but he was still plagued with his fear when later examinations came up.

What does this behavior accomplish? In the short run, individuals with anxiety disorders "solve" their problems by some kind of avoidance. In the long run, they persist in self-defeating behaviors. They typically react to a threatening situation by calling into play one or more of the **defense mechanisms** (see Chapter 9), usually in an exaggerated fashion.

Resorting to defense mechanisms is a prime example of allowing the tail (defense mechanisms) to wag the dog (the person's life).

Individuals with anxiety disorders usually do not require hospitalization and are not likely to be dangerous to themselves or others. In the sections that follow, we will look at specific types of anxiety disorders. We will be giving examples of "textbook" cases throughout this chapter. We should point out, however, that patients generally display various combinations of symptoms. Rarely, in real life, is there a "pure" type.

## Anxiety States

We may define **anxiety** as a fear reaction to unknown or unidentified stimuli, a premonition that something bad will happen. Box 14.3 presents the dimensions of anxiety. Persons suffering an **anxiety state** are usually in a constant state of anxiety and tension. Occasionally they may have "anxiety attacks" in which they experience intense and unbearable anxiety. These attacks are accompanied by widespread bodily symptoms, such as heart palpitations, profuse sweating, and breathing problems, as well as such psychological symptoms as inability to concentrate, difficulty in decision making, and a pervasive feeling of discouragement.

Anxiety is not in itself abnormal. Everyone experiences anxiety from time to time, but the individual in an anxiety state *constantly* feels threatened even though, to an outsider, there appears to be no real danger. For such an individual, the threat, although unidentifiable, is very real. The following case illustrates both the unfocused nature of anxiety and the acute phases of an anxiety attack:

## BOX 14.3

### Dimensions of Anxiety

**1. Realistic or pathological.** Anxiety is considered realistic when it is appropriate in degree to the objective threat; it is considered pathological when it is out of proportion to the actual threat.

**2. Specific or general.** Anxiety may be elicited by certain specific situations which the individual perceives as threatening; or it may be elicited by a view of the world as a generally dangerous and hostile place.

**3. Aware or unaware.** The individual may be acutely aware of his anxiety, as in an anxiety attack; he may feel vaguely apprehensive and anxious; or his anxiety may be repressed and kept out of awareness.

**4. Acute or chronic.** The individual may evidence sudden intense anxiety in the face of a threatening situation; or he may maintain a chronic, continuously high level of anxiety.

**5. Positive or negative.** At mild levels, anxiety may lead to increased effort and improved performance; at intermediate and higher levels, it may lead to the disorganization of behavior.

These dimensions of anxiety are not necessarily discrete, of course, but rather occur in varying combinations.

Adapted from Coleman, 1976.

© 1979 United Feature Syndicate, Inc.

**Free-floating anxiety**
Anxiety that is diffuse and without focus.

**Obsessive–compulsive disorder**
A type of disorder characterized by persistent and recurring thoughts or actions.

**Obsession**
A recurring thought or impulse that persistently intrudes itself into the individual's consciousness.

**Compulsive behavior**
The impulse to perform some act repeatedly.

*The 26-year-old wife of a successful lawyer came to a psychiatric clinic with the complaint that she had "the jitters." She said she felt that she was going to pieces. She had fears of being alone, of screaming, of running away, and of committing suicide. These fears were all intensified when she came near an open window. She suffered from constant headache, fatigue and nervousness, from episodes of abdominal cramps and diarrhea. Twice in the past year there had been "attacks," in which she had become dizzy and had broken out into a cold sweat. Her hands and feet became clammy, her heart pounded, her head seemed tight, she had a lump in her throat and could not get her breath. (Cameron and Magaret, 1951, p. 307)*

In the anxiety state, anxiety is diffuse and without focus **(free-floating).** In the other anxiety disorders to be discussed here, anxiety is at least partially alleviated by the development of specific symptoms that protect the individual against underlying anxiety. Except for incomplete repression, the individual in an anxiety state generally does not have these defenses.

## Obsessive–Compulsive Disorders

*The biggest thing I've got is this obsession which spoils everything I do. If I had the courage I'd kill myself and get rid of the whole lot—it goes on and on, day after day. The obsession governs everything I do from the minute I open my eyes in the morning until I close them at night. It governs what I can touch, and what I can't touch, where I can walk, and where I can't walk. It governs whatever I do. I can touch the ground but I can't touch shoes, can't touch hems of coats, can't use the toilet without washing my hands and arms half a dozen times—then they must be washed right up the arms. (Marks, 1965, p. 1)*

This case illustrates the pattern of symptoms in an **obsessive-compulsive disorder.** An **obsession** is a recurring thought or impulse that persistently intrudes itself into the individual's consciousness. The **compulsive behavior** is a means of suppressing the anxiety associated with the unpleasant persistent and recurring thoughts or impulses.

All of us at varying times have had obsessive thoughts and engaged in compulsive behaviors. For example, after an important exam, have you found yourself plagued with thoughts such as, "What was the third question?—How did I answer it? Did I leave anything out?" Have you ever engaged in such compulsive behaviors as knocking on wood, doodling, or counting telephone poles as you ride along in a car? We seem to have no control over even these relatively minor obsessions and compulsions. We usually recognize them as being foolish and irrational at the time they occur. It is only when these obsessive–compulsive behaviors seriously interfere with our daily lives that we classify them as obsessive–compulsive disorders. Individuals with such disorders may also recognize the irrationality of their behavior, but feel powerless to stop it. Moreover, they experience great anxiety if their compulsive actions are thwarted.

In later life, billionaire Howard Hughes was plagued by obsessions and compulsions, many of which centered around cleanliness and precision. For example, Hughes insisted that silverware be brought to him on a Kleenex, with the handles wrapped in more Kleenex fastened with tape.

**Phobic Disorders**

We all have moments when we irrationally fear and avoid an object or a situation. But imagine what it would be like to have fear as a constant companion. Imagine fear so overwhelming that it significantly interferes with everyday functioning.

**Phobias** are unreasonable, intense, and persistent fears of situations or objects that do not constitute any real danger to the person. Because they tend to occur under fairly specific circumstances, a large number of phobias have been identified and named according to the situations in which they occur (see Table 14.2). Although the **phobic disorder** may initially represent an intense fear of a specific object or situation, it may rapidly spread to a broad class of situations. The final result is an enormous constriction in one's life activities as virtually everything activates intense anxieties. Although the anxiety is elicited by a specific situation or class of objects, the individual is unaware of the reason for the fear. However, he or she is usually aware that the fear is exaggerated out of proportion to the actual danger.

Some theorists believe that the phobic object is symbolic of some underlying conflict. These theorists might search for some underlying sexual conflict, for example, to explain a phobic fear of snakes.

Other theorists use learning-theory principles to explain the phobic disorder. They argue that fear was originally conditioned to the phobic

Table 14.2

**Types of Phobias**

| | |
|---|---|
| Acrophobia | fear of high places |
| Agoraphobia | fear of open places |
| Astraphobia | fear of thunder and/or lightning |
| Cardiophobia | fear of heart attack |
| Claustrophobia | fear of closed spaces or confinement |
| Hemotaphobia | fear of the sight of blood |
| Hydrophobia | fear of water |
| Lalophobia | fear of (public) speaking |
| Mysophobia | fear of dirt or contamination |
| Nyctophobia | fear of darkness |
| Pathophobia | fear of disease or illness |
| Peccatophobia | fear of sinning |
| Phobophobia | fear of fear |
| Photophobia | fear of intense light |
| Thanatophobia | fear of death |
| Toxophobia | fear of being poisoned |
| Xenophobia | fear of strangers |
| Zoophobia | fear of animals (usually specific kinds) |

Source: Mahoney, 1980.

**Phobia**
An unreasonable, intense, and persistent fear of situations or objects that do not constitute real dangers.

**Phobic disorder**
A type of anxiety disorder characterized by intense fear of a situation or object which the individual realizes constitutes no real personal danger.

**Dissociative disorder**
A type of disorder that involves some impairment of memory functions, usually as a defense to avoid or escape from an anxiety-arousing situation.

object because of its direct or indirect association with a negative emotional state.

The following example describes a woman's fear of open spaces (agoraphobia) in which the initial phase of the disorder consisted of a panic attack:

*Agoraphobia? Fifteen years ago the word meant nothing to most people. Certainly, it meant nothing to the college girl about to sled down the hill in Vermont. As a cold wind hit the hill, she stood holding her chin, looking back at the house in the distance. Her friends heard her mutter something—that she had snow in her boot, or needed the bathroom— some such lie. Then she began to run looking down at the snow. She couldn't look at the house, it seemed too far away. She started to sweat and her legs went soft. She could not feel her feet, but they were running. Her heart was pounding, her face flushed. She began to panic. She felt as though she were coming apart, as if she had been running forever through the syrupy snow of a nightmare. Six Miltowns rattled against four Valiums in her pocket. The sweat on her body tripped triggers in her brain. The adrenalin signaled the nerves to further panic, "What if I die?" she thought. "Oh my God, I'm going crazy." Then she was at the house, the "safe" place, but she had added more fears to an already long list. She was afraid of snow. She was afraid of hills. And above all, she was afraid of ever again feeling the way she did running from that snowy hill in Vermont. (Baumgold, 1977)*

*. . . her panic attack was one of a series of such experiences that made the world around her an increasingly fearful place in which to live. She began to anticipate and avoid situations that might start still another panic attack. To avoid attacks, she shrank her world to situations that seemed "safe." She developed a terror of crowds; as she would drive into a tunnel, she would become terrified that it would not be possible to find an opening at the other end; entering an elevator became impossible. She could only go outside in the company of a friend who would reassure her and stay by her through what most of us think of as routine errands. She found she could not go above the first floor in a department store and often, unaccountably, bolted from games, dentist chairs, and restaurants. It became necessary to make excuses and to even lie to her friends when she missed appointments. Because of her crippling fear, her marriage relationship deteriorated and ultimately ended in divorce. (Price and Lynn, 1981, pp. 134–135)*

Box 14.4 presents several illustrations of phobic disorders with accompanying case examples. Although many of the fears may seem irrational, they are very real to those people who suffer from them.

## DISSOCIATIVE DISORDERS

Despite the fact that they are relatively rare, no form of emotional disorders has attracted such widespread attention as **dissociative disorders**. These involve some impairment of memory functions, perhaps as a defense to avoid or escape from an anxiety-arousing situation. Psychogenic

## BOX 14.4

### Case Examples of Phobic Reactions

**Acrophobia** . . . "Agnes W., an unmarried woman of 30, had been unable to go higher than the second or third floor of any building for a year. Whenever she tried to overcome her fear of height, she only succeeded in provoking intolerable anxiety. She remembered when it all began. One evening she was working alone at the office when she was suddenly seized with a terror lest she jump or fall out of the open eight story window. So frightened was Agnes by her impulse that she crouched behind a steel file for some time before she could trust herself to gather up her things and make for the street. She reached the ground level acutely anxious, perspiring freely, her heart pounding, and breathing rapid" (Cameron, 1963, p. 282).

**Claustrophobia** . . . "Bert C. entered therapy in part because of his fear of elevators. He walked the four flights to his office whenever possible. If he rode in the elevator, he was terrified over the possibility of being trapped and of being mutilated or killed in trying to escape. He often pictured these possibilities to himself" (Cameron, 1963, p. 287).

**Agoraphobia** . . . "Ethel H., a married woman of 26, had suffered her first acute anxiety attack two years before she began therapy. She was arriving alone by plane from England after visiting her parents there.

As she entered the high-ceilinged terminal where no one met her, she suddenly felt terrified by the huge, empty spaciousness. She began 'shaking like a leaf'; she could not get her bags through customs without constant help, she had the impulse to tell everyone around who she was in case she went mad. A porter, sensing her anxiety, expressed his concern over her openly, and this comforted her. She managed the rest of the trip by train without mishap, but reached home exhausted and unnerved, certain that something awful was happening to her" (Cameron, 1963, p. 291).

**Zoophobia** . . . Little Hans, a boy of five years old, refused to go into the street because he was afraid of horses. Actually he feared being bitten by them and no amount of rational persuasion could rid him of his fear.

**Ocholophobia** . . . "M's first phobic attack occurred when she was returning home by airplane. It was night and the place was crowded. The people pressed in around her, and M was seized by an overwhelming feeling of panic that seemed to come 'out of the blue.' Her stomach turned, she couldn't breathe, she was shaking and sweating and frightened by the very thought of the people pressing around her" (Baumgold, 1977.)

Price and Lynn, 1981, p. 137.

---

amnesia is a common example. The victim figuratively escapes a threatening situation by a partial or complete loss of memory of his or her "personal identity." Sometimes there is a special type of amnesia in which the individual literally escapes the situation by fleeing, at the same time forgetting his or her own identity and taking on a new identity. In this **fugue** state, the individual will frequently take on a new personality that has little in common with the person's prior life.

A relatively rare form of dissociative disorder occurs when two or more independent and often opposite personalities exist within the same individual, as in *Dr. Jekyll and Mr. Hyde* (a novel by Robert L. Stevenson) and the book and television movie *Sybil* (Schreiber, 1974). *Sybil* is an outstanding example of a dissociative reaction, in that the woman assumed 16 different and distinct personalities. In the following excerpt, one of the personalities (Vicky) engages in a logical conversation with her therapist

**Fugue**
A type of dissociative disorder in which the individual begins a new life and is amnesic about his prior identity.

Ingrid Bergman and Spencer Tracy in the film version of *Dr. Jekyll and Mr. Hyde.* **In the story, Dr. Jekyll, seeking to discover the secret of the good and evil sides of man's nature, creates a potion that transforms him into a bestial, immoral creature.**

concerning the advisability of informing another of the personalities (Sybil) of the existence of a whole family of personalities within the same skin.

*"And now," the doctor said as she looked steadily at Vicky, "I should like to ask your advice. I would like to tell Sybil about you and the others. What do you think?"*

*"Well," Vicky cautioned thoughtfully, "you can tell her. But be careful. Don't say too much."*

*In a confidential tone the doctor explained, "I think she ought to know. In fact, I don't see how the analysis can go anywhere if she doesn't."*

*"Be careful," Vicky reiterated. "Although the rest of us know about Sybil, she knows nothing about any of us, never has."*

*"I understand that, Vicky, but you see, I had planned to tell her about Peggy Lou when I thought she was a dual personality. But Sybil didn't give me a chance."*

*"Of course not," Vicky explained. "Sybil's always been afraid to reveal her symptoms—afraid of a diagnosis."*

*"Well," the doctor continued quietly, "I did tell Sybil that she is subject to fugue states during which she is unaware of what's happening."*

*"I know,"* Vicky asserted, *"but that's very different from telling her that she's not alone in her own body."*

*"I think it will reassure Sybil to know that she is functioning even though she doesn't know it."*

*"She, Doctor?"* Vicky asked quizzically. *"Isn't the pronoun we?"*

*The doctor paused and made no direct answer. It was a thoughtful Vicky who broke the silence, saying, "I suppose you can tell Sybil. But I repeat: is it* she *who is functioning?" Without waiting for the doctor to reply, Vicky asserted, "We're people, you know. People in our own right."\**

## SOMATOFORM DISORDERS

There are occasions when an individual will go to a physician with complaints of pain and/or loss of some physical function. Upon examination, no organic basis for the complaint is found, but there is reason to suspect that psychological factors, such as unresolved conflicts, are implicated. The individual may be suffering a **somatoform disorder.** It is important to note that the symptoms are not under the conscious control of the individual. Telling the person, "It's all in your head," will do nothing to relieve the condition.

## Somatization Disorders

*John M. was admitted to a psychiatric hospital following a history of job failure and an unstable family background. He made numerous complaints about his physical health. His concerns began when he experienced a swelling of his glands, which led him to seek help from numerous doctors, all of whom gave him treatments, but no treatment yielded relief. Ultimately, his physical complaints became so severe that he was unable to work.*

*He is a friendly, pleasant, docile person expressing deep concern about his physical health. He reports that he believes his sex glands are infected, that he has a hernia, suffers from constipation, and has continuous feelings of tightness and pain in his abdomen. While discussing his physical health, he shows deep preoccupation; but later, on another topic, seems relatively indifferent and even cheerful. (Adapted from Kisker, 1964)*

In this case example, we see all the features of a typical **somatization disorder:** John M. is preoccupied with the state of his health, he is constantly monitoring his body for signs of undesirable symptoms, and he rejects medical diagnoses that there is no physical disease. Indeed, like most people suffering a somatization disorder, John spends considerable time shopping around for a physician who will confirm his fear that there is something physically wrong.

---

**Somatoform disorder**
A type of disorder characterized by physical symptoms.

**Somatization disorder**
A type of disorder in which physical complaints are prominent.

**Conversion disorder**
A type of disorder characterized by sensory or motor impairment without any physical cause.

**Anesthesias**
Loss of sensitivity in some part of the body.

---

\*Reprinted from *Sybil* by Flora Rheta Schreiber, © 1973, with permission of Contemporary Books, Inc., Chicago, Illinois.

**Conversion**
**Disorders**

In **conversion disorders** (sometimes called *hysteria*), the individual suffers sensory or motor impairment (for example, blindness, paralysis, or **anesthesias** [see Fig. 14.1]) without any physical cause. However, the symptoms are not faked; they are genuine. In addition, some patients with conversion disorders seem to be indifferent to the disability and tend to resist treatment. This has been called *la belle indifference* ("beautiful indifference," or apathy). The following case shows both the defensive value of conversion disorders and the attitude of the patient toward his disability:

> *The patient was a young college student involved in a minor traffic accident on his way home from classes. Although he was slightly bruised, medical examination showed no serious physical involvement and the patient was discharged from the hospital. He awakened the next morning with a numbness in his legs and found himself unable to move them. He was returned by ambulance to the hospital for extensive neurological X-ray examinations with negative results.*
>
> *Throughout, the patient seemed bemused by the procedures, intrigued by the machinery, and taken by the nurses. The diagnosis: conversion reaction.*
>
> *This college student was interviewed by a psychologist and the following facts came to light. Just prior to the accident, he had another of many arguments with his family over his education. He preferred to seek employment in order to obtain an income. His parents, both from immigrant backgrounds, had forced him to continue his schooling in spite of constant bickering. He was on an allowance on the condition that he remain in school. Money had always been a problem since the patient*

Figure 14.1
**Hysterical anesthesias**

Individuals suffering from hysterical anesthesias (loss of feeling) typically report a lack of sensation in the areas shown in color. Note that this does not correspond to the normal neurological pattern indicated by the lines.

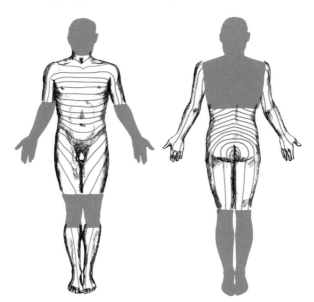

*tended to squander it on social activities, girl friends, and his motorbike. The patient admitted that he had not prepared himself for final examinations and was certain he would have failed them since he was incapable of successfully cramming. The draft had already taken some of his peers and he was positive that he would also be called once he lost his student deferment from the draft. The accident itself came as a surprise since he had always been reasonably cautious on his motorbike. Yet, he had driven in a carefree and even reckless fashion when the accident occurred. When he was first released from the hospital he felt "kinda lucky that I wasn't killed, but kinda sorry I wasn't scraped up more than I was." The impression was that a disabling injury would have been painful but useful. (Suinn, 1970, p. 238)*

## PERSONALITY DISORDERS

Unlike anxiety, dissociative, and somatoform disorders, personality disorders are disturbances without clear-cut physiological symptoms. Instead, individuals with personality disorders exhibit long-standing, inflexible, maladaptive ways of relating to the larger society. Table 14.3 shows the disorders in this category. We will focus our attention on the disorder most studied: the antisocial personality.

## The Antisocial Personality

Sometimes referred to as a psychopath or sociopath, the person with an **antisocial personality** is something of an enigma. Unlike those who are assailed by anxiety disorders, individuals with antisocial personalities are characterized by the absence of the extremes of anxiety and the various defenses against it. They lack impulse control and may engage in cheating, lying, or stealing with no apparent feeling of guilt or remorse. In extreme cases, they may kill, over and over, with no sense of doing wrong. Nevertheless, this is not to deny that they sometimes show signs of distress. They frequently evidence tension, difficulty in tolerating boredom, and depression, and they may feel (often rightly) that others are hostile toward them.

The successful ones may outwardly be extremely charming, possess engaging personalities, and impress people with disarming frankness. They often know how to say the right thing at the right time. But under this veneer of social desirability is an individual who does not hesitate to take advantage of others in the pursuit of goals. Perhaps because of this, individuals with antisocial personalities are characteristically incapable of maintaining good interpersonal relationships. However, because they are occasionally "successful" in their business, social, or sexual exploits, they see little reason to change. They are, therefore, highly resistant to all forms of therapy.

The majority of antisocial personalities are not successful in life. They fail to hold jobs or become independent and self-sustaining adults. Much of their time is spent in institutions, often penal rather than medical. They exhibit no respect for authority and seem incapable of learning from

**Antisocial personality** A personality disorder characterized by the absence of both anxiety and the various defenses against it.

Table 14.3

**Personality Disorders Described in *DSM*-III**

1. *Paranoid Personality Disorder:* Pervasive and unwarranted suspiciousness and mistrust of others

2. *Introverted Personality Disorder:* Inability and lack of desire to form social relationships

3. *Schizotypical Personality Disorder:* Tendency toward schizophrenic-type language, thought, and misperceptions without any sign of psychotic break with reality

4. *Histrionic Personality Disorder* (Hysterical Personality): Excitability, self-dramatization, attention-seeking behavior, shallowness, and lack of genuineness; frequently is manipulative of others by suicidal threats, gestures, or attempts

5. *Narcissistic Personality Disorder:* Self-centeredness with a grandiose sense of self-importance; exhibitionistic tendencies, requiring constant attention and admiration; lack of empathy for others and a tendency to exploit others for personal gain; vacillation of moods between over-idealization of self and extreme self-devaluation

6. *Antisocial Personality Disorder:* History of tantrums and chronic antisocial behavior (lying, thefts, vandalism, aggressive behavior, etc.), in which the rights of others are violated

7. *Borderline Personality Disorder:* Stormy personality who drifts into psychotic states under stress

8. *Avoidant Personality Disorder:* Low self-esteem, hypersensitivity to rejection, social withdrawal, and unwillingness to enter into relationships unless given strong guarantees of uncritical acceptance

9. *Dependent Personality Disorder:* Low self-confidence, fear of self-reliance, reliance on others to assume responsibility for major areas of life; feelings of intense discomfort when alone

10. *Compulsive Personality Disorder:* Many signs of obsessive–compulsive neurotic actions (indecisiveness, preoccupation, etc.)

past experience, feeling themselves to be immune from the consequences of their actions. Consider the following case of an antisocial personality:

> *Louis was considered by his family always to have been an "angry child." He simply would not mind. "Father would spank him and put him in a corner, but he would come out and do the same thing again and get spanked again." Both parents were extremely strict. They had come from deprived backgrounds and wanted their children to grow up to be "good citizens" and have a different life than they had had. Mother, who had been beaten by her father many times, felt some obligation to protect Louis when his father lost control in punishing him.*
>
> *Louis was particularly fatalistic in his attitude toward his problems when he came to the Clinic at age 15. He was aware of his lack of impulse*

Convicted thief, forger, pimp, and murderer, Charles Manson—like other antisocial personalities—has a talent for sensing the weaknesses of others and using them to his own advantage.

*control but had little hope of gaining control through his parents' way of "handling" him. He could envision only further antisocial behavior and eventual destruction of himself. He was unable to identify with a father whom he saw as passive and ineffectual but potentially destructive.*

*Louis was one of the older subjects seen in the follow-up. At 28, he was an unemployed truck driver. He had been fired for physically attacking his boss, an attack which he felt was justified because the boss was "unfair" to him. He had been discharged from military service a few years earlier as "incapable of adapting to military life."*

*His relationship to his family was still a hostile, dependent one. He and his father argued constantly. "Sometimes I don't talk to dad or mom at all for weeks at a time." His relationship with peers is equally poor. He described much rowdy, antisocial behavior with a gang of fellows who rode motorcycles in a group. "I used to get so smacked when I was out with them that the guys would put me on my cycle and head me toward my house." He is proud of his marksmanship with a gun. "I keep a pistol and it's loaded. Dad ordered me to get rid of it, but I wouldn't."*

*Louis' need to prove his masculinity in these symbolic ways is accompanied by an intense hatred of homosexual men. "I can't tolerate bisexual men and if I meet one in a dark alley, I'll smack them up. If they want their teeth, they'd better keep moving." (Cass and Thomas, 1979, p. 175)*

It is important to note that the antisocial personality does not always manifest itself in criminal activities, and not all criminals have antisocial personalities—in fact, most delinquents and criminals do not. A person may cheat, steal, and even murder and still have a code of ethics and maintain close interpersonal relationships. For example, members of the Mafia may commit a wide variety of crimes repulsive to many people, yet they have rules by which they live and show a high regard for loyalty to the group and family. Antisocial personalities owe allegiance only to themselves. Their only code is to get what they want; no one and nothing else matters.

## PSYCHOSEXUAL DISORDERS

The disorders covered in this category are extremely diverse, ranging from a variety of unconventional sexual behaviors to various sexual adjustment problems or dysfunctions. They include problems with gender identity, such as transsexualism, a disorder in which there is a persistent sense of discomfort and conflict between an individual's psychological gender and his or her biological sex.

Included also are a number of disorders characterized by an "unusual" choice of sexual object, such as in pedophilia, where an adult uses children for achieving sexual gratification. Most cases of pedophilia do not involve actual sexual intercourse or violence (Jaffe, 1976).

Another group of disorders involves unusual sexual activities such as exhibitionism, the act of exposing one's genitals to an unsuspecting observer; and sexual sadism, in which the individual inflicts physical or psychological suffering on another person in order to achieve sexual gratification.

**Ego-dystonic homosexuality** is also included in this category. It should be noted that this disorder does not include homosexuals who are comfortable with their sexual orientation. Box 14.5 discusses some of the controversies surrounding this classification.

**Ego-dystonic homosexuality** A disorder in which homosexual arousal is a persistent source of distress to the individual.

Of all the psychosexual disorders, psychosexual dysfunctions are probably the most common, particularly in their milder forms. In the following section we discuss a variety of these adjustment problems.

## Psychosexual Dysfunctions

*Over the years of our marriage my sexual desire for my wife has diminished gradually to the point that it is presently almost nonexistent. There have been too many disputes over how we raise the children, too many insensitive comments, too many demands, not enough freedom to be my own person. When I look at her I have to acknowledge that she is a remarkably beautiful woman, just as lovely as the day I was first attracted to her. I certainly feel no physical repulsion to her body. I guess it would be more accurate to say that I simply no longer have sexual feelings for her. One feeling I do have plenty of is hostility. I suspect it is this largely suppressed anger that has been the killer of my sexual interest. I wonder what it would be like if we could go back to the early years of our marriage when there were no children and the conflicts were few and the loving was good.\**

---

*Reprinted by permission from Crooks, R., and Baur, K., *Our Sexuality*, Menlo Park, California, The Benjamin/Cummings Publishing Company, Inc., 1980, p. 280.

## BOX 14.5

### Ego-dystonic Homosexuality

Ego-dystonic homosexuality is sexual desire toward a member of one's own sex that is "unacceptable to the ego" or a source of personal anxiety and conflict. The inclusion of this category in the DSM-III is a result of the continuing controversy between 1. those who consider homosexuality to be a maladaptive behavior resulting from pathological forces experienced during developmental stages and 2. clinicians, supported by members of the gay (organized homosexual) community, who see homosexuality as a normal variant of sexual expression. The longstanding controversy had previously been aired at a special session held at the 1973 meetings of the American Psychiatric Association to determine whether the classification of homosexuality as a mental disorder should be retained in the then-existing DSM-II (Stoller et al., 1973).

At that meeting, two well-known psychiatrists, Irving Bieber and Charles Socarides, supported the traditional view of homosexuality as a psychosexual disorder resulting from disturbed relationships between parents and their children and recommended that this classification should be retained in the DSM-II. When that proposal encountered opposition, Bieber suggested that homosexual behavior be reclassified as a category of sexual dysfunction, since "most homosexuals (especially those who are exclusively homosexual) cannot function heterosexually" (Stoller *et al.*, 1973). This too was considered inappropriate by many clinicians and practitioners. Most homosexuals function well in sexual relationships with members of the same sex, and many of them are bisexual. The issue was one of preference rather than function.

In the symposium devoted to this topic, Stoller, Marmon, and Spitzer (Stoller et al., 1973) supported the removal of homosexuality from the DSM-II nomenclature, preferring to consider it a normal variant of human sexual behavior.

After considering the issues, the trustees of the American Psychiatric Association voted on December

This case example illustrates the significance of personal and emotional factors in the human sexual response. It is not unusual for marital partners to find each other attractive after years of marriage. Indeed, as Box 14.6 illustrates, neither the length of marriage nor the age of the partners necessarily precludes a satisfying and healthy sexual relationship. However, constant bickering and fighting can erode any human relationship, particularly the most intimate. Hostility and sex make poor bedfellows.

What causes sexual problems? It's an easier question to ask than to answer. There are many factors that contribute to the quality of sexual experiences, such as learning during childhood; personal factors, including one's knowledge and attitudes; emotional considerations; interpersonal communication; and sexual orientation. In this section, we look at some of the more common sexual problems that plague both men and women. Although we will allude to some possible contributing factors, we will avoid the direct question of "cause."

*Imagine a man with a large light bulb on top of his head that lights up every time he has an erection. When he sees a sexy woman at the office the bulb starts to warm up. When he finds his wife at home in a slinky nightgown, the light gets even brighter. When she touches his [penis], it's top voltage and that bulb is shining like a beacon. Now imagine the*

15, 1973 to remove homosexuality from the DSM-II. A new category, Sexual Orientation Disturbance, was created and applied to those individuals who desired to change from a homosexual to a heterosexual orientation. DSM-III retained this compromise category, which is now called *ego-dystonic homosexuality*. Members of the gay community object to this category, however, because it means that some homosexuals may be viewed as "sick."

While the DSM-III states explicity that "homosexuality itself is not considered a mental disorder," it does state that "factors that predispose an individual to ego-dystonic homosexuality are those negative societal attitudes toward homosexuality that have been internalized" (p. 282). In other words, pressures to conform to societal standards and the desire to have children and a "socially sanctioned family life" may be incompatible with homosexuality. The diagnostic criteria for this category include "a persistent pattern of absent or weak heterosexual arousal" that interferes with establishing *desired* heterosexual relationships and a "sustained pattern of homosexual arousal" that is *unwanted* and distressing to the individual (DSM-III).

This diagnosis becomes inappropriate if an individual adjusts to his or her sexual orientation. There is some evidence that in time many individuals with homosexual inclinations give up the yearning to become heterosexual. In addition, the DSM-III points out that without intervention the development of heterosexual adjustment in these individuals "is rare" and that even with therapy the outcome is "disputed." It is obvious that this category was forged out of compromise. Whether or not this classification will prove helpful to clinicians and to the homosexuals who are unhappy with their sexual orientation must await its use in actual clinical practice.

Sue *et al.*, 1981, pp. 471–473.

---

*same bedroom scene, light bulb on head, but Nothing Happens. Zip. A complete blackout that you can't miss. That's what it feels like to have an erection problem. (Penney, 1981, p. 91)*

One author contends, "There probably isn't a man alive who has not, at some time or another in his life, been unable to have or to keep an erection" (Penney, 1981, p. 91). The ability to achieve and maintain an erection is not always under the individual's control. Many factors can serve as a "wet blanket" to this basic biological response. These include, but are not limited to, physical disorders, repressive sexual training, homosexual orientation, and a carry-over of psychological trauma associated with the first attempt at intercourse.

Physical illnesses are implicated in only a small percentage of sexual problems. These illnesses include diabetes, high blood pressure, and the aftereffects of surgery on the prostate gland. However, the use of drugs (such as "downers") and alcohol can temporarily suppress a man's ability to achieve and maintain an erection. Chronic abuse of drugs can lead to long-term difficulties.

By and large, however, sexual dysfunction is associated with nonbiological factors. To illustrate, repressive childhood training is frequently the culprit. A child who has been taught that sex is disgusting, sinful, dirty, and shameful cannot simply discard this training like a useless item

## BOX 14.6

### Upsetting an Old Taboo

Her face is lined, her hair white, her hands veined and bony. His features show the years of work, of children brought to adulthood, even of tragedy. Both of them are in their 70s.

But their walk has a snap as they stroll down the streets, backs straight. Their eyes sparkle when you talk to them, and they are more ready to smile than to grouse. Almost unconsciously, she grasps his upper arm. And if he thinks nobody is looking, he will let his hand slide slowly down her back.

Shocking? Only to those people who think that sexual activity among the elderly is ridiculous. Yet science is finding that as people get older, the majority seek and need sex as much as, and sometimes more than, young people. In fact, if older people stop having sex, it is mostly because they are physically sick or they have nobody willing to share intimacy with them.

Society at large shames many oldsters for their sexual longings. Dr. Eric Pfeiffer—professor of psychiatry and director of the Sun Coast Gerontology Center, University of South Florida—says that society places "a continuing taboo regarding sexual expression in old age." And this is happening in an era that is open to sex activity at all other ages.

. . . every survey shows that the vast majority like sex, want to have it and are sexually active. A 1980 study of 800 men and women over 60—by Drs. Bernard D. Starr and Marcella Bakur Weiner, psychologists at Brooklyn College in New York—revealed that 96 per cent like sex and 80 percent still have sexual relations. Of those in their 80s, two out of five still have sex.

Nevertheless, despite the evidence for continuing interest, more and more people abstain from sex in each decade of life. For men, impotence plays a big role—they simply can no longer become aroused. For women, opportunities disappear. Because women live eight years longer than men on the average, they soon outnumber men, which compounds their difficulties. Of every 10 older women, studies show, six have no mates; out of every 10 older men, only two are unmarried. Men, therefore, have the chance to be much more active sexually than women.

Most experts believe that if there were equal numbers of men and women, women would be the more active sex. "Women's sex drive continues to grow until they reach their 30s and remains the same throughout their lives," says Dr. Carol C. Flax, a New York City sex therapist. "For men, drive reaches a peak at 19 and then goes down, eventually disappearing for many."

Experts argue over whether to blame the decline

of clothing when adult status is achieved. As one young woman observed: "I dutifully followed the expectation to be chaste until marriage. However, a fifteen-minute ceremony did not make me instantly sexually responsive. My inhibition was a great disappointment to my husband and myself."*

The most common sexual complaint among women is the inability to achieve orgasm. Education and upbringing have been cited as the chief underlying causes of this female problem. However, not all failures of women to achieve orgasm can be laid at their feet. A female whose primary sexual experiences have been with men who reach orgasm too soon **(premature ejaculation)** may never have had the opportunity to experience an orgasm.

---

*Reprinted by permission from Crooks, R., and Baur, K., *Our Sexuality,* Menlo Park, California, The Benjamin/Cummings Publishing Company, Inc., 1980, p. 286.

in men on social or physical causes. Most agree that many older men who no longer seek sexual activity are in fact sexually potent and have just given up because they cannot perform as they did in their youth. Young men are quickly aroused, remain aroused and are aroused again quickly. As they grow older, many men believe they have lost potency because events go more slowly. They refuse to adapt.

In general, what you did sexually at 30 governs what you will do at 70. Dr. Mary Calderone—President of the Sex Information and Education Council of the U.S. (SIECUS) and one of the world's leading sexologists—says it is not true that you are born with a certain amount of sex capacity, which you can use up if you are too active in youth. "The more you use it," Calderone says, "the less you lose it—and that's not true of any bank account I've ever heard of." In other words, you can't save it for your old age. Men and women who start sex early and perform frequently do so into their later years.

If a man has an erection in the morning or during sleep, then no matter what his age, he is capable of sexual relations. In many medical centers, sleep laboratories measure sex-organ response during sleep. In the sex act, however, an older man may require more and longer physical stimulation. And it may take longer to achieve climax, a fact often appreciated by his partner.

As with women, older men stop having sex if they lack an interested partner. Both need someone to touch and to love. More than young people, they respond to cuddling, touching, perfumes and words of endearment. If there is someone around who is caring, the physical act follows. Older people are, in a way, more romantic than younger ones. The elderly seek and value intimacy more.

Many married couples get bored with each other not only sexually but intellectually and emotionally. To keep sex alive, experts say, it is important to find not only new things to do in bed, but new things to think about and to be concerned with.

Society has placed a heavy burden on older people. Sex for them, we say, is unseemly. We have equated sexiness with youth—the body smooth, rounded and unlined in women; tight, rippling muscles in men. Vigor equals virility. Old women are regarded as intrinsically ugly and unsexy, and old men are seen as repulsive. These attitudes make it all the more difficult for an older person to keep an interest in sex.

Sex for those getting older, the experts declare, is not only right and proper. It may be critical for their mental health. It should not be denied them.

Ubell, 1981, pp. 4–5.

---

**Premature ejaculation**
Consistently reaching orgasm so quickly as either to significantly lower subjective enjoyment of the experience and/or to impair the gratification of one's partner.

**Coitus**
The technical term for sexual intercourse.

**Retarded ejaculation**
The inability to ejaculate during intercourse.

What is premature ejaculation? It does not appear possible to define the term in a completely satisfactory way. For sexual partners accustomed to gaining satisfaction through **coitus,** it is easy to agree that a male who ejaculates prior to penetration is premature. But after penetration is achieved, how short a period is required to qualify as premature? To avoid putting a time clock on intercourse, some observers have included in the definition the partner's pleasure as well as the individual's subjective needs.

Like women who are unable to achieve orgasm, some males suffer from **retarded ejaculation.** They have no difficulty achieving and maintaining an erection. They just seem unable to ejaculate during intercourse. Psychological factors, such as guilt about sex, anxiety, and dislike of the partner appear to be contributory factors in this problem.

Worry about disappointing a sexual partner can also lead to sexual problems. As one observer has noted:

*Regardless of the nature of any particular sexual inadequacy, fears of performance are almost bound to affect both partners adversely. For example, if the male tends to be impotent, he will approach any opportunity for sexual intercourse with the fear that he will fail to obtain an erection, or that if he does he will be unable to retain it long enough to achieve coitus. This fear can be so intense that as such a man approaches a sexual situation, he loses all sense of the pleasure associated with this naturally occurring event, and may even break out in a cold sweat. Thus the fear itself destroys the nature of the sexual situation, and an erection becomes virtually impossible. On the other hand, the female partner of such a man is constantly worried not only on his behalf, but also that she will do something or behave in such a way as to embarrass him or aggravate his problem. Thus the sexual partners turn what should be a pleasurable and natural part of their relationship into a fear-ridden emotional nightmare. The same sort of situation can develop in reverse if the female has difficulty achieving orgasm—whatever the reason may be. She starts to worry that something is wrong with her, or that she is sexually inadequate. During sexual intercourse her fear of performance becomes the dominant aspect of the event, which of course only aggravates her problem. The concerned male partner, on the other hand, fears that it is his inadequacy which is responsible for her failure to reach orgasm. (Pengelley, 1978, pp. 104–105)*

## AFFECTIVE DISORDERS

**Manic state**
A mood characterized by excessive euphoria and excitement.

**Depressive state**
A mood characterized by excessive sadness and hopelessness.

Most of us have experienced fairly routine shifts in mood. At times we are cheerful, confident, and optimistic. At other times, we become blue, question our own abilities and accomplishments, and look to the next few hours of life with an uneasy feeling. These swings are commonplace among most of us and are not a cause for alarm. In some individuals, however, there is a marked disturbance in mood in which a prolonged emotion colors their entire psychic life. The most common mood changes involve either a highly agitated or a severely depressed state. In the agitated cycle, the **manic state,** the individual is usually cheerful, hyperactive, and distractable, and projects the image of an inflated self-esteem. In contrast, the **depressive state** involves a profound mood of sadness and hopelessness. This depressed mood is accompanied by appetite disturbances, loss of sleep, decreased energy, and feelings of worthlessness or guilt.

DSM-III describes three types of major affective disorders. In a *manic episode* the manic state prevails. The *major depressive episode* is dominated by a mood of deep depression. Finally, the *mixed bipolar disorder* involves both manic episodes and major depressive episodes, intermixed or alternating every few days (*DSM*-III, 1980, p. 217).

## Manic Episodes

*When I start going into a high, I no longer feel like an ordinary housewife. Instead I feel organized and accomplished and I begin to feel I am my most creative self. I can write poetry easily. I can compose melodies*

Abraham Lincoln was affected by a depressive disorder that was characterized by persistent feelings of sadness, hopelessness, and guilt or inadequacy.

*without effort. I can paint. My mind feels facile and absorbs everything. I have countless ideas about improving the conditions of mentally retarded children, of how a hospital for these children should be run, what they should have around them to keep them happy and calm and unafraid. I see myself as being able to accomplish a great deal for the good of people. I have countless ideas about how the environment problem could inspire a crusade for the health and betterment of everyone. I feel able to accomplish a great deal for the good of my family and others. I feel pleasure, a sense of euphoria or elation. I want it to last forever. I don't seem to need much sleep. I've lost weight and feel healthy and I like myself. I've just bought six new dresses, in fact, and they look quite good on me. I feel sexy and men stare at me. Maybe I'll have an affair, or perhaps several. I feel capable of speaking and doing good in politics. I would like to help people with problems similar to mine so they won't feel hopeless.*

*It's wonderful when you feel like this. . . . The feeling of exhilaration—the high mood—makes me feel light and full of the joy of living. However, when I go beyond this stage, I become manic, and the creativeness becomes so magnified I begin to see things in my mind that aren't real. For instance, one night I created an entire movie, complete with cast, that I still think would be terrific. I saw the people as clearly as if watching them in real life. I also experienced complete terror, as if it were actually happening, when I knew that an assassination scene was about to take place. I cowered under the covers and became a complete shaking wreck. As you know, I went into a manic psychosis at that point. My screams awakened my husband, who tried to reassure me that we were in our bedroom and everything was the same. There was nothing to be afraid of. Nevertheless, I was admitted to the hospital the next day. (Fieve, 1975, pp. 17–18)*

In this example of a manic episode, we see the high excitement, elation, and overactivity of the individual. The person may run wildly about the room, singing, shouting, and gesturing dramatically. His or her conversation is often erratic, reflecting confused thoughts and ideas. Occasionally, however, the dominating mood is one of irritability, especially when the individual is thwarted.

## Major Depressive Episodes

The symptoms in the depressive episode are almost the complete opposite of those in the manic state. Patients in the depressive state show an extreme slowing down of mental and physical activity. They feel dejected, worthless, and guilty. Frequently they attempt suicide (see Fig. 14.2).

The following excerpt describes the depressive episode of a 30-year-old single woman, Carol, right after learning that her male companion had accepted a promotion that involved his transfer to a new office about 30 miles away.

*Carol remained at home in bed for the next three days, not allowing John to visit her because she felt she was contagious. After she returned to work she continued to feel very lethargic, had difficulty concentrating, could not regain her appetite, "and felt quite depressed and tearful for no reason at all."*

*Convincing herself that she had not yet fully recovered from the "flu," she canceled several dates with John so that she could get more rest. She described him as being very understanding about this, even encouraging her to get some time off from work to take a short trip by herself and really rest and relax.*

**Figure 14.2**
**Suicide rates for men and women by age group**

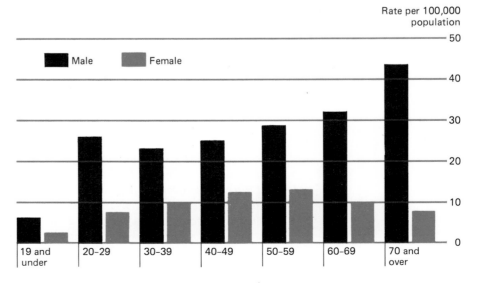

*During this same time, John had begun to spend increasing amounts of time at his new office. Their coffee-break meetings became very infrequent. Within the next week he expected to be moved completely.*

*The night before Carol came to the crisis center she had come home from work expecting to meet John there for dinner; instead she found a note under her door written by her neighbor. It said that John had telephoned him earlier in the day and left word for her that he had "suddenly been called out of town . . . wasn't sure when he would be back . . . but would get in touch with her later."*

*She told the therapist, "Suddenly I felt empty . . . that everything was over between us. It was just too much for me to handle. He was never going to see me again and was too damned chicken to tell me to my face! I went numb all over. . . . I just wanted to die." She paused a few minutes, head down and sobbing, then took a deep breath and went on. "I really don't remember doing it, but the next thing I was aware of was the telephone ringing. When I reached out to answer it, I suddenly realized I had a butcher knife in my right hand and my left wrist was cut and bleeding terribly! I dropped the knife on the floor and grabbed the phone. It was John calling me from the airport to tell me why he had to go out of town so suddenly—his father was critically ill."\**

## Mixed Bipolar Disorders

As previously indicated, a person suffering a mixed bipolar disorder displays the symptoms of both manic and depressive episodes intermixed or in rapid alternation every few days. The following excerpt from the history of Madeline K. illustrates the manic state:

*Her husband had returned home to find her twirling around the living room bizarrely draped in her wedding gown tied with a bathtowel and wearing a lampshade. She gaily greeted him, laughed and with an ear-piercing shrillness, invited him to stay for the exciting "coming-out" party she was giving. Strewn on the table were a thousand handwritten invitations signed with a flourish and addressed to such dignitaries as the President of the United States, the justices of the Supreme Court, the Emperor of Japan. She made incessant noises: singing her own ballads, shouting mottoes which she devised, reciting limericks, making rhyming sounds, and yelling obscenities. She had recorded her speech for presentation to the Library of Congress. The following is an excerpt:*

*"(Singing) By yon briefs—my briefs are entirely outrageous but God take me you'd best like it—(in normal voice) the world is round the world is crown'd—illusion of Georgie, once a porgie—can't you see?—I am worth more than all the cherries in the universe—red is beautiful, red is ripe—bow ye before me and receive my blessing—thank God I'm not the devil—the freshest thing on earth is a newborn clod—to work is to win—twin*

---

*From Aguilera, Donna C., and Messick, Janice M.: *Crisis Intervention*, ed. 4, St. Louis, 1982, The C. V. Mosby Co., pp. 117–119.

*is as twin does—I sing a song of sexpot—hand me your head on a platter and I will forgive you all your sins—my plan will earn you a hundred-thousand-fold—mishmoshmoneymash—slipperydickerypop—dam it all full speed abreast—my head is gold, my hands are silver, my tail is platinum—Where am I? What time is it? Who goes there?—Gee but it's marvelous to be alive. . . ." (Suinn, 1970, p. 367)*

The following presents a portrait of Madeline K. during a depressive state.

*An acquaintance had noticed her gradual refusal to leave her apartment and her apathetic attitude toward herself and the world around her. She looked immensely weary and had not slept soundly for days. She seemed mute, but would occasionally reply if a question were repeated long enough. Through careful probing it was found that she believed herself responsible for the "epidemics of the world" which she said was her punishment for earlier sickness. She felt an urge to do penance for a lifetime of sin but could not remember the exact nature of her sin. For the past three weeks she had remained indoors pondering her own evil nature, and fearful of going out and possibly infecting others through the sheer enormity of her evilness. Life looked hopeless, she felt as though she was living in a shadow of despondency, despair enveloped her very existence. In the hospital she typically retired to a dark corner and would sit motionless for hours, heaving an occasional deep sigh. She seemed on the verge of weeping but her sorrow was never able to break loose. She was easily led by the nursing aids to different rooms, but once there she resumed her previous posture and ruminating. (Suinn, 1970, pp. 367–368)*

## SCHIZO-PHRENIC DISORDERS

**Schizophrenia**
A type of psychosis characterized by personality disorganization, withdrawal from reality, disturbed thought processes, and emotional disorders.

**Delusion**
A belief that is contrary to reality.

**Hallucination**
A sensory experience in the absence of appropriate sensory stimulation.

Individuals suffering anxiety disorders or psychosexual dysfunctions are rarely so disturbed as to require hospitalization. In contrast, people suffering from some of the most extreme forms of emotional disturbance—such as **schizophrenia**—must often be admitted to institutions, at least temporarily.

What is schizophrenia? This is a highly controversial question. There is even considerable disagreement about whether schizophrenia is a single mental disorder or, instead, many different disorders with similar symptoms. Although patients diagnosed as schizophrenic share certain symptoms, such as loss of contact with reality and inability to function normally in society, they also display some distinctively different behaviors. These differences constitute the most widely accepted basis for differentiating the types of schizophrenia. Table 14.4 shows the five different types identified in *DSM*-III. We shall look more closely at three of these types: disorganized, catatonic, and paranoid.

*Disorganized schizophrenia* (formerly called hebephrenic schizophrenia) is characterized by the display of emotions that are inappropriate to the situation. Behavior is often silly and foolish; conversation is rambling and

Table 14.4
**Schizophrenic Subtypes Identified in *DSM*-III**

| Type | Characteristics |
|---|---|
| Disorganized type | Patients show disorganized thinking, shallow and inappropriate affect, unpredictable giggling, silly and regressive behavior and mannerisms, and frequent hypochondriacal complaints. Delusions and hallucinations, if present, are transient and not well organized. |
| Catatonic type | Patients show marked psychomotor disturbance, which may involve stupor, negativism, rigidity, excitement, or posturing. Sometimes there is rapid alternation between the extremes of excitement and stupor. Associated features include stereotypes, mannerisms, and waxy flexibility. Mutism is particularly common. During catatonic stupor or excitement the individual needs careful supervision to avoid hurting him- or herself or others, and medical care may be needed because of malnutrition, exhaustion, hyperpyrexia, or self-inflicted injury. |
| Paranoid type | This type is characterized primarily by the presence of persecutory or grandiose delusions, often associated with hallucinations. Excessive religiosity is sometimes seen. The patient's attitude is frequently hostile and aggressive, and his behavior tends to be consistent with his delusions. In general the disorder does not manifest the gross personality disorganization of the disorganized and catatonic types, perhaps because the patient uses the mechanism of projection, which ascribes to others characteristics he cannot accept in himself. Three subtypes of the disorder may sometimes be differentiated, depending on the predominant symptoms: hostile, grandiose, and hallucinatory. |
| Undifferentiated type | Patients show mixed schizophrenic symptoms and present definite schizophrenic thought, affect, and behavior not classifiable under the other types of schizophrenia. This type is distinguished from the schizoid personality. |
| Residual type | Patients show signs of schizophrenia but, following a psychotic schizophrenic episode, are no longer psychotic. |

Source: Adapted from Price and Lynn, 1981, p. 271; *DSM*-III, 1980, pp. 190–191.

incoherent and contains many neologisms (words made up by the individual). Victims sometimes have scattered and disorganized **delusions** (false beliefs) and **hallucinations** (sensory experiences in the absence of appropriate sensory stimulation). Many of the features of disorganized schizophrenia are discernible in the following case:

> *Edna K. was a 45-year-old wife of a laborer. Her illness had progressed rapidly and she was quite severely disturbed by the time of her admission to the hospital. It was impossible to obtain a meaningful description of her condition directly from her. The following is an excerpt from her intake interview:*
>
> ***Dr.:*** *I am Dr. _____. I would like to know something more about you.*
> ***Pt.:*** *You have a nasty mind. Lord!! Lord!! Cat's in a cradle.*
> ***Dr.:*** *Tell me, how do you feel?*
> ***Pt.:*** *London's bell is a long, long, dock. Hee! Hee! (Giggles uncontrollably.)*
> ***Dr.:*** *Do you know where you are now?*

> **Pt.:** *D ___ n! S ___ t on you all who rip into my internals! The grudgerometer will take care of you all! (Shouting) I am the Queen, see my magic, I shall turn you all into smidgelings forever!*
> **Dr.:** *Your husband is concerned about you. Do you know his name?*
> **Pt.:** *(Stands, walks to and faces the wall) Who am I, Who are we, Who are you, Who are they. (Turns) I . . . I . . . I . . . I!!! (Makes grotesque faces)*

*Edna was placed in the women's ward where she proceeded to masturbate. She always sat in a chosen spot and in a chosen way, with her feet propped under her. Occasionally, she would scream or shout obscenities. At other times she giggled to herself. She was known to attack other patients. She began to complain that her uterus was attached to a "pipeline to the Kremlin" and that she was being "infernally invaded" by Communism. (Suinn, 1970, p. 402)*

The most prominent feature of *catatonic schizophrenia* is an extreme disturbance of psychomotor activity. The individual may withdraw into muteness and physical immobility. Some catatonics assume and rigidly maintain a posture for long periods of time. Sometimes they exhibit "waxy flexibility," a state in which the body may be molded, like wax,

**This drawing by a schizophrenic patient fuses several strong images—including an ancient warrior, horse, mythical bird, mountains, and people—in an attempt to convey an ideal of strength and grandeur. The drawing is a good example of schizophrenic condensation, fusion, and abnormal cognition.**

From *Interpretation of Schizophrenia*, 2nd edition. Revised and expanded by Silvano Arieti, M.D. © 1974 by Silvano Arieti. © 1955 by Robert Brunner, Basic Books, Inc., N.Y.

into different positions. The following description of a catatonic patient illustrates these symptoms.

> *Manuel appeared to be physically healthy upon examination. Yet he did not regain his awareness of his surroundings. He remained motionless, speechless, and seemingly unconscious. One evening an aide turned him on his side to straighten out the sheet, was called away to tend another patient, and forgot to return. Manuel was found the next morning, still on his side, his arm tucked under his body, as he had been left the night before. His arm was turning blue from lack of circulation but he seemed to be experiencing no discomfort. Further examination confirmed that he was in a state of waxy flexibility. (Suinn, 1970, p. 403)*

*Paranoid schizophrenia* has received the greatest amount of attention from the mass media and the general public. When a severe psychotic condition is portrayed in a film, the symptoms shown are usually those of paranoid schizophrenia. The primary symptom is fragmented and illogical delusions. These are most often delusions of persecution ("They are out to get me"), but they are sometimes delusions of grandeur ("I am Napoleon," or "I am God"). Paranoid schizophrenics are sometimes dangerous because they may attempt to get revenge on those whom they perceive as threatening. "Mad Bombers" are frequently paranoid schizophrenics. Sirhan B. Sirhan, the convicted assassin of Senator Robert F. Kennedy, was diagnosed as a paranoid schizophrenic. Paranoid schizophrenics often have hallucinations in which they claim to be receiving orders, usually from outer space, God, or famous people in history. The following conversation illustrates the illogical delusions of a paranoid schizophrenic:

*Dr.:* What's your name?
*Pt.:* Who are you?
*Dr.:* I'm a doctor. Who are you?
*Pt.:* I can't tell you who I am.
*Dr.:* Why can't you tell me?
*Pt.:* You wouldn't believe me.
*Dr.:* What are you doing here?
*Pt.:* Well, I've been here to thwart the Russians. I'm the only one in the world who knows how to deal with them. They got their spies all around here though to get me, but I'm smarter than any of them.
*Dr.:* What are you going to do to thwart the Russians?
*Pt.:* I'm organizing.
*Dr.:* Whom are you going to organize?
*Pt.:* Everybody. I'm the only man in the world who can do that, but they're trying to get me. But I'm going to use my atomic bomb media to blow them up.
*Dr.:* You must be a terribly important person then.
*Pt.:* Well, of course.
*Dr.:* What do you call yourself?
*Pt.:* You used to know me as Franklin D. Roosevelt.
*Dr.:* Isn't he dead?
*Pt.:* Sure he's dead, but I'm alive.

*Dr.:* But you're Franklin D. Roosevelt?

*Pt.:* His spirit. He, God, and I figured this out. And how I'm going to make a race of healthy people. My agents are lining them up. Say, who are you?

*Dr.:* I'm a doctor here.

*Pt.:* You don't look like a doctor. You look like a Russian to me.

*Dr.:* How can you tell a Russian from one of your agents?

*Pt.:* I read eyes. I get all my signs from eyes. I look into your eyes and get all my signs from them.

*Dr.:* Do you sometimes hear voices telling you someone is a Russian?

*Pt.:* No, I just look into eyes. I got a mirror here to look into my own eyes. I know everything that's going on. I can tell by the color, by the way it's shaped.

*Dr.:* Did you have any trouble with people before you came here?

*Pt.:* Well, only the Russians. They were trying to surround me in my neighborhood. One day they tried to drop a bomb on me from the fire escape.

*Dr.:* How could you tell it was a bomb?

*Pt.:* I just knew.*

## ORGANIC MENTAL DISORDERS

**Organic mental disorders**
A category of disorders associated with known physiological causes.

**Dementia**
An organic mental disorder caused by deterioration of the brain.

Unlike the disorders we have been discussing, there is general agreement on the cause of **organic mental disorders**. According to *DSM*-III, in "all Organic Brain Syndromes, an underlying causative organic factor is always assumed" (*DSM*-III, 1980, pp. 107–108). The causes of the disorders in this category range from vitamin deficiencies to toxic chemicals, from infections and disease to brain tumors and injuries. Consider, for example, the following case:

*Mr. Leonard K., age 55, was referred to the hospital by his family after an episode of reckless promises, extravagant claims, and grandiose commitments. He had usually been a calm and reserved person, but gradually began to show a change in personality. Once a fastidious dresser, he had suddenly surprised his wife by neglecting to shave, wearing suits that had been wrinkled because he slept in them, and refusing to wash. He became more and more expansive, talkative, and occasionally violent. By the time he was committed for treatment he believed himself to be the state senator, and spoke of his planned travels to "executive emperor" (words he had difficulty in communicating). He was known to stand wherever a crowd was willing to listen and loudly pronounce his views on war, religion, birth control, and nearly any topic that was suggested.*

*His views were more on the order of "solutions" to world problems than opinions. His wife described him as having been an almost too mild person prior to the recent outbursts. His gradual loss of memory led him*

---

*From *Abnormal Psychology and Modern Life* by James C. Coleman, 5th ed., p. 276. Copyright © 1976, 1972, 1964 by Scott, Foresman and Company. Reprinted by permission of the publisher.

In spite of new drugs and therapy techniques that have enabled many mental patients to function in society, such patients still occupy approximately one-half of the hospital beds in the United States.

*to confabulation (filling in memory gaps by creating events to relate). His shift to grandiosity was believed to be an attempt to compensate for his lowered self-confidence and esteem. (Suinn, 1970, p. 332)*

Leonard K. was diagnosed as suffering from a disease of the brain associated with the final stages of syphillis. Early detection and treatment with drugs have greatly reduced the incidence of this condition today.

This is just one of the many types of organic brain disorders described in *DSM*-III. In this section, we will focus on **dementia,** an abnormal deterioration of the brain.

## Dementia

Each of us suffers from brain deterioration throughout life. We appear to be born with all the brain cells we will ever have; as cells die, there is no way to replace them. Fortunately, we seem to have more brain cells than we need, so these losses are inconsequential. But sometimes this deterioration accelerates, causing marked changes in thought and behavior. According to *DSM*-III: "The essential feature [of dementia] is a loss of intellectual abilities of sufficient severity to interfere with social or occupational functioning. The deficit is multifaceted and involves memory, judgment, abstract thought, and a variety of other higher cortical functions. Changes in personality also occur" (*DSM*-III, 1980, 107–108).

Affected persons typically show a *gradual* deterioration of mental abilities. Some become forgetful and confused, others hostile and irritable; a few become suspicious of even their closest relatives. Perhaps the most striking symptom involves impairment in memory functions. The affected person often confuses present-day happenings with past events. The following case illustrates such disturbances:

*During the past five years he had shown a progressive loss of interest in his surroundings and during the last year had become increasingly "childish." His wife and eldest son had brought him to the hospital because they felt they could no longer care for him in their home, particularly because of the grandchildren. They stated that he had become careless in his eating and other personal habits, was restless and prone to wandering about at night, and couldn't seem to remember anything that had happened during the day but was garrulous concerning events of his childhood and middle years. (Coleman, 1976, p. 550)*

Most typically, dementia occurs in those over 60 years of age, in which case it is referred to as *senile* dementia. Although the number of elderly afflicted with senile dementia is growing, this increase is directly related to the growing number of elderly persons. In fact, only about 5 percent of the elderly in the United States appear to have this disorder. Most older people are able to function quite well and show only minor decreases in mental ability.

Young people can also suffer from a form of dementia known as *presenile* dementia. In some cases, this appears to have a hereditary cause, as in Huntington's chorea, from which folksinger Woody Guthrie suffered. Unfortunately, there is currently no effective treatment for this disorder, which ultimately results in a complete loss of memory and the ability to reason. Further, because the symptoms are not apparent at a very early age and are often misdiagnosed when they do appear, individuals with Huntington's disease may unwittingly pass the disorder on to their children. Like senile dementia, though, presenile dementia is rare.

## Summary

1. The word "abnormal" means, literally, "away from normal." The normal–abnormal dimension is a continuum; there is no sharp dividing line between normal and abnormal. At times, an "abnormal" individual may behave quite normally; conversely, a "normal" person may, on occasion, engage in behavior that is considered abnormal.

2. Three different approaches to the definition of the abnormal are commonly used: the cultural definition, the adjustive significance of behavior, and the classification of certain types of behavior as abnormal. In this chapter we adhere to the *Diagnostic and Statistical Manual of Mental Disorders* (*DSM*-III, 1980) for the classification of various emotional disorders.

3. The individual suffering an anxiety disorder appears almost constantly unhappy, threatened, and anxious in situations most people would not view as dangerous, and characteristically responds to threatening situations with avoidance instead of coping with them.

4. Anxiety disorders include anxiety states, obsessive–compulsive disorders, and phobic disorders.

5. Dissociative disorders include amnesia, fugue states which involve inability to recall important information about oneself, and multiple personalities, in which individuals have two or more well-developed and distinct "people" within them who may or may not be aware of one another's existence.

6. Individuals suffering somatoform disorders complain of pain or loss of physical function when no organic basis for the complaint is found. Somatoform disorders include somatization and conversion disorders.

7. Personality disorders involve long-term maladaptive ways of relating to others in society. One form of personality disorder is the antisocial per-

sonality. Antisocial personalities usually have a difficult time holding jobs and taking on adult responsibilities. They can cheat, lie, and commit antisocial acts with little evidence of conscience.

8. Psychosexual disorders include unconventional sexual behaviors, problems of gender identity, sexual adjustment problems (such as ego-dystonic homosexuality, in which the homosexual is unhappy with his or her sexual orientation), and sexual dysfunctions.

9. Psychosexual dysfunctions are not commonly caused by physical disabilities. More frequently, psychological, social, cultural, and emotional factors are involved. Some common disorders include inability to achieve and maintain an erection, premature and retarded ejaculation, and inability to achieve orgasm.

10. Affective disorders involve pronounced disturbances in mood and are commonly accompanied by either a highly agitated (manic) or a severely depressed state. In mixed bipolar disorders, these two states may alternate in rapid succession.

11. Schizophrenic disorders involve severe breaks with reality and an inability to function normally in society. Five basic types of schizophrenic disorders have been described: (1) disorganized, (2) catatonic, (3) paranoic, (4) undifferentiated, and (5) residual.

## Terms to Remember

| | | |
|---|---|---|
| Abnormal | Obsessive–compulsive disorder | Premature ejaculation |
| Phobia | Phobic disorder | Coitus |
| Defense mechanisms | Dissociative disorder | Retarded ejaculation |
| Neurosis | Fugue | Manic state |
| Anxiety disorders | Somatoform disorder | Depressive state |
| Anxiety | Somatization disorder | Schizophrenia |
| Anxiety states | Conversion disorder | Delusion |
| Free-floating anxiety | Anesthesias | Hallucination |
| Obsession | Antisocial personality | Organic mental disorders |
| Compulsive behavior | Ego-dystonic homosexuality | Dementia |

**TECHNIQUES OF THERAPY**

Knowing only the following information about Mrs. C.,* can you hazard a guess concerning the dominant aspects of her personality?

She is 47 years old and has six children: Arlene, 17; Barry, 15; Charles, 13; Debra, 11; Ellen, 9; and Frederick, 7.

Do you imagine she is spontaneous, free, and easygoing? Or is her life likely to be highly organized, with a strong possibility of obsessive–compulsive characteristics? If you chose the second alternative, you are correct. The key clues to answering these questions are found in the facts that the children were born two years apart and they were named alphabetically. Perhaps it was no coincidence that Mrs. C. stopped having children when she got up to the first letter of her husband's name, George. We might imagine that such a woman would place a strong emphasis on orderliness. This is precisely the case.

For 10 years she has been plagued by a compulsive washing problem, 25 to 30 times a day for 5 to 10 minutes each time. In addition, her morning shower lasts for 2 hours, during which time every part of her body has to be washed in a precise order. If she forgets where she is in the sequence, she has to begin over again. George arises at 5 A.M. every morning and helps her keep track. Otherwise, he cannot hope to gain access to the shower by 7 o'clock.

She also has problems with underwear. No one can wear underwear more than one day and the underwear cannot be washed. As a result, underwear accumulates in all corners of the house by the thousands. George laments the fact that he has more than $500 invested in once-worn underwear.

Along with everything else, she has lost interest in her personal appearance. She often walks about the house bare from the waist up, a source of embarrassment to her teen-age sons. She refuses to buy new clothes for herself, and she has stopped setting her hair even though it is washed daily. Her constant washing of her body and hair gives her the appearance of a prune and a boiled lobster with the frizzies.

Mrs. C. comes from a strict, authoritarian home dominated by a huge father. After a date, he quizzed her in detail about what she had done. He permitted her no expression of anger or even of disagreement. Her mother constantly harped on the theme that sex is disgusting and that she must keep herself clean and disease-free. For her part, she derives no satisfaction from sex. She had sexual relations with her husband for 13 years, but only to satisfy him. For the past 2 years, she has had intercourse only twice.

The precipitating event in Mrs. C.'s compulsive concern with cleanliness apparently arose when one of her daughters contracted pinworms while the whole family was bedridden with the Asian flu. The doctor emphasized the need to keep the bedsheets and household linens completely sanitary in order to prevent the spread of the pinworm infestation. However, even after the illnesses had spent themselves, Mrs. C.'s need to keep things clean persisted.

---

*Adapted from Prochaska (1979) with permission.

In this example, we see the classic case of the tail wagging the dog. So overwhelmed is Mrs. C. by the problems that beset her daily that she is literally crippled in virtually every aspect of everyday existence. We shall return to Mrs. C. throughout the chapter to examine how various therapies might explain her preoccupations and how they might assist her in surmounting her problems.

## THERAPIES

Mrs. C. is not alone in her need for help. It has been estimated that one person in 10 will seek some form of treatment for emotional problems at some time in life. The range of problems that send people for psychological counseling may vary from severe to relatively minor adjustment problems.

Many medical disorders require fairly standard treatment, such as an antibiotic for a known bacterial infection. But the type of treatment given for emotional problems very often depends on the training, experience, and personality of the therapist, as well as on the problems the patient has. It has been said that there are as many forms of therapy as there are therapists. More than 130 different therapies have been identified (Parloff, 1976). Most therapists are identified with a specific school, or theoretical approach. When psychological methods are used, we refer to the treatment as **psychotherapy.** When medical methods are used, the treatment is called **medical therapy.** However, because different forms of therapy tend to overlap somewhat, they should not be considered separate and distinct entities. For example, schizophrenics may be given drugs (medical therapy) to make them more responsive to psychotherapy.

Whatever the techniques they employ, therapists share a common goal: to bring about changes in behavior. In fact, in many ways the similarities among the various types of therapies outweigh their differences. Although therapists may differ in particulars, most attempt to provide an environment in which the patients or clients feel free to reveal their innermost thoughts and feelings; most provide some opportunity for emotional release; most involve an attempt to bring about cognitive changes in the clients (better understanding of their own motives and feelings and improved comprehension of their relationships with significant people in their lives); most involve a great deal of talk (the so-called talk therapies); and most strive to bring about an improvement in the patients' self-esteem.

The objective of changing behavior is not unique to therapy. Salespeople, propagandists, advertisers, and teachers, to name a few, also have this objective. The therapy situation differs in the relationship between the parties involved. The patient is generally seeking help from the therapist, whom the patient perceives as having no motive other than a desire to help.

At one time or another, most of us have sought out a close friend, a relative, or a clergyman just to discuss personal problems. We may have been hoping to alleviate anxiety, fear, or guilt. These contacts are gener-

**Psychotherapy**
Treatment of emotional disturbance by psychological methods.

**Medical therapy**
Treatment of emotional disturbance by medical methods.

I've had something unusual happen to me this week
that I'd like to share with the group.

ally limited in duration, and usually occur in the context of a relationship other than psychotherapy. The "therapist" in these situations often has had no professional training in therapy and usually gives "off-the-cuff" advice.

When a person seeks professional help, the relationship between patient and therapist is usually restricted to the therapy situation. There are many different types of formal psychotherapy. They may differ in the methods employed or in their assumptions about the underlying purpose of therapy. For example, some therapies focus on the overt symptoms, whereas others view these symptoms as manifestations of deep unresolved unconscious conflicts. The various therapies differ also in the extent to which the therapist controls the course of therapy. Some therapies emphasize helping the patient achieve "insight" into personal problems. Others emphasize making the patients "happy" or able to function efficiently, or helping them make decisions and take responsibility for their own actions. Still others focus on changing the specific behavior that sent the person in search of help.

## INDIVIDUAL PSYCHO-THERAPIES

Although there are numerous kinds of individual therapies, we will restrict our discussion to four of the most widely practiced forms: psychoanalysis, person-centered therapy, rational–emotive therapy, and behavior therapy.

# Psychoanalysis

**Psychoanalysis**
A technique of psychotherapy in which the psychoanalyst endeavors to bring to the surface repressed impulses and thoughts so that the individual can deal with them.

**Psychosexual development**
Freud's theory that development takes place in stages in which the focus of pleasure shifts from one part of the body to another.

**Repression**
A defense mechanism in which the individual unconsciously excludes unpleasant thoughts, feelings, and impulses from conscious awareness.

**Free association**
A psychoanalytic technique for probing the unconscious; individuals report their thoughts and feelings as they occur spontaneously.

We have already seen that psychoanalytic theory is a theory of personality. Let us now look at **psychoanalysis** as a technique of psychotherapy. First, let's briefly review some aspects of the theory in order to understand its application to the therapeutic situation (see also Chapters 10 and 13).

During the critical stages of **psychosexual development,** a person may experience conflicts that are not successfully resolved. In the case of Mrs. C., a psychoanalyst might argue that she failed to resolve her conflict at the anal stage of psychosexual development. Her overstrict parents undoubtedly demanded that she control her bowels and not permit herself to become messy. This control was probably extended to include almost all aspects of her emotional life, including the tendency to express aggression. Her frequent hand washing, prolonged showers, and unwillingness to wash underwear are undoubtedly defenses against such anal pleasures as being dirty and openly expressing impulses.

The thoughts, feelings, and impulses associated with unresolved conflicts lead to anxiety. The person must find ways of dealing with or fending off the pain associated with this anxiety. One of the most common ways of accomplishing this is to **repress** unacceptable urges. Although repression alleviates the acute phase of the anxiety, it does not eliminate anxiety, but rather "buries it alive." In addition, a person often develops symptoms as a way of dealing with anxiety. Because the original source of the anxiety has been repressed, the individual is unaware of underlying conflicts. Thus Mrs. C. had no initial understanding of the causes of her overwhelming need to be clean and to avoid dirtiness, including sex, which she regarded as filthy. The psychoanalyst tried to bring her submerged (repressed) impulses and thoughts to the surface so that she could deal with them. Let's look at some of the techniques used in psychoanalysis.

In the classic psychoanalytic session, the patient, while sitting in a comfortable chair or lying on a couch, is required to **free-associate**—say anything that comes to mind. The patient is free to choose any topic, but must report all thoughts that go through his or her mind, as well as any associated feelings. Instructions are given not to try to construct a logical and coherent narrative, but simply to follow and report all thoughts as they occur spontaneously. The therapist usually sits behind the patient in order to avoid being distracting.

Think about the state you are in when you are completely relaxed, perhaps just before falling asleep. Your mind is filled with a multitude of disconnected thoughts, feelings, and desires. Psychoanalysts believe that the thoughts occurring during such periods of relaxation provide a fairly direct route to the unconscious. Over a number of sessions of free association (usually over a relatively long period of time), the patient will presumably achieve insight into the conflicts that have been thrust into his or her unconscious.

As much as the patient may want to be helped, he or she constantly fights for protection from anxiety-arousing experiences. As "dangerous" thematic material begins to emerge during the course of free association, the patient may resist further encroachments into the unconscious and suddenly "clam up," talk excessively about an unrelated topic, or deny something he or she previously said. For example, when told to lie on the couch and say whatever came into her mind, Mrs. C. became anxious. She would begin to talk about her obsessions rather than to free-associate. This **resistance** can also manifest itself in other ways. The patient may be late for the therapy appointment or forget it altogether. Or he or she may decide to discontinue therapy, as did the patient in the following example:

> *A young man had achieved a reputation for brave and dashing military exploits. For this, and because he was handsome and well-to-do, he was a romantic figure. But his physical relations with his wife were a disappointment to both him and her, and he began psychoanalytic treatment for this and some other symptoms. The early weeks of his analysis brought a sincere contrasting of the world's impression of him with his own realization of weakness. This encouraging phase was succeeded by a period of slowed up production culminating in a dream. He was exploring a house which looked very good on the outside. But as he went further through the halls of this interesting and handsome building he came to a corner of one room where he stopped short, horrified. For on the floor*

Psychoanalysis is a psychotherapeutic technique in which the patient expresses thoughts as they come to mind. Psychoanalysts can glean clues about conflicts in the patient's subconscious through these relaxed sessions. In a typical session, the patient lies on a couch while the analyst sits out of sight in order to minimize distraction.

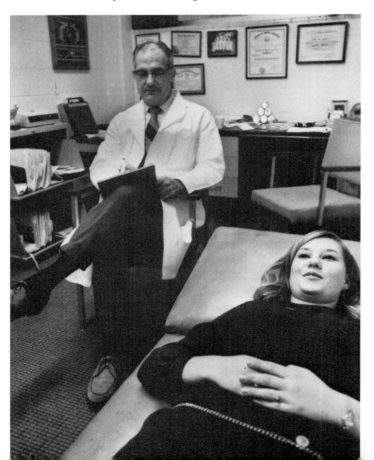

*in that corner lay something dreadful, disgusting, terrible—"too awful to look at. Perhaps it was a decaying dog—a cur—a beast—something of mine." He did not dare to look at it but turned and fled from the building.*

*A few days later the patient wrote that he was feeling better and believed he would discontinue his analysis. (Menninger, 1958, pp. 101–102)*

A psychoanalyst might interpret this case to indicate that when the patient came too close to the causes of his problem, his level of unconscious anxiety increased (as evidenced by his dream). The patient declared himself in need of no additional help (resisted therapy) so that he would not have to arouse this anxiety further.

Although the controls over unconscious processes are lessened during a state of relaxation, psychoanalysts believe that these controls are minimized during sleep. Thus unacceptable impulses that cannot find expression during waking hours may be expressed in dreams. Even in dreams, however, certain controls are still in effect. Consequently, some of the thematic material may take a disguised or symbolic form. When we speak of the **manifest content** of a dream, we mean the images and events that constitute the dream as it appears to the dreamer. The **latent content** is the actual meaning of the dream—the repressed motives seeking expression. The object of **dream analysis** is to uncover the unconscious wishes and impulses by studying the symbols as they appear in the manifest content of the dream. The following excerpt is taken from the fortieth hour of psychoanalytic therapy of an unmarried 28-year-old man:

*Cl.:* I had another of these dreams last night. I woke up in a sweat and was frightened almost to death.

*Th.:* Tell me about it.

*Cl.:* It's pretty much the same thing, I was driving a big truck along a dark country road at night. I saw a woman walking along it ahead of me, and I could have avoided her easily. But (great agitation) I didn't seem to want to! I just held the truck to the curve of the road on the right side, and I hit her! I hit her! and it was awful! I stopped and went around to her, and she was still alive but dying fast, and she was terribly battered!

*Th.:* Tell me about the woman. Just say whatever comes to mind now. Think about the woman and just say whatever occurs to you.

*Cl.:* Well, she was nobody I've ever known. She seemed small and sort of helpless. She was just walking along the road. It's not always the same woman in these dreams, but they're usually little old ladies like this one. She had dark hair and was terribly, terribly disfigured after the truck hit her. Mother's hair is almost snow white now, but this woman was dark. I've never known anybody like her. (pause)

*Th.:* It seems important to you not to know who this woman was. Go on.

*Cl.:* But I don't know who she was! She was just a little old woman on a dark country road. It was horrible! The accident messed her up so dreadfully! I felt nauseated and revolted by all the mess as well as by the horror of what I had done. But—and this is very strange—I didn't

---

**Resistance**
The tendency to resist or avoid treatment when anxiety-arousing material is being uncovered.

**Manifest content**
In psychoanalytic theory, the images and events that constitute the dream as it appears to the dreamer.

**Latent content**
In psychoanalytic theory, the actual meaning of a dream, the repressed motives that express themselves in the manifest content.

**Dream analysis**
A psychoanalytic technique aimed at uncovering the unconscious wishes and impulses as they appear in the manifest content of the dream.

feel any remorse in the dream, I don't think. I was terrified and sick at the sight but not really sorry. I think that's what wakes me up. I'm not really sorry.

*Th.:* Almost as if you were glad to have got rid of this little old lady. Go on. Just say whatever comes to mind.

*Cl.:* (after a long pause) I guess the horror of the sight is that she was so messy and bloody. Mother, the only older woman that I know really well, is always so neat and clean and well taken care of. This woman in the dream seemed, I don't know, evil somehow in spite of her being so helpless.

*Th.:* Your mother is quite a burden on you at times isn't she?

*Cl.:* Why, no! How can you say that? She's a wonderful person, and I'm glad to do what I can for her. She means more to me than anybody else.

*Th.:* These things are pretty painful to think about at times, but I'm pretty impressed by your knowing only your mother as a helpless little old lady and your dreaming so repeatedly about killing just such a person. And *you* are the one who dreams it! (Shaffer and Shoben, 1956, pp. 516–517)

In the course of psychoanalysis, patients usually form a complex emotional relationship with the therapist. They tend to identify the analyst with some adult figure who played a significant role in their childhood. They unconsciously transfer to the therapist the emotions and feelings they had toward that person; this process is called **transference.** Without understanding the reason, patients frequently alternate between attitudes of love and hate toward the therapist. Through the interpretation of this transference relationship, patients are helped to gain insight into the source of earlier conflicts and emotions.

Traditional psychoanalysis is a long, time-consuming, and expensive process. Patients may undergo as many as five psychoanalytic sessions a week over a period of many years. Recently, some psychoanalysts have attempted to shorten the total time required.

Box 15.1 presents a critical evaluation of psychoanalysis.

**Transference**
A process whereby patients project onto the therapist emotions and feelings they experienced in relation to another significant person.

**Person-cerented therapy**
A nondirective type of psychotherapy concerned primarily with the current adjustment of the individual.

## Person-Centered Therapy

Psychoanalysis is historical in the sense that it probes into the past experiences of the patient. It goes deep into the unconscious in its search for root causes and conflicts. It relies to a considerable extent on interpretations made by the psychoanalyst, and tends to stress intellectual rather than emotional factors. In contrast, **person-centered therapy** (formerly called client-centered therapy) is ahistorical in that it is concerned primarily with the current adjustment of the individual. It does not search deeply for underlying causes, but relies heavily on the patient to direct his or her own course of therapy. The goal of the person-centered therapy is the emotional, rather than intellectual, growth of the individual. The following excerpt is from the case history of an 18-year-old boy:

In his previous statements during the session, the client has said, "I don't want to be inferior in anything. . . ." "I try to cover the inferiority

## BOX 15.1

### A Critical Evaluation of Psychoanalysis

Psychoanalytic theory has had a tremendous impact on the field of psychology. Psychoanalysis and its variations are very widely employed. Nonetheless, the usefulness of the psychoanalytic view in explaining and treating behavior disorders has been challenged. Hall and Lindsey (1970) call attention to two major criticisms often leveled at psychoanalysis.

First, there are grave shortcomings in the empirical procedures by which Freud validated his hypotheses. His observations about human behavior were often made under uncontrolled conditions. For example, he relied heavily on case studies and his own self-analysis as a basis for the formulation of psychoanalytic theory. His patients, from whom he drew conclusions about universal aspects of personality dynamics and behavior, tended to be representative of a narrow spectrum of people. Although case studies are often an important and rich source of clinical data, the fact that Freud did not keep verbatim notes means his recollections were subject to distortions and omissions. Furthermore, he seldom checked the accuracy of the material related by his patients by any form of external corroboration (relatives, friends, test data, documents, or medical records). Such private and uncontrolled methods of inquiry are fraught with hazards. Freudian concepts have been difficult to define operationally.

Freud failed to make explicit the line of reasoning by which he drew inferences and conclusions. In his numerous writings he provided the end results of his thinking without the original data upon which they were based, his method of analysis, or any systematic presentation of his empirical findings. It is difficult, if not impossible, to replicate many of his investigations. Thus the reliability of his observations is impossible to evaluate. Did he really find a relationship between alcoholism and orality, between obsessive–compulsive behavior and anality? What safeguards did he use to control for subjectivism? His reluctance to follow the conventions of full scientific reporting leads many to view his concepts and explanations with skepticism.

A second major criticism leveled at psychoanalytic theory is that much of it cannot be empirically validated. The vagueness with which certain relationships are presented makes them virtually useless. What exactly is the relationship between the superego and the Oedipus complex? How intense must an experience be to become traumatic? Exactly how strong must instinctual forces be to overcome the ego?

Psychoanalysis also has limitations in its applicability. Individuals who have speech disturbances or are inarticulate (talking in therapy is important), people who have urgent, immediate problems (classical psychoanalysis requires much time), and people who are too young or old may not profit from psychoanalysis (Fenichel, 1945). Research studies have shown that psychoanalytic therapy is best suited to well-educated people of the middle and upper socioeconomic classes who exhibit neurotic rather than psychotic behavior. It is more limited in working with people of lower socioeconomic levels and with those who are less verbal, less intelligent, and more severely disturbed (Sloane *et al.*,1975).

Adapted from Sue *et al.*, 1981, pp. 66, 68.

up as much as possible." The following excerpt begins near the end of the interview.

*Cl.:* Yes, but you can never destroy the things you're inferior in. They always remain where everybody can see 'em, right on the surface. No matter how well you can talk, no matter how well you can dance, no matter how good a time you are to the persons who are with you, you certainly can't wear a veil.

*Th.:* M-hm. It's *looks* again, isn't it? . . .

*Cl.:* Yeah. I wish I was like my brother. He's dark just as the rest of the family is. Me—I'm light—puny. He's heavier-built than I am, too. Guess I was just made up of odds and ends. I'm too darn light. I don't like my face. I don't like my eyebrows and my eyes. Bloodshot, little cow-eyes. I hate my pimple chin and I detest the way my face is lopsided. One side is so much different from the other. One side, the chin bones stick out further and the jaw bones are more pronounced. My mouth isn't right. Even when I smile, I don't smile the way other people do. I tried and I can't. When other people smile, their mouths go up—mine goes down. It's me; backward in everything. I'm clumsy as the devil.

*Th.:* You feel sort of sorry for yourself, isn't that right?

*Cl.:* Yes, self-pity, that's me. Sure I know I pity myself, but I got something to pity. If there were two of me I would punch myself right in the nose just for the fun of it.

*Th.:* M-hm.

*Cl.:* Sometimes I get so disgusted with myself!

*Th.:* Sometimes you feel somewhat ashamed of yourself for pointing out all of those physical inadequacies, right?

*Cl.:* Yes, I know I should forget them—yeah, forget them—I should think of something else. And that's—I hate myself because I'm not sure. That's just another thing I can hate myself for.

*Th.:* You're sort of in a dilemma because you can't like yourself, and yet you dislike the fact that you don't like yourself.

*Cl.:* M-hm. I know it isn't natural for a person not to like himself. In fact, most people are in love with themselves. They don't know quite so much of themselves. I've known people like that.

*Th.:* M-hm.

*Cl.:* But not me. (Pause). I don't see how anybody loves me, even Mom. Maybe it's just maternal love. They can't help it, poor things. (Pause.)

*Th.:* You feel so worthless you wonder how anyone would think much of you.

*Cl.:* Yeah. But I'm not gonna worry about it. I've just gotta make up for it, that's all. I've just gotta forget it. And try to compensate for it.

*Th.:* M-hm. (Pause.)

*Cl.:* I've always tried to compensate for it. Everything I did in high school was to compensate for it.

*Th.:* M-hm. You've never had much reason to think that people really cared about you, is that right?

*Cl.:* That's right. Oh, if you only knew how they—

*Th.:* M-hm.

*Cl.:* Everything anyone ever said or ever did they were just trying to get something out of me. Or else they were—

*Th.:* It sort of made you feel inadequate not having the security of having people show that they cared a lot for you.

*Cl.:* That's right.

*Th.:* M-hm.

*Cl.:* No one ever did. . . . (Snyder, 1947, pp. 82–85)

Just as Sigmund Freud is considered the father of psychoanalytic theory, Carl Rogers is regarded as the progenitor of person-centered therapy. Rogers and his followers present a basically optimistic approach to life. Because they do not regard the people who seek their help as "sick," they use the term "client" instead of "patient." They believe that if people are not torn by conflicts, they will become productive and healthy human beings. Person-centered therapists provide a warm, friendly, and non-threatening environment that allows clients to accept aspects of themselves that they previously viewed negatively.

**Phenomenological (reality) self**
In Rogerian theory, the way the individual views him- or herself.

**Ideal self**
In Rogerian theory, the way the individual would like to be.

Rogers makes a key distinction between the **phenomenological** or **reality self** (the way individuals view themselves) and the **ideal self** (the way they would like to be). The way people view themselves may be at variance with the way they would like to be. The unhappy or maladjusted individual would probably show the greatest discrepancy between the phenomenological self and ideal self. The well-adjusted person might be expected to show less disparity.

A study was designed to test this important aspect of Rogers's theory. First, subjects were given a set of cards, each containing a sentence such as, "I am a submissive person," "I am a hard worker," or "I really am disturbed." The subjects were asked to pick out the cards that best described them. Then they were asked to go through the same cards again, and choose those that described the kind of person they would like to be. Two groups of subjects were employed in this study. One, the experimental group, was comprised of individuals seeking treatment for emotional problems. The other group, the control group, was made up of

Carl Rogers, shown here conducting a therapy session, emphasizes the importance of developing a client's positive self-concept in order to bring about constructive personality change.

people who were not looking for help. The subjects seeking therapy showed the least similarity between the way they viewed themselves (phenomenological self) and the way they would like to be (ideal self). The control subjects showed a high degree of similarity between phenomenological self and ideal self. After the experimental subjects received person-centered therapy, they showed a greater similarity between their phenomenological and ideal selves (Butler and Haigh, 1954).

In the case of Mrs. C., her adjustment was complicated by the fact that there was a wide disparity between the way she felt she must be in order to be worthy and the way her family wanted her to be. Her frequent washing, her emphasis on cleanliness, and her denial of sexuality was another way of saying, "Look at me. I am clean. Because I am not diseased, I am worthy and lovable." In contrast, she perceived her family as wanting her to stop washing. Only if she did so would they accept her and love her. Thus her self-esteem was threatened. If she did what was necessary to make her family happy, she would regard herself as unworthy. However, by continuing her preoccupation with cleanliness, she was in danger of losing their love.

A person-centered therapist would argue that caring is the basic issue, rather than whether or not Mrs. C. washes. She must first experience the esteem of another person who genuinely cares for her even when she washes to excess. She must know that others care for her even though, at any given moment or period of time, she may not feel that she warrants this caring.

Carl Rogers has stated that constructive personality change in the client depends on three fundamental attitudes of the therapist: (1) genuineness in the relationship, (2) acceptance of the client, and (3) an accurate understanding of the client's phenomenological world. These attitudes are more significant than the orientation, amount of training, and techniques of the therapist (Rogers, 1969).

## Rational– Emotive Therapy

*Although living a continent apart—Jim on the East Coast and Margo on the West—both were joined for a moment by the same bad news. Both had studied hard as undergraduates, and their efforts had seemed to pay handsome dividends. They both achieved 3.5 grade point averages on a 4 point scale. On the basis of their academic records, good scores on a qualifying test, and fine references from their professors, they had expected to be accepted into a school of veterinary medicine to which they had applied. But then the zinger came. Both received a tersely worded letter thanking them for applying to the veterinary school, but stating: "Due to the large number of highly qualified applicants, we are unable to accept you into the program." The immediate reaction of both Jim and Margo was the same—anger, an overwhelming sense of helplessness, and despair. They both suffered an injured self-esteem. As similar as their immediate reactions were, the aftermath was quite different. Jim's initial sense of despair gradually dissolved into a prolonged and profound state of depression. "There is something wrong with me," he lamented. "I am no good at anything I try. What good is a high grade point average if it can't get you into the career you want? My four years at college have been a meaningless sham, a waste of time and money. I am good for absolutely nothing.''*

*In contrast, Margo rebounded rapidly from her emotional down. ''Dammit,'' she said to herself, ''I took one of the toughest majors in the school and I'm in the upper five percent of my graduating class. I am a competent person. I refuse to let this thing derail me from my ambitions.'' Immediately, she began to make plans to enter a graduate program in biology. Even though the hour for graduate admissions was late, a call from one or two of her professors would surely open doors for her in programs that were not overenrolled. She would then have a full year to improve her credentials for admission into another school of veterinary medicine.*

These contrasting reactions to adversity can serve well to introduce the basic concepts of rational–emotive therapy. Its founder, Albert Ellis, agrees with psychoanalysts that irrational forces are at work in people suffering emotional disorders. However, he is convinced that the therapist need not delve deeply into childhood conflicts for causes and solutions. He has seen many patients who demonstrated remarkable insights into their childhood conflicts. Nevertheless, they remained unhappy and continued to get themselves into trouble. Ellis believes that therapy must become more active than free association on a couch. Rather, it must challenge people to examine their beliefs, and it must force them to repudiate irrational ideas and assumptions.

The rational–emotive theory of personality can be summarized by the first three letters of the alphabet. First there are Activating Events, such as loss of a loved one or rejection from enrollment in a professional school. These events activate the Belief Systems through which the activating events are processed and interpreted. These beliefs may be rational (rB) or irrational (iB). A rational belief activated by the rejection could be, ''It's a great disappointment but life must go on. Either I'll get into veterinary school next year or I'll find an alternative career goal.'' In contrast, an irrational belief might consist of nonproductive thoughts such as, ''They have rejected me. All I have striven for is being denied me. I am not good enough. I am a failure. The school that rejected me is making a shambles of my life.''

The Consequences of the Activating Events will be emotionally healthy and productive if processed through a rational belief system. There may be disappointment, sorrow, and other negative emotional reactions, but the overall thrust of the person's life is to increase that individual's determination to change whatever can be changed. When processed through an irrational belief system, the Consequences are continued unhappiness, lack of productivity, and futile, self-defeating behaviors. Box 15.2 summarizes twelve irrational ideas that Ellis believes are common to this culture.

According to Ellis, too many therapies have concentrated altogether too much time and effort on the Activating Event. To illustrate, psychoanalytic therapies probe ever deeper into the individual's history. But the past history cannot be changed. Historical knowledge may provide some

## · BOX 15.2

### Twelve "Irrational" Ideas

You might find it interesting to see which of these beliefs you have entertained at one time or another in your life. Since such ideas are so much a part of many people's thinking, it would not be at all unusual to agree with a number of the beliefs listed below.

1. The idea that you must, yes, must have sincere love and approval almost all the time from all the people you find significant.

2. The idea that you must prove yourself thoroughly competent, adequate, and achieving; or that you must at least have real competence or talent at something important.

3. The idea that people who harm you or commit misdeeds rate as generally bad, wicked, or villainous individuals, and that you should severely blame, damn, and punish them for their sins.

4. The idea that life proves awful, terrible, horrible, or catastrophic when things do not go the way you would like them to go.

5. The idea that emotional misery comes from external pressures and that you have little ability to control your feelings or rid yourself of depression and hostility.

6. The idea that if something seems dangerous or fearsome, you must become terribly occupied with and upset about it.

7. The idea that you will find it easier to avoid facing many of life's difficulties and self-responsibilities than to undertake some rewarding forms of self-discipline.

8. The idea that your past remains all-important and that, because something once strongly influenced your life, it has to keep determining your feelings and behavior today.

9. The idea that people and things should turn out better than they do; and that you have to view it as awful and horrible if you do not quickly find good solutions to life's hassles.

10. The idea that you can achieve happiness by inertia and inaction or by passively and uncommittedly "enjoying yourself."

11. The idea that you must have a high degree of order or certainty to feel comfortable; or that you need some supernatural power on which to rely.

12. The idea that you give yourself a global rating as a human and that your general worth and self-acceptance depend upon the goodness of your performance and the degree that people approve of you. (Ellis, 1977, p. 10)

---

Price and Lynn, 1981, pp. 498–499.

---

insights, but these insights do not necessarily alter irrational beliefs. Other therapies have set their sights on the other end of the scale, the Consequences. They may encourage people to express and discuss their emotions openly—tell what it feels like to be angry, depressed, or guilty. However, expressing emotions does little, if anything, about altering irrational beliefs. Similarly, getting people to change their behaviors, without corresponding alterations in their belief structure, will not lead to permanent benefits.

Rather, rational–emotive therapy concentrates its energies on analyzing, understanding, and attacking the irrational belief structure of the client. To illustrate, the following irrational beliefs in Mrs. C.'s system would be subject to challenge during the course of therapy: that she must be faultless—free of disease, dirt, and unclean desires—in order to be loved; that the consequences of pinworms are sufficiently severe to be treated as a major calamity; and that her carelessness contributed to her family's earlier episode with flu and pinworms. Understandably, rational–emotive therapy is not as easy as ABC because irrational beliefs do not die easily.

## Behavior Therapy

**Behavior therapy** is the application of the principles of conditioning (both classical and operant) to the modification of maladaptive behavior. The focus of behavior therapy is on the symptoms rather than the supposed "underlying causes." The adherents of this type of therapy regard anxiety disorders in a strikingly different way than psychoanalysts do. Psychoanalysts regard emotional disorders as the result of complex unconscious conflicts. Behavior therapists ignore the unconscious, and regard them as a collection of bad habits. Because all habits (good and bad) are learned, they can also be unlearned.

To illustrate, recall that Mrs. C.'s life is dominated by an aversion to dirt, disease, and sex. Behavioral therapists would *not* look to unconscious processes, such as unsatisfied anal impulses, for an explanation of her disturbed state. Rather, they would argue that she has been trained to avoid unclean situations through conditioning and/or modeling. Thus significant persons in her life (such as her mother and father) would reward her for avoiding situations that were unclean. Consequently, she avoids washing or even handling once-worn underwear, as well as the "messy" job of cooking. Sex, which her mother equated with disease, might also elicit aversive reactions for the same reason. Moreover, her mother provided a model of anxiety in the presence of dirt and sexual stimuli—a model from whom she learned all too well. From the point of view of the behavioral therapist, the emphasis of treatment must be directed toward uncoupling Mrs. C.'s associations of anxiety with dirt, disease, and sex. Only when this is accomplished will she be free to acquire other behaviors in the presence of these stimuli.

A variety of techniques are employed in behavior therapy, all of them based on the principles of conditioning discussed in Chapter 2. Let's look at several of these methods.

**Behavior therapy (behavior modification)**
A therapeutic technique based primarily on the application of the principles of conditioning to the modification of maladaptive behavior.

**Extinction therapy**
A technique of behavior therapy that consists of eliminating positive reinforcement for an undesired behavior.

**Extinction.**    Many undesirable habits are learned simply because positive reinforcement has unwittingly been associated with the occurrence of the response. For example, a parent may pay attention to a crying child only when the crying becomes extremely intense. Thus the parent is inadvertently providing positive reinforcement for loud crying. **Extinction therapy** would consist of eliminating the positive reinforcement for the undesired behavior. Experimental extinction procedures have been used successfully, for example, to tame overly aggressive children (Hamlin *et al.*, 1969), to reduce misbehavior in school (Madsen *et al.*, 1968), and to decrease delusional behavior in a psychotic patient (Ayllon and Michael, 1959). The following case history illustrates the application of extinction procedures in a hospital setting:

*The patient had weighed over 250 pounds for many years. She ate the usual tray of food served to all patients, but, in addition, she stole food from the food counter and from other patients. Because the medical staff regarded her excessive weight as detrimental to her health, a special diet had been prescribed for her. However, the patient refused to diet and continued stealing food. In an effort to discourage the patient from stealing, the ward nurses had spent considerable time trying to persuade her to stop stealing food. As a last resort, the nurses would force her to return the stolen food.*

*To determine the extent of food stealing, nurses were instructed to record all behavior associated with eating in the dining room. This record, taken for nearly a month, showed that the patient stole food during two thirds of all meals.*

PROCEDURE. *The traditional methods previously used to stop the patient from stealing food were discontinued. No longer were persuasion, coaxing, or coercion used.*

*The patient was assigned to a table in the dining room, and no other patients were allowed to sit with her. Nurses removed the patient from the dining room when she approached a table other than her own, or when she picked up unauthorized food from the dining room counter. In effect, this procedure resulted in the patient missing a meal whenever she attempted to steal food. (Ayllon, 1963)*

The withdrawal of food quickly eliminated the food-stealing response. In addition, the patient lost approximately 80 pounds over a 14-month period.

**Desensitization.** It is difficult to maintain two opposing emotional states at the same time. For example, can you be both anxious and relaxed? **Desensitization** procedures involve training the subject to relax in the presence of a situation that previously aroused anxiety or fear (see Chapter 8). These techniques have been particularly successful in the treatment of phobic fears.

For everyone there are certain things, situations, or events that arouse greater amounts of anxiety than other stimuli do. Each of us could probably construct a hierarchy in which we listed stimuli in order, from those that produce the least fear to those that produce the most. Desensitization therapy begins by teaching patients to relax. When this behavior is learned, they are told to imagine a situation that is low on their hierarchy (least fear-producing). If they continue to relax while imagining this situation, they are asked to imagine the next item on the hierarchy. As soon as a stimulus disturbs their state of relaxation, they are told to stop and concentrate on relaxing again. In this way, the patients are gradually led through a series of increasingly anxiety- or fear-arousing stimuli until they are able to tolerate the situation that is highest on their list.

You may recall the college student who was terrified of examinations (p. 512). Desensitization therapy was started with this patient:

**Desensitization**
A therapeutic technique that involves training an individual to relax in the presence of a situation that previously aroused anxiety or fear. In desensitization therapy, the individual is gradually led through a series of increasingly intense anxiety or fear-arousing stimuli until he or she is able to tolerate the situation that previously was the most anxiety-arousing.

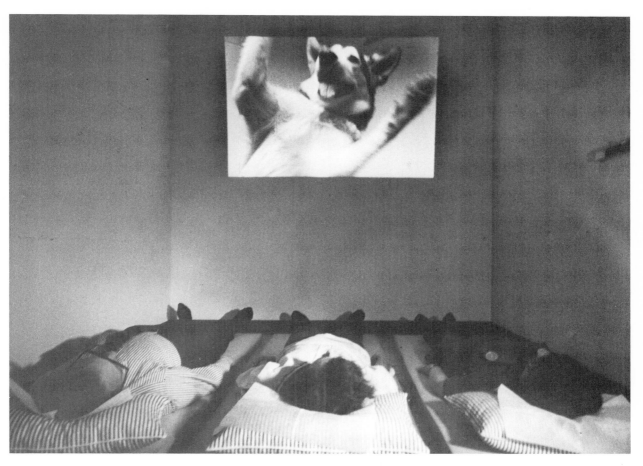

Film can be a useful medium in desensitization therapy. Here patients are undergoing treatment for their fear of dogs.

*He first made up a hierarchy of circumstances which he felt produced fear responses. He was then instructed in relaxation of muscle groups. The lowest item on his anxiety hierarchy list, being asked a question by his kid brother, was then presented while the patient was relaxing. When it was evident that this situation was well tolerated, the next item on the list was evoked, and so on. Within a month, the student reported being able to undertake examinations with only a modicum of tension. The patient returned, however, during final examinations with a recurrence of his paralyzing fear. Retraining continued with an emphasis on generalizing the relaxation responses to a wider variety of evaluational situations. Excellent progress has been noted and the student has recently been notified of his acceptability for graduate admissions. (Suinn, 1970, p. 242)*

One of the most successful techniques in behavior therapy has combined desensitization with modeling. In modeling, the patient observes another individual (the model) go through a series of responses to situations increasingly high on the patient's anxiety hierarchy. A considerable

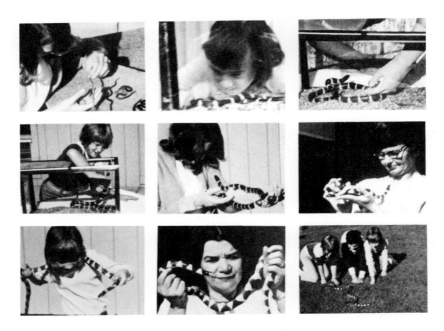

**Figure 15.1**
**Treating a snake phobia**

A combination of desensitization therapy and modeling was successfully used to treat snake phobia. The photographs show the models interacting with a live snake. Both live and film demonstrations were employed in the study. (Bandura *et al.,* 1969)

amount of research has been conducted with subjects suffering from phobic fears of snakes. In one study, the subjects observed a model handle and play with a snake. Gradually they were encouraged to participate in the handling of the snake (see Fig. 15.1). The combination of modeling and desensitization procedures resulted in a marked decrease in the subjects' fear of snakes (Bandura *et al.*, 1969).

From the point of view of the behavioral therapist, Mrs. C. is a prime candidate for the use of modeling and desensitization. We can substitute dirt (once-worn underwear) for the snake: She might first be told to imagine looking at dirty underwear. Using a carefully graded series of approximations to the final response of handling the underwear, she would gradually extinguish her extreme anxiety in the presence of objects she regarded as dirty. She might also benefit by watching a model perform the feared act without harmful consequences to the model. Once her fear of dirt had been conquered, the therapy could proceed to other fears, such as disease and sex. In fact, at some point in the course of her therapy, she might advantageously be introduced to sexual therapy as advocated by Masters and Johnson (see Box 15.3).

A criticism frequently leveled against desensitization, as well as other behavior therapy techniques, is that it treats the symptom without removing the underlying cause. The critics predict that **symptom substitution** may occur—that the patient may give up one symptom and substitute another in its place. Joseph Wolpe, a leader in the application of desensitization therapy, has countered this criticism by pointing to data he has collected. He studied 249 cases of emotional disorders, including many phobias, that had been successfully treated by the application of behavior therapy and found that only four patients had acquired new symptoms (Wolpe, 1969).

**Symptom substitution**
In psychoanalytic theory, the concept that a symptom is the result of an underlying conflict and that, unless the underlying conflict is resolved, removal of the symptom will merely result in a different symptom's appearing in its place.

**Positive reinforcer**
An event that strengthens the response that precedes it by virtue of its *presentation*.

**Contingent reinforcement**
Reward or reinforcement that is dependent upon making a given response.

**Token economy**
A reinforcement technique, sometimes used in hospitals, in which the individual is rewarded for socially accepted behavior with a token that can be exchanged for a desired object or activity.

*Positive reinforcement.*     You may recall (from Chapter 2) that pairing a **positive reinforcer** with a response that is to be learned is an extremely effective conditioning procedure. **Contingent reinforcement** (making a specific behavior a prerequisite for obtaining positive reinforcement) has been successfully employed in a variety of different settings. Mute psychotic children have acquired speech (Lovaas, 1968), and high school dropouts have learned academic skills (Clark *et al.*, 1968) as the result of the successful application of positive reinforcement techniques. The following case history illustrates the use of positive reinforcement in a hospital setting.

> *Shortly after the patient had been admitted to the hospital she wore an excessive amount of clothing which included several sweaters, shawls, dresses, undergarments and stockings. The clothing also included sheets and towels wrapped around her body, and a turban-like head-dress made up of several towels. . . .*
>
> *To determine the amount of clothing worn by the patient, she was weighed before each meal over a period of two weeks. By subtracting her actual body weight from that recorded when she was dressed, the weight of her clothing was obtained.*
>
> PROCEDURE. *The response required for reinforcement was stepping on a scale and meeting a predetermined weight. The requirement for reinforcement consisted of meeting a single weight (i.e., her body weight plus a specified number of pounds of clothing). Initially she was given an allowance of 23 pounds over her current body weight. The allowance represented a 2 pound reduction from her usual clothing weight. When the patient exceeded the weight requirement, the nurse stated in a matter-of-fact manner, "Sorry, you weigh too much, you'll have to weigh less." Failure to meet the required weight resulted in the patient missing the meal at which she was being weighed. (Ayllon, 1963)*

As a result of this treatment, the woman reduced the weight of her clothing from 25 pounds in the first week to 3 pounds in the ninth week, after which time it remained stable.

One of the most rapidly growing practices in institutional settings involves a slight variation of positive reinforcement techniques. Patients are permitted to earn varying numbers of tokens (secondary reinforcers) for engaging in specific constructive behaviors. These tokens may then be exchanged for various luxuries or privileges. We have already seen the successful application of a **token economy** in a study described in Chapter 3. Although the use of token economies in therapy began only recently, the practice has spread rapidly to many different settings. Perhaps the

## BOX 15.3

### Sexual Therapy

For a variety of reasons, some individuals of both sexes are unable to perform one or more of the behaviors required to achieve orgasm. It is illustrative to briefly examine the applications of learning techniques employed by Masters and Johnson to alleviate such sexual dysfunctions as impotence, premature ejaculation, retarded ejaculation, and inorgasmic potential in women (1970; 1974).

To begin with, a husband and wife are treated together. The reason is quite straightforward: sexual intercourse is an intense and intimate personal–social relationship in which the satisfaction of both partners is dependent upon their ability to work together as a team so as to achieve mutual sexual arousal and satisfaction. Indeed, mutual satisfaction is the foundation of the pleasure bond.

During the first few days of the two-week course, the partners are encouraged to spend periods of time in their room, unclothed. They are instructed to touch, fondle, and massage each other. The purpose is to allow each partner to discover the specific body areas which provide maximum sensual pleasure. However, touching the genital regions and the wife's breasts is specifically forbidden during this stage of therapy. The emphasis is completely upon exploration in giving pleasure without the imposition of overt sexual performance pressures that may be anxiety-producing to one or both of the partners. In many ways, the procedures are reminiscent of shaping . . . : "Instead of [its] being suggested . . . [that partners] go all the way from A to Z sexually on any specific occasion, it is suggested that marital units go from A to B one day, possibly from A to C or D the next . . ." (1970, p. 205).

The withholding of genital contact during the first few days of therapy serves an additional purpose—by increasing the deprivation level, the incentive value of the reinforcement increases.

In the Masters and Johnson sexual therapy, the

most dramatic results have been obtained in hospital settings. Patients who had previously shown little or no responsiveness to other people and things have become responsible and interested in their environment. Furthermore, they have been able to perform productive tasks within the hospital setting. A number of patients who had been hospitalized for long periods of time and had been considered hopeless have been released from the hospital after living for a time in a token economy. The effectiveness of token reinforcement on schizophrenics is shown schematically in Fig. 15.2.

Aversive conditioning.    Several years ago a young woman contracted a case of hiccoughs. Ordinarily, this would not be a cause for concern, because hiccoughs are rather common and generally harmless. In her case, however, the hiccoughs continued to plague her, and medical attention was sought. When she was unable to obtain relief through the use of various medical techniques, she was referred to traditional psychotherapists. The hiccoughs persisted to such extent that she suffered a severe loss of weight and was unable to sleep. It was clear that unless a way was found to stop her hiccoughs, she could not long survive. In desper-

period of nongenital contact also serves as encouragement for the dysfunctioning male and his marital partner. In the absence of performance expectations, penile erections occur quite spontaneously during the sensate focus phase of treatment. These spontaneous erections set the stage for manipulative play (teasing technique) with the erective reaction. In sessions lasting up to a half hour, the marital couple engages in slow, nondemanding sexual play during which the male may undergo several erections and losses of erections. Thus, the male gains some measure of control over his erective capacity and the female is sexually stimulated by the opportunity to produce an erection in her partner.

By the time the marital couple is ready for coital experience, they have become quite adept at communicating, often in a nonverbal fashion, their likes and dislikes, pleasures and aversions. They have, in effect, developed a feedback system which selectively rewards and encourages behavior that enhances each other's sexual pleasures. The female, for example, is encouraged to guide the hand of the male to the vaginal area that she wishes to have stimulated, thus obviating clumsy and sometimes painful manipulation.

Throughout all of the therapy period, one theme predominates: the individual should value sexual experiences. Unless each partner is able to internalize a value system that regards sex as pleasurable and desirable, the ability to perform the skills necessary for satisfactory sexual relations will be impaired. In short, the pleasure arising out of the activity is sufficient justification for the activity.

---

From *Principles of Personality* by J. S. Wiggins *et al.* (Reading, Mass.: Addison-Wesley, 1976), pp. 282–283. Reprinted with permission.

---

ation, the family of this young woman went to a psychologist who was practicing behavior therapy, then a relatively new form of therapy. He attached electrodes to her body that delivered a painful, but not physically damaging, electric shock. He made the delivery of the shock contingent upon her hiccoughing; that is, whenever she hiccoughed, she would receive a painful electric shock **(aversive conditioning)**. Within a short time, the hiccoughs disappeared. From the point of view of the behavior therapist, she was cured.

**Aversive conditioning**
A technique used in behavior therapy in which punishment or aversive stimulation is used to eliminate undesired behavior.

This case illustrates the successful application of aversive conditioning techniques. Aversive conditioning has also been used to cure a nine-month-old child of vomiting (Lang and Melamed, 1969), to eliminate stuttering (Goldiamond, 1965), and to treat bedwetting (Wickes, 1958). Though aversive conditioning appears to work in the short run, there are serious questions about its long-term effectiveness, particularly with adults. In addition, concerns about the ethics of its use generally limit it to cases where other methods have failed.

Aversive conditioning is often used in conjunction with positive reinforcement. The aversive stimulus is used to inhibit maladaptive behavior, and the positive reinforcement to strengthen constructive responses. This combination seems to offer a greater chance than either element

Hours spent in
appropriate
behavior
per week

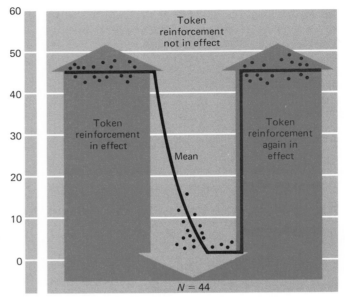

**Figure 15.2**
**The effect of token reinforcement on schizophrenia**

alone for effecting a long-lasting change in behavior, because the individual is given an opportunity to develop adaptive behaviors with which to replace maladaptive ones.

## GROUP PSYCHO-THERAPIES

So far, we have discussed therapeutic techniques involving the treatment of one patient at a time. A variety of techniques have been developed for the simultaneous treatment of several people. These **group therapies** have emerged for several reasons: economic necessity, shortage of trained therapists, and because some people seem to benefit from sharing and working out problems in a group situation.

Group approaches range from self-help groups like Alcoholics Anonymous and weight-control groups to groups that represent an extension of traditional psychotherapeutic techniques. For example, Rogerian and psychoanalytic therapists handle groups as well as individuals. Other groups represent a complete departure from these traditional techniques, to the extent that some groups have leaders who are not professionally trained, whereas others have no leader at all. But in spite of the diversity of group treatment methods, one observer has commented, "group therapy can help with most anything that individual therapy can, providing an appropriate group is available and the individual will accept the group as the mode of treatment" (Levine, 1979, p. 11).

**Group therapy**
Psychotherapy in which two or more people are treated simultaneously.

## Psychodrama

Have you ever thought of the amount of time you spend acting out various dramas in your mind? During these completely private scenarios, you play the parts of the protagonist and the antagonist, as well as the minor roles. These mental dramas revolve around our daily concerns, conflicts, frustrations, and feelings. Many of us are able to resolve our conflicts and work out solutions to life's crises; others are not. For those who are not, the psychodrama offers the opportunity to try out these internal plots in the external world. Psychodrama is a technique that a group therapy leader may utilize from time to time. Practitioners of psychodrama emphasize that the technique is regarded as a productive experience rather than a form of therapy.

There are a variety of therapeutic modalities available to people seeking greater self-awareness toward the goal of resolving their personal and interpersonal problems. The therapeutic process involves relating one's self to a system and interpreting behavior within the terms of a specific methodology. Most therapeutic systems, properly applied, do produce insights, self-awareness, and consequently, therapeutic progress. The difference between psychodrama and most other methodologies, however, is that psychodrama comes *closest* to the natural scenarios of people in everyday life.

**Group therapy has proved to be an effective form of treatment for many people who benefit from working out problems in a group situation.**

In psychodrama a person is encountering his or her conflicts and psychic pain in a setting that more closely approximates the real-life situation than do most other therapeutic approaches (Yablonsky, 1976, p. 4).

Unlike the "talk therapies," the technique of psychodrama encourages the protagonist to act out conflicts rather than discuss them. Moreover, the originator of psychodrama, J. L. Moreno, insisted that the action be "here and now." Thus, while acting out a role, you would not say, "My father used to look at me and say . . ." Rather, your words would be, "My father is looking at me and saying . . ."

The roles of important individuals are taken by other members of the psychodrama group. Thus one may be the mother, another the father, and another a lover. Those who remain may "double" with the antagonist. That is, they enter into the protagonist's world. If a severely disturbed individual sees a devil, they do not criticize that person by saying, "You're hallucinating." Rather, they join as if there really is a devil. Later, during the discussion, the reality of the situation may be presented along with the societal viewpoint. But first must come the enactment. Later comes the retraining.

The three phases of a psychodrama consist of the warm-up, the action, and the postdiscussion. The warm-up sets the stage for the drama. The action consists of the actual enactments. During the postdiscussion, members of the group share their feelings and personal experiences with the protagonist of the drama. Thus the protagonist learns that he or she is not alone. Moreover, the process produces group insight, increases cohesion, and enlarges interpersonal perceptions.

The following is a description of a psychodrama session in which a 40-year-old woman, Helen, is the protagonist:

> *Helen comes forward onto the psychodrama stage and begins to warm up to a session by exposing her inner drama to the group. She soliloquizes: "I keep reviewing over and over in my mind something I want to tell my mother. She's in the hospital with terminal cancer. I can't think of anything else. There are some things I feel compelled to tell her while she's still alive. She's very important to me. I hate her and I love her. I hate her because she's dominated my life and I've permitted it. I married a man I didn't love because I knew he was the kind of man she wanted me to marry. I love her because she has always given to me and at times was very good to me. Lately, I think about her constantly. In my mind I tell her off. This makes me feel guilty. So then I tell her how much I love her. In spite of this, when I'm with her I don't actually express any of my feelings. I feel it would be cruel to impose my problems on her at this time. After all, she is dying. I can't hurt her, yet I have this anger in me, and it's just eating me up." (Yablonsky, 1976, pp. 14–15)*

After the warm-up and during the action, Helen tells her "mother" how much she loves her, but she is totally unable to express any hostility. She interrupts to ask how she can tell a dying woman of her frustration and hatred. The director of the session says that, in real life, they wouldn't want her to say unpleasant things to her real mother. But because the woman playing her mother in the drama is not her mother, she can feel free to express herself openly. "Obviously, you can't hurt your mother because she really isn't here. I would strongly urge you to get these feelings out in the open" (p. 15).

Helen agrees and, getting into the mood of the psychodrama, tells her mother how much hatred she feels for her. As her anger increases, she grabs a foam rubber weapon and begins striking the table in front of her with it. She tells her mother of the pain and humiliation she has suffered at her hands. After openly expressing her hatred, she cries, "In spite of everything, I love you and want you to live" (p. 16).

Later, the group acted out her mother's death and funeral. Again Helen expressed her hatred and her forgiveness. A few days after the session, she visited her mother in the hospital. The following is her account of the visit:

*"The session and my last visit to my mother have lifted an enormous burden from my mind. I feel completely different about her. I could talk to her for the first time without guilt, pain, or anger. The session clarified my emotions and I felt freer to honestly talk to her. I believe I'm able to say goodbye to her now without rancor. Also, now that my mind is free from that pain and frustration, I can focus on other more positive things in my life." (Yablonsky, 1976, p. 17)*

## Encounter Groups

One of the most popular forms of group therapy today is the **encounter group.** This kind of group usually consists of 6 to 12 participants, and the members are encouraged to focus on their feelings and express them openly and honestly (see Box 15.4). There appears to be a move toward this type of group experience for individuals with no serious emotional disturbances. Many people consider encounter groups ideally suited for "normal" people who want to "grow, change, and develop" (Lieberman, 1976, p. 440).

Encounter groups can be found on college campuses throughout the country. Many of the studies concerned with the effects of encounter group experiences have been directed toward college students. In a comprehensive review of 14 such studies, the author concluded, "All but 2 of the 14 reported positive results—lower anxiety, increased **internal locus of control,** increased social interaction, increased self-esteem, value changes, and decreased discrepancy between self and ideal" (Lieberman, 1976, p. 219).

Nonetheless, some psychologists have expressed reservations about the widespread and indiscriminate use of encounter group therapy. For example, one extensive study reported that between 10 and 19 percent of the participants appeared to be adversely affected by the experience. Moreover, the study concluded that the positive changes were not as great as usually observed in individual psychotherapy, nor were they as long-lasting (Lieberman *et al.*, 1973).

Somewhat similar to the encounter groups are *training groups,* also called **T-groups.** At first, T-groups were used primarily in industrial and business settings. They are sometimes called **sensitivity groups,** because their aim is to develop more sensitive feelings and attitudes toward one's fellow workers.

**Encounter group**
A small therapy group that focuses on expressing feelings openly and honestly.

**Internal locus of control**
The orientation that the various outcomes in life are a direct consequence of forces within the individual.

**Sensitivity group (T-group)**
A type of small group that emphasizes the development of sensitive feelings and attitudes toward others.

## BOX 15.4

### Encounter Group Therapy for an Emotional Disorder

Mary, who was 27, had recently separated from her 29-year-old husband, Bill. Since Mary had tried to be the perfect wife, it came as quite a shock to her when Bill, after one year of marriage, told her he was no longer in love with her. Feeling responsible for the difficulties in her marriage, and anxious about her ability to establish meaningful marital or other interpersonal relationships, Mary joined an encounter group which met one evening a week for 2½ hours. The group was cofacilitated by two nonprofessional leaders who were being trained by and working under the local Growth Center, the group's sponsor. The male facilitator was a 27-year-old high school teacher and the female facilitator was a 35-year-old housewife with three children. The group consisted of 4 male and 5 female participants ranging in age from 19 to 40.

At first during the meetings, Mary remained relatively quiet and listened politely as others spoke. She made only positive comments when she did speak—avoiding saying anything negative to anyone.

During the fourth meeting, one of the members—Sid, aged 38—confronted Mary about her uniform politeness and seeming superficiality, an exchange in which the facilitator also took part:

*Sid:* Mary, I would like to get to know you better, but your polite sweet manner puts me off. Frankly, your sweetness makes me a little angry with you.

*Fcltr:* In your anger, Sid, what do you need to say to Mary?

*Sid:* (in a loud and moderately angry voice) Damn it, Mary, come out from behind that phony sweet facade of yours! Stop putting me off!

*Mary:* (with a polite smile and pleasant tone) Gee, I'm sorry, I really don't want to put you off.

*Fcltr:* Mary, become aware of your smile and tone of voice.

*Mary:* (again smiling) I guess I was smiling (followed by a childish chuckle).

*Sid:* Mary, you're impossible! (said in a tone implying that he did not think Mary capable of being aware of her pattern of behavior).

*Mary:* (in a more somber tone) I really don't understand, Sid, why you are angry at me. I'm trying to . . . (long pause followed by an embarrassed look).

*Fcltr:* Would you be willing to look at Sid and express your embarrassment to him?

*Mary:* Yes (then looking at Sid). I stopped my sentence because I was going to say . . . "I'm trying to be polite so that you'll like me."

*Sid:* Mary, that's the trouble. I don't like your politeness—it seems phony to me. I'd feel closer to you

---

## Family Therapy

"You're driving me crazy!" says a husband to his wife or a parent to his or her child. Although the words are usually not to be taken literally, the underlying sentiment may indeed reflect a state of agitation that can ultimately lead to emotional disturbances.

Only in recent years have therapists begun to recognize the importance of the family relationships to the mental health of the individual family members. Previously, a family with a depressed mother, an alcoholic father, or a child with behavioral problems would seek out therapy for the one "troubled" member. Now more and more families are participating in a form of counseling known as family therapy. In family therapy, the patient is not the *individual* but rather the *family unit* itself. The goal of the therapy process is to change the interactions among the family members.

Family therapists believe that the individual sees only part of what is happening. In order to effect changes, the whole family has to get together. Only then can they see the complete picture. Family therapists view an individual's problems as a signal that something is amiss in the

if I knew what you *really* were thinking and feeling.

*Mary:* You know it's true that I don't really feel all the nice things I say—but to imagine not being polite and sweet . . . just really scares me.

*Fcltr:* What is your fear?

*Mary:* I'm afraid nobody will like me.

*Sid:* I'm liking you right now.

*Mary:* You know when you said you like me, it made me feel anxious and confused. (She looks to facilitator.) I'm at a loss to figure out what's going on with me. Why do I feel confused?

*Fcltr:* Mary, right now the "why" of your confusion is secondary to the fact that you *are* feeling confused *right* now. Try to get the feel of your confusion. In other words, become aware of your sensations and let them emerge on their own.

*Mary:* (mildly distressed) I feel overcome by a growing sense of emptiness which I feel in my stomach.

*Fcltr:* Let your emptiness have its say. You're at the point at which you don't get support from others and you can't quite get it from yourself.

*Mary:* (mildly fearful) I feel awful. I feel like nothingness—I feel so empty.

*Fcltr:* (noting Mary's eyes becoming moist) What do your tears have to say to us, Mary?

*Mary:* (breaking into deep sobs) I feel unloved and unappreciated for what I am; I so much need everyone's approval. I really don't like myself. (Mary continues crying for several minutes, then adds as she looks down at the floor) Now I feel silly; everyone must think I'm a jerk!

*Fcltr:* Mary, you will get yourself into trouble by imagining what people are thinking. Right now, look at each person in the group and tell us what you see. (As Mary looks around the group, she sees the members looking at her sympathetically; several have been moved to tears by her outpouring of feeling.)

*Mary:* (responding to the warmth and support she sees around her) I feel so happy, so free right now. I want to express my warm feelings to all of you. (She goes around the group making contact by touching, holding, or talking to each member.)

As the group sessions continued, Mary became able to drop her "polite good-girl" role, to begin to understand and trust herself, and to improve her competence and authenticity in relating to others.

---

From Coleman, 1976.

family as a whole. Thus they are concerned with changes in relationships rather than changes in the individual. Toward this end, they will work with all members of the distressed family as well as in-laws and close friends, if necessary.

A variety of techniques such as one-way glass and video tape are employed in family therapy. Such techniques permit the family to see themselves in action and to examine some of the ways they interact. Another popular technique is "family sculpture." The therapist asks one member to position the family according to the way he or she perceives the group's relationships. Through the use of this method, family members can observe how each views the others and how they differ.

As one observer noted:

*The family-therapy method may indeed be the appropriate therapy for our times. Its rise in popularity coincides with the major changes in the structure of the American family that occurred in the 1960s. Therapists started seeing more and more cases of "families in transition," those*

**Family therapy is an effective form of treatment for the family as a unit. The goal of this type of therapy is to change the way family members interact.**

*traumatized by divorce or transformed by wives working or children leaving home. "Troubled families are everywhere," wrote the late Dr. Nathan W. Ackerman, a pioneer of family-therapy procedures. "Family relations are out of kilter. After an upset, the family seems less able to bounce back and regain its balance. It looks for all the world as if it is falling apart. Unlike Humpty Dumpty, however, it may well pull itself together."*

*Many studies over the years have suggested the importance of a healthy family structure to the mental and physical health of its members. A great French sociologist, Emile Durkheim, concluded in a study in the late 1800s that members of stable family structures experienced sharply reduced rates of suicide compared to those coming from broken homes. A Johns Hopkins School of Medicine study of 1,337 medical students from 1948 to 1964 suggested that subjects whose backgrounds indicated a lack of closeness to their parents were much more likely to develop suicidal patterns, mental illness, and tumors.*

*At the heart of the concept of family therapy is the optimistic belief that if spouses can lead each other and their children to illness, they can also learn to help each other regain health. (Simmons, 1981, pp. 81–82)*

## Community Mental Health

A few short decades ago, when people were judged to be mentally ill, many were placed in either private or public mental health facilities (often called insane asylums). Because private facilities were then and still are quite expensive, only the affluent could afford the private route to mental health care. The overwhelming majority of mentally disturbed wound up in the public tax-supported institutions. There the funds that were allocated could provide little more than minimum custodial care—a bed or cot, questionable food, and a small space to occupy during the waking hours. Treatment, when it was available, was hit-and-miss. Untold numbers of patients received little or no therapy for protracted periods of time. Many languished in these "prisons" for years and even decades, nameless and forgotten John and Jane Does discarded in the trash heap by "normal" society.

With the introduction of tranquilizers and other psychoactive drugs in the 1950s, the picture changed dramatically. Serious disturbances could often be brought under rapid control so that the patients were released from hospitals in record times. But they were released into communities poorly prepared to accept them and to integrate them into society. Moreover, relief provided by the various medications was often temporary, and many patients discontinued using them after their release. Many patients found themselves trapped in a revolving door: in, out, in again, out again.

The Community Health Center Act of 1963 ushered in the establishment of community mental health centers throughout the nation. This act established emergency mental health care in the community for individuals undergoing emotional crises, broader care for long-term mental patients, care for people discharged from institutional settings, and mental health education for the public. One of the impacts of this movement has been an emphasis on indirect rather than direct services (Price and Lynn, 1981). Thus psychiatrists and psychologists provide both education and support for individuals who interact daily with people suffering emotional problems—members of the clergy, teachers, and public health nurses. By assisting the helpers to help others, mental health professionals are able to multiply their impact on the community.

It is still too early to evaluate the success of the community health movement. As two professionals have noted:

> . . . history can be written in such a way as to lead us to believe that every new development is a victory in the march of progress. This march of progress view of history can lead to self-deception. A more judicious and thoughtful view of the recent history of mental health care is one that recognizes the . . . "revolution" as a real change in our orientation to treatment, but whether it reflects "progress" only time and careful research will tell. (Price and Lynn, 1981, p. 544)

## MEDICAL THERAPIES

A number of the techniques used with emotionally disturbed people do not involve direct behavioral manipulation. Instead, various kinds of medical treatment are used, either alone or in combination with certain psychotherapeutic techniques. It should be pointed out that these medical therapies can be administered only by physicians.

## Electro-convulsive Therapy

A patient, Nancy Twillings, is strapped to a hospital cart and wheeled into a room. Plainly visible is the machine that will deliver electroshock to the brain. Also present are a nurse, an attendant, an anesthesiologist, and a psychiatrist. Electrodes are attached to the patient's head. The psychiatrist says, "This won't hurt a bit." The anesthesiologist administers a drug to relax Nancy's muscles. A button is pushed, electrical impulses pass into the brain, and Nancy immediately goes into convulsions. When awakened later in a hospital room, Nancy is confused. She asks how she got there and wonders when she will get the treatment. Some alleviation of her symptoms may be noted, as well as some memory loss of the events immediately preceding the treatment. Nancy will again be wheeled into the room a number of times, and the same scenario will be repeated.

If she is suffering from a depressive state brought on by factors within herself (as opposed to external causes of depression, such as the loss of a loved one), she may show a remarkable improvement in her condition. We do not know why **electroconvulsive therapy (ECT)** works, when it works, but it does appear to be effective with various depressive states. In fact, in one extensive review of the literature, it was concluded that ECT was more effective than alternative procedures (e.g., drugs) in treating acute depressives (Scovern and Kilmann, 1980). Occasionally, ECT also appears to help some people suffering from schizophrenic disorders.

This patient is undergoing electroconvulsive therapy (ECT), a procedure that delivers electrical shocks to the brain. The technique has proved successful in treating various depressive states, but the reasons for its success are still unknown.

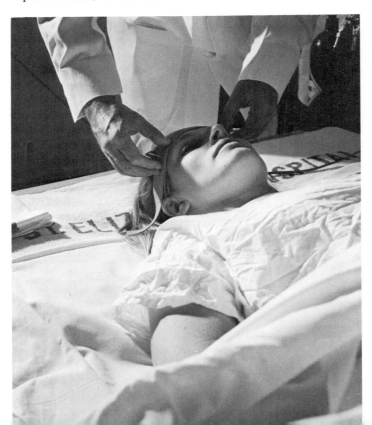

However, it does not seem to improve the disordered thought processes. Rather, it may alleviate the depressive symptoms that sometimes accompany the primary symptoms of schizophrenia.

## Chemotherapy

**Chemotherapy** is the use of various chemical substances (drugs) to treat disorders. Three main classes of chemotherapeutic agents are employed by psychiatrists: **minor tranquilizers, antipsychotic drugs,** and **antidepressants.**

**Minor tranquilizers.**   Certain disorders are characterized by hyperactivity, extreme anxiety, and hostile and destructive behavior. Individuals suffering from these disorders are usually not amenable to normal psychotherapy because their behavior interferes with the conduct of the therapy session. Such people have often been helped by the administration of *minor tranquilizers,* sometimes called *antianxiety drugs.*

Tranquilizers are commonly used by people to relieve feelings of tension and anxiety. Because they sometimes lead to undesired side effects, such as dizziness, nausea, and low blood pressure, and because many of them are potentially addictive, they should not be taken without medical advice.

**Antipsychotic drugs.**   The most dramatic effects of chemotherapy have been found with severely disturbed patients. In the 1950s, a drug called chlorpromazine (Thorazine) brought new hope to the psychiatric community. Used with schizophrenic patients, chlorpromazine reduced such symptoms as delusions, hallucinations, and disorganized thinking. Patients were calmer and more manageable but still remained alert, and there were no serious side effects. The atmosphere in mental hospitals was changed radically. Within a few years of its discovery, chlorpromazine and other antipsychotic drugs were being used as the primary form of treatment for many severely disturbed individuals, particularly schizophrenics.

Many studies have demonstrated the efficacy of antipsychotic drugs over placebos (Cole, 1964) and over other forms of treatment (May, 1968) for hospitalized schizophrenics. One measure of the impact of these drugs is the striking decline in the population of mental hospitals. In the 1950s approximately 560,000 mental patients resided in state mental institutions. At the beginning of the 1980s there are fewer than 200,000 patients inhabiting the state mental hospitals.

However, in spite of the dramatic changes in treatment, antipsychotic drugs have not provided the long-awaited cure for schizophrenia. Although many patients are able to leave the hospital and return to society, some still have residual symptoms and are never fully normal. Many have to be rehospitalized over and over again. One investigator (Hogarty, 1977) has cited a 37 percent relapse rate for patients receiving some form of maintenance antipsychotic drug therapy. Moreover, antipsychotic drug treatment can lead to side effects and complications that can be harmful

---

**Electroconvulsive therapy (ECT)**
A type of medical therapy in which electricity is used to produce convulsions and unconsciousness.

**Chemotherapy**
A therapeutic technique involving the treatment of disorders through the use of drugs.

**Minor tranquilizers**
A category of drugs that reduce feelings of tension and anxiety.

**Antipsychotic drugs**
A category of drugs that reduce the delusions, hallucinations, and disorganized thinking characteristic of patients with disorders such as schizophrenia.

**Antidepressants**
A category of drugs that relieve the despondency and agitation characteristic of patients with affective disorders.

to some patients. In spite of these limitations, there is no doubt that antipsychotic drugs are effective in reducing symptoms and have made an enormous difference in the environment of the hospitalized patient.

**Antidepressants.**    Other drugs known as *antidepressants* are used in the treatment of depressed, withdrawn, apathetic people. A review of studies employing a total of almost 6000 patients showed that four widely used antidepressants led to improvement in approximately 65 percent of the patients (Wechsler *et al.*, 1965).

One of the most interesting stories is that of lithium, an element found in small amounts in water throughout the world. A group of investigators noted a relationship between the amount of lithium found in water and the incidence of admissions to mental hospitals. Specifically, they noted that as the amount of lithium increased, the number of admissions decreased (Dawson *et al.*, 1970). Lithium appears to be particularly effective in the treatment of patients suffering manic episodes and bipolar disorders. One study reported an improvement rate of 70 to 80 percent among acutely agitated patients (Baldessarini, 1977). In the manic and depressive episodes of bipolar disorders, the mood swings occur less frequently. When they do occur, the debilitating effects are reduced (Van Praag, 1978).

However, lithium, like other chemotherapeutic agents, is a mixed blessing. It has a narrow safe range. If an overdose is administered, various body functions can be seriously impaired. It may even cause death. Furthermore, one practitioner has cautioned that "the decision [to prescribe lithium] should not be taken lightly as in most cases it is a life sentence as it often is with insulin in diabetes" (Holland, 1981, p. 147). Box 15.5 describes various possible psychological complications of drug treatment.

## Psychosurgery

The most dramatic form of medical therapy is **psychosurgery**—brain surgery used to treat emotional disturbances. The best known of these procedures is the prefrontal lobotomy, in which the frontal lobes of the brain are surgically detached from other parts of the brain.

When psychosurgery was first introduced it was greeted with enthusiastic claims for its success. However, later studies found that the effects were quite unpredictable. Some patients became more manageable, calmer, and less anxious. But many emerged from surgery little more than "vegetables" or "dehumanized zombies." Moreover, irreversible side effects such as seizures and impairments in intellectual and cognitive functioning were often observed (Barahal, 1958; Valenstein, 1973). Finally, because the effects of psychosurgery are permanent and irreversible, there have been both ethical and scientific objections to these procedures.

In spite of new advances in technical procedures, psychosurgery is still regarded as a "last resort" treatment. Because of recent advances in chemotherapy, psychosurgery is used only with the utmost care for those patients seemingly untreatable by other methods.

**Psychosurgery**
A type of medical therapy in which brain surgery is used to treat emotional disturbances.

# BOX 15.5

## Psychological Complications of Drug Treatment

Before the Food and Drug Administration (FDA) will grant approval for the marketing of a new drug, it first must undergo extensive clinical tests to insure its clinical value and safety. Even after a drug has met the rigorous licensing standards of the FDA, it still may produce side effects in certain patients. We have noted many of the physical side effects that are produced by drugs used to treat a variety of psychological disorders. But many of these drugs also induce psychological side effects that may change or compound the patient's symptoms. Such side effects are easily neglected or overlooked in a psychiatric population. A worsening of the patient's condition may be attributed to the "natural course" of the disorder, instead of drug-related complications.

Flaherty (1979) has summarized the psychological side effects of the antipsychotics, the antianxiety agents, and the antidepressant drugs. Let us now consider some of the major complications that can be induced by drugs in each of these classes.

**Antipsychotic drugs**  The major groups of antipsychotics are all capable of worsening the symptoms of psychosis by producing visual hallucinations, disorientation, and autonomic symptoms. In some cases antipsychotic medications can induce a fairly serious depression with insomnia, suicidal thoughts, and slowed motor activity. Reducing the dosage or substituting another drug may be helpful when such side effects are detected.

**Antianxiety agents**  Antianxiety drugs can heighten anxiety in patients with agitated depressions and increase the severity of depressed symptoms in patients who are depressed as well as anxious. Antianxiety drugs like the barbiturates have a fairly high abuse potential. If their use is abruptly discontinued for some reason in an addicted patient, a dangerous withdrawal syndrome may develop which requires prompt medical attention and treatment.

**Antidepressant drugs**  Tricyclic antidepressants can, in some patients, increase irritability. An acute manic episode may be triggered in patients with a history of mania. Schizophrenic symptoms may increase in severity if they are present during the course of administration of antidepressants (Flaherty, 1979).

These examples suggest that drug treatment for psychological disorders is not as straightforward as many people think. The very drugs that are used to treat a particular disorder may actually make the condition worse or create other problems for the patient. Over the entire course of treatment, careful monitoring of the psychological as well as the physical condition of the patient appears to be an absolute necessity.

Price and Lynn, 1981, pp. 516–517.

## A WORD ABOUT THERAPIES

As we noted earlier, many of us will seek professional psychological counseling at some point in our lives. For some people the need will carry with it a sense of urgency. The very core of their existence may feel threatened. For others, an acute but transitory crisis may precipitate a search for help. Still other people, with only minor adjustment problems, will immerse themselves in therapeutic programs in the hope of opening up new avenues of self-discovery and maximizing their own potential. But the menu of available therapies contains a smorgasbord of possible selections. How is a person to know where to turn for help?

If you read the theoretical statements of any therapeutic method, you will probably find them most convincing. When you read Freud, you may find his arguments insightful and reasonable—that is, until you read Rog-

## BOX 15.6

### Is Psychotherapy Effective?

For more than 25 years, psychologists have debated whether psychotherapy with neurotics is any more helpful than no therapy at all. The controversy about the effectiveness of psychotherapy can be traced to the publication of Hans Eysenck's review of studies of traditional therapeutic approaches to the treatment of neurosis (1952). Eysenck made the startling claim that patients who did not receive psychotherapy improved to the same extent as subjects who participated in the process. Eysenck's conclusion that traditional therapy was ineffective was based on his findings that 72 percent of patients appeared to improve without any special treatment ("spontaneous remission") after a two-year period, compared to a recovery rate of only 44 percent of patients in psychoanalysis and 66 percent of patients who participated in "eclectic" therapy. In later reviews, Eysenck argued forcefully against the notion that traditional therapy is effective and claimed that "uniformly negative" results extended to disorders other than neurotic conditions.

Eysenck's pessimism about the effectiveness of psychotherapy stimulated ardent defenses of its value. His conclusions were vigorously challenged. His reviews were criticized on both conceptual and statistical grounds. Furthermore, his opponents claim that he selected therapy studies and criteria of improvement which were biased against finding positive gains for traditional psychotherapy. It has also been argued that nontreated patients in control groups actually do receive support and advice (therapy) from friends, relatives, clergymen, and physicians. The qualities of effective psychotherapists may not be limited to licensed professionals. Individuals in the natural social environment may serve a therapeutic function for persons with neurotic disorders. Such spontaneous, unprogrammed therapy may account for some of the spontaneous remissions in nontreated individuals who seek and obtain therapeutic help from nontherapists. Thus, the recovery rates of nontreated individuals may have been inflated because neurotic persons may have received therapeutic aid in the natural environment (Bergin & Lambert, 1978).

Bergin and Lambert (1978) have argued that the rate of spontaneous remission is actually much lower than the statistic reported by Eysenck. Based on his recomputations of the data Eysenck drew from, Bergin concluded that a spontaneous remission rate of 43 percent may be more representative than the two-thirds estimate originally reported by Eysenck. Even if Eysenck's higher spontaneous remission rate were an accurate measure of improvement for nontreated neurotics, Bergin notes that the practice of psychotherapy would still be supported because patients in therapy improve in a much shorter time.

A number of more recent reviews support the conclusion that therapy is indeed effective. Mary Smith and Gene Glass (1977) at the University of Col-

ers or the proponents of any of a number of other contending therapies. As one observer noted:

*A book by a proponent of a particular therapy system can be quite persuasive. We may even find ourselves using the new ideas in therapy while reading the book. But when we turn to an advocate of a radically different approach, the confusion returns. Listening to proponents compare therapies does little for our confusion, except to confirm the rule that those who cannot agree on basic assumptions are often reduced to calling each other names. Thus, we unfortunately at times hear certain humanistic therapists refer to behavior therapists as cold, calculating controllers whose technological approaches to personal problems just add to the alienation of modern human beings. Some behaviorists counter by calling humanists tender-minded tearjerkers who are unscientific, anti-intellectual, and unable or unwilling to count. Meanwhile some psy-*

orado in Boulder analyzed the results of 375 controlled studies that reported the therapy outcomes of nearly 25,000 men and women. Smith and Glass found that regardless of the type of therapy they examined, psychotherapy always had some beneficial effect. Based on the studies they surveyed, they determined that the typical client who received treatment was better off in some way than three quarters of those who were untreated. Patients with symptoms of fear and anxiety showed even more impressive treatment gains over untreated control patients. These patients appeared to be more improved than 83 percent of the patients who did not receive psychotherapy.

Meltzoff and Kornriech (1970) compared the recovery rates of patients in 57 studies they considered to be well-designed, with 44 studies considered less adequate. The patients in the methodologically adequate studies showed higher rates of improvement than patients in the less well-designed studies (84 percent versus 75 percent).

The results of these studies lend some degree of confidence to the assertion that psychotherapy is effective [see Fig. 15.3]. It is unlikely, however, that even the positive findings of relatively large scale review efforts will quiet the voices of those who continue to debate the effectiveness of psychotherapy. We remain largely uncertain about which types of therapies work best with which types of patients and psychological disorders. Likewise, little is known

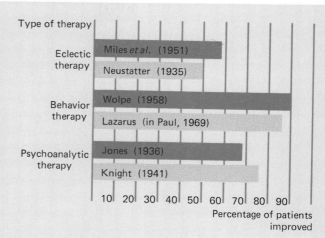

**Figure 15.3**
**Rates of improvement with psychotherapy**

about the specific therapeutic processes which lead to maximum change (Gottman & Markman, 1978). Answers to such questions will no doubt facilitate our understanding of the complex enterprise psychotherapy represents and improve our ability to better meet the needs of persons with problems in living.

Price and Lynn, 1981, pp. 455–456.

*choanalysts toss in their interpretative barbs by labeling behavior therapists naive, unanalyzed symptom treaters who are acting out their anal impulses to control; certain humanists are accused of acting out oedipal desires by playing touchy-feely games with taboo figures like patients.*
*(Prochaska, 1979, p. 2)*

Of course, psychoanalysis gets its share of criticism, too: It is perceived by some behaviorists as based on a questionable and unprovable theory and as having produced little substantiation of its effectiveness as a therapy; and it is perceived by humanists as time-consuming and expensive, to boot.

The truth of the matter is that many therapies may provide relief because of the features they share in common rather than because of the ways in which they differ. Most therapists do not practice only one style or theory of therapy. The effective therapist tailors the therapy to reflect

The sensitivity session is a form of therapy that helps people to achieve increased awareness of themselves and those around them.

the underlying structure according to which the client views the world, working to change whatever part of that structure has led the client to an inappropriate way of behaving. Many individuals beset by inner turmoil may require, more than anything else, a sympathetic ear, a soundboard that does not go "tsk! tsk!," an uninvolved but sympathetic observer, and a person who genuinely wishes them to bring order into their lives.

Is psychotherapy effective? This question has long been debated among mental health professionals as well as the general public. Box 15.6 on pages 576 and 577 explores some of the issues in this controversy.

# Summary

1. It has been estimated that 1 person in 10 will seek some form of treatment for emotional problems at some time in life. Psychological methods of treatment are called psychotherapy. Medical methods of treatment are referred to as medical therapy.

2. Four common forms of individual psychotherapy are psychoanalysis, person-centered therapy, rational–emotive therapy, and behavior therapy.

3. In classic psychoanalysis, the patient spends long sessions with the therapist free-associating and relating his or her dreams. The therapist remains detached, but assists the patient in seeing the unconscious meanings in the thoughts and actions described and through transference comes to represent the important people in the patient's life.

4. In person-centered therapy, the client directs the therapy. The therapist provides encouragement and emotional support to help the client minimize the disparity between the phenomenological self and the ideal self.

5. Rational–emotive therapy focuses on analyzing, understanding, and attacking the irrational belief systems of the client so that they may be repudiated and replaced with rational belief systems that will result in emotionally healthy and productive consequences.

6. Behavior therapists use techniques developed in learning research to help patients unlearn maladaptive behaviors and learn new, adaptive ones. Some specific methods employed include extinction, desensitization, modeling, positive reinforcement, and aversive conditioning.

7. Therapeutic techniques have been developed for the simultaneous treatment of several people. One of the most dramatic is psychodrama, which encourages the individual to act out conflicts rather than to discuss them.

8. Some groups represent an extension of traditional psychotherapeutic techniques, whereas others, such as encounter groups and sensitivity groups (T-groups), represent a departure from traditional methods.

9. In family therapy, the family unit, rather than the individual, is regarded as the patient. The goal of the psychotherapeutic process is to change the interactions among family members.

10. In the last few decades, primary care of even the severely disturbed has shifted from hospital settings to community mental health centers, in part because of improvements in chemical treatment of affective and schizophrenic disorders.

11. Some emotionally disturbed individuals are still treated with medical therapy, such as electroshock therapy or chemotherapy, used either alone or in combination with certain psychotherapeutic techniques. Although psychosurgery initially generated great enthusiasm among those working with the disturbed, because of its side effects and the improvement in chemotherapy its practice has been largely abandoned.

## Terms to Remember

| | | |
|---|---|---|
| Psychotherapy | Person-centered therapy | Group therapy |
| Medical therapy | Phenomenological (reality) self | Encounter group |
| Psychoanalysis | Ideal self | Internal locus of control |
| Psychosexual development | Behavior therapy (behavior modification) | Sensitivity group (T-group) |
| Repression | Extinction therapy | Electroconvulsive therapy (ECT) |
| Free association | Desensitization | Chemotherapy |
| Resistance | Symptom substitution | Minor tranquilizers |
| Manifest content | Positive reinforcer | Antipsychotic drugs |
| Latent content | Contingent reinforcement | Antidepressants |
| Dream analysis | Token economy | Psychosurgery |
| Transference | Aversive conditioning | |

16

# SOCIAL PSYCHOLOGY

## THE INDIVIDUAL IN SOCIETY

Do you think of yourself as a free and independent individual? Think for a moment about a typical day in your life. To what extent are you free of social pressures and restraints? Are the clothes you wear, the food you eat, your attitudes, your likes and dislikes truly and completely under your personal control?

If you think carefully, you will probably conclude that everything you do is influenced by the values, attitudes, and pressures of others. The very language you speak and the symbols with which you think are products of the **society** you live in. From the moment you get up in the morning, every aspect of your daily life is governed by the rules, regulations, and controls imposed on you by your parents, your friends, your teachers, and perhaps even the police officer on the corner.

How about people who have joined nonconformist groups? Are they any less subject to group pressures? Not necessarily. A member of the armed forces announced that he was a homosexual. He deviated from the heterosexual norm. The armed forces showed him that he was not free of social pressure: They abruptly and unceremoniously discharged him.

It is clear that social forces exert a compelling and pervasive influence on all aspects of our lives, from the cradle to Medicare. These influences are the concern of **social psychology.** Social psychologists study the individual in society—the ways in which the individual interacts with and modifies social groups to which he or she belongs and the various social forces that interact to influence the individual's behavior and thinking.

## Culture and Society

Societies differ from one another in what their members consider to be socially acceptable behavior. For example, do you consider it socially acceptable for a woman to run the household and be responsible for the economic activities of the family, while the man spends his time decorating himself, dancing, and gossiping with other men? If you were born and raised in the United States, you would probably question the appropriateness of this behavior. If you were a member of the Tchambuli tribe in New Guinea, however, you would find nothing extraordinary about it. Male children of the Tchambuli tribe are prepared for a life of dependence which, by Western standards, might be considered "feminine." The females are trained to be self-assertive and independent (Mead, 1939).

This example shows the effect of contrasting patterns of **culture** on human behavior. Studies of various cultures have shown the extreme malleability of human behavior. Margaret Mead, one of the foremost authorities on cultural differences and their effects on human behavior, made the following observation:

> The differences between individuals who are members of different cultures, like the differences between individuals within a culture, are almost entirely to be laid to differences in conditioning, especially during early childhood, and the form of this conditioning is culturally determined. Standardized personality differences between the sexes are of this order, cultural creations to which each generation, male and female, is trained to conform. (Mead, 1939, p. 191)

**Subcultures exist as segments of a larger culture and are distinguished by their own sets of values and traditions.**

The members of a given culture do not necessarily all behave and think in identical, prescribed ways. Nor do they all necessarily share common beliefs, values, and attitudes. Within any culture there may be various **subcultures;** these are segments of the larger culture that are characterized by their own customs, traditions, beliefs, values, and attitudes. For example, the rules governing eye contact vary according to one's subculture. Urban white Americans, for instance, avoid direct eye contact with a stranger once they are within recognition distance. On the other hand, many blacks look directly at one another, even if they are strangers. For some reason, differences in the way people of completely different cultures behave are much more easily accepted than differences in the behavior of individuals belonging to subcultures of one's own society. To black Americans, the eye behavior of whites gives the impression that they are being ignored, that they are not there. In fact, urban whites avoid eye contact with *anyone* with whom they are not familiar (Hall and Hall, 1971).

People may be influenced simultaneously by several different subcultures in the same society. They may live in a large metropolitan urban area, or a small rural community. They may be members of a particular ethnic group and observe a specific religious faith. They may belong to an academic, business, or professional community. Their behaviors and life-styles may reflect the influence of these many subcultures.

## Socialization and Roles

Some years ago the nation was stirred by the plight of a five-year-old girl, Anna, who was found locked up in an upstairs room. She had been there since infancy. The room was completely dark and unventilated, and had a chair for a bed. Anna's hands were tied above her head. Her mother occasionally provided a large quantity of milk but nothing else. No balanced diet. No love. No conversation. No instruction. This was Anna's punishment for making the supreme mistake of being illegitimate.

She was emaciated, both deaf and blind, totally listless and apathetic to everything. After many months of exposure to an enriched environment, it became apparent that she was neither deaf nor blind. She was able to acquire a few skills: toilet training, feeding herself, and walking. She even learned a few words and was able to call people by name. But it became clear, after years of effort, that five years of social isolation had wreaked irreversible damage. She would never become a warm, loving, intelligent human being (Davis, 1940, 1947).

Cases of this sort, no matter how extreme, remind us how much "becoming human" involves a combination of genetic potential and a social environment. Indeed, the human being is preeminently a social animal. Each of us is, in fact, the product of a social act—sexual intercourse. From the moment of birth, we and those around us are totally and inescapably enmeshed in a web of complex social interactions. Even when we are infants, our presence has a profound influence on the lives of those around us; we, in turn, are completely dependent on others for nurturance, support, and instruction. As we grow, we learn the language of our parents, what behaviors are acceptable to those about us, how to express certain emotions and feelings, and how and when to conceal them. In short, we learn to behave as other members of our society expect us to behave. This is referred to as **socialization.**

In childhood, socialization is largely accomplished by the operation of external forces—rewards applied to encourage appropriate behaviors and punishment administered to discourage undesired or inappropriate behaviors. In time we come to accept the **norms** and values of our society as guides for our own behavior. Incorporation of these norms and values into our internal "guidance system" is known as **internalization.**

Although internalization of values is obviously important in achieving and maintaining social order, it does not necessarily work in behalf of all members of a society. For many years both women and men have been subjected to an almost continuous assault of propaganda aimed at preparing them to assume their appropriate sex roles. The male has been expected to be aggressive, assertive, individualistic, inventive, and unemotional, and to exude self-confidence—the John Wayne type. However, strict adherence to this stereotyped role often leads to lowered self-esteem and anxiety in adulthood (Bem, 1975). In contrast, women have been expected to be compliant, warm, modest, and sensitive. These were felt to be desirable qualities for their roles as "helpmate," wife, and mother. However, many men and women in our society have devalued the traits defining "femininity." Acceptance of this sex-role stereotype means being dependent, emotional, and vulnerable, and these are characteristics we regard as immature (Bem, 1975).

**Socialization**
The process by which we acquire socially important behaviors.

**Norms**
Standards and expectations shared by a group.

**Internalization**
Incorporation of the norms and values of society into one's internal "guidance system."

**Androgyny**
The ability to express both feminine and masculine traits as the situation requires.

Thus strict adherence to the male sex-role stereotype by men and the female sex-role stereotype by women would leave neither men nor women completely fulfilled as adults. In recent years, it has been argued that members of both sexes would benefit by having available to them the full range of characteristics previously labeled as masculine or feminine. Thus expression of so-called masculine traits might be beneficial to a person, whether male or female, in certain situations. In other situations, expression of so-called feminine qualities might be advantageous. A person who is able to embrace the full range of qualities and to express them according to the demands of the situation would presumably be freer, more flexible, and more stable, emotionally. A person able to make such adjustments has been called **androgynous** (Bem, 1974).

Today many women are demanding that their horizons be expanded to encompass activities formerly the exclusive domain of the male. It is interesting that children's literature is already beginning to reflect these changing times and values. In contrast to a few decades ago, advocates of traditional roles for women are increasingly being portrayed as the "bad guys" (see Fig. 16.1).

One word of caution: The fact that individuals behave *as if* they have accepted the values of their society does not necessarily mean that they have internalized the norms. As one observer has noted:

> *If people were no longer threatened with punishment for their misdeeds, how many people would remain moral? Perhaps when all the shouting is done, people are more responsive to threats and rewards than is realized. Although it is valuable to preserve the idea of internalization, one should also recognize the strong possibility that people may behave in socially approved ways not so much because they have internalized norms, but because they have learned what consequences to expect for violating social norms. (Schneider, 1976, p. 189)*

This point is clearly made in the following excerpt from *Roots:*

> *It occurred to Kunta that these blacks masked their true feelings for the toubob [white man] . . . . He had by now many times witnessed the blacks' grinning faces turn to bitterness the instant a toubob turned his head away. He had seen them break their working tools on purpose, and then act totally unaware of how it happened as the "oberseer" bitterly cursed them for their clumsiness. And he had seen how blacks in the field, for all their show of rushing about whenever the toubob was nearby, were really taking twice as much time as they needed to do whatever they were doing.\**

In part, the socialization process is aimed at preparing each of us to occupy different positions in the social structure. These positions can be quite varied for any given individual. For example, a female in late adolescence may be a college student, a daughter, a part-time employee in

---

\*From *Roots* by Alex Haley. Copyright © 1976 by Alex Haley. Reprinted by permission of Doubleday & Company, Inc.

the school cafeteria, and a member of a woman's activist group. As a student, she is expected to attend classes, study, take examinations, and pass her courses. As a daughter, she is called upon to be helpful to her parents. As an employee, she is expected to be industrious and to submit to the authority of her employer. As a member of a woman's activist group, she is expected to be an articulate spokeswoman for women's rights.

The patterns of behavior expected in given social positions are called **roles.** Roles may vary in permanence. After students graduate, many of their roles as members of the college community will terminate, and they may assume new roles as husbands and wives, fathers and mothers, and professional workers.

At any given time, the different roles a person plays may be in conflict with one another. For example, the norms of the parents are frequently in conflict with those of the peer group. When they are, children

**Role**
The pattern of behavior expected in a given social position.

Figure 16.1    **Children's literature is beginning to reflect both the changing attitudes toward men and women and the changing expectations about what they are supposed to do. Here the boy holding traditional views about the appropriate behaviors of males and females is given a negative identification (Goofus). In contrast, the up-to-date boy who accepts these changes is identified as Gallant.**

Copyright © 1976, HIGHLIGHTS FOR CHILDREN, INC. Columbus, Ohio.

Many of us are faced with conflicting roles to play. Daniel Ellsberg was both a dedicated government employee and a concerned citizen who felt compelled to reveal the truth about the Vietnam War. He was dismissed from his duties at the Defense Department after leaking the Pentagon Papers to the public.

are more likely to be influenced by peers than by parents as they grow older (Torrance, 1969). Adherence to peer norms increases with age. In contrast, adherence to parent norms steadily declines with age (Berndt, 1979).

The patterns of behavior expected in a given role are not always clear-cut. The expectations depend on the social context. Whereas parents may expect their son or daughter to be respectful and obedient, the peer group may call upon the youngster to cut the ties of parental domination. Thus conflict may arise concerning manner of dress, hairstyle, and whether or not to try certain drugs. Conflicting roles continue to plague us throughout our lives. H. G. Wells, when surveying the many expectations people had of him in the roles of famous author, husband, and father, was reported to have proclaimed in despair, "I am not a person; I am a mob."

## JUDGING OTHERS— ATTRIBUTION THEORY

Imagine the following situation. You are a passive observer at a job interview of two candidates for a position at a munitions manufacturer. Candidate A is interviewed first. When asked the question, "How important is it that the United States maintain a strong military posture in the present day world?" Candidate A replies:

*Absolutely essential. The world is in a terrible state of tension. Numerous leaders of nations and terrorist groups are standing at our door looking for weaknesses, searching for signs of a wavering in our resolve to defend ourselves against aggression. We must remain strong so that other nations will not be tempted to test us on the battlefield. That's why I want the position. Your company plays a vital role in our national defense.*

In response to the same question, Candidate B says:

*I think we're overdoing this preparedness thing. We're spending hundreds of billions of dollars on defense each year while we're neglecting the needs of the people. For my part, I believe the threats of external aggression are largely trumped up as a means of feeding funds into the military–industrial complex. The position with this company interests me only from a management point of view. I deplore its mission.*

Having read the replies of the two candidates, answer the following question. "Was Candidate A or Candidate B more sincere in response to the interviewer's question?" If you were like most people, you selected Candidate B as more sincere. You may also have judged B as being self-defeating and perhaps a bit on the stupid side. But why might you consider Candidate B more sincere than A?

**Attribution theories**
Theories concerned with how people use information about behavior to make judgments about the cause of that behavior.

This question takes us into the core of **attribution theory.** Many social psychologists have suggested that we do not take the behavior of others at face value. Rather, before making a judgment about the behavior of others, we want to know *why* they behaved as they did. It is this attribution of cause that gives attribution theory its name. In general, we may attribute the behavior to internal characteristics of another person (that person's dispositions) or to external (situational) factors. The judgments we make about that person will depend on the attributions we make. Let's look at another example.

Franklin S. has asked Flora G. to marry him. Flora is extremely plain but very wealthy. Is Franklin proposing to Flora out of love for her (an internal disposition) or for her money (a situational factor)? What if she were both plain and poor? Would we change our judgment?

In the first case, where Flora is plain and wealthy, we are likely to attribute the marriage proposal to a situational factor—her enormous wealth. We are far less likely to judge this a case of true love because, in our society, we tend to value physical appearance very highly. We may reason, "If she's not attractive, then her money must be a factor." But when Flora is both plain and poor, we are more willing to accept the proposition that Franklin loves her. From this example, it should be clear that the underlying causes we attribute to behavior can often be extremely ambiguous. Very good-looking people are never sure why other people are attracted to them—for reasons of physical appearance alone or because of an engaging personality? Similar considerations apply to wealthy, or successful, or prominent people.

Because of this ambiguity, we are often forced to test our attributions in everyday life. If Flora loses all her wealth and Franklin remains steadfast in his attention to her, we would probably change our attribution.

"Why, he really does love her," we might say, somewhat surprised. In real life, much of the evidence we use to test the accuracy of our attributions falls into three broad categories: consistency, consensus, and freedom from external pressure.

## Consistency

When we first meet Fred, he is cheerful, carefree, warm, and friendly. But this is at a cocktail party, when moods are usually elevated. Nevertheless, we form a favorable first impression of him. But the nagging question remains: "Is it the ambience of the situation or does he possess a genuinely warm and friendly temperament?" The next time we see him, the situation is rife with tension and hostility. Two close friends have been in bitter conflict and a shouting match is going on. Fred is trying to intervene. He remains calm, warm, friendly, and optimistic throughout the exchange. We are now more inclined to attribute his behavior to dispositional factors (he really *is* a warm, friendly person). We see him again after he has suffered a personal tragedy. He is sad, somewhat subdued, but remains friendly and optimistic. The consistency of his behavior in three contrasting situations now convinces us that our first impression was essentially correct. However, had he responded with anger, hostility, or aggression in either of the two stressful situations, we might then attribute his behavior to situational factors: "Fred is a will-o'-the-wisp, changing with changed circumstances."

## Consensus

The search for consensus pervades many aspects of our lives. We often share our opinions of others with close friends. This is in part due to the fact that rarely is anyone an open book. There are always ambiguities and doubts. "From what I have seen of her, Sally appears to be extremely bright," we think, after engaging her in conversation. But when friends say, "Wow, that Sally is a smart one," we feel more confident in attributing high intelligence to her.

Much research on the role of consensus supports the following proposition: When we learn that others agree with us, we feel more confident in our judgments; when we find that others disagree with us, our confidence wanes (Wells and Harvey, 1977; Middlebrook, 1980). It is important to note that this is true as long as we feel that the others are free to express an honest judgment and when we do not perceive ulterior motives for their views.

## Freedom from External Pressure

Recall Candidate A, with whom we opened this discussion. Recall that, in the job interview, he or she said many favorable things about national defense, the need for a strong military posture, and the contribution of the munitions industry to national goals. Was the candidate sincere? We may feel some doubt because the situation demanded that favorable things be said if the candidate was to land the job. We may also question

At political conventions, large groups of followers affirm each other in backing the candidate of their choice.

the objectivity and integrity of a lobbyist who has much to gain by winning congressional legislative concessions. Similarly, we may discount confessions squeezed out of physical or mental torture chambers. Generally, whenever we perceive external pressures to be forcing others to behave in a given way, we tend to attribute the behavior to situational rather than dispositional factors. We question whether or not Galileo really did repent when his very life was at stake if he failed to comply with the demand for a confession.

## INTER- PERSONAL ATTRACTION

Our judgments of others are an important first step in deciding whom we do and do not like and love. But there are a great many other factors that influence this important aspect of social psychology, among them similarity, proximity, familiarity, and physical attractiveness. In this section, we will examine each of these elements in turn. First, however, we will examine how research on interpersonal attraction is conducted.

## Studying Interpersonal Attraction

Imagine that you enter a class at the beginning of the semester. You volunteer to participate in your instructor's study aimed at assessing the beliefs and attitudes of the incoming students. You are then administered a scale that consists of a number of items in which you either agree with or disagree with a number of statements, such as: "Religion is very important in my life." Later in the semester, you are asked to participate in a study in which you will be requested to judge the attractiveness of other people. The instructor does not indicate that the two activities are in any way related.

When you appear in the laboratory, you are asked to read an attitude scale that was purportedly filled in by another person (the stimulus person). You are then asked to fill out a scale about this stimulus person. Embedded in this scale are two items that assess your attraction to that person. In reality, no other person has filled out the attitude scale. Rather, the instructor has purposely constructed a set of answers that agree with yours (creating a similar stimulus person) or disagree with yours (creating a dissimilar stimulus person). The same procedures have been used with many other subjects. The results are then analyzed to determine to what extent, if any, similarity of subject and stimulus person affects the subject's rating of attraction.

In one classic study, it was found that the rating of attractiveness of the stimulus person was directly related to the proportion of items in the attitude scale on which the subject and the stimulus person agreed (Byrne and Nelson, 1965). In fact, this finding is so consistent that a group of researchers has shown that the relationship between proportion of agreement and attraction can be described mathematically by a straight line (Schoenemann *et al.*, 1976).

The procedures used to assess interpersonal attraction can be modified to find answers to other intriguing questions involving interpersonal attraction. For example, what's in a name? Apparently quite a bit. When college students were asked to select a beauty queen they voted for those with a desirable first name. Six photographs, ranked equivalent in physical attractiveness, were presented to 197 college students. Half the photographs were assigned a desirable first name, and half an undesirable one. The results: 158 to 39 in favor of the more attractive names (Garwood *et al.*, 1980).

## Similarity

We have all heard the expression "Opposites attract." In physical nature, this is a statement of fact. For example, opposite poles of a magnet do exert a strong attraction for one another, and like poles repel each other. By analogy, we have often applied this expression to human relationships. Thus when we observe strong alliances among individuals of different social, religious, or ethnic backgrounds, we may smile and smugly assert, "Aha, just as I have always said. Opposites attract."

Is this really true of human relationships? If anything, research on the subject of interpersonal attraction repudiates the notion of opposites attracting one another. Rather, people whom we perceive as similar to us are more likely to appeal to us than those we see as dissimilar.

In one study, a computer dating procedure was used to ascertain if religious or sexual attitudes were more important (Touhey, 1972). Some couples were matched according to sexual attitudes or religious attitudes. Others were *mismatched* on these variables. After an opportunity had been provided for the couples to interact, the attraction within each couple was measured. It was found that males felt sexual attitudes were more impor-

The membership patterns of various college sororities and fraternities typify the tendency to affiliate with people we perceive as similar to ourselves. These groups tend to recruit new members who, like these pledges at Berkeley, are similar in their interests, attitudes, and even physical attractiveness.

tant, whereas females were most attracted to men with similar religious views.

But what happens if you are shown a profile similar to yours, but the individual is identified as an undesirable person or belonging to a group that you do not favor? Under these circumstances, you are likely to dislike that person more than you would if he or she were dissimilar to you. It seems that we will go out of our way to dissociate ourselves from people similar to us who possess some undesirable characteristic (Novak and Lerner, 1968).

## Proximity

Even in this day of supersonic planes and rapid transit, **proximity** is one of the greatest determinants of who will be attracted to whom. Much research has been done in this area. A classic study by Festinger, Schachter, and Back (1950) found that, among residents of a university housing project for married students, individuals living right next door to each other were nearly twice as likely to be friends as those who lived even one apartment away. Physical nearness also appears to explain why students seated alphabetically tend to have close friends with the same last initial (Segal, 1974). In short, if you want to be emotionally close to someone, first get close to that person geographically.

## Familiarity

Proximity is closely linked to the influence of familiarity, the idea that the more you see someone, the more you will like that person—even if you don't know him or her. For example, Jorgensen and Cervone (1978) found that individuals shown pictures of strangers expressed more positive feelings toward a person when shown his or her picture on several occasions. It seems that, contrary to the old adage, familiarity does not breed contempt.

## Physical Attractiveness

Everywhere we turn we are assaulted with sights and sounds reminding us of the importance in our culture of being physically attractive. Advertisers spend enormous sums trying to persuade us that, if we use their products, we will be beautiful and thus attractive—especially to the opposite sex.

Physical attractiveness does appear to play a large role in interpersonal attraction. In one study (Byrne *et al.*, 1970), students attended a dance with partners they thought were computer-selected, but who were actually randomly assigned. The strongest predictor of satisfaction with one's date seemed to be that person's appearance. There appears to be a sexist component to this, however, with men being more influenced by the physical attractiveness of women than women are by the physical attractiveness of men (Krebs and Adinolfi, 1975).

For those of us who are less than "10s", it should be of some consolation to note that physical attractiveness appears to be less important in mate selection (Stroebe *et al.*, 1971) than in dating. Still, it seems that, at least initially, we "judge a book by its cover" when picking our friends and lovers.

## HOW GROUPS INFLUENCE BEHAVIOR

Now that we have looked at how we function in society as individuals and in one-to-one situations, we need to examine how we function in groups. Individuals may behave differently when they act as part of a group than when they act alone. Groups exert a continuing and pervasive influence on all aspects of our lives: our beliefs, attitudes, likes, and dislikes. Many investigators have demonstrated that a number of psychological processes are subject to group influences and pressures.

When we adapt our behavior or beliefs to be consistent with our perception of group values, we are **conforming.** The concept of conforming implies some conflict between the way we want to act and the way that group pressures expect us to behave. Thus if we behave as expected because we have internalized group values, we do not speak of this behavior as conformity (Worchel and Cooper, 1979). The group pressures involved in conforming behavior are implicit. The group does not *directly* demand that we behave in a given fashion. If the group does make its wishes explicit and command us to behave in a particular way, it is commanding our **obedience.** When we yield to pressures of those in authority ("just obeying orders"), our behavior is described as *obedient.* Both conformity and obedience have been the subject of extensive investigation.

**Proximity**
Physical nearness; propinquity.

**Conformity**
The process of adapting one's beliefs or behaviors so that they will be consistent with one's perception of group values.

**Obedience**
Yielding to the pressures of those in authority.

## Conformity

**Figure 16.2**
**Which of the lines matches line *X*?**

Percentage of
correct
estimates

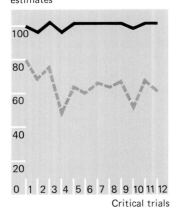

Critical trials

**Figure 16.3**
**Conformity**

When the subjects were not under pressure to conform, their judgments were virtually without error (solid line). When subjects made judgments in the face of group pressure, they made many errors (broken line). (Asch, 1955)

Look at the three lines in Fig. 16.2. Which line do you think matches line *X*? You have undoubtedly selected line *b* as the appropriate match. Do you think there are any conditions under which you could be convinced to select either line *a* or line *c*? Surprisingly, a series of investigations showed that, under certain experimental conditions, many individuals can be pressured into making an obviously incorrect judgment (Asch, 1951, 1955, 1956). Let's look at several of the experimental manipulations that have identified some of the factors involved in conformity behavior.

The basic experimental design involved groups consisting of several subjects who were required to match lines similar to those shown in Fig. 16.2. Only one of the subjects in each group was naive, that is, unaware of the design of the experiment. Unknown to this one person, the others were confederates working for the experimenter. The confederates were instructed to agree on an incorrect judgment on 12 of the 18 trials and to exert pressure on the naive subject to accept this judgment. The results are summarized in Fig. 16.3. As you can see, the average number of correct estimates given by the naive subjects is lower on all trials in which the confederates "ganged up" on the naive subjects. When the naive subjects were not exposed to group pressures, their judgments were virtually perfect.

Not all subjects were equally influenced by group pressures (see Box 16.1). Some subjects maintained their independence and never yielded to group pressures, whereas others agreed with the incorrect judgments of the majority almost all of the time. The naive subject in Fig. 16.4 was among the independent subjects. Note the obvious concern on his face as he leans forward to check his judgment.

In a variation of the original experimental design, the number of individuals pitted against the naive subject was systematically varied. The effect of group pressures rose rapidly from 3.6 percent errors with one confederate until, with three confederates opposing the judgment of the naive subject, the subject's errors were approximately 32 percent. Increasing the number of confederates beyond three did not appear to make a substantial difference in the number of errors the naive subject made. Thus the size of the opposition group appears to be important only up to a certain point.

In both of the situations just described, the naive subjects stood alone against a unanimous majority. What happens if the unanimity is disturbed by introducing a second subject (either a confederate instructed always to give correct answers or another naive subject)? In experiments, the effect of this manipulation was striking. The support of only a single individual was enough to decrease errors made by the naive subjects to about one-fourth of the errors made when they were pitted alone against the confederates. The errors remained relatively low even when the supporting partner left the room. But when the partner "defected" to the majority after the sixth trial, the error scores of the naive subjects showed an abrupt rise. Their frequency of errors increased to about the same level as in the original experimental session, in which the naive subject was opposed by the unanimous majority.

We previously indicated (see Box 1.2, Chapter 1) that all individuals do not appear to be equally susceptible to the influence of others. It has

## BOX 16.1

### Who's Fooling Whom?

After reading about the Asch procedure, you may be feeling a little sorry for the poor subjects. After all, they've been deceived, and if they conformed, they may be feeling embarrassed at their own plasticity.

But are all subjects so gullible that they accept the Asch procedure without question? Obviously, if some subjects become suspicious, the validity of the Asch procedure as a genuine conformity dilemma is greatly diminished. Thus assessing the frequency of the occurrence of suspicion among the subjects is of great importance. Unfortunately, relatively few studies have been done on the occurrence of suspicion, and the results of those that have been done are exceedingly mixed. Percentages of suspicion among subjects in the Asch procedure have varied all of the way from 2 percent (Vaughan, 1964) to 75 percent (Glinski *et al.*, 1970).

What might make subjects become suspicious? In one study in which junior and senior college students were used and a 75 percent rate of suspicion was obtained, a number of reasons emerged (Glinski *et al.*, 1970). Some of the students had prior knowledge of the Asch procedure. As one psychology student said, "I read this one, therefore I wasn't susceptible to the 'Asch' phenomenon." Aspects of the procedure itself seemed to raise the subject's suspicion. Out of twenty-eight subjects tested with a unanimous majority, twenty-six were suspicious of the prolonged unanimity of the majority. They felt that a consistent majority was simply incredible. Some students were suspicious because of information they had received from others who had already participated in the study. Although the usual request not to discuss the experiment with other students was made, five of the twenty-eight subjects "admitted that they had been given some information about the experiment" (p. 482).

Although the percentage of suspicious subjects among these advanced college students may be higher than that found in most conformity studies, the problem cannot be solved simply by using less "sophisticated" subjects. Conformity studies using high school students have also shown high percentages of suspicious subjects. In one study 55.7 percent of the boys tested and 38.8 percent of the girls tested were suspicious (Stricker *et al.*, 1967). The current emphasis on group conformity in the mass media may be alerting precollege subjects.

More work is needed to assess whether or not the high percentage of suspicion found in these two conformity studies is typical. However, the results do suggest that when future studies are done using the Asch procedure, investigators will have to be more concerned with the problem of the suspicious student. If students conform less when they are suspicious (Glinski *et al.*, 1970), and if suspicion has been more widespread than commonly thought, the true incidence of conformity may be even higher than that reported in the literature.

Middlebrook, 1980, p. 432.

---

**Internal locus of control**
The orientation that the various outcomes in life are a direct consequence of forces within the individual.

**External locus of control**
The orientation that the various outcomes in life are determined by forces outside the individual.

been suggested that susceptibility might be related to the **internal–external locus of control** dimension. In a comprehensive summary of research relating locus of control to conformity behavior one observer noted:

> . . . *evidence has been found which indicates that persons holding an internal locus of control withstand pressures directing them to behave in certain circumscribed manners. This is not true in all instances, although the exceptions to this generalization are revealing. Internals do yield to pressures, but not to the same pressures as externals. When acted upon as an object of experimentation, internals become almost playfully negativistic.*

**Figure 16.4**
**Asch conformity study**

*. . . However, internals do respond positively to reasoned argu-*
*ments, regardless of the status of the source, readily respond to directives*
*that seem congruent with their own perceptions, and shift in attitudes*
*and behavior when engaged in role playing, which allows more active*
*participation and self-direction. Externals appear to be responsive to the*
*status of the influencer and more ready to accept the suggestions and*
*directions of an experimenter. (Lefcourt, 1976, p. 48)*

Experiments on conformity behavior go beyond the laboratory into
real-life situations. In many business and industrial settings, workers often resist every effort by the management to introduce change. They frequently develop a set of norms that call for the maintenance of the status
quo. They express their resentment of change by various job actions:
work slowdowns, sick days, and sloppy and inefficient production. In a
sense, the management is in the position of the minority subject in the
conformity studies just discussed. How does it go about achieving orderly, nondisruptive, and acceptable change when the norms of the majority oppose it? In the conformity studies discussed so far, the object has
been to learn the conditions that influence an individual to conform to
group pressures. Other studies have been concerned with how group
norms may themselves be modified in order to permit change.

In one study conducted in a pajama factory, the company wished to
introduce several changes in production procedures. In order to determine the best method of overcoming worker resistance, an experiment
was conducted. In the control group, the workers were merely informed
that the changes were necessary to reduce cost and that a new piece-rate
schedule was being introduced. In two of the experimental groups, which
differed from each other in minor details, the workers and their leaders
were actively involved in a discussion of the cost problem. They agreed
that streamlining was possible, and even made constructive suggestions
of their own. In the subsequent 32-day observation period, the production levels of the control subjects fell below previous levels and remained
so throughout the experiment. All the experimental groups showed an
initial drop, but this was followed by an abrupt rise to levels that remained higher than those prevailing before the change (Coch and French,
1948).

## Obedience

If conformity raises questions about how far we should go to appease the group, obedience poses even more severe problems. To obey involves a certain measure of faith and trust in the source to be obeyed—faith that it has our best interests at heart and will do us no harm. It is thus the potential blindness of obedience that is its greatest danger.

From time to time, people are horrified when they learn of heinous crimes committed in the name of obedience. In Nazi Germany, for instance, millions of Jews were mutilated, raped, and executed by soldiers following orders. More recently, we were shocked by the revelations of the massacre at My Lai in Vietnam by soldiers who protested that they were just obeying orders. Are these atrocities bizarre departures from the norm performed by abnormal individuals, or can any responsible and respected person be persuaded to inflict punishment upon another human being?

Blind obedience to authority figures has caused many wartime crimes to be committed in the name of following orders.

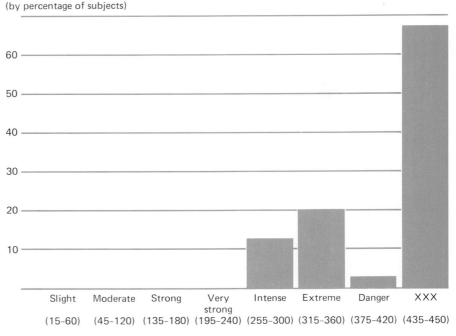

Maximum shock administered
(by percentage of subjects)

| | Slight | Moderate | Strong | Very strong | Intense | Extreme | Danger | XXX |
|---|---|---|---|---|---|---|---|---|
| | (15-60) | (45-120) | (135-180) | (195-240) | (255-300) | (315-360) | (375-420) | (435-450) |

Figure 16.5   **Subjects were told to administer increasing amounts of shock (voltages are given in**
Obedience   **parentheses) to a "learner." All 40 subjects administered shocks scaled "intense" or**
**higher. Only 35 percent of the subjects broke off before the end (see the text). (Milgram,**
**1963)**

In a dramatic study of destructive obedience, Stanley Milgram (1963) drew worldwide attention (see Fig. 16.5). He attempted to learn the extent to which a subject can be induced to inflict pain on another subject in response to an authority figure (the experimenter). The study was conducted under the pretext that the experimenter was trying to determine the effect of punishment on learning. Each of the 40 male subjects was told to test another subject (a confederate of the experimenter) on a learning task and to administer an increasing amount of punishment each time the "learner" made an error. Punishment was "administered" through a shock generator controlled by the subject. The intensity of the shock could be varied from slight (15 volts) through 30 different steps to severe shock (450 volts). Actually, the apparatus was not connected, but the "learner" was instructed to respond as if in pain. Whenever the subject hesitated to deliver punishment, he was prodded by the experimenter with such statements as, "Please continue," or "You have no other choice, you *must* go on" (Milgram, 1963).

Suppose you were a subject in this experiment. At what point would you stop administering the shock? Keep in mind that you have nothing to lose by stopping; you will incur only the displeasure of the authority figure. You might be surprised to learn that, in the actual experiment, 65 percent of the subjects obeyed the commands of the experimenter fully, and "administered" the highest amount of shock possible (see Fig. 16.5).

While doing this, however, many subjects reacted with acute discomfort and tension. The following observation was made of one of the subjects.:

> *I observed a mature and initially poised businessman enter the laboratory smiling and confident. Within 20 minutes he was reduced to a twitching, stuttering wreck, who was rapidly approaching a point of nervous collapse. He constantly pulled on his earlobe, and twisted his hands. At one point he pushed his fist into his forehead and muttered: "Oh God, let's stop." And yet he continued to respond to every word of the experimenter, and obeyed to the end. (Milgram, 1963, p. 377)*

In this study the subject was separated from the "victim" by being placed in a different room. What do you suppose would happen if they were both in the same room, so that the subject had a direct view of the agony being "inflicted"? Under these circumstances, the proportion of subjects who went "all the way" was reduced to 40 percent (Tilker, 1970). In another experiment, subjects were, in effect, given command authority. They could order somebody else to deliver the shocks, and thus could act as indirect rather than direct punishing agents. Under these circumstances, they were more likely to go "all the way" than were those who had to pull the switch themselves (Kilham and Mann, 1974).

Studies of this sort have provoked a great deal of criticism on ethical grounds (see Box 16.2). Milgram has replied:

> *I must say that I was totally astonished by the criticism that my experiment engendered. I thought what I was doing was posing a very legitimate question. How far would people proceed if they were asked to give increasingly severe shocks to another person? . . . I'm convinced that much of the criticism, whether people know it or not, stems from the results of the experiment. If everyone had broken off at slight shock or moderate shock, this would be a very reassuring finding and who would protest? (Milgram, 1977, p. 98)*

It should be emphasized that these experiments involved *destructive* obedience. Not all obedience is undesirable. Clearly the harmonious working of any group or society requires that its members obey certain rules and laws and conform to norms within acceptable ranges.

## Communication

Both conformity and obedience involve the influence of the group on the individual. Let us now examine one of the ways in which the individual influences the group—through communication.

All groups have a definite communication structure that specifies who may interact with whom and on what occasions. Some groups, such as seminar and encounter groups, permit a free flow of communication among all members. Other groups place a restriction on the direction of the communication. For example, in the traditional lecture class, the flow of communication is primarily from one person (the instructor) to the rest of the group. In organizations in which there is a centralized authority—the military, many large corporations, and various institutions—a top-to-bottom pattern prevails. In such hierarchical situations, individuals are

## BOX 16.2

### Ethics and the Obedience Experiment

Stanley Milgram's work on obedience is a classic demonstration of the extent to which we have been programmed to do as we're told by authorities.

The question that has been extensively debated is whether or not Milgram's work violated the rights of the subjects who participated in his study. One prominent critic of Milgram's work has argued forcefully that he did violate their rights (Baumrind, 1964). According to her, the self-respect of those who complied and administered the maximal shocks may have been irreparably harmed, and the subjects may have lost a certain amount of their ability to trust authority figures. Only if the results of a potentially dangerous experiment were of immediate and clear benefit to humanity—like a cure for cancer—*or* if the subjects were warned of the potential damage would such studies as Milgram's be defensible, according to this critic.

As you might imagine, Milgram has not remained silent while his work has been criticized. In rebuttal, he has advanced a number of arguments (Milgram, 1964). First, a careful postexperimental interview was conducted to dehoax the subjects and, at the same time, allow them to work out their feelings about the experiment. Subjects were told that many others had reacted as they had. Further, a questionnaire was sent to all of the subjects who had participated, and of the 92 percent who returned the questionnaire, 84 percent indicated that they were glad they had participated. For some subjects there was evidence that having gone through the trauma of the obedience experiment strengthened their belief in their own responsibility for their own actions. As a final precaution, a psychiatric interview was held with 40 of the subjects, who were thought to be most likely to have been affected by the experiment, and none of them showed any signs of having been psychologically harmed.

Thus Milgram has gathered an impressive array of rebuttals to his critics. But, of course, whether or not he has met ethical guidelines remains a question of personal values. How would you react if you heard that a well-trained psychologist was going to replicate the obedience test at a college that a very close friend of yours attends? If the test were done, what safeguards would you want to see implemented?

Adapted from Middlebrook, 1980, p. 25.

---

usually free to communicate only with people at their own level and those one level above or below.

Because of the complexity of many real-life group situations, most research is conducted under controlled laboratory conditions, where the number of participants can be limited and the flow of communication can be precisely controlled. These laboratory situations are somewhat artificial and do not necessarily permit generalization of the findings to real-world groups. Nevertheless, certain basic principles may be uncovered, which can then be tested in group situations outside the laboratory.

Many different patterns of communication have been described. In one study, subjects were separated from one another by partitions, but they could send messages to other subjects through slots in the partitions. The experimenter could control the flow of communications by opening and closing these slots. Several communication patterns were used to study the effect of interaction processes on the efficiency of five-member groups in arriving at solutions to relatively simple problems (see Fig. 16.6 for two of the patterns used). The most general finding was that the problem-solving efficiency of the group improved with increased centralization of structure (Leavitt, 1951). One of the criticisms leveled

Wheel

Circle

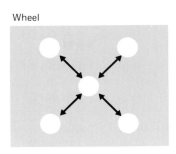
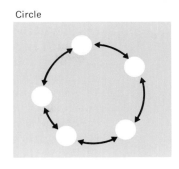

Figure 16.6
**Communication patterns**

Two patterns of communication involving small groups. In the "wheel" all communication is through a central figure. In the "circle" each group member may communicate only with two other members. These represent two different degrees of centralization in communication patterns that have been investigated in small-group situations. The "wheel" represents maximum centralization.

against the study was that the problem task was too simple, consisting primarily of sorting and exchanging information.

A review of studies that varied the complexity of the problem-solving task still suggests that centralized communication patterns appear to be superior (Shaw, 1964). The reviewer concluded that

> *centralized networks are generally more efficient when the task requires merely the collection of information in one place. Decentralized networks are more efficient when the task requires, in addition to the information collection process, that further operations must be performed on the information before the task can be completed. (Shaw, 1964, p. 144)*

Many recent studies have been directed at ascertaining the effects of communication on cooperation. Using a variety of subject populations, tasks, and degrees of communication, researchers have well established that communicating groups cooperate more than those not in communication (Dawes, 1980). Why is communication so successful in promoting cooperation? Three aspects of communication have been cited: humanization (subjects get to know one another); discussion (they have the opportunity to discuss possible solutions); and commitment (they are able to verbalize their commitment to find a solution) (Dawes *et al.*, 1977).

## Leadership

In many groups the direction of communications and often the structure of the communication system are directly related to the personality of the leader. But what is a leader?

Everyone knows that a leader is someone whom others follow. But do they follow that person all the time, under varying conditions and circumstances? If the leader is a supervisor at work and the supervisor tells you how he or she would like you to spend your leisure hours, would you conform? Is a person a leader by virtue of some special attributes that we call leadership qualities? Or are other factors involved, such as power by virtue of wealth or position or possession of some specialized knowledge or skills? Is leadership defined in terms of prosocial or helping activities? If so, how would you classify some of the "bad guys" in history, such as Adolph Schickelgruber (also known as Hitler)? Is leadership something so special that few of us ever achieve it? Or do most of us, at one time or another, assume leadership roles?

As you can see, arriving at a satisfactory definition of leadership is a monumental task. Indeed, it is probably not possible. This is because leadership is not a single unitary entity. It is many different things, for different people, in different situations.

For years, people interested in leadership have sought certain qualities thought to characterize effective leaders. In other words, they have looked for those traits possessed by leaders but not by nonleaders. Most of the studies using this approach have failed to find any single important characteristic that consistently defines successful leadership (Jenkins, 1947). This is not surprising when you consider the wide range of circumstances in which leaders emerge. Think of the many groups in which the leader is designated "president." Certainly, it is unlikely that there would be a common pattern of personality traits among the president of the United States, the president of the PTA, the president of a gay liberation movement, and the president of a nudist colony. Obviously, an effective leader must possess those qualities that permit both the individual members and the group as a whole to achieve their goals. Although the requisite qualities will vary somewhat from group to group, not all individuals are equally likely to assume leadership positions, and some people may become leaders of several different groups.

Although no specific personality trait will guarantee leadership in all situations, the results of various studies suggest that the possession of certain characteristics will increase the likelihood that an individual will become either a leader or a follower. A review of studies concerned with the personality characteristics of leaders revealed that certain traits are more likely to be found among leaders. Compared to other members of the group, they tend to be more intelligent, more dominant, better adjusted, and somewhat less conservative (Mann, 1959). Moreover, the amount of talking a person does during group discussions increases the likelihood that he or she will be selected by the group (Sorrentino and Boutillier, 1975). Interestingly, it is not the *quality* of the comments that are important but the *quantity* (Gentner and Lindskold, 1975). The reason is that members of the group are more likely to attribute willingness to work to quantity than to quality of verbal output. One reviewer concluded, "In short, anyone who wishes to become leader of a group had better talk more than others; it also helps if he knows what he is talking about" (Zander, 1979, p. 441). It should be emphasized than an individual who is able to function as a leader in one group is not necessarily able to become a leader in other situations. However, a leader in one group is more likely to become the leader of another group if the tasks are similar (Carter *et al.*, 1950).

In many group situations, two different leadership functions emerge: those of a *task specialist* and a *social specialist* (Bales, 1958). Task specialists organize and direct the group toward the achievement of its goals. They are not necessarily liked by the group members, but they perform a vital

**Cesar Chavez displays his flair for leadership in a demonstration supporting the rights of Hispanic Americans.**

function by keeping the group "on the job." In the performance of this function, many tensions and morale problems may arise. It is the social specialist who, through joking, cajolery, and generally heightening the esprit de corps, maintains harmony and dissipates tensions within the group. Occasionally, both of these functions are performed by a single individual, but more often they are allocated to different people.

## Group Action

Now that we have had an opportunity to examine the ways in which groups function, we are ready to look at some specific types of action characteristic of groups.

**Productivity.** The popular expression "Two heads are better than one" implies that two or more individuals working together toward the solution of a problem will be more successful than if they worked individually. The culmination of this point of view is found in the technique of *brainstorming*, which was widely practiced a number of years ago. Brainstorming is a technique that emphasizes group participation to elicit ideas and solve problems. The assumption is that the interaction among the group members will stimulate each individual to heights of creativity to which he or she could not aspire alone.

One investigator concluded that "the average person can think up twice as many ideas when working with a group [as] . . . when working alone" (Osborn, 1957). However, other studies using a diverse sampling of subjects have tended to refute this finding (Taylor *et al.*, 1957; Dunnette *et al.*, 1963). They report that individuals produce a greater number of ideas when working *alone*. These studies suggest that "a group tends to 'fall in a rut' and to pursue the same train of thought. The effect of this is to limit the diversity of approaches to a problem, thereby leading to the production of fewer different ideas" (Dunnette *et al.*, 1963). Individuals working alone appear to have a particular advantage where sustained creative effort is required.

You should not conclude, at this point, that individual performance is superior to a group effort in all types of situations. Certain tasks require a diversity of approaches for their solution. For example, the design of a new piece of equipment for use in an airplane might best be achieved by a team possessing many different skills—electronic, mathematical, psychological, and aeronautical. When the talents of a variety of different people can be pooled to contribute to the solution of a problem, group performance is likely to be superior to the performance of an individual working alone. A good example, with which you may already have had some experience, is the solution of crossword puzzles. Here the superiority of the group stems from the variety of verbal responses that are available for the solution (Thorndike, 1938).

**Decision making.**   In actual practice, most of the important decisions that are made in government, business, finance, and education are the products of group efforts. Because so many of the important decisions in life are in the hands of groups, we might ask, "What are the differences between the kinds of decisions made by groups and those made by individuals working alone?" One difference that has been observed is that decisions made by group consensus tend to be more risky than decisions made by the group members as individuals (Kogan and Wallach, 1967). This rather startling finding contradicts the common belief that groups tend toward more conservative courses of action.

In the original study of what is called the *risky shift* phenomenon, subjects were required to choose between a risky, but desirable, alternative and a more certain, but less desirable, alternative. The problems ranged over a wide variety of topics involving possible loss of money, prestige, and life. Box 16.3 provides an example. First, the subjects made their decisions while working alone. They were then placed in groups of six and required to arrive at a unanimous selection of a level of risk. Finally, each individual was again required to state his or her own risk preferences for each problem. A shift toward greater riskiness was found in both the group decisions and the subsequent individual decisions. This risky shift was not found in a control group that did not participate in the group discussions and decisions (Stoner, 1961). A number of subsequent

## BOX 16.3

### Risky Shift

☐ 1 in 10    ☐ 4 in 10    ☐ 7 in 10
☐ 2 in 10    ☐ 5 in 10    ☐ 8 in 10
☐ 3 in 10    ☐ 6 in 10    ☐ 9 in 10

**Figure 16.7**
**Odds of Mr. K's victory**

Mr. K. is a successful business man who has participated in a number of civic activities of considerable
value to the community. Mr. K. has been approached
by the leaders of his political party as a possible
congressional candidate in the next election. Mr. K.'s
party is a minority party in the district, though the
party has won occasional elections in the past. Mr. K.
would like to hold political office, but to do so would
involve a serious financial sacrifice, since the party
has insufficient campaign funds. He would also have
to endure the attacks of the political opponents in a
hot campaign.

Imagine that you are advising Mr. K.

Listed [in Fig. 16.7] are several probabilities or
odds of Mr. K's winning the election in his district.
Please check the lowest probability that you would
consider to make it worthwhile for Mr. K. to run for
political office.

**Sample problem situation employed to investigate the
"risky shift" phenomenon. The subjects could decide to
take no risk (Mr. K. should not run for office) or they
could state a willingness to take a risk when the chances
of success were 1, 3, 5, 7, or 9 chances in 10 that Mr. K.
would win. The lower the odds accepted by the subjects,
the greater the risk they are willing to take. Each subject
made twelve such decisions working alone both before
and after group discussion. Decisions made after group
discussion shifted toward greater riskiness. (Stoner, 1961)**

Madaras and Bem, 1968.

studies have verified this phenomenon with many different populations
and a variety of different problems (Kogan and Wallach, 1967).

In recent years, the term "polarization of position" has been substituted for "risky shift." This is because "all sorts of initial positions (opinions, judgments, preferences, etc.) become more polarized as a result of
relevant group discussion or simple exposure to the positions of others"
(Cialdini *et al.*, 1981, p. 386).

Although many hypotheses have been advanced to account for the
group polarization effect, two have received the most attention: social
comparison and persuasive argument. Advocates of the social-compari-
son explanation state that group discussion permits members to compare
their positions on an issue and/or their abilities with those of other
members. This comparison causes most individuals to move toward the initially favored position in order to place themselves in an esteemed position relative to others (Jellison and Arkin, 1977; Sanders and Baren, 1977).
The persuasive argument view is that group discussion generates a larger
proportion of arguments that support the group's initial dispositions. The
result is a shift, on the average, in the direction of the group predispositions (Vinokur and Burnstein, 1978). There is also the possibility that the

influence of a leader will sway the group in a direction it would not otherwise have taken.

Whatever the explanation, it is clear that the risky shift phenomenon may have extremely important implications in real-life situations. Governments are constantly making decisions in crisis situations where one of the risks may be war. Individuals who are unwilling to challenge authority on their own may do so as a member of a group. Even the irrational behavior sometimes found in crowds may involve the risky shift phenomenon.

## Anonymity and Bystander Apathy

Unfortunately, not all group actions are productively or constructively oriented. Sometimes the power of the group actually prevents action by enfolding its members in a cloak of anonymity.

People in large urban areas frequently live a life of virtual anonymity. It is quite common for neighbors not to know one another. Social and familial ties tend to be looser than in small rural communities. People living in big cities often complain that they have become little more than computer code numbers. Most of the people the urban dweller meets

*"Hold it! For all we know, he may be making a citizen's arrest."*

Drawing by Chas. Adams; © The New Yorker Magazine, Inc.

during the course of the day are complete strangers. People ride side by side on crowded buses and subways and rarely exchange a word or greeting. It is easy to feel anonymous and without identity in situations like these.

One of the unfortunate consequences of big city anonymity is what has come to be known as bystander apathy. People have been known to ignore accidents, crimes, and even murders that occurred right under their noses. A number of years ago, a young woman was brutally killed in the street during the early hours of the morning. Thirty-eight people viewed or heard the assault from their apartment windows. Although the attack continued for more than half an hour no one came to her rescue or even notified the police (Seedman and Hellman, 1974).

A number of incidents similar to this have been reported. In each case, there were large numbers of people who could have rendered assistance to the victim, and yet none did so. Such reports have led some people to conclude that the city dweller has become dehumanized and made callous by the environment. Obviously, some people do respond in emergencies. How, then, do we explain the behavior of those who do not?

A series of investigations has attempted to clarify some of the variables operating in bystander apathy. In one experiment, subjects (primarily female) were supposedly participating in a group discussion. Each subject was placed in a separate room containing a communication system. During the course of the discussion, one confederate (a stooge) simulated a seizure. The following is a verbatim account:

> I er um I think I I need er if if could er er somebody er er er er er er er give me a little er give me a little help here because er I er I'm er er h-h-having a a a a real problem er right now and I er if somebody could help me out it would it would er er s-s-sure be sure be good . . . because er there er er a cause I er I uh I've got a a one of the er sei———er er things coming on and and I could really er use some help so if somebody would er give me a little h-help uh er-er-er-er-er c-could somebody er er help er uh uh uh (choking sounds) . . . I'm gonna die er er I'm . . . gonna die er held er er seizure er (chokes, then quiet). (Latané and Darley, 1969, p. 261)

The communication system was set up in such a way that it was impossible for any subject to communicate with the others and to find out what, if anything, they were doing in this emergency. The experimenter recorded how soon the subject reported the emergency. The main independent variable in this experiment was the number of other people thought to be in the discussion group. Figure 16.8 shows that all the subjects who thought they were alone with the victim reported the emergency. When subjects thought that there were four others who could report the emergency, only 62 percent responded. Moreover, their responses were not as fast in this latter case (Latané and Darley, 1969). Evidently, the presence of other people inhibits an individual from intervening in an emergency. A wide variety of studies have consistently found that a person is more likely to render assistance when he or she is the only witness to an emergency (Latané and Nida, 1981).

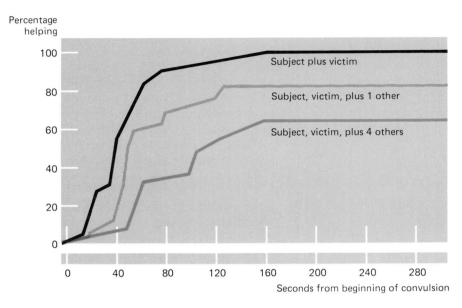

Figure 16.8
Bystander apathy

The fewer the bystanders, the greater is the likelihood that assistance will be offered to a presumed victim. Moreover, the assistance is rendered more quickly when there are few other onlookers. (Darley and Latané, 1968)

The experimenters note that glib labels, which are often used by the mass media to explain bystander apathy, may be misleading. They suggest that "situational factors, specifically factors involving the immediate social environment, may be of greater importance in determining an individual's reaction to an emergency than such vague cultural or personality concepts as 'apathy' or 'alienation due to urbanization' " (Latané and Darley, 1969, p. 268). Indeed, a bystander is affected by the reactions of others who are present. If they do not appear to regard the situation as an emergency, the bystander will perceive the situation as being less serious than if he or she were alone. In addition, the greater the number of people present, the more diffuse the responsibility of any one individual will be. Yet if the individual subject realizes that other bystanders are unable to render assistance, he or she is more likely to help (Ross and Braband, 1973).

These findings have been supported and extended in a more recent study (Schwartz and Gottlieb, 1980). In one situation, a confederate developed symptoms of physical discomfort that climaxed in convulsions. Ninety-two percent of the 52 subjects came to that person's aid, with lone bystanders responding faster than others. In another situation, a male confederate was apparently the victim of a violent attack. Eighty-nine percent of 127 bystanders offered the victim assistance. Again, a lone bystander responded more promptly than a bystander in the presence of others.

A critical factor in determining the speed of response of a bystander is whether or not the bystander is known to the other witnesses. If unknown, a bystander will respond as soon as the reality of the need and the appropriateness of the help are established. Anonymous bystanders are apparently less concerned about how others will react to their intervention than bystanders who are known to others.

Most of the research in this area has focused on bystander behavior to simulated emergencies and crimes. For the most part, these simulated situations were not extremely serious or dangerous (Shotland and Huston, 1979). One recent study (Huston *et al.*, 1981) examined bystander intervention in real-life criminal incidents. The investigators interviewed 32 people who had intervened in dangerous situations such as muggings, armed robberies, and bank holdups. In comparing this group who intervened with a group of noninterveners matched for age, sex, education, and ethnic background, they found:

*"Interveners, in contrast to noninterveners, reported considerably more exposure to crime in terms of personal victimization and witnessing the victimizations of others. Crime interveners also were taller, heavier, and better trained to cope with crimes and emergencies, having had significantly more life-saving, medical, and police training; and were more likely to describe themselves as physically strong, aggressive, emotional, and principled. In spite of an intensive search for personality differences between the two groups, none was found. Results suggest that crime interveners are not prompted to action by notably strong humanitarian purpose or by antisocial aggressiveness, but rather act out of a sense of capability founded on training experiences and rooted in their personal strength."* (Huston et al., 1981, p. 14)

## ATTITUDES

Attitudes are among the most important determinants of social behavior. They are acquired early in life during the course of socialization, and they continue to be modified throughout life as we interact with other people and the world around us. Attitudes largely determine our likes and dislikes, the stands we take on various issues, and the way we react to the various situations that we encounter in life. The remainder of this chapter is devoted to the ways in which attitudes are acquired and modified.

## The Nature of Attitudes

An **attitude** is a learned predisposition to respond in a specific way, negatively or positively, toward people, ideas, or situations. Attitudes typically involve an affective (or feeling) component, a cognitive (or thought) component, and a behavioral component. For example, when we endorse a candidate for political office, we are usually expressing positive feelings toward the candidate (affect), agreement with many of the candidate's ideas (cognition), and a decision to vote for that candidate at election time (behavior).

Although attitudes are somewhat similar to opinions and beliefs, we can make some distinctions. A **belief** is the acceptance of a proposition as fact. Beliefs are not necessarily in favor of or opposed to something;

they are simply statements that are assumed to have factual support. For example, you may believe that nuclear weapons have a tremendous capability to destroy and that both the United States and the Soviet Union have large stockpiles of such weapons. This belief does not necessarily predispose you to feel or act in any specific manner for or against nuclear weapons. If you hold certain attitudes, though, such as strong anti-Communism or concern for the environment, these attitudes, in conjunction with your beliefs, may influence your actions on this issue—you may join the army or picket the White House.

**Opinions** express judgments and feelings for which the factual support is far weaker than for beliefs. For example, you may hold an opinion that lobster is the tastiest food. Because your opinion is grounded on feelings more than facts, you may be willing to concede that chocolate cake is also delicious—perhaps as much so as lobster. But sometimes we are so convinced that our opinions are correct that we hold them to be beliefs. Because opinions more frankly express the feelings of an individual than beliefs do, they are more likely to reveal attitudes.

We are not always aware of our own attitudes. We may have acquired many of them early in life under circumstances that we have since forgotten. We are more aware of our beliefs, because we are able to express them verbally. As a consequence, attitudes may conflict with beliefs. For example, a person may assert a belief that all individuals in our society, regardless of race or creed, should have equal rights to live in any neighborhood they choose. The person may point to the Constitution and to Supreme Court rulings to support this belief. Yet this person may be uncomfortably disturbed upon learning that a member of some other group is planning to move into his or her neighborhood. This person's disturbed feelings are more indicative of the attitudes he or she holds than are the accompanying verbal statements.

If it is difficult to determine our own attitudes, how do we ascertain the attitudes of others? As advocates of attribution theory have pointed out, what a person says may not always be consonant with what he or she does. This will especially be the case when the person is under some external pressure to "say the right thing." Politicians are excellent cases in point. They are almost always "under the gun" to mirror sentiments of their constituencies or face defeat at the polls when election time comes around. Thus we are usually not surprised when a politician says one thing and then does the opposite.

When judging the attitudes of others, do we rely more on their verbal statements or on their actions? Two investigators (Ajzen and Fishbein, 1973) have suggested that actions speak louder than words. To learn if people hold prejudiced attitudes toward other groups we should not ask them how they feel about members of these groups. Rather, we should find out what acts or behaviors they are willing to direct toward these groups. In the view of these investigators, the answer to the question, "Would you join the same social club with a member of _____ group?" would be more revealing than the answer to the question, "Do you like the people in _____ group?"

This distinction is illustrated in a study in which landlords, in response to telephone inquiries, all stated that they would rent apartments

---

**Opinion**
A judgment or feeling for which the factual support is far weaker than for beliefs.

to blacks and interracial couples. Yet many of these same landlords would not even show the apartments to the couples when they appeared in person (McGrew, 1967).

## Development of Attitudes

The moment children are born, they are thrust into a social setting in which they will be learning attitudes. At first they will learn them primarily from their parents, who will reward them for expressing certain attitudes and punish them for others. During the first few years, the parents provide virtually the only input the children have for the formation of attitudes. Children act the way their parents do, and respond positively and negatively to the same things and situations. Indeed, when interview techniques are employed with children in order to determine their attitudes on various topics, the children very often cite their parents as the reason for behaving in a certain way. When children were asked about their selection of playmates, the following answers (Horowitz and Horowitz, 1938) were typical:

*First-grade girl:* "Mamma tells me not to play with black children. . . ."
*Second-grade boy:* ". . . mother and daddy tell me . . . not to play with colored people or colored persons' things."
*Fourth-grade boy:* "Mother and daddy tell me to play with white boys. . . ."

Many of these basic attitudes remain with the children throughout their lives. A study of political and religious attitudes of high school seniors showed high degrees of agreement with parental affiliations (Jennings and Niemi, 1968).

As children grow older and move out into other social situations, there is a marked broadening of outside influences as the children strive to be socially acceptable to these groups. During adolescence, this "moving out" is dramatic. Adolescents typically spend less time with their families than they did as children, and more time with their peer groups. These years of adolescence have been referred to, by some psychologists, as a period of storm and stress. The emerging adult attempts, unsuccessfully, to reconcile the many opposing social pressures and often contradictory attitudes that he or she encounters. What is often interpreted by parents as defiance of authority is merely compliance by the adolescent with the norms of his or her peer groups. Many of these changes are superficial, in that they do not represent deep-seated alterations of the basic elements of personality. They may involve new hairstyles, different forms of facial adornment, and new styles of dress. Other changes may reflect changing life-styles in the broader society, to which the older generations may be resistant. New patterns and norms governing sexual behavior exemplify this kind of change.

Some of the most striking changes in attitudes occur during the college years, when students are exposed to the many and varied attitudes and norms of the college community. Some of these new attitudes might diverge considerably from those the student held during high school. Many studies have demonstrated the impact of peer influence on the modification of attitudes during the college years. One study, conducted at a college noted for its "liberal" faculty, demonstrated that the attitudes held by students as freshmen showed a swing toward a more liberal viewpoint by the time there were seniors (Newcomb, 1943). Moreover, these more liberal attitudes tended to persist over a 20-year period (Newcomb, 1963).

## Cognitive Dissonance

**Cognitive dissonance**
Lack of agreement between one's beliefs, feelings, or behavior resulting in a state of tension.

**Prejudice**
Any kind of prejudgment, negative or positive; an attitude or opinion formed before examining all the facts.

**Discrimination**
Behavioral expression of prejudice.

People may sometimes behave in ways that are inconsistent with their existing attitudes, or they may hold contradictory attitudes. Such disparities take on many of the motivational characteristics that we discussed in relation to conflict behavior (Chapter 12). For example, some students are not able to modify their behavior and attitudes to conform to norms that are markedly different from their own. One of the colleges in this country has a reputation for encouraging students to adopt their own life-styles, to be independent, to show resourcefulness and initiative. One student at this school withdrew after her first year, complaining that the pressure to conform to the norm of "being different" was too much for her! The case of this student shows the contradictory pressures that characterize many adolescent conflicts: The pressure to conform to previously acquired norms and attitudes conflicts with the pressure to adopt new life-styles in conformity to peer-group norms. She "resolved" her conflict by withdrawing from the situation.

Although people differ in the amount of inconsistency they can tolerate, a basic assumption of **cognitive dissonance** theory is that inconsistency is intolerable to an individual. According to this theory, when two or more cognitions (such as beliefs and opinions) are in disagreement (are dissonant), a state of tension results. This inconsistency (dissonance) motivates the individual to adjust these cognitions so as to reduce the dissonance and thereby reduce the tension (Festinger, 1957). For example, suppose that a group of people who enjoy smoking are confronted with evidence that smoking is harmful. They are faced with two dissonant cognitions: "I enjoy smoking" and "Smoking is harmful." The dissonance (inconsistency between these two cognitions) results in a state of tension. How can they reduce the dissonance? They may reject or minimize the information ("Most people who smoke don't get lung cancer"); they may rationalize that by giving up smoking they will gain weight and excess weight is also harmful to health; or they may give up smoking.

When there is dissonance between attitudes and behavior, people usually modify their attitudes rather than their behavior. For example, when subjects were induced to lie to other subjects by telling them that an extremely tedious and boring task was, in fact, interesting, they subsequently rated the task as more interesting than did a control group of subjects who had not committed themselves to the lie (Festinger and Carlsmith, 1959). The experimental subjects reduced their cognitive dissonance by revising their attitude toward the task to fit their behavior. Another study showed that subjects tended to rate the task more positively if the person they had convinced was someone they liked rather than disliked (Cooper *et al.*, 1974).

If a person endures a lot of trouble or pain to attain something, he or she tends to view it as more valuable or important than if it had been attained through a minimum of effort. In one study, a group of female college students volunteered to participate in group discussions of sexual behavior. The subjects were randomly divided into three groups, which differed in the severity of initiation required for participation in the group discussion. In the group subjected to severe initiation, the girls were required to read some embarrassing material aloud to the experimenter. All the subjects then listened in on the discussions, which were designed to be extremely dull in order to maximize the dissonance of the subjects who had undergone severe initiation. The investigators found that subjects in the severe condition tend to have the most favorable attitudes toward the group's activities (Aronson and Mills, 1959).

A dramatic example of cognitive dissonance in a real-life situation was provided by the behavior of passengers who survived an air disaster. On October 13, 1972, a Uruguayan Air Force plane crashed into a remote and inaccessible peak in the Chilean Andes. Twenty-nine people died in the crash or shortly afterward; 16 survived 69 days of subzero temperatures and threatened starvation. The survivors later revealed that they had stayed alive by eating the flesh of the dead. With the strong prohibitions against cannibalism that exist in Western civilization, how were they able to convince themselves that eating human flesh was appropriate under these circumstances? One young man compared the cannibalism to a heart transplant, pointing out that the heart of a dead person is used to keep another person alive. Others found support for their behavior in the tenets of their religious faith, pointing to the communion ceremony, in which the individual symbolically drinks the blood and eats the flesh of Christ (Reed, 1974).

## Prejudice

Let's examine how attitudes develop and are related to behavior by looking at one specific type of attitude that has been studied extensively—*prejudice*.

**Prejudice** is defined as any kind of prejudgment, negative or positive. Social psychologists have generally been concerned with prejudice in the negative sense. Note that prejudice is an attitude (a predisposition to act that may or may not be associated with behavior). The behavioral expression of prejudice is **discrimination.**

Ordinarily, prejudice and discrimination are maintained by perceiving the person or group against whom the prejudice is directed as different from one's own group. This other group may be seen as having different status, ideals, and values, and as behaving in different ways.

Prejudices, like other attitudes, are wholly learned. They may be acquired early in life through interactions with other individuals who communicate, directly or indirectly, negative feelings and attitudes toward certain individuals or groups. Many parents directly teach their children to hold unfavorable attitudes toward certain groups, but there are also many indirect and subtle forces at work. A parent may communicate prejudices by a tone of voice or a gesture. Indeed, studies have found that

In addition to the more obvious manifestations of cultural and racial prejudice, we also discriminate between attractive and unattractive people. We tend to assign more positive personality traits to physically attractive individuals. In dating, couples are expected to have similar status ratings in the areas of physical attractiveness and popularity.

**Stereotype**
Preconceived idea about the attributes of people belonging to certain groups.

many children express racial and religious prejudices at early ages (Radke *et al.*, 1949; Ammons, 1950). These early attitudes are frequently superficial and may represent only the child's parroting of parental statements.

Prejudices are frequently supported by **stereotypes,** which are preconceived ideas about the attributes of people belonging to certain groups. For instance, in 1932, Princeton University students regarded Germans as scientifically minded, industrious, and stolid; Chinese as superstitious, sly, and conservative; and Turks as cruel, very religious, and treacherous (Katz and Braly, 1933). Yet stereotypes change, as you can see in Table 16.1, which compares the 1932 results with similar surveys conducted at Princeton in 1950 (Gilbert, 1951) and 1967 (Karlins *et al.*, 1969). Some caution is necessary in interpreting these results. Although the stereotypes may indeed have changed, we must also keep in mind that the type of student attending Princeton in 1932 may have been very different from the types attending in 1950 and 1967.

Is stereotyping all that bad? Actually, there is not much evidence that stereotypes are bad generalizations. A review of the research has shown that most of the arguments against stereotypes refer to specific stereotypes, not to stereotyping in general. The reviewers conclude that "what is wrong with stereotyping is no more and no less than what is wrong with human conceptual behavior in general" (McCauley *et al.*, 1980).

Prejudice occurs in all walks of life, and its victims range from the aged, the mentally ill, homosexuals, women, and ex-convicts to those who differ in religion and skin color. It has been suggested that one of the most pervasive effects of prejudice on the victim is the perceived lack of personal control over his or her own fate (Lefcourt, 1976). Blacks come to think that the white majority controls their lives; women believe that their destinies are largely in the hands of men; the emotionally disturbed see their lives as ruled by people in white coats; and gay people see their personal stability threatened by external forces over which they have no control. In extreme forms, then, the victims see little purpose in expending effort to improve their lot. They may become like unmotivated automatons, concerned with little more than the pleasure of the moment. Long-range planning is regarded as useless, since the majority can easily throw a "monkey wrench" in their best-laid plans. The feeling of helplessness can easily give way to despair.

In recent years, however, we have seen the formation of activist groups aimed at combating the constant harassment and discrimination directed against their members. The Gay Liberation Front, the National Organization of Women, and a group called Insane Liberation are some of the groups of this sort.

Of all the forms of prejudice, the one that has received the most attention in this country has been racial prejudice. The following observa-

Table 16.1

**Changes in Stereotypes Held by Princeton University Students
Toward Members of Three National Groups**

| National group | Trait | % of students checking trait | | |
|---|---|---|---|---|
| | | 1933 | 1951 | 1967 |
| Germans | Scientifically minded | 78 | 62 | 47 |
| | Industrious | 65 | 50 | 59 |
| | Stolid | 44 | 10 | 9 |
| | Intelligent | 32 | 32 | 19 |
| | Methodical | 31 | 20 | 21 |
| | Extremely nationalistic | 24 | 50 | 43 |
| | Progressive | 16 | 3 | 13 |
| Chinese | Superstitious | 34 | 18 | 8 |
| | Sly | 29 | 4 | 6 |
| | Conservative | 29 | 14 | 15 |
| | Tradition loving | 26 | 26 | 32 |
| | Loyal to family ties | 22 | 35 | 50 |
| | Industrious | 18 | 18 | 23 |
| Turks | Cruel | 47 | 12 | 9 |
| | Very religious | 26 | 6 | 7 |
| | Treacherous | 21 | 3 | 13 |
| | Sensual | 20 | 4 | 9 |
| | Ignorant | 15 | 7 | 13 |
| | Physically dirty | 15 | 7 | 14 |

Source: Katz and Braly, 1933; Gilbert, 1951; Karlins et al., 1969.

tion by a prominent psychologist depicts the pervasive effects of racial prejudice on the developing attitudes of the children who are its victims:

> *Human beings who are forced to live under ghetto conditions and whose daily experience tells them that almost nowhere in society are they respected and granted the ordinary dignity and courtesy accorded to others will, as a matter of course, begin to doubt their own worth. Since every human being depends upon his cumulative experiences with others for clues as to how he should view and value himself, children who are consistently rejected understandably begin to question and doubt whether they, their family, and their group really deserve no more respect from the larger society than they receive. These doubts become the seeds of a pernicious self- and group-hatred and the Negro's complex, debilitating prejudice against himself. (Clark, 1965, pp. 63–64)*

## Changing Attitudes

Although attitudes are relatively stable, they are not immutable; they can and do change, as we have seen. We have already discussed the three components of attitudes: affective, cognitive, and behavioral. Attempts to change attitudes have generally focused on changing one of these components. The assumption is that changing one component will create pressures to change the remaining components.

Many of the efforts of the United Nations and the mass media to reduce racial prejudice and stereotypes have focused on supplying information about the consequences of prejudice and facts that demonstrate that minority-group members have the same basic motivations and needs as everyone else. These efforts are an attempt to produce favorable attitudes by presenting informational material. The assumption behind this approach is that a favorable attitude will result in the desired behavior (lack of prejudice), and that changing the cognitive component will produce the favorable attitude. One study attests to the effectiveness of informational factors in changing attitudes (Eagly, 1974). Subjects were exposed to a tape recording that presented arguments in favor of sleeping less. Some tapes presented all of the information; others did not. The tapes presenting the greatest amount of information were maximally effective in producing attitude change.

Efforts have also been made to change attitudes by modifying behavior. If a person can be induced to behave in a way that is incompatible with certain attitudes he or she holds, those attitudes may change so as to become consonant with the behavior. It has often been noted by debaters that, when forced to defend a position with which they initially disagree, they are often finally swayed in the direction of that attitude. It is almost as if they "talk themselves into it." This aspect of attitude change has been studied in the laboratory. Students were given materials expressing attitudes that contradicted their own and were asked to give an informal talk defending the positions expressed in these materials. On two out of three issues, their own attitudes showed considerable change in the direction of the message in the prepared materials. There was little change on the third issue. Control subjects, who merely listened to the talk, showed far less attitude change (Janis and King, 1954).

The contrast between this World War II recruiting poster and the photo of a modern service academy graduate illustrates that attitudes can change over a period of time.

In another study, subjects in one group were provided with a script that they were to read to an audience. Subjects in a second group were given the same script, but were asked to improvise a talk based on it. In both groups, the subjects were defending positions at variance with their own attitudes. The subjects who improvised the talk showed greater change toward the position they were publicly advocating than did the subjects who merely read a prepared script (King and Janis, 1956).

In a study undertaken outside the laboratory, the attitudes of white housewives were ascertained before and after they moved into biracial housing projects, where circumstances forced them to adjust to the presence of blacks and to interact with them. In the fully integrated units, most of the attitudes changed in a favorable direction. In two units, however, there was considerable segregation, with black and white families living in separate buildings or separate parts of the project. White housewives living in these units showed little change one way or another (Deutsch and Collins, 1951).

It should not be assumed, however, that the solution to prejudice is simply to bring people holding prejudices into closer contact with members of the group against which the prejudice is directed. Much depends on the nature and quality of the contacts that subsequently develop.

As we have seen, some efforts at attitude change have focused on the cognitive component and others on the behavioral aspect of attitudes. In most cases, the changes in affective states have been viewed as consequences of altered behavioral or cognitive components. One investigator (Rosenberg, 1960) has concentrated his efforts on determining the extent to which the manipulation of affect, or feelings, will lead to cognitive changes. In one study, he administered a scale measuring the attitudes of the subjects on a number of issues: foreign aid, blacks moving into white neighborhoods, and so on. Then the subjects were hypnotized, and it was suggested to them that, upon awakening, they would feel differently about a particular issue. For example, one subject was told, "When you wake up, you will be very much in favor of Negroes moving into white neighborhoods. The mere idea of Negroes moving into white neighborhoods will give you a happy exhilarated feeling." The attitude scale was again administered a few days after the hypnotic session. It was found that the subjects changed their feelings in the direction suggested under hypnosis. Moreover, they now expressed changed cognitions that were in greater agreement with their changed feelings. For example, one subject who had favored foreign aid prior to hypnosis now argued that foreign aid would interfere with the development of self-reliance.

Of course, in a normal waking state, it is not possible to alter our affective condition without altering the cognitive component, but this study lends support to the idea that feelings are not the result of attitudes but, rather, are the foundation thereof.

**Persuasive communication.** In addition to the reactions to change of the three components of attitude, it is also necessary to consider the ways in which these components are commonly changed.

Much of human communication is devoted to influencing others and attempting to change their attitudes and beliefs. Hardly a day passes when we are not literally assaulted by countless efforts to influence our attitudes in one way or another. Open a magazine or newspaper, or turn on the television set. All the commercials you see and hear are designed to produce favorable attitudes toward various products. A political campaign is an expensive and concerted effort to influence attitudes. All of these deliberate attempts to influence attitudes may be regarded as **propaganda.** Although the word "propaganda" has acquired a negative connotation, it should not be considered, in and of itself, either good or bad.

**Propaganda**
Communication that deliberately attempts to influence attitudes.

Although propaganda has much in common with education, because both processes are designed to affect attitudes and behavior, they differ both in their objectives and in the types of appeals that they use. The primary goal of education is to impart information and knowledge (the cognitive component), whereas propaganda more frequently appeals to the emotions (the affective component). Moreover, the objective of propaganda is to persuade you to *the propagandist's* way of thinking, whereas the educator attempts to bring your ideas into line with facts. This distinction is not always clear-cut, because propagandists serve as educators insofar as they impart knowledge and information. Likewise, educators may employ persuasive appeals to convince students to adopt their points of view on a particular issue. Indeed, many educators may turn out to be more successful propagandists than those who make their careers in the field of propaganda.

One factor that has frequently been investigated with respect to persuasive communication is the *source* of the communication. It has been found that the status and prestige of the individual advocating a position is often an important determinant of attitude change.

In one study, high school students were asked to rate the fairness of arguments attributed to three different sources. All subjects listened to the same speech, which advocated greater leniency in the treatment of juvenile delinquents. One group was told that the speaker was a judge in the juvenile courts (positive source); a second group was told that the speaker was drawn from the audience (neutral source); and a third group was also told that the speaker was drawn from the audience, but that a preliminary interview revealed the speaker to have a criminal record (negative source). The investigators (Hovland *et al.*, 1953) found that the presentation was rated fair about twice as often when it was delivered by the positive source as when it was presented by the negative source. Moreover, greater attitude changes were found in connection with the "judge's" speech.

Another study confirmed these results when the subjects were tested immediately, but revealed an interesting effect when they were retested weeks later. In this study, all subjects read the same communication. One

Advertisers, who are experts in propaganda, know celebrity endorsements of their products can significantly increase sales. Here Farrah Fawcett meets with Boston reporters to promote Fabergé's Farrah Fawcett Hair Care Collection.

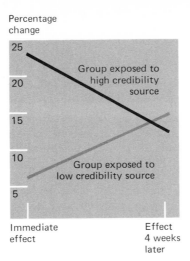

Percentage change

25

20 — Group exposed to high credibility source

15

10 — Group exposed to low credibility source

5

Immediate effect          Effect 4 weeks later

**Figure 16.9**
**The sleeper effect**

When subjects are tested immediately, a high-credibility source produces greater attitude change than a low-credibility source. With the passage of time, however, the amount of change is about the same regardless of the original source. This is known as the "sleeper" effect. (Hovland and Weiss, 1951)

**Sleeper effect**
The phenomenon that communication ascribed to a low-credibility source initially has little effect on attitude change, but may have a greater effect once the source is forgotten.

group was given a high-credibility source for the communication; another group was given a low-credibility source, such as a Hollywood gossip columnist. When the subjects were tested immediately after reading the communication, the attitudes of the first group (given the high-credibility source) were found to have changed far more than the attitudes of the second group. When the subjects were retested four weeks later, however, the attitudes of both groups were found to have changed about the same amount (see Fig. 16.9). It appears that the subjects in the second group had forgotten the source but remembered the content and were influenced by it. This change over time is known as the **sleeper effect** (Hovland and Weiss, 1951).

The practical implications of the sleeper effect, if valid, are enormous. A completely irresponsible person could make the wildest charges and feel confident that, with the passage of time, many people would forget the source of the message but would be influenced by its content. A more recent study would appear to reduce this danger. It was found that the high-credibility source did, in fact, lose its effectiveness over time; however, contrary to the previous finding, the low-credibility source showed little or no gain (Gillig and Greenwald, 1974). On the basis of this finding, Gillig and Greenwald argued that social psychology should "lay the sleeper effect to rest." More recent studies have suggested that the sleeper effect is "a living phenomenon" as long as certain conditions occur (Cook *et al.*, 1979). For example, they note that the attitude change among subjects exposed to a low-credibility source creates a decay force that operates against the sleeper effect. When the effect of this decay force was removed, they found evidence of the sleeper effect.

The content of the message has also been shown to be a factor in the effectiveness of a persuasive communication. One question that has been explored is the efficacy of presenting both sides of an issue, rather than only one side. It was found that a one-sided argument is more effective for reinforcing a person's original attitudes, but that presenting both sides is more effective for changing a person's attitudes (Hovland *et al.*, 1949).

The content of a message may vary in a number of different ways. You have probably all seen commercials on television promoting the use of safety belts. Some of these commercials show the consequences of failure to wear safety belts by portraying broken bodies. Others give statistics concerning the number of injuries and deaths attributed to the failure to wear seat belts. Which of these two types of commercials do you think is more successful? Research on the effect of fear-arousing messages has led to conflicting results. For example, one study demonstrated that fear-producing messages were more effective than informational messages (Berkowitz and Cottingham, 1960). Another study obtained the opposite result (Janis and Feshback, 1953). These conflicting findings were possibly reconciled in a more recent study (Krisher *et al.*, 1973). The persuasive communication attempted to convince male students to obtain a vaccination for mumps. The low-fear group merely received factual information concerning the possible complications of mumps. An intermediate-fear group viewed pictures that showed these complications. A third group was given false information concerning their increased rate of heartbeat when attending the message. This group was highly aroused. The intermediate-fear message obtained the best results. Sixty percent of these subjects were eventually vaccinated, whereas only 20 and 30 percent in the low- and high-fear groups submitted to vaccination.

Why do you suppose high-fear messages do not produce the great changes one might expect? One proposal is that if the audience is already very concerned and fearful about an issue, a fear-arousing message may trigger defensive reactions that will reduce anxiety, and thus cancel the effectiveness of the message. For example, doctors report that patients who fear they may be suffering a serious or incurable illness often do not seek medical advice because they are afraid of a confirming diagnosis, whereas patients whose worst fears have been confirmed by diagnosis seek other medical advice in the hope of receiving a more favorable report. On the other hand, the fear-arousing message may be more successful in changing attitudes when the audience is not already concerned about an issue (McGuire, 1960).

Another possibility is that the relationship between attitude change and fear is an inverted U (see Fig. 16.10). From this point of view, increas-

**Figure 16.10**
**Relationship between fear and attitude change**
(Worchel and Cooper, 1979)

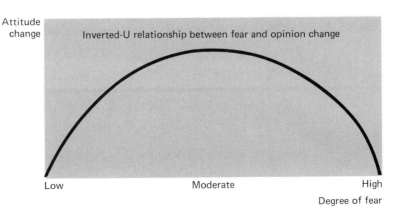

Amish communities still live in much the same way as they did over a century ago. Isolation from the larger society helps protect their culture from the intrusion of unwanted ideas and values.

ing fear arousal from low to moderate leads to increased attitude change; further increases in fear arousal lead to decreased changes in attitude (Worchel and Cooper, 1979).

**Resistance to change.** It may seem that attitudes are susceptible to so many influences that they should be in a constant state of flux. In fact, most attitudes are highly resistant to change. Remember that we have many mechanisms that defend us against the intrusion of unwanted ideas or attitudes. We may selectively attend to only those elements of a message with which we agree. Or we may distort our perception of a message in such a way as to make it conform to the attitudes we hold. The tendency to perceive and distort selectively may have a far-reaching impact on diplomatic relations. Suppose representatives from one nation believe that another nation is unfriendly, warlike, and hostile. When they meet with representatives of that nation, they may perceive any gesture, including genuine peaceful overtures, as threatening and as betraying some ulterior motive.

Charles Darwin, a great nineteenth-century biologist, always carried a pencil and pad with him in case he made observations that contradicted his theory of evolution. He recognized his tendency to selectively forget conflicting evidence.

We have seen that close contact with a group against which a person holds unfavorable attitudes may, under certain circumstances, alter these attitudes in a favorable direction. Many people make every effort to avoid this contact. Segregation, in part, represents just such an effort. Information that contradicts views that we hold also tends to produce tension. Thus we usually avoid information and attitudes inconsistent with our own. A heavy smoker will probably avoid reading the latest scientific report linking smoking to lung cancer and heart disease. How often does a person committed to a particular political ideology attend lectures or read statements presenting opposing views?

Finally, contrary to the popular maxim that "opposites attract," people generally associate with others who hold and support similar views (see Fig. 16.11). In general, results of various studies have shown that people tend to like, and be attracted to, others who hold attitudes similar to their own (Byrne, 1971; Griffitt and Veitch, 1974).

Contemporary directions in attitude research. One of the most clearly discernible trends in current attitude research is the distinction between processing communications via the central (cognitive) route and processing them via the peripheral route (Cialdini *et al.*, 1981). The cognitive approach to attitude change paints a very thoughtful picture of persuasion. We are not always motivated or able to engage in effortful thinking about a message; nevertheless, attitude changes do occur. It has been suggested that we take the cognitive or central route when our abilities permit us to reflect on the message and when we are motivated to do so. The central route emphasizes a thoughtful consideration of the issues. In contrast, the peripheral route is taken when either ability or motivation is low. The peripheral route is likely to emphasize factors that are irrelevant

**Figure 16.11
Similarity of attitudes**

**When individuals perceive the attitudes of a stranger as highly similar to their own, they tend to rate the stranger as attractive. (Byrne and Nelson, 1965)**

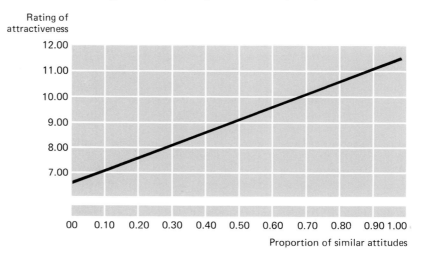

to the message, such as, the reward for advocating a view or the attractiveness of the source. A review of this distinction led the reviewers to conclude:

> *The accumulated literature on persuasion indicates that persuasion via the central route is likely to produce an enduring attitude change, but persuasion via the peripheral route is likely to produce a change that lasts only if the change is subsequently bolstered by supportive cognitive argumentation. (Cialdini et al., 1981, p. 365)*

## Summary

1. Social psychology is concerned with the individual in society—the social forces that interact to influence the individual's behavior and thinking, and the ways in which the individual interacts with and modifies social groups to which he or she belongs.

2. Societies themselves differ from one another in what their members consider to be socially acceptable behavior. Studies of various cultures have demonstrated the extreme malleability of human behavior.

3. Socialization refers to learned ways of behaving according to the expectations of other members of society.

4. Internalization represents the acceptance of norms and values of a society as guides for our own behavior.

5. When judging the causes of the behavior of others, we may attribute the behavior to internal characteristics of the individual (dispositions) or to external (situational) factors. Attribution theory is concerned with the ways in which people use information about behavior to make judgments about the causes of that behavior. In everyday life, we use consistency, consensus, and freedom from external pressure to test the accuracy of our attributions.

6. Many factors are involved in the interpersonal attraction process. Some of the most important include similarity, proximity, familiarity, and physical attractiveness.

7. People are said to be conforming when they adapt their behavior to be consistent with their perception of group values. When they yield to the pressures of those in authority, they are said to be obedient. In both cases, going along can have negative consequences, yet refusing to conform or obey may make the individual extremely uncomfortable—to the point where he or she gives in.

8. Groups differ in their modes of communication, types of leadership, and bases for making decisions and taking action. These actions can vary greatly, from productive or creative problem solving to individual apathy as a result of the anonymity of the group situation.

9. Attitudes—learned predispositions to respond in specific ways toward people, ideas, or situations—are important determinants of an individual's social behavior. Attitudes typically involve an affective, a cognitive, and a behavioral component.

10. During the early years of life, attitudes are primarily influenced by the child's parents. With increasing age and exposure to a wider variety of social situations, there is a broadening of outside influences on the formation of attitudes.

11. A basic assumption of the theory of cognitive dissonance is that inconsistency is intolerable to an individual. When two or more cognitions are dissonant, a state of tension results. The dissonance motivates the individual to adjust these cognitions so as to reduce the dissonance, and thereby reduce the tension.

12. Prejudice is defined as any kind of prejudgment, positive or negative.

13. Efforts to alter attitudes have often been directed toward one of the components of attitudes: cognitive, behavioral, and affective.

14. Many attitudes remain highly resistant to change. There are many mechanisms that defend the individual against the intrusion of unwanted ideas or attitudes. We may selectively attend to only those elements of a message with which we agree, or we may distort our perception of the message in such a way that it conforms to attitudes that we hold.

# Terms to Remember

Society

Social psychology

Culture

Subculture

Socialization

Norms

Internalization

Androgyny

Role

Attribution theories

Proximity

Conformity

Internal locus of control

External locus of control

Obedience

Attitude

Belief

Opinion

Cognitive dissonance

Prejudice

Discrimination

Stereotype

Propaganda

Sleeper effect

# APPENDIX ON STATISTICS

## WHAT IS STATISTICS?

**Statistics**
A collection of numerical facts expressed in summarizing statements; or a method of dealing with data: a tool for collecting, organizing, and analyzing numerical facts or observations.

**Descriptive statistics**
Procedures employed to organize and present data in a convenient, usable, and communicable form.

**Inferential or inductive statistics**
Procedures employed to arrive at broader generalizations or inferences from sample data to populations.

**Variable**
A characteristic or phenomenon that may take on different values.

**Data**
Numbers or measurements that are collected as a result of observations.

**Population** or **universe**
A complete set of individuals, objects, or measurements having some common observable characteristic, or a theoretical set of potential observations.

**Parameter**
Any characteristic of a population that is measurable.

**Sample**
A subset of a population or universe.

**Random sample**
A subset of a population or universe selected in such a way that each member of the population has an equal opportunity to be selected.

**Measurement**
The assignment of numbers to objects or events according to sets of predetermined (or arbitrary) rules.

**Nominal scale**
Observations of unordered variables.

Think for a moment of the thousands of incredibly complex things you do during the course of a day, and then stand in awe at the marvel you represent. Imagine you are driving in heavy traffic. You are continuously scanning the road conditions, noting the speed of cars in front of you relative to your speed, the position and rate of approach of vehicles to your rear, and the presence of automobiles in the oncoming lane. If you are an alert driver, you are constantly summarizing this descriptive information—usually without words or awareness. Imagine next that, without warning, the car in front of you suddenly jams on its brakes. In an instant, you are summoned to act upon this prior descriptive information. You must brake the car, turn left, turn right, or pray. Your probability mechanism instantly assesses alternative courses of action: If you jam on the brakes, what is the likelihood that you will stop in time? Is the car behind you sufficiently distant to avoid a rear-end collision? Can you prevent an accident by turning into the left lane or onto the right shoulder? Most of the time, the decision made from sensory data is correct. It is for this reason that most of us grow up to reach a ripe old age. And we make such decisions uncounted thousands of times each and every day of our lives. It is for this reason that you should regard yourself as a sublime mechanism for generating statistical decisions. In this sense, you are already a statistician.

In this section we shall attempt to provide you with some of the formal procedures for collecting and analyzing data, and making decisions or inferences based upon these analyses. Because we shall frequently be building upon your prior experiences, you will often feel you are in familiar territory: "Why, I have been calculating arithmetic means almost all my life—whenever I determine my test average in a course or the batting average of my favorite baseball player!" If you constantly draw upon your previous knowledge and relate materials to what is familiar in daily life, statistics need not, and should not, be the bugaboo it is often painted to be.

What, then, is statistics all about? Although it would be virtually impossible to obtain a general consensus on the definition of **statistics**, it is possible to make a distinction between two distinct definitions:

1. Statistics is commonly regarded as a *collection* of numerical facts that are expressed in terms of summarizing statements and that have been collected either from several observations or from other numerical data. From this perspective, statistics constitutes a collection of statements such as, "The average IQ of eighth-grade children is . . . ," or "Seven out of 10 people prefer brand X to brand Y," or "The New York Yankees hit 25 home runs over a two-week span during . . ."
2. Statistics may also be regarded as a *method* of dealing with data. This definition stresses the view that statistics is a tool concerned with the collection, organization, and analysis of numerical facts or observations.

Adapted from *Fundamentals of Behavioral Statistics*, 4th ed., by Richard P. Runyon and Audrey Haber (Reading, Mass.: Addison-Wesley Publishing Co., 1980).

We shall focus our discussion on the second definition.

A distinction may be made between the two functions of the statistical method: **descriptive** statistical techniques and **inferential** or **inductive** statistical techniques.

The major concern of descriptive statistics is to present information in a convenient, usable, and understandable form. Inferential statistics, on the other hand, is concerned with generalizing this information or, more specifically, with making inferences about populations that are based upon samples taken from those populations.

In describing the functions of statistics, certain terms have already appeared with which you may or may not be familiar. Before we elaborate on the differences between descriptive and inductive statistics, it is important for you to learn the meaning of certain terms that will be employed repeatedly throughout the text.

## Definitions of Terms Commonly Used in Statistics

A **variable** is any characteristic of a person, environment, or experimental situation that can vary from person to person, environment to environment, or experimental situation to experimental situation. A variable is contrasted with a constant, the value of which never changes.

**Data** are numbers or measurements that are collected as a result of observations.

**Population** or **universe** refers to a complete set of individuals, objects, or measurements having some common observable characteristic.

A **parameter** is any characteristic of a population that is measurable.

**Sample** refers to a subset of a population or universe.

A **random sample** is a subset of a population or universe selected in such a way that each member of the population has an equal opportunity to be selected.

## Qualifying the Data

**Measurement** is the assignment of numbers to objects or events according to sets of predetermined (or arbitrary) rules. The different levels of measurement that we shall discuss represent different levels of numerical information contained in a set of observations (data), such as a series of house numbers, the order of finish in a horse race, a set of IQ scores, or the price per share of various stocks. The type of scale obtained depends on the kinds of mathematical operations that can be legitimately performed on the numbers. In the social sciences, we encounter measurements at every level.

**Nominal scales.** Observations of unordered variables constitute a very low level of measurement and are referred to as a **nominal scale** of measurement. We may assign numerical values to represent the various classes in a nominal scale, but these numbers have no quantitative properties. They serve only to identify the class. The data employed with nominal scales consist of frequency counts, or tabulations of the number of occurrences in each class of the variable under study.

If we were to study the sex of the offspring of female rats that had been subjected to atomic radiation during pregnancy, sex would be the variable that we would observe. There are only two possible values of this variable: male and female (barring an unforeseen mutation that produced a third sex!). If we were using a computer to analyze our results, we might assign a number to each value of the variable. Thus male might be assigned a 0 and female a 1. Our data would consist of the number of observations in each of these two classes. Note that we do not think of this variable as representing an ordered series of values, such as height, weight, speed, etc. An organism that is female does not have any more of the variable, sex, than one that is male.

**Ordinal scales.**   When we move into the next higher level of measurement, we encounter variables in which the classes *do* represent an ordered series of relationships. Thus the classes in **ordinal scales** not only are different from one another (the characteristic defining nominal scales) but also stand in some kind of *relation* to one another. The numerals employed in connection with ordinal scales are nonquantitative. They indicate only position in an ordered series and not how much of a difference exists between successive positions on the scale.

Examples of ordinal scaling include: rank ordering of baseball players according to their "value to the team," rank ordering of potential candidates for political office according to their "popularity" with people, and rank ordering of officer candidates in terms of their "leadership" qualities. Note that the ranks are assigned according to the ordering of individuals within the class. It does not in fact make any difference whether we give the most popular candidate the highest numerical rank or the lowest, so long as we are consistent in placing the individuals accurately with respect to their relative position in the ordered series.

**Interval and ratio scales.**   Finally, the highest level of measurement in science is achieved with scales employing cardinal numbers **(interval and ratio scales)**. In interval and ratio scales, equal differences between points on any part of the scale are equal. Thus the difference between 4 feet and 2 feet is the same as the difference between 9231 feet and 9229 feet.

The interval scale differs from the ratio scale in terms of the location of the zero point. In an interval scale the zero point is arbitrarily determined. It does not represent the complete absence of the attribute being measured. Our calendar is an example of an interval scale: The year zero does not mean that there was no time before this year. In contrast, the zero in a ratio scale does represent the complete absence of the attribute of interest. Zero length means no length. As a consequence of this difference in the location of the zero point, only the ratio scale permits us to make statements concerning the ratios of numbers in the scale; for example, 4 feet are to 2 feet as 2 feet are to 1 foot.

---

**Ordinal scale**
A scale in which the classes stand in a relationship to one another that is expressed in terms of the algebra of inequalities: $a$ is less than $b$, or $a$ is greater than $b$ (this statement in algebraic notation is written $a < b$, or $a > b$).

**Interval scale**
A quantitative scale that permits the use of arithmetic operations. The zero point in this scale is arbitrary.

**Ratio scale**
The ratio scale is the same as the interval scale, except that there is a true zero point.

Apart from the difference in the nature of the zero point, interval and ratio scales have the same properties.

It should be clear that one of the most sought-after goals of the behavioral scientist is to achieve measurements that are at least interval in nature. Although it is debatable that many of our scales achieve interval measurement, most behavioral scientists are willing to make the assumption that they do.

## DESCRIPTIVE STATISTICS

Let us imagine that you have just accepted a position as curriculum director in a large senior high school. Your responsibility is to develop curricula that not only agree with the students' needs and motivations but also provide maximum challenges to their intellectual capacities. The total solution to such a complex and provoking problem is beyond the scope of this text. However, it is clear that no steps toward a solution can be initiated without some assessment of the intellectual capacities of the student body. Accordingly, you go to the guidance office and pull out at random (i.e., in such a way that every member of the population shares an equal chance of being selected) 110 student dockets containing a wealth of personal and scholastic information. Because your present concern is to assess intellectual ability, you focus your attention on the entry labeled "IQ estimate." You write these estimates down on a piece of paper, with the results listed in Table A.1.

As you mull over these figures, it becomes obvious to you that you cannot make heads or tails out of them unless you organize them in some systematic fashion. It occurs to you to list all the scores from highest to lowest and then place a slash mark alongside each score every time it

Table A.1
**IQ Scores of 110 High School Students Selected at Random**

| | | | | | | | | | |
|---|---|---|---|---|---|---|---|---|---|
| 154 | 131 | 122 | 100 | 113 | 119 | 121 | 128 | 112 | 93 |
| 133 | 119 | 115 | 117 | 110 | 104 | 125 | 85 | 120 | 135 |
| 116 | 103 | 103 | 121 | 109 | 147 | 103 | 113 | 107 | 98 |
| 128 | 93 | 90 | 105 | 118 | 134 | 89 | 143 | 108 | 142 |
| 85 | 108 | 108 | 136 | 115 | 117 | 110 | 80 | 111 | 127 |
| 100 | 100 | 114 | 123 | 126 | 119 | 122 | 102 | 100 | 106 |
| 105 | 111 | 127 | 108 | 106 | 91 | 123 | 132 | 97 | 110 |
| 150 | 130 | 87 | 89 | 108 | 137 | 124 | 96 | 111 | 101 |
| 118 | 104 | 127 | 94 | 115 | 101 | 125 | 129 | 131 | 110 |
| 97 | 135 | 108 | 139 | 133 | 107 | 115 | 83 | 109 | 116 |
| 110 | 113 | 112 | 82 | 114 | 112 | 113 | 142 | 145 | 123 |

Table A.2

**Frequency Distribution of IQ Scores of 110 High School Students Selected at Random**

| X | f | X | f | X | f | X | f |
|---|---|---|---|---|---|---|---|
| 154 | \| | 135 | \|\| | 116 | \|\| | 97 | \|\| |
| 153 | | 134 | \| | 115 | \|\|\|\| | 96 | \| |
| 152 | | 133 | \|\| | 114 | \|\| | 95 | |
| 151 | | 132 | \| | 113 | \|\|\|\| | 94 | \| |
| 150 | \| | 131 | \|\| | 112 | \|\|\| | 93 | \|\| |
| 149 | | 130 | \| | 111 | \|\|\| | 92 | |
| 148 | | 129 | \| | 110 | \|\|\|\|\| | 91 | \| |
| 147 | \| | 128 | \|\| | 109 | \|\| | 90 | \| |
| 146 | | 127 | \|\|\| | 108 | \|\|\|\|\|\| | 89 | \|\| |
| 145 | \| | 126 | \| | 107 | \|\| | 88 | |
| 144 | | 125 | \|\| | 106 | \|\| | 87 | \| |
| 143 | \| | 124 | \| | 105 | \|\| | 86 | |
| 142 | \|\| | 123 | \|\|\| | 104 | \|\| | 85 | \|\| |
| 141 | | 122 | \|\| | 103 | \|\|\| | 84 | |
| 140 | | 121 | \|\| | 102 | \| | 83 | \| |
| 139 | \| | 120 | \| | 101 | \|\| | 82 | \| |
| 138 | | 119 | \|\|\| | 100 | \|\|\|\| | 81 | |
| 137 | \| | 118 | \|\| | 99 | | 80 | \| |
| 136 | \| | 117 | \|\| | 98 | \| | | |

occurs (Table A.2). The number of slash marks, then, represents the frequency of occurrence of each score.

When you have done this, you have constructed an ungrouped **frequency distribution** of scores. Note that in the present example the scores are widely spread out and a number of scores have a frequency of zero. Under these circumstances it is customary for most researchers to *group* the scores and then obtain a frequency distribution of "grouped scores" (see Table A.3).

## Graphical Statistics

The next step usually is to present the data in pictorial form so that readers may readily apprehend the essential features of a frequency distribution and compare one with another if they desire. Such pictures, called graphs, should be thought of *not* as substitutes for statistical treatment of data but rather as *visual aids* for thinking about and discussing statistical problems.

Table A.3

**Grouped Frequency Distribution of IQ Scores**

| Class interval | $f$ | Class interval | $f$ | Class interval | $f$ |
|---|---|---|---|---|---|
| 150–154 | 2 | 125–129 | 9 | 100–104 | 12 |
| 145–149 | 2 | 120–124 | 9 | 95–99 | 4 |
| 140–144 | 3 | 115–119 | 13 | 90–94 | 5 |
| 135–139 | 5 | 110–114 | 17 | 85–89 | 5 |
| 130–134 | 7 | 105–109 | 14 | 80–84 | 3 |
| | | | | | $N = 110$ |

Source: Based upon data appearing in Table A.2.

**Frequency distribution**
When the values of a variable are arranged in order according to their magnitudes, a frequency distribution shows the number of times each score occurs.

**Bar graph**
A form of graph that employs bars to indicate the frequency of occurrence of observations within each nominal or ordinal category.

**Histogram**
A form of bar graph used with interval- or ratio-scaled frequency distributions.

**Frequency curve**
A form of graph representing a frequency distribution, in which a continuous line is used to indicate the frequency of the corresponding scores.

**Bar graphs.**   As illustrated in Fig. A.1, the **bar graph**, is a graphic device employed to represent data that are either nominally or ordinally scaled. A vertical bar is drawn* for each category, and the *height* of the bar represents the number of members of that class.

The bars should be separated rather than touching, so that any implication of continuity among the categories is avoided.

**Histograms.**   It will be recalled that interval- and ratio-scaled variables differ from ordinally scaled variables in one important way; that is, in interval and ratio scales, equal differences in scale values are equal. This means that we may permit the vertical bars to touch one another in graphic representations of interval- and ratio-scaled frequency distributions. Such a graph is referred to as a **histogram** (see Fig. A.2).

**Frequency curves.**   We can readily convert the histogram into another commonly employed form of graphic representation, the **frequency curve**, by joining the midpoints of the bars with straight lines. However, it is not necessary to construct a histogram prior to constructing a frequency curve. All you need to do is place a dot where the tops of the bars would have been and join these dots. When two or more frequency distributions are compared, the frequency curve provides a clearer picture. Figure A.3 shows a frequency curve based upon the grouped frequency distribution appearing in Table A.3.

Frequency curves may take on an unlimited number of forms. However, many of the statistical procedures discussed here assume a particu-

---

*Bar graphs are sometimes drawn horizontally (this has an advantage in cases where the number of cases [or classes] is large and the list may occupy a full page in length). Nevertheless, the vertical array (as shown in Fig. A.1) is more often used (and more easily understood at sight) because of its adaptability to a histogram or a frequency curve (cf. Fig. A.2).

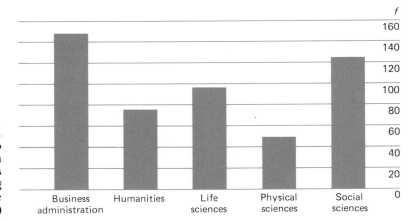

**Figure A.1**
**Number of students who are enrolled in introductory economics courses and are majoring in the various academic fields (hypothetical data)**

**Normal curve**
A frequency curve with a characteristic bell-shaped form.

**Skewed distribution**
A distribution that departs from symmetry and tails off at one end.

lar form of distribution, namely, the "bell-shaped" **normal curve** (see Fig. A.4). The normal curve is referred to as a symmetrical distribution, because, if it is folded in half, the two sides will coincide.

When a distribution is not symmetrical, it is said to be **skewed.** If we say that a distribution is **positively skewed**, we mean that the distribution tails off at the high end of the horizontal axis and there are relatively fewer frequencies at this end. If, on the other hand, we say that the distribution is **negatively skewed**, we mean that there are relatively fewer scores associated with the left-hand, or low, side of the horizontal axis.

## Measures of Central Tendency

We have already stated that the behavioral scientist is frequently called upon to compare the measurements obtained from two or more groups of subjects for the purpose of drawing inferences about the effects of an independent variable. **Measures of central tendency** greatly simplify the

**Figure A.2**
**Frequency distribution of the number of children per family among 389 families surveyed in a small suburban community (hypothetical data)**

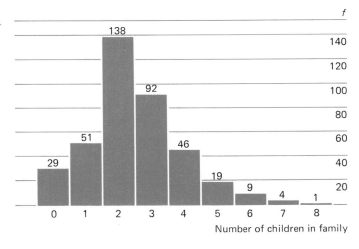

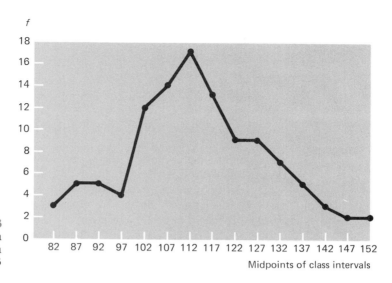

**Positively skewed distribution**
A distribution that has relatively fewer frequencies at the high end of the horizontal axis.

**Negatively skewed distribution**
A distribution that has relatively fewer frequencies at the low end of the horizontal axis.

**Measure of central tendency**
An index of central location employed in the description of frequency distributions.

**Mean**
The sum of the scores or values of a variable divided by their number.

**Median**
A score or potential score in a distribution of scores above and below which one-half of the frequencies fall.

**Mode**
The score that occurs with the greatest frequency.

task of drawing conclusions. We shall define a measure of central tendency as an *index of central location employed in the description of frequency distributions*. The center of a distribution may be defined in different ways; we shall concern ourselves with three of the most frequently employed measures of central tendency: the mean, the median, and the mode.

**The mean.**    You are probably intimately familiar with the arithmetic **mean**, for whenever you obtain an average of grades by summing the grades and dividing by the number of grades, you are calculating the arithmetic mean. In short, *the mean is the sum of the scores or values of a variable divided by their number*. So, for example, using the figures in Table A.1, 12,540/110 = 114.

**The median.**    With grouped frequency distributions, the **median** is defined as *that score or potential score in a distribution of scores above and below which one-half of the frequencies fall*. By using the data as arranged in Table A.2, we can easily determine that 113 is the median in this particular instance.

**The mode.**    Of all measures of central tendency, the **mode** is the most easily determined because it is obtained by inspection rather than by computation. The mode is simply *the score that occurs with the greatest frequency*. In Table A.2, the mode is 108. For grouped data, the mode is designated as the midpoint of the interval containing the highest frequency count. In Table A.3 the mode is a score of 112, because 112 is the midpoint of the interval (110–114) containing the greatest frequency.

## Measures of Dispersion

A score by itself is meaningless. It takes on meaning only when it is compared with other scores or other statistics. Thus if we know the mean of the distribution of a given variable, we can determine whether a particular score is higher or lower than the mean. But how much higher or lower? It is clear at this point that a measure of central tendency such as the mean provides only a limited amount of information. To describe a distribution more fully, or to interpret a score more fully, we require additional information concerning the **dispersion** of scores about our measure of central tendency.

Consider Fig. A.5 (a) and (b). In both examples of frequency curves, the mean of the distribution is exactly the same. However, note the difference in the interpretations of a score of 128. In (a), because the scores are widely dispersed about the mean, a score of 128 may be considered only moderately high. Quite a few individuals in the distribution scored above 128, as indicated by the area to the right of 128. In (b), on the other hand, the scores are compactly distributed about the same mean. Consequently, the score of 128 is now virtually at the top of the distribution, and it may therefore be considered a very high score.

It can be seen, then, that in interpreting individual scores, we must find a companion to the mean or the median. This companion must in some way express the degree of dispersion of scores about the measure of central tendency. We shall discuss two such measures of dispersion or variability: the *range* and the *standard deviation*. Of these, we shall find the standard deviation to be our most useful measure of dispersion in both descriptive and inferential statistics.

**The range.** When we calculated the various measures of central tendency, we located a *single point* along the scale of scores and identified it as the mean, the median, or the mode. When our interest shifts to measures of dispersion, however, we must look for an index of variability that indicates the *distance* along the scale of scores.

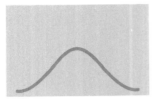

Figure A.4
**The normal curve**

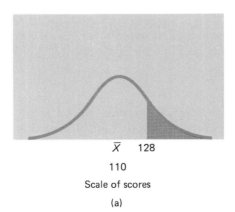

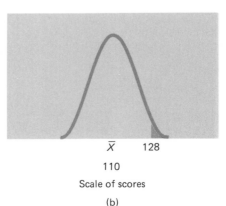

Figure A.5
**Two frequency curves with identical means but differing in dispersion or variability**

(a)                (b)

One of the first measures of distance that comes to mind is the **range**. The range is by far the simplest and the most straightforward measure of dispersion. It consists simply of the scale distance between the largest and the smallest score. Thus if the highest score is 140 and the lowest is 30, the range is 110.

Although the range is meaningful, it is of little use because of its marked instability. Note that if there is one extreme score in a distribution, the dispersion of scores will appear to be large when in fact the removal of that score may reveal an otherwise "compact" distribution. Several years ago, an inmate of an institution for retarded persons was found to have an IQ score in the 140s. Imagine the erroneous impression that would result if the range of scores for the inmates was reported as, say, 140–20, or 120! Stated another way, the range reflects only the two most extreme scores in a distribution.

*The standard deviation.* As we have seen, when we are dealing with data from normally distributed populations, the mean is our most useful measure of central tendency. We obtained the mean by adding together all the scores and dividing them by the number of scores *(N)*. If we carried these procedures one step further, we could subtract the mean from each score, sum the deviations from the mean, and thereby obtain an estimate of the typical amount of deviation from the mean. By dividing by *N*, we would have a measure that would be analogous to the arithmetic mean except that it would represent the dispersion of scores from the arithmetic mean. However, the sum of the deviations of all scores from the mean must add up to zero. If we square each deviation from the mean, we legitimately rid ourselves of the minus signs, while still preserving the information that is inherent in these deviation scores. Then, by taking the square root, we arrive at the **standard deviation**. The standard deviation is of immense value in three different respects:

1. The standard deviation reflects dispersion of scores, so that the variability of different distributions may be compared in terms of the standard deviation.
2. The standard deviation permits the *precise* interpretation of scores within a distribution.
3. The standard deviation, like the mean, is a member of a *mathematical system* that permits its use in more advanced statistical considerations.

The standard deviation for the scores given in Table A.1 is 15.77 (see Table A.4).

*The standard normal distribution.* A great many events in everyday life as well as in experimental situations fall within the **standard normal distribution**. The standard normal distribution has a mean of 0, a standard deviation of 1, and a total area equal to 1.00. There is a fixed proportion of cases between a vertical line (ordinate) erected at any one point

Table A.4
**Standard Deviation**

| IQ | Mean (114) minus IQ | Squared* |
|----|---------------------|----------|
| 154 | 114 − 154 = −40 | 1600 |
| 133 | 114 − 133 = −19 | 361 |
| 116 | 114 − 116 = −02 | 4 |
| 128 | 114 − 128 = −14 | 196 |
| 85 | 114 − 85 = 29 | 841 |
| 100 | 114 − 100 = 14 | 196 |
| 105 | 114 − 105 = 09 | 81 |
| 150 | 114 − 150 = −36 | 1296 |
| 118 | 114 − 118 = −04 | 16 |
| . . . | . . . | . . . |
| 98 | 114 − 98 = 16 | 256 |
| 142 | 114 − 142 = −28 | 784 |
| 127 | 114 − 127 = −13 | 169 |
| 106 | 114 − 106 = 08 | 64 |
| 110 | 114 − 110 = 04 | 16 |
| 101 | 114 − 101 = 13 | 169 |
| 110 | 114 − 110 = 04 | 16 |
| 116 | 114 − 116 = −02 | 4 |
| 123 | 114 − 123 = −09 | 81 |

*Total of squares = 27,360; 27,360 ÷ 110 = 248.72727; $\sqrt{248.72727}$ = 15.771089.

and an ordinate erected at any other point. Taking a few reference points along the normal curve, we can make the following statements:

1. Between the mean and 1 standard deviation above the mean are found 34.13 percent of all cases. Similarly, 34.13 percent of all cases fall between the mean and 1 standard deviation below the mean. Stated in another way, 34.13 percent of the *area* under the curve is found between the mean and 1 standard deviation above the mean, and 34.13 percent of the *area* falls between the mean and −1 standard deviation.

2. Between the mean and 2 standard deviations above the mean are found 47.72 percent of all cases. Because the normal curve is symmetrical, 47.72 percent of the area also falls between the mean and −2 standard deviations.

3. Finally, between the mean and 3 standard deviations above the mean are found 49.87 percent of all cases. Similarly, 49.87 percent of the cases fall between the mean and −3 standard deviations. Thus 99.74 percent of all cases fall between ±3 standard deviations. These relationships are shown in Fig. A.6.

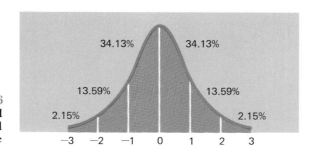

**Figure A.6**
**Areas between selected points under the normal curve**

## THE CONCEPT OF CORRELATION

Up to this point, we have been interested in calculating various statistics that permit us to describe thoroughly the distribution of the values of a single variable and to relate these statistics to the interpretation of individual scores. However, as you are well aware, many of the problems in the behavioral sciences go beyond the description of a single variable in its various and sundry ramifications. We are frequently called upon to determine the relationships among two or more variables. For example, college administration officers are vitally concerned with the relationship between high school averages or Scholastic Aptitude Test (SAT) scores and performance at college. Do students who do well in high school or who score high on the SAT also perform well in college? Conversely, do poor high school students or those who score low on the SAT perform poorly at college? Do parents with high intelligence tend to have children of high intelligence? Is there a relationship between the declared dividend on stocks and their paper value in the exchange? Is there a relationship between socioeconomic class and recidivism in crime?

As soon as we raise questions concerning the relationships among variables, we are thrust into the fascinating area of **correlation.** In order to express quantitatively the extent to which two variables are related, it is necessary to calculate a **correlation coefficient.** There are many types of correlation coefficients. The decision about which one to employ with a specific set of data depends upon such factors as (1) the type of measurement scale in which each variable is expressed, (2) the nature of the underlying distribution, and (3) the characteristics of the distribution of the scores.

No matter which correlational technique we use, all have certain characteristics in common:

1. Two sets of measurements are obtained on the same individuals (or events), or on pairs of individuals who are matched on some basis.
2. The values of the correlation coefficients vary between $+1.00$ and $-1.00$. Both extremes represent perfect relationships between the variables, and $0.00$ represents the *absence* of a relationship.
3. A **positive relationship** means that individuals obtaining high scores on one variable tend to obtain high scores on a second variable. The

**Correlation**
The relationship between two variables.

**Correlation coefficient**
A measure that expresses the extent to which two variables are related.

**Positive relationship**
Variables are said to be positively related when a high score on one is accompanied by a high score on the other. Conversely, low scores on one variable are associated with low scores on the other.

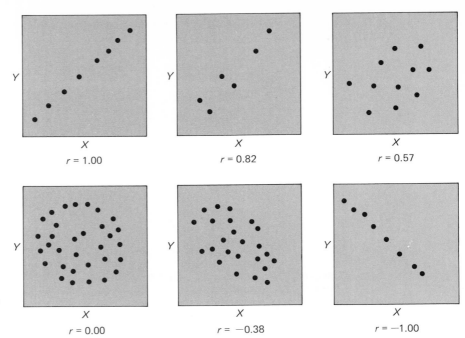

**Figure A.7**
**Scatter diagrams showing various degrees of relationship between two variables**

r = 1.00    r = 0.82    r = 0.57

r = 0.00    r = −0.38    r = −1.00

**Negative relationship**
Variables are said to be negatively related when a high score on one is accompanied by a low score on the other. Conversely, low scores on one variable are associated with high scores on the other.

**Scatter diagram**
A graphic device employed to represent the variation in two variables.

converse is also true; that is, individuals scoring low on one variable tend to score low on a second variable.*

4. A **negative relationship** means that individuals scoring low on one variable tend to score high on a second variable. Conversely, individuals scoring high on one variable tend to score low on a second variable.

Figure A.7 shows a series of **scatter diagrams** illustrating various degrees of relationships between two variables, $X$ and $Y$. In interpreting the figures it is important to remember that every dot represents two values: an individual's score on the $X$-variable and the same person's score on the $Y$-variable.

---

## INFERENTIAL STATISTICS

As a behavioral scientist, your task has just begun when you have completed your descriptive function. In fact, you are often nearer to the beginning than to the end of your task. The reason for this is obvious when we consider that the purpose of your research is often to explore hypotheses of a general nature, rather than simply to compare limited samples.

Let us imagine that you are interested in determining the effects of a given drug upon the performance of a task involving psychomotor coordination. Consequently, you set up a study involving two conditions, *experimental* and *control*. You administer the drug to the experimental subjects at specified time periods before they undertake the criterion task.

---

*These characteristics are true for correlation coefficients that measure linear relationship, but not for all correlation coefficients.

To rule out "placebo effects," you administer a pill containing inert ingredients to the control subjects. After all subjects have been tested, you perform your descriptive function. You find that "on the average" the experimental subjects did not perform as well as the controls. In other words, the arithmetic mean of the experimental group was lower than that of the control group. You then ask the question, "Can we conclude that the drug produced the difference between the two groups?" Or, more generally, "Can we assert that the drug has an adverse effect upon the performance of the criterion task under investigation?" To answer these questions, it is not sufficient to rely solely upon descriptive statistics.

"After all," you reason, "even if the drug has *no effect*, it is highly improbable that the two group means would have been *identical*. Some difference would have been observed." The operation of uncontrolled variables (sometimes referred to rather imprecisely as "chance factors") is certain to produce some disparity between the group means. The critical question, from the point of view of inferential statistics, becomes: "Is the difference great enough to rule out uncontrolled variation in the experiment as a sufficient explanation?" Stated another way: "If we were to repeat the experiment, would we be able to predict with confidence that the same differences (i.e., the control group mean being greater than the experimental group mean) would systematically occur?"

As soon as we raise these questions, we move into the fascinating area of statistical analysis that is known as *inductive* or *inferential statistics*.

## Sampling

Earlier we defined a *population* as a *complete* or theoretical set of individuals, objects, or measurements having some common observable characteristic. It is frequently impossible to study *all* the members of a given population because the population as defined either has an infinite number of members or is so large that it defies exhaustive study. Moreover, when we refer to "the population," we are often dealing with a hypothetical entity. In the typical experimental situation the actual population does not exist. We attempt to find out something about the characteristics of that population *if it did exist*. For example, when we administer a drug to a group of subjects (the *sample*), we wish to generalize our results to everyone who could potentially receive the drug. This population is, of course, hypothetical.

Because populations can rarely be studied exhaustively, we must depend on samples as a basis for arriving at a hypothesis concerning various characteristics, or parameters, of the population. Note that our interest is not in descriptive statistics per se, but in making inferences from data. Thus if we ask 100 people how they intend to vote in a forthcoming election, our primary interest is not in knowing how these 100 people will vote, but in estimating how the members of the entire voting population will cast their ballots.

Almost all research involves the observation and the measurement of a limited number of individuals or events. These measurements are presumed to tell us something about the population.

**Significance**

Once we have selected a sample, performed an experiment, and described our results, how can we decide the significance of our results?

Let us say that you have a favorite coin that you use constantly in everyday life as a basis of either–or decision making. For example, you may ask, "Should I study tonight for the psychology quiz, or should I relax at the movies?" Your solution: "Heads, I study; tails, I don't." Over a period of time, you have sensed that the decision has more often gone against you than for you (in other words, you have to study more often than relax!). You begin to question the accuracy and the adequacy of the coin. Does the coin come up heads more often than tails? How might you find out?

One thing is clear. The true proportion of heads and tails characteristic of this coin can never be known. You could start tossing the coin this very minute and continue for a million years (granted a long life and a remarkably durable coin) and you would not exhaust the population of possible outcomes. In this instance, the true proportion of heads and tails is unknowable because the universe, or population, is unlimited.

In order to determine whether or not the coin is biased, we will have to obtain a sample of the "behavior" of that coin and arrive at some generalization concerning its possible bias. For example, if we toss the coin 10 times and obtain 5 heads and 5 tails, would we begin to suspect our coin of being biased? Of course not, because this outcome is exactly a 50–50 split, and is in agreement with the hypothesis that the coin is not biased. What if we obtained 6 heads and 4 tails? Again, this is not an unusual outcome. In fact, we can answer the question how often, given a theoretically perfect coin, we may expect an outcome at least this much different from a 50–50 split. Reference to Fig. A.8, which represents the theoretical probability distribution of various numbers of heads when $N = 10$, reveals that departures from a 50–50 split are quite common. Indeed, whenever we obtain either 6 or more heads, or 4 or fewer heads, we are departing from a 50–50 split. Such departures will occur fully 75.4 percent of the time when we toss a perfect coin in a series of trials with 10 tosses per trial.

What if we obtained 9 heads and 1 tail? Clearly, we would begin to suspect the honesty of the coin. Why? At what point do we change from an attitude accepting the honesty of the coin to an attitude rejecting its honesty? This question takes us to the crux of the problem of inferential statistics. We have seen that, the more unusual or rare the event, the more prone we are to look for nonchance explanations of the event. When we obtained 6 heads in 10 tosses of our coin, we felt no necessity to find any other explanation for its departure from a 50–50 split than a statement that such a departure would occur frequently by chance. However, when we obtained 9 heads, we had an uncomfortable feeling concerning the honesty of the coin. Nine heads out of 10 tosses is such a rare occurrence that we begin to suspect that the explanation may be found in the characteristics of the coin rather than in the so-called laws of chance. The critical question is, "Where do we draw the line that determines what inferences we make about the coin?"

The answer to this question reveals the basic nature of science: its probabilistic rather than absolutistic orientation. In the social sciences,

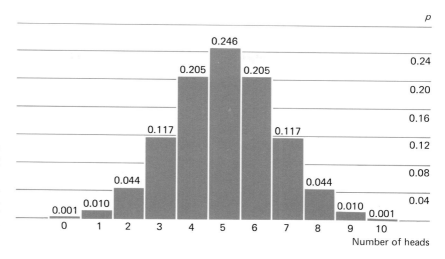

**Significance level**
A probability value that is considered so rare in the sampling distribution that one is willing to assert the operation of nonchance factors. Common significance levels are 0.05 and 0.01.

most researchers have adopted one of the following two cutoff points as the basis for *inferring the operation of nonchance factors.*

1. When the event or one more deviant would occur *5 percent of the time or less, by chance,* some researchers are willing to assert that the results are due to nonchance factors. This cutoff point is known variously as the 0.05 **significance level,** or the 5.00 percent significance level.

2. When the event or one more deviant would occur *1 percent of the time or less, by chance,* other researchers are willing to assert that the results are due to nonchance factors. This cutoff point is known as the 0.01 significance level, or the 1.00 percent significance level.

In the example of the coin test, we can show mathematically that the chances of 9 heads in 10 tosses occurring naturally is only 2.2 percent. Either the coin is "lucky," or it's weighted.

## Terms to Remember

| | | |
|---|---|---|
| Statistics | Interval scale | Median |
| Descriptive statistics | Ratio scale | Mode |
| Inferential or inductive statistics | Frequency distribution | Dispersion |
| Variable | Bar graph | Range |
| Data | Histogram | Standard deviation |
| Population or universe | Frequency curve | Standard normal distribution |
| Parameter | Normal curve | Correlation |
| Sample | Skewed distribution | Correlation coefficient |
| Random sample | Positively skewed distribution | Positive relationship |
| Measurement | Negatively skewed distribution | Negative relationship |
| Nominal scale | Measure of central tendency | Scatter diagram |
| Ordinal scale | Mean | Significance level |

**Ablation.** Surgical removal of a part of the brain.

**Abnormal.** (1) Those behaviors that fail to comply with cultural values or standards (cultural definition); (2) behaviors that interfere with the individual's ability to achieve goals or to resolve motivational conflicts (adjustment definition); (3) certain types of behaviors, for example, disordered thought processes.

**Absolute refractory period.** A short period of time after a neuron discharges a nervous impulse during which it will not fire again, regardless of the intensity of stimulation.

**Absolute threshold.** The minimum amount of stimulation that can be detected 50 percent of the time by a given sense.

**Accommodation.** (1) A monocular cue to depth perception; the lens bulges for near objects and flattens out for far objects. (2) Piaget's term for the alteration of an existing schema to allow for new stimuli.

**Achievement motive.** The desire to do well and achieve success.

**Achievement stage.** According to Schaie, the initial application of cognitive skills to real-life problems and solutions; it is characteristic of early adulthood.

**Acquisition.** The stage of conditioning during which the organism learns the association between the US and the CS.

**Acquisitive stage.** According to Schaie, the acquisition of the intellectual skills we will need throughout life; it is characteristic of childhood and adolescence.

**Addiction.** Physiological dependence on (need for) a drug.

**Adrenal gland.** An endocrine gland, one of whose secretions is adrenalin.

**Adrenalin.** A hormone secreted by the adrenal glands that activates bodily structures and systems during an emergency.

**Affect.** An internal state or feeling.

**Afferent neurons.** Sensory neurons that transmit nervous impulses from the sensory receptors to the brain and spinal cord.

**Affiliation.** The tendency or desire to associate with and form attachments to other people, to depend upon them.

**Aggression.** Physical or verbal behavior intended to inflict harm or injury.

**Agonistic.** Agonistic behavior is behavior involving either fight or flight.

**All-or-none law.** The principle that a neuron fires at full charge or not at all, no matter how intense the stimulation, so long as it is at or above the threshold level.

**Alpha waves.** Brain waves typical of a relaxed waking state.

**Ambivalence.** Mixed feelings (both positive and negative) toward a person or situation.

**Amniocentesis.** The procedure used to remove amniotic fluid from a pregnant woman. This fluid is then analyzed to determine whether there are genetic defects in the fetus.

**Amplitude.** The height of a wave, indicative of the strength of a wave.

**Analgesia.** Anything producing an insensitivity to pain.

**Anal stage.** In psychoanalytic theory, the stage of psychosexual development during which the infant is

# GLOSSARY

preoccupied with sensations from the anal area.

**Androgyny.** The ability to express both feminine and masculine traits as the situation requires.

**Anesthesias.** Loss of sensitivity in some part of the body.

**Antidepressants.** A category of drugs that relieve the despondency and agitation characteristic of patients with affective disorders.

**Antipsychotic drugs.** A category of drugs that reduce the delusions, hallucinations, and disorganized thinking characteristic of patients with disorders such as schizophrenia.

**Antisocial personality.** A personality disorder characterized by the absence of both anxiety and the various defenses against it.

**Anxiety.** A fear reaction to unknown or unidentified stimuli; a premonition that something bad will happen.

**Anxiety disorders.** Emotional disturbances characterized by maladaptive behavior aimed at avoiding anxiety.

**Anxiety state.** A type of disorder characterized by constant anxiety and tension.

**Approach–approach conflict.** A conflict in which the individual is simultaneously motivated to approach two desirable but incompatible goals.

**Approach–avoidance conflict.** A conflict in which the individual is simultaneously motivated both to approach and to avoid a goal object.

**Approach gradient.** A change in the strength of the approach tendency with decreasing distance from the goal object.

**Aptitude tests.** Instruments designed to measure an individual's capacity to achieve proficiency in a given activity or occupational field.

**Assimilation.** Piaget's term for the incorporation of new stimuli into an existing schema.

**Association neurons.** Neurons usually found in the central nervous system that connect afferent and efferent neurons.

**Associative cortex.** The parts of the brain concerned with such complex behaviors as thinking, speech, and memory.

**Attitude.** A learned predisposition to respond in a specific way, negatively or positively, toward people, ideas, or situations. Attitudes typically involve an affective (or feeling) component, a cognitive (or thought) component, and a behavioral component.

**Attribution theories.** Theories concerned with how people use information about behavior to make judgments about the cause of that behavior.

**Auditory area.** An area in the temporal lobes that is responsible for auditory sensations.

**Auricle.** The external part of the ear.

**Autokinetic effect.** The apparent movement of a stationary pinpoint of light in a dark room.

**Autonomic nervous system.** The part of the peripheral nervous system that regulates such inner organs of the body as the heart, the stomach, and the glands.

**Aversive conditioning.** A technique used in behavior therapy in which punishment or aversive stimulation is used to eliminate undesired behavior.

**Avoidance–avoidance conflict.** A conflict in which the individual is simultaneously motivated to avoid two undesirable alternatives.

**Avoidance conditioning.** A form of conditioning in which the organism can avoid an aversive stimulus by making the appropriate response to a warning signal.

**Avoidance gradient.** A change in the strength of the avoidance tendency with decreasing distance from the goal object.

**Axon.** A long fiber extending from the cell body of a neuron that carries nervous impulses away from the cell body.

**Bar graph.** A form of graph that employs bars to indicate the frequency of occurrence of observations within each nominal or ordinal category.

**Behavior.** In the most general sense, anything an organism does.

**Behaviorism.** A school of psychology (associated with J. B. Watson) that maintains that psychologists should study only what is observable—behavior, not conscious experience.

**Behavior therapy (behavior modification).** A therapeutic technique based primarily on the application of the principles of conditioning to the modification of maladaptive behavior.

**Belief.** The acceptance of a proposition as fact.

**Binocular cues.** Cues to distance and depth that require the use of both eyes.

**Biofeedback.** Information about a bodily response from either the senses or an outside source. On the basis of this information, the organism can adjust and modify its bodily responses.

**Biological drive.** A motive that stems from the physiological state of the organism, for example, hunger.

**Blind spot.** The spot on the retina where the optic nerve leaves the eye. Because it contains no receptors, it leaves a gap in the field of vision.

**Brightness.** How dark or how light a color is; it is determined by the intensity of the light at the wavelength.

**Brightness constancy.** The tendency to perceive objects in their correct brightness, regardless of the conditions of illumination.

**Cannon–Bard theory.** The theory that a physiological state and the emotional experience of it are triggered simultaneously by the hypothalamus.

**Case-history method.** Data assembled about the past history of an individual or group in order to understand present behavior.

**Castration anxiety.** A boy's fear that his father will castrate him in retaliation for his Oedipal feelings.

**Central nervous system.** The brain and spinal cord.

**Cerebellum.** A brain structure located under the rear portion of the cerebral cortex that plays a key role in muscle coordination.

**Cerebral cortex.** The layer of nervous tissue beneath the skull that is the outer covering of the cerebral hemispheres and that plays a major role in intellectual processes such as thought and language.

**Cerebral hemispheres.** The two symmetrical halves of the brain.

**Change-of-environment method.** A method of breaking habits in which the individual is removed from all cues that normally elicit the undesired behavior.

**Chemotherapy.** A therapeutic technique involving the treatment of emotional disorders through the use of drugs.

**Chromosomes.** Complex chemical substances within the cell nucleus that carry the determiners of heredity called genes. The normal human cell has 46 chromosomes, arranged in pairs.

**Clairvoyance.** A form of extrasensory perception; the presumed ability to perceive things without the use of the sense organs.

**Classical conditioning (Pavlovian conditioning).** A type of learning in which a previously neutral stimulus, through repeated pairings with an unconditioned stimulus, acquires the capacity to evoke the response originally made to the unconditioned stimulus.

**Clinical psychologist.** A psychologist who is involved in diagnosis, assessment, and treatment of emotionally disturbed individuals.

**Closure.** In perception, the tendency to perceive broken lines as continuous, and incomplete figures as complete and closed.

**Cognitive appraisal theory.** The theory that an emotional experience is a result of cognitive interpretation of a situation triggering physiological arousal.

**Cognitive dissonance.** Lack of agreement between one's beliefs, feelings, or behavior resulting in a state of tension.

**Cognitive processes.** Mental processes involved in thinking, reasoning, and problem solving.

**Cognitive psychology.** A branch of psychology dealing with thoughts, knowledge, and ideas.

**Cohabitation.** Living together in a sexual relationship without marriage.

**Coitus.** The technical term for sexual intercourse.

**Collective unconscious.** In Jung's theory, a portion of the unconscious containing certain shared experiences, predispositions, and symbols that are inherited and found in all members of a given race or species.

**Compensation.** A defense mechanism in which individuals make up for a real or imagined deficiency or weakness in one area by striving to excel in another.

**Complexity.** The presence of frequencies other than the

fundamental frequency; the number and strength of these other frequencies determines the timbre of a sound.

Compulsive behavior. The impulse to perform some act repeatedly.

Computer-assisted instruction. Programmed instruction in a computer.

Concept. An abstract idea or representation of the common characteristics of objects that are otherwise different.

Concept formation. Learning to attach a symbol to objects that share a common characteristic, while ignoring their differences.

Concrete operational stage. Piaget's third stage of cognitive development, in which the child develops logical thinking toward concrete objects.

Concurrent validity. The extent to which scores on one measure compare to scores on an already existing criterion.

Conditioned response (CR). The learned response to a conditioned stimulus.

Conditioned stimulus (CS). A stimulus that, through repeated pairings with an unconditioned stimulus (US), acquires the capacity to evoke a response it did not originally evoke.

Conduction deafness. Impairment of hearing due to impaired functioning of the bones in the middle ear.

Cones. One of the two types of receptors for vision located in the retina; the cones mediate color vision.

Conflict. The simultaneous arousal of two or more incompatible motives or attitudes.

Conformity. The process of adapting one's beliefs or behaviors so that they will be consistent with one's perception of group values.

Conscious mind. In psychoanalytic theory, that part of the mind which is aware of the individual's feelings and behaviors.

Conscious self. That part of the organismic self concerned with individuals' perceptions of themselves and of their relationships with others.

Conservation. A term used by Piaget to refer to the ability of the child to recognize that certain properties of objects (e.g., weight, quantity) remain the same despite changes in their appearance.

Construct. A term that refers to a set of ideas, not directly observed, by which we organize and interpret the world. Many of the terms used in psychology are constructs. For example, learning, attitude, personality, and intelligence are not directly observed; but we use these terms to organize the ways we think about people and events.

Constructive memory. The transformation of a memory to reflect the inclusion of new information.

Consummatory response. The final response in a sequence of goal-directed behaviors.

Contingent reinforcement. Reward or reinforcement that is dependent upon making a given response.

Continuity. In perception, the tendency to see elements as grouped together if they appear to be a continuation of a pattern.

Continuous reinforcement. Reinforcement of a response every time it occurs.

Control group. In an experiment, that group of subjects *not* given the independent variable.

Convergence. A binocular cue to depth perception; in viewing a near object, the eyes tend to turn toward each other to focus.

Convergent thinking. Thinking that involves the ability to arrive at a conclusion "in accordance with truth and fact."

Conversion disorder. A type of disorder characterized by sensory or motor impairment without any physical cause.

Corpus callosum. A connective fiber bridge through which the two cerebral hemispheres communicate.

Correlation. The relationship between two variables.

Correlation coefficient. A measure that expresses the extent to which two variables are related.

Counseling psychologist. A psychologist who focuses on minor adjustment problems or assists in vocational and educational guidance. Counseling psychologists typically work with people whose problems are less serious and less deep-rooted than those treated by clinical psychologists.

**Creativity.** Productive thinking that is directed toward new relations and solutions to problems.

**Critical period.** The time period during which the capacity to benefit from experiences is optimal.

**Culture.** The customs, traditions, beliefs, values, and attitudes that characterize a social group.

**Data.** Numbers or measurements that are collected as a result of observations.

**Defense mechanisms.** Behavior patterns, presumed to be unconscious, aimed at reducing anxiety in the individual.

**Delusion.** A belief that is contrary to reality.

**Dementia.** An organic mental disorder caused by deterioration of the brain.

**Dendrites.** Hairlike structures of a neuron that receive nervous impulses from other neurons and carry them toward the cell body.

**Denial.** A defense mechanism in which the individual unconsciously denies the existence of events that have aroused his or her anxiety.

**Dependent variable.** Behavior that is being observed and measured and that depends upon changes in the independent variable.

**Depressive state.** A mood characterized by excessive sadness and hopelessness.

**Derived IQ score.** The average score on an intelligence test for a given age group is set equal to 100; individ-

uals who score on a par with their age level will obtain an IQ score of 100.

**Descriptive statistics.** Procedures employed to organize and present data in a convenient, usable, and communicable form.

**Desensitization.** A therapeutic technique that involves training an individual to relax in the presence of a situation that previously aroused anxiety or fear. In desensitization therapy, the individual is gradually led through a series of increasingly intense anxiety- or fear-arousing stimuli until he or she is able to tolerate the situation that previously was the most anxiety arousing.

**Developmental psychologist.** A psychologist who studies the behavior and behavioral changes of the individual from the prenatal period through maturity and old age.

**Difference threshold.** The minimum increase or decrease of stimulation necessary for a person to detect a change in stimulation.

**Diffusion of responsibility concept.** A theory to account for the observation that we become less likely to help a person in distress as the number of other people available to render assistance increases.

**Directed thinking.** Controlled purposeful thinking that is directed toward a specific goal or outcome, as in problem solving.

**Discrimination.** Behavioral expression of prejudice;

learning to respond differentially to similar stimuli.

**Dispersion.** The spread or variability of scores about the measure of central tendency.

**Displaced aggression.** Aggression directed toward a source other than the original cause of frustration.

**Displacement.** A defense mechanism in which individuals transfer reactions or energy from one object to another, "safer" object.

**Dissociative disorder.** A type of disorder that involves some impairment of memory functions, usually as a defense to avoid or escape from an anxiety-arousing situation.

**Distributed practice.** Learning material with rest periods intervening between practice sessions.

**Disuse theory of forgetting.** The theory that learning produces a memory trace that automatically fades or decays with the passage of time.

**Divergent thinking.** Thinking that involves seeing new and unusual relationships that are appropriate to a problem situation.

**Dominant gene.** A member of a gene pair that takes precedence over the remaining gene in determining inherited characteristics.

**Double blind.** An experimental design in which neither the experimenter nor the subjects know what treatment is being administered.

**Down's syndrome.** A genetic defect resulting in mental

retardation and certain physical characteristics.

**Dream analysis.** A psychoanalytic technique aimed at uncovering the unconscious wishes and impulses as they appear in the manifest content of the dream.

**Drug abuser.** A person who uses drugs to excess and is unable to function without them.

**Drug user.** A person who uses drugs, but not to excess.

**Ecological validity.** Taking into account the natural setting in which the behavior being interpreted occurs.

**EEG.** A recording of brain wave activity obtained from an electroencephalograph.

**Effector.** A muscle or gland.

**Efferent neurons.** Motor neurons that transmit nervous impulses from the brain and spinal cord to the muscles and glands.

**Ego.** In psychoanalytic theory, the aspect of the personality that regulates and controls the impulsive expressions of the id and deals with the demands of reality.

**Egocentrism.** An early state in the child's cognitive development in which he or she does not clearly distinguish between the self and the world other than the self.

**Ego-dystonic homosexuality.** A disorder in which homosexual arousal is a persistent source of distress to the individual.

**Ego ideal.** In psychoanalytic theory, the perfect self one would like to be.

**Eidetic imagery.** Visual imagery that is so clear and detailed that the objects represented seem to be actually present; sometimes called photographic memory.

**Electra complex.** Unconscious sexual feelings of a girl for her father.

**Electroconvulsive therapy (ECT).** A type of medical therapy in which electricity is used to produce convulsions and unconsciousness.

**Electroencephalograph.** An instrument for recording the electrical activity of the brain.

**Embryo.** The developing organism from about the second to the eighth week after conception.

**Emotion.** A complex state involving cognitions, overt responses, internal changes, and motivational aspects.

**Empiricism.** The theoretical position that behavior is determined by experience and that human nature can be understood best by *observing* people and their behavior.

**Encounter group.** A small therapy group that focuses on expressing feelings openly and honestly.

**Endocrine glands.** A group of glands that maintain body functioning by secreting chemical substances directly into the bloodstream.

**Erogenous zones.** The various sensitive areas of the body.

**ESB.** Electrical stimulation of the brain.

**Escape conditioning.** A form of aversive conditioning in which the organism can terminate an aversive stimulus by making the appropriate response.

**Eustress.** The "good" stress beneficial to the individual, according to Selye.

**Excitatory nucleus.** A group of neurons that activate the behavior for which this nucleus is responsible. For example, activation of the excitatory nucleus for eating leads to increased eating.

**Executive stage.** According to Schaie, the development of high-level problem-solving skills not related to day-to-day job or family responsibilities; it is characteristic of the thirties to the sixties.

**Exhaustion method.** A method of breaking habits in which the individual makes the undesired response, in the presence of the stimuli that normally evoke it, so often that the response is finally extinguished.

**Experiment.** A scientific method in which the experimenter systematically alters a variable so that observed changes in another variable (behavior) may be attributed to changes in the first.

**Experimental group.** In an experiment, that group of subjects given the independent variable.

**Experimental neurosis.** Disturbed behavior in animals that results when they are required to make extremely difficult discriminations.

**Experimental psychologist.** A psychologist involved in the experimental investigation of psychological phenomena.

**Expressive function of language.** Communication of meanings to others, for example, by speech or writing.

**External locus of control.** The orientation that the various outcomes in life are determined by forces outside the individual.

**Exteroceptors.** Sensory receptors that provide information about the external world (for example, the receptors involved in sight).

**Extinction.** The reduction in response that occurs in operant conditioning when the conditioned response (CR) is no longer followed by reinforcement and in classical conditioning when the conditioned stimulus (CS) is presented *without* the unconditioned stimulus (US).

**Extinction therapy.** A technique of behavior therapy that consists of eliminating positive reinforcement for an undesired behavior.

**Extrasensory perception (ESP),** sometimes called Psi. A form of perception that does not rely on the use of any of the known senses.

**Extrinsic motivation.** Desire to perform a behavior based on the expectation of external reward.

**Extroversion.** The tendency to be outgoing and to engage in occupations or activities in which there is much contact with people.

**Fetus.** The developing organism from about the end of the second month after conception until birth.

**Figure and ground.** In perception, the tendency to see things as objects against a background.

**Fissure of Rolando (central fissure).** The crevice or groove that separates the frontal from the parietal lobes of the brain.

**Fixed-interval schedule (FI).** A schedule for reinforcing operant behavior in which reinforcement is administered after a fixed period of time.

**Fixed-ratio schedule (FR).** A schedule for reinforcing operant behavior in which reinforcement is administered after the organism emits a fixed number of responses.

**Formal operational stage.** Piaget's final stage of cognitive development, in which the child develops the ability to deal with abstract relationships.

**Fovea.** The central region of the retina; it contains only cones.

**Free association.** A psychoanalytic technique for probing the unconscious; individuals report their thoughts and feelings spontaneously as they occur.

**Free-floating anxiety.** Anxiety that is diffuse and without focus.

**Frequency.** The number of vibrations, or cycles, per second; it determines the pitch we hear.

**Frequency curve.** A form of graph representing a frequency distribution, in which a continuous line is used to indicate the frequency of the corresponding scores.

**Frequency distribution.** When the values of a variable are arranged in order according to their magnitudes, a frequency distribution shows the number of times each score occurs.

**Frontal lobe.** The lobe in the front portion of the brain, in front of the fissure of Rolando; it is involved in fine motor activities and possibly in almost every complex behavioral process.

**Frustration.** A blocking or thwarting of goal-directed activities.

**Frustration tolerance.** The amount of frustration that an individual is able to cope with effectively.

**Functionalism.** A school of psychology that raised questions concerning the functions or purposes served by the mind, consciousness, and so forth in the adjusting organism.

**Fugue.** A type of dissociative disorder in which the individual begins a new life and is amnesic about his or her prior identity.

**General adaptation syndrome.** A three-stage physiological reaction to prolonged stress, consisting of an alarm stage, a resistance stage, and an exhaustion stage.

**Genes.** The basic unit of hereditary transmission, located on the chromosomes.

**Genetic counseling.** Providing people with information about the risks and consequences of inheriting or transmitting various genetic disorders.

**Genital stage.** In psychoanalytic theory, the stage of psychosexual development in which the focus of erotic pleasure returns to the genital zone and the individual achieves mature heterosexual relations.

**Genotype.** The underlying genetic makeup of an individual.

**Germ cells.** The sperm in males and egg in females that unite during fertilization to produce a new organism. Germ cells contain half the chromosomes found in other body cells.

**Gestalt psychology.** A school of psychology that stresses the view that we see things as unified wholes rather than as discrete, independent parts.

**Gonads.** Sex glands; testes in males and ovaries in females.

**Gradient.** A change in the strength of the response tendency, as shown by a rising or falling curve in a graph.

**Grammar.** The rules that determine how to combine words into meaningful sentences.

**Group therapy.** Psychotherapy in which two or more people are treated simultaneously.

**Habituation.** Psychological dependence on (need for) a drug.

**Hallucination.** A sensory impression in the absence of an appropriate environmental stimulus.

**Hallucinogens.** Psychoactive drugs that usually produce hallucinations.

**Halo effect.** The tendency, when making judgments about a particular trait, to be influenced by an overall impression of the individual being rated.

**Higher-order conditioning.** Conditioning of a response to a stimulus by pairing the neutral stimulus with another stimulus that was previously conditioned to elicit the response.

**Histogram.** A form of bar graph used with interval- or ratio-scaled frequency distributions.

**Homeostasis.** A mechanism whereby the body maintains a state of physiological equilibrium. There are homeostatic mechanisms for virtually every bodily function.

**Hormones.** Chemical substances secreted by the endocrine glands directly into the bloodstream.

**Hue.** Scientific term for color; a specific wavelength is seen as a specific hue.

**Humanism.** An approach to psychology that emphasizes the self, internal experiences, and natural growth toward good mental health.

**Hypertension.** A medical disorder characterized by chronically high blood pressure.

**Hypnosis.** A means of achieving a trancelike state of increased suggestibility.

**Hypothalamus.** A subcortical structure that plays an important role in hunger, thirst, sex, emotion, and other physiological functions.

**Hypothesis.** A proposed explanation of the relationship between events or variables that can be tested.

**Id.** In psychoanalytic theory, the primitive and instinctual drives of the individual; the id is concerned only with immediate satisfaction of basic biological drives.

**Ideal self.** In Rogerian theory, the way the individual would like to be.

**Identification.** The process of incorporating into one's own personality the values and beliefs of another person, usually a parent.

**Illusion.** A perception that is a distortion of an actual sensory experience.

**Imprinting.** A learning process that occurs with extreme rapidity during a critical period in the organism's life—for example, the process by which a young duckling learns to follow its mother or any moving object.

**Incompatible-response method.** A method of breaking habits that involves the extinction of an undesirable response and the acquisition of a new response that is incompatible with the original undesired response.

**Independent variable.** A variable that is examined in order to determine its effects on behavior (the dependent variable).

**Industrial psychologist.** A psychologist who functions in an industrial setting in an effort to find solutions to practical, business-related problems.

**Inferential** or **inductive statistics.** Procedures employed to arrive at broader generalizations or inferences from sample data to populations.

**Inhibitory nucleus.** A group of neurons that suppress or curb the behavior for which this nucleus is responsible. For example, activation of the inhibitory nucleus for eating leads to decreased eating.

**Insight.** A sudden solution to a problem.

**Insomnia.** A sleep disorder characterized by difficulty attaining or maintaining sleep three or more nights a week over long periods of time.

**Instinctive behavior.** Unlearned patterns of behavior characteristic of every member of a species or every member of a sex within a species. The behavior appears to be inherited and conforms to a complex, fixed pattern.

**Intellectualization.** A defense mechanism in which individuals defend themselves against the anxiety produced by a conflict by cutting off their emotional

involvement and dealing with the conflict on a strictly intellectual level.

**Intelligence.** The ability to adapt to new situations and to profit from previous experiences when confronted with new situations or problems; some people define intelligence as what intelligence tests measure.

**Intelligence quotient (IQ).** The individual's mental age divided by his or her chronological age and multiplied by 100: $IQ = (MA/CA) \times 100$.

**Intensity.** The amplitude of the sound waves; it determines the loudness of sound.

**Interference theory of forgetting.** The theory that events intervening after the original learning may interfere with the retention of this learning.

**Internalization.** Incorporation of the norms and values of society into one's internal "guidance system."

**Internal locus of control.** The orientation that the various outcomes in life are a direct consequence of forces within the individual.

**Interoceptors.** Sensory receptors that provide information about internal states of the organism.

**Interposition.** A monocular cue to distance perception; it occurs when one object partially obscures another in our field of vision.

**Interpretive area.** A portion of the temporal lobes that, when electrically stimulated, sometimes produces

vivid memories of past events.

**Interval scale.** A quantitative scale that permits the use of arithmetic operations. The zero point in this scale is arbitrary.

**Intervention procedures.** Attempts to correct unfavorable aspects of a child's environment by modifying this environment at a sufficiently early age.

**Intrinsic motivation.** Desire to perform a behavior based on factors other than external rewards.

**Introspection.** A method of looking within and describing one's conscious experience.

**Introversion.** The tendency to look inward, to prefer being alone, and to engage in activities in which there is little contact with people.

**Inventory.** A series of objective questions designed to measure a single trait or several aspects of personality simultaneously.

**Iris.** The colored part of the eye; it restricts the amount of light admitted.

**James-Lange theory.** The theory that an emotional experience results from perception of bodily changes.

**Latency stage.** In psychoanalytic theory, the stage of psychosexual development in which sexual urgings become dormant.

**Latent content.** In psychoanalytic theory, the actual meaning of a dream, the repressed motives that express themselves in the manifest content.

**Lateral fissure.** The crevice or groove that separates the temporal and frontal lobes.

**Learned motive.** A motivational state in which learned, rather than biological, factors appear to be the primary determinant.

**Learning.** A relatively permanent change in behavior resulting from experience or practice.

**Learning how to learn.** Developing certain strategies that can be transferred from one situation to comparable situations.

**Learning set.** A general approach to the solution of similar problems.

**Lesion.** Any destruction or damage to tissue.

**Libido.** In psychoanalytic theory, the psychological energy associated with sexual impulses.

**Limbic system.** A group of interrelated structures involved in emotional and motivated behavior.

**Linear perspective.** Distance perception through the apparent convergence of parallel lines.

**Lipostat.** A proposed mechanism in the hypothalamus that sets the amount of fat that the organism needs to maintain.

**Locus of control.** A broad concept that relates to the point at which controls are exercised over an individual's life.

**Long-term memory (LTM).** A type of memory of extremely long duration.

**Loudness.** The hearing sensation determined by the amplitude of the sound wave.

**Manic state.** A mood characterized by excessive euphoria and excitement.

**Manifest content.** In psychoanalytic theory, the images and events that constitute the dream as it appears to the dreamer.

**Mantra.** A smooth-flowing word or phrase, drawn from an ancient Indian language, that is repeated over and over again during a meditative period.

**Massed practice.** Learning material by crowding practice into long, unbroken time intervals.

**Maturation.** Biological changes that occur in the normal course of development after birth.

**Maturational readiness.** The time interval during which the organism is first physically capable of acquiring a particular function or skill.

**Mean.** The sum of the scores or values of a variable divided by their number.

**Measurement.** The assignment of numbers to objects or events according to sets of predetermined (or arbitrary) rules.

**Measure of central tendency.** An index of central location employed in the description of frequency distributions.

**Median.** A score or potential score in a distribution of scores above and below which one-half of the frequencies fall.

**Medical therapy.** Treatment of emotional disturbance by medical methods.

**Meditation.** A state of consciousness achieved by concentrating on some re-petitive activity and characterized by relaxation, heightened sensory awareness, intense emotional states, and altered perceptions of time and space.

**Medulla.** A subcortical structure that plays an important role in vital functions such as breathing and blood circulation.

**Meissner's corpuscles.** Sensory receptors for touch located in hairless skin regions.

**Memory.** Retention of prior experiences in such a way that they influence later behavior.

**Memory span.** The amount of information that an individual can absorb in short-term memory and recall immediately.

**Memory trace.** A modification of nervous tissue presumed to underlie memory. This is a construct used to explain retention.

**Menarche.** First menstruation; the beginning of puberty for females.

**Mental age (MA).** The individual's score on an intelligence test based on a norm; an MA of 7 means that the individual has performed as well as the average seven-year-old child.

**Mental retardation.** Below-normal intelligence; generally an IQ of 70 or less.

**Mental telepathy.** A form of extrasensory perception in which one person "reads" the mind of another.

**Minor tranquilizers.** A category of drugs that reduce feelings of tension and anxiety.

**Mnemonic devices.** Techniques for organizing material to be learned in order to maximize efficiency in remembering.

**Mode.** The score that occurs with the greatest frequency.

**Monocular cues.** Cues to distance and depth that require the use of only one eye.

**Motion parallax.** When we move, near objects appear to move across our visual field more rapidly than far objects.

**Motivated forgetting.** A theory maintaining that we forget certain events or experiences because we are unconsciously motivated to do so.

**Motive.** A condition that serves to energize and direct behavior toward specific classes of goal objects.

**Motor area.** The region of the brain concerned with the regulation of voluntary motor activities.

**Multiple approach–avoidance conflict.** A conflict in which the individual is simultaneously motivated both to approach and to avoid two or more goal objects.

**Myelin sheath.** A fatty insulation surrounding many axons.

**Nanometer.** A measure of electromagnetic wavelength: one-billionth of a meter.

**Naturalistic observation.** A scientific method that involves careful observations of behavior in a natural setting.

**Negatively skewed distribution.** A distribution that has relatively fewer frequencies at the low end of the horizontal axis.

**Negative reinforcement.** An event that strengthens the response that precedes it by virtue of its *removal* or *termination.*

**Negative relationship.** Variables are said to be negatively related when a high score on one is accompanied by a low score on the other. Conversely, low scores on one variable are associated with high scores on the other.

**Negative transfer.** The interference of prior experience in an earlier situation with learning in a new situation.

**Nerve deafness.** Deafness caused by damage to or destruction of the auditory nerve.

**Neural impulse.** A temporary electrochemical reaction of the neuron when it has been activated.

**Neuron.** A nerve cell consisting of a cell body, an axon, and dendrites.

**Neurosis.** The term formerly used to denote emotional disturbances characterized by maladaptive behavior aimed at avoiding anxiety.

**Night terrors.** A sleep disorder characterized by episodes in which the individual awakens from an NREM state, screaming in terror. The victim frequently is unable to recall the source of the terror and, after returning to sleep, may awaken with no recall of the entire episode.

**Nominal scale.** Observations of unordered variables.

**Nondirected thinking.** A form of thinking that is controlled more by the individual's desires and needs than by reality, as in daydreaming.

**Nonsense syllables.** Three-letter combinations that do not make a word—for example, ZEB.

**Noradrenalin.** A hormone secreted by the adrenal glands that produces the physiological changes associated with anger.

**Normal curve.** A frequency curve with a characteristic bell-shaped form.

**Norms.** Standards and expectations shared by a group.

**Obedience.** Yielding to the pressures of those in authority.

**Objectivity.** In a test, the degree to which scoring is free of the influence of subjective and personal factors. One of the characteristics of the professional psychologist's approach to the study of behavior; studying behavior without allowing personal prejudices and opinions to affect one's judgment.

**Object permanence.** A concept of Piaget's that refers to the child's realization that an object continues to exist even though it is not physically present.

**Observational learning.** Learning that takes place by observing models.

**Obsession.** A recurring thought or impulse that persistently intrudes itself into the individual's consciousness.

**Obsessive–compulsive disorder.** A type of disorder

characterized by persistent and recurring thoughts or actions.

**Occipital lobe.** The lobe occupying the extreme rear portion of the brain and primarily concerned with vision.

**Oedipus complex.** Unconscious sexual feelings of a boy for his mother.

**Operant conditioning.** A type of learning in which the response is instrumental in obtaining rewards or in escaping (or avoiding) aversive stimuli.

**Operational definition.** A definition of terms or concepts by the way in which they are measured.

**Opinion.** A judgment or feeling for which the factual support is far weaker than for beliefs.

**Optic chiasma.** The point at which the optic nerves meet and the fibers from each separate before heading for the left and right hemispheres of the cerebral cortex.

**Optic nerve.** Those fibers that transmit information about what is seen from the eye to the brain.

**Oral stage.** In psychoanalytic theory, the first stage of psychosexual development, during which the mouth is the principal source of sexual or erotic pleasure.

**Ordinal scale.** A scale in which the classes stand in a relationship to one another that is expressed in terms of the algebra of inequalities: $a$ is less than $b$, or $a$ is greater than $b$ (this statement in algebraic no-

tation is written $a < b$, or $a > b$).

**Organic mental disorders.** A category of disorders associated with known physiological causes.

**Organismic self.** In Roger's theory of self, the total, organized awareness, or potential awareness of the mind.

**Organismic variable.** Such naturally occurring characteristics of the organism as sleep levels, age, and gender.

**Overlearning.** Continued practice after mastery has been achieved.

**Overregulation.** A type of error in which rules are applied more widely than they should be.

**Paired-associate learning.** A type of learning in which items (words, syllables) are learned in pairs. The subject must respond with the appropriate word or syllable when presented with the associated stimulus.

**Pancreas.** A gland that secretes digestive enzymes into the small intestine and insulin into the bloodstream.

**Parameter.** Any characteristic of a population that is measurable.

**Parapsychology.** The scientific study of phenomena such as extrasensory perception that are usually considered outside the realm of scientific psychology.

**Parasympathetic branch.** The division of the autonomic nervous system that is dominant when the organism is placid. This system decreases heart rate and

blood pressure and regulates normal digestive processes.

**Parietal lobe.** One of the lobes occupying the rear portion of the brain, located between the fissure of Rolando and the occipital lobe; it is concerned with sensation of body feelings.

**Partial reinforcement.** Reinforcement of a response only some of the times that it occurs.

**Part-method.** A method of learning in which the individual separates the material to be learned into parts, and learns one part at a time.

**Penis envy.** In Freudian theory, the female's unconscious desire to have a penis.

**Perception.** The organization and interpretation of sensory experiences.

**Perceptual constancy.** The tendency to see the world as relatively stable and unchanging, despite the wide variations in information received by the senses.

**Peripheral nervous system.** The part of the nervous system that connects the central nervous system with the receptors and effectors.

**Personal construct.** Kelly's term for each individual's unique categories for classifying people and events.

**Personality.** Persistent and enduring behavior patterns of an individual, which tend to be expressed in a wide variety of life situations.

**Person-centered therapy.** A nondirective type of psychotherapy concerned primarily with the current adjustment of the individual.

**Phallic stage.** In psychoanalytic theory, the stage of psychosexual development in which the focus of erotic pleasure is the sex organs.

**Phenomenological (reality) self.** In Rogerian theory, the way the individual views him- or herself.

**Phenotype.** The characteristics that we can observe, as distinguished from those traits carried genetically but not necessarily displayed.

**Phi phenomenon.** An illusion of motion produced by a rapid succession of stationary images, as in electric signs.

**Phobia.** An unreasonable, intense, and persistent fear of situations or objects that do not constitute real dangers.

**Phobic disorder.** A type of anxiety disorder characterized by intense fear of a situation or object which the individual realizes constitutes no real personal danger.

**Phonemes.** The basic sounds that constitute the building blocks of language.

**Physiological psychology.** The study of the biological mechanisms underlying behavior.

**Physiology.** The study of functions of bodily systems.

**Pitch.** Highness or lowness of a sound; it is determined by the frequency of the sound wave.

**Pituitary gland.** An endocrine gland whose secretions regulate other endocrine glands; sometimes called the master gland.

**Placebo.** An inactive substance used instead of an active substance and given to the control group in an experiment.

**Placebo effect.** An improvement or change resulting from faith or belief that a given substance has curative powers.

**Pleasure principle.** The tendency to seek immediate satisfaction of basic urges; it is characteristic of the id.

**Polygraph.** An apparatus, commonly known as the lie detector, for recording several physiological measures simultaneously, such as galvanic skin response, heart rate, blood pressure, and rate of breathing.

**Pons.** Subcortical structures that serve as a bridge connecting various parts of the brain.

**Population** or **universe.** A complete set of individuals, objects, or measurements having some common observable characteristic, or a theoretical set of potential observations.

**Positive reinforcement (positive reinforcer).** An event that strengthens the response that precedes it by virtue of its *presentation*.

**Positive relationship.** Variables are said to be positively related when a high score on one is accompanied by a high score on the other. Conversely, low scores on one variable are associated with low scores on the other.

**Positive transfer.** The facilitation of learning in a new situation by prior experience in another situation.

**Positively skewed distribution.** A distribution that has relatively fewer frequencies at the high end of the horizontal axis.

**Precognition.** A form of extrasensory perception; the ability to perceive events that have not yet occurred.

**Predictive validity.** The extent to which a test predicts performance in a criterion situation.

**Prejudice.** Any kind of prejudgment, negative or positive; an attitude or opinion formed before examining all the facts.

**Premature ejaculation.** Consistently reaching orgasm so quickly as to significantly lower subjective enjoyment of the experience and/or to impair the gratification of one's partner.

**Prenatal.** The prenatal period is the period of life before birth.

**Preoperational stage.** Piaget's second stage of cognitive development. During this period the child develops symbolic thinking and language but not logical thinking.

**Primary reinforcement.** Any event that has reinforcing properties that directly fulfill physical needs and that depend little, if at all, on previous learning.

**Proactive interference.** The interference of one task with the retention of a second.

**Problem solving.** Behavior directed toward overcoming an obstacle or adjusting to a situation by using new ways of responding.

**Programmed instruction.** A method of instruction that systematically applies the principles of operant conditioning to the learning situation.

**Projection.** A defense mechanism in which individuals attribute their own unacceptable desires, impulses, traits, and thoughts to others.

**Projective techniques.** Methods of assessing personality in which the individual is confronted with ambiguous materials and asked to interpret them.

**Propaganda.** Communication that deliberately attempts to influence attitudes.

**Proximity.** Physical nearness; propinquity. In perception, the tendency to see things that are close together as a pattern or an organized whole.

**Psychiatrist.** A medical doctor who has received specialized training in treating emotional disturbances.

**Psychoactive drugs.** Those drugs that have psychological effects—that is, that affect the user's perceptual, cognitive, or emotional state.

**Psychoanalysis.** A school of psychology, founded by Sigmund Freud, that emphasizes the unconscious determinants of behavior; a theory of personality and the diagnosis and treatment of psychopathology.

**Psychoanalyst.** A psychologist or psychiatrist whose approach to treatment of the

emotionally disturbed is based upon psychoanalytic theories.

**Psychokinesis.** A form of extrasensory perception; the ability to move objects without physically touching them.

**Psycholinguistics.** The study of language acquisition and use, as well as the formal structure of language.

**Psychology.** The science of behavior.

**Psychosexual development.** Freud's theory that development takes place in stages in which the focus of pleasure shifts from one part of the body to another.

**Psychosexual stages.** Freud's theory of developmental stages in which the focus of pleasure shifts from one part of the body to another.

**Psychosocial stages.** Erikson's theory of eight developmental stages, in each of which the individual must resolve a different crisis.

**Psychosomatic disorders.** Physical disorders such as ulcers, asthma, and hypertension that have their origins in, or are aggravated by, emotional factors.

**Psychosurgery.** A type of medical therapy in which brain surgery is used to treat emotional disturbances.

**Psychotherapy.** Treatment of emotional disturbance by psychological methods.

**Psychotic.** Displaying a severe form of emotional disturbance that involves loss of

contact with reality, disturbed thought processes, and personality disorganization.

**Psychotocism.** As postulated by Eysenck, an ingredient of personality that includes a deficiency in loyalty toward people, groups, or social standards.

**Puberty.** The time when children achieve sexual maturity, marked by menstruation in females and the appearance of live sperm in males.

**Pupil.** The opening in the eye through which light passes.

**Pupillometer.** A device used to measure changes in pupil size.

**Random sample.** A subset of a population or universe selected in such a way that each member of the population has an equal opportunity to be selected.

**Range.** A measure of dispersion; the scale distance between the largest and the smallest score.

**Rapid eye movement (REM).** Rapid movements of the eyes occurring during sleep. Subjects awakened during the REM stage, generally report that they have been dreaming.

**Rating scale.** A device for making judgments about oneself or others on certain defined traits.

**Rationalization.** A defense mechanism in which individuals find socially acceptable but false reasons for their behavior.

**Ratio scale.** The ratio scale is the same as the interval scale, except that there is a true zero point.

**Reaction formation.** A defense mechanism in which individuals protect themselves from unacceptable motives or feelings by repressing them and assuming the opposite attitudes and behaviors.

**Reality principle.** The principle of adapting the demands of the id to the realities of the environment.

**Recall.** A method of measuring retention whereby the individual must reproduce a previously learned response with a bare minimum of cues.

**Receptive function of language.** Understanding of language.

**Recessive gene.** A member of a gene pair that is expressed only when combined with a like gene. If a recessive gene is paired with a dominant gene, the effect of the recessive gene is masked.

**Recitation.** In learning, active repetition (or recitation) of material one is trying to recall (as opposed to passive reading).

**Recognition.** A method of measuring retention whereby the individual must demonstrate the ability to identify previously learned material.

**Reflex.** An unlearned automatic bodily response to stimulus.

**Reflex arc.** The pathway from a receptor to an effector that a nervous impulse follows to produce a reflex.

**Regression.** A defense mechanism in which individuals revert to an immature form of behavior that once brought satisfaction.

**Reinforcement.** An event that serves to strengthen the response that precedes or produces it.

**Reintegrative stage.** According to Schaie, the refocusing of cognitive skills to deal with the problems of old age and retirement.

**Relative refractory period.** A brief interval following the absolute refractory period during which the neuron will respond only to intense stimulation.

**Relearning.** A method of measuring retention whereby the individual relearns material that has been partially or completely forgotten. The difference in the amount of practice required to achieve the original point of mastery provides a measure of the degree of retention.

**Reliability.** The degree to which a test yields consistent results each time it is taken.

**REM rebound.** A period of increased REM activity following previous REM suppression or deprivation.

**Repression.** A defense mechanism in which the individual unconsciously excludes unpleasant thoughts, feelings, and impulses from conscious awareness.

**Resistance.** The tendency to resist or avoid treatment when anxiety-arousing material is being uncovered.

**Responsible stage.** According to Schaie, the improving of cognitive skills in order to deal with the greater complexity of life characteristic of the thirties to the sixties.

**Retarded ejaculation.** The inability to ejaculate during sexual intercourse.

**Reticular activating system (RAS).** A network of cells in the center of the brain that is involved in activating and arousing higher brain centers.

**Retina.** Photosensitive surface of the eye; it acts much like the film in a camera.

**Retinal disparity.** A binocular cue to depth perception; both eyes get slightly different images of an object because the eyes are separated from each other.

**Retrieval.** The process of sifting through materials in long-term memory to find the specific information needed at a particular time.

**Retroactive interference (retroactive inhibition).** Loss in retention caused by the nature of the activity intervening between learning and remembering.

**RNA (ribonucleic acid).** A complex molecule presumed to play an important role in the physiological basis of memory.

**Rods.** One of the two types of receptors for vision located in the retina. No color is experienced with rod vison, only black, white, and gray.

**Role.** The pattern of behavior expected in a given social position.

**Rooting.** A reflex in infants. The baby's head turns toward the cheek that is stimulated.

**Rorschach test.** A projective test of personality consisting of a series of ink blots to be interpreted.

**Rote learning.** Verbatim learning that does not require a logical understanding of the material to be learned.

**Sample.** That part of a population (all possible subjects) selected for study.

**Saturation.** The richness of a color; it is determined by the purity of the light at that wavelength.

**Savings score.** A measure of retention, this is the percentage score indicating the time saved in relearning material.

**Scapegoat.** An innocent victim who becomes the target of displaced aggression.

**Scatter diagram.** A graphic device employed to represent the difference between two variables.

**Schedule of reinforcement.** An established plan for allotting reinforcements under partial reinforcement.

**Schema** (plural: **schemata**). Piaget's term for a mental framework for classification or conceptualization of information.

**Schizophrenia.** A type of psychosis characterized by personality disorganization, withdrawal from reality, disturbed thought processes, and emotional disorders.

**School psychologist.** A psychologist who evaluates learning and emotional problems and also administers and interprets tests in a school setting.

**Secondary reinforcement.** Any event that acquires reinforcing properties through association with a primary reinforcer.

**Self-actualization.** The tendency to strive to realize one's full potential.

**Self-ambulation.** The ability to walk on one's own.

**Semantically related.** Stimuli are semantically related if the words representing them share similar meanings (for example, "like" and "love"; "dislike" and "hate").

**Semantics.** The study of meaning in language.

**Sensation.** Information taken in by the senses but not yet interpreted.

**Sensitivity group (T-group).** A type of small group that emphasizes the development of sensitive feelings and attitudes toward others.

**Sensorimotor stage.** Piaget's first stage of cognitive development, occurring during the first two years of life, when the child learns to know the world through sensory and motor activities.

**Sensory adaptation.** With most of our senses, continued exposure to a given level of stimulation will lead to an inability to detect that stimulation.

**Sensory deprivation.** A condition in which the individual receives a minimum of sensory stimulation; this condition sometimes leads to hallucinations.

**Sensory receptor.** A specialized surface that is sensitive to a particular type of stimulus.

**Sensory register.** A system for holding stimulus information in its original form (sound as sound, vision as image, etc.) for brief periods of time. It is presumed that there is a separate sensory register for each sense modality.

**Separation anxiety.** Fear experienced by the infant when the caretaker leaves; it is usually seen at about 10 to 12 months of age.

**Serial-anticipation learning.** A type of learning in which the subject is required to memorize a list of words or syllables in a fixed order.

**Set.** A readiness to perceive or respond in a certain way because of prior experience or expectations.

**Shape constancy.** The tendency to perceive objects that are familiar to us as retaining their shape, even though a variety of different visual images are received by the retina.

**Shaping.** Modifying behavior by reinforcing only those responses that successively approximate the final desired behavior.

**Short-term memory (STM).** A type of memory of extremely short duration and limited capacity.

**Significance level.** A probability value that is considered so rare in the sampling distribution that one is willing to assert the operation of nonchance factors. Common significance levels are 0.05 and 0.01.

**Similarity.** In perception, the tendency to see objects that are similar as forming subgroups.

**Size constancy.** The tendency to perceive objects as their correct size, regardless of the size of the retinal image they produce at varying distances.

**Skewed distribution.** A distribution that departs from symmetry and tails off at one end.

**Sleeper effect.** The phenomenon that communication ascribed to a low-credibility source initially has little effect on attitude change, but may have a greater effect once the source is forgotten.

**Socialization.** The process by which we acquire socially important behaviors.

**Social psychologist.** A psychologist who studies the individual's interactions with groups and the ways in which groups influence the individual's feelings, attitudes, and beliefs.

**Social psychology.** The study of the individual in society—the various social forces that interact to influence the individual's behavior and thinking, and the ways in which the individual interacts with and modifies social groups to which he or she belongs.

**Society.** A group of people, dependent on one another, who are regarded as forming a single community.

**Somatic nervous system.** The part of the peripheral nervous system that serves the sense organs and the skeletal muscles.

**Somatization disorder.** A type of disorder in which physical complaints are prominent.

**Somatoform disorder.** A type of disorder characterized by physical symptoms.

**Sound threshold.** The minimum sound intensity that can be heard under standardized testing conditions.

**Source traits.** Underlying variables that are determinants of observed behavior.

**Spinal cord.** The part of the central nervous system that serves primarily to relay messages back and forth between the brain and the other parts of the body.

**Split-brain surgery.** A surgical procedure whereby the structures connecting the cerebral hemispheres are severed.

**Spontaneous recovery.** The recurrence of the previously extinguished conditioned response following a rest period.

**SQ 3R method.** A method of studying that involves five stages: survey, question, read, recite, and review.

**Standard deviation.** An extremely useful measure of dispersion defined as the square root of the sum of the squared deviations from the mean, divided by $N$.

**Standardization.** The process by which norms, or standards, are obtained for comparing individual scores. A test is administered under comparable conditions to some large and representative group.

**Standard normal distribution.** A normal distribution that has a mean of 0, a standard deviation of 1, and a total area equal to 1.00.

**Statistics.** A collection of numerical facts expressed in summarizing statements; or a method of dealing with data; a tool for collecting, organizing, and analyzing numerical facts or observations.

**Stereotype.** A preconceived idea about the attributes of people belonging to certain groups.

**Stimulus generalization.** Once an organism has learned to associate a given behavior with a specific stimulus, it tends to show this behavior toward similar stimuli.

**Stimulus needs.** A class of motivational states, involving a need for stimulation, for which no underlying physiological basis has been discovered.

**Stranger anxiety.** A fear of unfamiliar or strange faces that develops in the infant somewhere around the sixth month.

**Stress.** Changes, pressures, threats, and other conditions in life that make physical and emotional demands on a person.

**Structuralism.** A school of psychology (associated with Wilhelm Wundt) that emphasized the structure of conscious experience.

Subcortical structures. Masses of nerve fibers and clusters of cell bodies located below the cerebral cortex and responsible for such vital functions as breathing, heart rate, and blood pressure.

Subculture. A segment of a larger culture, characterized by its own customs, traditions, beliefs, values, and attitudes.

Sublimation. A defense mechanism in which individuals transform ''shameful'' motives into socially acceptable, creative ones.

Superego. In psychoanalytic theory, internal controls and standards derived from early influences; the superego corresponds to the ''conscience.''

Superstitious behavior. Behavior learned simply by virtue of the fact that it happened to be followed by reinforcement, even though this behavior was not instrumental in producing the reinforcement.

Suppression. Conscious inhibition of anxiety-producing thoughts, feelings, and impulses (contrasted with repression, which is unconscious).

Surface traits. Clusters of behavior that appear to go together.

Survey method. A method of collecting data through the use of interviews and questionnaires.

Symbol. Anything that stands for something else.

Sympathetic branch. The division of the autonomic nervous system that mobilizes the body during emergencies by increasing heart rate and blood pressure, accelerating secretion of adrenalin, and inhibiting digestive processes.

Symptom substitution. In psychoanalytic theory, the concept that a symptom is the result of an underlying conflict and that, unless the underlying conflict is resolved, removal of the symptom will merely result in a different symptom's appearing in its place.

Synapse. The point of transmission of a nervous impulse from the axon of one neuron to the dendrites of another.

Synesthesia. The translation of one sensory experience into another, such as feeling an odor or seeing a sound.

Systematic observation. Planning and preparing well in advance and controlling the conditions under which observations are made.

Tabula rasa. A ''blank slate''; the term used to describe the theory that a baby's mind at birth is blank and that all that appears upon it is ''written'' by experience.

Teaching machine. A device for presenting programmed instruction.

Temporal lobe. The lobe of the brain located below the lateral fissure and concerned with hearing.

Thalamus. A subcortical structure that serves primarily to relay sensory impulses from all parts of the body to the cerebral cortex.

Thematic Apperception Test (TAT). A projective test of personality in which the subject makes up stories for a set of pictures.

Thinking. The internal manipulation of symbols.

Threshold of excitability. Minimum intensity of stimulation necessary to activate a neuron.

Thyroid gland. An endocrine gland whose secretions regulate body metabolism.

Timbre. The richness of a sound; it is determined by the complexity of the sound.

Token economy. A reinforcement technique, sometimes used in hospitals, in which the individual is rewarded for socially accepted behavior with a token that can be exchanged for a desired object or activity.

Tolerance. The body's ability to withstand a given amount of a drug and its need for increased dosages of that drug to produce the desired effects.

Toleration method. A method of breaking habits in which the stimulus eliciting the undesired response is introduced gradually.

Trace transformation theory of forgetting. The theory that explains distortions in memory in terms of changes in the pattern of the memory trace.

**Trait.** A characteristic used to describe a basic personality dimension.

**Transference.** A process whereby patients project onto the therapist emotions and feelings they experienced in relation to another significant person.

**Two-factor theory.** The theory that an emotional experience is a result of cognitive interpretation of a situation that has produced physiological arousal.

**Type theories.** Theories of personality that attempt to classify people into broad categories, using primary characteristics to describe the whole personality.

**Unconditioned response (UR).** A response that automatically occurs to an unconditioned stimulus without any learning being required.

**Unconditioned stimulus (US).** A stimulus that naturally and automatically elicits an unconditioned response.

**Unconscious mind.** In psychoanalytic theory, the part of the mind that is unaware of the individual's feelings and behaviors.

**Validity.** The extent to which a test measures what it purports to measure.

**Variable.** A characteristic or phenomenon that may take on different values.

**Variable-interval schedule (VI).** A schedule for reinforcing operant behavior in which reinforcement is administered after a variable interval of time.

**Variable-ratio schedule (VR).** A schedule for reinforcing operant behavior in which the number of responses required for each reinforcement varies.

**Vicarious.** Experienced through imagining the experience of another.

**Visual area.** The rear portion of the occipital lobes of the brain; it controls visual activity.

**Whole-method.** A method of learning in which the individual learns the material as a whole unit.

**Yerkes–Dodson law.** A general rule stating that there is an optimal level of arousal at which performance of a task is most effective and that that level is related to the difficulty of the task, with high arousal best for easy tasks and low arousal best for difficult ones.

Abood, L. G. (1960). "A Chemical Approach to the Problem of Mental Disease" In *The Etiology of Schizophrenia*, edited by D. D. Jackson. New York: Basic Books.

Adler, A. (1964). *Social Interest: A Challenge to Mankind*. Translated by J. Linton and R. Vaughn. New York: Capricorn Books.

Agvilera, D., and Messick, J. M. (1978). *Crisis Intervention*. 3rd ed. St. Louis: Mosby.

Aiken, L. R., Jr. (1971). *Psychological and Educational Testing*. Boston: Allyn & Bacon.

Ajzen, I., and Fishbein, M. (1973). "Attitudinal and Normative Variables as Predictors of Specific Behaviors." *Journal of Personality and Social Psychology* **27**, 41–57.

Aleksandrowicz, M. K. (1974). "The Effect of Pain-Relieving Drugs Administered during Labor and Delivery on the Behavior of the Newborn: A Review." *Merrill-Palmer Quarterly* **20**, 2.

Allen, K. E., and Harris, F. R. (1966). "Elimination of a Child's Excessive Scratching by Training the Mother in Reinforcement Procedures." *Behavior Research and Therapy* **4**, 79–84.

Alper, T. G. (1974). "Achievement Motivation in College Women: A Now-You-See-It-Now-You-Don't Phenomenon." *American Psychologist* **29**, 194–203.

Ammons, R. B. (1950). "Reactions in a Projective Doll-Play Interview of White Males Two to Six Years of Age to Differences in Skin Color and Facial Features." *Journal of Genetic Psychology* **76**, 323–341.

Anastasi, A. (1958). *Differential Psychology*. New York: Macmillan.

Anderson, B., and McCann, S. M. (1955). *Acta Physiologica Scandinavica* **33**, 333–346.

Archer, E. J. (1960). "A Re-evaluation of the Meaningfulness of All Possible CVC Trigrams." *Psychological Monographs* **74**.

Arkin, A. M.; Hastey, J. M.; and Reiser, M. F. (1966). "Post-Hypnotically Stimulated Sleep-Talking." *Journal of Nervous Mental Disease* **142**, 293–309.

Arnold, M. B. (1960). *Emotion and Personality*. Vols. 1 and 2. New York: Columbia University Press.

Aronfreed, J., and Leff, R. (1963). "The Effects of Intensity of Punishment and Complexity of Discrimination upon the Learning of an Internalized Inhibition." Unpublished manuscript, University of Pennsylvania.

Aronson, E., and Mills, J. (1959). "The Effect of Severity of Initiation on Liking for a Group." *Journal of Abnormal and Social Psychology* **59**, 177–181.

Aronson, E., and Rosenbloom, S. (1971). "Space Perception in Early Infancy: Perception within a Common Auditory–Visual Space." *Science* **172**, 1161–1163.

Asch, S. E. (1956). "Studies of Independence and Conformity: A Minority of One against a Unanimous Majority." *Psychological Monographs* **70**(9).

——— (1955). "Opinions and Social Pressure." *Scientific American* **193**, 31–35.

——— (1951). "Effects of Group Pressure upon the Modification and Distortion of Judgment." In *Groups, Leadership, and Men*, edited by M. H. Guetzkow. Pittsburgh: Carnegie Press.

Aserinsky, E., and Kleitman, N. (1953). "Regularly Occurring Periods of Eye Motility and Concomitant Phenomena during Sleep." *Science* **118**, 273.

Ashley, W. R.; Harper, R. S.; and Runyon, D. L. (1951). "The Perceived Size of Coins in Normal and Hypnotically Induced Economic States." *American Journal of Psychology* **64**(4), 564–572.

Averill, J. R. (1976). "Emotion and Anxiety: Sociocultural, Biological, and Psychological Determinants." In *Emotions and Anxiety*, edited by M. Zuckerman and C. D. Spielberger. New York: Wiley.

Ax, A. (1953). "The Physiological Differentiation between Fear and Anger in Humans." *Psychosomatic Medicine* **15**, 433–442.

Ayllon, T. (1963). "Intensive Treatment of Psychotic Behavior by Stimulus Satiation and Food Reinforcement." *Behavior Research and Therapy* **1**, 53–61.

Ayllon, T., and Michael, J. (1959). "The Psychiatric Nurse as a Behavioral Engineer." *Journal of the Experimental Analysis of Behavior* **2**, 323–334.

Bachrach, A. J. (1965). *Psychological Research*. 2nd ed. New York: Random House.

Bachrach, A. J.; Erwin, W. J.; and Mohr, J. P. (1965). "The Control of Eating Behavior in an Anorexic by Operant Conditioning Techniques." In *Case Studies in Behavior Modification*, edited by L. P. Ullmann and L. Krasner. New York: Holt, Rinehart & Winston.

Bahrick, H. P., and Bahrick, P. O. (1964). "A Re-examination of the Interrelations among Measures of Retention." *Quarterly Journal of Experimental Psychology* **16**, 318–324.

Bakan, P. (1969). "Hypnotizability, Laterality of Eye Movements, and Functional Brain Asymmetry." *Perceptual Motor Skills* **28**, 927–932.

Balagura, S. (1973). *Hunger: A Biopsychological Analysis*. New York: Basic Books.

# BIBLIOGRAPHY

Baldessarini, R. J. (1977). *Chemotherapy in Psychiatry*. Cambridge, Mass.: Harvard University Press.

Bales, R. F. (1958). "Task Roles and Social Roles in Problem-Solving Groups." In *Readings in Social Psychology*, edited by E. Maccoby, J. M. Newcomb, and E. L. Hartley. New York: Holt, Rinehart & Winston.

Baltes, P. B. (1979). "Life-Span Developmental Psychology: Some Conveying Observations on History and Theory." In *Life-Span Development and Behavior*, vol. 2, edited by P. B. Baltes and O. G. Brim. New York: Academic Press.

Baltes, P. B.; Reese, H. W.; and Lipsitt, L. P. (1980). "Life-Span Developmental Psychology." *Annual Review of Psychology* **31** 65–110.

Baltes, P. B., and Schaie, K. W. (1976). "On the Plasticity of Intelligence in Adulthood and Old Age: Where Horn and Donaldson Fail." *American Psychologist* **31**,(10), 720–725.

Bandura, A. (1973). *Aggression: A Social Learning Analysis*. Englewood Cliffs, N.J.: Prentice-Hall.

———— (1967). "The Role of Modeling Processes in Personality Development." In *The Young Child*, edited by W. W. Hartup and N. L. Smothergill. Washington, D.C.: National Association for the Education of Young Children.

Bandura, A.; Blanchard, E. B.; and Ritter, B. (1969). "Relative Efficacy of Desensitization and Modeling Approaches for Inducing Behavioral, Affective, and Attitudinal Changes." *Journal of Personality and Social Psychology* **13**, 173–179.

Bandura, A., and Menlove, F. L. (1968). "Factors Determining Vicarious Extinction of Avoidance Behavior through Symbolic Modeling. *Journal of Personality and Social Psychology* **8**, 99–108.

Bandura, A.; Ross, D.; and Ross, S. A. (1963). "Imitation of Film-Mediated Aggressive Models." *Journal of Abnormal and Social Psychology* **66**, 3–11.

———— (1961). "Transmission of Aggression through Imitation of Aggressive Models." *Journal of Abnormal and Social Psychology* **63**, 575–582.

Bandura, A., and Walters, R. H. (1963). *Social Learning and Personality Development*. New York: Holt, Rinehart & Winston.

———— (1959). *Adolescent Aggression*. New York: Ronald Press.

Banquet, J. P. (1973). "Spectral Analysis of the EEG in Meditation." *Electroencephalography and Clinical Neurophysiology* **35**, 143–151.

Barahal, H. S. (1958). "100 Prefrontal Lobotomies: Five-to-Ten-Year Follow-Up Study." *Psychiatric Quarterly* **32**, 653–678.

Barber, T. X.; Spanos, N. P.; and Chavez, J. F. (1974). *Hypnosis, Imagination, and Human Potentialities*. New York: Pergamon Press.

Bard, P., and Mountcastle, V. B. (1947). "Some Forebrain Mechanisms Involved in the Expression of Rage with Special Reference to Suppression of Angry Behavior." *Research Publications of the Association for Research on Nervous and Mental Diseases* **27**, 362–404.

Barker, R. G.; Dembo, T.; and Lewin, K. (1943). "An Experiment with Young Children." In *Child Behavior and Development*, edited by R. G. Barker, I. S. Kounin, and H. F. Wright. New York: McGraw-Hill.

———— (1941). "Frustration and Regression: An Experiment with Young Children." *University of Iowa Studies in Child Welfare* **18**(1): xv + 314.

Baron, R. A. (1974). "Aggression as a Function of Victim's Pain Cues, Level of Prior Anger Arousal, and Exposure to an Aggressive Model." *Journal of Personality and Social Psychology* **29**, 117–124.

———— (1973). "Threatened Retaliation from the Victim as an Inhibitor of Physical Aggression." *Journal of Research in Personality* **7**, 103–115.

Barron, F. (1958). "The Psychology of Imagination." *Scientific American* **3**, 150–166.

Barron, F., and Harrington, D. M. (1981). "Creativity, Intelligence, and Personality." *Annual Review of Psychology* **32**, 439–476.

Bartlett, F. C. (1954). *Remembering: A Study in Experimental and Social Psychology*. Cambridge: Cambridge University Press.

Batchelor, I., and Campbell, R. (1969). *Henderson and Gillespie's Textbook of Psychiatry for Students and Practitioners*. 10th ed. New York: Oxford University Press.

Battle, E. S., and Lacey, B. (1972). "A Context for Hyperactivity in Children, Over Time." *Child Development* **43**, 757–773.

Baumgold, J. (1977). "Agoraphobia: Life Ruled by Panic." *New York Times Magazine*, December 4, p. 46.

Baumrind, D. (1964). "Some Thoughts on the Ethics of Research: After Reading Milgram's 'Behavioral Study of Obedience.'" *American Psychologist* **19**, 421–423.

Baur, S. (1975). "First Message from the Planet of the Apes." *New York*, February 24, pp. 30–37.

Beck, A. T. (1967). *Depression: Causes and Treatment*. Philadelphia: University of Pennsylvania Press.

Becker, H. S. (1963). *Outsiders: Studies in the Sociology of Deviance*. New York: Free Press.

Bem, S. L. (1980). "Beyond Androgyny: Some Presumptuous Prescriptions for a Liberated Sexual Identity." In *The Future of Woman: Issues in Psychology*, edited by J. Sherman and F. Denmark. New York: Psychological Dimensions.

———— (1979). "Theory and Measurement of Androgyny: A Reply to the Pedhazer-Tetenbaum and Locksley-Colten Critiques." *Journal of Personality and Social Psychology* **37**, 1047–1054.

———— (1975). "Probing the Promise of Androgyny." Keynote address for the APA-HIMH Conference on the Research Needs of Women. Madison, Wis., May 31.

———— (1974). "The Measurement of Psychological Androgyny." *Journal of Consulting and Clinical Psychology* **42**, 155–162.

Bem, S. L., and Daryl, J. (1970). "We're All Nonconscious Sexists." *Psychology Today* **4**(6), 22–26.

Benson, H. (1975). *The Relaxation Response*. New York: Morrow.

Berger, R. (1969). "The Sleep and Dream Cycle." In *Sleep: Physiology and Pathology*, edited by A. Kales. Philadelphia: Lippincott.

Bergin, A. E., and Lambert, M. J. (1978). "The Evaluation of Therapeautic Outcomes." In *Handbook of Psychotherapy and Behavior Change*, 2nd ed., edited by S. L. Garfield and A. E. Bergin. New York: Wiley.

Berko, J. (1958). "The Child's Learning of English Morphology." *Word* **14**, 150–177.

Berkowitz, L. (1974). "Some Determinants of Impulsive Aggression: Role of Mediated Associations with Reinforcements for Aggression." *Psychological Review* **81**(2), 165–176.

———— (1968). "Impulse, Aggression, and the Gun." *Psychology Today* **2**(4), 18–22.

———— (1965). "The Concept of Aggressive Drive: Some Additional Considerations." In *Advances in Experimental Social Psychology,* vol. 2, edited by L. Berkowitz. New York: Academic Press.

Berkowitz, L., and Cottingham, D. R. (1960). "The Interest Value and Relevance of Fear Arousing Communications." *Journal of Abnormal and Social Psychology* **60,** 37–43.

Berlyne, D. E. (1958). "The Influence of Complexity and Novelty in Visual Figures on Orienting Responses." *Journal of Experimental Psychology* **55,** 289–296.

Berndt, T. J. (1979). "Developmental Changes in Conformity to Peers and Parents." *Developmental Psychology* **15,** 608–616.

Berscheid, E., and Walster, E. H. (1969). *Interpersonal Attraction.* Reading, Mass.: Addison-Wesley.

Bexton, W. H.; Heron, W.; and Scott, T. H. (1954). "Effects of Decreased Variation in the Sensory Environment." *Canadian Journal of Psychology* **8,** 70–76.

Bird, B. L.; Cataldo, M. F.; and Cunningham, C. (1977). "Single-Subject Experimental Analysis of EMG Biofeedback Effects in Treating Cerebral Palsied Children." *Proceedings of the Biofeedback Society.* Orlando, Fla.

Birren, J. E.; Kinney, D. K.; Schaie, K. W.; and Woodruff, D. S. (1981). *Developmental Psychology: A Life-Span Approach.* Boston: Houghton Mifflin.

Blackford, L. (1974). *Student Drug Use Surveys, San Mateo County, California.* Preliminary Report, County Department of Health and Welfare, San Mateo, Calif.

Blehar, M. C.; Lieberman, A. F.; and Ainsworth, M. D. (1977). "Early Face-to-Face Interaction and Its Relation to Later Infant–Mother Attachment." *Child Development* **48,** 182–194.

Block, J. H. (1973). "Conception of Sex Role: Some Cross-Cultural and Longitudinal Perspectives." *American Psychologist* **28,** 512–526.

Bolles, R. C., and Fanselow, M. S. (1982). "Endorphins and Behavior." *Annual Review of Psychology* **33,** 87–103.

Boring, E. G., ed. (1945). *Psychology for the Armed Services.* Washington, D.C.: Combat Forces Press.

Bower, G. H. (1978). "Experiments on Story Comprehension and Recall." *Discourse Process* **1,** 211–231.

Bower, G. H., and Clark, M. C. (1969). "Narrative Stories as Mediators for Serial Learning." *Psychonomic Science* **14,** 181–182.

Bowlby, J. (1969). *Attachment and Loss,* vol. 1: *Attachment.* New York: Basic Books.

Bowles, N.; Hynds, F.; and Maxwell, J. (1978). *Psi Search: The New Investigation of Psychic Phenomena That Separates Fact from Fiction.* New York: Harper & Row.

Braaten, L. J. (1963). "Some Reflections on Suicidal Tendencies among College Students." *Mental Hygiene* **47,** 562–568.

Brady, J. V. (1958). "Ulcers in 'Executive' Monkeys." *Scientific American* **199**(4), 95–100.

Braine, M.D.S. (1963). "The Ontogeny of English Phrase Structure: The First Phase." *Language* **39,** 1–13.

Brazelton, T. B.; Tronick, E.; Adamson, L.; Als, H.; and Wise, S. (1975) "Early Mother–Infant Interaction." In *Parent–Infant Interaction,* Ciba Symposium. Amsterdam: Associated Science Publishers.

Brenner, J. M., and Kleinman, R. A. (1970). "Learned Control of Decreases in Systolic Blood Pressure." *Nature* **226**(5250), 1063–1064.

Bridges, K.M.B. (1932). "Emotional Development in Early Infancy." *Child Development* **3,** 324–341.

Brierly, H. (1967). "The Treatment of Hysterical Spasmodic Torticollis by Behavior Therapy." *Behavior Research and Therapy* **5,** 139–142.

Brody, N. (1980). "Social Motivation." *Annual Review of Psychology* **31,** 143–168.

Bronson, G. (1971). "Infants' Reactions to an Unfamiliar Person." Paper presented at Meetings of the Society for Research in Child Development.

Broughton, W. J. (1968). "Sleep Disorders: Disorders of Arousal?" *Science* **159,** 1070–1078.

Brown, H. (1976). *Brain and Behavior.* New York: Oxford University Press.

Brown, R. (1970). *Psycholinguistics: Selected Papers of Roger Brown.* New York: Free Press.

Brown, R. W., and Lennenberg, E. H. (1954). "A Study in Language and Cognition." *Journal of Abnormal and Social Psychology* **49,** 454–462.

Buckhout, R. (1974). "Eyewitness Testimony." *Scientific American* **231,** 23–31.

Buckhout, R., and 81 Concerned Berkeley Students, eds. (1971). *Toward Social Change.* New York: Harper & Row.

Bulatov, P. K. (1963). "The Higher Nervous Activity in Persons Suffering from Bronchial Asthma." In *Problems of Interrelationship between Psyche and Soma in Psychoneurology and General Medicine.* Institute Bechtereva. (Reprinted in *International Journal of Psychiatry,* September 1967, p. 245.)

Buros, O. K., ed. (1972). *The Seventh Mental Measurement Yearbook.* Highland Park, N.J.: Gryphon Press.

Burt, C. (1958). "The Inheritance of Mental Ability." *American Psychologist* **13,** 5–10.

Buss, A. H. (1966). *Psychopathology.* New York: Wiley.

Butler, J. M., and Haigh, G. V. (1954). "Changes in the Relation between Self-concepts and Ideal Concepts Consequent upon Client-Centered Counseling." In *Psychotherapy and Personality Change,* edited by C. R. Rogers and R. F. Dymond. Chicago: University of Chicago Press.

Byrne, D. (1971). *The Attraction Paradigm.* New York: Academic Press.

Byrne, D.; Ervin, C. R.; and Lamberth, J. (1970). "Continuity between the Experimental Study of Attraction and 'Real Life' Computer Dating." *Journal of Personality and Social Psychology* **16,** 157–165.

Byrne, D., and Nelson, D. (1965). "Attraction as a Linear Function of Proportion of Positive Reinforcements." *Journal of Personality and Social Psychology* **1**(6), 659–663.

Cameron, N. (1963). *Personality Development and Psychopathology: A Dynamic Approach.* Boston: Houghton Mifflin.

Cameron, N., and Magaret, A. (1951). *Behavior Pathology.* Boston: Houghton Mifflin.

Campbell, C. (1974). "Transcendence Is as American as Ralph Waldo Emerson." *Psychology Today,* April, pp. 37–38.

Cannon, W. B. (1929). *Bodily Changes in Pain, Hunger, Fear and Rage.* 2nd ed. New York: Appleton-Century-Crofts.

Canter, A.; Kondo, C. V.; and Knott, J. R. (1975). "A Comparison of EMG Feedback and Progressive Muscle Relaxation Training in Anxiety Neurosis." *British Journal of Psychiatry* **127**, 470–477.

Carrington, P. (1977). *Freedom in Meditation*. New York: Anchor Press/Doubleday.

Carter, L. F.; Haythorn, W.; and Howell, M. (1950). "A Further Investigation of the Criteria of Leadership." *Journal of Abnormal and Social Psychology* **45**, 350–358.

Cartwright, R. D. (1978). *A Primer of Sleep and Dreaming*. Reading, Mass.: Addison-Wesley.

Cass, L. K., and Thomas, C. B. (1979). *Childhood Pathology and Later Adjustment: The Question of Prediction*. New York: Wiley.

Cattell, R. B. (1971). *Abilities: Their Structure, Growth, and Action*. Boston: Houghton Mifflin.

———— (1965). *The Scientific Analysis of Personality*. Baltimore: Penguin Books.

———— (1950). *Personality: A Systematic, Theoretical, and Factual Study*. New York: McGraw-Hill.

———— (1946). *Description and Measurement of Personality*. Yonkers, N.Y.: World Book.

Chance, J. E. (1965). "Internal Control of Reinforcements and the School Learning Process." Paper presented at the Convention of the Society for Research in Child Development.

Cherry, R., and Cherry, L. (1974). "Showing the Clock of Age." *New York Times Magazine*.

Chomsky, N. (1969). "Language and the Mind." In *Readings in Psychology Today*. Del Mar, Calif.: CRM Books.

Cialdini, R. B.; Petty, R. E.; and Cicioppo, J. T. (1981). "Attitude and Attitude Change." *Annual Review of Psychology* **32**, 357–404.

Clark, E. V. (1975). "Knowledge, Context, and Strategy in the Acquisition of Meaning." In *Georgetown University Round Table on Languages and Linguistics*, edited by D. P. Dato. Washington, D.C.: Georgetown University Press.

Clark, K. B. (1965). *Dark Ghetto: Dilemmas of Social Power*. New York: Harper & Row.

Clark, M.; Lachowitz, T.; and Montrose, I. B. (1968). "A Pilot Basic Education Program for School Dropouts Incorporating a Token Reinforcement System."

*Behavior Research and Therapy* **6**, 183–188.

Cleeland, C. S. (1973). "Behaviour Technics in the Modification of Spasmodic Torticollis." *Neurology* **23**, 1241–1247.

Coates, J. (1980). "Pot More Perilous Than We Thought." *Chicago Tribune*. March 26, pp. 1, 14.

Coates, T. J., and Thoresen, C. E. (1978). "Treating Obesity in Adolescents: A Behavioral Approach." In *Advances in Behavioral Medicine*, edited by J. M. Ferguson. Cited in Krumboltz, J. D.; Becker-Haven, J. F.; and Burnett, J. D. (1979). "Counseling Psychology." *Annual Review of Psychology* **30**, 555–602.

Coch, L., and French, J.R.P., Jr. (1948). "Overcoming Resistance to Change." *Human Relations* **1**, 512–532.

Cohen, L. D.; Kipnis, D.; Kunkle, E. C.; and Kubzansky, P. E. (1955). "Observations of a Person with Congenital Insensitivity to Pain." *Journal of Abnormal and Social Psychology* **51**, 333–338.

Cohen, S. (1973). "Infant Attentional Behavior to Face–Voice Incongruity." Unpublished Ph.D. dissertation, University of California at Los Angeles.

Coile, N. (1981). "Sex Roles." *Tucson Citizen*, August 14, p. 1B.

Cole, J. O. (1964). "Phenothiazine Treatment in Acute Schizophrenia: Effectiveness." *Archives of General Psychiatry* **10**, 246–261.

Coleman, J. C. (1979). *Contemporary Psychology and Effective Behavior*. 4th ed. Glenview, Ill.: Scott, Foresman.

———— (1976). *Abnormal Psychology and Modern Life*. 5th ed. Glenview, Ill.: Scott, Foresman.

———— (1972). *Abnormal Psychology and Modern Life*. 4th ed. Glenview, Ill.: Scott, Foresman.

———— (1949). "Facial Expression of Emotion." *Psychological Monographs* **329**(296).

Conrad, R. (1972). "Speech and Reading." In *The Relationships between Speech and Reading*, edited by J. F. Kavanagh and I. G. Mattingly. Cambridge, Mass.: MIT Press.

———— (1964). "Acoustic Confusion in Immediate Memory." *British Journal of Psychology* **55**, 75–84.

Cook, T. D.; Gruder, C. L.; Henningan, K. M.; and Flay, B. R. (1979). "History of the Sleeper Effect: Some Logical Pitfalls in Accepting the Null

Hypothesis." *Psychological Bulletin* **35**, 140–158.

Cooper, C. J. (1964). "Some Relationships between Paired-Associate Learning and Foreign Language Aptitude." *Journal of Educational Psychology* **55**(3), 132–138.

Cooper, J.; Zann, M. P.; and Goethals, G. R. (1974). "Mistreatment of an Esteemed Other as a Consequence Affecting Dissonance Reduction." *Journal of Experimental Social Psychology* **10**, 224–233.

Corballis, M. C., and Beale, I. L. (1971). "On Telling Left from Right." *Scientific American* **224**(3), 96–104.

Corbett, A. T. (1977). "Retrieval Dynamics for Rote and Visual Image Mnemonics." *Journal of Verbal Learning and Verbal Behavior* **16**(2), 233–246.

Cousins, S. (pseud.) (1938). *To Beg I Am Ashamed*. New York: Vanguard Press.

Cowles, J. T. (1937). "Food-Tokens as Incentives for Learning by Chimpanzees." *Comparative Psychology Monographs* **14**(71).

Crandall, V. C.; Good, S.; and Crandall, V. J. (1964). "Reinforcement Effects of Adult Reactions and Nonreactions on Children's Achievement Expectations: A Replication Study." *Child Development* **35**, 485–497.

Crisp, A. H. (1970). "Premorbid Factors in Adult Disorders of Weight, with Particular Reference to Primary Anorexia Nervosa (Weight Phobia)." *Journal of Psychosomatic Medicine* **14**(1), 1–22.

Cronbach, L. J. (1970). *Essentials of Psychological Testing*. New York: Harper & Row.

Crooks, R., and Baur, K. (1980). *Our Sexuality*. Menlo Park, Calif.: Benjamin/Cummings.

Darley, J. M., and Latané, B. (1968). "Bystander Intervention in Emergencies: Diffusion of Responsibilities." *Journal of Personality and Social Psychology* **8**(4), 377–383.

Davis, K. (1947). "Final Note on a Case of Extreme Social Isolation." *American Journal of Sociology* **52**, 432–437.

———— (1940). "Extreme Social Isolation of a Child." *American Journal of Sociology* **45**, 554–565.

Davis, R.; Sutherland, N. S.; and Judd, B. R. (1961). "Information Content in Recognition and

Recall." *Journal of Experimental Psychology* **61**, 422–429.

Dawes, R. M. (1980). "Social Dilemmas." *Annual Review of Psychology* **31**, 169–193.

Dawes, R. M.; McTavish, J.; and Shaklee, H. (1977). "Behavior, Communication, and Assumptions about Other People's Behavior in a Common Dilemma Situation." *Journal of Personality and Social Psychology* **35**, 1–11.

Dawson, E. B.; Moore, T. D.; and McGanity, W. J. (1970). "The Mathematical Relationship of Drinking Water, Lithium, and Rainfall to Mental Hospital Admissions." *Diseases of the Nervous System* **31**, 811–820.

deCharms, R. (1972). "Personal Causation Training in the Schools." *Journal of Applied Social Psychology* **2**, 95–113.

Deci, E. L. (1972). "The Effects of Contingent and Non-contingent Rewards and Controls on Intrinsic Motivation." *Organizational Behavior and Human Performance* **8**, 217–229.

Deikman, A. J. (1973). "Deautomatization and the Mystic Experience." In *The Nature of Human Consciousness*, edited by R. E. Ornstein. San Francisco: Freeman.

———. (1966). "A Deautomatization and the Mystical Experience." *Psychiatry* **29**, 329–343.

Delgado, J.M.R. (1963). "Cerebral Heterostimulation in a Monkey Colony." *Science* **141**, 161–163.

Dement, W. C. (1965). "An Essay on Dreams: The Role of Physiology in Understanding Their Nature." In *New Directions in Psychology*, vol. II, edited by F. Barron *et al.* New York: Holt, Rinehart & Winston.

———. (1960). "The Effect of Dream Deprivation." *Science* **131**, 1705–1707.

Dement, W. C., and Kleitman, N. (1957). "The Relation of Eye Movements during Sleep to Dream Activity: An Objective Method for the Study of Dreaming." *Journal of Experimental Psychology* **53**, 339–346.

Dennis, W. (1960). "Causes of Retardation among Institutional Children: Iran." *Journal of Genetic Psychology* **96**, 47–59.

Derlega, V. J., and Janda, L. H. (1981). *Personal Adjustment*. 2nd ed. Glenview, Ill.: Scott, Foresman.

Deutsch, M., and Collins, M. E. (1951). *Interracial Housing: A Psychological Evaluation of a Social Experiment*. Minneapolis: University of Minnesota Press.

Dewan, E. (1970). "The Programming (P) Hypotheses for REM Sleep." In *Sleep and Dreaming*, edited by E. Hartmann. Boston: Little, Brown.

*Diagnostic and Statistical Manual of Mental Disorders*. 3rd ed. (1980). Washington, D.C.: American Psychiatric Association.

Diamond, E. (1969). "The Most Terrifying Psychic Experience Known to Man." *New York Times Magazine*, December 7, pp. 56–57.

Di Lollo, V. (1977). "Temporal Characteristics of Iconic Memory." *Nature* **267**, 241–243.

Dohrenwend, B. S., and Dohrenwend, B. P., eds. (1974). *Stressful Life Events: Their Nature and Effects*. New York: Wiley.

Dollard, J., and Miller, N. E. (1950). *Personality and Psychotherapy*. New York: McGraw-Hill.

Douvan, E., and Adelson, J. (1966). *The Adolescent Experience*. New York: Wiley.

Dunbar, F. (1943). *Psychosomatic Diagnosis*. New York: Harper & Row.

Dunn, A. J. (1980). "Neurochemistry of Learning and Memory: An Evaluation of Recent Data." *Annual Review of Psychology* **31**, 343–390.

Dunnette, M. D.; Campbell, J.; and Jaastad, K. (1963). "The Effect of Group Participation on Brainstorming Effectiveness for Two Industrial Samples." *Journal of Applied Psychology* **47**, 30–37.

Dusek-Girdano, D., and Girdano, D. A. (1980). *Drugs: A Factual Account*. 3rd ed. Reading, Mass.: Addison-Wesley.

Duska, R., and Whelan, M. (1975). *Moral Development: A Guide to Piaget and Kohlberg*. New York: Paulist Press.

Eagly, A. H. (1974). "Comprehensibility of Persuasive Arguments as a Determinant of Opinion Change." *Journal of Personality and Social Psychology* **29**, 758–773.

Ebbinghaus, H. (1913). *Memory*. New York: Columbia University Teachers College. (Reprinted by Dover, New York, 1964.)

Eckberg, D. L. (1979). *Intelligence and Race: The Origins and Dimensions of the IQ Controversy*. New York: Praeger.

Ehrlich, A. (1964). "Neural Control of Feeding Behavior." *Psychological Bulletin* **61**, 100–110.

Ehrmann, W. (1961). "Premarital Sexual Intercourse." In *The Encyclopedia of Sexual Behavior*, vol. II, edited by A. Ellis and A. Abarbanel. New York: Hawthorn Books.

Eibl-Eibesfeldt, J. (1973). "The Expressive Behavior of the Deaf-and-Blind-Born." In *Social Communication and Movement*, edited by M. von Cranach and I. Vine. New York: Academic Press.

Elkind, D. (1970). *Children and Adolescents: Interpretive Essays on Jean Piaget*. New York: Oxford University Press.

Elkind, D., and Dabek, R. F. (1977). "Personal Injury and Property Damage in the Moral Judgments of Children." *Child Development* **48**, 518–522.

Ellis, A. (1977). "The Basic Clinical Theory of Rational-Emotive Therapy." In *Handbook of Rational-Emotive Therapy*, edited by A. Ellis and R. Grieger. New York: Springer Publishing.

Elmadjian, F. (1959). "Excretion and Metabolism of Epinephrine." *Pharmacological Review* **11**, 409–415.

Emde, R. N., and Harmon, R. J. (1972). "Endogenous and Exogenous Smiling Systems in Early Infancy." *Journal of the American Academy of Child Psychiatry* **11**, 177–200.

Engler, B. O. (1979). *Personality Theories: An Introduction*. Boston: Houghton Mifflin.

Epstein, S. (1980). "The Self-Concept: A Review of the Proposal of an Integrated Theory of Personality." In *Personality: Basic Aspects and Current Research*, edited by E. Staub. Englewood Cliffs, N.J.: Prentice-Hall.

Erdelyi, M. H., and Becker, J. (1974). "Hypermnesia for Pictures: Incremental Memory for Pictures but Not Words in Multiple Recall Trials." *Cognitive Psychology* **6**, 159–171.

Erdelyi, M. H., and Goldberg, B. (1979). "Let's Not Sweep Repression under the Rug: Toward a Cognitive Psychology of Repression." In *Functional Disorders of Memory*, edited by J. F. Kihlstrom and F. J. Evans. Hillsdale, N.J.: Erlbaum.

Erdelyi, M. H., and Kleinbard, J. (1978). "Has Ebbinghaus Decayed with Time? The Growth of Recall (Hypermnesia) over Days." *Journal of Experimental Psychology: Human Learning and Memory* 4(4), 275–289.

Erikson, E. H. (1963). *Childhood and Society.* 2nd ed. New York: Norton.

——— (1951). *A Healthy Personality for Every Child. A Fact Finding Report: A Digest.* Mid-Century White House Conference on Children and Youth. Raleigh, N.C.: Health Publications Institute.

Erwin, J., and Kuhn, D. (1979). "Development of Children's Understanding of the Multiple Determination Underlying Human Behavior." *Developmental Psychology* 15(3), 352–353.

Eysenck, H. J. (1975). *The Inequality of Man.* San Diego: Edits Publishers.

——— (1971). *The IQ Argument: Race, Intelligence, and Education.* LaSalle, Ill.: Open Court.

——— (1970). *The Structure of Human Personality.* 3rd ed. London: Methuen.

——— (1967). *The Biological Basis of Personality.* Springfield, Ill.: Thomas.

——— (1952). "The Effects of Psychotherapy: An Evaluation." *Journal of Consulting Psychology* 16, 319–324.

Farberow, N. L., and Shneidman, E. S. (1955). "A Study of Attempted, Threatened, and Completed Suicide." *Journal of Abnormal and Social Psychology* 50, 230.

Feinberg, I.; Jones, R.; Walker, J. M.; Cavness, C.; and Mark, J. (1975). "Effects of High Dosage Delta-9-Tetrahydrocannabinol on Sleep Patterns in Man." *Clinical Pharmacology and Therapeutics* 17(4), 458–464.

Fenichel, O. (1945). *The Psychoanalytic Theory of Neuroses.* New York: Norton.

Ferguson, J. M., and Taylor, C. B., eds. (1980). *The Comprehensive Handbook of Behavioral Medicine.* Vols. 1–3. Jamaica, N.Y.: SP Medical & Scientific Books.

Festinger, L. (1957). *A Theory of Cognitive Dissonance.* Stanford, Calif.: Stanford University Press.

Festinger, L., and Carlsmith, J. M. (1959). "Cognitive Consequences of Forced Compliance." *Journal of Abnormal and Social Psychology* 58, 203–211.

Festinger, L.; Schachter, S.; and Back, K. (1950). *Social Pressures in Informal Groups: A Study of Human Factors in Housing.* New York: Harper.

Fieve, R. R. (1975). *Moodswing: The Third Revolution in Psychiatry.* New York: Morrow.

Firestone, I. J.; Kaplan, K.; and Russell, J. C. (1973). "Anxiety, Fear, and Affliction with Similar-State versus Dissimilar-State Others: Misery Sometimes Loves Nonmiserable Company." *Journal of Personality and Social Psychology* 26, 409–414.

Flaherty, J. A. (1979). "Psychiatric Complications of Medical Drugs." *Journal of Family Practice* 9, 243–254.

Fleck, S. (1960). "Family Dynamics and Origin of Schizophrenia." *Psychosomatic Medicine* 22, 337–339.

Flor-Henry, P. (1969). "Temporal Lobe Epilepsy: Etiological Factors." *American Journal of Psychiatry* 126(3), 400–403.

Ford, M.; Bird, B.; Newton, F.; and Sheer, D. (1977). "Follow-Up on Voluntary Control of 40 EEG, Maintenance of Control during Problem Solving, and Generalization of Effect." Paper delivered at the Fourteenth Annual Meeting of the Federation of Western Societies of Neurological Sciences, February.

Fosdick, H. E. (1941). *Living under Tension.* New York: Harper & Bros.

Foulkes, D. (1962). "Dream Reports from Different Stages of Sleep." *Journal of Abnormal and Social Psychology* 65, 14–28.

Foulkes, D., and Fleisher, S. (1975). "Mental Activity in Relaxed Wakefulness." *Journal of Abnormal Psychology* 84, 66–75.

Fox, L. (1962) "Effecting the Use of Efficient Study Habits." *Journal of Mathematics* 1, 75–86.

Francke, L. (1978). "Going It Alone." *Newsweek,* September 4, p. 76.

Frankenburg, W. K., and Dodds, J. B. (1967). "The Denver Developmental Screening Test." *Journal of Pediatrics* 71(2), 181–191.

Freeman, F. S. (1962). *Theory and Practice of Psychological Testing.* New York: Holt, Rinehart & Winston.

French, J. D. (1957). "The Reticular Formation." *Scientific American* 196(5), 54–60.

Freud, S. (1957). "The Unconscious." In *The Standard Edition of the Complete Psychological Works of Sigmund Freud,* vol. 14, edited by J. Strachey. London: Hogarth Press. (Originally published 1915.)

Fromm, E. (1970). "Age Regression with Unexpected Appearance of a Repressed Childhood Language." *International Journal of Clinical and Experimental Hypnosis* 18(2), 79–88.

Funkenstein, D. H. (1955). "The Physiology of Fear and Anger." *Scientific American* 192, 74–80.

Galin, D., and Ornstein, R. E. (1975). "Hemispheric Specialization and the Duality of Consciousness." In *Human Behavior and Brain Function,* edited by H. J. Widroe. Springfield, Ill.: Thomas.

Gallup, G. (1970). *Generation Gap Shown in Sex View.* American Institute of Public Opinion.

Gamper, E., and Krall, A. (1934). "Weitere Experimentell-Biologische Untersuchungen zum Schizophrenic Problem." *Zeitschrift für die Gesamte Neurologie und Psychiatrie* 150, 252–271.

Gardner, B. T., and Gardner, R. A. (1971). "Two-Way Communication with an Infant Chimpanzee." In *Behavior of Nonhuman Primates,* edited by A. M. Schrier and F. Stollnitz. New York: Academic Press.

Gardner, R. A., and Gardner, B. T. (1975). "Early Signs of Language in Child and Chimpanzee." *Science* 187, 752–753.

Garmezy, N. (1978). "Never Mind the Psychologist: Is It Good for the Children?" *Clinical Psychologist* 31(1), 4–6.

Garnica, C. K. (1975). "Some Characteristics of Prosodic Input to Young Children." Unpublished Ph.D. dissertation, Stanford University.

Garry, R., and Kingsley, H. L. (1970). *The Nature and Conditions of Learning.* 3rd ed. Englewood Cliffs, N.J.: Prentice-Hall.

Garten, S. (1908). "Veränderungen der Netzhaut durch Licht. In *Graefe-Saemisch Handbuch der Augenheilkunde,* 2nd ed.

Garwood, S. G., et al. (1980). "Beauty Is Only 'Name' Deep: The Effect of First-Name on Ratings of

Physical Attraction." *Journal of Applied Social Psychology* **10**(5), 431–435.

Gates, A. J. (1917). "Recitation as a Factor in Memorizing." *Archives of Psychology* **6**, 40.

Gellhorn, E., and Kiely, W. F. (1972). "Mystical States of Consciousness: Neurophysiological and Clinical Aspects." *Journal of Nervous Mental Disease* **154**, 399.

Gericke, O. L. (1965). "Practical Use of Operant Conditioning Procedures in a Mental Hospital." *Psychiatric Studies and Projects* **3**(5), 3–10.

Geschwind, N. (1979). "Specializations of the Human Brain." *Scientific American* **241**(3), 180–199.

Getzels, J. W., and Csikszentmihalyi, M. (1976). *The Creative Vision: A Longitudinal Study of Problem Finding in Art.* New York: Wiley.

Gilbert, G. M. (1951). "Stereotype Assistance and Change among College Students." *Journal of Abnormal and Social Psychology* **46**, 245–254.

Gillie, O. (1979). "Burt's Missing Ladies." *Science* **204**, 1035–1039.

———— (1976).

Gillig, P. M., and Greenwald, A. G. (1974). "Is It Time to Lay the Sleeper Effect to Rest?" *Journal of Personality and Social Psychology* **29**, 132–139.

Ginsburg, H., and Koslowski, B. (1976). "Cognitive Development." *Annual Review of Psychology* **27**, 29–61.

Gintner, G., and Lindskold, S. (1975). "Rate of Participation and Expertise as Factors Influencing Leader Choice." *Journal of Personality and Social Psychology* **32**, 1085–1089.

Girdano, D. A., and Girdano, D. D. (1976). *Drugs—A Factual Account.* 2nd ed. Reading, Mass.: Addison-Wesley.

Glaros, A. G. (1977). "Subjective Reports in Alpha Feedback Training." Paper delivered at the Fourteenth Annual Meeting of the Federation of Western Societies of Neurological Sciences, February.

Glaros, A. G.; Freedman, R.; and Foureman, W. C. (1977). "Effects of Perceived Control on Subjective Reports in Alpha." Paper delivered at the Fourteenth Annual Meeting of the Federation of Western Societies of Neuro-logical Sciences, February.

Glass, A. L.; Holyoak, K. J.; and Santa, J. L. (1979). *Cognition.* Reading, Mass.: Addison-Wesley.

Glass, D. O. (1976). "Stress, Competition, and Heart Attacks." *Psychology Today,* December, p. 54.

Glaze, J. A. (1928). "The Association Value of Nonsense Syllables." *Journal of Genetic Psychology* **35**(2), 255–269.

Glinski, R. J.; Glinski, B. C.; and Slatin, G. T. (1970). "Nonnaivity Contamination in Conformity Experiments: Sources, Effects, and Implications for Control." *Journal of Personality and Social Psychology* **16**, 478–485.

Glucksberg, S., and King, L. J. (1967). "Motivated Forgetting Mediated by Implicit Verbal Chaining: A Laboratory Analogy of Repression." *Science* **58**, 517–519.

Goldberg, P. (1968). "Are Women Prejudiced Against Women?" *Trans-Action* **5**, 28–30.

Goldenson, R. M. (1970). *The Encyclopedia of Human Behavior,* vol. 2. *Psychology, Psychiatry, and Mental Health.* New York: Doubleday.

Goldiamond, I. (1965). "Fluent and Nonfluent Speech (Stuttering): Analysis and Operant Techniques for Control." In *Research in Behavior Modification,* edited by L. Krasner and L. P. Ullmann. New York: Holt, Rinehart & Winston.

Goodman, L. (1968). *Sunsigns.* New York: Bantam Books.

Goorney, A. B. (1968). "Treatment of a Compulsive Horse Race Gambler by Aversion Therapy." *British Journal of Psychiatry* **114**, 329–333.

Gottman, J., and Markman, H. (1978). "Experimental Designs in Psychotherapy Research." In *Handbook of Psychotherapy and Behavior Change,* 2nd ed., edited by S. L. Garfield and A. E. Bergin. New York: Wiley.

Griffitt, W., and Veitch, L. (1974). "Preacquaintance Attitude Similarity and Attraction Revisited: Ten Days in a Fall-Out Shelter." *Sociometry* **37**, 163–173.

Grinspoon, L. (1969). "Marihuana." *Scientific American* **221**(6), 17–25.

Grinspoon, L.; Ewalt, J. R.; and Shader, R. (1968). "Psychotherapy and Pharmacotherapy in Chronic Schizophrenia." *American Journal of Psychiatry* **124**, 67–74.

Gross, L. (1972). "A Parents' Primer on Pot." *Los Angeles Times, West,* May 7.

Grossman, S. P.; Dacey, D.; Halaris, A.; Collier, T.; and Routtenberg, A. (1978). "Aphagia and Adipsia

after Preferential Destruction of Nerve Cell Bodies in the Hypothalamus." *Science* **202**, 537–539.

Gubar, G. (1969). "Drug Addiction: Myths and Misconceptions." *Pennsylvania Psychiatric Quarterly* **8**, 24–32.

Guilford, J. P. (1967). *The Nature of Human Intelligence.* New York: McGraw-Hill.

———— (1959). *Personality.* New York: McGraw-Hill.

———— (1954). "A Factor Analytic Study across the Domains of Reasoning, Creativity, and Evaluation: I. Hypotheses and Description of Tests." *Reports from the Psychological Laboratory.* Los Angeles: University of Southern California.

Haber, A.; and Kalish, H. I. (1963). "Prediction of Discrimination from Generalization after Variations in Schedule of Reinforcement." *Science* **142**(3590), 412–413.

Haber, A., and Runyon, R. P. (1983). *Psychology of Adjustment.* Homewood, Ill.: Dorsey Press.

Hale, E. (1981). "Growing Old Can Be Graceful." *Tucson Citizen,* September 14, p. 1A.

Haley, A. (1976). *Roots.* New York: Doubleday.

Hall, C. S., and Lindsey, G. (1970). *Theories of Personality.* New York: Wiley.

Hall, E., and Hall, M. (1971). "The Sounds of Silence." *Playboy,* June.

Halmi, K. A.; Powers, P.; and Cunningham, S. (1975). "Treatment of an Anorexia Nervosa with Behavior Modification." *Archives of General Psychiatry* **32**, 93–96.

Halstead, W. C., and Rucker, W. B. (1968). "Memory: A Molecular Maze." *Psychology Today* **2**(1), 38–41.

Hamlin, R. L.; Buckholdt, D.; Bushell, D.; Ellis, D.; and Ferritor, D. (1969). "Changing the Game from 'Get the Teacher' to 'Learn.' " *Trans-Action* **6**, 20–31.

Harlow, H. F. (1965). "Sexual Behavior in the Rhesus Monkey." In *Sex and Behavior,* edited by F. Beach. New York: Wiley.

———— (1959). "Love in Infant Monkeys." *Scientific American* **200**(6), 68–74.

———— (1949). "The Formation of Learning Sets." *Psychological Review* **56**, 51–65.

Harlow, H. F., and Harlow, M. K. (1966). "Learning to Love." *American Scientist* **54**, 244–272.

Harlow, H. F., and Suomi, S. J. (1970). "Nature of Love Simplified." *American Psychologist* **25**, 161–168.

Harlow, H. F., and Zimmerman, R. R. (1959). "Affectional Responses in the Infant Monkey." *Science* **130**, 421–432.

Harrison, A., and Connolly, K. (1971). "The Conscious Control of Fine Levels of Neuromuscular Firing in Spastic and Normal Subjects." *Developmental Medicine and Child Neurology* **13**, 762–771.

Hartmann, E.; Baekeland, F.; and Zwilling, G. (1972). "Psychological Differences between Long and Short Sleepers." *Archives of General Psychiatry* **26**, 463–468.

Hartmann, E. L. (1973). *The Functions of Sleep.* New Haven, Conn.: Yale University Press.

Hastorf, A. H., and Cantril, H. (1954). "They Saw a Game: A Case Study." *Journal of Abnormal and Social Psychology* **29**, 129–134.

Havighurst, R. J. (1972). *Developmental Tasks and Education.* New York: McKay.

Hayes, C. (1951). *The Ape in Our House.* New York: Harper & Row.

Haynes, S. N.; Moseley, D.; and McGowan, W. T. (1975). "Relaxation Training and Biofeedback in the Reduction of Frontalis Muscle Tension." *Psychophysiology* **12**, 547–552.

Hayter, J. (1980). "The Rhythm of Sleep." *American Journal of Nursing*, March, pp. 457–461.

Heath, R., and Mickle, W. (1960). "Evaluation of Seven Years' Experience with Depth Electrode Studies in Human Patients." In *Electrical Studies on the Unanesthetized Brain,* edited by E. R. Ramey and D. O'Doherty. New York: Hoeber Medical Division, Harper & Row.

Heath, R. G. (1960). "A Biochemical Hypothesis on the Etiology of Schizophrenia." In *The Etiology of Schizophrenia,* edited by D. D. Jackson. New York: Basic Books.

Heidbreder, E. (1947). "The Attainment of Concepts: III. The Problem." *Journal of Psychology* **24**, 93–138.

——— (1946). "The Attainment of Concepts: I. Terminology and Methodology." *Journal of General Psychology* **35**, 173–189.

Heron, W. T., and Skinner, B. F. (1937). "Changes in Hunger during Starvation." *Psychological Record* **1**, 51–60.

Hess, E. H. (1958). "Imprinting in Animals." *Scientific American* **198**(3), 81–90.

Hess, E. H., and Polt, J. M. (1960). "Pupil Size as Related to Interest Value of Visual Stimuli." *Science* **132**, 349–350.

Hess, E. H.; Seltzer, A. L.; and Shlien, J. M. (1965). "Pupil Response of Hetero- and Homosexual Males to Pictures of Men and Women: A Pilot Study." *Journal of Abnormal Psychology* **70**(3), 165–168.

Hilgard, E. R. (1979). *Mysteries of the Mind.* National Geographic Film.

——— (1977). *Divided Consciousness: Multiple Controls in Human Thought and Action.* New York: Wiley-Interscience.

——— (1973). "A Neodissociation Interpretation of Pain Reduction in Hypnosis." *Psychological Review* **80**(3), 396–411.

——— (1965). *Hypnotic Susceptibility.* New York: Harcourt, Brace and World.

Hilgard, E. R., and Hilgard, J. R. (1975). *Hypnosis in the Relief of Pain.* Los Altos, Calif.: Kaufmann.

Hilgard, J. R. (1974). "Imaginative Involvement: Some Characteristics of the Highly Hypnotizable and Non-hypnotizable." *International Journal of Clinical and Experimental Hypnosis* **22**, 138–156.

Hogarty, G. E. (1977). "Treatment and the Course of Schizophrenia." *Schizophrenia Bulletin* **3**, 587–599.

Holland, P. J. (1981). "Lithium Capsule." *American Family Physician* **24** (9), 147–148.

Holmes, D. S. (1972). "Repression or Interference? A Further Investigation." *Journal of Personality and Social Psychology* **22**, 163–170.

Holmes, T. H., and Rahe, R. H. (1967). "The Social Readjustment Rating Scale." *Journal of Psychosomatic Research* **11**, 213–218.

Holvey, D. N., and Talbott, J. H., eds. (1972). *The Merck Manual of Diagnosis and Therapy.* 12th ed. Rahway, N. J.: Merck, Sharp, & Dohme Research Laboratories.

Horn, J. L. (1976). "Human Abilities: A Review of Research and Theory in the Early 1970s." *Annual Review of Psychology* **27**, 437–485.

Horner, M. S. (1969). "Fail: Bright Women." *Psychology Today* **3**, 36–38.

Horowitz, E. L., and Horowitz, R. E. (1938). "Development of Social Attitudes in Children." *Sociometry* **1**, 301–338.

Horowitz, M. J. (1969). "Flashbacks: Recurrent Intrusive Images after the Use of LSD." *American Journal of Psychiatry* **126**(4), 147–151.

Horton, D. L., and Turnage, T. W. (1976). *Human Learning.* Englewood Cliffs, N. J.: Prentice-Hall.

Hovland, C. I. (1938). "Experimental Studies in Rote-Learning Theory: III. Distribution of Practice with Varying Speeds of Syllable Presentation." *Journal of Experimental Psychology* **23**, 172–190.

Hovland, C. I.; Janis, I.; and Kelly, H. (1953). *Communication and Persuasion.* New Haven, Conn.: Yale University Press.

Hovland, C. I., Lumsdaine, A., and Scheffield, F. (1949). *Experiments on Mass Communication.* Princeton, N.J.: Princeton University Press.

Hovland, C. I., and Weiss, W. (1951). "The Influence of Source Credibility on Communication Effectiveness." *Public Opinion Quarterly* **15**, 635–650.

Howe, K. G., and Zanna, M. P. (1975). "Sex-Appropriateness of the Task and Achievement Behavior." Paper presented at the Meeting of the Eastern Psychological Association.

Hudspeth, W. J.; McGaugh, J. L.; and Thompson, C. W. (1964). "Aversive and Amnesic Effects of Electroconvulsive Shock." *Journal of Comparative and Physiological Psychology* **57**, 61–64.

Hunt, J. McV. (1979). "Psychological Development: Early Experience. *Annual Review of Psychology* **30**, 103–143.

Hunt, J. McV.; Mohandessi, K.; Ghodssi, M.; and Akiyama, M. (1976). "The Psychological Development of Orphanage-Reared Infants: Intervening with Outcomes (Tehran). *Genetic Psychology Monographs* **94**, 177–226.

Hunt, M. (1974). *Sexual Behavior in the 1970s.* Chicago: Playboy Press.

Huston, T. L.; Ruggiero, M.; Conner, R.; and Geis, G. (1981). "Bystander Intervention into Crime: A Study Based on Naturally-Occurring Episodes." *Social Psychology Quarterly* **44**(1), 14–23.

Huxley, J. (1953). *Evolution in Action.* New York: Harper & Row.

Hyden, H. (1969). "Biochemical Aspects of Learning and Memory." In *On the Biology of Learning*, edited by K. Pribram. New York: Harcourt Brace Jovanovich.

Iversen, L. L. (1979). "The Chemistry of the Brain." *Scientific American* **241**(3), 134–150.

Jaffe, A. C. (1976). "Child Molestation." *Medical Aspects of Human Sexuality*, pp. 73, 96.

James, W. (1890). *The Principles of Psychology*. Vols. 1 and 2. New York: Holt.

Janis, I. L., and Feshback, S. (1953). "Effects of Fear-Arousing Communications." *Journal of Abnormal and Social Psychology* **48**, 78–92.

Janis, I. L., and King, B. T. (1954). "The Influence of Role Playing on Attitude Change." *Journal of Abnormal and Social Psychology* **99**, 211–218.

Janis, I. L.; Mahl, G. R.; Kagan, J.; and Holt, R. (1969). *Personality: Dynamics, Development, and Assessment*. New York: Harcourt Brace Jovanovich.

Jankel, W. R. (1977). "EMG Feedback in Bell's Palsy." *Proceedings of the Biofeedback Society*. Orlando, Fla.

Jasper, H., ed. (1969). *Basic Mechanisms of the Epilepsies*. Boston: Little, Brown.

Jeannaret, P., and Webb, W. (1963). "Strength of Grip on Arousal from Full Night's Sleep." *Perceptual and Motor Skills* **17**, 759–761.

Jellison, J. M., and Arkin, R. (1977). "Social Comparison of Abilities: A Self-Presentational Approach to Decision Making in Groups." In *Social Comparison Processes: Theoretical and Empirical Perspectives*, edited by J. M. Suls and R. L. Miller. Washington, D.C.: Hemisphere.

Jenkins, J. G., and Dallenbach, K. M. (1924). "Oblivescence during Sleep and Waking." *American Journal of Psychology* **35**, 605–612.

Jenkins, W. O. (1947). "A Review of Leadership Studies with Particular Reference to Military Problems." *Psychological Bulletin* **44**, 54–79.

Jenkins, W. O.; McFann, H.; and Clayton, F. L. (1950). "A Methodological Study of Extinction Following Aperiodic and Continuous Reinforcement." *Journal of Comparative and Physiological Psychology* **43**, 155–167.

Jennings, M. K., and Niemi, R. G. (1968). "The Transmission of Political Values from Parent to Child." *American Political Science Review* **62**, 169–184.

Jensen, A. R. (1969). "How Much Can We Boost I.Q. and Scholastic Achievement?" *Harvard Educational Review* **39**, 1–123.

John, E. R. (1967). *Mechanisms of Memory*. New York: Academic Press.

Johnson, H. E., and Garton, W. H. (1973). "Muscle Re-education in Hemiplegia by Use of Electromyographic Device." *Archives of Physical Medicine* **54**, 320–322.

Johnson, H. M.; Swan, T. H.; and Weigand, G. E. (1930). "In What Position Do Healthy People Sleep?" *Journal of the American Medical Association* **94**, 2058–2068.

Jones, M. C. (1924). "The Elimination of Children's Fear." *Journal of Experimental Psychology* **7**, 382–390.

Jones, W. H.; Chernovetz, M. E.; and Hansson, R. O. (1978). "The Enigma of Androgyny: Differential Implications for Males and Females?" *Journal of Consulting and Clinical Psychology* **46**, 298–313.

Jorgensen, B. W., and Cervone, J. C. (1978). "Affect Enhancement in the Pseudorecognition Task." *Personality and Social Psychology Bulletin* **4**, 285–288.

Jouvet, M. (1962). "Recherches sur les Structures Nerveuses et les Mecanismes Responsables de Différentes Phases du Sommeil Physiologique." *Archives Italiennes de Biologie* **100**, 125–206.

Jung, C. G. (1923). *Psychological Types*. New York: Harcourt Brace Jovanovich.

Kagan, J. (1979). "Overview: Perspectives on Human Infancy." In *Handbook of Infant Development*, edited by J. Osofsky. New York: Wiley.

Kahn, M. (1966). "The Physiology of Catharsis." *Journal of Personality and Social Psychology* **3**, 278–286.

Kales, A. (1972). "The Evaluation and Treatment of Sleep Disorders: Pharmacological and Physiological Studies." In *The Sleeping Brain*, edited by M. Chase. Los Angeles: Brain Information Service, 447–491.

Kales, A., and Kales, J. (1973). "Recent Advances in the Diagnosis and Treatment of Sleep Disorders." In *Sleep Research and Clinical Practice*, edited by D. Usdin. New York: Brunner/Mazel.

Kales, A. F.; Hoedmaker, F.; Jacobson, A.; and Lichtenstein, F. (1964). "Dream Deprivation: An Experimental Reappraisal." *Nature* **204**, 1337–1338.

Kamin, L. J. (1974). *The Science and Politics of I.Q.* New York: Halstead.

Kamiya, J. (1969). "Operant Control of the EEG Alpha Rhythm and Some of Its Reported Effects on Consciousness." In *Altered States of Consciousness*, edited by C. Tart. New York: Wiley.

Kanin, G. (1978). *It Takes a Long Time to Become Young*. New York: Doubleday.

Kaplan, A. (1974). *The New Sex Therapy: Active Treatment of Sexual Dysfunction*. New York: Brunner/Mazel.

Karlins, M.; Coffman, T. L.; and Walters, G. (1969). "On the Fading of Social Stereotypes: Studies in Three Generations of College Students." *Journal of Personality and Social Psychology* **13**, 1–16.

Kastenbaum, R. (1977). *Death, Society, and Human Behavior*. St. Louis: Mosby.

Katona, G. (1940). *Organizing and Memorizing*. New York: Columbia University Press.

Katz, D., and Braly, K. W. (1933). "Racial Stereotypes of 100 College Students." *Journal of Abnormal and Social Psychology* **28**, 280–290.

Kellogg, W. N., and Kellogg, L. A. (1967). *The Ape and the Child: A Study of Environmental Influence on Early Behavior*. New York: Hafner Publishing, 1967. (Originally published by McGraw-Hill, New York, 1933.)

Kelley, H. H., and Michela, J. L. (1980). "Attribution Theory and Research." *Annual Review of Psychology* **31**, 457–501.

Kermis, M.; Monge, R.; and Dusek, J. (1975). "Human Sexuality in the Hierarchy of Adolescent Interests." Paper presented at the Annual Meeting of the Society for Research in Child Development.

Kerner Commission (1968). *Report of the U.S. National Advisory Commission in Civil Disorders*.

Washington, D.C.: U.S. Government Printing Office.

Kilham, W., and Mann, L. (1974). "Level of Destructive Obedience as a Function of Transmitter and Executant Roles in the Milgram Obedience Paradigm." *Journal of Personality and Social Psychology* **29**, 696–702.

King, B. T., and Janis, I. L. (1956). "Comparison of the Effectiveness of Improvised versus Nonimprovised Role-Playing in Producing Changes." *Human Relations* **9**, 177–186.

Kinsey, A. C.; Pomeroy, W. B.; and Martin, C. E. (1948). *Sexual Behavior in the Human Male.* Philadelphia: Saunders.

Kinsey, A. C.; Pomeroy, W. B.; Martin, C. E.; and Gebhard, P. H. (1953). *Sexual Behavior in the Human Female.* Philadelphia: Saunders.

Kirsner, J. B. (1971). "Acid-Peptic Disease." In *Textbook of Medicine,* edited by P. B. Beeson and W. McDermott. Philadelphia: Saunders.

Kisker, G. W. (1964). *The Disorganized Personality.* New York: McGraw-Hill.

Klatzky, R. L. (1975). *Human Memory: Structures and Process.* San Francisco: Freeman.

Klineberg, O. (1938). "Emotional Expression in Chinese Literature." *Journal of Abnormal and Social Psychology* **33**, 517–520.

Kogan, N., and Wallach, M. A. (1967). "Risk Taking as a Function of the Situation, the Person, and the Group." In *New Directions in Psychology,* vol. 3., edited by G. Mandler *et al.* New York: Holt, Rinehart & Winston.

Kohlberg, L. (1980). "The Meaning and Measurement of Moral Development." Heinz Werner Memorial Lecture.

——— (1969). "Stage and Sequence: The Cognitive-Developmental Approach to Socialization." In *Handbook of Socialization Theory and Research,* edited by D. A. Goslin. Chicago: Rand McNally.

Kohn, M. L. (1963). "Social Class and Parent–Child Relationships: An Interpretation." *American Sociological Review* **68**, 471–480.

Korman, A. K.; Greenhaus, J. H.; and Badin, I. J. (1977). "Personal Attitudes and Motivation." *Annual Review of Psychology* **28**, 175–196.

Krebs, D., and Adinolfi, A. A. (1975).

"Physical Attractiveness, Social Relations, and Personality Style." *Journal of Personality and Social Psychology* **31**, 245–253.

Krisher, H. P.; Darley, S. A.; and Darley, J. M. (1973). "Fear-Provoking Recommendations, Intentions to Take Preventive Actions, and Actual Preventive Action." *Journal of Personality and Social Psychology* **26**, 301–308.

Kroger, W. S., and Fezler, W. D. (1976). *Hypnosis and Behavior Modification: Conditioning.* Philadelphia: Lippincott.

Krueger, W. C. F. (1929). "The Effect of Overlearning on Retention." *Journal of Experimental Psychology* **12**, 71–78.

Kübler-Ross, E. (1969). *On Death and Dying.* New York: Macmillan.

Kuder, G. Frederic (1950). *Kuder Preference Record.* Chicago: Science Research Associates.

Kuhne, W. (1878). Cited in Wald, G. (1950). "The Eye and Camera." *Scientific American* **183**(2), 32–41.

Kunzel, M. G.; Sovak, M.; Sternbach, R. A.; and Dalessio, D. J. (1977). "Biofeedback Techniques in the Treatment of Chronic Headache." Paper delivered at the Fourteenth Annual Meeting of the Federation of Western Societies of Neurological Sciences, February.

Labov, W. (1972). *Language in the Inner City: Studies in Black English Vernacular.* Philadelphia: University of Pennsylvania Press.

Lally, J. R. (1971). *Development of a Day Care Center for Young Children.* Syracuse University Children's Center Progress Report, February.

Landreth, C. (1967). *Early Childhood: Behavior and Learning.* New York: Knopf.

Lang, P. (1970). "Autonomic Control." *Psychology Today* **4**(5), 37–41.

Lang, P. J., and Melamed, B. G. (1969). "Avoidance Conditioning Therapy of an Infant with Chronic Ruminative Vomiting." *Journal of Abnormal Psychology* **74**, 1–8.

Latané, B., and Darley, J. M. (1969). "Bystander 'apathy.'" *American Scientist* **57**, 244–268.

Latané, B., and Nida, S. (1981). "Ten Years of Research on Group Size and Helping." *Psychological Bulletin* **89**(2), 308–324.

Laughlin, H. P. (1967). *The Neuroses.* Washington, D.C.: Butterworths.

Lazarus, R. S., interviewed by D. Goleman (1979). "Positive Denial:

A Case for Not Facing Reality." *Psychology Today.*

Lazarus, R. S.; Kanner, A. D.; and Folkman, S. (1980). "Emotions: A Cognitive-Phenomenological Analysis." In *Emotion: Theory, Research and Experience,* vol. 1, edited by R. Plutchik and H. K. Kellerman. New York: Academic Press.

Leavitt, H. J. (1951). "Some Effects of Certain Communication Patterns on Group Performance." *Journal of Abnormal and Social Psychology* **46**, 38–50.

Lee, E. S. (1951). "Negro Intelligence and Selective Migration: A Philadelphia Test of the Klineberg Hypothesis." *American Sociological Review* **16**, 227–233.

Lefcourt, H. M. (1976). *Locus of Control.* Hillsdale, N.J.: Erlbaum.

LeGros, J. J.; Gilot, P.; Seron, X.; Claessens, J.; Adam, A.; Moeglen, J. M.; Audibert, A.; and Berchier, P. (1978). "Influence of Vasopressin on Learning and Memory." *Lancet* **1**, 41–42.

Lennenberg, E. H. (1969). "On Explaining Language." *Science* **164** (3880), 635–643.

Lepper, M. R., and Greene, D., eds. (1978). *The Hidden Costs of Reward: New Perspectives on the Psychology of Motivation.* Hillsdale, N.J.: Erlbaum.

Lepper, M. R.; Greene, D.; and Nisbett, R. E. (1973). "Undermining Children's Intrinsic Interest with Extrinsic Reward: A Test of the 'Overjustification' Hypothesis." *Journal of Personality and Social Psychology* **28**, 129–137.

Levenstein, P. (1976). "The Mother–Child Home Program." In *The Preschool in Action,* 2nd ed., edited by M. C. Day and R. K. Parker. Boston: Allyn & Bacon.

Levin, R., and Levin, A. (1975). "A Sexual Pleasure: The Surprising Preferences of 100,000 Women." *Redbook,* September, p. 38.

Levine, B. (1979). *Group Psychotherapy: Practice and Development.* Englewood Cliffs, N.J.: Prentice-Hall.

Levine, F. J., and Tapp, J. L. (1973). "The Psychology of Criminal Identification: The Gap from Wade to Kirby." *University of Pennsylvania Law Review* **121**, 1079–1131.

Levine, F. M., and Fasnacht, G. (1974). "Token Rewards May Lead to Token Learning." *American Psychologist* **29**(1), 816–820.

Lewin, K. (1935). *A Dynamic Theory of Personality*. New York: McGraw-Hill.

Lewis, W. E.; Mishikim, M.; Bragin, E.; Brown, R. M.; Pert, C. B.; and Pert, A. (1981). "Opiate Receptor Gradients in Monkey Cerebral Cortex: Correspondence with Sensory Processing Hierarchies." *Science* **211**, 1166–1169.

Lieberman, M. (1975). "Survey and Evaluation of the Literature on Verbal Psychotherapy of Depressive Disorders." Report prepared for the Clinical Research Branch, National Institutes of Health.

Lieberman, M. A. (1976). "Change Induction in Small Groups." *Annual Review of Psychology* **27**, 217–250.

Lieberman, M. A.; Yalom, I. D.; and Miles, M. B. (1973). *Encounter Groups: First Facts*. New York: Basic Books.

Lieberman, P. (1968). "Primate Vocalizations and Human Linguistic Ability." *Journal of the Acoustical Society of America* **44**, 1574–1584.

Liebert, R. M.; Poulos, R. W.; and Strauss, G. D. (1974). *Developmental Psychology*. Englewood Cliffs, N.J.: Prentice-Hall.

Liebert, R. M., and Spiegler, M. D. (1978). *Personality: Strategies and Issues*. 3rd ed. Homewood, Ill.: Dorsey Press.

Liebman, R.; Minuchin, S.; and Baker, L. (1974). "An Integrated Treatment Program for Anorexia Nervosa." *American Journal of Psychiatry* **131**(4), 432–436.

Lindgren, H. C. (1956). *Educational Psychology in the Classroom*. New York: Wiley.

Lobsenz, N. (1974). "Sex and the Senior Citizen." *New York Times Magazine*, January 20, pp. 87–91.

Loftus, E. F. (1979). "The Malleability of Human Memory." *American Scientist* **67**(3), 312–320.

Lovaas, O. I. (1968). "Some Studies on the Treatment of Childhood Schizophrenia." In *Research in Psychotherapy*, edited by J. M. Shuen. Washington, D.C.: American Psychological Association.

Luchins, A. S. (1942). "Mechanization in Problem Solving: The Effect of Einstelling." *Psychological Monographs* **54**(248).

Luria, A. R. (1970). "The Functional Organization of the Brain." *Scientific American* **222**(3), 66–78.

Lyon, D. O. (1914). "The Relation of Length of Material to Time Taken for Learning and the Optimum Distribution of Time." *Journal of Educational Psychology* **5**, 1–9.

MacLeish, K. (1972). "Stone-Age Cave Men of Mindaneo." *National Geographic*, August.

Maccoby, E., and Jacklin, C. (1974). "What We Know and Don't Know about Sex Differences." *Psychology Today* **8**, 109–112.

Madaras, G. R., and Bem, D. J. (1968). "Risk and Conservation in Group Decision-Making." *Journal of Experimental Social Psychology* **4**(3), 350–365.

Madsen, C. H., Jr.; Becker, W. C.; Thomas, D. R.; Koser, L.; and Plager, E. (1968). "An Analysis of the Reinforcing Function of 'Sit Down' Commands." In *Readings in Educational Psychology*, edited by R. K. Parker. Boston: Allyn & Bacon.

Mahoney, M. J. (1980). *Abnormal Psychology*. New York: Harper & Row.

Mallick, S. K., and McCandless, B. R. (1966). "A Study of Catharsis of Aggression." *Journal of Personality and Social Psychology* **4**, 591–596.

Mann, R. D. (1959). "A Review of the Relationship between Personality and Performance in Small Groups." *Psychological Bulletin* **56**, 241–270.

Marinacci, A. A., and Horande, M. (1960). "Electromyogram in Neuromuscular Re-education." *Bulletin of the Los Angeles Neurological Society* **25**, 57–71.

Marks, J. M. (1965). *Patterns in Meaning in Psychiatric Patients*. London: Oxford University Press.

Marler, P. (1967). "Animal Communication Signals." *Science* **157**, 769–774.

Marshall, M. (1981). "Why Our Children Are Killing Themselves." *Ebony*, September, pp. 36–38.

Martindale, C. (1981). *Cognition and Consciousness*. Homewood, Ill.: Dorsey Press.

Maslach, C. (1979). "Negative Emotional Biasing of Unexplained Arousal." *Journal of Personality and Social Psychology* **37**, 359–369.

Maslow, A. H. (1971). *Farther Reaches of Human Nature*. Esalen Institute Book Publishing Program. New York: Viking.

——— (1962). *Toward a Psychology of Being*. Princeton, N.J.: Van Nostrand.

———, ed. (1954). *Motivation and Personality*. New York: Harper & Row. (Reprinted 1970).

Masserman, J. H. (1961). *Principles of Dynamic Psychiatry*. Philadelphia: Saunders.

Masters, W. H., and Johnson, V. E. (1974). *The Pleasure Bond*. Boston: Little, Brown.

——— (1970). *Human Sexual Inadequacy*. Boston: Little, Brown.

——— (1966). *Human Sexual Response*. Boston: Little, Brown.

Maugh, T. H., II (1974a). "Marijuana: The Grass May No Longer Be Greener." *Science* **185**, 683–685.

——— (1974b). "Marijuana (II): Does It Damage the Brain?" *Science* **185**, 775–776.

May, P. R. (1968). *Treatment of Schizophrenia: A Comparative Study of Five Treatment Methods*. New York: Science House.

McCarthy, D. (1954). "Language Development in Children." In *Manual of Child Psychology*, 2nd ed., edited by L. Carmichael. New York: Wiley.

McCary, J. L. (1967). *Human Sexuality*. Princeton, N.J.: Van Nostrand.

McCauley, C.; Stitt, C. L.; and Segal, M. (1980). "Stereotyping: From Prejudice to Prediction." *Psychological Bulletin* **87**(1), 195–215.

McClelland, D. C. (1962). "Business Drive and National Achievement." *Harvard Business Review*, July–August, pp. 99–112.

McConnell, J. V.; Jacobson, A. L.; and Kimble, D. P. (1959). "The Effect of Regeneration upon Retention of a Conditioned Response in the Planarian." *Journal of Comparative and Physiological Psychology* **52**, 1–5.

McFadden, E. R., Jr.; Luparello, T.; Lyons, H. A.; and Bleeker, E. (1969). "The Mechanisms of Action of Suggestion in the Induction of Acute Asthma Attacks." *Psychosomatic Medicine* **31**(2), 134–143.

McFarland, R. A., and Campbell, C. (1975). "Precise Heart-Rate Control and Heart-Rate Perception." *Perceptual and Motor Skills* **41**(3), 730.

McGaugh, J. L., and Herz, M. J., eds. (1970). *Controversial Issues in Consolidation of Memory Trace*. New York: Atherton Press.

McGeoch, J. A. (1930). "The Influence of Associative Value upon the Difficulty of Nonsense-Syllable Lists." *Journal of Genetic Psychology* **37**, 421–426.

McGlothlin, W. (1975). "Drug Use and Abuse." In *Annual Review of Psychology*, edited by M. R. Rosenzweig and L. W. Porter. Palo Alto, Calif.: Annual Reviews.

McGlothlin, W. H., and Arnold, D. O. (1971). "LSD Revisited: A Ten Year Follow-Up of Medical LSD Use." *Archives of General Psychiatry* **24**, 35–49.

McGrew, J. (1967). "How Open Are Multiple Dwelling Units?" *Journal of Social Psychology* **72**, 233–236.

McGuire, W. J. (1960). "A Syllogistic Analysis of Cognitive Relationships." In *Attitude Organization and Change*, edited by C. I. Hovland and I. L. Janis. New Haven, Conn.: Yale University Press.

McKay, H.; Sinisterra, L.; McKay, A.; Gomez, H.; and Lloreda, P. (1978). "Improving Cognitive Ability in Chronically Deprived Children." *Science* **200**, 270–278.

McNemar, Q. (1942). *The Revision of the Stanford–Binet Scale*. Boston: Houghton Mifflin.

Mead, M. (1939). "Sex and Temperament." In *From the South Seas*. New York: Morrow.

Medinnus, G. R., and Johnson, R. C. (1976). *Child and Adolescent Psychology*. 2nd ed. New York: Wiley.

Mees, C.E.K. (1934). "Scientific Thought and Social Reconstruction." *Electrical Engineering* **53**, 383–384.

Megargee, E. I. (1970). "The Prediction of Violence with Psychological Tests." In *Current Topics in Clinical and Community Psychology*, edited by C. Spielberger. New York: Academic Press.

Meltzoff, J., and Kornriech, M. (1970). *Research in Psychotherapy*. New York: Atherton Press.

Menninger, K. (1958). *Theory of Psychoanalytic Technique*. New York: Basic Books.

Middlebrook, P. N. (1980). *Social Psychology and Modern Life*. 2nd ed. New York: Alfred A. Knopf.

Milgram, S. (1977). *The Individual in a Social World: Essays and Experiments*. Reading, Mass.: Addison-Wesley.

———— (1964). "Issues in the Study of Obedience." *American Psychologist* **19**, 848–852.

———— (1963). "Behavioral Study of Obedience." *Journal of Abnormal and Social Psychology* **67**, 371–378.

Miller, G. A. (1956). "The Magical Number Seven, Plus or Minus Two: Some Limits on Our Capacity for Processing Information." *Psychological Review* **63**, 81–97.

———— (1951). *Language and Communication*. New York: McGraw-Hill.

Miller, N. E. (1975). "Application of Learning and Biofeedback to Psychiatry and Medicine." In *Comprehensive Textbook of Psychiatry*, 2nd ed., edited by A. M. Freedman, H. I. Kaplan, and B. J. Sadock. Baltimore: Williams & Wilkins.

———— (1969). "Learning of Visceral and Glandular Responses." *Science* **163**, 434–445.

———— (1958). "Central Stimulation and Other New Approaches to Motivation and Reward." *American Psychologist* **13**, 100–108.

———— (1957). "Experiments on Motivation: Studies Combining Psychological, Physiological and Pharmacological Techniques." *Science* **126**, 1271–1278.

———— (1944). "Experimental Studies of Conflict." In *Personality and the Behavior Disorders*, vol. I, edited by J. McV. Hunt. New York: Ronald Press.

———— (1941). "The Frustration–Aggression Hypothesis." *Psychological Review* **48**, 337–342.

Miller, N. E., and Bugelski, R. (1948). "Minor Studies in Aggression: II. The Influence of Frustrations Imposed by the In-Group on Attitudes Expressed toward Out-Groups." *Journal of Psychology* **25**, 437–442.

Milner, B. (1959). "The Memory Deficit in Bilateral Hippocampal Lesions." *Psychiatric Research Reports* **11**, 43–52.

Mischel, W. (1981). *Introduction to Personality*. 3rd ed. New York: Holt, Rinehart & Winston.

Mollon, J. D. (1982). "Color Vision." *Annual Review of Psychology* **33**, 41–85.

Monahan, J., ed. (1975). *Community Mental Health and the Criminal Justice System*. New York: Pergamon Press.

Monahan, L.; Kuhn, D.; and Shaver, P. (1974). "Intrapsychic versus Cultural Explanation of the 'Fear of Success' Motive." *Journal of Personality and Social Psychology* **29**, 60–64.

Montagu, A. (1974). "Aggression and the Evolution of Man." In *Advances in Behavioral Biology*, vol.

12: *The Neuropsychology of Aggression*, edited by R. S. Whalen. New York: Plenum.

More, A. J. (1969). "Delay of Feedback and the Acquisition and Retention of Verbal Materials in the Classroom." *Journal of Educational Psychology* **60**, 339–342.

Munsterberg, H. (1908). *On the Witness Stand: Essays on Psychology and Crime*. New York: Clark, Boardman.

Musante, G. J. (1976). "The Dietary Rehabilitation Clinic: Evaluative Report of a Behavioral and Dietary Treatment of Obesity." *Behavioral Therapy* **7**, 198–204.

"The Mystique of the Older Woman" (1977). *Playboy Magazine* (May).

Myers, B. M., and Baum, M. J. (1980). "Facilitation of Copulatory Performance in Male Rats by Naloxone: Effects of Hypophysectomy, 17Alpha-entradial, and Lateinizing Hormone Releasing Hormone." *Pharmacol. Biochem. Behav.* **12**, 365–370.

Myers, R. D., and Melchior, C. L. (1977). "A Chemical Cause for Alcoholism." *Science News*, May 21, p. 327.

"Mysteries of the Mind" (1979). *National Geographic*.

Nakazima, S. A. (1966). "A Comparative Study of the Speech Developments of Japanese and American English in Childhood: II. The Acquisition of Speech." *Studia Phonologica* **4**, 38–55.

National Clearing House for Drug Abuse Information (1974). *Amphetamines*. Series 28, No. 1.

National Institute of Mental Health (1969). *The Mental Health of Urban America*. Washington, D.C.: Public Health Service Publication No. 1906.

Navarick, D. J. (1979). *Principles of Learning: From Laboratory to Field*. Reading, Mass.: Addison-Wesley.

Nebes, R. D. (1974). "Hemispheric Specialization in Commissurotomized Man." *Psychological Bulletin* **81**(1), 1–14.

———— (1973). "Perception of Dot Patterns by the Disconnected Right and Left Hemisphere in Man." *Neuropsychologia* **11**, 285–290.

———— (1972). "Dominance of the Minor Hemisphere in Commissurotomized Man in a Test of Figural Unification." *Brain* **95**, 633–638.

——— (1971). "Superiority of the Minor Hemisphere in Commissurotomized Man for the Perception of Part–Whole Relations. *Cortex* **7**, 333–347.

Nelson, K. (1974). "Concept, Word and Sentence: Interrelations in Acquisition and Development." *Psychological Review* **81**, 267–285.

Neugarten, B. L., interviewed by E. Hall (1980). "Acting One's Age: New Rules for Old." *Psychology Today*, April, pp. 66–80.

Newcomb, T. M. (1963). "Persistence and Regression of Changed Attitudes: Long Range Studies." *Journal of Social Issues* **19**, 3–14.

——— (1943). *Personality and Social Change*. New York: Dryden Press.

Newman, B. M., and Newman, P. R. (1979). *Development through Life: A Psychosocial Approach*. Homewood, Ill.: Dorsey Press.

Newman, H. H.; Freeman, F. N.; and Holzinker, K. J. (1937). *Twins: A Study of Heredity and Environment*. Chicago: University of Chicago Press.

*Newsweek* (1971). "Drugs on Campus." January 25, p. 52.

Neymann, C., and Yacorzynski, G. (1942). "Studies of Introversion–Extraversion and Conflict of Motives in Psychoses." *Journal of Genetic Psychology* **27**, 241–255.

Nickel, T. W. (1974). "The Attribution of Intention as a Critical Factor in the Relation between Frustration and Aggression." *Journal of Personality* **42**, 482–492.

Noble, G. (1973). "Effects of Different Forms of Filmed Aggression on Children's Constructive and Destructive Play." *Journal of Personality and Social Psychology* **26**, 54–59.

Norman, W. T. (1967). *2800 Personality Trait Descriptors: Normative Operating Characteristics for a University Population*. Ann Arbor: Department of Psychology, University of Michigan.

Novak, D., and Lerner, M. (1968). "Rejection as a Consequence of Perceived Similarity." *Journal of Personality and Social Psychology* **9**, 147–152.

Nowlis, D. P., and Rhead, J. C. (1968). "Relation of Eyes-Closed Resting EEG Alpha Activity to Hypnotic Susceptibility." *Perceptual Motor Skills* **27**, 1047–1050.

Noyes, A. P., and Kolb, L. C. (1963). *Modern Clinical Psychiatry*. Philadelphia: Saunders.

Olds, J., and Milner, P. (1954). "Positive Reinforcement Produced by Electrical Stimulation of Septal Area and Other Regions of Rat Brain." *Journal of Comparative and Physiological Psychology* **47**, 419–427.

Oliveros, J. C.; Jandali, M. K.; Timsit-Berthier, M.; Remy, R.; Benghezal, A.; Audibert, A.; and Moeglin, J. M. (1978). "Vasopressin in Amnesia." *Lancet* **1**, 42.

Ornstein, R. E. (1977). *The Psychology of Consciousness*. 2nd ed. New York: Harcourt Brace Jovanovich.

——— (1975). *The Psychology of Consciousness*. New York: Penguin Books.

———, ed. (1973). *The Nature of Human Consciousness: A Book of Readings*. San Francisco: Freeman.

Osborn, A. F. (1957). *Applied Imagination*. 2nd ed. New York: Scribner.

Osgood, C. E. (1953). *Method and Theory in Experimental Psychology*. New York: Oxford University Press.

Owen, D. R. (1972). "The 47, XYY Male: A Review." *Psychological Bulletin* **78**, 209–233.

Pagano, R. R.; Rose, R. M.; Stivers, R. M.; and Warrenburg, S. (1976). "Sleep during Transcendental Meditation." *Science* **191**(4224), 308–310.

Page, J. (1977). *The Other Awkward Age*. Berkeley, Calif.: Ten Speed Press.

Paivio, A. (1969). "Mental Imagery in Associative Learning and Memory." *Psychological Review* **76**, 242–263.

Palmer, R. J., and Masling, J. (1969). "Vocabulary for Skin Color in Negro and White Children." *Developmental Psychology* **1**, 396–401.

Pankove, E., and Kogan, N. (1968). "Creative Ability and Risk-Taking in Elementary School Children." *Journal of Personality* **36**, 420–439.

Papalia, D. E. (1972). "The Status of Several Conservation Abilities across the Life Span." *Human Development* **15**, 229–243.

Paris, S. G., and Carter, A. Y. (1973). "Semantic and Constructive Aspects of Sentence Memory in Children." *Developmental Psychology* **9**, 109–113.

Parke, R. D. (1969). "Effectiveness of Punishment as an Interaction of Intensity, Timing, Agent Nurturance and Cognitive Structuring." *Child Development* **40**(1), 213–235.

Parke, R. D., and Walters, R. H. (1967). "Some Factors Determining the Efficacy of Punishment for Inducing Response Inhibition." *Monographs of the Society for Research in Child Development* **32**(109).

Parloff, M. B. (1976). "Shopping for the Right Therapy." *Saturday Review*, February 21, pp. 14–16.

Parmelee, A. H. (1973). "Diagnostic and Intervention Studies of High-Risk Infants." Third Year Contract Proposal (NIH-NICHD 71-2447), March.

Parmelee, A. H., and Haber, A. (1973). "Who Is the Risk Infant?" *Clinical Obstetrics and Gynecology* **16**(1), 376–387.

Patterson, G.; Littman, R.; and Bricker, W. (1967). "Assertive Behavior in Children: A Step toward a Theory of Aggression." *Monographs of the Society for Research in Child Development* **32**(5).

Pavlov, I. P. (1927). *Conditioned Reflexes*. New York: Oxford University Press.

Peck, M. L., and Schrut, A. (1971). "Suicidal Behavior among College Students." *HSMHA Health Reports* **86**(2), 149–156.

Pedersen, E.; Faucher, T. A.; and Eaton, W. W. (1978). "A New Perspective on the Effects of First-Grade Teachers on Children's Subsequent Adult Status." *Harvard Educational Review* **48**(1), 1–31.

Penfield, W. (1959). "The Interpretive Cortex." *Science* **129**, 1719–1725.

——— (1958). *The Excitable Cortex in Conscious Man*. Springfield, Ill.: Thomas.

Pengelley, E. T. (1978). *Sex and Human Life*. 2nd ed. Reading, Mass.: Addison-Wesley.

Penney, A. (1981). *How to Make Love to a Man*. New York: Potter.

Perry, D., and Perry, L. (1974). "Denial of Suffering in the Victim as a Stimulus to Violence in Aggressive Boys." *Child Development* **45**, 55–62.

Pert, A. (1981). "The Body's Own Tranquilizers." *Psychology Today*, September, p. 100.

Peterson, L. R., and Peterson, M. T. (1959). "Short-Term Retention of Individual Verbal Items." *Journal of Experimental Psychology* **58,** 193–198.

Peterson, R. C. (1931). *Scale of Attitude toward War.* Chicago: University of Chicago Press.

Pfeifer, W. D., and Bookin, H. D. (1978). "Vasopressin Antagonizes Retrograde Amnesia in Rats Following Electroconvulsive Shock." *Pharmacol. Biochem. Behav.* **9,** 261–263.

Piaget, J. (1972). "Intellectual Evolution from Adolescence to Adulthood." *Human Development* **15,** 1–12.

————— (1952). *The Origins of Intelligence in Children.* New York: International Universities Press.

————— (1932). *The Moral Judgment of the Child.* London: Kegan Paul.

Pierrel, R., and Sherman, J. G. (1963). "Train Your Pet the Barnabus Way." *Brown Alumni Monthly,* February.

Pines, M. (1971). "A Child's Mind Is Shaped before Age 2." *Life,* December 17, p. 63.

Plutchik, R. (1980a). "A General Psychoevolutionary Theory of Emotion." In *Emotion: Theory, Research and Experience,* vol. 1, edited by R. Plutchik and H. Kellerman. New York: Academic Press.

————— (1980b). *Emotion: A Psychoevolutionary Synthesis.* New York: Harper & Row.

————— (1977). "Cognitions in the Service of Emotions: An Evolutionary Perspective." In *Emotions,* by D. K. Candland, J. P. Fell, E. Keen, A. I. Leshner, R. Plutchik, and R. M. Tarpy. Monterey, Calif.: Brooks/Cole.

Pollard, J. C.; Uhr, L.; and Stern, E. (1965). *Drugs and Phantasy.* Boston: Little, Brown.

Pomerantz, J. R.; Sager, L. C.; and Stoever, R. J. (1977). "Perception of Wholes and Their Component Parts: Some Configural Superiority Effects." *Journal of Experimental Psychology: Human Perception and Performance* **3,** 422–435.

Prechtl, H., and Beintema, D. (1964). "The Neurological Examination of the Fullterm Newborn Infant." In *Little Club Clinics in Developmental Medicine.* No. 12. London: Spastics Society Medical Information Unit and William Heinemann Medical Books.

Premack, A. J., and Premack, D. (1972). "Teaching Language to an Ape." *Scientific American* **226,** 92–99.

Prescott, J. W. (1979). "Alienation of Affection." *Psychology Today,* December, p. 124.

Price, R. H., and Lynn, S. J. (1981). *Abnormal Psychology in the Human Context.* Homewood, Ill.: Dorsey Press.

Prince, M. (1921). *The Unconscious.* 2nd ed. New York: Macmillan.

Prochaska, J. O. (1979). *Systems of Psychotherapy: A Transtheoretical Analysis.* Homewood, Ill.: Dorsey Press.

Pryse-Phillips, W. (1969). *Epilepsy.* London: Bristol-Wright.

Quanty, M. B. (1976). "Aggression Catharsis: Experimental Investigations and Implications." In *Perspectives on Aggression,* edited by R. G. Geen and E. C. O'Neal. New York: Academic Press.

Radke, M. J.; Trager, H. G.; and Davis, H. (1949). "Social Perceptions and Attitudes of Children." *Genetic Psychology Monographs* **40,** 327–347.

Reed, P. P. (1974). *Alive.* New York: Lippincott.

Reid, J. E., and Inbau, F. E. (1966). *Truth and Deception.* Baltimore: Williams & Wilkins.

Rest, J. (1968). "Developmental Hierarchy in Preference and Comprehension of Moral Judgment." Unpublished Ph.D. dissertation, University of Chicago.

Reynolds, G. S. (1968). *Primer of Operant Conditioning.* Glenview, Ill.: Scott, Foresman.

Rheingold, H. L. (1961). "The Effect of Environmental Stimulation upon Social and Exploratory Behavior in the Human Infant." In *Determinants of Infant Behavior,* edited by B. M. Foss. New York: Wiley.

Rice, B. (1978). "The New Truth Machines." *Psychology Today,* June, pp. 61–77.

Rice, R. A. (1972). "System Energy and Future Transportation. *Technological Review,* January, 35–36.

Ridenour, M. V., ed. (1978). *Motor Development: Issues and Applications.* Princeton, N.J.: Princeton Book Co.

Ritchie, D. D., and Carola, R. (1979). *Biology.* Reading, Mass.: Addison-Wesley.

Roberts, D. F., and Bachen, C. M. (1981). "Mass Communication Effects." *Annual Review of Psychology* **32,** 307–356.

Roberts, M. J., and Canfield, M. (1980). "Behavior Modification with a Mentally Retarded Child." *American Journal of Nursing* **28**(4), 679.

Robinson, F. P. (1961). *Effective Study.* Rev. ed. New York: Harper & Row.

Rocks, L., and Runyon, R. P. (1972). *The Energy Crisis.* New York: Crown.

Rodin, E. A. (1973). "Psychomotor Epilepsy and Aggressive Behavior." *Archives of General Psychiatry* **28**(2), 210–213.

Roffwarg, H.; Muzio, J.; and Dement, W. (1966). "Ontogenetic Development of the Human Sleep–Dream Cycle." *Science* **152,** 604–619.

Rogers, C. R. (1969). "The Therapeutic Relationship: Recent Theory and Research." In *Contemporary Research in Personality,* edited by I. G. Sarason. Princeton, N.J.: Van Nostrand.

————— (1959). "A Theory of Therapy, Personality and Interpersonal Relationships." In *Psychology: A Study of a Science,* vol. 3: *Formulations of the Person and the Social Context,* edited by S. Koch. New York: McGraw-Hill.

————— (1951). *Client-Centered Therapy.* Boston: Houghton Mifflin.

Rorvik, D. (1972). "How to Relieve Headaches by Warming Your Hands." *Journal,* June, pp. 82–83.

Rosen, E., and Gregory, I. (1965). *Abnormal Psychology.* Philadelphia: Saunders.

Rosenberg, M. S. (1960). "Cognitive Reorganization in Response to the Hypnotic Reversal of Affect." *Journal of Personality* **28,** 39–63.

Rosenthal, R. (1966). *Experimenter Effects in Behavioral Research.* New York: Appleton-Century-Crofts.

Rosenthal, R., and Jacobson, L. (1968). *Pygmalion in the Classroom.* New York: Holt, Rinehart & Winston.

Rosenthal, T. L., and Carroll, W. R. (1972). "Factors in Vicarious Modification of Complex Grammatical Parameters." *Journal of Educational Psychology* **63,** 174–178.

Rosenthal, T. L., and Kellogg, J. S. (1973). "Demonstration versus Instructions in Concept Attainment by Mental Retardants." *Behavior Research and Therapy* **11,** 299–302.

Ross, A., and Braband, J. (1973). "Effect of Increased Responsibility on Bystander Intervention: II. The Cue Value of a Blind Person." *Journal of Personality and Social Psychology* **25**, 254–258.

Routtenberg, A., and Lindy, J. (1965). "Effects of the Availability of Rewarding Septal and Hypothalamic Stimulation on Bar-Pressing for Food under Conditions of Deprivation." *Journal of Comparative and Physiological Psychology* **60**, 158–161.

Rubin, I. (1967). "Increased Self-Acceptance: A Means of Reducing Prejudice." *Journal of Personality and Social Psychology* **5**, 233–238.

Rubin, K. H.; Attewell, P. W.; Tierney, M. C.; and Tumolo, P. (1973). "Development of Spatial Egocentrism and Conservation across the Life Span." *Developmental Psychology* **9**, 432.

Runyon, R. P. (1981). *How Numbers Lie: A Consumer's Guide to the Fine Art of Numerical Deception.* Brattleboro, Vt.: Lewis Publishing.

Runyon, R. P., and Rocks, L. (1973). "The Energy Crisis: A Perspective." Address given before the Academy of Political Science, July 19.

Sachs, J. S.; Brown, R.; and Salerno, R. A. (1976). "Adults' Speech to Children." In *Baby Talk and Infant Speech* (Neurolinguistics 5), edited by W. van Raffler Engel and Y. Lebrum. Amsterdam: Sevets & Zerthlinger, B. V.

Sanders, G. S., and Baron, R. S. (1977). "Is Social Comparison Irrelevant for Producing Choice Shifts?" *Journal of Experimental Social Psychology* **13**, 303–314.

Sarason, I. G., and Sarason, B. R. (1980). *Abnormal Psychology.* 3rd ed. Englewood Cliffs, N.J.: Prentice-Hall.

Sarason, I. G., and Sarason, B. (1957). "Effects of Motivating Instructions and Reports of Failure on Verbal Learning." *American Journal of Psychology* **70**, 92–96.

Sawin, D. B., and Parke, R. D. (1979). "The Effects of Inter-agent Inconsistency on Aggression in Children." Unpublished manuscript, University of Texas.

———— (1972). "Father's Affectionate Stimulation and Caregiving Behaviors in Early Infancy." *Journal of the American Academy of Child Psychiatry* **28**, 509–513.

Scanlon, J. W., and Alper, M. H.

(1974). *Perinatal Pharmacology and Evaluation of the Newborn.* Boston: Little, Brown.

Scarr, S., and Weinberg, R. A. (1976). "I.Q. Test Performance of Black Children Adopted by White Families." *American Psychologist* **31**, 726–739.

Schacht, R., and Nathan, P. E. (1977). "But Is It Good for the Psychologists? Appraisal and Status of DSM-III." *American Psychologist* **32**, 1017–1025.

Schachtel, E. G. (1959). *Metamorphosis.* New York: Basic Books.

Schachter, S. (1965). "Obesity and Eating." *Science* **150**, 971–979.

———— (1959). *The Psychology of Affliction.* Stanford, Calif.: Stanford University Press.

Schachter, S., and Gross, L. (1968). "Manipulated Time and Eating Behavior." *Journal of Personality and Social Psychology* **10**, 98–106.

Schachter, S., and Singer, J. E. (1962). "Cognitive, Social, and Physiological Determinants of Emotional State." *Psychological Review* **69**, 379–399.

Schaefer, E. S., and Aaronson, M. (1970). "Infant Education Research Project." Paper presented at the Conference on Conceptualizations of Preschool Curricula, Center for Advanced Study in Education, City University of New York, May.

Schaffer, H. R., and Emerson, P. (1965). "Patterns of Response to Physical Contact in Early Human Development." *Journal of Child Psychology and Psychiatry* **5**, 1–13.

Schaie, K. W. (1979). "The Primary Mental Abilities in Adulthood: An Exploration in the Development of Psychometric Intelligence." In *Life-Span Development and Behavior,* vol. 2, edited by P. B. Baltes and O. G. Brim. New York: Academic Press.

Schaller, G. B. (1963). *The Mountain Gorilla.* Chicago: University of Chicago Press.

Schlosberg, H. (1954). "Three Dimensions of Emotion." *Psychological Review* **61**, 81–88.

———— (1952). "The Description of Facial Expressions in Terms of Two Dimensions." *Journal of Experimental Psychology* **44**, 229–237.

Schneider, D. J. (1976). *Social Psychology.* Reading, Mass.: Addison-Wesley.

Schoenemann, P.; Byrne, D.; and Bell, P. A. (1976). "A Statistical

Reinterpretation of an Attraction Model." Unpublished manuscript, Purdue University.

Schreiber, F. R. (1973). *Sybil.* Chicago: Contemporary Books.

Schwartz, G. E. (1974). "TM Relaxes Some People and Makes Them Feel Better." *Psychology Today,* April, pp. 3–44.

Schwartz, G. E., and Weiss, S. M., eds. (1978). *Proceedings of Yale Conference on Behavioral Medicine.* Washington, D.C.: U.S. Government Printing Office. Department of Health, Education, and Welfare No. NIH, 78-1424.

Schwartz, S. H., and Gottlieb, A. (1980). "Bystander Anonymity and Reactions to Emergencies." *Journal of Personality and Social Psychology* **39**: 418–430.

Sclafani, A. (1976). "Appetite and Hunger in Experimental Obesity Syndrome." In *Hunger: Basic Mechanisms and Clinical Implications,* edited by D. Novin, W. Wyrwicka, and G. Bray. New York: Raven Press.

Sclafani, A., and Kluge, L. (1974). "Food Motivation and Body Weight—Level I. Hypothalamic Hyperphagic Rats: A Dual Lipostat Model of Hunger and Appetite." *Journal of Comparative and Physiological Psychology* **86**, 28–46.

Scott, J. (1969). "Performance after Abrupt Arousal from Sleep: Comparison of a Simple Motor, a Visual-Perceptual and a Cognitive Task." *Proceedings: 77th Annual Convention of the APA,* pp. 225–226.

Scott, J. P. (1980). "The Function of Emotions in Behavioral Systems: A Systems Theory Analysis." In *Emotion: Theory, Research and Experience,* vol. 1, edited by R. Plutchik and H. Kellerman. New York: Academic Press.

———— (1962). "Critical Periods in Behavior Development." *Science* **138**, 949–958.

Scovern, A. W., and Kilmann, P. R. (1980). "Status of Electroconvulsive Therapy: Review of the Outcome Literature." *Psychological Bulletin* **87**, 260–303.

Sears, R. R. (1936). "Experimental Studies of Projection: I. Attribution of Traits." *Journal of Social Psychology* **7**, 151–163.

Sears, R. R.; Maccoby, E. E.; and Levin, H. (1957). *Patterns of Child Rearing.* Evanston, Ill.: Row, Peterson.

Sears, R. R.; Whiting, J.W.M.; Nowlis, V.; and Sears, P. S. (1953). "Some Child Rearing Antecedents of Aggression and Dependency in Young Children." *Genetic Psychology Monographs* **47**, 135–234.

Seedman, A., and Hellman, P. (1974). "Why Kitty Genovese Haunts New York: The Untold Story." *New York* **7**(July 29), 32–41.

See, C. (1975). "Anorexia Nervosa is Starvation by Choice." *Today's Health* **53**(5) (May), 46–50.

Seer, P. (1979). "Psychological Control of Essential Hypertension: Review of the Literature and Methodological Critique. *Psychological Bulletin* **86**, 1015–1043.

Segal, M. W. (1974). "Alphabet and Attraction: An Unobtrusive Measure of the Effect of Propinquity in a Field Setting." *Journal of Personality and Social Psychology* **30**, 654–657.

Seiden, R. H. (1970). "We're Driving Young Blacks to Suicide." *Psychology Today* **4**, 24–28.

———— (1966). "Campus Tragedy: The Study of Student Suicide." *Journal of Abnormal Psychology* **71**, 389–399.

Seligman, M.E.P. (1974). "Submissive Death: Giving Up on Life." *Psychology Today* **7**, 80–85.

———— (1971). "Phobias and Preparedness." *Behavior Therapy* **2**, 307–320.

Seligman, M.E.P.; Maier, S. F.; and Solomon, R. L. (1969). "Unpredictable and Uncontrollable Aversive Events." In *Aversive Conditioning and Learning,* edited by F. R. Brush. New York: Academic Press.

Selye, H. (1978). *The Stress of Life.* Rev. ed. New York: McGraw-Hill.

———— (1973). "The Evolution of the Stress Concept." *American Scientist* **61**, 692–699.

———— (1956). *The Stress of Life.* New York: McGraw-Hill.

Shaffer, L. F., and Shoben, E. J. (1956). *The Psychology of Adjustment.* 2nd ed. Boston: Houghton Mifflin.

Shapiro, D.; Tursky, B.; Gershon, E.; and Stern, E. (1969). "Effects of Feedback and Reinforcement on the Control of Human Systolic Pressure." *Science* **163**, 588–590.

Shatz, M., and Gelman, R. (1973). "The Development of Communication Skills: Modifications in the Speech of Young Children as a Function of

Listener." *Monographs of the Society for Research in Child Development* **38**(152).

Shaw, M. E. (1964). "Communication Networks." In *Advances in Experimental Social Psychology,* vol. 1, edited by L. Berkowitz. New York: Academic Press.

Sheehy, G. (1976). *Passages.* New York: Dutton.

Sheldon, W. (1944). "Constitutional Factors in Personality." In *Personality and the Behavior Disorders,* edited by J. McV. Hunt. New York: Ronald Press.

———— (1940). *The Varieties of Human Physique.* New York: Harper & Row.

Sherman, M. C., and Sherman, I. C. (1929). *The Process of Human Behavior.* New York: Norton.

Shiffrin, R. M. (1970). "Forgetting: Trace Erosion or Retrieval Failure?" *Science* **168**, 1601–1603.

Shirley, M. M. (1933). *The First Two Years.* Institute of Child Welfare, Monograph No. 7. Minneapolis: University of Minnesota Press.

Shoben, E. J., Jr. (1957). "Toward a Concept of the Normal Personality." *American Psychologist* **12**, 183–189.

Shotland, R. L., and Huston, J. L. (1979). "Emergencies: What Are They and Do They Influence Bystanders to Intervene?" *Journal of Personality and Social Psychology* **37**, 1822–1834.

Shultz, T. R., and Horibe, F. (1974). "Development of the Appreciation of Verbal Jokes." *Developmental Psychology* **10**, 13–20.

Sigerist, H. E. (1951). *A History of Medicine.* Vol. 1. New York: Oxford University Press.

Simmons, R. C. (1981). *Understanding Human Behavior in Health and Illness.* 2nd ed. Baltimore: Williams and Wilkins.

Simon, C. W., and Emmons, W. H. (1956). "Responses to Material Presented during Various Levels of Sleep." *Journal of Experimental Psychology* **51**, 89–97.

Skeels, H. M. (1966). "Adult Status of Children with Contrasting Early Life Experiences: A Follow-Up Study. *Monographs of the Society for Research in Child Development* **31**(105), 1–65.

Skinner, B. F. (1957). *Verbal Behavior.* New York: Appleton-Century-Crofts.

Sloane, R. B.; Staples, F. R.; Cristol, A. H.; Yorkston, N. J.; and Whipple, K. (1975). *Psychotherapy*

*versus Behavior Therapy.* Cambridge, Mass.: Harvard University Press.

Smith, B. M. (1971). *The Polygraph in Contemporary Psychology.* San Francisco: Freeman.

Smith, D. E. (1970). *Journal of Psychedelic Drugs.* Vol. 3, no. 1 San Francisco: Haight-Ashbury Free Medical Clinic.

Smith, M. L., and Glass, G. V. (1977). "Meta-Analysis of Psychotherapy Outcome Studies." *American Psychologist* **32**, 752–760.

Snow, C. E. (1977). "The Development of Conversation between Mothers and Babies." *Journal of Child Language* **4**, 1–22.

———— (1972). "Mothers' Speech to Children Learning Language." *Child Development* **43**, 549–565.

Snyder, F. (1966). "Toward an Evolutionary Theory of Dreaming." *American Journal of Psychiatry* **123**, 1221–1236.

Snyder, S., and Lampanella, V. (1969). "Psychedelic Experiences in Hysterical Psychosis and Schizophrenia." *Communications in Behavioral Biology* **3**, 85–91.

Snyder, S. H. (1970). "What We Have Forgotten about Pot—A Pharmacologist's History." *New York Times Magazine,* December 13.

Snyder, W. U. (1947). *Casebook of Non-Directive Counseling.* Boston: Houghton Mifflin.

Sontag, S. (1972). "The Double Standard of Aging." *Saturday Review,* September 23, pp. 29–38.

Sorrentino, R. M., and Boutillier, R. G. (1975). "The Effect of Quantity and Quality of Verbal Interaction on Ratings of Leadership Ability." *Journal of Experimental Social Psychology* **11**, 403–411.

Spence, J. T., and Helmreich, R. L. (1979). "The Many Faces of Androgyny: A Reply to Locksley and Colten." *Journal of Personality and Social Psychology* **37**, 1032–1046.

———— (1978). *Masculinity and Femininity: Their Psychological Dimensions, Correlates, and Antecedents.* Austin: University of Texas Press.

Sperry, R. W. (1968). "Hemisphere Deconnection and Unity in Conscious Awareness." *American Psychologist* **23**, 723–733.

Spiegel, H. (1970). "A Single-Treatment Method to Stop Smoking Using Ancillary Self-Hypnosis." *International Journal of Clinical Hypnosis* **18**, 235–250.

Spiro, M. E. (1958). *Children of the Kibbutz.* Cambridge, Mass.: Harvard University Press.

Stachnik, T. J. (1980). "Priorities for Psychology in Medical Education and Health Care Delivery." *American Psychologist* **35,** 8–15.

Stark, R., and McEvoy, J., III (1970). "Middle-Class Violence." *Psychology Today* **4**(6), 52–54.

Stearman, M. B. (1973). Cited in "Controlling Epilepsy by Biofeedback" (1973). *Science News* **104**(9), 132–133.

Stein, A. H., and Bailey, M. M. (1973). "The Socialization of Achievement Orientation in Females." *Psychological Bulletin* **80,** 345–366.

Stephans, J. H.; Harris, A. H.; Brady, J. V.; and Shaffer, J. W. (1975). "Psychological and Physiological Variables Associated with Large Magnitude Voluntary Heart Rate Changes." *Psychophysiology* **12,** 381–387.

Sterman, M. B. (1973). "Neurophysiological and Clinical Studies of Sensory Motor EEG Biofeedback Training: Some Effects on Epilepsy." In *Seminars in Psychiatry,* edited by L. Birk. New York: Grune & Stratton.

Sternbach, R. (1963). "Congenital Insensitivity to Pain." *Psychological Bulletin* **60,** 252–264.

Stevens, C. F. (1979). "The Neuron." *Scientific American* **241**(3), 54–66.

Stoller, R. J.; Marmon, J.; Bieber, I.; Gold, R.; Socarides, C. W.; Green, R.; and Spitzer, R. I. (1973). "A Symposium: Should Homosexuality Be in the APA Nomenclature?" *American Journal of Psychiatry* **130,** 1207–1216.

Stone, L. J., and Church, J. (1973). *Childhood and Adolescence.* 3rd ed. New York: Random House.

Stoner, J.A.F. (1961). "A Comparison of Individual and Group Decisions Involving Risk." Unpublished master's thesis, Massachusetts Institute of Technology.

Stricker, E., and Zigmond, M. (1976). "Brain Catecholamines and the Lateral Hypothalamic Syndrome." In *Hunger: Basic Mechanisms and Clinical Implications,* edited by D. Novin, W. Wyrwicka, and G. Bray. New York: Raven Press.

Stricker, L. J.; Messick, S.; and Jackson, D. N. (1967). "Suspicion of Deception: Implications for Conformity Research." *Journal of Personality and Social Psychology* **5,** 379–389.

Stroebe, W.; Insko, C. A.; Thompson, V. D.; and Layton, B. D. (1971). "Effects of Physical Attractiveness, Attitude Similarity, and Sex on Various Aspects of Interpersonal Attraction." *Journal of Personality and Social Psychology* **18,** 79–91.

Sue, D.; Sue, D. W.; and Sue, S. (1981). *Understanding Abnormal Behavior.* Boston: Houghton Mifflin.

Suinn, R. M. (1971). "The Application of Short-Term Video-Tape Therapy for the Treatment of Test Anxiety of College Students." Unpublished report, Colorado State University.

――― (1970). *Fundamentals of Behavior Pathology.* New York: Wiley.

Suls, J., and Kalle, R. J. (1979). "Children's Moral Judgments as a Function of Intention, Damage, and an Action's Physical Harm." *Developmental Psychology* **15**(1), 93–94.

Suomi, S. J.; Harlow, H. F.; and McKinney, W. T. (1972). "Monkey Psychiatrists." *American Journal of Psychiatry* **128,** 927–932.

Supa, M.; Cotzin, M.; and Dallenbach, K. M. (1944). "Facial Vision: The Perception of Obstacles by the Blind." *American Journal of Psychology* **57,** 133–183.

Surwillo, W. W. (1963). "The Relation of Simple Response Time to Brain Wave Frequency and the Effects of Age." *Electroencephalography and Clinical Neurophysiology* **15,** 105–114.

Sussman, H. M., and MacNeilage, P. F. (1975). "Studies of Hemispheric Specialization for Speech Production." *Brain and Language* **2**(2), 131–151.

Sutherland, J. M., and Trait, H. (1969). *The Epilepsies: Modern Diagnosis and Treatment.* Edinburgh: Livingstone.

Szondi, L.; Moser, U.; and Webb, M. W. (1959). *The Szondi Test.* Philadelphia: Lippincott.

Szyrynski, V. (1973). "Anorexia Nervosa and Psychotherapy." *American Journal of Psychotherapy* **27**(4), 492–505.

Tanner, J. M. (1973). "Growing Up." *Scientific American* **229**(3), 35–43.

Tapp, J. L. (1976). "Psychology and the Law: An Overture." *Annual Review of Psychology* **27,** 359–404.

Tarjan, G., and Eisenberg, L. (1972). "Some Thoughts on the Classification of Mental Retardation in the United States of America. *American Journal of Psychiatry,* supplement, **128**(11), 14–18.

Tarler-Benlolo, L. (1978). "The Role of Relaxation in Biofeedback Training: A Critical Review of the Literature." *Psychological Bulletin* **85**(4), 727–755.

Tassinari, C. A.; Peraita-Adrados, M. R.; Ambrosetto, G.; and Gastaut, H. (1974). "Effects of Marijuana and Delta-9-THC at High Doses in Man: A Polygraphic Study." *Electroencephalography and Clinical Neurophysiology* **36**(1), 94.

Taylor, D. W.; Berry, P. C.; and Block, C. H. (1957). "Does Group Participation When Using Brainstorming Facilitate or Inhibit Creative Thinking?" Technical Report No. 1, Yale University, Department of Psychology, Office of Naval Research.

Taylor, I. (1977). *Introduction to Psycholinguistics.* New York: Holt, Rinehart & Winston.

Taylor, S., and Mettee, D. (1971). "When Similarity Breeds Contempt." *Journal of Personality and Social Psychology* **20,** 75–81.

Teitlebaum, P. (1964). "Appetite." *Proceedings of the American Philosophical Society* **108,** 464–472.

Terman, L. M., ed. (1925). *Genetic Studies of Genius.* Vol. 1. Stanford, Calif.: Stanford University Press.

Terman, L. M., and Merril, M. A. (1960). *Stanford–Binet Intelligence Scale.* Boston: Houghton Mifflin.

Terman, L. M., and Oden, M. H. (1959). *Genetic Studies of Genius,* vol. 5: *The Gifted Child at Midlife.* Stanford, Calif.: Stanford University Press.

――― (1947). *The Gifted Child Grows Up.* Stanford, Calif.: Stanford University Press.

Terrace, H. (1979). *Nim.* New York: Alfred A. Knopf.

Thomas, A., and Chess, S. (1977). *Temperament and Development.* New York: Brunner/Mazel.

Thomas, A.; Chess, S.; and Birch, H. G. (1970). "The Origin of Personality." *Scientific American* **223,** 102–109.

Thomas, D. W., and Mayer, J. (1973). "The Search for the Secret of Fat." *Psychology Today,* September, pp. 74–79.

Thomas, W. I. (1937). *Primitive Behavior: An Introduction to the Social Sciences.* New York: McGraw-Hill.

Thompson, T. (1972). "Richie." *Life,* May 5, pp. 58–72.

Thorndike, R. L. (1938). "The Effect of Discussion upon the Correctness of Group Decisions When the Factor of Majority Influence Is Allowed For." *Journal of Social Psychology* **9,** 343–362.

Tilker, H. A. (1970). "Socially Responsible Behavior as a Function of Observer Responsibility and Victim Feedback." *Journal of Personality and Social Psychology* **14,** 95–100.

*Time* (1980). "Are Those Apes Really Talking?" March 10, pp. 50–57.

———— (1971). "Redefining Violence." June 14, p. 49.

Torrance, E. P. (1969). "Peer Influences on Preschool Children's Willingness to Try Difficult Tasks." *Journal of Psychology* **72,** 189–194.

Touhey, J. C. (1972). "Comparison of Two Dimensions of Attitude Similarity on Heterosexual Attraction." *Journal of Personality and Social Psychology* **23,** 8–10.

Trevarthen, C., and Kinsbourne, M. (1974). Unpublished study cited in Nebes, R. D. (1974). "Hemispheric Specialization in Commissurotomized Man." *Psychological Bulletin* **81**(1), 1–14.

Turnbull, J. W. (1962). "Asthma Conceived as a Learned Response. *Journal of Psychosomatic Research* **6,** 59–70.

Tyler, L. E. (1981). "More Stately Mansions—Psychology Extends Its Boundaries." *Annual Review of Psychology* **32,** 1–20.

Tyler, R. W. (1933). "Permanence of Learning." *Journal of Higher Education* **4**(April), 204, Table 1.

Ubell, E. (1981). "Upsetting an Old Taboo." *Parade,* November 1, pp. 4–5.

Ullmann, L. P., and Krasner, L. (1969). *A Psychological Approach to Abnormal Behavior.* Englewood Cliffs, N.J.: Prentice-Hall.

Underwood, B. J. (1961). "Ten Years of Massed Practice on Distributed Practice." *Psychological Review* **68,** 229–247.

Ungerstedt, U. (1971). "Sterotaxic Mapping of the Monomine Pathways in the Rat." *Acta Physiologica Scandinavica* **367,** 1–48.

Vachon, L., et al. (1976). "Bronchial Effects of Marijuana Smoke in Asthma." In *Pharmacology of Marijuana,* edited by M. Braude and S. Szarn. New York: Raven Press.

Valenstein, E. S. (1973). *Brain Control.* New York: Wiley.

Van Praag, H. M. (1978). "Neural-endocrine Disorders in Depression and Their Significance for the Monoamine Hypothesis of Depression." *Acta Psychiatrica Scandinavica* **57,** 389–404.

Vaughan, G. M. (1964). "The Trans-Situational Aspect of Conforming Behavior." *Journal of Personality* **32,** 335–354.

Vinokur, A., and Burnstein, E. (1978). "Depolarization of Attitudes in Groups." *Journal of Personality and Social Psychology* **36,** 872–885.

Vogel, G.; Thurmond, A.; Gibbons, P.; Sloan, K.; Boyd, M.; and Walker, M. (1975). "REM sleep Reduction Effects on Depression Syndromes." *Archives of General Psychiatry* **32,** 765–777.

Wahler, R. G. (1969). "Infant Social Development: Some Experimental Analysis of an Infant–Mother Interaction during the First Year of Life." *Journal of Experimental Child Psychology* **7,** 101–113.

Wallace, R. K., and Benson, H. (1972). "The Physiology of Meditation." *Scientific American,* February.

Wallace, W. H.; Turner, S. H.; and Perkins, C. C. (1957). "Preliminary Studies of Human Information Storage." *Signal Corps Project No. 1320.* Institute for Cooperative Research, University of Pennsylvania.

Wallach, M. A. (1970). "Creativity." In *Carmichael's Manual of Child Psychology,* 3rd ed., edited by P. H. Mussen. New York: Wiley.

Wallach, M. A., and Wing, C. W., Jr. (1969). *The Talented Student: A Validation of the Creativity–Intelligence Distinction.* New York: Holt, Rinehart & Winston.

Warren, W. (1968). "A Study of Anorexia Nervosa in Young Girls." *Journal of Child Psychology and Psychiatry and Allied Disciplines* **9**(1), 27–40.

Watson, W. C. (1981). *Physiological Psychology.* Boston: Houghton Mifflin.

Webb, W. (1968). *Sleep: An Experimental Approach.* New York: Macmillan.

Wechsler, D. (1958). *The Measurement and Appraisal of Adult Intelligence.* 4th ed. Baltimore: Williams & Wilkins.

Wechsler, H.; Grosser, G. H.; and Greenblatt, M. (1965). "Research Evaluating Anti-depressant Medications on Hospitalized Mental Patients: A Survey of Published Reports during a 5-Year Period." *Journal of Nervous and Mental Disease* **141,** 231–239.

Weil, A. T.; Zinberg, N. E.; and Nelson, J. M. (1969). "Clinical and Psychological Effects of Marijuana in Man." *Science* **162,** 1234–1242.

Weiss, J. M. (1971). "Effects of Coping Behavior in Different Warning Signal Conditions on Stress Pathology in Rats." *Journal of Comparative and Physiological Psychology* **77,** 1–13.

———— (1968). "Effects of Coping Responses on Stress." *Journal of Comparative and Physiological Psychology* **65,** 251–260.

Weiss, J. M.; Glazer, H. I.; and Pohorecky, L. A. (1974). "Neurotransmitters and Helplessness: A Chemical Bridge to Depression?" *Psychology Today* **8,** 58–62.

Weiss, T., and Engel, B. T. (1975). "Evaluation of an Intracardiac Limit of Learned Heart Rate Control." *Psychophysiology* **12,** 310–312.

Wells, G. L., and Harvey, J. H. (1977). "Do People Use Consensus Information in Making Causal Attributions?" *Journal of Personality and Social Psychology* **35**(5), 279–293.

Whalen, R., and Edwards, D. (1966). "Sexual Reversibility in Neonatally Castrated Male Rats." *Journal of Comparative and Physiological Psychology* **62,** 307–311.

Whalen, R. G. (1949). "Where Were You the Night of April 23, 1935?" *New York Times Magazine,* December 18, p. 18.

White, B. L. (1972). "Fundamental Early Environmental Influences on the Development of Competence." In *Third Symposium on Learning: Cognitive Learning,* edited by M. E. Meyer.

White, W. A. (1932). *Outline of Psychiatry.* New York: Nervous and Mental Disease Publishing Co.

Whorf, B. L. (1956). *Language, Thought and Reality.* New York: Wiley.

———— (1947). "Science and Linguistics." In *Readings in Social Psychology,* edited by T. M. Newcomb and E. L. Hartley. New York: Holt.

Wickelgren, W. A. (1981). "Human

Learning and Memory." *Annual Review of Psychology* **32**, 21–52.

———— (1977). *Learning and Memory.* Englewood Cliffs, N.J.: Prentice-Hall.

Wickes, I. G. (1958). "Treatment of Persistent Enuresis with the Electric Buzzer." *Archives of Diseases in Childhood* **33**, 160–164.

Wiggins, J. S.; Renner, K. E.; Clore, G. L.; and Rose, R. J. (1976). *Principles of Personality.* Reading, Mass.: Addison-Wesley.

Wilson, W. C. (1975). "The Distribution of Selected Sexual Attitudes and Behaviors among the Adult Population of the United States." *Journal of Sex Research* **11**(1), 46–64.

Winterbottom, M. R. (1953). "The Relation of Childhood Training in Independence to Achievement Motivation." Unpublished Ph.D. dissertation, University of Michigan. Abstract in University Microfilms, Publication No. 5113.

Wold, C. I. (1970). "Characteristics of 26,000 Suicide Prevention Center Patients." *Bulletin of Suicidology* **6**, 24–28.

Wolf, S., and Wolff, H. G. (1947). *Human Gastric Functions.* New York: Oxford University Press.

Wolff, P. H. (1963). "Observations on the Early Development of Smiling." In *Determinants of Infant Behavior,* vol. 2, edited by B. M. Ross. New York: Wiley.

Wolpe, J. (1969). "For Phobia: A Hair of the Hound." *Psychology Today* **3**(1), 34–37.

Wood, F., and Kinsbourne, M. (1974).

Paper in *Symposium on Pathological Forgetting.* Boston: International Neuropsychology Society, February 8.

Woodruff, D. S. (1975). "Relationships among EEG Alpha Frequency, Reaction Time and Age: A Biofeedback Study." *Psychophysiology* **12**(6), 673–681.

Worchel, S., and Cooper, J. (1979). *Understanding Social Psychology.* Rev. ed. Homewood, Ill.: Dorsey Press.

World Health Organization (1974). Cited in Tuohy, W. (1974). "World Health Agency Zeroes in on Suicide." *Los Angeles Times,* October 25, pp. 1–3.

Wortis, J. (1972). "Comments on the ICD Classification of Mental Retardation." *American Journal of Psychiatry,* supplement, **128**(11), 21–24.

Yablonsky, L. (1976). *Psychodrama: Resolving Emotional Problems through Role-Playing.* New York: Basic Books.

Yang, R. K.; Zweig, A. R.; Douthitt, T. C.; and Federman, E. J. (1976). "Successive Relationships between Maternal Attitudes during Pregnancy, Analgesic Medication during Labor and Delivery, and Newborn Behavior." *Developmental Psychology* **12**(1), 6–14.

Yarrow, M. R., and Scott, P. M. (1972). "Imitation of Nurturant and Nonnurturant Models." *Journal of Personality and Social Psychology* **23**, 259–270.

Yarrow, M. R.; Scott, P. M.; and Wexler, C. Z. (1973). "Learning Concern for Others." *Developmental Psychology* **8**, 240–260.

Young, P. (1981). "Psychologist Has People Figured." *Arizona Daily Star,* December 3, p. 7c.

Zajonc, R. B. (1975). "Dumber by the Dozen." *Psychology Today,* January, pp. 37–43.

Zander, A. (1979). "The Psychology of Group Processes." *Annual Review of Psychology* **30**, 417–451.

Zelazo, N. A.; Zelazo, P. R.; and Kolb, S. (1972). "Walking in the Newborn." *Science* **176**, 314–315.

Zelnik, M., and Kantner, J. (1972). Survey of Female Adolescent Sexual Behavior. Conducted for the Commission on Population, Washington, D.C.

Zelson, C.; Rubio, E.; and Wasserman, E. (1971). "Neonatal Narcotic Addiction: 10 Year Observation." *Pediatrics* **48**, 178–189.

Zimmerman, B. J., and Pike, E. O. (1972). "Effects of Modeling and Reinforcement on Acquisition and Generalization of Question-Asking Behavior." *Child Development* **43**, 892–907.

Zimmerman, W. (1970). "Sleep Mentation and Auditory Awakening Thresholds." *Psychophysiology* **6**, 540–549.

Zubin, J. (1977/1978). "But Is it Good for Science?" *Clinical Psychologist* **31**, 1.

**Text credits (by page number)**

**16:** Box 1.2, excerpt from *Roots* by Alex Haley. Copyright © 1976 by Alex Haley. Reprinted by permission of Doubleday & Company, Inc.

**24–25:** Box 1.4, from *Psychological Research: An Introduction,* 2nd ed., by Arthur J. Bachrach. Copyright © 1962 by Random House, Inc. Reprinted by permission of the publisher.

**45–46:** From *Behavior Pathology,* by Norman Cameron and Ann Magaret. Copyright © 1951 by Houghton Mifflin Company, renewed 1979. Used by permission.

**55:** From *Contemporary Psychology and Effective Behavior,* 4th ed., by J. C. Coleman. Copyright © 1979 Scott, Foresman and Company.

**76–77:** Box 2.5, from J. S. Wiggins *et al., Principles of Personality.* Reading, Mass.: Addison-Wesley, © 1976 Reprinted by permission.

**86:** Box 3.1, from Arnold L. Glass, Keith J. Holyoak, and J. L. Santa, *Cognitive Psychology.* Reading, Mass.: Addison-Wesley, © 1979. Reprinted by permission.

**99:** Box 3.3, excerpt from *Roots* by Alex Haley. Copyright © 1976 by Alex Haley. Reprinted by permission of Doubleday & Company, Inc.

**102–103:** From Arnold L. Glass, Keith J. Holyoak, and J. L. Santa, *Cognitive Psychology.* Reading, Mass.: Addision-Wesley, © 1979. Reprinted by permission.

**120–121:** From *American Scientist,* Journal of Sigma Xi, The Scientific Research Society. **67:**312 (1979). Loftus, E. F., "The Malleability of Human Memory."

**147:** Jean Berko, "The Child's Learning of English Morphology," *Word* **14,** 1958, pp. 154–155. Reprinted by permission.

**180–181:** Box 5.2, from *Abnormal Psychology and Modern Life,* 5th ed., by J. C. Coleman. Copyright © 1976 Scott, Foresman and Company.

**270:** Box 7.4, from *Contemporary Psychology and Effective Behavior,* 4th ed., by J. C. Coleman. Copyright © 1979 Scott, Foresman and Company.

**274–275:** Box 7.5, from "Marijuana (II): Does it Damage the Brain?", Maugh, T. H., II, *Science* Vol. 185, pp. 775–776, August 30, 1974. Copyright © 1974 by the American Association for the Advancement of Science.

**292:** Box 8.1, from *Abnormal Psychology and Modern Life,* 5th ed., by J. C. Coleman. Copyright © 1976 Scott, Foresman and Company.

**347:** From *Abnormal Psychology and Modern Life,* 5th ed., by J. C. Coleman. Copyright © 1976 Scott, Foresman and Company.

**350:** From *Abnormal Psychology and Modern Life,* 5th ed., by J. C. Coleman. Copyright © 1976 Scott, Foresman and Company.

**354:** From *Behavior Pathology,* by Norman Cameron and Ann Magaret. Copyright © 1951 by Houghton Mifflin Company, renewed 1979. Used by permission.

**356:** From *Behavior Pathology,* by Norman Cameron and Ann Magaret. Copyright © 1951 by Houghton Mifflin Company, renewed 1979. Used by permission.

**371:** From James E. Birren *et al.: Developmental Psychology: A Life-Span Approach.* Copyright © 1981 by Houghton Mifflin Company, pp. 123–124. Used by permission.

**372–373:** Box 10.1, from Ritchie and Carola, *Biology,* © 1979. Reading, Mass.: Addison-Wesley, pp. 302–303. Reprinted with permission.

**380:** Box 10.2, from James E. Birren *et al.: Developmental Psychology: A Life-Span Approach.* Copyright © 1981 by Houghton Mifflin Company. Used by permission.

**426–427:** Box 11.3, from Marshall, "Teenage suicides: Why our children are killing themselves." *Ebony,* September, 1981, pp. 36–38.

**506:** Box 14.1, from *Abnormal Psychology and Modern Life,* 5th edition, by James C. Coleman. Copyright © 1976, 1972, 1964 by Scott, Foresman and Company. Reprinted by permission of the publisher.

**509:** Box 14.2, adapted from *Understanding Abnormal Behavior,* by David Sue *et al.* Copyright © 1981 by Houghton Mifflin Company. Used by permission.

**512:** From *Fundamentals of Behavior Pathology,* by R. M. Suinn. Copyright 1970, John Wiley and Sons, Inc. p. 242. Used by permission.

**513:** Box 14.3, from *Abnormal Psychology and Modern Life,* 5th edition, by James C. Coleman. Copyright © 1976, 1972, 1964 by Scott, Foresman and Company. Reprinted by permission of the publisher.

**514:** From *Behavior Pathology,* by Norman Cameron and Ann Magaret. Copyright © 1951 by Houghton Mifflin Company, renewed 1979. Used by permission.

**517:** From *Abnormal Psychology in the Human Context,* by R. H. Price and S. J. Lynn. Copyright © 1981, The Dorsey Press. Used by permission.

**518:** Box 14.4, from Norman Cameron: *Personality Development and Psychopathology: A Dynamic Approach,* pp. 282, 287, 291, 294. Copyright © 1963 by Houghton

# ACKNOWLEDGMENTS

Mifflin Company. Used by permission. Also from *Abnormal Psychology in the Human Context,* by R. H. Price and S. J. Lynn. Copyright © 1981, The Dorsey Press. Used by permission.

**521–522:** From *Fundamentals of Behavior Pathology,* by R. M. Suinn. Copyright 1970, John Wiley and Sons, Inc., p. 238. Used by permission.

**523–524:** From *Childhood Pathology and Later Adjustment: The Question of Prediction,* by L. K. Cass and C. B. Thomas. Copyright 1979, John Wiley and Sons, Inc., p. 175. Used by permission.

**526–527:** Box 14.5, adapted from *Understanding Abnormal Behavior,* by David Sue et al. Copyright © 1981 by Houghton Mifflin Company. Used by permission.

**528–529:** Box 14.6, from Ubell, E., "Upsetting an old taboo." *Parade,* November 1, 1981.

**530:** From *Sex and Human Life,* 2nd edition, by E. T. Pengelley, copyright © 1978. Reading, Mass.: Addison-Wesley, pp. 104–105. Reprinted with permission.

**530–531:** From *Moodswing: The Third Revolution in Psychiatry,* by Ronald R. Fieve, M.D. Copyright © 1975 by Ronald R. Fieve. By permission of William Morrow & Company.

**533–539:** From *Fundamentals of Behavior Pathology,* by R. M. Suinn. Copyright 1970, John Wiley and Sons, Inc. Reprinted by permission.

**540:** From *Abnormal Psychology and Modern Life,* 5th edition, by James C. Coleman, p. 550. Copyright © 1976, 1972, 1964 by Scott, Foresman and Company. Reprinted by permission of the publisher.

**544–545:** From *Systems of Psychotherapy,* by J. O. Prochaska. Copyright © 1979 by The Dorsey Press. Reprinted with permission.

**549–550:** From L. F. Shaffer and E. J. Shoben: *The Psychology of Adjustment,* 2nd edition, pp. 516–517. Copyright © 1956 by Houghton Mifflin Company. Used by permission.

**551:** Box 15.1, adapted from *Understanding Abnormal Behavior,* by David Sue et al. Copyright © 1981 by Houghton Mifflin Company. Used by permission.

**551–552:** From William U. Snyder: *Casebook of Non-directive Counseling,* pp. 82–85. Copyright

© 1947, renewed 1974 by Houghton Mifflin Company. Used by permission.

**556:** Box 15.2, From *Abnormal Psychology in the Human Context,* by R. H. Price and S. J. Lynn. Copyright © 1981, The Dorsey Press. Used by permission.

**558:** Reprinted with permission from *Behaviour Research and Therapy,* 1963 (I), T. Ayllon, "Intensive treatment of psychotic behaviour by stimulus satiation and food reinforcement." Copyright 1963, Pergamon Press, Ltd.

**559:** From *Fundamentals of Behavior Pathology,* R. M. Suinn. Copyright 1970 by John Wiley and Sons, Inc. Reprinted with permission.

**561:** Reprinted with permission from *Behaviour Research and Therapy,* 1963 (I), T. Ayllon, "Intensive treatment of psychotic behaviour by stimulus satiation and food reinforcement." Copyright 1963, Pergamon Press, Ltd.

**568–569:** Box 15.4, from *Abnormal Psychology and Modern Life,* 5th edition, by James C. Coleman. Copyright © 1976, 1972, 1964 by Scott, Foresman and Company. Reprinted by permission of the publisher.

**571:** From *Abnormal Psychology in the Human Context,* by R. H. Price and S. J. Lynn. Copyright © 1981, The Dorsey Press. Used by permission.

**575:** Box 15.5, From *Abnormal Psychology in the Human Context,* by R. H. Price and S. J. Lynn. Copyright © 1981, The Dorsey Press. Used by permission.

**576–577:** From *Systems of Psychotherapy,* by J. O. Prochaska. Copyright © 1979 by The Dorsey Press. Reprinted with permission.

**576–577:** Box 15.6, from *Abnormal Psychology in the Human Context,* by R. J. Price and S. J. Lynn. Copyright © 1981, The Dorsey Press. Used by permission.

**Table credits**

**Table 9.1:** From T. H. Holmes and R. J. Rahe, "The social readjustment rating scale." *Journal of Psychosomatic Research,* 1967, **11,** pp. 213–218.

**Table 10.2:** Reprinted with permission of Macmillan Publishing Co., Inc. from *Psycholinguistics* by Roger Brown. Copyright © 1970 by The Free Press, a Division of Macmillan Publishing Co., Inc.

**Table 12.1:** Reproduced by permission of Riverside Publishing Company.

**Table 12.3:** James E. Birren et al.: *Developmental Psychology: A Life-Span Approach.* Copyright © 1981 by Houghton Mifflin Company. Used by permission.

**Figure credits**

**Fig. 1.2:** Wide World Photos

**Fig. 2.7:** Pfizer, Inc.

**Fig. 2.9:** Teaching Machines, Incorporated—A Division of Grolier Incorporated

**Fig. 2.10:** Elizabeth Hamlin/Stock, Boston.

**Fig. 2.13:** Stephen Wicks

**Fig. 2.16:** Yerkes Regional Primate Research Center

**Fig. 2.17:** After W. O. Jenkins, H. McFann, and F. L. Clayton, "A Methodological Study of Extinction Following Aperiodic and Continuous Reinforcement," *Journal of Comparative and Physiological Psychology* **43,** 1950, pp. 155–167. Copyright © 1950 by the American Psychological Association. Used by permission.

**Fig. 2.19:** Elliott Erwitt/Magnum

**Fig. 2.22:** Albert Bandura

**Fig. 3.1:** Mindy Jassenoff

**Fig. 3.2:** Mindy Jassenoff

**Fig. 3.9:** Courtesy of Ralph Gerbrands Co., Arlington, Mass.

**Fig. 3.20:** Elizabeth Loftus, University of Washington

**Fig. 3.21:** Customtime Corporation, Philadelphia, Pa.

**Fig. 3.24:** Courtesy of Dr. Harry F. Harlow, University of Wisconsin Primate Laboratory

**Fig. 4.3:** Photo Courtesy of R. A. and B. T. Gardner

**Fig. 4.6:** E. Sue Savage-Rumbaugh, Yerkes Regional Primate Research Center

**Fig. 4.7:** From Jean Berko, "The Child's Learning of English Morphology," *Word* **14,** 1958, pp. 154–155. Reprinted by permission.

**Fig. 4.12:** Mindy Jassenoff

**Fig. 5.5:** E. R. Lewis, T. E. Everhart, and Y. Y. Zeevi, *Science* 165, 1140–1143, September 12, 1969.

**Fig. 5.7(a):.** Courtesy of Dr. Neal E. Miller, The Rockefeller University

**Fig. 5.8:** Dr. José M. R. Delgado, 1963, courtesy Yale University News Bureau

**Fig. 5.9:** Dr. José M. R. Delgado, 1963, courtesy Yale University News Bureau

**Fig. 5.10(a):** Courtesy of Dr. Wilse B. Webb

**Fig. 5.11:** Kimball, *Biology*, © 1978. Reading, Mass.: Addison-Wesley. Figure 27.9. Reprinted by permission.

**Fig. 5.13:** Courtesy of Dr. Ivan Beale

**Fig. 5.16:** Freedman, *Introductory Psychology*, Second Edition, © 1982. Reading, Mass.: Addison-Wesley. Figure 2.7. Reprinted by permission.

**Fig. 5.18:** Freedman, *Introductory Psychology*, Second Edition, © 1982. Reading, Mass.: Addison-Wesley. Figure 2.6. Reprinted by permission.

**Fig. 5.19:** Levy, *Elements of Biology*, © 1982. Addison-Wesley, Reading, MA. Figure 10.25. Reprinted with permission.

**Fig. 5.20:** After A. R. Luria, *The Functional Organization of the Brain*, copyright © 1970 by Scientific American, Inc. All rights reserved.

**Fig. 5.22:** Dr. M. E. Olds

**Fig. 5.24:** The Bettmann Archive

**Fig. 6.2:** Kimball, *Biology*, © 1978. Reading, Mass.: Addison-Wesley. Figure 26.7. Reprinted with permission.

**Fig. 6.3:** Courtesy of Dr. George Wald, Harvard University

**Fig. 6.8:** Freedman, *Introductory Psychology*, Second Edition, © 1982. Reading, Mass.: Addison-Wesley. Figure 3.5. Reprinted by permission.

**Fig. 6.13:** Liz Muller

**Fig. 6.14:** Jeff Albertson/Stock, Boston

**Fig. 6.23:** Liz Muller

**Fig. 6.24:** Liz Muller

**Fig. 6.25:** Freedman, *Introductory Psychology*, Second Edition, © 1982. Reading, Mass.: Addison-Wesley. Figure 3.13. Reprinted by permission.

**Fig. 6.28(b):** Camerique Photos

**Fig. 6.29:** K. C. Dendooven

**Fig. 6.30:** Bruce Anderson

**Fig. 6.32(a):** Ron Hirshman

**Fig. 7.1:** Kleitman, N. "Patterns of dreaming." *Scientific American* **203;** pp. 82–88. © 1960. Adapted by permission of William C. Dement.

**Fig. 7.7:** NIH Gerontology Photo

**Fig. 7.8:** Reprinted with permission from D. D. Girdano and D. A. Girdano, *Drugs, A Factual Account*, 2nd ed. Reading, Mass.: Addison-Wesley, 1976, p. 62.

**Fig. 7.9:** Reprinted with permission from D. D. Girdano and D. A. Girdano, *Drugs, A Factual Account*, 2nd ed. Reading, Mass.: Addison-Wesley, 1976, p. 60.

**Fig. 8.4:** Courtesy of Dr. Philip Teitelbaum

**Fig. 8.7:** Myron Davis

**Fig. 8.8:** Liz Muller

**Fig. 8.10:** From D. E. Berlyne, "The Influence of Complexity and Novelty in Visual Figures on Orienting Responses," *Journal of Experimental Psychology* **55**, 1958, pp. 289–296. Copyright © 1958 by the American Psychological Association. Reprinted by permission.

**Fig. 8.13:** U.P.I.

**Fig. 8.14:** U.P.I.

**Fig. 8.18:** C. Martindale, *Cognition and Consciousness*. Homewood, Ill.: The Dorsey Press, 1981, p. 247.

**Fig. 8.20:** Liz Muller

**Fig. 8.21:** Schlosberg, 1952.

**Fig. 9.4:** "Frustration and Aggression," University of Iowa Press Child Welfare Series.

**Fig. 9.7:** Courtesy of Dr. Joseph V. Brady

**Fig. 10.2:** Janice Fullman/The Picture Cube (photo of woman); Frank Siteman/The Picture Cube (photo of man)

**Fig. 10.4:** Ritchie and Carola, *Biology*, © 1979. Reading, Mass.: Addison-Wesley, pp. 302–303. Reprinted with permission.

**Fig. 10.6:** Life Nature Library, *Animal Behavior*. Photograph by Nina Leen, © 1980, Time-Life Books Inc.

**Fig. 10.8:** Courtesy of Dr. Harry F. Harlow, University of Wisconsin Primate Laboratory

**Fig. 10.9:** Courtesy of Dr. Harry F. Harlow, University of Wisconsin Primate Laboratory.

**Fig. 10.11:** All photos except "2 days," "2 months," and "3 months" by Liz Muller

**Fig. 10.12:** Courtesy of Dr. Arthur H. Parmelee

**Fig. 10.13:** Courtesy of Dr. Arthur H. Parmelee

**Fig. 10.14:** Mindy Jassenoff

**Fig. 11.2:** After "Growing Up," by J. M. Tanner. Copyright © 1973 by *Scientific American*, Inc. All rights reserved.

**Fig. 12.2:** Reproduced by permission of Houghton Mifflin Company.

**Fig. 12.4:** Reprinted with permission of Macmillan Publishing Co., Inc. from *Differential Psychology* by A. Anastasi. Copyright © 1958 by Macmillan Publishing Co., Inc.

**Fig. 12.10:** Reproduced by permission. Copyright © 1980 by the Psychological Corporation, New York, N.Y. All rights reserved.

**Fig. 12.11:** Diagram "Kuder Profile of Mary Thomas" from *Essentials of Psychological Testing*, 3rd edition, by Lee J. Cronbach, Harper & Row, 1970. Based on *Kuder Preference Record*, Vocational Form C, copyright 1950 by G. Frederic Kuder.

**Fig. 12.14(a):** Photo courtesy of The Psychological Corporation, 304 E 45th St., New York, N.Y. 10017. **(b):** From *Personality* by J. P. Guilford, copyright 1959 by McGraw-Hill Book Company; used with permission. **(c):** Reproduced by permission from the Rosenzweig P-F Study, copyright 1948. **(d):** After a test devised by L. Szondi, copyright 1959 by the J. B. Lippincott Company.

**Fig. 13.1:** 16 Personality Factor Questionnaire. Copyright 1949–1967 by The Institute for Personality and Ability Testing, Champaign, Illinois. Reproduced by permission.

**Fig. 13.2:** National Library of Medicine, Bethesda, Maryland

**Fig. 15.1:** Courtesy of Albert Bandura, Stanford University

**Fig. 16.1:** "Goofus and Gallant" by Garry Cleveland Myers. Pictures by Marion Hull Hamel. *Highlights for Children*, June/July 1976. Copyright © 1976, *HIGHLIGHTS FOR CHILDREN, INC.* Columbus, Ohio.

**Photograph credits**

**4:** Left, M. Shostak/Anthro-Photo; center, Diego Goldberg/Sygma; right, Hella Hammid/Photo Researchers

**8:** The Bettmann Archive

**11:** Culver Pictures

**13:** Historical Pictures Service, Chicago

**16:** Top, Van Bucher/Photo Researchers, Inc.; bottom, Van Bucher/Photo Researchers, Inc.

**22:** Paul Fusco/Magnum

**35:** Right, Clif Garboden/Stock, Boston; left, Massillon Museum

**36:** Boston Globe

**43:** Left, U.P.I.; center, Anwar Hussein; right, Gilles Peress/Magnum

**62:** Wide World Photos

**72:** Alex Webb/Magnum

**75:** Mindy Jassenoff

**85:** Left and right, Jean Boughton, Boston

**91:** National Library of Medicine, Bethesda, Maryland

**93:** Cary Wolinsky/Stock, Boston

**98:** Michael Evans/Liaison
**104:** Jean Boughton, Boston
**111:** Wide World Photos
**113:** Martha Swope
**132:** Rich Smolan—Photography
**134:** Peter Vandermark/Stock, Boston
**154:** Paul Conklin/Monkmeyer Press Photo Service
**155:** Owen Franken/Stock, Boston
**203:** The Bettmann Archive
**210:** Left, Toni Angermayer/Photo Researchers; right, Gordon Smith/ Photo Researchers
**214:** George N. Peet/The Picture Cube
**217:** *The New York Times*
**218:** U.P.I.
**236:** Institute for Parapsychology, Durham, N.C.
**241:** Stephen J. Sherman
**244:** © Michael Heron, 1980/Woodfin Camp and Associates
**252:** Cris Springmann © 1982/Black Star
**261:** U.P.I.
**263:** Culver Pictures
**271:** Triangle, *Sandoz Journal of Medical Science*, 1955, II, 119–123
**277:** Cary Wolinsky/Stock, Boston
**278:** Dr. Peter M. Witt
**285:** U.P.I.
**291:** Hella Hammid/Photo Researchers
**292:** Photographic Laboratory, Naval Medical Research Institute, Bethesda, Maryland
**300:** Rapho/Photo Researchers
**303:** Giansanti/Sygma
**306:** Jeff Albertson/Stock, Boston
**311:** *Boston Globe* Photo
**312:** Stoelting Company of Chicago
**319:** David Austen/Stock, Boston

**330:** U.P.I.
**334:** Hope Alexander/Woodfin Camp
**336:** Ellis Herwig/Stock, Boston
**339:** Eric L. Brown/Monkmeyer
**340:** John Nance/Magnum
**342:** Editorial Photocolor Archives
**346:** The Bettmann Archive
**354:** Movie Star News, New York, N.Y.; © 1980 by Paramount Pictures Corp.
**360:** Brown Brothers
**366:** *Boston Globe* Photo
**376:** Mimi Forsyth/Monkmeyer
**383:** Abigail Heyman/Archive Pictures
**386:** Left, Merrim/Monkmeyer; right, Ellis Herwig/Stock, Boston
**399:** Kennerly/Liaison Agency
**406:** Peter Vandermark/Stock, Boston
**407:** G. Marshall Wilson, courtesy *Ebony* magazine and the Johnson Publishing Co.
**410:** Left, Photo Researchers, Inc.; right, Burk Uzzle/Magnum
**412:** Picture Cube
**414:** Anna Kaufman Moon/Stock, Boston
**418:** Left, Weisbrot/Stock, Boston; right, Jerry Berndt/Stock, Boston
**421:** Photo Researchers
**425:** Roger Lubin/Jeroboam, Inc.
**430:** Thomas Hopker/Woodfin Camp & Associates
**435:** Van Bucher/Photo Researchers
**438:** National Library of Medicine, Bethesda, Maryland
**446:** National Archives
**451:** Cornell Capa/Magnum
**454:** Bob Adelman/Magnum
**459:** Sybil Shelton/Monkmeyer
**467:** The Bettmann Archive

**480:** René Burri/Magnum
**481:** Charles Gatewood
**492:** U.P.I.
**495:** Stock, Boston
**507:** Peter Carmichael/Woodfin Camp & Associates
**511:** U.P.I.
**515:** Brown Brothers
**519:** Culver Pictures
**524:** U.P.I.
**531:** Brown Brothers
**536:** From *Interpretation of Schizophrenia*, 2nd Edition. Revised and expanded by Silvano Arieti, M.D. © 1974 by Silvano Arieti. © 1955 by Robert Brunner (Basic Books, Inc., N.Y.)
**539:** Burk Uzzle/Magnum
**548:** Van Bucher/Photo Researchers
**553:** Carl Rogers
**559:** *The New York Times*
**565:** Alex Webb/Magnum
**570:** Andrew Sacks/Editorial Photocolor Archives
**572:** National Institute of Mental Health
**578:** Michael Meadows/Editorial Photocolor Archives
**583:** Henri Cartier Bresson/Magnum
**587:** Wide World Photos
**590:** Goldberg/Sygma
**592:** U.P.I.
**597:** U.P.I.
**603:** Bettye Lane
**614:** Abigail Heyman/Archive Pictures
**617:** Left, Library of Congress; right, Wide World Photos
**619:** *Boston Globe* Photo
**622:** John Launois/Black Star

**Definitions of terms can be found on the pages indicated by bold type.**